SPLENDID VISION, UNSWERVING PURPOSE

DEVELOPING AIR POWER FOR THE UNITED STATES AIR FORCE DURING THE FIRST CENTURY OF POWERED FLIGHT

History Office
Aeronautical Systems Center
Air Force Materiel Command
Air Force History and Museums Program
United States Air Force
Wright-Patterson Air Force Base, Ohio

2002

DEDICATION

To all the U.S. Air Force civilian and military personnel—directors, program managers, scientists, engineers, technicians, logisticians, and support people
—whose untiring efforts "keep 'em flying"

Front Cover: (Top) Lieutenant James H. "Jimmy" Doolittle pilots a DH-4 advertising the 1924 Air Show held in Dayton, Ohio; Lieutenant Henry "Hap" Arnold, who learned to fly at the Wright School of Aviation; and the 10th Infantry Band, Ohio National Guard, performs in front of the headquarters building during the dedication of Wright Field in 1927. (Center) "This Field Is Small – Use It All," McCook Field motto emblazoned on the main hangar; main gate of McCook Field. (Below) The 1909 Wright Military Flyer; Orville and Wilbur Wright.

Back Cover: (clockwise from upper left) Aircraft: Northrop B-2 Spirit, AGM-129 Advanced Cruise Missile, Lockheed F-117 Nighthawk, Teledyne Ryan RQ-4A Global Hawk, Boeing's X-35A Joint Strike Fighter prototype; Lieutenant General James T. Stewart Hall, part of the James H. Doolittle Acquisition Management Complex at Wright-Patterson Air Force Base; special operations forces board an MC-130 Combat Talon en route home from Grenada following Operation Urgent Fury in 1983; graduating class of Air Force test pilot school pose in front of an F-80A at Patterson Field; Air Force Security Policeman Adam Wilson, 1950s; Army Air Corps aircraft mechanics during World War II, (back row) Mike Pezzuti, "Finks," Roy Boarman, (front row) John Stephen, Bernie Freeman; General James T. Stewart; General Bernard A. Schriever.

FOREWORD

During the winter of 1934, I was a pilot in the Air Corps and found myself flying the mail across the country in an open cockpit biplane. President Franklin D. Roosevelt had annulled government contracts with private airmail carriers and given the job to the Air Corps. If patriotism and heroism were enough to get the job done, this would have been a wonderful story, but the bravery and determination of the pilots were not enough to compensate for the inadequate airplanes we were flying, and we suffered many tragic losses. Aircraft in 1934 had engines, wings, and landing gear, but that was about it. During those long, cold flights across the heartland of the nation I had plenty of time to think about improvements that could and should be made to airplanes. Unfortunately, aeronautical research and development (R&D) was a low national priority and funding was always meager. Ironically, it was the death of so many Air Corps pilots during that cold winter of 1934 that drew attention to the sad state of Army aviation and motivated our leadership to increase funding for aeronautical research and development. That proved to be a critical and very timely decision because the technologies developed in the late 1930s were soon needed for thousands of aircraft flown by Allied forces to fight and win World War II.

Several years and a world war later, I found myself in a position to truly appreciate the complex business of developing and incorporating advanced technologies into new weapon systems. In the post-World War II era, these processes became infinitely more complicated than they had been in the past. The war had stimulated aeronautical research and development in Europe, as well as in the United States. We saw amazing advances in the areas of propulsion, electronics, materials, and every other technical area. Technologies advanced to the point where we no longer were developing airplanes and rockets; we were creating complex aeronautical and aerospace weapon systems. Each system consisted of a vast array of highly complex subsystems neatly configured onto a platform that worked in perfect harmony—when the engineers got it right. The trick, of course, was getting it right. The complexity and number of component systems presented engineers and program managers with some very interesting challenges. We had come a long way since the old days—only 20 years previous—when we could fly practically anything if we had enough lift, thrust, and piano wire.

Within the Air Force, Dayton has always been synonymous with aeronautical research and development. Of course, Dayton was the home of Wilbur and Orville Wright, who made the first practical use of a wind tunnel in order to obtain reliable data for achieving the world's first heavier-than-air, controlled, and powered flight in 1903. The Wrights refined their invention sufficiently by 1905 to offer a military version of their airplane to the U.S. Signal Corps. Unfortunately, Army brass failed to comprehend the enormous potential of military aviation, although many European nations had embraced the new technology and were investing heavily in aeronautical R&D.

Although the Signal Corps finally purchased the Wright Military Flyer in 1909, they saw no role for military aircraft beyond that of observation, and the flying program was poorly supported. Finally, with America's entry into World War I, the need for an organized approach to aeronautical R&D became apparent, and the Army established McCook Field in Dayton, Ohio. McCook was the nation's first installation whose purpose was to develop state-of-the-art airplanes, engines, air armament, and associated equipment. More than this, McCook Field brought together in one location many of the nation's and the world's leading aeronautical engineers and researchers. After World War I, many of these individuals went on to positions in industry and higher education, while others remained in government service. Thus was laid the foundation of that vital partnership between government, industry, and academe that led to such outstanding advances in American aerospace power in the second half of the twentieth century.

In 1927, tiny McCook closed. The Army Air Corps had looked nationwide for a new site to house its R&D organization. Dayton was eventually chosen primarily because community leaders offered free land. Also, much of the aircraft industry at the time was either already in, or relatively near, Dayton and transportation routes were excellent. So McCook engineers, scientists, and test pilots were relocated several miles east of the city in newly constructed, state-of-the-art R&D facilities named after both Wright brothers. Wright Field's laboratories and shops quickly became world-renowned.

Unfortunately, Wright Field soon saw investment in aeronautical R&D dwindle during the Great Depression. The funding shortage did not stop the pace of R&D, but it did adversely impact the number of military airplanes that were eventually purchased. Much ingenuity and creativity went into developing advanced technologies that were tested and validated on one or two aircraft but never put into production. Even when aircraft were purchased for the active inventory, the numbers were very low. We found ourselves, in the mid-1930s, in a relatively advanced state of aeronautical development—but it existed only at Wright Field, not at airfields around the nation.

I reported to the Air Corps Engineering School at Wright Field in 1939, the year that Hitler invaded Poland, and there was growing concern that the world was heading towards another world war. That fear translated into increased funding for R&D, and the pace of development was accelerating. At the Engineering School, I got a theoretical introduction to aeronautics. More than this, I developed an understanding of the problems confronting the Air Corps' intrepid band of engineers and project officers: problems of funding, recruitment, facilities, and organization. Upon graduation, I became a test pilot and learned that Wright Field was becoming a test pilot's idea of heaven. For those of us who had flown little more than World War I-era open cockpit biplanes, Wright Field gave us our first practical acquaintance with the latest combat airplanes. I can recall days when I tested five or six new aircraft. When I served at Wright Field, it was a very exciting place. The dedicated engineers who had worked there during the lean years were energized because they finally had the money and support they needed to explore advanced technologies and build new aircraft in partnership with a revitalized aircraft industry. Funding made R&D possible, and the threat of war made it imperative.

I served in the Pacific during World War II and was keenly aware that it was Wright Field that brought U.S. forces and our Allies an amazing number of specialized aircraft. Commanders in the theater of operations sent their requirements for aircraft and modifications to Dayton, and Wright Field delivered. We saw daily combat and, of course, we thought that Wright could have delivered faster and a bit better, but then we were constantly sending Wright new and ever more complex requirements. Some requirements were conflicting; some were ambiguous; and some were simply impossible. Warfighters are very picky customers because lives are on the line every time a warplane takes off. We always want more and better airplanes. The fact is, during World War II, Wright Field did deliver—splendidly.

Wright Field excelled to such a great extent during World War II largely because it was able to rapidly escalate a precise process of R&D that was perfected by its scientists, engineers, and test personnel in the 1930s. They used tried-and-true techniques to insert known technologies into aircraft designed for a myriad of special purposes and developed new technologies and solutions to problems. Then, American industry supported the war effort by devoting all possible resources to production of wartime materiel, including thousands of warplanes.

World War II was a turning point in aeronautical development. The remarkable advances of the British in airborne radar and jet engines and of the Germans in operational jet aircraft and guided missiles jolted many in the Army Air Forces' command structure into realizing not only the importance but also the preeminence in R&D in achieving and maintaining air superiority. We in the Air Force are indeed fortunate that the commanding general of the Army Air Forces was General Hap Arnold.

General Arnold is one of those pivotal figures in the history of great nations. Realizing the importance of British and German aeronautical achievements, he took the first steps toward making R&D an integral part of postwar Air Force planning and funding. Arnold's objectives were frustrated at first by the precipitate demobilization following the war and his retirement due to ill health. However, he left behind devoted colleagues and disciples who spent the next five years working toward enlarging the role of Air Force R&D. The first step was the establishment of the Air Research and Development Command (ARDC) in 1951.

In the 1950s, at a time when it appeared that the Soviet Union was beating us in the space race, I was at ARDC's Western Development Division (WDD) charged with the job of rapidly developing numerous advanced missile systems to counter the Soviet challenge. Sending ballistic missiles into outer space was not a simple process. We achieved success because we developed new processes, cut through a lot of red tape, and approached each new challenge with creativity, determination, and courage to experiment and try out new ideas. We also had sufficient funding and, perhaps more importantly, the ears of senior leaders who were always available when we called and who trusted us to act independently.

The formation of ARDC was only a first step in protecting the role of military R&D in the Air Force. A second, more decisive step was taken in 1961 with the establishment of the Air Force Systems Command (AFSC). While ARDC gave organizational status to R&D, AFSC combined R&D with procurement and production and, most importantly, with funding authority. At the same time, the Air Force's laboratories, engineering cadres, and system program offices were fundamentally reorganized.

I was fortunate to serve as the final commander of ARDC, where I had the opportunity to bring the weapon system management approach developed at WDD to the aircraft programs at the Wright Air Development Division and other acquisition centers. I served as the first commander of AFSC, when the Air Force finally achieved the unified research and development organization that Hap Arnold had envisioned. As commander of AFSC, I had full authority to control the entire development cycle of weapon systems to include research, development, test, evaluation, procurement, and production.

For the next 30 years, Systems Command was synonymous with excellence in aerospace product acquisition. During those years, the groundwork for the Air Force as we know it today was laid. With a few notable exceptions, such as the C-130 and B-52, virtually every fighter, bomber, trainer, and transport aircraft in today's inventory was envisioned, designed, built, and deployed between the early 1960s and early 1990s. And, indeed, systems only recently or not yet fielded were on the drawing boards during those years—systems like the F/A-22, the Joint Strike Fighter, and unmanned aerial vehicles. The end of the Cold War in the late 1980s and early 1990s brought about a number of reorganizations within the Air Force. Among them was the merger of Air Force Systems Command and Air Force Logistics Command (AFLC) to form the Air Force Materiel Command (AFMC).

Today, our nation is once again at war—a war on terrorism. Our military is being called upon to fight a new kind of war, a war never before envisioned and a war that quite conceivably may never end. The weapons of this war are those developed for traditional warfare and the measures of their success and failure are quite different than those in past conflicts. One thing has not changed, however. Our warfighters are being supported strongly by the AFMC laboratories as well as the acquisition, product, logistics, and test centers within AFMC, which are carrying on a tradition begun in 1917. This is the arm of the Air Force that keeps 'em flying by evolving new technologies, developing and acquiring new weapon systems, maintaining and updating existing systems, and providing the tools for our warfighters. To a large measure our troops on the front line live and die by the products of AFMC.

This fascinating book tells the story of the warfighter from a unique perspective and one that is seldom highlighted. This is the story of those who support the fighting forces by developing and acquiring new and better weapon systems. The brave pilots and flight personnel put their lives on the line for us each time they go into combat. It was comforting to me to know, when I wore the uniform and even more so today, that the tools our troops are fighting with are the products of engineers, scientists, test pilots, administrative personnel, contract and finance experts who are the best in the business when it comes to developing new warplanes. They come to their jobs every day with as much enthusiasm and determination as a pilot scrambling in response to a threat. I salute our men and women on duty in the operational Air Force and take my hat off to the dedicated acquisition personnel who labor in relative anonymity to bring state-of-the-art weapon systems to our warfighters.

It has been a great pleasure for me to devote my career to working with the good people from the world of acquisition, and I am honored to put my name on a book that celebrates their vital role in defending our nation.

GENERAL BERNARD A. SCHRIEVER
U.S. Air Force, Retired

The Creed of Wright Field

Here on this ground where Wilbur and Orville Wright brought to full life man's age-old dream of rising in flight above the earth, we of Wright Field consecrate ourselves to the splendid vision and unswerving purpose which motivated those great and honored pioneers of the sky. Their patience, their firm determination, their untiring devotion to their aim--- these we take as a light to guide and inspire us.

We hold in all humility to the faith that man can if man will. We believe that there is no true failure save the failure of the human spirit. We have met uncounted times, and shall meet uncounted times again, the little failures that try and break the souls of little men. We have tried; and we have failed. We shall try again tomorrow, and again tomorrow fail. But these defeats we shall meet undaunted, as we have met the defeats of the past. We know that at last we shall have a measure of success; and in that moment all the failures shall become paltry things indeed.

Yet even in success shall our humility be maintained. For it is the essence of our creed that perfection is an elusive myth that never shall man do well but that he may do better--- that success is but the stepping-stone to new trial and new success--- that there shall be no final triumph, but only the long and glorious record of those who have given themselves, in life and death, to the pursuit of knowledge and advancement, to the crusade of learning which shall never end.

Our hands and eyes lifted, in war and in peace, toward the heavens which alone shall measure our hopes and aspirations--- we make this solemn confession of our faith.

This creed, which has guided Army Air Forces research and experimental work since its inception in 1917, has been inscribed and is officially attested this 17 day of DECEMBER in the year 1942 at the Army Air Forces Materiel Center, Wright Field, Ohio.

A W Vanaman
BRIGIDIER GENERAL, U.S.A.
COMMANDING GENERAL, A.A.F. MATERIEL CENTER

Ralph O Brownfield.
COLONEL, AIR CORPS
COMMANDING OFFICER WRIGHT FIELD

PREFACE

Splendid Vision, Unswerving Purpose, the title of this book, is taken from a document called "The Creed of Wright Field." The creed was hammered out in 1942, when this nation was in the depths of World War II. It served the purpose of what today would be called a "vision statement." Unlike modern vision statements, however, the creed cast a glance backward as well as forward. While candidly owning up to occasional failures, the creed reaffirmed the "can-do" spirit that has been the hallmark of America's aeronautical enterprise from the very beginning.

The purpose of this book is to recapture, in words and pictures, some of the spirit that has infused those charged with developing this nation's aerial weapons and weapons platforms over the past century.

This has been a century of achievement without parallel. The century began when Daytonians Wilbur and Orville Wright designed, built, and flew the world's first powered, controllable, manned airplane. In 1917, the U.S. Army established McCook Field in Dayton, Ohio, for the development of aircraft and aeronautical materiel in World War I. In 1927, the Army moved McCook's engineering staff to newly opened Wright Field east of Dayton. During the 1920s and 1930s, Wright Field laid the technical and materiel foundations for the air force that won air superiority for the armies of America and its Allies in World War II while devastating the military and industrial infrastructure of America's foes. In the postwar period, Wright Field became part of Wright-Patterson Air Force Base, the epicenter of the United States Air Force's aerospace enterprise during the Cold War and after. The half century since the end of World War II has witnessed multiple, and in many cases concurrent, revolutions in propulsion, electronics, materials, manufacturing, and human factors that have resulted in aircraft, missiles, and spacecraft undreamt of during the prewar era. In the lifetime of a single individual, we have passed from the Barling bomber to the B-2, from the Kettering Bug to Unmanned Combat Aerial Vehicles.

During the past century we have, in short, traveled from Huffman Prairie, where the Wright brothers perfected the practicality of their flying machine, *to the moon*. In 1986, Wright-Patterson's air base wing history office published a book that celebrated this achievement in its title. The present book is the first of a two-volume sequel to that highly regarded work. This book details the science and engineering accomplishments of the aeronautical acquisition enterprise, from the Wright brothers to the present. Its companion volume, scheduled for publication next year, will survey the often unsung history of base support activities without which the technical achievement would not have been possible.

This project originated in 1998 when the ASC History Office team began planning history products to commemorate the centennial of flight. Planning is easy, but turning plans into reality can be a challenge. This book would not have been completed without the strongest possible support of ASC commanders during the ensuing years, Lieutenant General Robert F. Raggio and Lieutenant General Richard V. Reynolds; Executive Directors Mr. Jerome P. Sutton and Dr. Vincent J. Russo; and staff directors Colonel Scott W. McLaughlin and Colonel Ward T. Willis, and their deputy, Mr. Tom Owens, who gave us virtually unlimited resources, talented personnel, and unfailing support in order for us to succeed. Then a wonderful thing happened: they all stood back and empowered us to do our best, which was a powerful incentive for the history team. Their advocacy of this project and faith in our history team led Lieutenant General Joseph H. Wehrle of the U.S. Air Force Centennial of Flight Office to recommend this book as one of the Air Force's centerpiece projects for 2003.

In addition to management support, we also needed uniquely talented people with creativity, enthusiasm, and a positive attitude. ASC's History Team has these qualities in abundance. First and foremost are the historians, archivists, and support personnel of the ASC History Office staff: Dr. Jim Aldridge, Mr. Jim Ciborski, Ms. Charmaine Dunn, Mr. Bruce Hess, Dr. Henry Narducci, Ms. Robin Smith, and last only in the alphabet, Ms. Lori Tagg. In addition to these "full-time" staff members are our intrepid and multi-talented reservists, notably, Senior Airman Michael "Micky" Cordiviola, Captain Elizabeth Langwell, Senior Airman Stan Parks, and Senior Master Sergeant Jim Sturm. We have been further honored by the expert assistance of retired members of the Wright-Patterson family who have volunteered their services on behalf of this project and others, namely, Ms. Helen Kavanaugh-Jones, Master Sergeant Dave Menard (U.S. Air Force, retired), and Dr. Squire Brown. Finally, we must thank Mr. Thomas P. Richards from the National Air Intelligence Center for generously providing us the services of Mr. Curtis Alley, graphics designer extraordinaire, whose artistry is evident literally from cover to cover; and Lieutenant Colonel Edward G. Worley, chief of the ASC Public Affairs Office, for providing us the publishing expertise of Mr. Donald R. Yates. Every one of these individuals contributed in some respect to this project. Without his or her contribution, this book could not have been accomplished in so timely or professional a manner.

Last but not least, we would like to thank retired General Bernard A. Schriever, a man whose life was devoted to the Air Force's research, development, and acquisition activities over the past half century. General Schriever reviewed the entire text and graciously agreed to write the Foreword. He has long inspired teams to excel, take chances, and develop creative solutions to problems. This is something the ASC History Team did, and General Schriever's willingness to give this work his stamp of approval is humbling. We hope this book brings back fond memories for some, enlightens others, and educates those who have never really known what the word "acquisition" means. Hopefully, we have provided useful definition.

Past is but prologue. "Team History" is moving on to new challenges.

Diana G. Cornelisse

DIANA G. CORNELISSE
Chief Historian

CREDITS AND ACKNOWLEDGEMENTS

This book is the work of many individuals. The first four chapters were researched and written over a decade and a half ago by Ms. Lois E. Walker and Mr. Shelby E. Wickham of the 2750th Air Base Wing History Office, Wright-Patterson Air Force Base. It was a monumental task that those of us who followed in their footsteps fully appreciated. Members of the ASC History Team who later edited the original chapters were Dr. Henry Narducci, Ms. Lori Tagg, Ms. Robin Smith, Mr. Jim Ciborski, and Ms. Diana Cornelisse. Dr. Jim Aldridge wrote chapters 5 and 7 and chapter 6 was written by Ms. Lori Tagg. Sidebars were contributed to various chapters by Ms. Robin Smith, Ms. Lori Tagg, Mr. Jim Ciborski, Senior Airman Stan Parks, Ms. Diana Cornelisse, Mr. Andrew Kididis (ASC Engineering Directorate), and Mr. George Cully (Air Force Materiel Command History Office). Ms. Lori Tagg, Mr. Jim Ciborski, and Ms. Charmaine Dunn assembled the appendices; Ms. Robin Smith compiled and edited the glossary, endnotes, and bibliography; and Captain Elizabeth Langwell, Ms. Lori Tagg, Mr. Jim Ciborski, Ms. Robin Smith, and Senior Airman Stan Parks compiled the extensive index. Mrs. Helen Kavanaugh-Jones performed the herculean task of editing the entire book from cover to cover. Lieutenant Coby Leslie (ASC's Commander's Staff Operations) and Mr. Dave Cornelisse (National Archives and Records Administration) also provided editorial oversight prior to publication. We were most fortunate to have the services of Mr. Curtis Alley (National Air Intelligence Center) to provide graphic support. He created the attractive graphics design, formatted the entire volume, and patiently suffered through what seemed like a never-ending series of text changes. Photographs used in this book, unless otherwise noted, are from the official U.S. Air Force photograph collection of the ASC History Office archives.

A special debt of thanks is owed to the "enforcers" of this project. Ms. Lori Tagg served as senior project manager of this book. She kept the project on track and on schedule as well as undertaking the grueling task of coordinating the completion of each portion of the history (text, sidebars, photo captions, front and back matter) with the various authors, finalizing all text, and ensuring that the formatted book was properly arranged. Ms. Diana Cornelisse conducted overall management of the project, making assignments, and orchestrating the diverse, always unpredictable, and uniquely creative talents of the extended History Team. She worked with Mr. Mark Frazier, Senior Consultant at BearingPoint, and the excellent people in Lieutenant General Joseph H. Wehrle's Air Force Centennial of Flight Office to ensure that their expectations for this book were fully realized. Assisted by Captain Elizabeth Langwell and Staff Sergeant Stan Parks, Ms. Cornelisse conspired to beg, borrow, and steal resources from all corners of Wright-Patterson Air Force Base while assuring one and all that, despite appearances, the book was progressing quite well.

As the historians and archivists worked on the book Mr. Bruce Hess was left to manage the ASC Archive and answer the dozens of reference requests that were received weekly. He performed his duties admirably, receiving much advice but little assistance from management. He counted on his trusty reservists, Technical Sergeant Melissa Rich and Technical Sergeant Bob Mack to report for duty when needed. Ms. Charmaine Dunn prepared charts and graphs for the book and handled all other activities required to maintain a government office for the full year that this book was in production. Her quiet efficiency, calming presence, and stoic manner saved her boss from a panic attack on more than one occasion. The History Team was further inspired by Shiloh Smith, our fearless canine mascot, who most nobly represented his breed and the thousands of mascots who have faithfully served aviators throughout the past century. Shiloh led our pack.

The History Office owes a special debt to the ASC Reserve Program, which has for nearly a decade provided the office with outstanding reservists. Those supporting this project included Captain Elizabeth Langwell, Senior Airman Micky Cordiviola (our webmaster), Senior Airman Stan Parks, Senior Master Sergeant Jim Sturm, Technical Sergeant Melissa Rich, Technical Sergeant Bob Mack, and Lieutenant Colonel (sel) Ruthie Williamson. Reservists performed numerous research and writing projects and were there to help with the dozens of miscellaneous situations that arose during the course of a normal business day.

In addition to the contributions of the aforementioned, the completion of this book would have been impossible without the assistance of numerous individuals who complemented the History Team with their knowledge, experience, and enthusiastic support. Those who reviewed parts or all of individual chapters included: Mr. Albert E. Misenko, retired chief historian of the ASC History Office; Mr. Jerome P. Sutton, retired program manager and executive director of ASC; Mr. Ralph Johnston, Mr. William Laubendorfer, Colonel Ron Thurlow, and Mr. J. Arthur Boykin, all retired ASC program managers; Dr. Squire L. Brown, retired chief of the Flight Mechanics Branch, Engineering Directorate; Master Sergeant Dave Menard, retired researcher, United States Air Force Museum; Mr. Jim Plymyer, ASC

Reconnaissance System Program Office (SPO); Ms. Tressie Easterwood, ASC F-16 SPO; Mr. Mike Patterson, ASC RC-135 Deputy Program Manager; Chaplain Lieutenant Colonel Lawrence V. Tagg, U.S. Air Force retired; and Mr. Martyn D. Tagg, Air Force Materiel Command Headquarters Environmental Management Division. Numerous people within ASC's Engineering Directorate reviewed all or parts of the text, including Mr. Jon Ogg, director, Mr. Robert B. "Scott" Kuhnen, Mr. Joseph J. Lusczek, and Mr. Andrew Kididis. Mr. Steve Cloyd, Air Force Research Laboratory Propulsion Directorate, and Mr. Fred Oliver, deputy director of that organization, also reviewed portions of the text.

The "Century of Air and Space Power Timeline" insert is the work of Dr. George Watson of the Air Staff History Support Office, Washington, D.C.; Dr. Richard P. Hallion, former Air Force Historian; and Mr. Tom Segars, Pentagon Graphics. Master Sergeant Dave Menard (U.S. Air Force, retired) reviewed the timeline in addition to photographs throughout the book and the index to ensure their proper identification. Mr. Milton C. Ross, director of ASC Contracting, and Ms. Maureen Beech, Universal Technology Corporation, provided cogent advice on production issues. Ms. Audrey Gee, Commander's Staff Operations, handled the all-important financing arrangements.

Finally, thanks go to Lieutenant Colonel Edward G. Worley, Director of ASC Public Affairs, whose entire staff provided the History Team with outstanding support. Most notably, the services of Mr. Don Yates who put on his old printer's cap to serve as our liaison with the Government Printing Office. Mr. Bill Meers and Ms. Patti Traylor of ASC Public Affairs Security Review expedited the formal security review of the final draft by the appropriate organizations within ASC and the Air Force Research Laboratory. Lieutenant Tana Hamilton and Ms. Susan Barone provided media coverage and served as our link with the general public on this and other Centennial of Flight projects.

Many others contributed everything from insight and advice to photographs and inspiration. This group includes: Dr. Richard P. Hallion, former Air Force Historian, who has been a source of much inspiration, guidance, and support to us in the ASC History office for the past 20 years, and the current acting Air Force Historian, Mr. William C. Heimdahl, who made the resources of the U.S. Air Force History and Museums Program available to the ASC staff. We also received tremendous support from Colonel Carol Sikes and her staff at the Air Force History Support Office, most notably Mr. Jacob Neufeld and Dr. Richard Wolf. Other notable contributions were made by Mr. John D. Weber, Chief of the Air Force Materiel Command History Office; Mr. Clay Fujimura, Air Force Research Laboratory Sensors Directorate; Mr. Joseph J. Lusczek, ASC Engineering Directorate; Dr. Jeffrey Underwood and Mr. Jeffrey Duford, United States Air Force Museum Research Division; Dr. Timothy Warnock and Mr. Jay Godwin, U.S. Air Force Historical Research Agency; Mr. William Head, chief historian, Warner Robins Air Logistic Center History Office; Lieutenant Michael Scales and Chief Master Sergeant Melvin Fore, ASC B-2 SPO; Ms. Dawne Dewey, head of Special Collections and Archives, Wright State University, Dayton, Ohio; Mr. Randy Parker, 88th Air Base Wing Civil Engineering; Dr. Jan Ferguson, 88th Air Base Wing Historic Preservation Office; Mr. Larry Davis, Squadron-Signal Publications; Dr. Paul Ferguson and Mr. George Cully, Air Force Materiel Command History Office; Mr. James O. Young, chief historian, Air Force Flight Test Center; Mr. Derek Linder, GrummanGoose.com; Mr. Donald Davidson, historian, Indianapolis Motor Speedway; and Ms. Melba Hunt, Kettering-Moraine Museum. Special thanks go to Colonel Richard E. Cole (U.S. Air Force, Ret.), Jimmy Doolittle's co-pilot on the Tokyo Raid, for sharing personal photographs of his childhood in Dayton and his memories of McCook Field.

Among the organizations and institutions at Wright-Patterson Air Force Base that assisted in this project are the United States Air Force Museum; Air Force Materiel Command History Office; Air Force Institute of Technology; National Air Intelligence Center; and the Air Force Research Laboratory. Other Air Force organizations that were of assistance include the Air Staff History Support Office, United States Air Force Headquarters, Bolling Air Force Base, Washington, D.C.; U.S. Air Force Historical Research Agency, Maxwell Air Force Base, Alabama; and the Air Force Flight Test Center History Office, Edwards Air Force Base, California.

Organizations and institutions outside the Air Force that provided valuable support were the Wright State University Library, the Kettering-Moraine Museum, and the Dayton-Montgomery County Historical Society, which houses the National Cash Register (NCR) Archive. Very special thanks go to Mr. Steve Boortz, assistant manager of the U.S. Government Printing Office (GPO) in Columbus, Ohio, and Mr. Jim Cameron in GPO's Washington, D.C. marketing office. Both were exceptionally helpful in getting this book published on time and on budget. This is the most recent in a long series of publications that Mr. Boortz, working with our printing liaison, Mr. Don Yates, has produced for the History Team.

We wish to thank Colonel Mark C. Christian, the commander of the National Air Intelligence Center (NAIC), as well as Colonel Gregory J. O'Brien and Mr. Tom P. Richards, also of NAIC. Also, a special mention to Mr. Curtis A. Alley for his artistic expertise in the layout and design work for this book. His creative energy and good humor were appreciated by all.

Perhaps most significantly we thank the leadership of Aeronautical Systems Center for giving the History Team the resources and support we needed to complete this book. Nothing good happens without strong leadership from the top. Lieutenant General Robert F. Raggio requested this book be written the week he reported to ASC as commander. He was followed by Lieutenant General Richard V. Reynolds, whose strong patriotism, love of the Air Force, enthusiasm for history, and highest standards of excellence inspired us to do our best. Advocate-in-Chief for this book was Dr. Vincent J. Russo, ASC's Executive Director. His love of the Dayton community and the legacy of Wright-Patterson were contagious and served to further motivate the History Team to produce a book that did justice to the heritage that we at the Aeronautical Systems Center and all of the Air Force Materiel Command share. Daily support came from the Commander's Staff Directorate, the office where resources are controlled. Colonel Scott W. McLaughlin, followed by Colonel Ward T. Willis, ensured that that the History Office was adequately housed, equipped, and staffed for a project of this scope and for our upcoming Centennial of Flight books. Both directors were well served by their deputy, Mr. Tom M. Owens, a true master of maneuvering through the bureaucracy. From resolving personnel issues to acquiring IT equipment, Tom Owens was the man who made things happen. Without his personal assistance in removing barriers, resolving problems, and turning lemons into lemonade, this book would not have been published.

Lieutenant General Joseph H. Wehrle, Assistant Vice Chief of Staff and the dedicated members of his Air Force Centennial of Flight Office provided tremendous support, cogent advice, and the all-important funding needed to produce this publication. Locally, Wright-Patterson Air Force Base's 2003 Celebration Team, headed first by Ms. Kee Kee Schuh followed by Ms. Catherine Peterson, served as advocates of our book project and ensured that senior leadership was constantly reminded that *Splendid Vision, Unswerving Purpose* would be an appropriate and lasting contribution to the Centennial of Flight commemoration. Finally, we thank General Bernard Schriever for his advice, guidance and inspiration and, his secretary, Ms. Sue Task, for her graciousness and assistance.

To all the above, we owe a heavy debt of gratitude. The authors alone are responsible for any errors of fact or interpretation.

TABLE OF CONTENTS

List Of Tables

List Of Plans, Drawings, And Graphs

List Of Charts

List Of Maps

List Of Aerial Photographs

THE VIEW FROM HUFFMAN PRAIRIE—THE WRIGHTS AND THEIR FLYING MACHINE

A small herd of black and white cows and two brown plow horses standing in a small lot gazed across the barbed wire fence and regarded with mild concern the odd contraption nestled outside a small shed. The machine was too large to be a corn planter. Although steam-driven agricultural equipment often had small canvas covers to shade operators, this strange machine had two huge canvas covers on its body, at some distance from the ground. Moreover, the thing had an odd-looking beak and a ridiculous twin tail. Its claws seemed to be missing. In general profile the machine resembled a big bird—many times larger than the familiar chicken hawk.

As the animals watched, two men came from the open end of the shed where they had been awaiting the passage of a brief but heavy thundershower. The rain had lowered the temperature to 81° F, but the humidity remained at 66 percent. Swarms of mosquitoes and horseflies taunted and tormented their targets.

It was early afternoon, May 26, 1904. Despite the heat and humidity each man was dressed for business, in heavy, high-top, laced leather shoes; dark wool trousers; a white, long-sleeved shirt with a high, stiff collar; a vest; and a bow tie. One wore a derby. The other sported a cap. Turning his visor rakishly to the rear, 33-year-old Orville Wright wedged his lean body into a prone position in the V-shaped cradle on the white, muslin-covered lower wing of a 700-pound biplane. He lay well forward of the leading edge of the wing, with his face about 36 inches above the ground. His shoes pushed against a footrest on the trailing edge of the left wing. He held tightly to the leading edge of the wing with his right hand while using his left to work the horizontal elevator out front. This position was awkward, uncomfortable, and potentially dangerous, but it reduced wind resistance. Within a few inches of his right ear, the four-cylinder, homemade engine sputtered and crackled. The 16-horsepower engine turned two eight-foot, counter-rotating, pusher-type propellers set 10 feet apart. Sweat poured down Orville's face. Every thread of clothing was soaked. He glanced to the left wing where 37-year-old Wilbur Wright gripped a strut to help steady the biplane. Its 21-foot length was supported by wooden skids on a yoke that ran freely on two small, tandem wheels along a wooden monorail.

Conditions at 2 p.m. were far from ideal, but there had been enough delays. Orville nodded to Wilbur, who dropped his hand from the strut. The fragile biplane gathered speed as it wavered along the monorail.

Huffman Prairie, 1904 ***(Wright State University Archives, Wright Brothers Collection)***

In the air over Huffman Prairie. The pilot lay prone on the lower wing.

Orville's head and shoulders leaned forward over the edge of the wing like the bowsprit on a sleek sailing vessel. At the end of the monorail the airplane's speed was about 25 mph. The craft leaped upward to a height of eight feet and covered a distance of 25 feet before dropping to the ground.

It skidded over the sodden pasture, spraying its pilot with black mud and brown muck. It landed with sufficient force to crack several of the six-foot, white-pine spars that separated the upper and lower wings, and nearly catapulted Orville from his precarious perch.

Notwithstanding aching muscles and a sore neck, Orville smiled broadly and his blue eyes sparkled as he climbed from the wing. Wilbur grinned with delight and relief. They had flown again! They had established far better marks during their historic first flights at Kitty Hawk, North Carolina, but again they had prevailed. And a Huffman Prairie tradition was established.

Wilbur Wright, born April 16, 1867, died May 30, 1912 *(Wright State University Archives, Wright Brothers Collection)*

Orville Wright, born August 19, 1871, died January 30, 1948 *(Wright State University Archives, Wright Brothers Collection)*

CHARLES E. TAYLOR

(Federal Aviation Administration Aviation News)

Charles "Charlie" E. Taylor was born on May 24, 1868, near Cerro Gordo, Illinois. After his family moved to Lincoln, Nebraska, he attended school and then worked at several kinds of mechanical jobs. In 1894 he married Henrietta Webbert, a woman from Dayton, Ohio, and two years later he decided to relocate to her hometown in search of better job opportunities. Henrietta's uncle owned the building that housed the Wright Cycle Company in Dayton, and through him Taylor became acquainted with the Wright brothers. By the time Taylor met the Wright brothers, he had his own machine shop, and the Wrights asked for his help in making wheel hubs and coaster brakes for their bicycles. Taylor eventually went to work full-time for Wilbur and Orville because they offered him good money (30 cents an hour) and because he liked them. Katharine Wright did not care for Taylor's excessive cigar smoking (up to 20 cigars a day!), but Wilbur and Orville knew they could always count on him. They trusted Taylor to watch their bicycle shop while they were busy working on their airplane, and later they turned to him for help with their plane. Taylor helped the Wrights build a wind tunnel that could measure the lift and drag of a wide variety of wing designs. When Wilbur and Orville were finally satisfied with the design of their airplane, they discovered that they could not buy a suitable engine for it, so they told Taylor what they needed and he built it from scratch. He delivered a 12-horsepower engine that would successfully carry, for the first time in history, a man and a glider through the air. The Wright brothers' airplane flew at Kitty Hawk, North Carolina, through the power of Charlie Taylor's engine.

After the Wright brothers' first successful flight, Taylor was put in charge of the maintenance of the airplanes kept and tested at Huffman Prairie. Later, when the Wrights began manufacturing airplanes, Taylor was responsible for the manufacture of the engines. In 1911, Cal Rodgers came to town, took flying lessons from the Wrights, and signed Taylor on as his chief mechanic in his bid to become the first person to ever fly coast to coast. After the long, arduous, but ultimately successful flight of Rodgers and his Vin Fiz (a plane that had to be constantly rebuilt by Taylor and his assistants because it crashed 16 times as it made its way across the country), Taylor returned to Dayton, but in 1928 he decided to move to California. He was working as a machinist there when he was contacted by Henry Ford about going to Greenfield Village in Dearborn, Michigan, to help in the reconstruction of the Wright home and the Wright Cycle shop (both of which Ford had saved from almost certain demolition in Dayton). Taylor worked on the reconstruction for several years and even built a replica of his engine. After World War II broke out, he took a job in a factory making cartridge shells. During the last years of his life, Taylor suffered from poor health, but he also started receiving recognition for the vital role he had played in the Wright brothers' historic flight. When the public became aware of Taylor's failing health, people from all over the country sent him letters and gifts to show their gratitude, and the Aircraft Industries Association volunteered to pay for his long-term care. On January 30, 1956, the last surviving direct contributor to the First Flight passed away. He was inducted posthumously into the National Aviation Hall of Fame in 1965.

Close-up of the four-cycle Wright engine, built by Charlie Taylor, used in 1910 *(Wright State University Archives, Wright Brothers Collection)*

Sources: "Charles Edward Taylor – 1965," *National Aviation Hall of Fame Enshrinees*, online at http://www.nationalaviation.org/enshrinee/taylor.html; Tom Crouch, *The Bishop's Boys: A Life of Wilbur and Orville Wright* (New York, Norton, 1989); Howard R. DuFour, *Charles E. Taylor: The Wright Brothers Mechanician* (New Carlisle, Ohio, DuFour, 1997).

Flyer I, first flight on December 17, 1903, Kitty Hawk, North Carolina ***(NCR Archives, Montgomery County Historical Society)***

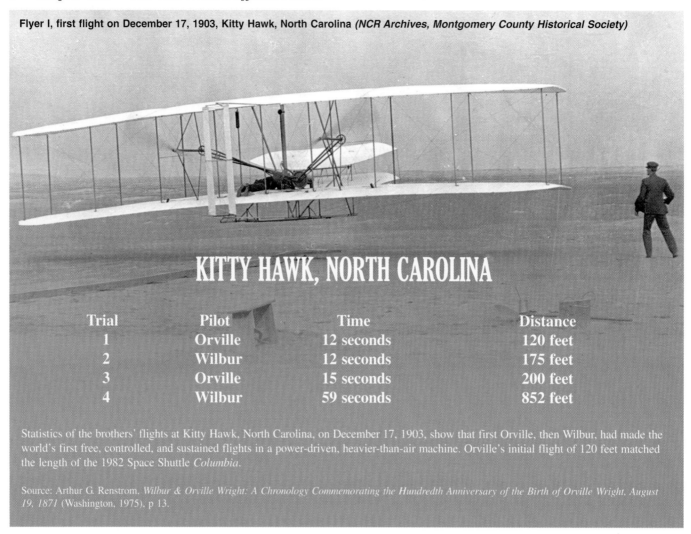

KITTY HAWK, NORTH CAROLINA

Trial	Pilot	Time	Distance
1	Orville	12 seconds	120 feet
2	Wilbur	12 seconds	175 feet
3	Orville	15 seconds	200 feet
4	Wilbur	59 seconds	852 feet

Statistics of the brothers' flights at Kitty Hawk, North Carolina, on December 17, 1903, show that first Orville, then Wilbur, had made the world's first free, controlled, and sustained flights in a power-driven, heavier-than-air machine. Orville's initial flight of 120 feet matched the length of the 1982 Space Shuttle *Columbia*.

Source: Arthur G. Renstrom, *Wilbur & Orville Wright: A Chronology Commemorating the Hundredth Anniversary of the Birth of Orville Wright, August 19, 1871* (Washington, 1975), p 13.

HUFFMAN PRAIRIE: A LOGICAL CHOICE

According to Fred Kelly, the Wright brothers' close friend and biographer, the pioneers' initial incentive had been "to gain the distinction of being the first of mankind to fly." They had not envisioned any practical use for their invention. But after their success at Kitty Hawk, they began to think the airplane "could be developed into a machine useful for scouting in warfare; for carrying mail to isolated places; for exploration; and that it would appeal to those who could afford it for sport."[1]

Their airplane, however, required considerable refinement before production models could be manufactured and sold. They also needed a great deal more experience in actual flying before they could demonstrate the machine or train pilots. "Much practice would be required . . . and that would mean more expense in proportion to income for they would have less time for building and repairing bicycles," their primary source of income.[2]

Thus, financial circumstances dictated the need to locate a site for flying and experimental work close to Dayton. The brothers selected an 84-acre farm along the eastern shore of the Mad River (a tributary of the Great Miami River) in Greene County, about eight miles east of Dayton and two miles from the Village of Fairfield.[3] Since Mr. Torrence Huffman, a prominent Dayton banker, owned the property, it was known as "Huffman Prairie." The land was mostly flat land in the river bottom or flood plain. Adjacent to the pasture's northern border were the Dayton-Springfield Pike and the track of the Dayton-Springfield-Urbana electric interurban rail system (known locally as the "Damned Slow and Uncertain"). Trolleys stopped every 30 minutes at the small depot, known as Simms Station, adjacent to Huffman Prairie. Surrounding the depot lay open farm country composed of large fields, most of them grassy and bordered by fences and clusters of tall, spreading trees. Here and there, widely separated, a house or a barn lifted a gray roof amid the lush greenery.

The site held several advantages for the struggling pioneers. Mr. Huffman allowed them to use the land rent-free with the sole restriction that the Wrights keep the farm gates closed to prevent the horses and cattle from wandering away. The trolley and the short ride from their bicycle shop solved their logistical concerns. And the field's relative isolation gave the Wrights the privacy they desired while they perfected their invention and waited for the United States government to grant them a patent.

During April and May 1904, the Wright brothers, nattily attired in business suits, commuted daily (but never on Sundays) between their workshop in Dayton and Simms Station, bringing lumber, airplane materials, and parts. They cleared the tall prairie grass with scythes. Then they erected a shed-like hangar in the southeast portion of the field, far from Simms Station, to give them privacy from prying eyes and curious spectators. When they finished, they had, as one writer noted, "erected the first airport in the world."[4]

Although the site offered comparatively flat terrain and convenient, economical transportation, it was hardly an ideal test facility. Poles and power lines ran along the northern border; a high bluff lay to the west; and 50-foot-high trees dotted the landscape. In a June 21, 1904 letter to the brothers' mentor, Octave Chanute, Wilbur wrote:[5]

> We are in a large meadow of about 100 acres. It is skirted on the west and north by trees. This not only shuts off the wind somewhat but also gives a slight downtrend. However, this matter we do not consider anything serious. The greater troubles are the facts that in addition to cattle there have been a dozen or more horses in the pasture and as it is surrounded by barbwire fencing we have been at much trouble to get them safely away before making trials. Also the ground is an old swamp and is filled with grassy hummocks some six inches high so that it resembles a prairie dog town. This makes the track-laying slow work. While we are getting ready the favorable opportunities slip away, and we are usually up against a rainstorm, a dead calm, or a wind blowing at right angles to the track.

Progress was measured in seconds and in feet. On August 4, for example, Wilbur was airborne for 20 seconds (including the run down the monorail), and traveled 272 feet.

In September, the fledgling aviators installed a catapult launching device to counter the erratic winds and increase lift at takeoff. The pyramidal tower, or "derrick" to use Wilbur's term, consisted of four 30-foot poles erected teepee-fashion at one end of the monorail. Inside the tower a heavy weight was lifted to the top and linked to the airplane by a series of pulleys and ropes. After considerable experimentation, a single weight of 1,600 pounds was found to be the most effective. Falling some 16 feet, the weight exerted a forward pull equal to 350 pounds, enough to get the aircraft into the air with "a run of only 50 feet even in a dead calm."[7] When the catapult was used for the first time, Wilbur flew over 2,000 feet.[8]

Thus, well and truly into the air, the brothers set about learning to fly and mastering flight dynamics, being always cautious to remain within the confines of Mr. Huffman's prairie in the belief that property rights extended vertically. They flew over the cows and collided with birds. On September 20, Wilbur made history's first controlled circle during a flight lasting 1 minute 3.8 seconds. On November 9, he completed four circles, covering a distance of nearly three miles in 5 minutes 4 seconds. Orville duplicated the record on December 1. By December 9, 1904, their flight log stood at 105 launches for a total flight time of 50 minutes, and a top landing speed approaching 50 mph.[9]

When the flying season ended in December, the Wrights disassembled the airplane, packed it and all their tools and gear into crates and boxes, and moved them into winter quarters in their West Dayton bicycle shop. The vacated hangar became a shelter for livestock. During the winter of 1904-1905, the aviation pioneers began working on the Wright Flyer III, the aircraft that would become the world's first practical airplane.

In spring 1905, the brothers built a slightly larger hangar closer to the Simms Station depot. Orville opened the flying season on June 23 with a flight of 272 feet in 9.5 seconds. While landing, the left wing struck the ground and cracked four corner ribs. This was hardly an auspicious start for a new campaign. Nonetheless, with the 1905 Flyer III, the Wrights finally solved the mystery of powered flight and developed the first truly practical airplane.[10]

The Wright brothers' primary source of income was a bicycle manufacturing and repair business located at 1127 W. Third Street in Dayton. This seasonal business allowed them ample time in autumn and winter for flight experimentation with gliders and the first Wright Flyers. ***(Wright State University Archives, Wright Brothers Collection)***

Milton Wright, a bishop in the Church of the United Brethren in Christ and a loyal supporter of his sons' activities, chronicled their successes in his personal diary. The first flight over Huffman Prairie was entered laconically, "Went at 9:00 [trolley] car to Huffman's farm. At 2:00 Orville flew about 25 feet. I came home on 3:30 [trolley] car. It rained soon after." ***(Photo and diary from Wright State University Archives, Wright Brothers Collection)***

EARLY WRIGHT AIRPLANES

All of the Wrights' early powered airplanes were named Flyers:

Flyer I (1903) was called the *Kitty Hawk*. After Wilbur's final flight the afternoon of December 17, 1903, a gust of wind upended the fragile aircraft. The wreckage was disassembled and the parts shipped to Dayton. In 1916, the components were reassembled, replacement parts were inserted, and the restored *Kitty Hawk* was exhibited at the Massachusetts Institute of Technology. On January 31, 1928, Orville shipped the machine to the Science Museum in London on indefinite loan for exhibition. On December 17, 1948, the 1903 airplane was installed formally in the Smithsonian Institution, Washington, D.C.

Flyer II (1904) was the first airplane over Huffman Prairie. In it, the brothers executed the first controlled circles. After the 1904 flying season ended, the engines, propellers, and other parts were used in the construction of the more powerful 1905 Flyer III.

Flyer III (1905) taught the Wrights "the secrets of powered flight," according to historian Charles Gibbs-Smith. Disassembled after the 1905 season, it was restored in June 1950 and placed on permanent exhibit at the Carillon Historical Park in Dayton, Ohio.

Military Flyer (1909), also known as Signal Corps Airplane No. 1, was the first heavier-than-air vehicle purchased by the Army. On August 2, 1909, the Aeronautical Board formally accepted the airplane at a cost of $25,000 plus a $5,000 bonus for exceeding the specified minimum speed of 40 mph by 2 mph in speed trials. For the next two years, this airplane was the only one in the Army inventory. In 1911, Signal Corps Airplane No. 1 was sent to the Smithsonian Institution for exhibition.

The 1903 Flyer I ready for its first flight, November 24, 1903 ***(Wright State University Archives, Wright Brothers Collection)***

The Flyer III over Huffman Prairie in 1905

Orville and Wilbur discuss the Flyer II at Huffman Prairie in May 1904. ***(Wright State University Archives, Wright Brothers Collection)***

The Military Flyer meets Army specifications for wagon transport, Fort Myer, August 1908. ***(Wright State University Archives, Wright Brothers Collection)***

The pioneers learned to bank, turn, and make circles and figure eights with ease. Their longest flight of the year came on October 5, when Wilbur was airborne for 39 minutes 23 seconds. He flew over 24 miles at an average speed of 38 mph while making 29 circuits of the pasture.[11]

For the next three years, Dayton remained home base while the brothers traveled to Washington and Europe and captured the attention of both. During this time their genius produced both the vehicle and the spirit that launched the U.S. Army Signal Corps into heavier-than-air flight.

THE SIGNAL CORPS MACHINE

On February 10, 1908, the newly established Aeronautical Division of the Signal Corps accepted the Wrights' bid to provide the Army with its first heavier-than-air flying machine. The proposed machine was to weigh 1,100 to 1,250 pounds and be capable of remaining in the air for at least one hour carrying two men, with a total weight of 350 pounds. It also had to achieve a speed of at least 40 mph. The

Dignitaries inspect the Wright Flyer prior to the beginning of the trials. As noted on the photo, they included: 1) Colonel Hatfield, 13th Cavalry; 2) Secretary Truman H. Newberry, U.S. Navy; 3) Major Fournier, French Military Attaché; 4) Lieutenant George Sweet, U.S. Navy; 5) General Luke Wright, [Office of the] Secretary of War; 6) Major George Squier, Signal Corps; 7) Lieutenant Richard B. Creecy, Marine Corps; 8) Mr. Funciulli. ***(Wright State University Archives, Wright Brothers Collection)***

Katharine Wright, sister of Orville and Wilbur, was the brothers' staunchest supporter and constant companion, accompanying them on their travels in the United States and Europe. ***(Wright State University Archives, Wright Brothers Collection)***

The Wright family home at 7 Hawthorn Street, Dayton, about 1900. The house, as well as the Wright Cycle Shop located at 1127 W. Third Street, was relocated to Henry Ford's Greenfield Village, Dearborn, Michigan. The dedication ceremony was held on Wilbur Wright's birthday, April 16, in 1938. Dayton inventor and General Motors executive, Charles F. Kettering, delivered the toast, and Wright-trained pilots, Frank Lahm and Walter "Brookie" Brookins, as well as Orville's good friend, English writer Griffith Brewer, addressed the crowd. ***(Wright State University Archives, Wright Brothers Collection)***

ORVILLE WRIGHT, FORT MYER, VIRGINIA, SEPTEMBER 1908

Date	Record	Statistics
September 9	Flight Endurance	1 hour 2 minutes, circling field 55 times at altitude of 80 feet
September 11	Flight Endurance	1 hour 10 minutes, circling field 57.5 times
September 12	Two-Man Flight*	9 minutes 6.33 seconds; Passenger: Major George O. Squier, president, Signal Corps Aeronautical Board
	Flight Endurance	1 hour 14 minutes, circling field 71 times at altitude of 300 feet

*The first passenger in a powered airplane had been Charles W. Furnas, a Wright brothers' mechanic who flew with Orville on May 14 at Kitty Hawk, North Carolina. The first military passenger was Lieutenant Frank P. Lahm who flew during the acceptance trials at Fort Myer on September 3, 1908.

Lieutenant Thomas Etholen Selfridge was commissioned in the Artillery Corps in 1903. In May 1908, he flew an airplane he helped design with the assistance of Alexander Graham Bell and Glenn H. Curtiss, thus making him the first military person to pilot a heavier-than-air machine. With his tragic demise at Fort Myer in September 1908, Selfridge was also the first military person to lose his life in an airplane.

price was to be $25,000, and delivery was scheduled for August 28, 1908.

The Wrights based their bid on the capabilities of their 1908 model aircraft. Designed as a military vehicle for both training and reconnaissance functions, the new airplane contained two major improvements over earlier models, one in the engine and one in the airframe. The engine had four vertical (rather than horizontal) cylinders, which raised its output to 35 horsepower, continuously.[12] The new airframe allowed for two people and, since "manifestly, for military purposes it was essential that both pilot and passenger should sit upright," the frame was fitted with two side-by-side seats.[13] Thus, the new airplane was designed to fly faster and longer, and to carry two people, upright, either of whom could control the aircraft.[14]

Before the Army would accept it, the airplane had to pass endurance and speed tests at Fort Myer, Virginia, in September 1908. The brothers decided that Orville would fly the tests. On May 17, Wilbur departed for Europe, where he spent the next year demonstrating Wright airplanes, promoting sales, and training other pilots. Orville, after extensive spring practice at Kitty Hawk, North Carolina, and summer refitting in Dayton, shipped the airplane to Fort Myer in August.

According to one observer, "when the official flight trials at Fort Myer began, the public journeyed there by the thousands to see the mystery of flight dissolved and the skeptics at last proved wrong."[15] Afternoon visitors from nearby Washington, D.C., included President William Howard Taft and many of the Cabinet members. The starting track and wooden tower for hoisting the catapult weight were erected on the Fort Myer drill ground, surrounded by buildings and tall trees. These limitations constrained straight flight, without turns, to only "a few hundred yards at the most."[16] Nevertheless, Orville treated spectators to new world's records, day after day, in flight endurance.[17]

The tests were suspended on a tragic note on September 17, when Orville and a passenger, Lieutenant Thomas E. Selfridge, crashed from an altitude of 125 feet. The accident occurred "when one of the propellers split, causing it to lose pushing power, and a stay wire to the tail was then torn loose, making the tail uncontrollable." Lieutenant Selfridge sustained a fatal skull fracture when he struck one of the wooden uprights of the framework.[18] Orville suffered a fractured left leg and four cracked ribs. He remained hospitalized at Fort Myer until late October, returning to Dayton on November 1.

The Army, however, was impressed with the airplane's overall performance prior to the crash and granted an extension of the contract delivery date until the summer of 1909.

The interim period was a productive one for the Wrights. Orville recuperated in Dayton and, in January, he and sister Katharine joined Wilbur in Europe. Wilbur had been seeking European contracts, flying in exhibitions, and training pilots in France and Italy. He flew before European heads of state, including King Edward VII of England, King Alfonso XIII of Spain, and King Victor Emmanuel III of Italy. Government and military leaders of every major power took personal note. The Wrights were celebrated and honored wherever they appeared. Their return to the United States was marked by presidential honors in Washington and the largest, most impressive homecoming Dayton could arrange.

The celebrations did not stop their progress, however. June 1909 was spent in Dayton, testing propellers to determine the cause of the accident at Fort Myer and to

THE WRIGHT BROTHERS HOMECOMING CELEBRATION JUNE 17-18, 1909

(Dayton and Montgomery County Public Library)

Daytonians came out in force to greet the Wright brothers at Union Station upon their return from Europe in 1909. The city welcomed them with a grand, two-day homecoming celebration. The festivities included the formation of a giant U.S. flag by 2,500 Dayton school children.

One of the two local medals presented to the Wrights by the Honorable Edward E. Burkhart, mayor of Dayton, at the June 18, 1909, celebration held in Dayton. The brothers also received state of Ohio medals and a special United States Congressional Medal: "In recognition of their ability, courage and success in navigating the air."

Source: Fred C. Fisk and Marlin W. Todd, *From Bicycle to Biplane* (West Milton, Ohio, 1990)

Preparing for flight at Fort Myer. The airplane is mounted on the launching rail and is being connected to the weight in the starting derrick in the background. ***(Wright State University Archives, Wright Brothers Collection)***

Poised for takeoff, June 1909. Fort Myer soldiers pull the rope raising the drop-weight to the derrick peak. ***(Wright State University Archives, Wright Brothers Collection)***

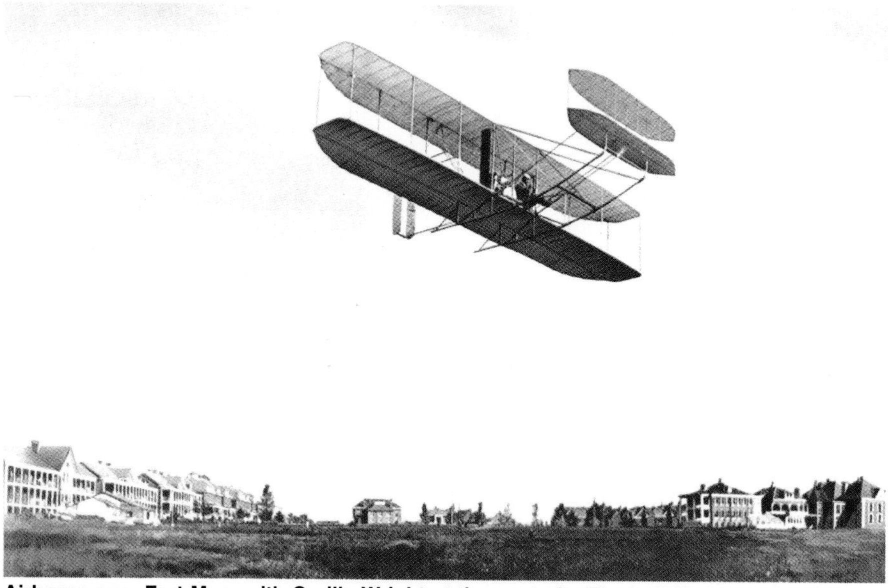

Airborne over Fort Myer with Orville Wright at the controls. The buildings surrounding the drill grounds constrained straight flight. ***(Wright State University Archives, Wright Brothers Collection)***

preclude similar problems in the upcoming flight tests.

The Wright family returned in force to Fort Myer on June 20, 1909, to resume flight tests. Wilbur was present, along with sister Katharine, but Orville did all the flying. Presumably as a matter of pride, he wanted to finish what he had started the year before.

The Wrights brought with them an improved version of their "Signal Corps machine." Overall design changes included a "combination of a front movable rudder with a fixed horizontal plane in the rear of the machine in contrast to the front horizontal rudder" of the 1903-1908 models.[19] Orville flew a series of short test flights with the new model between June 29 and July 19, then prepared for the two crucial tests of endurance and speed. To demonstrate endurance, the aircraft had to remain aloft for one hour carrying two persons. On July 27, with Lieutenant Frank P. Lahm aboard, Orville flew for 1 hour 12 minutes 37.8 seconds, thereby exceeding the Army standard and setting a new world record. President William Howard Taft was among the 10,000 cheering spectators as the airplane circled the drill field almost 80 times at an altitude of 150 feet.[20]

The speed test was flown on July 30. Orville and Lieutenant Benjamin D. Foulois, his passenger, flew a cross-country speed course between Fort Myer and Shuter's (sometimes spelled Shooter's) Hill, near Alexandria, Virginia. This first-

Officers of The Wright Company included Orville, left, and Wilbur as chief executives. ***(Wright State University Archives, Wright Brothers Collection)***

ever cross-country flight covered a round-trip distance of 10 miles.

Seven thousand witnesses, again including the president, cheered as the airplane lifted from the monorail at 6:46 a.m., then watched as it twice circled the drill field to gain altitude. Cheers dissolved into hushed murmurs as the aircraft disappeared from view in the direction of Alexandria. Even Wilbur and Katharine Wright were tight-lipped, although they had the utmost confidence in both man and machine. The airplane popped up momentarily, then disappeared again between two ridges.

When it reappeared heading straight for the drill field, the crowd waved hats, handkerchiefs, and anything else at hand. The roar of cheers and applause "was loud enough to be heard by the two air travelers despite the noise of the engine alongside them."[21] The 10-mile flight was clocked at a speed of 37.735 mph outbound, and 47.431 mph on the return, for an average speed of 42.583 mph. They had flown more than 2 mph faster than their goal of 40 mph, and had done so at an altitude of 450 to 500 feet, an exceptional height.[22]

On August 2, the Aeronautical Board formally accepted the Wright machine. Brigadier General James Allen, chief signal officer of the Army, appointed the members of the "Board of Officers Convened by Office Memorandum No. 18, Office of the Chief Signal Officer of the Army, dated June 21, 1909, for the Purpose of Observing Trials of Aeronautical Devices, Etc." Major George O. Squier, Signal Corps, was the Board's president. Lieutenant Frederic E. Humphreys, Corps of Engineers, served as the recorder. The members of the Board were Lieutenant George C. Sweet, U.S. Navy; Major Charles Saltzman, Signal Corps; Lieutenant Frank P. Lahm, Signal Corps; and Captain C. deForest Chandler, Signal Corps. Upon payment of $25,000 for the airplane and a bonus of $5,000 for exceeding by 2 mph the specified minimum speed of 40 mph, Signal Corps Airplane No. 1 entered the Army inventory.

To complete the terms of their contract, the Wrights were required to instruct two men in the handling and operation of their flying machine. (No extra payment was allowed for this purpose.)[23] Since the Fort Myer commander insisted that his drill field be returned to its primary purpose, the Army leased suitable acreage from the Maryland Agricultural College at nearby College Park, Maryland. Wilbur gave flight instruction to three Signal Corps officers:

MAJOR GENERAL BENJAMIN D. FOULOIS

Lieutenant Benjamin D. Foulois was the Army Signal Corps' official observer in the passenger seat of the Wright Flyer when Orville Wright passed the all-important speed trial on July 30, 1909, at Fort Myer, Virginia. Based on the successful completion of the speed test and a previous endurance test, the Army ordered its first airplane, Signal Corps Airplane No. 1. Foulois later described his role in that historic flight: "I would like to think that I was chosen on the basis of my intellectual and technical ability, but I found out later that it was my short stature, light weight, and map-reading experience that tipped the decision in my favor."

After returning from an aeronautical congress in France in late 1909, Lieutenant Foulois started to take flying lessons with Wilbur Wright, but after other trainees damaged Signal Corps Airplane No. 1, it and Foulois were reassigned to Fort Sam Houston in Texas where Foulois was ordered to teach himself to fly. There he became the Army's only active pilot, navigator, instructor and observer before he had even soloed in an airplane. He completed flight training on his own, writing to Orville Wright for advice. Foulois later joked that he was the world's first correspondence-school pilot.

Benjamin Foulois served as chief of the Materiel Division at Wright Field from June 1929 to July 1930 and resided in the commander's official residence, a nineteenth-century farm house located near Huffman Prairie, the field where the Wright brothers experimented with their flying machine and where they later established a flying school. During his career Foulois held numerous leadership positions. He won the prestigious Mackay Trophy for his command of the 1931 Air Corps' maneuvers that were based out of Wright Field and went on to command the U.S. Army Air Corps during the years leading up to World War II. Foulois was one of the few brave men who chose to endure personal and professional retaliation for his outspoken support for an air force independent of Army control. In later years he received belated recognition for his numerous contributions to military aviation and was honored at Wright-Patterson Air Force Base in 1989 when Building 88, his former home and now the official residence of the Aeronautical Systems Center commander, was memorialized in his honor.

Source: John F. Shiner, "Benjamin D. Foulois: In the Beginning," *Makers of the United States Air Force,* John L. Frisbee, ed. (Washington, D.C., United States Air Force, 1987).

The 1910 Wright hangar at Simms Station housed both the Wright Exhibition Company and the Wright School of Aviation. General Henry H. Arnold wrote, in 1949: "The Simms Station is gone today ... It would have been a fine exhibit in the midst of what is now sprawling Patterson Field, with Wright Field just over the hill—virtually in the center of the modern United States Air Force's technical proving ground." *(United States Air Force Museum)*

Both buildings of The Wright Company factory in West Dayton were completed in 1911. *(Wright State University Archives, Wright Brothers Collection)*

The Wright brothers experiment with pontoon hydroplanes on the Miami River, Dayton, Ohio, March 21, 1907. *(Air Force Historical Research Agency)*

Lieutenants Lahm and Foulois, both of whom had flown with Orville during the acceptance flights, and Lieutenant Frederic E. Humphreys (on special duty from the Corps of Engineers). When flight instruction ended on November 5, Wilbur was ready to join Orville in a bold, new venture.

THOSE DARING YOUNG MEN ...

Aviation became an industry in Dayton with the incorporation of The Wright Company on November 22, 1909, with Wilbur Wright as president and Orville as one of two vice presidents. The company listed a capital stock of $1 million, a New York corporate office, and a planned manufacturing facility in Dayton. It was time. Since Wilbur's European tour in 1908, airplanes designed and licensed by the Wrights had been sold abroad by French, British, and German companies.

By November 1910, construction was complete on the first of two factory buildings in West Dayton, and the company was turning out two airplanes a month. The company also leased Mr. Huffman's land, where a large, new hangar near Simms Station advertised to all that the Wrights had returned to fly over Huffman Prairie. The 1910 hangar housed two branches of the Wright corporation: the Wright Exhibition Company and the Wright School of Aviation. The exhibition company, managed by Roy Knabenshue, flew airplanes at county fairs, aero shows and exhibits, speed races, and other large public gatherings to display Wright aircraft and attract potential customers. Pilots received a salary of $20 per week, plus $50 for every day they flew. The Wright Company received any prize money earned and charged $1,000 per day each time one of the team members performed. The exhibition company, however, was short-lived. The Wrights dissolved the company and abandoned the exhibition business in 1911 due to the heavy loss of life associated with exhibition flying. Of the original nine team members, five died in airplane crashes.[24]

The second branch made Simms Station famous as the site of the Wright School of Aviation, which operated from 1910 through 1916. Other Wright schools for training "operators" were instituted at Montgomery, Alabama, now the location of Maxwell Air Force Base, in 1910; at Augusta, Georgia, in 1911; and at Belmont

PIONEER FLYERS TRAINED ON HUFFMAN PRAIRIE FLYING FIELD

Henry H. Arnold
A. Roy Brown
Cal P. Rodgers
Arch Hoxsey
P. O. Parmelee
O. A. Brindley
Harry N. Atwood
L. E. Norman
C. LaQ. Day
O. A. Danielson
Rose Dougan
Verne Carter
Maurice Coombs
Percy E. Beasley
W. E. Orchard
Louie Mitchell
Andrew Drew
C. Couturier
Farnum T. Fish
William Kabitzke
Howard M. Rinehart
W. E. Bowersox
W. J. Sussan
James L. Gordon
P. S. Kennedy
G. A. Magor
George Breadner
A. C. Harland
Harry Swan
W. E. Robinson
Kenneth Whiting
Frank T. Coffyn
C. J. Peterson
Robert E. Lee
K. G. MacDonald
Albert Elton
Charles Wald
M. B. Galbraith
Robert McC. Weir
S. T. Edwards
Frank Lahm
Charles deF. Chandler
Robert G. Fowler
Duval LaChappelle
J. C. Turpin
J. C. Henning
H. V. Hills
C. E. Utter
Marjorie Stinson
Lyle H. Scott
J. M. Alexander
E. P. Beckwith
George H. Simpson
A. G. Woodward
J. A. Harman
O. G. Simmons
A. A. Merrill
Wilfred Stevens
F. J. Southard
Maurice Priest
Al A. Bressman
L. E. Brown
C. J. Creery
Edward A. Stinson
Lloyd S. Breadner
N. A. Magor
C. E. Neidig
Harley Smith
L. B. Ault
M. S. Beal
Griffith Brewer
L. W. Bonney
C. A. Terrell
Goroku Moro
Paul Gadbois
George A. Gray
Bernard L. Whelan
Basil D. Hobbs
G. S. Harrower
C. McNicoll
John Rodgers
Thomas DeW. Milling
Walter Brookins
A. L. Welsh
Howard Gill
Harold H. Brown
A. B. Gaines Jr.
Mrs. Richberg Hornsby
C. Ando
Ferdinand Eggena
J. A. McRae
T. D. Pemberton
Gordon R Ross
A. Y. Wilks
T. C. Wilkinson
C. L. Webster
Philip W. Page
Arch Freeman
Grover C. Bergdoll
John A. Bixier
M. T. Schermerhorn
K. F. Saunders
John Galpin
M. C. Dubuc
W. H. Chisam
J. R. Bibby
A. W. Briggs
J. C. Watson
J. C. Simpson
C. G. Bronson
Ralph Johnstone
R. J. Armor
Frank Kitamura
B. B. Lewis
L. G. Ireland
J. G. Klockler
R. M. Wright
J. A. Shaw
H. B. Evans

Marjorie Stinson was one of three women who learned to fly at Huffman Prairie. She was also the only woman granted a pilot's license by the Army and Navy Committee of Aeronautics. *(War Department Records, National Archives and Records Administration)*

Some of the Canadians who earned their wings at the Wright School of Aviation are pictured at Simms Station in 1915. *(Wright State University Archives, Wright Brothers Collection)*

Lieutenant Henry H. Arnold at the Wright School of Aviation, 1911

A Model A skims down the monorail . . . *(Wright State University Archives, Wright Brothers Collection)*

and takes off . . . *(Wright State University Archives, Wright Brothers Collection)*

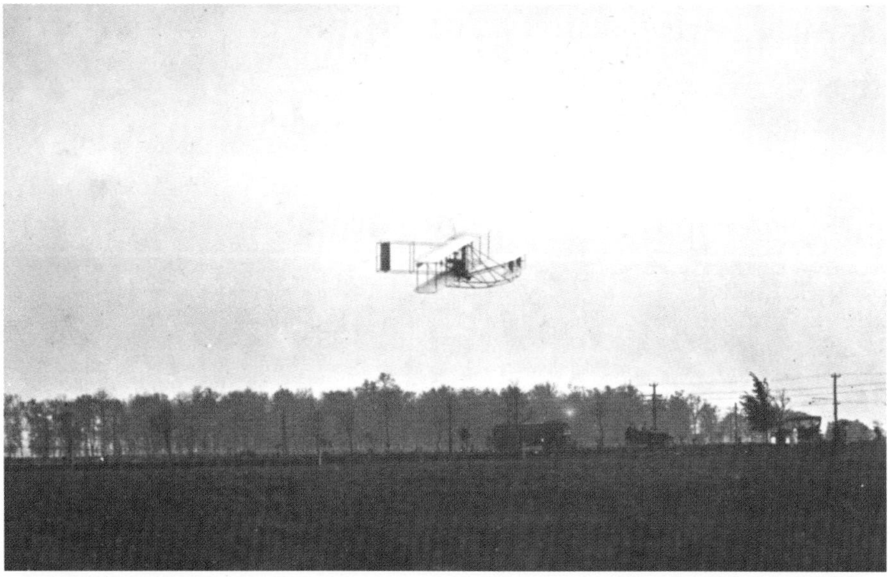

into flight over Simms Station, 1910. Model As, built between 1907 and 1909, were the first Wright machines with two seats and the first in which the crew sat upright. Orville flew a Model A during the first military trials at Fort Myer, September 1908. *(Wright State University Archives, Wright Brothers Collection)*

Park, New York, in 1911. The Simms Station School advertised "four hours of actual practice in the air and such instruction in the principles of flying machines as is necessary to prepare the pupil to become a competent and expert operator." Instruction in these necessary principles occupied students for most of their 10 days of training, with 5 to 15 minutes of each day spent in the air.

Tuition was $250 per pupil, payable at the time of enrollment, and covered any incidental "breakage to the machine." However, the airplanes used in training were equipped with duplicate controls so that the instructor could immediately assume control "should the student make any serious mistake."[25]

Diverse groups of students came to Simms Station: civilians learning to fly their own purchases, Army officers heading for instructorships at Signal Corps Aviation Schools like the one at College Park, and even officers from the Navy. (The brothers offered to train a U.S. Navy pilot if the service would order a hydroplane from The Wright Company. The Navy agreed; the airplane was delivered July 15, 1911.) The May 1911 class, for example, included three civilian students and three military officers, Lieutenant John Rodgers, U.S. Navy, and Lieutenants Henry H. Arnold and Thomas DeWitt Milling, both of the Army Signal Corps. In all, 119 pilots trained at Huffman Prairie. Many of them were Canadians en route to the Great War, including A. Roy Brown who would receive the aerial credit for downing Germany's "Red Baron" (Captain Manfred von Richthofen).

Students at the Wright School of Aviation learned about the airplane from the inside out: how to maintain, repair, and modify the machine, as well as how to fly it. Exchanging aspiration for perspiration, Arnold, Milling, Rodgers, and their classmates took off their coats and neckties, rolled up their sleeves, and got to work, skinning their knuckles and smearing oil, grease, and dirt on their shirts, trousers, and shoes. After this indoctrination on the field and in the West Dayton factory, students knew the function of every part of an airplane and understood the principles followed in putting wood, fabric, and a source of power together in a combination that permitted man to leave the ground and control his journey through the air.

Such familiarization was especially valuable to the military students. In his autobiography, *Global Mission*, Arnold commented:

> Milling and I were soon grateful for the days spent in the factory, for in addition to learning how to fly we found we would have to master the construction and maintenance features of the Wright machine well enough to teach our own mechanics the ABC of a ground crew's job when we went to our first station. There were no crew chiefs nor aircraft mechanics in the Army in those days.[26]

The schedule for Arnold's training typified the Aviation School pattern. On May 9, 1911, Lieutenant Arnold made his first flight. Chief instructor Art L. Welsh, who had earned his own wings just a year earlier, gave the seven-minute lesson. By his nineteenth flight, Arnold could land the airplane without assistance. After 28 flights and a cumulative flying time of 3 hours 48 minutes, Arnold was graduated and certified as a qualified military aviator.

The Wrights taught their students more than the mechanics of flight; they imbued them with a "can-do" spirit. As Arnold wrote in his autobiography, "More than anyone I have ever known or read about, the Wright brothers gave me the sense that nothing is impossible. I like to think—and during World War II—often did, that the Air Force has rooted its traditions in that spirit."[27]

The brothers maintained an active relationship with the Army Signal Corps aviation program, serving as consultants and teaching both pilots and instructors. These included Lieutenant Lahm and Captain Charles deForest Chandler, commandant of the Signal Corps Aviation School at College Park.[28]

The Wright Company used Huffman Prairie for other purposes as well. It served as a flight testing range for their aircraft and a staging area for several significant flights. The most noteworthy of these occurred in November 1910 when Phil Parmalee, one of their exhibition team pilots, took off in a Wright aircraft en route to Columbus, Ohio. On board was a cargo of silk for delivery to the Morehouse-Martens Company, which had paid almost $5,000 for the shipment. The one-hour flight was the first time an airplane carried commercial freight.[29]

Although they did not know it, the brothers' career as a team was drawing to a close. On May 2, 1912, Wilbur fell gravely ill with typhoid fever during a trip to Boston, Massachusetts. He returned to Dayton two days later and his condition worsened. He died May 30, 1912, at the age of 45. The entire nation mourned. President William Howard Taft, in his message to the Wright family, eulogized Wilbur as "deserving...to stand with Fulton, Stephenson, and Bell" in America's Hall of Fame for inventors.

Orville succeeded his brother as president of The Wright Company. He also carried on the tradition of invention with his development of the automatic stabilizer. Using a "special experimental machine Model E with very thick surfaces," Orville demonstrated his automatic stabilizer to three official representatives of the Aero Club of America. Seven circles of Huffman Prairie with "hands off controls" earned him the prestigious Aero Club of America Trophy of 1913 for this contribution to aviation.[30] Orville continued his personal flying career for only six years after his brother's death. On May 13, 1918, he flew the 1911 model Flyer one last time, alongside the first DeHavilland DH-4 manufactured by the Dayton Wright Company at Moraine City, south of Dayton.

Orville Wright piloting the Wright Model E. The Model E carried the automatic stabilizer that earned Orville the Aero Club of America Trophy for 1913. It also was one of only two Wright models with a single propeller. *(Wright State University Archives, Wright Brothers Collection)*

END OF AN ERA

Huffman Prairie fell silent in February 1916. It was the end of an era. Although aviation pioneers no longer flew there, their names were not forgotten. Between May 1910 and February 1916, 119 pilots earned their wings at Simms Station. Most were civilians; one even came from Japan. Several were from the U.S. Army and U.S. Navy. There were also three daring young women who defied both gravity and convention. More than a third of the graduates were Canadians. Eager for World War I duty, they bypassed over-subscribed Canadian flying schools to earn the wings required for acceptance into the Royal Flying Corps or the Royal Naval Air Service. All of their names are embossed on one of the special plaques that surround the Wright Memorial located in a 27-acre wooded park known as Wright Brothers Hill in Area B of Wright-Patterson Air Force Base. It sits atop a 100-foot bluff overlooking Huffman Prairie and Simms Station. Dedicated August 19, 1940, the memorial was conveyed to the U.S. Air Force on September 9, 1978, in honor of the 75th anniversary of the Wright's first powered flight. The part of Huffman Prairie where the original 1904 hangar stood was entered on the National Register of Historic Places on May 6, 1971, as the "world's first flying and landing field for airplanes."

DAYTON'S FLOOD OF 1913

Huffman Dam, shown here on March 25, 1922, was one of five earthen dams built to prevent another disastrous flood in downtown Dayton.

In March 1913, melting snow and a three-day-long rainstorm deluged the Miami Valley and swelled Loramie Creek and the Great Miami, Mad, and Stillwater rivers, all of which converged and ran through the heart of Dayton. Portions of downtown Dayton were flooded to a depth of 10 feet. The disaster killed nearly 400 people in the Miami Valley and caused $100 million in damages. The Miami Conservancy District, formed and led by John H. Patterson, president of National Cash Register (NCR), immediately outlined a plan to build retarding dams to control the amount of water flowing through urban areas. The Conservancy District purchased land along the rivers and proceeded to construct five earthen dams. One of the dams was along the Mad River near Huffman Prairie, where the Wright brothers had made many of their famous flights. Construction of Huffman Dam was completed in 1922, leaving Huffman Prairie in the flood plain.

The Signal Corps recognized the value of Huffman Prairie for a pilot training school and negotiated with the Miami Conservancy District to purchase the tract. This tract included Simms Station and the land on which The Wright Company established its School of Aviation between 1910 and 1916. At that time, the district did not own the land, but they immediately purchased the property from landowners and then leased it to the Signal Corps. On June 6, 1917, the Army established Wilbur Wright Field, one of four United States aviation schools for training pilots during World War I.

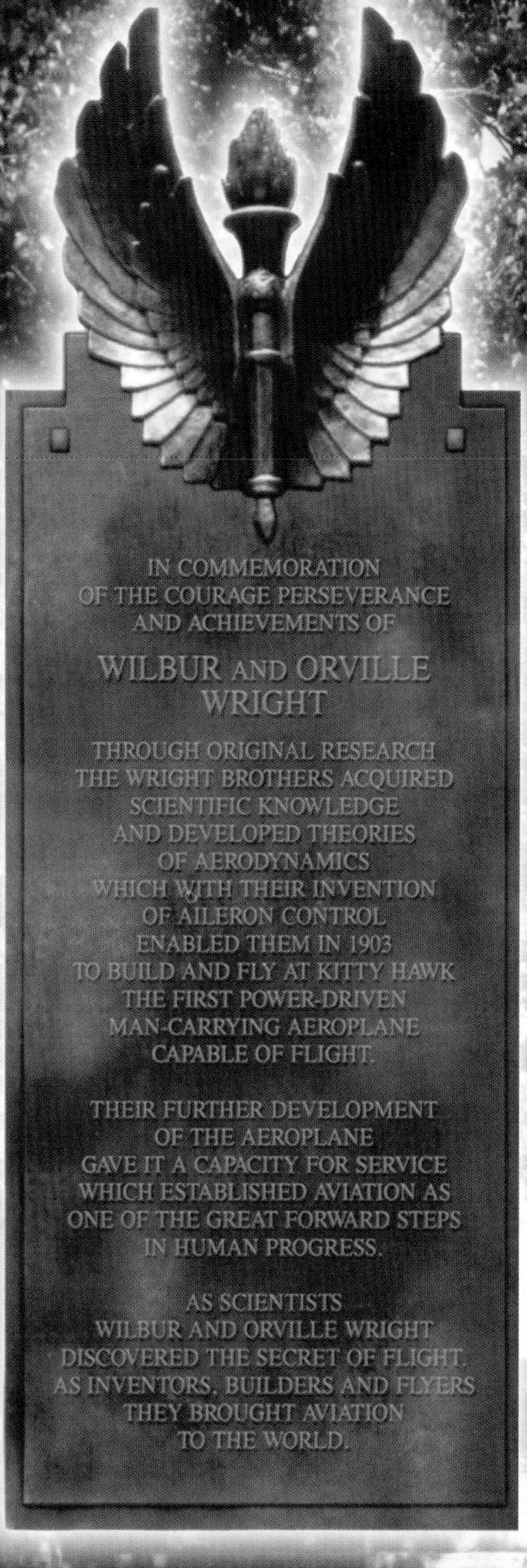
IN COMMEMORATION
OF THE COURAGE PERSEVERANCE
AND ACHIEVEMENTS OF
WILBUR AND ORVILLE
WRIGHT
THROUGH ORIGINAL RESEARCH
THE WRIGHT BROTHERS ACQUIRED
SCIENTIFIC KNOWLEDGE
AND DEVELOPED THEORIES
OF AERODYNAMICS
WHICH WITH THEIR INVENTION
OF AILERON CONTROL
ENABLED THEM IN 1903
TO BUILD AND FLY AT KITTY HAWK
THE FIRST POWER-DRIVEN
MAN-CARRYING AEROPLANE
CAPABLE OF FLIGHT.
THEIR FURTHER DEVELOPMENT
OF THE AEROPLANE
GAVE IT A CAPACITY FOR SERVICE
WHICH ESTABLISHED AVIATION AS
ONE OF THE GREAT FORWARD STEPS
IN HUMAN PROGRESS.
AS SCIENTISTS
WILBUR AND ORVILLE WRIGHT
DISCOVERED THE SECRET OF FLIGHT.
AS INVENTORS, BUILDERS AND FLYERS
THEY BROUGHT AVIATION
TO THE WORLD.

Inscription on the Wright Memorial oblesque

Orville Wright and Major General Henry H. "Hap" Arnold chat at the dedication of the Wright Memorial, August 19, 1940. *(Wright State University Archives, Wright Brothers Collection)*

Dayton dedicated its memorial to the Wright brothers on Orville Wright's sixty-ninth birthday, August 19, 1940. The 30-foot monument, made of pink North Carolina marble, overlooks the vast expanse of land that is Wright-Patterson Air Force Base and includes Torrence Huffman's Huffman Prairie.

One of the National Aeronautics and Space Administration's (NASA) latest ideas for improving aircraft performance is actually based on an old idea borrowed from the inventors of flight, Wilbur and Orville Wright. In a joint program with engineers from the Air Vehicles Directorate of the Air Force Research Laboratory (AFRL) at Wright-Patterson Air Force Base, NASA researchers based their Active Aeroelastic Wing project on the Wright brothers' system of "wing warping." In order to make a Wright Flyer turn, the Wrights "warped" or twisted the wings, as birds do in flight. Later it was discovered that aerodynamic forces naturally wreak havoc on an airplane's wings and, in an effort to reduce the lack of flight control, airplane wings were shortened and made less flexible—and less efficient.

NASA and AFRL scientists hope to "harness" aerodynamic forces and use them to maneuver planes with less drag and increased fuel efficiency. An F/A-18 was modified by Boeing Phantom Works to be the research vehicle for the Active Aeroelastic Wing project. The wings of the F/A-18 were modified to enable them to make slight twisting movements that control the roll of the plane without the use of ailerons and flaps. Data from this research project, based upon early twentieth-century know-how, will streamline many types of twenty-first century commercial and military aircraft.

Sources: "Wing innovation takes NASA back to future," *Dayton Daily News*, March 27, 2002, Business Section, pp 1E, 6E. Photographs from the NASA Dryden Flight Research Center Photo Collection, online at http://is2.dfrc.nasa.gov/gallery/photo/index.html.

This close-up of the Model A used at Simms Station in 1910 shows the wing warp that was essential for flight stability. *(Wright State University Archives, Wright Brothers Collection)*

Boeing Phantom Works modified the wings on this F/A-18 to enable them to warp. Research data from the flight test of this aircraft provides NASA and the AFRL Air Vehicles Directorate at Wright-Patterson Air Force Base with information needed to make Active Aeroelastic Wing technology practical. *(NASA)*

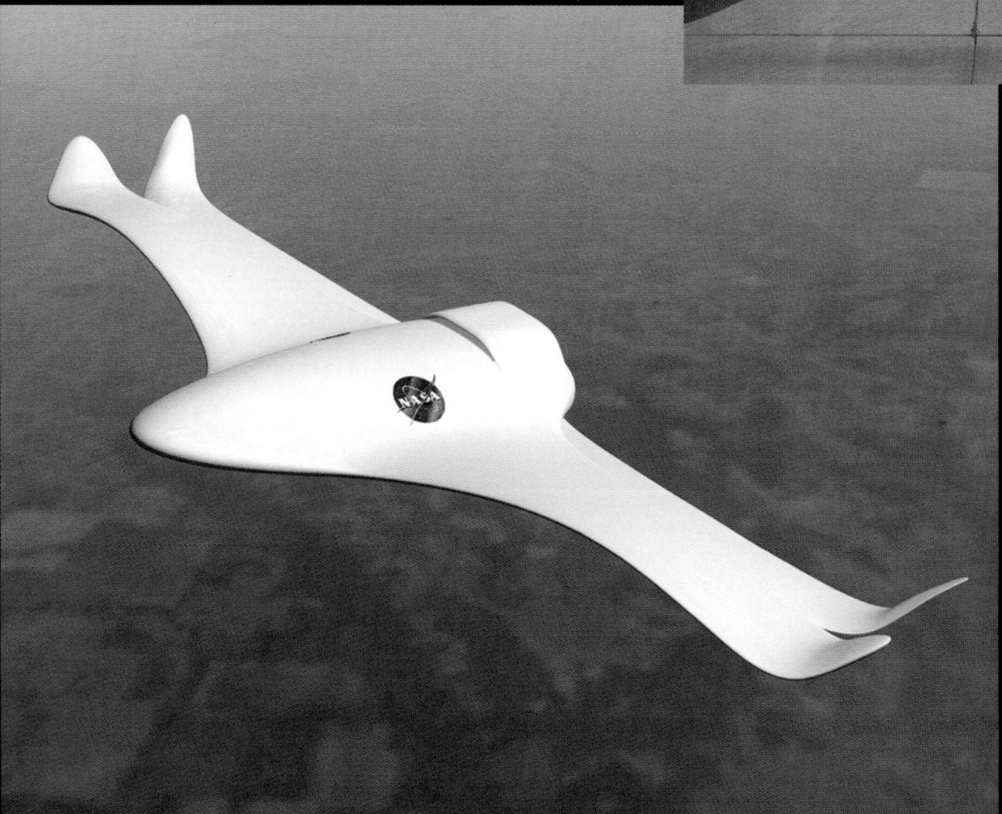

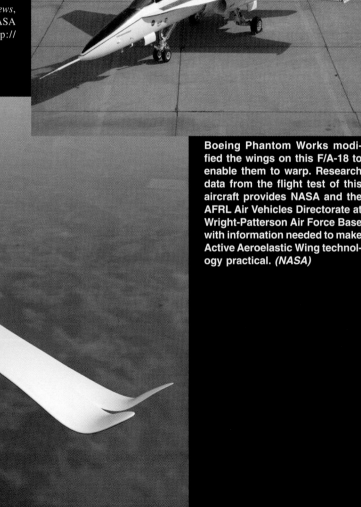

A NASA illustration of a possible future aircraft with active aeroelastic wings that make a tail unnecessary. *(NASA)*

THE CRADLE OF AVIATION—MCCOOK FIELD

The story of McCook Field began several years prior to U.S. entry in World War I. On March 3, 1915, eight months after the Aviation Section of the Signal Corps was created, Congress established a National Advisory Committee for Aeronautics (NACA). This committee, composed of representatives from the War, Navy, Treasury, Commerce, and Agriculture departments, was tasked to direct studies that would generate data vital to the improvement of American military aviation. NACA's foremost concern was the war in Europe. Although America was not yet directly involved, leading members of the military establishment thought it prudent to assess American aviation capabilities. Should America enter the war, they believed an effective aerial force might be the deciding factor in an Allied victory.

The Aviation Section in 1916 could claim only a handful of aeronautical engineers and draftsmen. It was no secret that the United States lagged far behind the rapid developments taking place in Europe due to wartime demands. U.S. engineers had little experience with military aircraft design and aircraft production was performed basically one airplane at a time. NACA members were determined to rectify these deficiencies.

Congress granted NACA authority to conduct research and experimentation "in any laboratory, in whole or in part, which may be assigned to it."[1] What the committee discovered, however, was that no such facility existed. In the summer of 1916, the committee concluded it had no alternative but to construct its own research facility, one that would be shared jointly by

McCook Field, "Cradle of Military Aviation Development," along the eastern bank of the Great Miami River in Dayton *(Mrs. Darlene Gerhardt)*

NACA, the Army, and the Navy. Property was purchased near Hampton, Virginia, and in April 1917 construction began on the installation that would become Langley Field.

These efforts, however, were quickly overcome by events. The United States declared war against Germany on April 6, 1917. Although appropriations for aviation had been increased five months earlier (to $14 million on November 16, 1916), the engineering and aircraft manufacturing industries lacked sufficient time to gear up for the tremendous demands of wartime production. Nor could NACA help them.

Six days after the declaration of war, Congress appointed a second body to work specifically within the area of aircraft production. The Aircraft Production Board was created to coordinate all activities of the nation's aircraft manufacturers during the massive build-up to follow. It was also to ensure that the resources and raw materials required by the manufacturers were available to them. The Board worked on behalf of both the War Department and the Department of the Navy, directing the completion of contracts let by both departments.

The expectations made of the Aircraft Production Board were staggering. Signal Corps records show that in the eight years prior to 1916 only 59 airplanes had been ordered and received. During 1916, 366 airplanes had been requisitioned, but only 83 had been delivered.[2] The United States government was, therefore, woefully unprepared when an urgent cable arrived from Premier Alexandre Ribot of France on May 26, 1917. The premier requested 16,500 aircraft, 5,000 trained pilots, and 50,000 "mechanicians" as America's contribution to the Allied effort for the first six months of the 1918 campaign.[3] Although this goal was far greater than the United States ever hoped to accomplish, it did spark action in Congress. Between May 12 and July 24, 1917, President Woodrow Wilson signed a series of three bills appropriating a total of $694,250,000 for military aeronautics.[4] In a spirit of enthusiasm, a program was proposed calling for the production of 12,000 service airplanes; 4,900 primary, advanced, and fighting airplanes; and 24,000 service engines by June 30, 1918.[5]

Even these goals were out of reach. America's aeronautical engineers were not versed in mass production techniques. They knew very little about the special equipment needed to fit an airplane for military use, and even less about writing technical manufacturing specifications for mass production of that equipment. Aerial machine guns, bombing equipment, lights for night flying, aviators' clothing, compasses used in flying, and other aviation instruments had not been studied and developed to the extent they had been by the Europeans. Moreover, the Allied nations involved in the development of military aviation were extremely secretive about their efforts. The United States, by not participating earlier in the war, had been excluded from access to these contemporary research findings. As Newton D. Baker, former secretary of war, wrote in 1919:[6]

> Probably no military secrets were more closely guarded in Europe than developments in aircraft. As a consequence, when we entered the war, airplane construction in the United States was upon a most limited scale, and our knowledge of developments which had taken place in Europe was largely hearsay.

Attention was suddenly focused on the need for the intensive program of fundamental research and experimentation forecast earlier by the members of the National Advisory Committee for Aeronautics. Progress at Langley, unfortunately, was painfully slow. After war was declared, the civilian contractor constructing the facilities received urgent orders to increase his workforce and accelerate operations. This extra pressure only served to cause confusion and inefficiency. Construction actually slowed, and Langley played only a limited role in World War I.[7] The Navy grew impatient with these construction delays and moved its operations to experimental bases elsewhere. The Aviation Section of the Signal Corps decided to pursue a similar course.

AN ALTERNATIVE TO LANGLEY FIELD

Industrialist Edward A. Deeds was a key member of the Aircraft Production Board and a prominent member of the Dayton business community. He was president of the Delco Company, past president of The National Cash Register Company, and a director of the Dayton Metal Products Company (which made fuses for the Russian government).[8] His interest in aviation

Distinguished Dayton aviation supporters and Army Air Service leaders attended a testimonial dinner on February 22, 1919, honoring Colonel Edward A. Deeds who was instrumental in establishing Wilbur Wright Field and McCook Field. Prominent guests were (front row, left to right) Orville Wright; Major General George O. Squier, and Colonel Deeds; (back row, left to right): Charles F. Kettering, Lieutenant Harold H. Emmons, Lieutenant Colonel Leonard S. Homer, Harold E. Talbott, Walter S. Kidder, Colonel Thurman H. Bane, Colonel M. F. Davis, and Dr. S. W. Stratton. ***(NCR Archives, Montgomery County Historical Society)***

An amphibious Grumman G-21 Goose sits at South Field on Colonel Edward A. Deeds' Moraine Farm. (*Kettering-Moraine Museum*)

and his understanding of the need to develop America's air power stemmed from his personal friendship with Wilbur and Orville Wright, nurtured from their early days on Huffman Prairie.

Deeds was well known in Washington circles by virtue of his service on the Munitions Standards Board. He served on the Aircraft Production Board from May 17 to August 2, 1917. On August 2, he was appointed acting chief of the newly created Equipment Division of the Signal Corps. Three weeks later, on August 24, he was commissioned as a colonel in the Signal Corps Reserve and was officially promoted to the position of chief of the Equipment Division. In order to accept a commission, Deeds relinquished his ties with private business and his financial connections, retaining only the presidency of the Board of Directors of the Miami Conservancy District (a non-partisan, state-chartered public organization).[9]

The Equipment Division oversaw the production of thousands of airplanes and engines within only a few months. Under Colonel Deeds' leadership, the division was authorized to spend upwards of $350 million. Deeds initially was assigned 14 officers and 111 civilians. His staff grew to 300 officers and 2,700 civilians within six months.[10] When he assumed command of the Equipment Division, the colonel found a fragmented engineering program. Pending completion of Langley Field, Signal Corps engineering projects were being conducted in several different locations, including Washington, Detroit, Chicago, and Buffalo.[11] Deeds was constantly frustrated by the slow progress of the dispersed aviation program. It was evident that production problems were exacerbated by the absence of a strong, supportive central engineering and experimental facility. He gave top priority to establishing a temporary facility, aside from Langley Field, where shops, laboratories, hangars, a flying field, offices, and other appropriate facilities could be centralized in one location.

The area of the country most familiar to Deeds was Dayton, Ohio. He also knew a good deal about the potential for aviation development in Dayton. In 1916, Deeds had established one of the first private flying fields in the United States—South Field, at his south Dayton estate, Moraine Farm. He had equipped it with a hangar and a research laboratory, and permitted its later use as a testing ground for airplanes manufactured by the Dayton Wright Airplane Company (which Deeds helped to establish).[12]

During 1916, Colonel Deeds also had invited Dayton inventor Charles F. Kettering and Orville Wright to inspect "a plot of 120 acres adjoining Triangle Park in the outskirts of Dayton," a tract lying between the Miami River and present-day Keowee Street, to determine its suitability for use as a public aviation field.[13] When asked if he felt the land would make a good landing field, Orville Wright allegedly replied:[14]

> This is admirably adapted for use in cross-country flights which are sure to come. The long curved stretch of land admits of landing from every direction. With coast-to-coast flying the southern route . . . through Dayton must be taken.

Mr. Wright also believed that the field, once cleared and leveled, would be useable as a training field for light airplanes. Thus encouraged, Deeds secured options on the land and purchased it with Kettering in March 1917. This site became known as North Field. Initial leveling work at North Field began on March 13 but was not completed, most likely because Deeds and Kettering almost immediately became engrossed in wartime work.[15]

When the chief of the Equipment Division was asked to locate an appropriate site for a temporary Signal Corps experimental station, Colonel Deeds' thoughts turned first to the South Field property in Dayton. Many people, including engineers at the

In 1918, Charles F. Kettering, a Dayton Wright Company board member, designed the Kettering Aerial Torpedo, nicknamed the "Bug." The $400 torpedo was a 300-pound papier-mâché airplane with 12-foot cardboard wings and a 40-horsepower engine. It could carry 300 pounds of explosives at 50 mph. First tested on October 2, 1918, the flying bomb had impressive range and accuracy. The Army ordered a number of "Bugs," but the bombs were not used in combat because officials worried about their reliability, especially when carrying explosives over Allied troops. Lessons learned from the "Bug," hailed as the world's first guided missile, later contributed to radio-controlled drones. (*Montgomery County Historical Society*)

Equipment Division, considered Dayton to be a nearly ideal site for such a facility. It was in the middle of the nation's industrial region, had a centralized position with respect to the major aeronautical manufacturing agencies, and boasted a local pool of trained labor. Since time was of the essence and Dayton possessed facilities that were already partially developed, there seemed little need to search further.

The engineers of the Equipment Division presented a formal request to the Aircraft Production Board to locate a temporary facility in Dayton at South Field. The Aircraft Production Board appointed a committee to evaluate the site and assess its suitability. Lieutenant Colonel Virginius E. Clark and Majors Jesse G. Vincent and E. J. Hall were selected to represent the Signal Corps. They were dispatched to Dayton to meet with the other committee members, Albert Kahn, an architect from Detroit, and Charles F. Kettering, who represented the Dayton Wright Airplane Company. Another Dayton Wright executive, Harry E. Talbott, Sr., also joined the committee for its Dayton meeting.[16]

COUNCIL OF NATIONAL DEFENSE

Aircraft Production Board
Washington

RESOLUTION passed at meeting of Board on September 27, 1917.

WHEREAS, great delays are being incurred in starting production of the army combat program because of lack of central engineering and experimental facilities, engineering now being done in Washington at the Bureau of Standards, Smithsonian Building and Old Southern Railway Building; at Mineola; New Haven; Dayton; Detroit; Chicago; and Buffalo, and

WHEREAS, a Board of Engineers, consisting of Lieutenant Colonel Clark, Major Vincent, Major Hall, and Captain Marmon, have asked that immediate steps be taken to provide for the proper facilities to meet their requirements, and

WHEREAS, after investigation they have recommended that temporary arrangements be made in Dayton where this work can be centralized, Dayton being located within a night's ride of Indianapolis, Detroit, Buffalo, Cleveland, Chicago, Pittsburgh, Washington, and the East, and

WHEREAS, a favorable location is immediately available, being in daily use by the Wright Field Company for private training and experimental work; some hangars and small repair shops already constructed, all of which can be taken over by the Government on a satisfactory basis, the field itself being particularly suitable for experimental test work, and is located within convenient distance of the Wilbur Wright Field, on which field it is possible to test out the largest and fastest machines, and

WHEREAS, this field is conveniently served by City service with water, gas, electricity, street car facilities, with an abundant supply of highly skilled labor available, and

WHEREAS, it will be perhaps considerable time before the permanent construction at Langley Field will be in effective operation, and suitable mechanics secured and housed,

NOW THEREFORE BE IT RESOLVED: that the request of the engineers be approved and the Aircraft Production Board recommend to the Chief Signal Officer that the Construction Division be instructed to provide at once such additional temporary facilities as are necessary to meet the emergency now existing.

AIRCRAFT PRODUCTION BOARD
By

(signed)
Executive Secretary
Captain Signal Corps, U.S.A.

WILBUR WRIGHT FIELD, 1917-1925

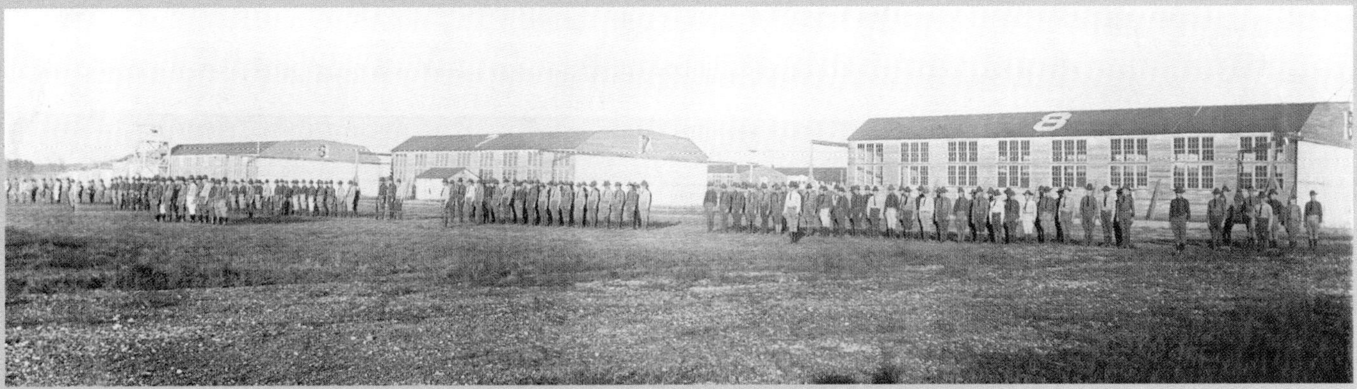

Signal Corps Aviation School flying cadets stand roll call behind Wilbur Wright Field hangars, spring 1918.

Wilbur Wright Field, Ohio, officially opened in June 1917. Named after Wilbur Wright, who died of typhoid fever in 1912, the airfield played a significant role in training men destined for combat operations in Europe. The new field, situated on 2,000 acres of flood plain leased from Dayton's Miami Conservancy District, included the original Huffman Prairie used as a flying field by the Wright brothers. The new field's primary mission was to administer the Signal Corps Aviation School, one of the largest aviation schools in the nation. The first class of flying cadets began instruction on June 28, 1917. By the end of the year, 796 students attended the school, and of those, 82 graduated with a rating of Reserve Military Aviator and were given commissions as second lieutenants in the Reserve Corps. Flight instruction shifted to schools in warmer climates during the winter months, but resumed at Wilbur Wright Field the following April.

During the winter lull, Wilbur Wright Field accepted several additional administrative responsibilities. The Aviation Mechanics' School opened in December 1917 to fill a critical need for airplane mechanics in the Allied forces. Three-week-long courses at the school provided training in three specialties: airplane, airplane motor, and motor transport. By the time the school closed in April 1918, it had graduated 1,181 students. The Aviation Armorers' School opened at Wilbur Wright Field in March 1918 to train officers and enlisted men in the new field of aerial armament. Six-week-long courses provided instruction in machine guns, gun sights, synchronization methods, and the storage and mounting of bombs. Wilbur Wright Field also established a program for testing and inspecting machine guns to insure all armament remained in proper working condition. Finally, the field provided hangar space and maintenance support for airplane testing initiated at nearby McCook Field.

World War I ended on November 11, 1918, and the Aviation School and Armorers' School demobilized soon thereafter. In January 1919, Wilbur Wright Field administratively merged with the Fairfield Aviation General Supply Depot and the two installations became the Wilbur Wright Air Service Depot. At that time, the field primarily served as a storage site for war surplus materiel. Airplane testing associated with McCook Field continued, and testing facilities expanded to include a high-altitude bombing range; a two-mile, electrically timed speed course; and equipment for testing machine gun butts. In August 1924, the city of Dayton donated 4,500 acres, including the leased land on which Wilbur Wright Field stood, to the United States government. One year later, the designation "Wilbur Wright" was discontinued and the new expanded facility became Wright Field, in honor of both Wright brothers. Orville Wright attended the formal dedication ceremony held in 1927.

Wilbur Wright Field, July 1923
(United States Air Force Museum)

Many pilots who flew so courageously with the Air Service, American Expeditionary Forces, in France during World War I received their primary flight training at Wilbur Wright Field. The biplane trainers most frequently used were the Curtiss JN-4D Jenny (left) and the Standard SJ-1. These single-engine airplanes featured two open cockpits in tandem and fabric-covered fuselages and wings. They each cost approximately $6,000. *(United States Air Force Museum)*

Officials of the Dayton Wright Airplane Company pose in front of a DeHavilland DH-4 observation airplane at the Moraine facility, April 27, 1918. The company manufactured these British-designed airplanes for the U.S. Army Air Service and the Royal Flying Corps. (*NCR Archives, Montgomery County Historical Society*)

DeHavilland DH-4 airplane fuselages awaiting wings at the Dayton Wright Airplane Company, August 24, 1918. Dayton Wright produced nearly three-fourths of the more than 4,500 British-designed DH-4 airplanes manufactured in the United States between 1917 and 1918.

Although the Aircraft Production Board had not yet received a report from its committee in Dayton, it adopted a resolution on September 27, 1917, approving the request of the Equipment Division engineers. The resolution then went forward to Brigadier General George O. Squier, chief signal officer, for action.

THE ESTABLISHMENT OF MCCOOK FIELD

Events in the closing days of September 1917 moved swiftly. The Aircraft Production Board resolution was adopted and forwarded on September 27. On the 28th, General Squier directed a memo to the adjutant general of the Army recommending approval for construction of temporary buildings "on former Wright Flying Field" (South Field, not to be confused with nearby Wilbur Wright Field). The cost was set at $350,000 plus $25,000 to pay for existing buildings.[17]

Later the same day (September 28), however, Lieutenant Colonel C. G. Edgar of the Construction Division received a telegram from J. K. Grannis, the superintendent of construction. Grannis, who was in Dayton examining the site, stated that the evaluation committee's decision was to change the location of the experimental station "from South Field to Triangle Park."[18] Undaunted, General Squier immediately sent a second memo to the adjutant general, worded identically to the first memo, except that it recommended approval for construction of temporary buildings "in Triangle Park" (North Field). Estimated cost was still $350,000.[19] As it turned out, events in Dayton had not unfolded as planned. The Dayton Wright Airplane Company objected to the Equipment Division's proposal to locate its facility at South Field. If the Equipment Division took over use of the flying field, it would be impossible for the Dayton Wright Company to fulfill its defense contract obligations for engineering work on the DeHavilland DH-4 and the DeHavilland DH-9.[20]

Yet Kettering and Talbott of the Dayton Wright Company had a genuine desire to assist the war effort. Considering the urgency of the situation, they suggested to the committee that North Field might be an equally acceptable site for the station. They pointed out that North Field was closer to the city than the Moraine site and more easily reached by municipal transportation. Its terrain better lent itself to the

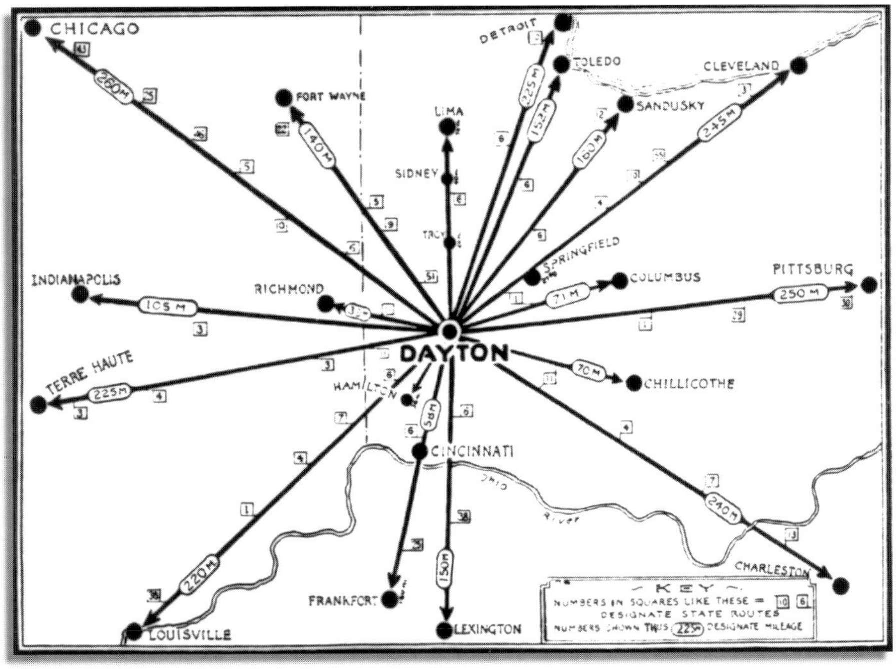

Dayton was viewed as a central location for Air Service engineering activities, being "within a night's ride of Indianapolis, Detroit, Buffalo, Cleveland, Pittsburgh, Washington, and the East."

The "Fighting McCooks," often spoken of as one family, were the collective sons of two brothers, Major Daniel McCook (top) and Dr. John McCook. Every son of both families, a total of 15, was a commissioned officer during the Civil War, except Charles Morris McCook, who declined a commission in the regular army, preferring to serve as a private in a regiment of volunteers. Charles was killed in the first battle of Bull Run. General Alexander McDowell McCook (below) was one of Daniel McCook's sons. *(National Archives and Records Administration)*

construction of buildings, and it had more ready access to gas, electric, and, especially, sewer facilities.

The committee immediately visited the North Field location. After determining that this alternate site would fit the bill, Mr. Grannis submitted his telegram to Washington. In a confirmation letter posted the same day, Grannis quoted the plans that Colonel Clark and Major Vincent had outlined already for a main building of "two stories, Workshop below, Office and Drafting room above, 60 ft wide and 600 ft long," and for an airplane assembly building "90 ft wide and 270 ft long, having two 135 ft doors, 30 ft high on the longface."[21] Colonel Deeds gave his immediate approval to the selection of the North Field site.

By the first of October all confusion had been cleared up. A memo from Deeds to Colonel Edgar, dated October 1, stated: "Chief Signal Officer on Saturday signed the paper setting aside the appropriation for the construction work at North Field in Dayton for the experimental engineering work. Mr. Craighead, the attorney from Dayton, will be here Wednesday to close up the lease."[22]

On the same date (October 1), the Aircraft Production Board adopted a resolution to name the new temporary field:[23]

> WHEREAS, the field which has been selected for temporary experimental and engineering purposes at Dayton, Ohio, has been until recently in possession of the "Fighting McCook" family for over one hundred years, and,
>
> WHEREAS, Major Daniel McCook, the head of this family and his nine sons, were all officers in the Civil War, all but one being wounded and six being killed, one of the survivors being Major General Alexander McDowell McCook, who did such distinguished service both during and after the war,
>
> THEREFORE BE IT RESOLVED: that this temporary experimental and engineering field be called the "McCook Field" in honor of the McCook family.

The terms of the lease agreement were worked out in Washington. Colonel Deeds first conveyed his interest in North Field to his co-owner, Charles F. Kettering. Mr. Kettering, in turn, conveyed the property to the Dayton Metal Products Company (Deeds had withdrawn his interest in this company at the time he went to work for the government). An agreement was then drawn up whereby the Dayton Metal Products Company would lease the acreage to the government. The amount of rent agreed upon for the property was $9,493.26 from October 4, 1917, to June 30, 1918, with an annual lease of $12,800 per year commencing July 1, 1918, renewable from year to year until June 30, 1921.[24]

Main Street, McCook Field, 1918

The area occupied by McCook Field officially measured 254.37 acres. It was located geographically one and one-half miles from the center of the city of Dayton, bounded by Herman Avenue on the south, Keowee Street on the east, and the Miami River on the north and west. The girth of the field was 14,677 feet.[25]

On October 13, 1917, Signal Corps Office Memorandum No. 22 formalized the existence of McCook Field. The memo announced that in order to "centralize engineering work and fix responsibility," the Engine Design Section and the Plane Design Section from Langley Field were being merged into a single organization, to be known as the Airplane Engineering Department. Its headquarters were to be located in temporary facilities at Dayton, "where its activities would be within a night's ride of Indianapolis, Detroit, Buffalo, Cleveland, Pittsburgh, Washington, and the East."[26] It was clearly stated that McCook Field was to be a temporary experimental station for engineering purposes only, and not a military post.

THE CONSTRUCTION PROCESS

Although the lease for the McCook Field property was not signed until October 4, 1917, the crucial decisions had been made and plans were under way. Albert Kahn had finished the architectural studies and drawings. Contracts for construction of the first group of buildings at McCook were awarded two days before the signing of the lease, on October 2, to the Dayton Lumber and Manufacturing Company.[27] To expedite matters, Superintendent Grannis was authorized by the Construction Division to purchase all necessary materials from local sources.

The first order of business before buildings could be erected and the runway constructed was to prepare the land. Some work had been done already. When Deeds and Kettering began developing the site as a public flying field, they had ordered preliminary grading, including removal of an old river embankment. The experimental flying anticipated at McCook, however, required that the field be graded absolutely flat, rolled, and sodded.[28] Inadequate site drainage complicated grading problems. The natural topography of the land constituted the primary difficulty, compounded by the fact that the storm sewers surrounding the field were too high for drainage. A French drain had to be constructed to handle storm drainage, and sink pumps had to be installed in the gravel stratum underlying the field to drain particularly difficult sections.[29]

According to Captain H. H. Blee in his "History of Organization and Activities of Airplane Engineering Division," actual construction work was started on October 10, 1917, "and pushed ahead with astonishing rapidity. Large forces of workmen were employed working in shifts day and night, seven days a week."[30] Construction was carried out by two shifts of men daily, with a total of 900 men in both shifts. This pace continued for 24 working days. At that time the first building was sufficiently complete to allow the wood and metal shops to install some machinery and begin work. Subsequently, 100 men spent an additional 28 days in finishing the building. Construction of the Final Assembly building began on October 25. It also used two shifts of men, totaling 400 in both shifts, for 35 working days. Final work was completed in 60 more days with a crew of 120 men.[31]

The initial buildings erected at McCook Field in the fall of 1917 were the engineering and shops building, the Final Assembly building, main hangar, garage, barracks, mess hall, cafeteria, transformer house, and engine test stands. Two existing structures at the field housed the dynamometer laboratory and the engine assembly building. Upon its completion, a central heating plant provided heat to nearly all buildings on station.[32] Because many of these buildings were designed as "temporary construction," special precautions were taken to provide fire protection to them. Modern

The motto emblazoned on McCook's main hangar cautioned all pilots to plan ahead. At 100 feet wide and 1,000 feet long, the macadamized runway barely accommodated the successively heavier and more powerful Air Service airplanes designed by engineers at McCook Field. *(Dayton and Montgomery County Public Library)*

fire equipment on station and a standby fire protection system using the Dayton water mains came into existence.[33]

The runway at McCook Field was a definite improvement over the bumpy grass strips to which most pilots of the day were accustomed. The special macadam-and-cinder runway was 1,000 feet long and 100 feet wide to allow the best possible conditions for flight testing. The runway had to be laid across the short expanse of the field, however, in order to take advantage of the prevailing winds. This resulted in extremely short approach and takeoff distances due to surrounding obstacles (trees, the river, etc.). It also led to the coining of McCook Field's motto, "This Field Is Small—Use It All," which was emblazoned on the front of one of the hangars. (As aircraft grew in size and power, this constraint became one of the major factors that forced McCook's activities to relocate to Wright Field in 1927.) The macadamized runway was the principal runway used, especially under poor weather conditions or when the ground was soggy, but aircraft also made use of other portions of the flying field that were heavily rolled and sodded.

A high fence with lookout towers encircled the installation. Once research and experimentation activities commenced, military armed guards stood watch 24 hours a day "in order to protect activities at McCook from the machinations of spies."[34]

Taxiway to the McCook Field runway (center right), spring 1919 *(Air Force Wright Aeronautical Laboratory Technical Library)*

Administrative building which housed the offices of the chief of the Airplane Engineering Division, the assistant chief, and the adjutant, as well as the Divisional Planning Section

Air Service officers assigned to McCook Field in 1919 included many who went on to distinguish themselves in Air Force history. Among those pictured are: Colonel Thurman Bane, Lieutenant Muir S. Fairchild, Lieutenant John Macready, Lieutenant Leigh Wade, Lieutenant Harold Harris, Lieutenant Albert Hegenberger, and Captain George Kenney.

OPERATIONS BEGIN

As stated earlier, McCook Field was created as the main facility of the Airplane Engineering Department, a consolidation of the Plane Design Section and the Engine Design Section from Langley Field. Lieutenant Colonel Clark of the Plane Design Section was designated officer in charge of the new department and thus became the first commanding officer of McCook Field. Major Vincent, chief of the Engine Design Section, became executive officer.

As executive officer, Major Vincent immediately went to Dayton to begin transfer arrangements for those activities relocating to McCook.[35] In late October, Lieutenant H. E. Blood (Engine Design Section) joined Major Vincent in Dayton, bringing with him the first contingent of personnel and equipment. Because construction at the field was only in its initial stages, the engineering personnel set up temporary headquarters in downtown Dayton, leasing two floors of the Lindsey Building at 25 South Main Street for department offices.[36]

Major General George O. Squier served as chief signal officer, U.S. Army, from 1917 to 1923 *(United States Air Force Museum)*

On November 5, 1917, Chief Signal Corps Officer Major General Squier signed Office Memorandum 53 assigning functional responsibility to the Airplane Engineering Department at McCook for all technical and experimental work previously conducted at Langley.[37] On November 22, General Squier further specified the division of work between Langley and the Airplane Engineering Department. Responsibility for engine and plane development, installation of cameras on experimental airplanes, and work on the synchronization of machine guns was assigned to McCook. Work continued at Langley under other commands included instruction and experimentation in bombing, photography, radio, telegraphy, and all demonstrations of foreign airplanes.[38]

The first troops assigned to McCook arrived in Dayton on November 14, 1917.[39] The 246th Aero Squadron from Kelly Field, Texas, consisted of 90 men and came to McCook to perform both guard duty and fire patrol. The squadron's arrival gave a certain military air to the new engineering and experimentation facility. A letter from McCook Field in 1918 indicates that a number of these troops spent their first year at the new field in tents until sufficient barracks could be constructed. The letter noted that permanent indoor living space "was badly needed on account of the sickness among the soldiers at McCook Field."[40]

By the first week in December 1917, enough buildings at McCook had been completed to allow key personnel of the Airplane Engineering Department to move from downtown Dayton to the new installation. On December 4, 1917, operations officially commenced at McCook.[41] There was not room at the field to accommodate all the employees from the downtown location, and some sections continued their work at the Lindsey Building in Dayton. In fact, for the duration of the war there was always more staff assigned to McCook than there was office space to house them, and the Signal Corps, as well as the Army Air Service, was forced to lease office space in several Dayton structures. The Dayton Savings Building at 25 North Main Street, the Mutual Home Building at 40 North Main Street, and the Air Service Building (later known as the Knott Building) were all used to make up for the lack of space at McCook.

One month after McCook opened, Signal Corps Office Memorandum 11 transferred full responsibility to McCook for the design of all airplanes and accessories.[42] This resolved a good deal of confusion that had existed since America entered the war in April 1917. At that time, responsibility for aircraft design and production was fragmented among a variety of organizations. This process of drawing diverse industries together, compounded by the haste and anxieties of wartime, took a full nine months. The end result, however, was an efficient operation established at McCook Field. For the remaining 10 months of the war "a rare combination of men, money, and a sense of national urgency created, almost overnight, the single most influential agency in the early years of American air power."[43] As one aviation historian has noted, "In many respects it [McCook Field] was the single most influential organization in the history of American aviation, for it not only provided a start for some of the most talented men in the industry, but it set standards which they have continued to live up to."[44]

McCook Field, from its very beginnings, was different from all other World War I Army installations because it was essentially a business institution rather than a military post. McCook was administered in the same manner as the Signal Corps aviation general supply depots and Army Regulation No. 191 exempted it from the control of the secretary of war. All civilian employees at the field came under Schedule A of the Civil Service, which exempted them from competitive examinations.[45] This arrangement had a profound effect on the functioning and business-like operation of the installation, and freed it to a large extent from the complexities of military inter-agency bureaucracy.

The fact that McCook Field functioned, by and large, in a fashion similar to private industry was due not only to its independent status, but also to the nature of the employees who administered the installation and directed its principal research. The critical shortage of aeronautical engineers in the military had forced the Signal Corps to seek production and engineering expertise in the private sector. Men like Deeds with experience in industry—particularly the automotive industry—were recruited, and in some cases commissioned, to lend vital support to the aircraft development program. For example, Major Vincent, executive officer at McCook, was a former executive of the Packard Motor Car Company. E. J. Hall, who assisted in reorganization of the Engine Design Section, came to the Signal Corps from the Hall-Scott Motor Car Company, and drew with him experts from Cadillac, Dodge, Packard, Durant, and Pierce.[46] The membership of the Aircraft Production Board itself included Sidney D. Waldon, a former vice president of the Packard Motor Car Company, Howard E. Coffin of the Hudson Motor Car Company, and Robert L. Montgomery of the J. F. Brill Company of Philadelphia. Other men applied their industrial experience to supervisory positions in the various shops at McCook. W. J. Rueger, in charge of the Shop Order Department in 1918, was an 11-year veteran of the Chalmers Motor Company production department. R. J. Myers, head of the Wood Shop, brought with him extensive experience with the Curtiss Airplane Corporation and the U.S. Navy Yards. H. L. Bill of the Factory Department had been employed by the Springfield Body Corporation, the Chalmers Motor Company, and Hayes Manufacturing, all of Detroit. C. F. Simmons, factory manager, had worked at the American Blower Company, Detroit Gear and Machine, and the King Motor Car Company.[47] The contributions these men made are perhaps no better exemplified than in the development of the Liberty engine, the productive genius of Vincent and Hall.[48]

During its early years, McCook Field became a meeting ground for the foremost engineers of aviation-related industries, both from the United States and abroad.[49] Among other noted accomplishments, these men solved the many problems associated with adapting existing European aircraft designs to American mass production techniques. (See Chapter 4: Forging an Air Force for details of the specific engineering developments of this period.)

McCook Field experienced rapid growth during 1918. This further crowded conditions in the already limited space. Sketchy reports from the Factory Branch in 1918

McCook Field fire department in full dress. A combined guard and fire department of about 35 civilian employees protected the installation in the years after World War I. World War I-vintage trucks had solid rubber tires and wheels with wooden spokes.

General John J. Pershing (center) inspects McCook Field, December 16, 1919, escorted by McCook Field commander, Colonel Thurman H. Bane (right).

indicate that at least one barrack, a sand test building, a mess hall, a hospital, and hangars to house foreign and exhibition airplanes were constructed that year. The lumber storage facility and cafeteria were relocated, and the macadam-and-cinder runway was extended to a total length of 1,340 feet.[50] Workers completed an auxiliary heating plant near the end of the field that, together with the central heating plant, supplied all buildings with steam heat.[51] In all, 47 buildings occupied 371,914 square feet. By the end of the war in November 1918, the government had more than $2,352,000 invested in the buildings, machinery, and equipment located at McCook Field proper.[52]

The government leased additional real estate during and immediately after the war to support McCook operations. Leases included 212 lots from the city of Dayton for an annual rent of $3,200; 60 lots from the Dayton Savings and Trust Company for $1,461 per year; and 14 lots from individual citizens for approximately $561 per year, total.[53] (By mid-1919, nearly all operations had been reduced in size and centralized at the field.)

There were two military support units at McCook during 1918. The 246th Aero Squadron, previously mentioned, had arrived in November 1917. On January 9, 1918, it was redesignated the 807th Aero Squadron. On July 1, 1918, the 881st Aero Squadron was organized at McCook. On July 12, the squadrons were further designated as Squadron A (807th) and Squadron B (881st). On August 1, 1918, the two squadrons merged into "Detachment No. 10, A.S.A.P."[54]

In January 1918, the Signal Corps created the Department of Production Engineering to work in concert with the Airplane Engineering Department, providing the engineering information necessary for the manufacture of airplanes, engines, and accessories. The new department moved to Dayton so that the two functions would be in close proximity. Insufficient space existed in the Lindsey Building, however, to accommodate the new department. On April 15, 1918, the Department of Production Engineering transferred to Washington, although it retained its mandate to support the Airplane Engineering Department.[55]

Earlier reference was made to the monumental problems the United States faced in gearing up its aircraft production program in the spring of 1918. Delays in the program soon provided the impetus for a major restructuring of the aeronautical sections of the War Department. The Overman Act established authority for this reorganization on May 20, 1918. The Act gave the president full discretionary authority to redistribute functions of top government agencies for the duration of the war, plus an additional six months. President Wilson, in conjunction with ranking War Department officials, created two new branches of the War Department to assume, respectively, the operations and equipment phases of the aeronautical program. A Division of Military Aeronautics was designated to assume all aeronautical functions previously assigned to the Office of the Chief Signal Officer. A Bureau of Aircraft Production was established to assume the duties previously assigned to the Equipment Division and was placed under direct supervision of the secretary of war (thereby entirely independent of the Signal Corps). On May 24, 1918, the War Department officially recognized the Division of Military Aeronautics and the Bureau of Aircraft Production as constituting the Air Service.[56]

Within the Bureau of Aircraft Production, the Production Engineering Department and the Airplane Engineering Department were frequently at odds with each other. These two departments (the latter at McCook and the former in Washington) had been established as separate units and had a tendency to work in isolation without properly consulting each other.[57] As a result, on June 24, 1918, a special division of the Bureau of Aircraft Production was created to centralize and coordinate their efforts. General Memorandum 23 combined the two departments with the Science and Research Department and the Technical Information Department, to form a new Engineering and Research Division within the Bureau of Aircraft Production.[58] To further stimulate cooperation, the Production Engineering Department once more relocated to Dayton. This time, it was housed in the Air Service Building, and remained there for the duration of the war.

The two agencies created by President Wilson which had not functioned successfully as separate entities, the Bureau of Aircraft Production and the Division of Military Aeronautics, were also merged on August 1, 1918. The head of the new organization was designated Director of the Air Service and Assistant Secretary of War. On August 27, the position was filled by the appointment of John D. Ryan, prominent banker, president of the Anaconda Copper Company, and former chairman of the Aircraft Board (which succeeded the Aircraft Production Board).[59]

A further refinement was effected on August 31, when the Airplane Engineering Department and the Production Engineering Department were withdrawn from control of the Bureau of Aircraft Production and merged to become a separate Airplane Engineering Division of the new Air Service. This action was made official with the issuance of Bureau of Aircraft Production General Memorandum No. 166, dated September 13, 1918, which laid responsibility for "complete supervision of all engineering for the Bureau of Aircraft Production" upon the new division.[60] Lieu-

MAJOR GENERAL WILLIAM MITCHELL

Brigadier General William Mitchell

Major General "Billy" Mitchell has been called the "Prophet of Air Power" because of his astonishingly accurate ideas about the potentiality of military aviation. When Mitchell became assistant chief of the Air Service in 1921, he tried to convince U.S. Army leaders to establish an air service independent of the Army. He told them (to no avail) that airplanes could do more than just provide cover for ground troops. Another one of his goals as assistant chief of the Air Service was the acquisition of a bomber capable of sinking a battleship. He turned to the Engineering Division at McCook Field to design such an aircraft, and McCook engineers sought manufacturers' bids for constructing it. The result was the XNBL-1 Barling bomber, a 42,000 pound airplane assembled at Wilbur Wright Field and first flown on August 22, 1923.

Mitchell believed so strongly in the potential of air power that he sacrificed his career for it. He hoped that by forcing the Army to court-martial him, he would draw public attention to his cause. His refusal to keep quiet about the need for change in military doctrine regarding the use of air power forced the court to find him guilty of conduct that discredited the military service, and he was suspended from active duty. He resigned from the Army in February 1926 and lived long enough to see Benito Mussolini use, for the first time in history, a combined force of land and air operations to launch a savage and surprise attack on an unsuspecting country. Mitchell also had warned about Pearl Harbor's vulnerability to attack in 1923; his death in 1936 spared him the pain of seeing his warnings tragically ignored. In 1948 he was awarded a special Medal of Honor posthumously in recognition of the foresight he had shown in the use of air power.

Source: Program from "Dedication of the Lieutenant General Kenneth B. Wolfe Hall, Major General William L. Mitchell Hall, and the Frederick T. Rall, Jr. Hall" (Wright-Patterson Air Force Base, Ohio, April 30, 1997).

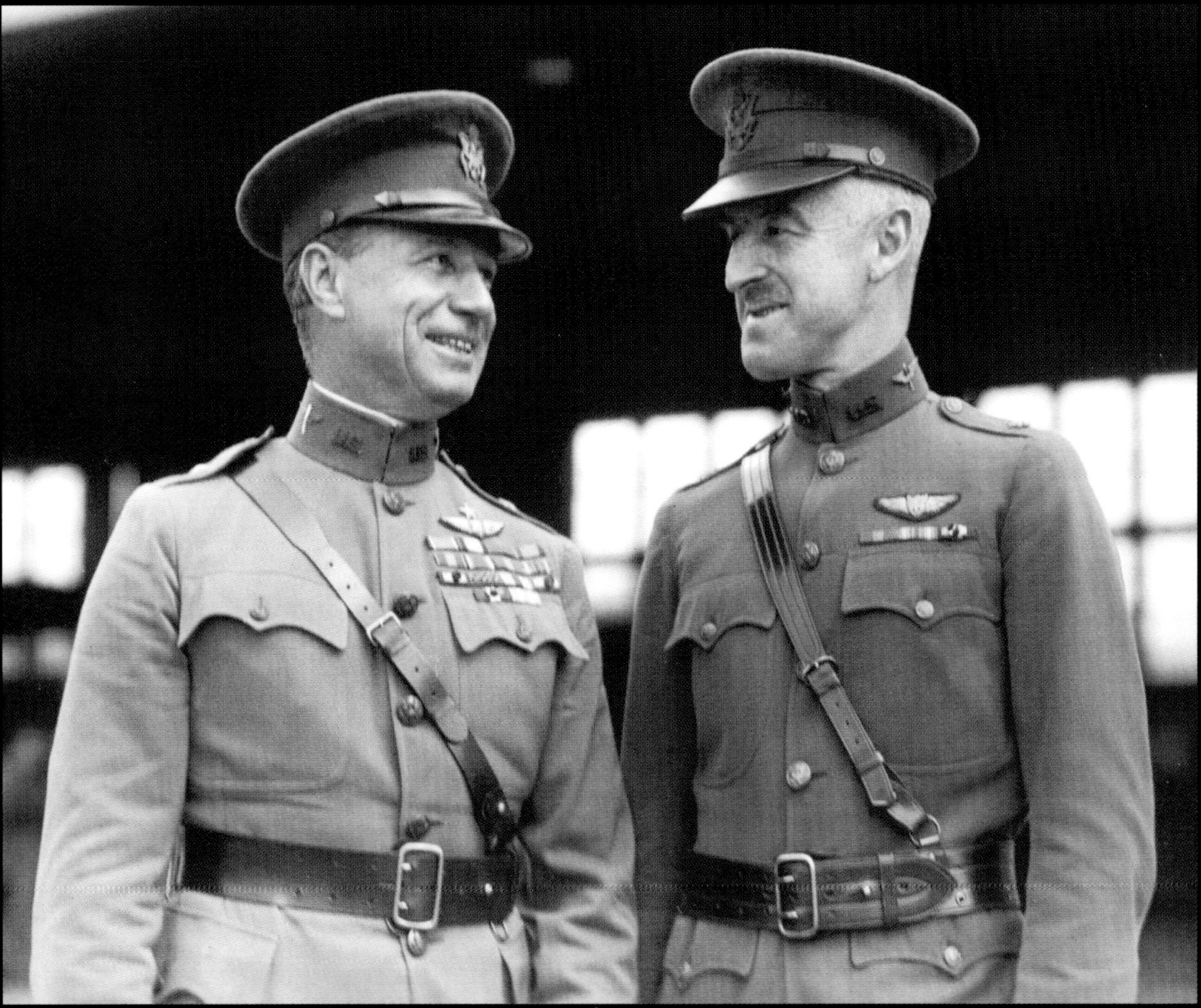

Brigadier General William Mitchell, assistant chief of the Air Service, confers with Colonel Thurman Bane, post commander, during one of his frequent inspection trips to McCook Field, 1919. (*NCR Archives, Montgomery County Historical Society*)

Civilian guards at the main gate of McCook Field

McCook Field adjutant's office (base administration), about 1920

tenant Colonel Vincent became chief of engineering in charge of the combined division, with headquarters in the Air Service Building in Dayton. The title "Engineering Division, Air Service," became the permanent designation for the organization at McCook Field and was retained until 1926.

On September 18, 1918, the Bureau of Aircraft Production directed that the Armament Section of the Ordnance Department also should move to McCook so that the ordnance engineers and draftsmen could work directly with the aircraft engineers in designing and installing bomb sights and bomb racks. The Armament Section left Washington for Dayton on October 3, under the command of Major Harry D. Weed. This change represented the last addition to the experimental facilities at McCook prior to the armistice on November 11, 1918.[61]

In addition to the complications caused by these organizational changes, McCook came under the direction of four different commanders during 1918. Lieutenant Colonel Clark was relieved as commander on January 24, 1918, by Major Frederick T. Dickman. This enabled Lieutenant Colonel Clark to devote his entire energies to the development of original airplane designs. In the meantime, Lieutenant Colonel Vincent had suggested an entirely new organization for the Airplane Engineering Department aimed at improving operations. The Equipment Division approved his plan on February 6, 1918, and the resulting reorganization of the Airplane Engineering Department placed Lieutenant Colonel Vincent in charge effective the same day. He served as commander until November 24, 1918, when Colonel Thurman H. Bane, the first postwar commander of McCook, became chief of the Airplane Engineering Division.

Despite these many changes, the engineering work at McCook Field continued unabated. Historian Edward O. Purtee stated, "Before the end of hostilities the Bureau of Aircraft Production had succeeded in accelerating airplane production to the extent of producing more than 11,700 airplanes and 32,400 engines in America."[62] The record achieved by the aeronautical engineers associated with McCook Field became known around the world as the standard of excellence.

MCCOOK AFTER THE WAR

Colonel Thurman H. Bane actually assumed two hats when he became the first postwar commander of McCook Field. In addition to his new position as chief of the Airplane Engineering Division, he also continued to serve as chief of the Technical Section of the Division of Military Aeronautics, a position he had held since August 1918. The Engineering Division at McCook Field after the war was a consolidation of the Airplane Engineering Division, the Technical Section of the Division of Military Aeronautics, and the Testing Squadron at Wilbur Wright Field.[63]

It became Colonel Bane's job to combine the work of the Bureau of Aircraft Production and the Division of Military Aeronautics on a permanent peacetime basis. He merged the facilities and personnel of the two units, consisting of 2,300 scientists, engineers, technicians, and support officers assigned to 19 sections and 75 branches, into an efficient organization. Colonel Bane's vision was instrumental in seeing McCook Field through the difficult years of the postwar period, fraught with inadequate funding and compounded by apathy toward the goals of the Engineering Division. It was through his personal efforts that the division was able to accomplish its mission in a relatively unfettered fashion.

MCCOOK FIELD COMMANDERS

Lieutenant Colonel Virginius E. Clark	Oct 1917	-	Jan 1918
Major Frederick T. Dickman	Jan 1918	-	Feb 1918
Lieutenant Colonel Jesse G. Vincent	Feb 1918	-	Nov 1918
Colonel Thurman H. Bane	Nov 1918	-	Dec 1922
Major Lawrence W. McIntosh	Jan 1923	-	Jun 1923
Major John F. Curry	Jul 1923	-	Mar 1927

In 1918, Colonel Thurman Harrison Bane was placed in charge of McCook Field, where he organized the Air Service's Engineering Division. While commanding at McCook, Bane introduced modern industrial methods of research, design, and manufacture. At the same time, he founded an Air Service School of Application—the forerunner of the Air Force Institute of Technology. In December 1922, Colonel Bane retired from the Army due to ill health. He died February 22, 1932, and was buried at West Point. *(United States Air Force Museum)*

1100 HOURS, NOVEMBER 11, 1918
THE "WAR TO END ALL WARS" HAD ENDED.

U.S. Army Air Service strength stood at 195,023 officers and enlisted men. Airplane inventories reflected 7,800 biplane trainers (largely Curtiss JN-4 Jennys), 1,000 service airplanes (primarily DH-4s manufactured in American factories), and 5,000 combat-type airplanes (purchased abroad from English, French, and Italian companies).

Air Service strength in Europe totaled 5,707 officers and 74,237 enlisted men. Combat training had been completed by 1,674 pilots and 841 observers. Of these, 1,402 pilots and 769 observers had flown combat sorties over enemy lines.

The Air Service lost 818 brave men during the war in Europe: 164 aircrewmen were killed in action or died as a result of wounds received in action, 319 were killed in airplane accidents, and 335 died from other causes. Other Air Service casualties included 200 missing in action, 102 prisoners of war, and 133 wounded.

U.S. Army soldiers march up Main Street, Dayton, Ohio, during a World War I victory parade, November 1918. ***(Dayton and Montgomery County Public Library)***

Sources: "An Air Force Almanac," *AIR FORCE Magazine*, May 1982, p 171; Maurer Maurer, ed., *The U.S. Air Service in World War I*, Vol. 1: *The Final Report and a Tactical History* (Washington, 1978), 67.

"Entire personnel of the Engineering Division of the Air Service, McCook Field, Dayton, Ohio," 1920 (approximately 50 officers and 1,200 civilian employees)

In May of 1919, the responsibilities of the Engineering Division expanded to encompass all of the aircraft experimental activities previously conducted at Langley Field in Virginia.[64] This further complicated the problem of crowded facilities which McCook already faced. With this centralization, however, McCook became the nerve center of the aircraft and engineering activities of the Air Service. It was at McCook that virtually all significant developments took place. These major engineering developments and achievements included controllable and reversible pitch propellers, aircraft engine superchargers, bullet-proof and leak-proof gasoline tanks, the radio beam, a non-magnetic aircraft clock, an ambulance airplane, the air-cooled radial engine, mapping and night observation cameras, and the free-fall parachute. Also developed at McCook and refined at Wilbur Wright Field were night-flying techniques and a model airway which was the forerunner of today's network of continental and intercontinental commercial air routes. (See Chapter 4: Forging an Air Force for the story of the technological advancements in aviation made at both McCook and Wright fields.)

Both manpower and funds to carry out the Engineering Division's mission after World War I were in ever-dwindling quantity. At the end of the war, the population at McCook totaled 58 officers, 267 enlisted men, and 1,915 civilians.[65] These wartime numbers soon dwindled, though, and from 1920 to 1926 the work of the Engineering Division was normally carried out by a personnel force of about 50 officers and from 1,100 to 1,500 civilians.[66] Additionally, in 1919 the Air Service appropriations were severely cut to $25 million from the $55 million requested.[67] The Engineering Division's share of this budget was proportionately small, and continued to decline over the next several years, from $5 million in 1921, to $3 million in 1924, reaching low ebb in 1927.[68] As one historian stated, however:[69]

> Ironically, the lean years . . . produced the greatest achievements at McCook Field, for during the mid-1920s the scientists and engineers of the Engineering Division had little to work with but their own genius, and it was this ingenuity alone that kept the Air Service from becoming completely obsolete.

Colonel Thurman Bane (seated), commanding officer of McCook Field, 1919

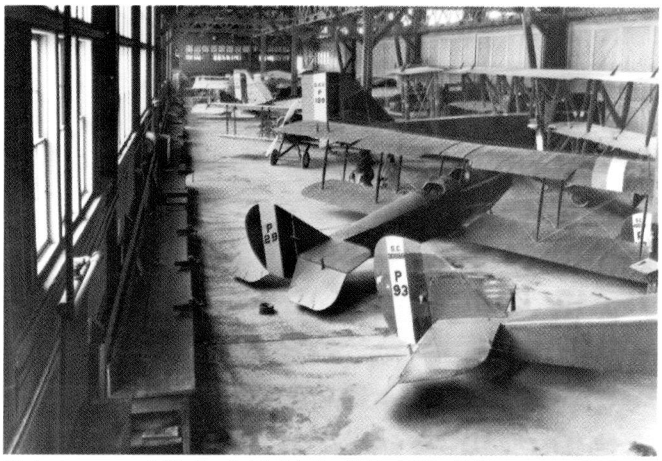

Main hangar at McCook Field, April 5, 1920. Tail number P93 belongs to a DeHavilland DH-4 observation airplane. P29 is a Curtiss JN-4H Jenny trainer. On the other side of the trainer is GAX P129, a three-winged, experimental, armored ground attack airplane powered by two pusher engines. *(Wright State University Archives)*

MAJOR RUDOLPH W. SCHROEDER

Major Rudolph W. Schroeder

In 1916 Rudolph W. Schroeder enlisted in the U.S. Army and served in the Aviation Section of the Signal Corps. Rising to the rank of major by the end of World War I, "Shorty" Schroeder came to McCook Field in 1918 to command test pilots. At 6 feet 4 inches, Major Rudolph Schroeder already stood at an altitude head and shoulders taller than most of his contemporaries at McCook Field. But standing tall wasn't enough for "Shorty," as his friends liked to call him. He served as the Army's chief test pilot between 1919 and 1920. In two years Schroeder set five world altitude records, and his fifth record-breaking flight nearly ended in his death. On February 27, 1920, Schroeder decided to pilot his Packard-LePere LUSAC-11 to a record-breaking altitude. Short of oxygen at the then unheard of height of 33,114 feet, and overcome by carbon monoxide from the engine exhaust, he passed out at the controls and the airplane entered a sharp dive. At 2,000 feet he regained consciousness and made an almost miraculous landing saving life, limb, and plane but not, unfortunately, his eyesight. Due to the extreme cold at high altitude, Schroeder's eyes had frozen open when he lifted his fogged-up goggles to see the instrument panel, and his vision was permanently damaged. He spent the remainder of his life promoting the cause of flight safety.

Source: ASC History Office, *Birthplace, Home, and Future of Aerospace* (Wright-Patterson Air Force Base, Ohio, 1999), p 26; "Pioneers and Heroes," ASC Background Papers.

The Packard-LePere LUSAC-11 biplane in which Schroeder made his last world altitude record

CONTROVERSY WITH THE AIRCRAFT INDUSTRY

The greatest challenge faced by the Engineering Division was its mandate to act as a clearinghouse between the Air Service and the aircraft industry. If the Air Service had been hamstrung by lack of appropriations, the American aircraft industry had been similarly crippled by the cessation of wartime production. European nations, after the war, had adopted programs to rechannel their aviation momentum into commerce and well-organized national defense systems. No such plan operated in the United States to soften the blow sustained by the American aircraft industry or to develop alternative solutions.[70]

The Engineering Division at McCook acted as a middleman, interpreting Army specifications and standards for manufacturers, testing products when they were completed, and suggesting improvements if products did not fully meet specifications. Members of the aircraft industry, in dire economic straits, complained that the operations at McCook Field infringed upon their development rights by concentrating control of all military aircraft design and testing into one organization. They feared that the Air Service was in essence forming a general "brain trust" at McCook, composed of government employees, to perform all of the work connected with design of airplanes and aeronautical equipment. They demanded that the Army transfer some of the Engineering Division's work to private enterprise.[71]

The battle that ensued between McCook and the aircraft industry, as both fought for their very existence, caused severe cutbacks in the work at McCook. Few additional airplanes were being developed for the Air Service, and there was constant pressure in the postwar period for the Air Service to "make do" with equipment and supplies left over from the war. At best, this surplus equipment was obsolete, and thus hampered experimental development; at worst, it jeopardized the safety of all who worked with it. The accusations and complaints registered by the aircraft industry finally provoked action. An American aviation mission was dispatched to Europe in the spring of 1919 to investigate progress being made there in aircraft production. The report of this mission ultimately sparked a measure of increased government support for the U.S. aircraft industry aimed at encouraging development of civil aeronautics.[72]

IN A STATE OF READINESS

On December 1, 1921, newly appointed chief of the Air Service, Major General Mason M. Patrick, directed basic organizational changes in the Engineering Division at McCook Field. Eight newly established sections reflected the alignment of responsibilities: Planning, Technical, Factory, Flying, Procurement, Supply, Patents, and Military.[73]

General Patrick had assumed command of the Air Service on October 15, 1921, following Major General Charles T. Menoher, and was a more direct advocate of engineering development than his predecessor. General Patrick had definite ideas about the job that the Engineering Division should be accomplishing. He purportedly defined the division's duties in one sentence: "To have in readiness for immediate production and service, the most advanced types of aircraft, engines, armament and other miscellaneous equipment."[74] General Patrick initiated operation of a "Production Model Room" at McCook, which contained models of actual equipment necessary to outfit a fighting air force. Each model was complete with drawings, specifications, parts lists, and bills of materials necessary to begin production of the item in quantity, within 24 hours if necessary.

This radio-controlled "tank" was a popular novelty during a 1923 air show and exhibition at McCook.

Major General Mason M. Patrick, chief of the Air Service, 1924. General Patrick commanded the Air Service and its successor, the Air Corps, from 1921 to 1927, and was a strong supporter of the 1924 Round-the-World Flight. At age 60 General Patrick became the oldest general ever to win his wings. While stationed at McCook Field, General Patrick put a carefully planned acquisition process in place; convinced that aviation would play a key role in future wars, Patrick was determined that the aviation resources of the United States would never again be found deficient during wartime as they were during World War I.

A captured Fokker biplane still bears its German Air Force cross insignia as it flies over McCook Field. Many foreign aircraft, both from Allied and enemy nations, were tested at McCook. *(United States Air Force Museum)*

John Arthur Macready served as chief test pilot and chief of the Flying Section at McCook Field. He became one of the best known test pilots of the era, earning three Mackay trophies for setting world records for altitude, duration, and non-stop transcontinental flight (the latter made with Lieutenant Oakley G. Kelly). Macready also performed the first successful crop-dusting demonstration, the first aerial photographic survey of the United States (made with Lieutenant Albert W. Stevens), and the first night parachute jump. He retired from military service in 1946.

In a typical exercise, General Patrick would send a "problem" message to Colonel Bane at the Engineering Division such as, "Congress meets on the 20th for the purpose of declaring war—I will visit McCook on the 18th to review items ready for production." Materials in the Production Model Room were constantly maintained in three classifications: "Ready for Immediate Production," "Experimental," or "Obsolete." On his visits to McCook, General Patrick could thus easily review samples of fully developed products and see experimental items being tested in the field. The goal of the Air Service was to preclude, at all costs, the problems of unpreparedness that the nation had experienced in World War I, so that there would never again be the need to ask, "What shall we build? How shall we build it?"[75]

THE AIR SERVICE ENGINEERING SCHOOL

One of the most important corollaries of the work at McCook was the education of a solid corps of Air Service officers to manage new Air Service programs resulting from the tremendous growth in aeronautical engineering and aviation technology. In November 1918, Colonel Bane, as chief of the Technical Section of the Division of Military Aeronautics, wrote to the director of the division in Washington requesting permission to establish an Air Service School of Application at McCook. He proposed a school similar to the Ordnance School of Application at Sandy Hook Proving Ground, New York, with which he had previously been associated. The stated purpose for this school was to provide "proper technical training" to permanent officers of the Air Service. All officers in command of air stations, Colonel Bane asserted, should receive extensive technical training to more effectively and efficiently direct their operations training in such fields as maintenance of airplanes and motors, machine-shop installation, shop management and cost accounting, power plant installation and operation, laboratory testing of fuels and raw materials, and principles of elementary aerodynamics.[76] The best remedy for the Air Service's lack of technical experts, to Colonel Bane's way of thinking, was for the Air Service to train its own, and the logical place to accomplish this was at McCook.

Although formal approval had not yet been received, Colonel Bane began drawing a teaching staff together. Among the first was Lieutenant Edwin E. Aldrin, who had served on the staff of the aeronautical engineering school for Army and Navy pilots at the Massachusetts Institute of Technology during World War I. In February 1919, Lieutenant Aldrin transferred to McCook along with other former personnel from the school. Colonel Bane capitalized upon his experience, appointing him chief of the School Section. As Lieutenant Aldrin put it, he "had the job of starting a school from nothing."[77]

The first unofficial classes in June 1919 were attended by approximately 10 Air Service lieutenant colonels and majors under the tutelage of Lieutenant Aldrin. Under Colonel Bane's strong guidance, however, the school was carefully developed. Aldrin, as secretary and later assistant commandant at McCook, shouldered most of the responsibility for getting the school under way and continued to run the school for the first few years. (Aldrin's son, astronaut Major Edwin E. "Buzz" Aldrin Jr., would graduate from the Air Force Institute of Technology in 1963.)

Authorization for the first official course of instruction was received from the Air Service director just prior to the start of classes on November 10, 1919. Colonel Bane was of course appointed commander of the new school in addition to his other duties. As described in a later history of the Air Force Institute of Technology:[78]

> The group that gathered for the first official class on 10 November 1919 was small: Aldrin, another lieutenant, two majors, and four lieutenant colonels. They assembled in a hangar. Aldrin read them an introduction to the course and gave a copy of it to each officer. In the months that followed, the course envisioned by Col Bane became a reality. The classrooms were small frame buildings and hangars clustered along McCook's small grass runway, and the main educational tools were the blackboard and practical experience. On some evenings, prominent men from colleges and commercial plants delivered lectures illustrated by lantern slides.

The students in those early years took advantage of all the resources available to them—books, civilian engineers, strategic and tactical experts, research findings, and extensive laboratory training and equipment. The first class graduated in September 1920, by which time the school had been officially named the Air Service Engineering School.

The daily activities at McCook provided an ideal atmosphere for learning and participating first-hand in the development of aeronautics. When Colonel Bane retired at the end of 1922, the school was firmly established and its graduates were beginning to make their mark in the world.

By 1923, the Air Service Engineering School curriculum had four courses of instruction, three for Air Service officers and one for employees of the Engineering Division. The most professional of these was the one-year course in General Aeronautical Engineering, primarily airplane design and aircraft engine design. This core course was supplemented by a five-month course in Maintenance Engineering for officers. A three-month course in Maintenance Engineering for reserve officers and a group of six evening courses in aerodynamics, metals, and other subjects for employees and officers at McCook completed the curriculum.[79]

The class of 1927 was the last to receive instruction in the crowded classrooms "clustered along McCook's small grass runway," as facilities at McCook were dismantled for the move to Wright Field (see Chapter 3: Building a Firm Foundation). The Air Corps Engineering School, as it

AFIT graduates piloted the X-15 to record speeds and altitudes.

THE AIR FORCE INSTITUTE OF TECHNOLOGY

The Air Force Institute of Technology (AFIT), located at Wright-Patterson Air Force Base, Ohio, educates USAF personnel in the military sciences and defense technologies to enable the Air Force to remain on the cutting edge of aerospace development.

Tracing its roots to 1919 when the Air Service established the Air Service School of Application at McCook Field in Dayton, AFIT underwent many organizational changes. The school moved to Wright Field in 1927 and became the Air Corps Engineering School. It became the Army Air Force Institute of Technology in 1946 and, with the establishment of the Air Force as a separate service the following year, it received its current designation. In 1950 the Air Force administratively reassigned AFIT to Air University. Several years later, in 1954, the 83d Congress authorized the commander of Air University to confer degrees upon graduates of the AFIT Resident College. The Air Force Institute of Technology is accredited by the Higher Learning Commission and holds membership in the North Central Association.

As a result of the latest restructure in 1999, AFIT's two graduate schools combined to form the Graduate School of Engineering and Management. This school, along with the School of Systems and Logistics and the Civil Engineer and Services School, comprise AFIT's resident program. The Graduate School of Engineering and Management produces engineers with a broad education capable of directing future aerospace research and development programs.

Some AFIT students directly contribute to the Air Force mission through their research projects that deal with current technological and medical issues pertinent to air power. The Institute also manages the Civilian Institution Programs, which provide other educational opportunities for Air Force personnel enrolled in civilian universities, research centers, hospitals, and industrial organizations throughout the country.

The Air Force Institute of Technology continually modifies its curriculum to meet the ever changing needs of the twenty-first century Air Force. Most recently, AFIT accepted a group of senior noncommissioned officers into its master's degree programs.

Sources: *Air Force Institute of Technology Graduate School of Engineering and Management: Academic Year 2001-2002 Catalog*, pp 2-3; Fact Sheet, AFIT/SC, "The Air Force Institute of Technology"; News Release, Air Force Print News, "Air Force selects 8 senior NCOs for AFIT," July 2, 2002.

Air Service Engineering School, Class of 1920, McCook Field. Front row (left to right): Lieutenant Edwin E. Aldrin, assistant commandant; Lieutenant Colonel Benedict, Lieutenant Colonel Rader, and Major Sneed, students. Back row (left to right): Mr. LaBaie, instructor; Lieutenant Wilcox, Lieutenant Colonel Dargue, Major Frank, and Lieutenant Colonel McIntosh, students; Private Perkins, administration. Lieutenant Aldrin was in charge of the school's operations, although Colonel Thurman H. Bane, McCook Field commander, served officially as commandant. This was the school's first group of students, who began their studies in November 1919.

During the early 1920s, the Air Service Engineering School moved its classes to more spacious quarters. Lieutenant Aldrin (standing second from right) and Mr. LaBaie, instructor (standing third from right), were still active in school affairs.

Modern AFIT facilities (*Air Force Institute of Technology)*

GENERAL JAMES HAROLD DOOLITTLE

James H. Doolittle, early in his career

Doolittle was a daredevil test pilot at McCook and Wright fields.

James H. "Jimmy" Doolittle was a true pioneer in aviation history. Born in California in 1896, he grew up in Alaska, where his first experience with flying came at the age of 13 when he built a glider. Upon America's entry into World War I he enlisted in the Aviation Section of the Signal Corps. In 1918 he was commissioned a second lieutenant and by 1922 he entered the history books as the first pilot to fly the United States coast-to-coast in less than a day.

A few days after that flight, Doolittle received orders to report to the Engineering School at McCook Field. Upon graduation in 1923 he enrolled at the Massachusetts Institute of Technology and became one of the first Americans to earn advanced degrees in aeronautical sciences (MA in 1924 and PhD in 1925.) His thesis was supported by a series of grueling flight acceleration tests at McCook Field in a Fokker PW-7, which he drove to the point of structural failure in order to determine the breaking point of the wings under combat conditions. Following graduation he continued his flight test career at McCook Field (later Wright Field) and became one of the nation's best known pilots.

Doolittle left active duty in 1930 and entered the Air Corps Reserve. He was employed by Shell Oil Company where he achieved what he considered to be his most important contribution to World War II, although the world would know him better as the leader of the Tokyo Raid. He persuaded Shell Oil's management to develop and produce 100-octane aviation fuel in 1934, although no commercial market for it existed at that time. Doolittle accurately predicted that high octane fuel was fundamental to future aeronautical progress and its early development gave Allied aircraft an important edge over the Axis forces during the war.

In the postwar years Doolittle returned to Shell Oil and for the next 50 years served as a senior aeronautical advisor to numerous administrations. He added his voice to the call for an independent air force (established in 1947) and, over the years, served as an influential member of numerous committees and commissions. He served as chairman of the Air Force Scientific Advisory Board and the National Advisory Committee for Aeronautics and was a member of the President's Foreign Intelligence Advisory Board, Defense Science Board, Atomic Energy Commission, and the Air Force Space Systems Advisory Group, to mention only a few.

In 1985 President Ronald Reagan nominated Doolittle to be promoted to the rank of full general. He pinned on his fourth star in 1985 and in 1989 was further honored to receive the Presidential Medal of Freedom for his extraordinary contributions to aerospace progress and over 70 years of service to the nation. Doolittle died on September 27, 1993, in Pebble Beach, California.

Source: James H. Doolittle with Carroll V. Glines, *I Could Never Be So Lucky Again* (New York, 1991).

'Admiral' Doolittle returns in triumph to McCook Field, having bested the Navy in the Schneider Cup seaplane race, 1925.

Doolittle, front, pilots a flying advertisement for the 1924 International Air Races in Dayton.

A CHILDHOOD FANTASY COMES TRUE

As a child growing up in Dayton, Ohio, during the 1920s, Richard E. Cole often rode his bicycle to a levee of the Miami River to watch and admire the daring aerobatics of a McCook Field pilot named James H. Doolittle. Although children often conjure up fantasies about going on exciting adventures with their heroes, young Dick Cole could scarcely have dreamed that one day he would be flying with his hero on a mission that would go down in American aviation history as one of the most daring air attacks of all time.

After graduating from Steele High School in Dayton and attending Ohio University for two years, Cole enlisted in the Air Corps and received his wings and a commission as a second lieutenant in the Army Air Forces in July 1941. After the Japanese bombed Pearl Harbor and the United States entered World War II, U.S. military and government leaders decided to plan an attack on Japan to boost the morale of the American people and to show the Japanese they were not invulnerable. Legendary pilot Jimmy Doolittle was chosen to lead an air raid on mainland Japan, and he in turn asked for volunteers to accompany him on the very dangerous, almost suicidal, mission. When Doolittle took off from the short runway of the carrier *Hornet* to lead the famous raid of the 16 B-25 bombers on Tokyo, at his side was his copilot, Dick Cole. Although Doolittle and his men had to crash-land in China after the raid because their planes did not have enough fuel to make it back to the carrier, most of the raiders—including Dick Cole—survived the mission and continued to serve their country throughout the duration of the war.

Dick Cole's school picture from Jefferson Grade School

Source: *Doolittle's Tokyo Raiders 60th Anniversary Reunion,* online at http://www.thestateonline.com/doolittle/doolittle.htm; *60th Doolittle Raiders Reunion*, online at http://www.doolittleraidersreunion.com/attend.html.

From the time he was a small child, Dick Cole loved airplanes of all kinds. Whenever he got the chance, he would go to McCook Field (right) and check out the planes being tested there. Cole was also an avid member of the Model Airplane League of America (below, right).

The crew of the first B-25 to depart the USS *Hornet*, prior to the Tokyo Raid. Copilot Lieutenant Richard E. Cole (right, front row) stands alongside raid commander Lieutenant Colonel James H. Doolittle. Their crewmates are (from left to right, back row) navigator Lieutenant Henry A. Potter, bombardier Sergeant Fred A. Braemer, and gunner Sergeant Paul J. Leonard. Doolittle is wearing the Wright Field patch on his flight jacket.

MCCOOK FIELD SUPPORTED THE 1924 ROUND-THE-WORLD FLIGHT

One of the most spectacular achievements of the U.S. Army Air Service was an around-the-world flight performed from April to September 1924. It was the first globe-circling flight in aviation history.

As the vehicle for this historic mission, the Air Service selected a specially designed biplane: the single-engine (400 horsepower) Douglas World Cruiser with a top speed of 102 mph. McCook Field pilot and engineer Lieutenant Erik Nelson helped design the prototype World Cruiser, then test flew it at McCook. He also piloted one of the global mission World Cruisers. Four of the new aircraft, with highly experienced pilots and copilots/mechanics took part in the flight:

"Seattle" – Major Frederick Martin (mission commander) and Sergeant Alva Harvey;
"New Orleans" – Lieutenant Erik Nelson and Lieutenant John Harding;
"Chicago" – Lieutenant Lowell Smith and Lieutenant Leslie Arnold; and
"Boston" – Lieutenant Leigh Wade and Staff Sergeant Henry Ogden.

The "world tour" route—which began and ended at Seattle, Washington—was divided into six sections (called divisions), each covering a specific area of the globe. These divisions and their assigned areas were as follows (listed in order flown):

Division 1 – Seattle, British Columbia, Alaska, the Aleutian Islands
Division 2 – Kurile Islands and Japan
Division 3 – China, Indo-China (Vietnam/Laos/Cambodia), Siam (Thailand), Burma, India
Division 4 – India, Persia (Iran), Iraq, Syria, Turkey
Division 5 – Rumania, Serbia, Hungary, Austria, France, England
Division 6 – England, Orkney Islands, Faroe Islands, Iceland, Greenland, Labrador, Newfoundland, Nova Scotia, Massachusetts, Washington, D.C.

Fuel, supplies, spare parts, crew accommodations, and maintenance support for the flight were pre-positioned at many of these locations. McCook Field became the main logistics base, with subordinate depots located in each division. Fairfield Air Intermediate Depot was responsible for obtaining, packaging, and shipping parts and supplies to the various airfields within the divisions. The four-plane flight took off from Lake Washington, near Seattle, at 8:47 a.m., April 6, 1924. Weight restraints prohibited the carrying of radios, parachutes, life preservers, and rafts. Unfortunately, only two of the planes — "New Orleans" and "Chicago" — returned to Seattle six months later at the completion of their globe-circling journey. "Seattle" crashed at Dutch Harbor, Alaska, on April 30, and "Boston" ditched in the North Atlantic on August 2. Luckily, no injuries or losses occurred in these mishaps.

Upon their return to the United States in September after the grueling, six-month odyssey, President Calvin Coolidge and his cabinet met the weary crews of "New Orleans" and "Chicago." Continuing on from the nation's Capitol, the two aircraft stopped at McCook Field for three days (September 14-16). En route to the field, they were met near Columbus by McCook test pilot Lieutenant Harold Harris flying a six-engine Barling bomber triplane. Over Wilbur Wright Field, the crews were greeted by the words "Welcome World Fliers" painted in huge letters on the ground. Upon landing at McCook, an estimated crowd of 75,000 people cheered the planes and crews. McCook technicians serviced and repaired the aircraft while flight surgeons examined the crews and declared them fit to continue their journey.

The final landing of "New Orleans" and "Chicago" took place at Seattle before a crowd of 50,000 enthusiastic fans at 1:28 p.m. on September 28—175 days after their takeoff. The record-setting mission had covered 26,300 miles in a total flight time of 363 hours—the equivalent of 15 days, 3 hours, and 7 minutes in the air at an average speed of 80 mph.

After the post-flight festivities, ferry crews flew the two remaining World Cruisers back to McCook Field. The world flight crewmen were decorated by Congress with the Distinguished Service Medal and also received several foreign awards. In 1957 "New Orleans" went on permanent display at the United States Air Force Museum. "Chicago" was put on display at the National Air and Space Museum in Washington, D.C. A Navy admiral said of the flight: "Other men will fly around the earth but never again will anybody fly around it first." Another page of aviation history had been written in red, white, and blue ink.

Major J. F. Curry (left), chief of the Engineering Division and future commander of McCook Field, greeted three of the four World Flight crews upon their arrival in Dayton. They were (left to right): Lieutenant Lowell Smith, Staff Sergeant Henry Ogden, and Lieutenants Erik Nelson, Leigh Wade, John Harding, and Leslie Arnold. *(Dayton and Montgomery County Public Library)*

1924 INTERNATIONAL AIR RACES

A special edition of the McCook Field publication *The Slipstream Monthly* highlighted events at the Air Races.

On October 2-4, 1924, Wilbur Wright Field and Fairfield Air Intermediate Depot hosted the International Air Races. The event encompassed 12 major races (with prestigious trophies and prize money at stake), skywriting exhibitions, balloon flights, parachute demonstrations, freak flying, aerial combat, and formation flying. Although the foreign contestants cancelled their entries prior to the opening ceremonies, allegedly because they knew their planes were no match for American aircraft, the races attracted more than 100,000 spectators. Pilots from Air Service fields across the nation, including Wilbur Wright and McCook fields, took part. The Chief of the Air Service, Major General Mason M. Patrick, personally selected 23 skilled officers to fly in the most prestigious trophy races, each for a separate class of airplane. The winners of the trophies were:

Liberty Engine Builders Trophy (Observation-type airplanes)
Lieutenant D. G. Duke (Office of the Chief of the Air Service)

Dayton Chamber of Commerce Trophy (Large capacity airplanes)
Lieutenant D. M. Myers (Phillips Field)

Pulitzer Trophy (Speed classic)
Lieutenant H. H. Mills (McCook Field)

John L. Mitchell Trophy (Pursuit-type aircraft)
Lieutenant Cyrus Bettis (Selfridge Field)

The International Air Races were not without tragedy, however. Lieutenant Alexander Pearson (McCook Field) and Captain Burt E. Skeel (Selfridge Field) were killed when their airplanes crashed during the three-day event.

Lieutenant James H. Doolittle (left), famed McCook Field test pilot, his wife Josephine, and Major General Mason M. Patrick, chief of the Air Service, at the International Air Races in 1924

Parade at McCook Field publicizing the 1924 International Air Races held at nearby Wilbur Wright Field *(Air Force Wright Aeronautical Laboratory Technical Library)*

was then known, resumed classes at the new installation in 1928 under the auspices of the Air Corps Materiel Division. Classes were held in the Materiel Division headquarters building, now Building 11 in Area B of Wright-Patterson Air Force Base.[80]

Members of the "First Bombardment Board," July 9, 1926, meet to test and make recommendations on procurement of bombardment airplanes for the Air Corps. Included are (left to right): Lieutenant Harold L. George, Lieutenant John DeF. Barker, Major Louis H. Brereton (president of the Board), Lieutenant E. W. Dichman, Lieutenant Muir S. Fairchild, and Lieutenant Odas Moon. *(United States Air Force Museum)*

CREATION OF THE AIR CORPS MATERIEL DIVISION

The most significant reorganization of activities at McCook Field took place in 1926. In July of that year, the Air Service became the Air Corps. Under provisions of the Air Corps Act, the activities of the Air Corps were divided into three major branches, each headed by an assistant chief of the Air Corps. Brigadier General William E. Gillmore was appointed chief of the newly designated Materiel Division, with headquarters at McCook Field. Brigadier General James E. Fechet assumed command of the Operations Division, with headquarters at Washington, D.C., and Brigadier General Frank P. Lahm headed the Air Corps Training Center, with headquarters at Kelly Field.[81]

The Materiel Division was an expansion of the Engineering Division, and included not only engineering, but also supply, procurement, and maintenance of aircraft. (See Chapter 3: Building a Firm Foundation for more comprehensive coverage of this reorganization.) The mission of the Materiel Division was to furnish all aircraft and aeronautical equipment used by the Air Corps. This encompassed five basic responsibilities, widely expanded from the relatively specialized mission of the Engineering Division:[82]

- Development, procurement, and test of aircraft and concomitant equipment
- Distribution and maintenance of materiel in the field
- Planning of industrial preparedness
- Maintenance of an adequate engineering plant and test facility
- The dissemination of technical information for the good of the service, the industry, and the general public.

The Materiel Division, in fact, comprised most of the major functions of the new Air Corps, with the exception of training. Many of those functions have remained at Wright-Patterson to the present day. Modern-day research and development, weapon systems acquisition, and supply and maintenance of current systems are carried on by "descendants" of the Engineering Division, such as the Aeronautical Systems Center, the Air Force Research Laboratory, and their higher headquarters, the Air Force Materiel Command. The missions are the same; only the organizations, people, and technology have changed.

Light truck used to transport aerial bombs from storage igloos to the flightline, about 1925. Spare wheels were mounted on the front of the truck. Note the hand crank to start the engine.

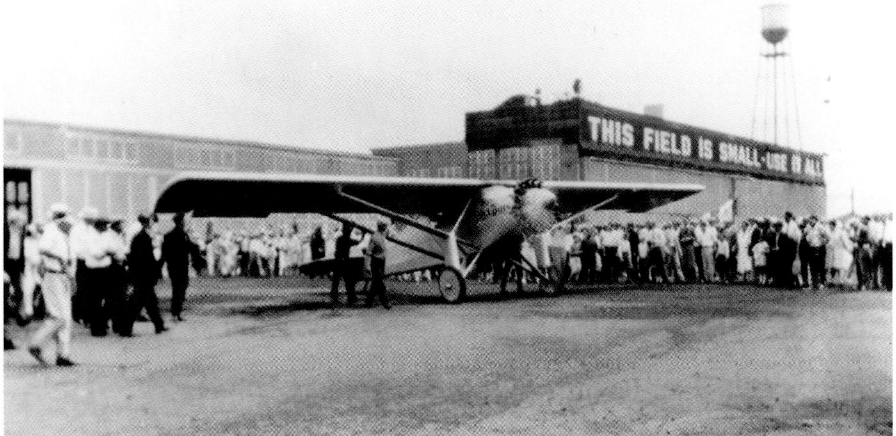

Charles A. Lindbergh briefly landed his *Spirit of St Louis* at McCook Field on June 17, 1927, during the return leg of his historic transatlantic flight. After taking off, he passed over the Fairfield Air Depot, where he was met by aircraft from the 1st Pursuit Group, Selfridge Field, Michigan, and escorted back to St. Louis. Lindbergh returned to Dayton five days later and spent the night as a guest of Orville Wright.

FAIRFIELD AIR DEPOT—1917-1946

The Fairfield Air Depot, Dayton, Ohio, began as the Fairfield Aviation General Supply Depot in 1917 as a wartime supply center for the Signal Corps Aviation Schools at Wilbur Wright Field, Scott and Chanute fields in Illinois, and Selfridge Field in Michigan. The depot supplied everything from airplane parts and engines to shoelaces. Over the next three decades, the depot underwent various name changes until its inactivation in 1946 as part of the postwar demobilization. At that time, it was a part of Patterson Field, created on July 1, 1931, and named in honor of Lieutenant Frank Stuart Patterson, a native Daytonian test pilot killed in the crash of his DH-4 while testing a machine gun synchronizer over Wilbur Wright Field in 1918. The new Patterson Field incorporated Huffman Prairie, Wilbur Wright Field, and Fairfield Air Depot Reservation. Although located on Patterson Field, the Fairfield Air Depot retained its title and continued as a major function of the new installation.

The Fairfield depot's normal supply function included furnishing parts and equipment to repair shops and other Air Service installations. By 1927, the Fairfield depot served all Air Service installations east of the Mississippi River, and those in a few states west of the river, as well as depots in the Panama Canal Zone, Hawaiian Islands, and the Philippines. At various times throughout its history, it accepted additional roles. Following World War I, it took on the huge task of inventorying, discarding, and storing war surplus materiel. It also assumed responsibility for overhauling airplane engines when the Engineering Repair Section from the Aviation Repair Depot in Indianapolis moved to Fairfield in 1920. The depot established the supply system and maintenance schedule for the 1924 Round-the-World Flight, controlled the experimental Model Airway System from 1925-1926 (the first airline to provide regularly scheduled flights between fixed points), modified the airplanes used for flying the United States air mail in 1934, and installed and maintained special equipment used during exercises to perfect new bombing techniques and tactics.

The depot's most significant contribution, however, was its role in logistics during World War II when the need for emergency maintenance, repair, and supply work skyrocketed. From the employment of 500 people in 1939, the depot expanded to more than 19,000 workers at its height in 1943. It operated 24 hours a day, seven days a week, supplying, maintaining, and repairing all types of war materiel for stateside depots and remote field depots around the world. As one of the oldest depots in the nation, Fairfield was a proving ground for new ideas to streamline the supply system and was selected to train military and civilian employees in repair and supply procedures. Through the Air Service Command, it provided expertise to the establishment, layout, and manning of new depots and sub-depots around the nation. Until the day it closed in January 1946, the depot provided the backbone of the logistics function that Air Force Materiel Command, headquartered at Wright-Patterson Air Force Base, manages to this day.

An engine ready for overhaul, moved by an overhead electric hoist

Fairfield Air Depot on Patterson Field, Ohio. The largest building at lower right was the original depot headquarters.

The logo of the McCook Field Engineering Division was retained by the Air Corps Material Division in 1926. The Dayton Stamp Club honored the logo and McCook Field in 1980.

The organization of the Materiel Division and its component agencies were outlined in 1926 as follows: the headquarters at McCook Field; six air depots located at Fairfield (Ohio), Little Rock (Arkansas), Middletown (Pennsylvania), Rockwell Field (California), San Antonio (Texas), and Scott Field (Illinois); three procurement districts with centers in Dayton (Central), New York City (Eastern), and Santa Monica, California (Western); and six procurement planning districts under the Industrial War Plans Section.[83]

This massive reorganization and its consequent shifts in personnel made evident, more than ever, the inadequacy of the facilities at McCook Field. Fortunately, by 1926, definite plans for relocation of the Materiel Division had been approved and implementation was under way.

A NEW HOME IS SOUGHT

McCook Field originally was established as a temporary, experimental site for wartime testing, and earned a notable reputation during World War I. As early as December 1918, however, only one month after the armistice, rumors were afoot concerning relocation of the Engineering Division to a more permanent home. Originally, that permanent home was to have been Langley Field in Virginia, as discussed earlier. In fact, on December 5, 1918, Colonel Bane received a memo from Colonel Arthur Woods, assistant director of Military Aeronautics, stating in part that, "You will be safe in assuming that your work will stay where it is for six months and some time after that it will be moved to Langley [Field]."[84]

Several thousand guests attended this static exhibition and air show at McCook Field on July 4, 1923. Proceeds were donated to the Soldiers' Emergency Relief Fund (similar to today's Air Force Aid Society).

Thurman Bane himself was the first to admit that the setup at McCook was far from ideal. Growth of the Engineering Division had been so rapid and extensive during the war that the initial facilities were inadequate to house its expanded functions. Bane was not entirely pleased with the prospect of moving the entire division and its operations to Langley because moving would mean the loss of many well-trained and hard-to-replace men and significant disruption of operations, but he recognized that the problems at McCook were legion. They could not be compensated for and worked around indefinitely.

Because of the immediate press for wartime facilities, buildings at McCook had not been erected according to any master plan. As additional buildings were required and constructed, they slowly encroached upon the flying field itself. The majority of these buildings were of temporary construction, posing a great fire hazard and necessitating constant, costly maintenance.

The macadamized runway at McCook, oriented to take advantage of the prevailing winds, lay across the smallest dimension of the field—less than 2,000 feet. At the end of the runway was a dike topped with trees, which protected the field from the river.[85] Although small World War I pursuit and trainer airplanes had been able to negotiate this tight approach, it proved entirely inadequate for the larger, postwar aircraft being developed at McCook. Those airplanes tested at McCook posed a very real danger to Dayton citizens living in the surrounding neighborhoods because of the field's location in the very heart of the city. A number of emergency landings during the 1920s terminated in treetops in the vicinity of McCook or in the (usually) shallow Great Miami River. Consequently, larger airplanes from McCook were flight-tested at Wilbur Wright Field near Fairfield.

In addition to these safety and space considerations, the lack of a rail line to the field posed another limitation. Supplies and equipment (284 carloads in 1923) had to be hauled two miles from the station in Dayton.[86]

One final limitation was the fact that rent on the McCook Field property increased each year. McCook Field stood in a prime location, and the original owners were anxious to convert the land to more profitable use. Annual rental of McCook Field after 1924 was quoted at $60,000 per year. In times of tight money, the Air Service felt that this was an exorbitant and unjustifiable sum to pay for facilities that were far from adequate.[87]

Although the climate of opinion in the United States during the 1920s opposed the concept of increasing the country's offensive capability and the development of air power for military purposes, it was more than evident that the science of aeronautical engineering was only beginning to show its real potential. The impetus given to development of aeronautics during the war unveiled an unlimited future for the airplane, and ignited a spark in the imagination and spirit of American ingenuity. According to one contemporary historian: "With the signing of the armistice, civilization awoke to find the infant of aviation already a growing child upon her hands. It would never again be hushed to sleep and its crib pushed out of sight."[88] The sky was literally the limit.

The fact that the Engineering Division would continue its exploration was assured, and clamor for a suitable facility reverberated on all sides. The unanswered question remained, "Where?" Many, including Colonel Bane, anticipated that Langley was the prime candidate. Langley did offer certain advantages, mainly its proximity to Washington (so that congressmen and officers of the Air Service could be near the actual work), more ample facilities for bombing and firing from the air, and a permanent physical plant. There is evidence, however, that the Virginia installation was never seriously considered.

Facilities of the Dayton Wright Airplane Company at Moraine were considered the most logical site for the relocation of the Engineering Division. The airplane pictured is most likely an early experiment in radio control, a product of research by Charles F. Kettering. (*NCR Archives, Montgomery County Historical Society*)

The National Advisory Committee for Aeronautics had been one of the only agencies to establish operations at Langley during the war. The Navy had contravened its original plans and never used Langley. Perhaps partially for status reasons, after the war, the Air Service felt that it, too, should have its own independent research facilities. Colonel Bane evidently was not partial either way. His only concern was that a location be selected and a decision made so that the division could get on with its work. In the end, relocation to Langley was vetoed and the colonel was forced to exercise patience with the decision to leave the Engineering Division at McCook until a more suitable location could be obtained.[89]

As mentioned previously, in May of 1919 all aircraft experimentation activities conducted at Langley during the war transferred to McCook (providing further evidence that Langley was never seriously considered).[90] In 1920 the War Department established the Air Service Field Officers School (later the Air Corps Tactical School) at Langley. Providing facilities for this school created crowded conditions at the installation. Relocating the Engineering Division from McCook after that time would have called for a major reorganization.[91]

Sites in New Jersey, Maryland, and Michigan were reportedly considered as locations for the Air Service Engineering Division, but finding a site that already possessed adequate facilities and that would require little capital expenditure was next to impossible. One site that held a degree of promise, however, was the old Dayton Wright Airplane Company at South Field, south of Dayton.

At the conclusion of the war, Dayton Wright was in the process of making final settlements with the government. It was proposed that after the final settlement of contracts with the manufacturer, the government would take over the plant and relocate the Air Service Engineering Division there. The primary argument for the move was that the War Department had invested over $634,000 in the property for additions to the plant and $366,000 in roads and other improvements, all of which would be sacrificed unless the government purchased the plant and converted it to another use. As a plus, the Dayton Wright

Langley Field was one alternative considered for the permanent home of the Engineering Division. (*United States Air Force Museum*)

factory buildings were of permanent, modern industrial construction and serviced by adequate rail and land transportation. The flying field was of a suitable shape and size, and there was a corps of the highest-grade mechanics, who were familiar with operations, available for hire. Relatively little government money would need to be expended in order to render the facility suitable for the experimental work.[92] The choice was logical, but appropriations to fund the move were not forthcoming.

The proposal to assume ownership of the Dayton Wright facility was only one of a series of proposals to move the Engineering Division submitted to a Congress reluctant to approve any military appropriations. The fiscal year 1920 Report of the Air Service to the Secretary of War stated

> The Air Service has failed in its endeavors to secure from Congress an appropriation to provide a home for its Engineering Division.... A suitable location . . . was offered the Air Service by the Dayton Wright Airplane Company at a price which the Air Service representatives considered very reasonable. This proposition was submitted to Congress, but permission for the consummation of the project was refused.

This report further concluded:[93]

> The Air Service has been unable to date to find a suitable location for the Engineering Division on Government-owned land. The search for a location will be continued, but it is hardly believed that the Government now owns land which will be suitable for a plant of this kind. ...At any rate, it is now clear that at its next session Congress must take the necessary legislative action for this primary and most important requirement of the Air Service.

By 1922 McCook Field's critical need for new facilities had become an irresistible force and Congress, the proverbial immovable object. It was during this crucial impasse, when federal agencies remained deadlocked, that the citizens of Dayton rallied to take matters into their own hands to provide a solution to the problem.

JOHN H. PATTERSON

John H. Patterson, founder and chairman of the Board, The National Cash Register (NCR) Company, and a long-time supporter of the Air Service, was a man of insight as well as a man of action. According to Samuel Crowther, Patterson's biographer, it was during one of Brigadier General Billy Mitchell's visits to Dayton that Mitchell, then assistant chief of the Air Service, and Patterson first discussed taking more aggressive steps to keep the McCook Field operations in Dayton. Of primary importance was the pride Dayton claimed as the birthplace of aviation and as the center of aviation technology in the United States. It was equally important to maintain the economic initiative by keeping the experimental aircraft industry and its highly skilled work force in Dayton. In the recessionary period immediately following the war, the promise of a sizeable, steady federal payroll, certain to expand as the field of aviation grew, was an opportunity to be seized.

Lieutenant Frederick B. Patterson (left) and his father, John H. Patterson, founder of The National Cash Register Company, 1918. John Patterson is recognized as the father of modern salesmanship and an American pioneer in industrial relations. Mr. Patterson identified strongly with Brigadier General Billy Mitchell's support of the engineering work at McCook Field. He had an ardent desire to help strengthen and expand the operations conducted at McCook so that they might make a dynamic and lasting contribution to Dayton (the birthplace of aviation), to the military, and eventually to commercial aviation. *(Mrs. Howell Jackson)*

Mr. Patterson was already known in Washington for his support of the Air Service. He now focused his considerable energies on two specifics: increasing congressional appropriations to the Air Service so that essential work such as that done at McCook would continue, and negotiating with War Department officials to permanently relocate McCook activities to some other site near Dayton.

On the local level, Patterson began examining various sites in the Dayton vicinity and methodically charting their advantages and disadvantages. In Washington, two NCR representatives, John F. Ahlers and Horace W. Karr, spent five weeks applying persuasive leverage in Congress on behalf of Air Service appropriations. They spoke to the Military Affairs Committee, the House Appropriations Committee, and the Ohio delegation to Congress. At Patterson's direction they also interviewed 400 congressmen and 96 senators. The efforts of the two NCR representatives weighed significantly in the passage of increased Air Service appropriations for the coming year.[94]

No funds existed in the budget, however, to relocate McCook Field. Mr. Patterson would not admit defeat or countenance delays, and resolved to stage an independent campaign to save McCook Field. On May 5, 1922, Patterson and the Dayton Chamber of Commerce hosted a gala luncheon at the Gibbons Hotel in Dayton in honor of General Mitchell and Colonel Bane. Mr. Patterson outlined his plans for keeping McCook Field in Dayton. General Mitchell spoke on the valuable work being performed by the Engineering Division. He particularly urged Dayton citizens to take advantage of their opportunity to visit the field and become familiar with the government's activities in the development of the Air Service.[95]

Unfortunately, John H. Patterson did not live to see the fruits of his efforts. The next morning, Mitchell and Patterson met in the latter's office to discuss strategy and progress toward their mutual goal of retaining McCook Field in the Dayton area. That same afternoon Mr. Patterson departed by train for Atlantic City. Dayton was shocked and saddened two days later by the news that John H. Patterson had passed away on the train while en route from Philadelphia to Atlantic City on May 7, 1922.[96] Patterson had laid the essential foundation, however, and formulated specific goals and objectives for the campaign to save

Flying cadets from the Signal Corps Aviation School, Wilbur Wright Field, enjoy a reception on the lawn at the Far Hills estate of John H. Patterson, president of The National Cash Register Company, 1918. (*NCR Archives, Montgomery County Historical Society*)

McCook Field. His plans had only to be implemented.

THE DAYTON AIR SERVICE COMMITTEE

John Patterson's only son, Frederick Beck Patterson, assumed leadership of The National Cash Register Company after his father's untimely death. Frederick had served as president of NCR under his father's tutelage since July of 1921. As such, he had been involved in the strategy meeting held in his father's office on the morning of May 6 and also had a personal interest in the McCook Field project. During World War I, Frederick Beck Patterson was commissioned as a second lieutenant in the Army Air Service and served with the 15th Photographic Air Squadron in France. He remained active in aviation affairs after the war, eventually serving as chairman of the National Aeronautic Association.

Shortly after John H. Patterson's death, it was rumored that a definite decision had been made by the Air Service to move the Engineering Division out of Dayton. Upon personal investigation, Frederick discovered the story to be true and acted quickly. From May until October, Patterson conducted extensive negotiations with the secretary of war, the attorney general, and officers of the Air Service. He also enlisted the aid of numerous prominent Daytonians. The organization formed under Patterson's direction was named the Dayton Air Service Committee and was composed of distinguished citizens who spent freely of their time and money in support of the McCook Field project:[97]

Frederick B. Patterson, President
Frederick H. Rike, Vice President
Ezra M. Kuhns, Secretary
W. M. Brock, Treasurer
W. R. Craven
Valentine Winters
Harry H. Darst
Irvin G. Kumler
Colonel Frank T. Huffman
Colonel Edward A. Deeds
George W. Shroyer
F. J. Ach
John C. Haswell
Horace W. Karr
Edward Wuichet
George B. Smith
H. D. Wehrley
John F. Ahlers
C. E. Comer

In essence, what Mr. Patterson learned from Air Service officials was that if Dayton wished to retain McCook Field it would have to donate land for relocation of the Engineering Division. A number of other cities was vying for the same honor and had made offers of land; so if Dayton was seriously interested, it would have to equal or better the incentive. This was not an unusual suggestion at the time, for during World War I Congress had passed legislation encouraging patriotic groups and individuals to make free and clear donations of land to the federal government.[98]

Frederick Patterson arranged for Air Service officials to view a site near Riverside (formerly Harshmanville), just outside of Dayton, that had been high on John H. Patterson's list of potential sites. The property consisted of 4,988 acres, and spread across two counties. In Greene County the available property included the site of former Wilbur Wright Field and land later occupied by areas A and C of Wright-Patterson Air Force Base. (The government already owned 40 acres adjacent to this tract, occupied by the Fairfield Air Intermediate Depot.) In Montgomery County, an additional 550 contiguous acres to the southwest were available near Riverside. A large portion of the available land (4,325 acres) was owned by the Miami Conservancy District. The remaining acreage proposed for the site was composed of seven parcels owned by the following individuals:[99]

Jannie Harshman	172.129 acres
Charles & Susan Beckel	171.260 acres
Alice Tobey	22.976 acres
William Stickle	21.000 acres
Louis Gradsky	37.023 acres
William Mathers	143.310 acres
William Mays	96.000 acres

Charts publicized by the Dayton Air Service Committee showed that a total of $325,000 would be required to purchase the eight parcels.

First meeting of the Dayton Air Service Committee, October 25, 1922, at the Dayton Country Club. The committee subsequently organized a campaign that yielded over $425,000 in public contributions to purchase a permanent home for McCook Field activities. Committee members, all prominent Dayton business leaders, are (from left): Irvin G. Kumler, H. W. Karr, G. W. Shroyer, Dr. D. F. Garland, Edward Wuichet, Frederick H. Rike, Frederick B. Patterson, W. R. Craven. John C. Haswell, H. D. Wehrley, Valentine Winters, and John F. Ahlers. Seated in the back row are Ezra M. Kuhns and Harold E. Talbott. (*NCR Archives, Montgomery County Historical Society*)

Captain Edward Rickenbacker, World War I Air Service ace, and Frederick B. Patterson, president of NCR (*NCR Archives, Montgomery County Historical Society*)

The Air Service officials who viewed this vast tract of land were impressed and thrilled at the thought of obtaining enough land to comprise "the largest flying field in the world." Their response was so optimistic that the Dayton Air Service Committee proceeded immediately to secure options on all of the land. Meanwhile, Frederick Patterson continued to press the issue in Washington in order to obtain official approval of the project from the Air Service, and an iron-clad commitment from the government to accept the land when the Dayton Air Service Committee raised money to purchase it.

On October 25, 1922, Patterson announced that he had received a letter from the Air Service confirming its commitment to accept the land. With the government's approval of the proposed site also came word that the Air Service was contemplating the establishment of an air academy at the same location, a school that would eclipse both West Point and Annapolis in enrollment and importance.[100]

Patterson's response was swift and decisive. A dinner meeting of the Dayton Air Service Committee convened at the Dayton Country Club on Wednesday evening, October 25, to discuss specific strategies for raising money to purchase the land. It was decided to advertise creation of the new aviation facility as a lasting monument to the Wright brothers. The committee believed this concept would appeal to the sentiment of the entire community. Dayton citizens at the time were sorely aware of the fact that France was the only country to erect a monument commemorating the achievements of the Wrights. They felt that the most logical location in the United States for a similar memorial was Dayton, Ohio.

A massive public campaign was planned for the very next week, to be conducted on October 31 and November 1, 1922. The goal of the campaign was to raise $400,000. This would be enough to ensure purchase of the new lands, with a nest egg of at least $25,000 left over to erect an official memorial to the Wright brothers. It was imperative that money be raised quickly, because options on the land expired January 1, 1923.

H. D. Wehrley, executive secretary of the Community Chest, was named campaign manager. General headquarters for the campaign were established at the Chamber of Commerce offices in the Mutual Home Building at 40 North Main Street.[101] Twenty-five team captains were appointed to head teams of five men each.

Frederick Patterson hosted a dinner at NCR for more than 200 Daytonians involved in the campaign on Friday evening, October 27, at which time the entire project was explained in detail. Major General Patrick and Colonel Bane attended. In addition, the campaigners were treated to movies of the Pulitzer aerial race in Detroit and of Lieutenants John Macready and Oakley Kelly making their record-breaking, cross-country flight.[102]

By October 31, all of Dayton was aware of the immensity and importance of the campaign. At noon on the first day of the campaign a spectacular aerial exhibition was held over Dayton by crews from McCook Field. Factory whistles sounded simultaneously throughout the town to signal the beginning of the campaign.[103] Contributions were solicited from all major businesses, and intensive door-to-door canvassing resulted in many contributions from private citizens. Pledges were for a period of three years, collectable every six months commencing January 1, 1923, in order to encourage sizable donations.

The strategy carefully planned by Frederick Patterson worked. By sundown on October 31, $278,573 had been pledged, only $50,000 short of the amount needed to purchase the land. The second day of active campaigning terminated with a victory dinner for team captains and workers at the Miami Hotel. Patterson

More than 200 team captains and workers received campaign plans from the Dayton Air Service Committee at this dinner, October 27, 1922, hosted by Mr. Frederick B. Patterson in the NCR employee dining room. (*NCR Archives, Montgomery County Historical Society*)

announced that the response from the citizens of Dayton far exceeded the committee's expectations and that the fund had already passed the goal of $400,000.[104] In fact, pledges continued to flow in until November 10. Dayton historian Charlotte Reeve Conover wrote of the campaign:[105]

> For two days everybody thought and talked Wright Field. Not a man was left unapproached. All the arguments were aired; all our civic loyalty was drawn upon. When the final count of contributions to the fund was made it showed that Dayton "had gone over the top" to the tune of $425,673.

Once the final count of contributions had been tallied, Patterson wired General Patrick that the money had been raised and that steps were being made to expedite the legal transfer of land titles to the U.S. government. His telegram read, in part:[106]

> The spirit which dominated this campaign will ever mark the attitude of Dayton toward the United States Air Service. Our citizens always will extend a hearty hand of fellowship to its members. We are not unmindful of the kindly interest you have taken in this great project, and desire to thank you for your many courtesies and kind consideration.
>
> With best wishes for the continued wonderful progress of the United States Air Service, and assurance that Dayton always may be depended upon to do its share in furthering such a splendid and necessary cause, we are,
>
> The Dayton Air Service Committee
> F. B. Patterson, General Chairman

FROM DAYTON WITH PRIDE

The technicalities involved in purchasing land and presenting it to the government required that the Dayton Air Service Committee incorporate. Articles of incorporation for the committee were filed with the Ohio secretary of state on November 16, 1922. The articles listed, as committee officers: President, Frederick Beck Patterson, president of NCR; Secretary, Ezra M. Kuhns, general counsel of NCR; and Treasurer, W. M. Brock, secretary of the Gem City Building and Loan Association. The articles of incorporation empowered the committee to acquire and hold property intended for use by the government, to receive and enforce payment of subscriptions, and to borrow money on the faith and credit of those subscriptions. A finance committee was formed to implement plans for financing these transactions, headed by W. R. Craven, Valentine Winters, and Harry H. Darst.[107]

Negotiations for the land took place over several ensuing months, as did debate in Congress over the funds necessary to construct a new home for the Engineering Division and to complete the division's transfer from McCook Field. The Air Service decided not to carry the name of McCook to the new installation. The name "Wright Field" was deemed appropriate considering the size and location of the new field, and the direct link that would thus be forged between the new installation and aviation's founding fathers.

On August 9, 1924, 428.50 acres of Montgomery County (Mad River Township) land and 4,091.97 acres of Greene County (Bath Township) land were conveyed to the United States government by the Dayton Air Service Committee for the consideration of one dollar ($1.00) for each tract.[108] Frederick B. Patterson traveled to Washington, D.C., on August 17, 1924, to personally present Secretary of War John Weeks with the deeds to the acquired lands. Secretary Weeks insisted, due to the significance of the occasion, that Patterson have an audience with President Calvin Coolidge to make the presentation. Following the audience, President Coolidge addressed a very warm letter to Patterson recognizing and praising the sacrifices made by the people of Dayton.

The exact wording of the Warranty Deed presented to the government read as follows:[109]

> KNOW ALL MEN BY THESE PRESENTS:
>
> That THE DAYTON AIR SERVICE INCORPORATED COMMITTEE, a corporation organized under the laws of the State of Ohio, with principal offices at Dayton, Ohio, hereinafter referred to and styled the grantor, in consideration of One ($1.00) Dollar to it paid by the United States of America, receipt whereof is hereby acknowledged, does hereby GRANT, BARGAIN, SELL AND CONVEY to the UNITED STATES OF AMERICA, its successors and assigns forever, subject to the limitations hereinafter mentioned, the following real estate: (DESCRIPTION)

The original deeds recorded that the land was sold to the government for use as an aviation field, or for such other service of the United States as the government considered desirable. Upon abandonment or discontinuance of the use of the land, how-

72 PAGES TODAY

Main News Section
Second News Section
Society Section
Sport Section
Comic and Magazine Sections

DAYTON DAILY NEWS

MAIN NEWS SECTION

Fair Sunday and Monday; moderate temperature.

VOL. XXXVIII. No. 363 (SUNDAY EDITION Established Nov. 2, 1913) DAYTON, OHIO, SUNDAY, AUGUST 17, 1924. PRICE FIVE CENTS

U. S. ACCEPTS AIR FIELD GIFT

Military Home May Have New Hospital

OLD STRUCTURE FOUND UNSAFE AS PROBE ENDS

Fire Officials Are Called Into Congressional Inquiry.

MANY COMPLAINTS ARE TOSSED ASIDE

Evidence Fails to Support Rumors—Recommendations Outlined.

That a movement toward the erection of a new general hospital at the Dayton National Military home would be started at once, was the statement made Saturday night by Congressman Roy G. Fitzgerald as he, with Congressman Alfred Bulwinkle, finished a congressional probe of affairs at the Dayton institution.

Remodeled and altered innumerable times, the present structure housing all sick patients with the exception of tubercular, was declared to be a fire hazard that would within the next few years, fail to meet the ordinary code specifications for a building of this kind.

This will necessitate the construction of a new hospital and to bring it about when it will be urgently needed, the movement will be started at once, Congressman Fitzerald declared.

Assistant Fire Chief William H. Carver and Chief Inspector Joseph Kirby, made an examination of the building Saturday afternoon and while not classing it as a fire trap, pointed out many conditions that

ALLIED, GERMAN DELEGATES SIGN DEBT PROTOCOL

Reparations Problem Finally Settled Along Plan of Dawes.

HEAVY OBLIGATION TAKEN BY BERLIN

French Promise to Withdraw Soldiers as Soon as Possible.

TELEGRAM OF THANKS IS SENT TO DAWES

LONDON, Aug. 16.—Gen. Charles Gates Dawes sent a congratulatory message to the reparations conference this evening upon the happy conclusion of its labors. A reply was sent to Gen. Dawes, thanking him for his own work in behalf of reparations settlement.

LONDON, Aug. 16.—The German reparations problem which has kept Europe in a ferment for nearly five years,

MILLIONS TO BE SPENT HERE

The map shows the location of the new McCook field, the name of which may be changed to Wright Field, deed for which has been presented to the govern-

YOUTH OF LOEB, LEOPOLD IS PUT TO FOREGROUND

Ages of Two Slayers Are

MAN SHOT IN BOX CAR FIGHT

Four Arrested in Raid by Constables on Big Four Near Moraine City.

DAVIS TO MAKE 2 SPEECHES IN BUCKEYE STATE

To Discuss Issues in Hall

DAYTON LAUDED AS PATTERSON SUBMITS DEEDS

President, in Letter, Acknowledges Patriotism of Citizens.

WRIGHT MEMORIAL PROVISION IS MADE

Monumnt to Stand Among Costly Buildings to Go Up on Site.

Dayton's gift of 4988 acres of land, lying east of the city to be used in the relocation of McCook field, has been accepted by the government, it was announced Saturday by Frederick B. Patterson, head of the N. C. R., president of the National Aeronautic association and chairman of the Dayton Air Service committee which raised a fund to purchase the land.

This means that Dayton will continue to be the center of experimental work of the U. S. air service and forecasts the expenditure of millions of dollars in erecting buildings and otherwise equipping the new field.

Deeds for the land, given to the government, were recorded this week in Montgomery and Greene county courts.

The deeds then were taken to Washington by Mr. Patterson who presented them to the government through Secretary of War John W. Weeks, on behalf of the citizens of Dayton, who made the new air field possible.

Impressed by the nature of Mr. Patterson's mission, war department officials arranged that he be taken to the White House, where President Coolidge was told of the land gift.

M'COY FIGHTS SANITY PROBE OF ALIENISTS

Two-Hour Grill Leaves Former Boxer Completely Crushed.

EXPERTS REFUSE TO COMMENT ON TEST

Battler to Be Indicted For Murder by Jury, Tuesday.

LOS ANGELES, Aug. 16.—Weeping, ashamed, completely crushed, Norman Selby, professionally known as "Kid McCoy," emerged tonight from a two-hour examination by three alienists employed by the district attorney to fight the announcement of defense attorneys that the former ring champion is insane.

Jeering and twisting his lips so that he shouted out words from the corners of his mouth, McCoy bitterly resented the questioning at the hands of the trio of alienists, Dr. Victor Parkin, Dr. Louis Weber and Dr. Paul Bowers.

McCoy was given the army psychological tests, was asked scores of questions regarding his career and his eight marriages and at last examined physically.

The three alienists refused to comment on their tests or to indicate in any way their results.

They will submit a complete re-

ever, title to the lands, according to the deeds, would *ipso facto* revert to the grantors, with the government having the period of one year to remove or dispose of any buildings, structures, or improvements on the land, to which it would still hold title. From this original deed has undoubtedly sprung the popular misconception that the property occupied by Wright-Patterson Air Force Base today would revert to the city of Dayton or other original owners were the government to abandon the site or cease to employ civilian workers.

On December 18, 1924, however, the Dayton Air Service Committee reversed its position on the controversial clause by means of the following resolution:[110]

RESOLUTION:

This is to certify that at a special meeting of the Board of Trustees of the Dayton Air Service Incorporated Committee, held pursuant to notice, and at which a quorum was present, the following resolution was unanimously adopted. "Resolved: that this Committee does hereby waive and release its reversionary right in and to the lands conveyed to the United States Government lying in Montgomery and Greene Counties, Ohio, as described in deeds to the United States dated February 4, 1924 and August 9, 1924 respectively, and the President and Secretary of this Committee are hereby authorized and instructed to execute, acknowledge and deliver on behalf of the Committee, Quit Claim Deeds to the United States in and to the lands referred to, thereby releasing to the United States the Reversionary Right of this Committee to said lands, as contained in the former deeds.

IN WITNESS WHEREOF, I have hereunto set my name and the Corporation Seal of said Committee, on this 18th day of December, 1924.

The Dayton Air Service Incorporated Committee,
Ezra M. Kuhns, Secretary

A Quit Claim Deed stated that the Dayton Air Service Committee did "Remiss, release, and forever quit-claim to the United States of America, its successors and assigns forever, the above mentioned reversionary rights" to the donated lands.[111] The Dayton Air Service Committee, over the next six years, continued to donate small parcels of land to the government. These were, by and large, sections of land that had been exempted in the original deeds because of existing railroad and traction line rights-of-way. As these became available for sale, the committee purchased and donated them to the government—always for the consideration of $1.00. In all instances, following the December 1924 resolution, the property was sold to the government outright, with no reversionary rights attached.[112]

While negotiations were under way to secure the land for Wright Field, Congress debated over appropriations for the new field. A bill submitted to Congress in December 1922 by Representative Roy Fitzgerald of Ohio allowed the president, through the secretary of war, to sell and dispose of land, buildings, machinery, and equipment at air sites owned by the government when such were no longer of use to the Air Service, and deposit the proceeds thereof with the treasurer of the United States. The entire sum, not to exceed $5 million, would then be appropriated for the erection of buildings, for gas and electric systems, machinery, and equipment at the new field.[113] Senator Frank B. Willis of Ohio introduced a similar bill in the Senate. Both bills were subsequently referred

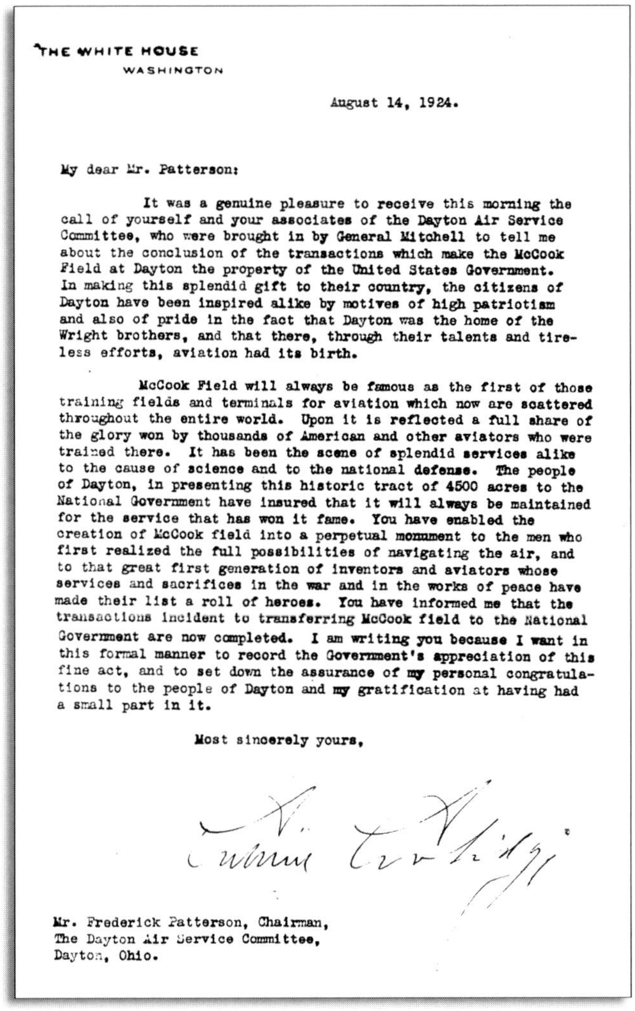

THE WHITE HOUSE
WASHINGTON

August 14, 1924.

My dear Mr. Patterson:

It was a genuine pleasure to receive this morning the call of yourself and your associates of the Dayton Air Service Committee, who were brought in by General Mitchell to tell me about the conclusion of the transactions which make the McCook Field at Dayton the property of the United States Government. In making this splendid gift to their country, the citizens of Dayton have been inspired alike by motives of high patriotism and also of pride in the fact that Dayton was the home of the Wright brothers, and that there, through their talents and tireless efforts, aviation had its birth.

McCook Field will always be famous as the first of those training fields and terminals for aviation which now are scattered throughout the entire world. Upon it is reflected a full share of the glory won by thousands of American and other aviators who were trained there. It has been the scene of splendid services alike to the cause of science and to the national defense. The people of Dayton, in presenting this historic tract of 4500 acres to the National Government have insured that it will always be maintained for the service that has won it fame. You have enabled the creation of McCook field into a perpetual monument to the men who first realized the full possibilities of navigating the air, and to that great first generation of inventors and aviators whose services and sacrifices in the war and in the works of peace have made their list a roll of heroes. You have informed me that the transactions incident to transferring McCook field to the National Government are now completed. I am writing you because I want in this formal manner to record the Government's appreciation of this fine act, and to set down the assurance of my personal congratulations to the people of Dayton and my gratification at having had a small part in it.

Most sincerely yours,

Mr. Frederick Patterson, Chairman,
The Dayton Air Service Committee,
Dayton, Ohio.

to the respective Military Affairs committees of each house. The Air Service was poised to begin construction as soon as the land was officially transferred and funds made available.

These efforts were strongly backed by the Dayton Air Service Committee. Additionally, Frederick B. Patterson reinstituted publication of a journal entitled *Aviation Progress*, first published by the Dayton Chamber of Commerce at the direction of John H. Patterson in March 1922, to educate members of Congress about achievements taking place at McCook Field and thereby influence them to pass the critical appropriations legislation. A special notice posted on the front cover of various issues of the journal stated:

> To Every Member of Congress:
>
> Development of the United States Air Service is one of the urgent needs of our nation. Bills supporting the program for its progress will come before you during the next session. Yours is a grave responsibility, and this booklet has been prepared to help you in careful study of the subject. Aviation must have your support.

Numerous large photographs with bold, clearly-worded text and impressive statistics were designed for at-a-glance reading by congressmen. To broaden the image of the contributions being made by the Air Service, *Aviation Progress* also elaborated on the brilliant future of aviation in general, illustrating such potential commercial applications as crop-dusting, air-mail service, passenger service, freight transport, medical relief, and the use of

AVIATION PROGRESS

Congress should provide enough money for scientific research in aviation.

This remarkable picture was taken by the official photographer of the U. S. Army Air Service at McCook Field, Dayton, Ohio. The picture shows Lt. Macready, holder of the world's altitude record, flying through the clouds over Dayton. All of the military research work of the country is done at McCook Field.

THE sub-committee of the House Military Appropriations Committee of Congress is considering the advisability of reducing the appropriation for aviation research work. The appropriation should not be reduced. The report of the sub-committee is to be made in the next few days.

The request of the United States Air Service for an appropriation of $4,200,000 for aviation research has been approved by Gen. Chas. G. Dawes, Director of Budgets. When the matter came up before the sub-committee of the House Military Appropriations Committee, it was intimated that the recommendation would be ignored. The sub-committee talked about reducing the appropriation to $2,000,000.

The cost of a modern battleship is $40,000,000. Can America afford to sacrifice its opportunity to make the country safe in war and also lead the world in civil aviation just to save $2,000,000—one-twentieth the cost of a single battleship?

United States needs brains of experts.

In the event that such action is taken, aviation research will be greatly retarded. It will result in the dismissal of half of the expert air men who are now devoting their time and brains to the development of aviation to the highest degree. The country needs their brains and their efforts.

Aviation research must be continued. The significance of aviation as a protective measure was emphasized in the discussions at the recent Limitation of Arms Conference. It was agreed that through the air service a country may have maximum defense at minimum expense.

War proved value of airplane.

What the airplane may do in warfare was demonstrated to a large degree in the late world conflict. Then, again, following the war, the supremacy of airplane attacks was most graphically demonstrated in the bombing experiments off the Virginia capes. As a result of this demonstration, military men agreed that military airplanes can destroy any type of surface craft now afloat.

Research makes for progress.

Aviation research has been carried on in a most commendable way during the past four years. Remarkable progress has been made. But to continue the work, Congress must provide sufficient funds.

Aviation preparedness is not a question of soldiers idly sitting by waiting for war, battleships eating up public funds tied to docks. It is a question of active scientific research to develop the military and commercial aviation resources of this country.

The present wave of economy—justifiable and desirable in the extreme—must not sweep away in its money-saving operations the United States air service research organization.

How the United States compares with other countries in aviation.

Authorized strengths in airplanes of leading countries.		Actual strength on October 1, 1921.		Aeronautical appropriations of the principal powers for 1922.	
United States	1229	United States	537	United States (Fiscal year 1921-1922)	$31,613,431
France	2163	France	1722	France, 435,926,595 francs	84,383,770
Great Britain	1077	Great Britain	1048	Great Britain, 20,033,400 pounds	97,161,990
Italy	1288	Italy	494	Italy, 64,760,000 lires	12,535,811
Japan	1101	Japan	537	Japan, Press Report	19,798,940

Banner of the Saturday, March 11, 1922, issue of *Aviation Progress*, published by the Dayton Air Service Committee (*NCR Archives, Montgomery County Historical Society*)

aerial photography to facilitate mapping, surveying, and city planning.

The battle to secure funding was long and controversial. The Fitzgerald bill and other efforts were blocked, and Congress adjourned without taking action. In 1925, however, and in succeeding years, Congress did make appropriations both for construction of buildings and for purchase of equipment for Wright Field:[114]

FISCAL YEAR	APPROPRIATIONS BUILDINGS AND GROUNDS	APPROPRIATIONS NEW EQUIPMENT
1926	$500,000	$297,600
1927	$1,000,000	$715,200
1928	$600,000	$792,300
1929	$300,000	$488,200

In April 1925, an initial $5,000 was transferred to the Engineering Division at McCook so that grading of the new flying field could start immediately.[115]

On August 21, 1925, the War Department discontinued the designation "Wilbur Wright Field." All of the land that had been donated to the government by the Dayton Air Service Committee in 1924 (including Wilbur Wright Field), combined with the government-owned acreage belonging to the Fairfield Air Intermediate Depot, became known officially as "Wright Field," honoring both Wilbur and Orville.[116]

Progress at the new site was rapid. In less than one year, the residents of McCook Field were prepared to transfer operations to their new home. Many important chapters in air advancement had been written at McCook Field. Even more startling chapters in aeronautical history would be recorded at Wright Field in the years to come.

GROUNDBREAKING AT WRIGHT FIELD

Official groundbreaking ceremonies were held at Wright Field on April 16, 1926. More than 100 citizens of Dayton, officials from McCook and Wilbur Wright fields, members of the Dayton Air Service Committee, and Orville and Katharine Wright, witnessed the auspicious event. Several local dignitaries took turns operating a steam shovel provided by the construction company to symbolically break ground. They included Frederick B. Patterson, Major John F. Curry, commander of McCook Field, and Major Augustine Warner Robins, commander of the Fairfield Air Intermediate Depot.

Members of the Dayton Air Service Committee, local Air Service officers, and distinguished guests attend groundbreaking ceremonies for Wright Field on April 16, 1926. (*NCR Archives, Montgomery County Historical Society*)

Frederick B. Patterson, at the controls, lifts the first bucket of earth at the site of Wright Field. *(Mrs. Howell Jackson)*

Distinguished guests at the Wright Field groundbreaking included Orville and Katharine Wright. *(Mrs. Howell Jackson)*

Frederick B. Patterson (left), Secretary of War Dwight F. Davis, and Chief of the Air Service Major General Mason M. Patrick at the Wright Field groundbreaking ceremonies *(Mrs. Howell Jackson)*

Construction at Wright Field gets under way *(Mrs. Howell Jackson)*

BUILDING A FIRM FOUNDATION—THE ESTABLISHMENT OF WRIGHT FIELD

Wright Field has been described as a kaleidoscope of aerospace science, engineering, technology, and education. As home of the Materiel Division and later the Materiel Command, Wright Field was the scene of engineering development and procurement, as well as the heart of Air Corps/Army Air Forces logistical support. As home of the Air Corps School of Engineering, Wright Field hosted countless young officers seeking advanced education in the developing fields of military aviation and logistics.

In the two decades between the dedication of Wright Field in 1927 and the designation of Wright-Patterson Air Force Base in 1948, the name of Wright Field was synonymous with military aeronautical development. Wright Field engineers and logisticians explored concepts that provided the impetus for a modern Air Force, and guided the technical development of aeronautical equipment that was at the time the most sophisticated in the world. Officers like Clinton Howard, Leslie MacDill, Franklin O. Carroll, Orval Cook, Kenneth B. Wolfe, George Goddard, Grandison Gardner, Albert Stevens, and Laurence Craigie, and outstanding civilian scientists such as John B. Johnson, Ralph Ferguson, Ezra Kotcher, Adam Dickey, Opie Chenoweth, Clarence Clawson, Samuel Burka, and John Lamphier helped the Wright Field laboratories achieve international renown. Military leaders such as William E. Gillmore,

Wright Field, 1929

Augustine Warner Robins, Oliver P. Echols, George C. Kenney, Hugh J. Knerr, William F. Volandt, Alfred J. Lyon, Elmer E. Adler, and Edward M. Powers made vital contributions to the logistical progress of the Air Corps.

Air-cooled radial engines, superchargers and turbosuperchargers, high-octane fuels, self-sealing fuel tanks, controllable-pitch and full-feathering propellers, cantilever and flying wings, pressurized cabins, automatic landing gear, blind-flying instrumentation, free-fall parachutes, autogiros, gliders, helicopters, and jet airplanes all have their special place in Wright Field history.

The roster of Wright Field test pilots included Air Force pioneers famous for their courage and skill: James H. Doolittle, Stanley M. Umstead, Benjamin Kelsey, Fred Bordosi, Frank G. Irvin, Ann Baumgartner, Albert Boyd, and J. S. Griffith. Some gave their lives in the path of progress at Wright Field: Hugh M. Elmendorf, Irvin A. Woodring, Ployer P. Hill, Perry Ritchie, Robert K. Giovannoli, Hezekiah McClellan, and Richard Bong.

It is appropriate that Wright Field, named in honor of Dayton's most famous native sons, has been a continuous center of American aeronautical development. The achievements that unfolded at Wright Field have perpetuated the Wright brothers' legacy of aeronautical ingenuity and their spirit of engineering excellence.

THE DEDICATION OF WRIGHT FIELD

The sun dawned in a gray and rainy sky on the morning of October 12, 1927. Twenty-four pilots from the 1st Pursuit Group had flown to Dayton from Selfridge Field, Michigan, to perform at the dedication ceremonies for Wright Field. All through the morning, they wandered about restlessly, eyes cast on the skies, for it seemed that the flying program would most certainly be cancelled.

At an early hour, distinguished guests and officials began arriving at the field. Orville Wright, the first gentleman of flight, Secretary of War Dwight F. Davis, Assistant Secretary of War F. Trubee Davison, Air Corps Chief Major General Mason M. Patrick, and Dayton industrialist and former Chief of the Signal Corps Equipment Division Colonel Edward A. Deeds headed the list of visiting dignitaries.

At 9:30 a.m. the new and modern Wright Field laboratories were opened for public inspection. For several days the different departments, recently relocated from McCook Field, had been occupied in arranging an impressive array of their experimental equipment for display. Materiel Division engineers from the Armament, Propeller, Parachute, Photographic, Radio, and Lighter-than-Air laboratories kept busy throughout the day answering a battery of questions about the complicated and unusual equipment with which they worked.

Parachutes, tow targets, bombs, machine guns, airship models, aviators' clothing, and countless other items on display captured the attention of Dayton's air-minded citizens.

The earth-induction compass was of particular interest to many aviation enthusiasts. A facsimile of the Hegenberger-Maitland instrument board used on the Air Corps California-Hawaii flight in June 1927 was on display, complete with B-5 compass, vertical flight indicator, engine gauge, airspeed indicator, and special tachometer. (See Chapter 4: Forging an Air Force for details of this exciting flight.) The non-freezing, pitot-static tube developed by Materiel Division engineers at the suggestion of the United States Air Mail Service was also available for close inspection. Thrilled groups of high school students surrounded the Ruggles Orientator to take turns simulating the maneuvers of flight.

Rain forced the official dedication ceremonies indoors to the new auditorium of the administration building. The band of the 10th Infantry, Ohio, opened the ceremony at 12:30 p.m. The dedication of the new installation as Wright Field, in honor of both Wilbur and Orville Wright, established two precedents. It marked the

Administration building, Wright Field. Known today as Building 11, Area B, it originally served as headquarters for the Air Corps Materiel Division when the division moved from McCook Field in 1927.

DEDICATION OF WRIGHT FIELD, OCTOBER 12, 1927

(Clockwise from top left) Members of the 10th Infantry Band, Ohio National Guard, prepare to play at the dedication of Wright Field. Curtiss P-1 Hawks from the 1st Pursuit Group, Selfridge Field, Michigan, thrilled spectators with low-level formation flying. Distinguished visitors at the dedication of Wright Field, October 12, 1927; front row (left to right): Orville Wright, Dwight Davis, Judge Kenesaw Mountain Landis, F. Trubee Davison, and Major General Mason M. Patrick; second row (from the left): Brigadier General William E. Gillmore, Dr. Joseph Ames, and Colonel Edward A. Deeds. (*Wright State University Archives*) Official dedication ceremony for Wright Field, held in the auditorium of Building 11. Wright Field civilian police secure the halyard of the first flag flown at Wright Field after it was raised by aviation pioneer Orville Wright. Secretary of War Dwight Davis is handing Mr. Wright his hat.

OFFICIAL MESSAGE FROM THE CHIEF, MATERIEL DIVISION

Brigadier General William E. Gillmore, who served as chief of the Air Corps Materiel Division, Wright Field, from October 1926 to June 1929. Building 262, Area A, the Air Force Materiel Command headquarters at Wright-Patterson Air Force Base, was dedicated in his honor on October 27, 1976.

The establishment of a permanent home for the headquarters of the Materiel Division, and suitable laboratories for prosecuting the engineering and scientific work necessary in procuring satisfactory flying and fighting equipment for our Air Corps, is a matter that should react with general pride and satisfaction to all people of our great country, and in particular to the people of Dayton, who through their generosity and understanding cooperation have helped to make these plans possible.

It is a fortuitous circumstance that the magnificent tract of land given to the government by the citizens of Dayton, should also be the scene of the first flying experiments of Wilbur and Orville Wright.

It is particularly fitting that this historic site should for all time be devoted to further experimentation in aviation, and maintained as an active and useful monument to their great gift to mankind. The dedication of this field in honor of the Wright brothers, and of the people of Dayton who presented the site to the Government, should be splendid inspiration to the men who must carry on this important work, which in spite of the wonderful progress made in the near past, is but in its infancy.

It is pleasing to think that the name of Wright, in addition to the glory already won, will hereafter be directly associated with the future developments of aviation.

WILLIAM E. GILLMORE
Brigadier General, Air Corps
Chief, Materiel Division

first time that an Army installation was named for two civilians who had never been in military service, and the first time an installation was named for a living individual. In all likelihood, it was also the first time that an individual so honored by the military service was present at his own memorialization.

Principal speakers at the event included Dwight Davis, F. Trubee Davison, Major General Patrick, Colonel Deeds, and Brigadier General William E. Gillmore, chief of the Materiel Division. Orville Wright occupied the seat of honor on the stage although, as was his custom, he declined to address the audience.

The central theme of the dedicatory addresses was the vital role played by the Materiel Division and its forerunner, the Engineering Division at McCook Field, in the progress of American aviation. The very existence of Wright Field, however, was a tribute to the citizens of Dayton. It was their persistence, prescience, and philanthropy that had persuaded the War Department to keep the Materiel Division in Dayton, Ohio, the cradle of aviation. The official dedication program listed more than 600 individual donors who had given concrete expression to their aviation enthusiasm.

Each of the distinguished speakers made reference to the great significance of the achievements of Dayton's famed native sons. The remarks of Secretary Davis were particularly salient:[1]

> So far as aviation is concerned, we are today on historic ground. Not very far from here stands the ramshackle structure which nearly a generation ago housed the first airplanes built by the Wright brothers—Wilbur and Orville. We are, therefore, in more than one sense, building upon the foundation laid by the Wright brothers and it is only fitting that we in this hour should recollect and honor the courage, patience and ability that made those first flying machines possible.

General Gillmore, in concluding the indoor portion of the ceremony, announced that Mr. Wright had consented to raise the first flag upon Wright Field. All adjourned to the flagpole in front of the administration building where, under the guiding hand of the world's first aviator, the Stars and Stripes was raised to the sound of the national anthem and honored with a 21-gun salute.

Symbol of the Air Corps Materiel Division, mounted above both main entrances of the headquarters building. Modeled after the famous Rodin sculpture *The Thinker*, the symbol was originally adopted by the Engineering Division at McCook Field and was retained after the 1926 reorganization creating Materiel Division.

Although it had been announced earlier that the flying program would be cancelled, a sudden clearing of the skies led officials to reverse their decision. Crowds began to gather at the flying field near Fairfield (formerly known as Wilbur Wright Field) immediately after lunch to inspect airplanes on display and to witness the flying exhibition.

The afternoon program opened with skilled acrobatic flying by McCook Field test pilots Lieutenants James Doolittle, James Hutchison, and Reuben Moffat. The acrobatic flying was followed by a tactical demonstration in which an unmanned observation balloon went down in flames.

The 1st Pursuit Group from Selfridge Field demonstrated 24-plane formation flying and other tactical formations. Parachute jumps were made by M. H. Clair of Wright Field and F. G. Manson, William Moore, and Owen Kindred of Fairfield, Ohio. Two of the parachutists side-slipped so that they landed impressively close to the crowd of spectators.

A free balloon, piloted by Major R. A. Hale and Lieutenant Malcolm S. Lawton, ascended from the field and landed some 45 minutes later in Clifton, Ohio. Shortly after 2:00 p.m., the Army's non-rigid dirigible, Airship RS-1, appeared overhead. A photographic airplane next impressed the crowd as an observer took pictures over the field, developed them in flight, and dropped the finished prints to earth before landing. Spectators were delighted to hear voices from a radio airplane in flight over the field broadcasting information on all the activities.

The final event of the day was the John L. Mitchell Trophy Race for pilots of the 1st Pursuit Group. Fifteen Curtiss P-1 Hawk biplanes entered. When all had finished the race, it was announced that there had been just one minute and 23 seconds difference in time between the first and last airplanes. The Mitchell Trophy was awarded to the winner, Lieutenant Irvin A. Woodring, to hold for one year. (Lieutenant Woodring later lost his life while testing an airplane at Wright Field on January 20, 1933.) Silver trophies for the first-, second-, and third-place winners were donated by Daytonians.

After the flying program, many of the spectators drifted over to the visiting commercial airplanes display. These included the Brock and Schlee *Pride of Detroit*, its fuselage adorned with an international collection of autographs; a Huhl Airster, in which Louis Meister had piloted a party down from Marysville, Michigan; a Stinson; a Waco; and many others. Near dusk, the three Wright Whirlwind engines on the visiting Ford Trimotor began to warm up. All passengers aboard, it headed north to reach Detroit in time for a late dinner. "It would probably strike darkness before landing, but the plane was equipped for night flying, so what was the difference? Somehow, that great monoplane winging its way into the dusk, about the ordinary business of flying home, was a fitting and symbolic finale to the Wright Field Dedication Ceremonies," by far the most elaborate dedication held in the long history of Wright-Patterson Air Force Base.[2]

MOVING MCCOOK FIELD

The topography of the land upon which Wright Field was located divided the field naturally into two parts. The 750 acres lying on the protected west side of Huffman Dam (later Area B) provided a logical site for the experimental plant and the main flying field of the Materiel Division. The remainder of Wright Field, approximately 3,800 acres, lay in the flood control basin of the Mad River. This larger portion included the site of the former Wilbur Wright Field and the 40-acre tract occupied by the Fairfield Air Depot (later Areas A and C). An old hangar in this area still stood as evidence of the flying school operated by Wilbur and Orville Wright at Huffman Prairie from 1910 to 1916. This larger area of the field was well suited for conducting air maneuvers on a large scale.

The process of moving Materiel Division operations from McCook Field to Wright Field began in the spring of 1927, prior to the official dedication. Most of the McCook Field operations were to relocate directly to new buildings on the smaller portion of the base. The Test Flight Section, however, planned to ship part of its equipment to the Fairfield Air Depot (FAD), closer to where its operations would be established.

In the early morning hours of March 25, 1927, the first trucks assembled at McCook Field in preparation for loading. A total of 69 buildings at McCook were to be emptied. Their contents ranged from airplanes, airplane engines, extremely

By June 1927, construction at Wright Field had progressed sufficiently to allow the Materiel Division to begin moving its mission, personnel, and equipment from McCook Field. Offices in the administration building (foreground) and in the laboratories behind it were occupied earlier.

Dismantling McCook for the move to Wright Field. Per terms of the McCook Field lease, buildings were razed and foundations were torn up. Materials such as steel girders were salvaged for use in construction at the new installation.

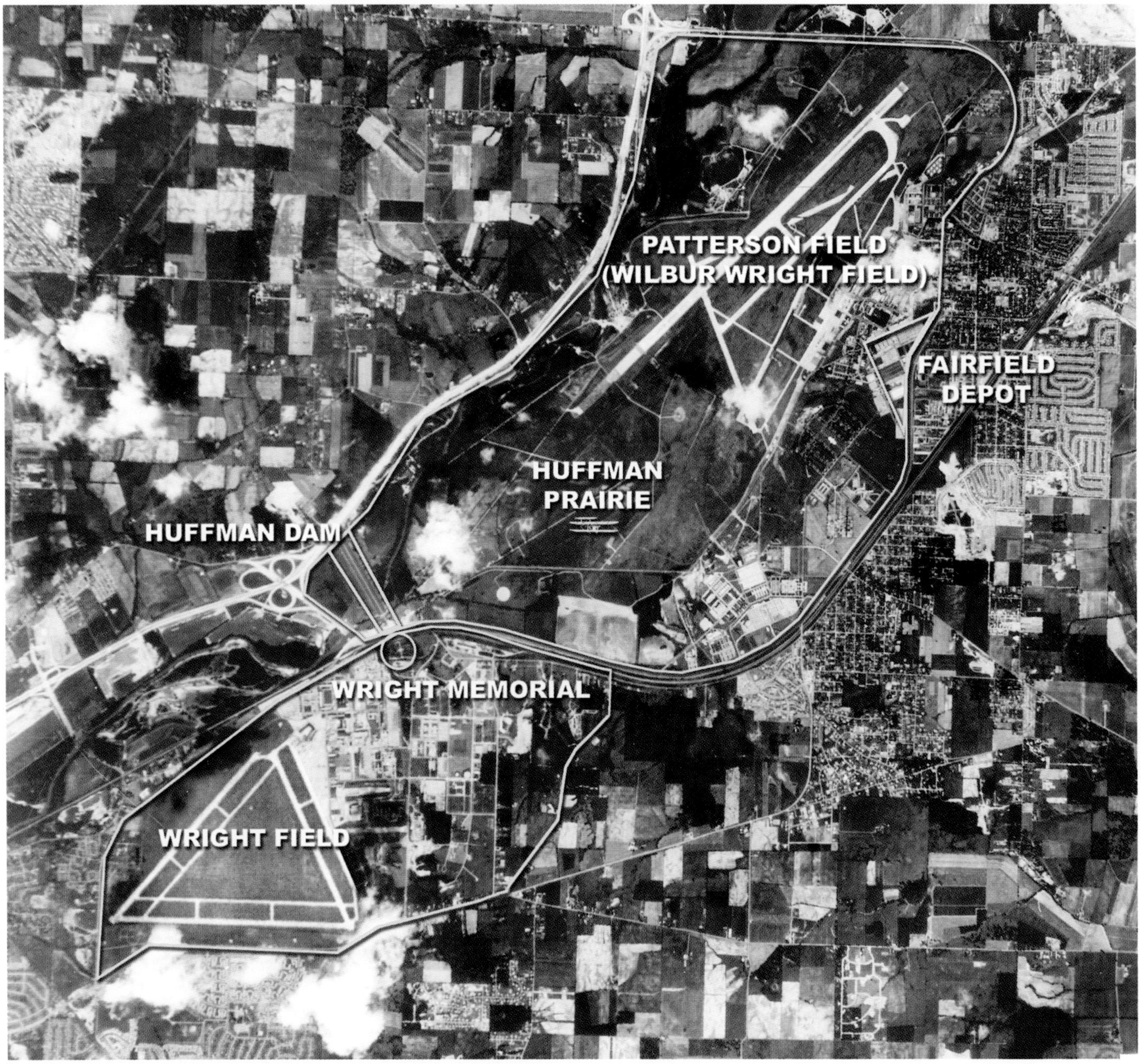

Aerial view of Wright-Patterson Air Force Base illustrating the spatial relationships of significant historical portions of the base

sensitive instruments used in flying and precision testing, a 14-inch wind tunnel, and an 11,000-pound punch press for stamping out metal tips used on propellers, to the 1,052 steel file cabinets, 600 desks, and other office equipment used in day-to-day operations. Also included were the McCook Field Aeronautical Reference Library and artifacts from the Army Aeronautical Museum. In all, it was estimated that more than 4,500 tons would be moved from the old field to the new.[3]

State highway regulations prohibited moving excessive tonnage by road during the spring season when the ground was soft. Thus, only lighter equipment could be hauled in McCook field trucks and the 28 trucks and trailers on loan from the Quartermaster Corps at Jeffersonville, Indiana. Spur tracks were laid at both McCook and Wright fields that connected with the electric railroad and standard railroad lines. Heavier equipment was loaded onto regular, flat-bottomed freight cars and transported by rail.

At the McCook Field site, provisions of the lease required that all buildings be removed and the ground restored to useable condition. The largest portion of the demolition program involved some 35 major buildings, mostly of standard Air Service, steel-hangar construction. The chief of the Repair and Maintenance Section directed demolition operations, using Quartermaster trucks and temporary labor crews. Some of the wooden buildings at McCook were sold to a local wrecking firm for removal.

Some salvaged materials from the demolished buildings were used to construct buildings at Wright Field, although the principal structures at the new field had been completed. Doors, door frames, and window sashes were salvaged, along with piping and sanitary fixtures, lighting fixtures, radiators, conduit and wire, and sheet metal work such as ventilators and cowling. The main salvage process was aimed at the steel framework of the McCook Field buildings. They contained nearly 900 tons of steel, representing a current market value of about $81,000. The steel was dismantled and transported to Wright Field.

Three important activities of the Materiel Division—the dynamometer laboratory, the propeller test building and test stands, and the 5-foot wind tunnel—remained in operation at McCook Field until new quarters could be completed at Wright Field. A lease was arranged with

THE MCCOOK FIELD 14-INCH WIND TUNNEL

McCook's 14-inch wind tunnel on display at the United States Air Force Museum

The first wind tunnel constructed for testing purposes at McCook Field was patterned after one designed by Orville Wright, though it was much larger. It consisted of 2,100 pieces of propeller-quality walnut, taken from the trimmings of propeller laminations, as well as quantities of mahogany and birch woods. Each three-quarter-inch length consisted of six segments glued and nailed in a circular shape before being turned on a lathe. The tunnel's interior surface was highly polished enamel. It had a diameter of 14 inches at the choke and 60 inches near the exit. The tunnel was slightly less than 22 feet long and was mounted on a massive wooden base.

A 24-blade fan with a diameter of 60 inches drew air through the tunnel. Driven through a jack-shaft, the fan was mounted on ball bearings and flexibly connected to a Sprague electric dynamometer, rated at 200 to 300 horsepower. The dynamometer drove the fan at a maximum speed of 2,000 rpm, producing an airspeed of 453 mph at the choke of the tunnel.

The tunnel was used to test or calibrate airspeed instruments and to study the aerodynamic properties of different shapes. Objects to be tested were mounted in the choke of the tunnel through a plate glass observation door at the side. Smoke pictures could be taken to help study how air flowed around a body of a given shape at different speeds.

This wind tunnel, a vital part of McCook Field research, is now on permanent display at the United States Air Force Museum.

The McCook Field baseball team became the Wright Flyers when it moved to Wright Field. The team won the Cosmopolitan League Championship with a 13-2 record the first year it wore Wright Flyer jerseys.

the General Motors Company, then owner of the section of McCook Field on which these labs stood, permitting use of the site until September 30. The lease was let in consideration of $1 and title to the buildings, thus allowing the division virtually free use of the grounds.[4] When facilities were still not complete in the fall, General Motors extended the lease. The new dynamometer lab at Wright Field was finally finished during fiscal year 1929. The 5-foot wind tunnel relocated during that year, too, together with installation of sufficient equipment to begin operations. The propeller testing activity transferred permanently to Wright Field on May 22, 1929.[5]

CONDITIONS AT THE NEW WRIGHT FIELD

With passage of the Air Corps Act and creation of the Air Corps Materiel Division in 1926, Wright Field was forced to accommodate a larger number of organizations than originally anticipated. To further complicate the matter, austere funding for military aviation delayed the construction schedule at Wright Field and plans for some of the new laboratories had to be delayed indefinitely. In all, conditions at the site were far from ideal for many of the incoming organizations.

One of the larger testing laboratories, the Materials Branch, was housed in a building that had been constructed for office use (Building 16). The associated heat-treating operation and all foundry operations, however, were set up at a separate site (Building 46) across the street from the main laboratory. This building, like many others at the time, was originally a temporary structure. At that point, it had a permanent concrete floor and steel-girder framework, but the roof and walls were covered with corrugated sheet steel, and the windows had wooden frames. Years later, brick walls, metal-frame windows, and permanent roofs were added.[6] Facilities yet to be erected included the airplane hangars, the firehouse, guard house, boiler house, gymnasium, school, and a civilian cafeteria. Many other buildings were of temporary construction and lacked permanent-type walls and roofs.[7]

No paved streets, sidewalks, or street lighting existed at Wright Field in the beginning months. Likewise, grading of the flying field and of grounds around the buildings had yet to be accomplished.[8]

Officer and enlisted housing remained on the list of projected construction. The buildings at McCook Field used for housing enlisted men had been vacated and demolished on April 1, 1927, as part of the move. In the interim, enlisted men were either attached to FAD for rations and quarters or paid a separate allowance. Officers were placed on commutation status, occupying privately owned housing in or about the city of Dayton, with the exception of officers of the Field Service Section and the Flying Branch, who occupied government quarters at FAD.[9]

A Caterpillar tractor (pulling a road-grader) and a wood-fired steam engine roller level the streets at Wright Field.

Perhaps most discouraging of all were the frequent curtailments of work due to lack of personnel. Government pay scales in the middle and late 1920s could not compete with salaries in the private sector. The Materiel Division experienced a high attrition rate as skilled scientists succumbed to the lure of better-paying jobs in private industry or simply tired of the heavy workloads and insufficient funding that beset military aviation. Austerity at the time prohibited filling positions left vacant, thus further increasing the workload for those who remained.

Moreover, no money was available for new equipment or lab furniture. Lab personnel helped plan, cut, assemble, and erect such necessary items as room partitions, chemical hoods and worktables, benches, and cabinets at the new location.

Despite these many difficulties, much excitement and a blossoming faith in the glorious future of the new installation surrounded the move to Wright Field. Once back to working capacity, the laboratories of the Materiel Division were, in fact, the equal of other top-level research laboratories in the world.

By July 1928, practically all activities of the Materiel Division were housed in their new facilities. The only exceptions were the flight test operations at Fairfield and the propeller test facility still at McCook. Principal units added during fiscal year 1927 were the assembly shops building, the dynamometer laboratory, the torque stands, the generator house, foundations for the first propeller test rig, and the building for the 5-foot wind tunnel.[10] As fiscal year 1927 came to a close, contracts were awarded for construction of the flight hangars. Hangars 2 and 3, their headhouse (later Hangar 10), and Hangar 4 were completed and occupied in fiscal year 1929.[11]

A concrete ramp, shown under construction in 1931, surrounded the hangars at Wright Field. For nearly a decade, this ramp served as a "runway" for pursuit airplanes such as the Curtiss Hawk biplanes. Wright Field's runways were not paved until 1941.

Civilian firefighters pose in front of the newly completed Wright Field firehouse in 1931. A plaque mounted on the front of the building dedicated it to the memory of Mr. Frank A. Smith, who lost his life during construction of the station.

The stone gatehouses at Wright Field's entrance were completed in September 1931. At left is Building 11, Materiel Division headquarters.

THE MISSION OF THE MATERIEL DIVISION

The Materiel Division, as mentioned briefly in Chapter 2, was established at McCook Field on October 15, 1926, nearly one year prior to the dedication of Wright Field. The division was one of three major activities of the newly designated Air Corps, as established under provisions of Public Act 446 (69th Congress). This legislation, approved July 2, 1926, amended the national defense act to change the name of the Air Service to "Air Corps" and provided the chief with three assistants, each with the rank of brigadier general. Brigadier General James E. Fechet was placed in charge of the Operations Division with headquarters at Washington, D.C., and Brigadier General Frank P. Lahm was assigned as head of the Air Corps Training Center headquartered at Kelly Field, Texas. Brigadier General William E. Gillmore was appointed to direct the diverse and complex workings of the Materiel Division at Dayton.

The Materiel Division assumed responsibility for all functions previously performed by the Engineering Division, the Supply Division, the Industrial War Plans Division, and the Materiel Disposal Section of the Air Service, leaving only a materiel liaison office in Washington in the Office of the Chief of the Air Corps. When the Supply Division moved to Dayton in the fall of 1926, all materiel activities of the Air Corps became centralized in Dayton, with temporary headquarters at McCook Field pending completion of the permanent headquarters at Wright Field.[12]

Despite initial difficulties, this reorganization led to a more efficient and economical system of operation and placed the logistics organization of the Air Corps on a firmer footing. To accomplish the goals of the five-year Air Corps expansion program authorized in 1926, procurement, supply, and engineering functions worked closely together, even if relations between them were not entirely harmonious.

Under the direction of General Gillmore, six major sections conducted the operations of the Materiel Division. All six moved to Wright Field during the spring and summer of 1927. These sections were:[13]

- Procurement
- Engineering
- Administration
- Field Service
- Industrial War Plans
- Repair and Maintenance

The first three of these are discussed below. Because the functions of the Repair and Maintenance Section were divided in the late 1920s, with repair operations assigned to the Engineering Section and maintenance carried out as a function of the Administration Section, that section is not covered separately.

In addition to materiel and engineering functions, the chief of the division also directed operations of the Air Corps Engineering School and the Army Aeronautical Museum at Wright Field.

Panoramic view of Wright Field, 1930. In the foreground is the boiler plant that provided steam heat for all major buildings. On the right are laboratories and administrative offices of the Materiel Division. Beyond them are hangars and the concrete ramp. To the left are shops, test facilities, and warehouses.

Procurement Section

Relations between the military and the civilian aircraft industry, which were somewhat strained in the early 1920s, became more amicable in the late 1920s and early 1930s. A major factor was increased public awareness of aviation, resulting in wider interest in aeronautical development and a willingness to support it. Increased procurement activity under the five-year Air Corps development program was also instrumental in restoring health to the American aircraft industry, which had struggled under financial difficulties since the end of World War I.

The Procurement Section of the Materiel Division was responsible for purchasing practically all equipment and supplies used by the Air Corps, from new airplanes to necessary operating and maintenance supplies. In the rapidly developing field of aviation, the Materiel Division often found itself seeking parts not yet available commercially, or ones with more stringent requirements than could be met by existing products. Such needs taxed the patience and ingenuity of both the Procurement Section and cooperating manufacturers. Batteries, carburetors, spark plugs, generators, starters, radiators, radio tubes, and incandescent lamps, for example, were all commercially available for automotive purposes. Off-the-shelf auto parts did not transfer successfully to airplanes, however, because of the more severe environmental conditions to which the parts were routinely subjected. The job of the Procurement Section was to identify the specialized aspects of thousands of items needed by the Air Corps, locate or oversee the adaptation of suitable items, and establish reliable sources of supply for them. Procurement became a process of persistent, creative problem solving.[14]

The major work of the Procurement Section was performed by its four branches. Contract Administration compiled information about individual contractors' plant facilities, resources, and finances. The Purchase Branch, with two contracting officers and approximately 60 civilians, secured bids, awarded contracts, administered purchase orders, and followed contracts until delivery was made. The Legal Branch addressed the many legal questions involved in making awards and administering contracts.

Perhaps the most important and difficult work of the Procurement Section, however, was performed by the Inspection Branch. The procurement inspection program was organized into three major districts, with centers in New York City (Eastern District), Dayton (Central District), and Santa Monica (Western District). Six Air Corps officers were designated as Air Corps inspection representatives under the jurisdiction of the Materiel Division and were assigned to airplane contractors' plants in an on-site inspection capacity. At different times, Materiel Division representatives were stationed at the following manufacturing plants:[15]

- Consolidated Aircraft Company, Buffalo, New York
- Curtiss Aeroplane and Motor Company, Buffalo and Garden City, New York
- Keystone Aircraft Corporation, Bristol, Pennsylvania

Major General Benjamin D. Foulois, head of the Materiel Division from July 1929 to June 1930, hosted the second class of the special Navigation School at Wright Field. From left: Captain Clyde V. Finter, instructor, Lieutenant Odas Moon, Lieutenant Westside Larson, Lieutenant Lloyd Blackburn, General Foulois, Lieutenant Harry Halverson, Lieutenant Edgar Selzer, Lieutenant Uzal Ent, and Lieutenant Bradley Jones.

Attendees at a 1936 Engineering and Supply Conference sponsored by the Procurement Section of the Materiel Division. Those destined to play a future role in Wright-Patterson history include, by number: (3) Lieutenant Colonel Junius H. Houghton, (4) Colonel Frank M. Kennedy, (7) Brigadier General Augustine W. Robins, (18) Colonel Joseph T. McNarney, (24) Captain Joseph T. Morris, (35) Major Bennett E. Meyers, and (38) Lieutenant Edwin W. Rawlings.

- Douglas Company, Santa Monica, California
- Boeing Company, Seattle, Washington
- Goodyear-Zeppelin Corporation, Akron, Ohio
- Northrop Company, Inglewood, California

In addition, some 110 civilian inspection employees operated from district inspection offices located strategically throughout the country, with responsibility for inspecting contracted items wherever necessary. At Wright Field, a staff of approximately 50 civilians controlled and coordinated requirements for inspections conducted at division facilities or in the field. By 1937, equipment and supplies purchased by the Air Corps involved approximately $60 million in contracts, all requiring approval and acceptance by the Procurement Section.[16]

The work of the Procurement Section also supported advancements of the Materiel Division in other areas. Engineering work carried on by the Materiel Division at Wright Field, while devoted entirely to the development of military aircraft, resulted in great benefit to civil and commercial aeronautics, especially in the solution of basic problems, the development of standards, and the dissemination of technical information.

The Procurement Section served as liaison between the Materiel Division and manufacturers of airplanes and aircraft equipment. Every effort was made to impress contractors with the necessity of furnishing equipment that functioned reliably with only a moderate amount of maintenance. The standards maintained by the Materiel Division thus ensured the high quality of equipment for military application and also engendered improvements in civil aeronautics.

The Procurement Section made a conscientious effort to promote standardization in several arenas. It furthered Air Corps policy to develop more than one source of supply by encouraging competing manufacturers to develop the same article. Samples of each company's product were tested for contract specifications, and several manufacturers might be listed as acceptable suppliers for the item.

The Materiel Division also worked closely with the Bureau of Aeronautics in adopting common standards, the goal being to facilitate reduction in stocks and increase use of identical processes by aircraft manufacturers. As part of this liaison, a conference devoted to developing standards was held each year, attended by representatives of the Materiel Division, the Bureau of Aeronautics, and interested manufacturers. Resulting policies were of special benefit to aircraft manufacturers doing joint work for the Army and the Navy.[17]

Standardized accounting procedures for contractors were established by the Procurement Section in the early 1930s. Prior to that time, individual manufacturers set up their accounts and determined their costs in discretionary fashion. This resulted in a diversity of methods for determining engineering costs, special tool costs, depreciation costs, and other overhead expenses. The Procurement Section made an effort to apply cost statements to each contract in order to compare the different manufacturers' costs. Comparisons could not be made on any equitable basis, however, until allowances were made for the different methods of distributing overhead expenses—a difficult process.

The Materiel Division rectified this situation by initiating a system that went a long way toward standardization of the industry. Division personnel drafted a chart of accounts that fit the needs of industry and ensured uniformity in accounting and cost finding. A conference was convened for contractors' representatives at which the accounts were discussed and the final form

Main entrance to Wright Field, looking north, October 1932. The flagpole and ceremonial 75-mm field artillery piece sit in front of Materiel Division headquarters (Building 11, not visible). The cannon fired salutes during reveille and retreat ceremonies.

South side of the Wright Field Assembly Building (Building 31). Virtually every type of aircraft in the Air Corps' inventory visited this hangar at one time or another during the 1930s.

of the chart was agreed upon. The provisions of these accounts went into effect on January 1, 1933, and were conscientiously applied by the contractors concerned. The new system permitted direct comparisons of the costs of different types of airplanes, considerably simplifying the process.[18]

In addition to this new way of processing cost information, Wright Field also provided direct benefit to civil aeronautics in an ambitious program of disseminating technical information to the industry. Instruction books and numerous reports were made available dealing with approaches and solutions to structural, aerodynamic, design, and maintenance problems.

Engineering Section

The work of the Engineering Section was the most complex and the most exciting of all the activities at Wright Field. The Engineering Section consisted of seven main engineering branches: Aircraft, Power Plant, Engineering Procurement, Equipment, Materials, Armament, and Shops. Overall, the role of the Engineering Section was to initiate experimentation, design, testing, and development of airplanes, engines, propellers, accessories, and associated ground equipment.

The responsibilities of the individual branches of the Engineering Section provide a composite view of engineering activities at Wright Field in the period from the dedication of the installation in 1927 until 1939, at which time the rapid buildup associated with World War II necessitated a reorganization of the Materiel Division.

Aircraft Branch

The Aircraft Branch was concerned with the development of new types of aircraft and with the improvement of those already accepted as standard. It included the former Airplane and Lighter-than-Air branches that had been consolidated under its jurisdiction during fiscal year 1932.[19] When an entirely new airplane was contemplated, the Aircraft Branch made a thorough study of the qualifications desired and drew up proper specifications. These specifications were then submitted to manufacturers across the country for their use in drafting tentative designs. Completed design proposals including, in the case of procurement competitions, actual prototype airplanes were submitted to the branch for examination.

After delivery of a prototype airplane from the manufacturer, the engineers of the Aircraft Branch submitted it to rigorous test and evaluation. Wright Field housed the most extensive and modern aircraft test facilities available, representing an equipment investment of approximately $10 million by 1938.[20] These facilities were divided into six major laboratory functions, all reporting to the chief of the branch.

The *Structures Development and Test Laboratory* conducted stress analysis of all aircraft submitted to the Air Corps, tested the structural strength of aircraft after purchase, and developed new methods of assembling aircraft structures. It is to this group that the world owes the development of the all-metal monocoque airplane and also the first sub-stratosphere airplane, complete with pressurized cabin. This Wright Field laboratory, building on early developmental work at McCook Field, perfected the sciences of static and dynamic testing to the state-of-the-art levels used through the 1930s. The purpose of this testing was to calculate the maximum strength of a particular structure, both at rest and in motion. In static testing, airplane structures were kept at rest and

Superstructure of the craneway for the propeller test rigs at Wright Field, under construction in 1926. The railroad-type car that traveled along the top of the craneway housed the 20-ton crane used to carry aircraft engines to and from the test stands.

Propeller mounted on electric whirl rig No. 2 for testing, 1944. The test rigs were enclosed during World War II.

weighted down with lead bars or shot-filled bags. In dynamic testing, the structures being tested were supported by a jig and then dropped. The height and angle of the drop were mathematically computed to give the same shock or jar to the assembly that it would actually sustain under specific landing conditions.

The structural test laboratory at Wright Field in the 1930s was one of the best equipped in existence. (The structures laboratory should not be confused with the "static test" facility, Building 65, completed in 1944 to perform structural tests on the B-36 bomber.) The weight of the jig and its auxiliary members used in dynamic testing was 52 tons, supported on a 228-ton base of reinforced concrete and steel. Two traveling cranes of five-ton and 15-ton capacity, respectively, made easy work of picking up a complete airplane or an entire static test setup, steel scaffolding and all.

The *Special Research and Test Laboratory* of the Aircraft Branch prepared airplane design studies from which military characteristics were established; prepared final design specifications for new airplanes; evaluated new airplanes submitted on competition to the Air Corps; and, once an airplane was placed in service, corrected unsatisfactory design features. Many of these projects were of a strictly experimental nature.[21]

The *Propeller Research and Test Laboratory* conducted exhaustive tests to determine the characteristics of each type of propeller accepted by the Air Corps. During the 1930s, the Materiel Division possessed the largest propeller test rigs in the world. Propellers up to 45 feet in diameter could be whirl-tested for endurance at speeds up to 4,300 rpm. Electric motors, the largest being one of 6,000 horsepower, powered the propeller rigs. When the propeller lab and the power plant lab conducted tests, the demands for electric power were so terrific that a special Dispatcher's Office at Wright Field coordinated testing schedules with attendants at the Dayton Power and Light Company. Personnel in the propeller lab performed this duty, and designed the outdoor electric substation at the field. The Propeller Research Lab also engaged in continuous research and development of new types of propellers. The introduction of controllable-speed and variable-pitch metal propellers was the result of thousands of hours of study and testing at Wright Field. The propeller lab also conducted all propeller tests for the Navy and the Department of Commerce.[22]

WRIGHT FIELD'S 5-FOOT WIND TUNNEL

The initial Wright Field wind-tunnel building

Inside the permanent Wright Field 5-foot wind tunnel building, 1936

The 5-foot wind tunnel was one of the last items moved from McCook Field to Wright Field because the building specially constructed for it was not completed until 1929.

In 1921, engineers at McCook Field, Ohio, began construction of a 5-foot wind tunnel for use in testing the aerodynamic qualities of airplane designs. McCook Field already had a 14-inch tunnel, but it proved too small for larger models and could not work with the lower wind speeds needed to test some components. Elisha Noel Fales, an aeronautical engineer at McCook, recommended an 8-foot tunnel, but the design was scaled back to five feet to fit within existing facilities (a steel hangar) at the small airfield. Working without detailed design drawings or specifications, the Wood Shop at McCook, directed by R. J. Myers, constructed the tunnel in little more than a year.

The finished tunnel measured 96 feet long and five feet in diameter at the throat or test section. Two 12-foot-diameter, 12-bladed, counter-rotating fans powered by four Sprague dynamometers produced wind speeds up to 260 mph. The tunnel could be used for both high- and low-speed tests, and accommodated airplane models with wingspans up to 40 inches. Rated as the most efficient tunnel in the world at that time, the 5-foot wind tunnel was immediately put to use testing airplane components and models, such as the XNBL-1 Barling bomber and dirigible designs.

In 1929, the wind tunnel was moved to a new facility at Wright Field. The brick structure allowed the wind tunnel to operate more efficiently by stabilizing internal air pressure. In the 1930s, nearly every airplane procured was tested for its aerodynamic characteristics in the tunnel. Additional tests contributed to the solution of dangerous flutter problems and the effectiveness of ailerons on airplane control. Even after larger tunnels were built at Wright Field during World War II, the 5-foot tunnel continued to be used for aircraft and missile tests, including designs of the X-24B, the X-29, the F-4C, the F-15, the C-130, and the EC-135.

The Air Force Institute of Technology assumed operation of the tunnel in 1958, and unlike the larger tunnels built during World War II, the tunnel continued to operate as a teaching and research tool into the twenty-first century. In 1992, the American Society of Mechanical Engineers dedicated it as a National Historic Mechanical Engineering Landmark. It remains the oldest operational wind tunnel in the world.

Sources: James F. Aldridge, *Wright Field's Five Foot Wind Tunnel* (Wright-Patterson Air Force Base, Ohio, 1997); Emma J. H. Dyson, Dean A. Herrin, and Amy E. Slaton, The *Engineering of Flight: Aeronautical Engineering Facilities of Area B, Wright-Patterson Air Force Base, Ohio* (Washington, D.C., 1993), pp 84-86.

The *Aerodynamics Research and Test Laboratory* developed methods for calculating aerodynamic performance of new airplanes through predictive measurements taken in wind tunnels, as well as actual performance measurements of the airplane in flight. This laboratory made major contributions to the science of aerodynamics and to the establishment of design criteria for the best aerodynamic shapes for control surfaces, fairings, fillets, and the like.

Two wind tunnels, 14 inches and 60 inches in diameter, respectively, operated at Wright Field prior to World War II. The smaller tunnel was used for testing small airfoils or propellers, the larger for complete airplane models. Both contained highly sensitive instruments for precise measures of performance criteria. The 5-foot wind tunnel, 90 feet in length, could test components at air speeds up to 275 mph.[23]

The *Accessory Design and Test Laboratory* developed and tested wheels, brakes, tires and tubes, landing gear complete with retracting mechanism, skis, floats, hulls, and other aircraft parts. Wheels and brakes were constantly tested to produce correct drum and brake-lining combinations. Oleo struts and retracting mechanisms were evaluated for each type of airplane. Hydraulic and pneumatic mechanisms were tested and perfected, as was landing gear designed for instrument landings and takeoffs.

The *Lighter-than-Air Unit* of the Aircraft Branch developed and refined Air Corps balloons, balloon accessories, and non-rigid airships. In the 1920s, for example, this unit was largely responsible for the development of the TC-13, a non-rigid airship designed for patrol and reconnaissance. Produced by Goodyear, the TC-13 was 196 feet long, had a capacity of 200,600 cubic feet of helium or hydrogen gas, and could cruise at 47 mph for 1,650 miles, powered by two 150-horsepower Wright engines.

The Aircraft Branch also concerned itself with the development of the "pressure cabin." Early experiments conducted at McCook Field between 1919 and 1923 attempted to solve one of the major human problems associated with high-altitude flying: in the low air pressure above 30,000 feet, pilots could not assimilate sufficient oxygen to function. The goal was to develop a pressurized compartment that maintained a constant air pressure regardless of the airplane's altitude. These experiments were suspended around 1923 because they involved greater complication and expense than was warranted.

By February 1935, however, the need for a pressurized cabin had increased significantly and Wright Field engineers initiated a renewed effort. In the summer of 1937, their energetic program of research and experimentation produced the world's first airplane with a pressurized cabin. The invention proved successful when operated over several hundred hours at altitudes where oxygen was usually required, and soon became a feature of both new military and commercial aircraft.[24]

The Lockheed XC-35, developed at Wright Field, was the first successful, pressurized-cabin airplane. In 1937, the Air Corps received the Aero Club of America Trophy (renamed the Robert J. Collier Trophy in 1944) for designing, supervising construction, and completely equipping the airplane.

Power Plant Branch

The second major component of the Engineering Section of the Materiel Division was the Power Plant Branch. Activities of this branch were housed in the dynamometer laboratory, the torque stands, and the fuel test laboratory. Visitors to Wright Field could not ignore the roar of engines under test, either on torque stands or in the dynamometer laboratory. The refinement of airplane engines represented the heart of aviation development. The work of the Power Plant Branch concentrated primarily on increasing the power output of engines in service, developing new types of engines, improving fuels to permit greater power output and lower fuel consumption, and extending supercharging to higher power and altitudes. The exhaust gas turbine supercharger and other types of turbine superchargers with greater capacity were successfully adapted to radial, air-cooled engines.

The development of engine accessories paralleled and supported this work. The Power Plant Branch made progress during the 1930s in developing such accessories as vacuum pumps, long-reach spark plugs, magnetos and fielding, engine-driven gearboxes for accessory drives, hydraulic fuel-pump drives, fuel pressure regulators, automatic oil temperature control valves, automatic supercharger regulators, automatic mixture controls, fuel injectors and controls, and hydraulic engine controls. The general trend of these improvements was to reduce the great mass of control handles and gadgets in the cockpit by replacing as many as possible with proven automatic controls.[25]

Each model of an engine submitted for evaluation to the Power Plant Branch was first subjected to a 50-hour Development Test. After completing necessary modifications, the engine was subjected to a 150-hour Type Test. Successful completion of this test established that particular model as satisfactory for use in military aircraft, and it was assigned an Air Corps model designation. The duration and severity of the Type Test usually revealed any major problem with an engine, although subsequent Service Test results were the basis of its final evaluation. If, during the evaluation process, an engine was judged to possess unusual military value, it was normally a year or more before release was granted for its use on commercial airliners or export to foreign countries.[26]

Wright Field torque stand complex

The *Dynamometer Laboratory* was equipped with instruments to compute and measure performance of high-powered aircraft engines and their components. These sophisticated instruments included high-speed dynamometers for measuring output or driving torque, gauges for determining fuel consumption, scales for measuring oil consumption, revolution counters, and tachometers for measuring engine speed.

The *Torque Stand* complex was one of the more imposing structures at Wright Field. A series of 40-foot stacks, joined by enclosed passages, was built to contain seven torque stands, six for engine endurance tests and one for propeller tests. The stacks were open to the sky to take in fresh air from above and discharge air upward to be carried away by the wind. High-powered engines tested on the torque stands produced almost deafening noise, for up to 150 hours at a time. So intense was this noise that pilots flying over the stacks at altitudes up to 600 feet reported hearing it over the roar of their own engines.[27] Each engine support pier consisted of a huge block of concrete sunk 20 feet into the ground and completely encased in cork to absorb vibration. Observation rooms full of instruments enabled engineers to study engine performance under various tests.

The *Fuel Test Laboratory* contained six single-cylinder engines especially designed and constructed for testing fuels and lubricants. This laboratory worked to improve quality standards for fuels and lubricants to effect significant increases in aircraft engine performance. An oil dilution system for cold weather starting, for example, became standardized for all types of aircraft.[28]

The Power Plant Branch made many significant contributions to overall engine development during the 1930s. Not only did it conduct extensive experimentation with high-powered, air-cooled engines, for example, but it also revitalized the potential of liquid-cooled engines. The development of an antifreeze solution (commonly called Prestone) to replace water as a coolant made it possible to reduce the

Refrigeration equipment in the laboratories of the Power Plant Branch was used in the development of cold-weather accessories and temperature controls for aircraft.

size of the radiator in liquid-cooled engines by 60 percent. With Prestone cooling, supercharging, and propeller gearing, liquid-cooled engines remained a promising technology for many more years.

Engineering Procurement Branch

During fiscal year 1933, all engineering procurement activities transferred from the Procurement Section to the Engineering Section to simplify administration of contracts. In a further refinement, the Engineering Section created an Engineering Procurement Branch in May 1935 to handle the engineering work pertaining to aircraft acquisition.[29]

The work of the Engineering Procurement Branch included assembling and coordinating all technical data required for the procurement of a complete aircraft. The branch was responsible for following a complete contract, from preparing initial specifications to making necessary adjustments during the course of the contract. These adjustments might extend well beyond the delivery date of the last contracted airplane, depending on the contractor's degree of responsibility.

As a sample of its operations, during 1936 the Engineering Procurement Branch handled the procurement work involved in the manufacture of about 1,230 airplanes, including three autogiros. These airplanes were of 30 distinct types, which could be further broken down into 40 different models. These contracts covered both production and modification. In addition, myriad other processes were carried on, such as the handling of data submitted informally, the examination of foreign and racing plane data, and the completion of the many special studies, reports, and investigations required for the information of the chief engineer or for transmittal to higher authority.

The project officer for any given contract carried a heavy load of responsibilities. Typically, he maintained a file of data on corresponding foreign airplanes, as well as data on similar, previously constructed domestic aircraft. Acting as the direct representative of the chief engineer, the project officer visited the manufacturing plants and the tactical units operating "his" airplanes. He flew demonstration airplanes as soon as they were available and obtained other pilots' comments on the demonstration model. Coordinating with the Air Corps' representative at the manufacturer's plant, he usually ferried the first model of a contracted airplane to Wright Field. He further monitored the Wright Field tests. He was a member of the Mock-Up Board and an observer at static testing. He watched inspections and initiated any order affecting "his" airplanes that came to Wright Field for demonstration, test, acceptance, or modification. The project officer thus followed the production of a given type from the inception, in the form of basic "military characteristics," through all procedures, to the delivery of the last airplane.[30]

Equipment Branch

The Equipment Branch of the Engineering Section consisted of six laboratories: Instrument and Navigation, Electrical, Parachute and Clothing, Aerial Photographic, Miscellaneous Equipment, and Physiological Research. This branch was responsible for research and development as well as standardization of approximately 500 items of ground and air equipment. Flight indicators, turn indicators, artificial horizons, directional gyroscopes, altimeters, airspeed indicators, compasses,

Wright Field facilities, 1934. To the right of hangars, in a line, are the Power Plant torque stands, the wind-tunnel building, the power house for the Propeller Laboratory, and the propeller test rigs and craneway.

DEVELOPMENT OF THE PARACHUTE

Following World War I, Major Edward L. Hoffman, an engineer and pilot, and his Parachute Branch in the Equipment Section of the Engineering Division at McCook Field, worked to develop an acceptable personnel emergency escape parachute for use with aircraft. Although American balloon crewmen had carried parachutes during the war, those in aircraft had not. On April 28, 1919, Leslie L. Irvin jumped from a USD-9 biplane flying at approximately 80 mph at 1,500 feet to become the first American to complete a jump after manually opening the parachute in midair. Irvin deployed his chute at an altitude of approximately 1,000 feet. Irvin broke his ankle on landing, but the test proved the suitability of the new parachute. Hoffman's assistant, James Floyd Smith, with the help of others in the branch, had developed the new chute.

Smith, himself a veteran aviator, made the second jump followed by two other civilian "parachute mechanics," James Russell and James Higgins. Sergeant Ralph Bottriell became the fifth jumper with the 30-foot diameter chute. Each man used the same type of chute equipped with 40 suspension lines. Although the last of the test group to test the new chute, Bottriell had more experience at parachuting than any other known individual. Starting as a teenager jumping from balloons, he executed over 500 jumps! During these jumps Bottriell parachuted from balloons and airplanes with his chute being deployed by a static line. Sergeant Bottriell thus became the first military member to perform a free-fall jump. The new parachute developed by Smith allowed the jumper to free-fall and elect when to pull the ripcord. Bottriell later received the Distinguished Flying Cross for his contributions to aerial flight and parachute development.

Not everyone supported the idea of carrying parachutes, however. Some pilots of the era felt that parachutes should not be carried because it was their duty to try to save their aircraft during emergencies. One pilot thought parachutes would foster "faintheartedness" and lead to unnecessary crashes which could have been prevented if the pilot simply landed the plane. Others believed that a parachutist would lose consciousness or that carrying a parachute implied that the pilot did not have confidence in his airplane. Some pilots at McCook Field did not share this opinion.

The Air Service conducted more than 1,500 successful parachute jumps before adopting "seat-pack" chutes as regular equipment. In 1922, the adjutant general directed that parachutes were mandatory for Air Service fliers. In 1920 William O'Conner became the first person to save his own life with a free-fall parachute. He was testing another type of free-fall parachute that failed to deploy, but luckily he had a standard Air Service chute as a backup.

Leslie Irvin and others eventually founded the "Caterpillar Club" for anyone who bailed out under emergency conditions. Upon verification of the successful jump, the recipient was awarded the gold Caterpillar Pin.

Sources: Maurer Maurer, *Aviation in the U.S. Army, 1919-1939* (Washington, D.C., 1987), pp 161-164; Air Force Enlisted Heritage Research Institute, File 19-10, "Enlisted Firsts: MSgt Ralph Bottriell;" Andrew S. Kididis,"The Art of Drag, A History of U.S. Air Force Parachute Technology Development," manuscript, 2002.

Live jump from a Martin bomber over McCook Field (*Mrs. Darlene Gerhardt*)

Colonel Edward L. Hoffman models the quick-attachable chest parachute with a triangle-type canopy known as the Hoffman Triangle Parachute, about 1931.

Prototype Model "A" parachute modeled by James Floyd Smith. Leslie Irvin used this chute in the first live, free-fall jump on April 28, 1919.

drift sights, and engine instruments were under constant improvement and development.

The *Instrument and Navigation Laboratory* was assigned full use of a twin-engine Douglas C-33 to conduct experimental flight tests. The airplane was used in testing such devices as improved gyro octants, drift sights and signals, automatic pilots, and navigation computers. In addition, the instrument lab tested improved versions of tachometers that also recorded engine running time and controls to synchronize engine speed in multi-engine aircraft.

The *Electrical Laboratory* specialized in aircraft and ground lighting systems. It developed advanced equipment to keep pace with the requirements of modern aircraft and newly constructed landing field installations. Specific projects included development of portable-by-air lighting equipment for landing fields and experimentation with alternating current for aircraft application.

The *Parachute and Clothing Laboratory* developed and tested parachutes and designed safer and more efficient flight clothing. The principal efforts at Wright Field revolved around the development of the Hoffman Triangle Parachute, designed by Colonel Edward L. Hoffman, former head of the Parachute Board at McCook Field. In 1930, Hoffman was granted two patents associated with the development of this parachute, which featured a highly stable and guidable canopy. This development represented one of the first formal attempts to apply engineering principles to canopy design. The concept of the triangle parachute was refined throughout the 1930s. The parachute itself was expected ultimately to replace the flat-circular parachute then being used. The Hoffman Triangle Parachute canopy of 1931 resembled a flat isosceles triangle with two rounded corners and one corner cut off in a straight line. Suspension lines were attached to canopy attachment loops, formed at the end of tapes that ran over the canopy in a pattern engineered by Hoffman. The horizontal airstream captured by this unique canopy imparted a "drive" or glide of about five mph. It was then possible to "steer" the parachute by turning it through proper riser manipulation, and thus affect safer landings. The final version of the triangle parachute (about 1932) had a canopy configured basically like a cloverleaf, and was called the 25.0-foot canopy.

As lives continued to be saved by individual use of parachutes, a radical idea emerged—that of lowering an entire airplane by the use of large parachutes. This would alleviate the inherent problems in equipping a large number of airplane passengers with individual parachutes. Numerous experiments were conducted in the development of this concept, including several years of work at Wright Field under Hoffman's direction. Hoffman's early experiments with large parachutes started in the 1920s. His initial attempts in 1929 involved a 96-gore, 84-foot circular parachute, which successfully carried 1,600-pound test bombs safely to the ground. With the advent of the triangle parachute design, experiments continued with a triangle parachute of the same size, intended ultimately to land a complete airplane. Although these plane-chute experiments had little impact on air safety in the years that followed, they demonstrated that extremely large parachutes could be manufactured without fabrication problems, and that such large parachutes could be conveniently packed, deployed, and used to safely land large payloads.

Despite its many advantages as a personnel parachute, the smaller version of

Night aerial photographic techniques developed by Lieutenant George W. Goddard produced this photograph of Wright Field during the 1931 Air Corps Maneuvers.

The Physiological Research Laboratory at Wright Field in 1937 had three altitude pressure chambers. This was the largest at 31 feet in length and 8 feet in diameter. It could simulate conditions at altitudes up to 80,000 feet above sea level, including temperatures to –65° F.

the triangle parachute was discontinued because of its complex design and the fact that it was extremely costly to manufacture and maintain. Subsequently, the Parachute and Clothing Laboratory concerned itself with the development of hemispherical canopies and rapid-opening parachutes for use in the faster military airplanes.[31]

The clothing section of the Parachute and Clothing Laboratory worked to modify and standardize flight clothing, especially winter and high-altitude clothing. Its projects included electrically heated clothing and rubber-soled winter shoes lined with sheep shearing. A shoulder-type safety belt, which operated in conjunction with a lap-type belt, was developed to minimize pilot injury in a crash.

The *Aerial Photographic Laboratory* was able to build on the impressive reputation achieved when the Materiel Division was still at McCook Field. The first night cameras were developed at McCook and later improved at Wright Field, primarily under the impetus of aerial photography pioneer Lieutenant George W. Goddard (later brigadier general).

One of the most productive applications of aerial photography was in mapmaking. Air Corps officers and engineers, assisted by officers of the Corps of Engineers stationed at Wright Field, produced accurate maps of the entire United States from aerial photographs. Mapmakers traditionally divided the United States into quadrangles, each covering an average area of 225 square miles, according to the Geological Survey. Formerly, it had taken several seasons to map each quadrangle. By airplane, this territory was covered in a few hours with great accuracy and reduced cost. In another project with the Corps of Engineers, the entire area inundated by the Ohio River in 1937 was photographed as an aid in planning future flood control.[32]

Often new photographic equipment had to be developed to handle the specific requirements of the project at hand. The flood-control project mentioned above used the Air Corps Type T-3A camera. Different types, however, were required by bombers taking pictures through haze above 10,000 feet, or by swift, low-flying reconnaissance airplanes. Both types of cameras were successfully developed at Wright Field and used sensitive films created by commercial laboratories at the instigation of the Air Corps. Processing equipment was perfected for in-flight use, making it possible to develop negatives exposed during a flight before the airplane landed. Air Corps photographers used equipment developed by experts at the Materiel Division to obtain the highest-altitude and longest-distance photographs of their day. Electrical heating systems for both the cameras and the clothing worn by aviators for high-altitude work also were developed at Wright Field.

A self-contained, mobile photographic laboratory trailer designed and built during the late 1930s featured one room equipped for printing and another for film processing and print finishing. This unit housed its own ventilation system, water supply, electric power plant, and chemical and material supply, together with all the photographic accessories necessary to produce complete photo-mosaics.[33]

The *Miscellaneous Equipment Laboratory*, the fifth laboratory of the Equipment Branch, designed ancillary equipment to support work accomplished by the other laboratories. A steam-operated external energizer, for example, was designed especially for use in cold weather. It consisted of a small, automatically controlled steam generator weighing about 100 pounds and a steam-driven external energizer. Other miscellaneous equipment the laboratory developed included devices for preventing ice formation on the outside of windshields and fogging on the inside; a portable, canvas-covered maintenance shelter supported by a rigid tubular framework; and lightweight, portable, collapsible wing jacks for large airplanes. The Miscellaneous Equipment Laboratory also did research and development work on transportation equipment and oxygen apparatus for use at high altitudes.[34]

The *Physiological Research Laboratory* established at Wright Field on May 18, 1935, operated under the direction of an Army medical officer and applied itself specifically to medical aspects of modern military flying. The laboratory designed experimental equipment to measure the effects of increased speeds, altitudes, and durations on aviators, with a view to designing equipment capable of alleviating the ill effects caused by these conditions. Prominent among this equipment were three pressure chambers, the largest being 31 feet in length and eight feet in diameter, designed to simulate the extraordinary pressures and temperatures of high altitudes. The chambers could simulate altitudes to 80,000 feet above sea level and temperatures to -65° F.[35]

One of the most interesting projects of the Physiological Research Lab in the late 1930s was its investigation of centrifugal force effects on pilots. The centrifuge used in this research consisted of a long rotating arm with a seat bolted to its outer end. Powered by a large electric motor, this arm rotated at speeds up to 80 rpm, generating a force equal to 20 times the pull of gravity (20 g's). Members of the laboratory acted as experimental subjects at forces up to eight g's, although pure research continued to much higher levels.[36] The laboratory also waged war against aeroembolism, the same painful disability that deep-sea divers call "the bends," in which bubbles of nitrogen form in the bloodstream during violent climbs.

Materials Branch

The Materials Branch of the Engineering Section tested and refined the multiplicity of materials connected with flight. Many of these materials were used directly in aircraft, such as fuels, oils, paints, varnishes, fabrics, rubber, and steel, and necessarily carried high standards. Specifications had to be developed, however, for hundreds of other specialized items commonly used in maintenance work, from paper and cleaning rags to sawdust and soaps. Competition was keen in the field of materials science, as new and improved substances were developed with increasing frequency. Each new material posed fresh problems in terms of manufacture, and often in the study of fundamental properties as well. The Materials Branch often conducted extensive chemical analysis of the substances being developed.

The branch pioneered development of welded steel structures and fostered the application of chrome-molybdenum alloy steel to this type of construction. Similar experiments were conducted in connection with aluminum, magnesium, and beryllium-base alloys.[37]

Although both water- and air-cooled airplane engines were used during the 1930s, primary attention was given to the development of the air-cooled type. The Materials Branch was responsible in large part for developing aluminum alloys suitable for pistons and cylinder heads in air-cooled engines. The Materials Branch foundry made hundreds of different castings of each new alloy to ensure proper design, not only from the cooling standpoint but for ease of production.[38]

Interest in magnesium alloy development remained active throughout the 1930s. This material was attractive because of the substantial weight savings compared to aluminum, and because of its ready availability. In later years, development of a process to extract magnesium from sea water made it especially attractive. Magnesium castings were used on production engines for such parts as cover plates, nose pieces, housings, and practically all landing wheels in the late 1930s. Cooperative programs were carried on with the two magnesium producers of this period, the Aluminum Company of America and the Dow Chemical Company.

Materials for innumerable small airplane parts, such as tires, wing ribs, metal wing spars, cables, and propeller blades, were the subjects of constant experimentation. Of critical importance was the development of a glass substitute for windows and windshields that offered better visibility and impact-resistance than shatterproof glass. A methyl methacrylate plastic material introduced in 1937 successfully met these requirements.

Natural rubber was another material for which a more durable and versatile synthetic substitute was sought. Thiokol and Duprene were the principal synthetics studied. Thiokol found application in refueling hoses, balloon-valve seats, and dope-and-lacquer hoses. Duprene was used extensively for fuel, oil, water, and ethylene glycol connector hoses, in tires and tubes, as cement in balloon seams, and as a balloon-cloth coating to reduce gas permeability. Synthetic rubber also was used for hydraulic system components and for seals and gaskets.[39]

A zinc chromate primer was accepted, after extensive testing, for use on early aluminum-skinned airplanes. In 1933, an atmospheric exposure rack and a tidewater rack were erected at Chapman Field, near Miami, Florida, to obtain accelerated exposure performance data. Two or three months' exposure in that environment was considered equivalent to one year in Dayton. An aluminum alloy for coating exterior surfaces was introduced after exhaustive laboratory investigation of its mechanical properties at Wright Field and corrosion tests in the bay at Chapman Field. It proved to reduce the requirements for aircraft painting appreciably.[40]

A reliable technique for spot-welding of both stainless steel and aluminum-alloy structures was also developed during the 1930s. The Materials Branch issued the first specification covering a complete spot-welding procedure for stressed aluminum-alloy parts in fiscal year 1935. By 1938, an experimental, spot-welded aluminum-alloy wing for an A-17 airplane was flight tested at Wright Field. As a result, magnesium sheet alloys were included in the spot-welding program for the following year.[41]

Workers in the Materials Branch monitor instruments in the cold chamber control room during a simulated –70° F cold weather test.

Another research activity conducted at Wright Field during the 1930s was development of a non-destructive inspection technique known as magnetic particle inspection. Small cracks and other surface-connected defects in steel parts were notoriously difficult to detect, posing a serious problem for inspection personnel. A trained eye and a hand-held magnifying glass were the usual tools used. Since lives and expensive property were at stake, priority was given to developing reliable techniques of flaw detection. By 1935, specifications existed for a magnetic particle inspection apparatus. It used a system of magnets and dry powder and detected minute flaws by analysis of residual magnetic particles. This equipment was procured for some repair depots and was considered suitable for inspection of all ferrous aircraft and engine parts. The automotive, marine, and railroad industries adopted the magnetic particle inspection method in 1937. The process was further developed and refined in later years.[42]

The Materials Branch expanded its fuel and lubrication activities during the 1930s. Two particularly thorny problems were resolved, in collaboration with the Power Plant Branch, in the areas of gum formation in gasoline and vapor lock. The branch also concentrated on improving performance of lubricants under high- and low-temperature conditions. Paraffin, naphthalene, and vegetable-oil bases were studied to determine how their coefficients of friction changed with variations in temperature. Improvements in high-viscosity engine oils resulted in engines that started easier at low temperatures without excessive oil consumption.[43]

One of the most interesting facilities of the Materials Branch was the laboratory known as the "cold room." Approximately 20 tons of cooling coils regulated environmental conditions in this laboratory. The sub-freezing temperatures experienced at high altitudes could be simulated, allowing study of their effects on fuels, engine and instrument lubricants, fluids for hydraulic control mechanisms, oil coolers, fuel systems, and engine operating parts. Starting and operating characteristics of both liquid- and air-cooled engines were tested at temperatures as low as –50° F. Such tests were absolutely necessary to ensure that the engine that operated at 85° F at ground level would operate just as efficiently at –75° F during high-altitude flight. Tensile, impact, and fatigue properties of aircraft materials were tested by equipment installed permanently in the "cold room." Additional tests were made using portable equipment. Engineers conducting experiments in the "cold room" were furnished with electrically heated flight clothing.[44]

Armament Branch

The Armament Branch of the Engineering Section was tasked with designing armament equipment to increase the tactical efficiency of Army bombardment, attack, and pursuit airplanes. The branch designed systems to ensure proper mounting and efficient functioning of machine guns, bombs, and ammunition on all new and modified Army models, taking into consideration the numerous installation limitations and operational conditions involved. The Armament Branch also prepared the portions of airplane specifications that dealt with armament.

Revisions in the design of bomb racks and release-control mechanisms occurred at Wright Field. In bomber cockpits, an electrically illuminated panel represented the loaded bomb rack, showing the arrangement of bombs on the different stations. A special unit in the wiring system allowed a pre-selected, timed release of bombs at successive intervals. The design process for these instruments required the careful calculation of such factors as air speed, pitch and yaw, wind speed, altitude, and bomb trajectory. The Armament Branch also was responsible for advances in pyrotechnics, including parachute flares, signal pistols, wingtip flares, smoke signals, and certain articles of equipment used on the ground, such as pyrotechnic beacons and position lights.[45]

The increased ground speed of modern attack airplanes necessitated improvements in fixed-gun installations to increase firepower against ground targets. The design of special equipment for cooling machine guns extended the burst of fire. Gun sights for fixed and flexible guns and machine-gun synchronizers also underwent many improvements.

Service tests were conducted at Wright Field on the equipment used to flexibly mount .30-caliber and .50-caliber machine guns in various positions on bombardment, attack, and observation airplanes. The adoption of .50-caliber machine guns as flexible weapons gave rise to further refinements, such as the use of power-driven mechanisms to operate machine gun turrets in bombardment airplanes. The service test program at Wright Field also extended to synchronized gun equipment, pyrotechnic devices, and various items of bombing equipment, as well as practice and service bombs and other items of ammunition supplied by the Ordnance Department.[46]

Shops Branch

The Engineering Shops Branch acted as a service laboratory for the Engineering Section. Skilled mechanics assigned to this branch were responsible for the inspection, modification, and repair of both experimental airplanes and the prototype airplanes submitted to Wright Field by manufacturers. When necessary equipment was not available, the Shops Branch created it, an example being the design and fabrication of a jack powerful enough to raise the largest of airplanes. The shops also designed, fabricated, and installed many of the parts and accessories required in the experimental work of the various other laboratories of the Engineering Section.[47] This branch performed a major role, for example, in preparing propellers for both experimental and routine use on aircraft and in repairing them after damage by erosion or accident.

A 20-ton wing jack developed by the Shops Branch undergoes tests in the Materials Branch cold chamber.

Administration Section

The Administration Section of the Materiel Division had two important functions: administration of the Materiel Division itself and operation of Wright Field as a military post. For the first 10 years, from 1927 until 1937, the chief of the Administration Section served simultaneously as the commanding officer of Wright Field. The assistant chief of the Administration Section also performed a dual function as the Wright Field adjutant.[48] In May 1937, the Administration Section was removed from the organizational chart and its functions consolidated directly under the Materiel Division Executive Office. The executive officer thus assumed a second "hat" as the commanding officer, with the assistant executive serving as adjutant.

The Administration Section supervised the many branches that performed actual day-to-day operations at the field. This included management of all military and civilian personnel assigned to the Materiel Division, as well as such routine affairs as mail distribution, central files, transportation, and the functions of the Quartermaster and Station Supply.

The section also was responsible for a host of additional duties that today would be considered beyond the scope of a base administrative office. The mandate of the Administration Section, as stated in the 1927 Annual Report of the Materiel Division, called for it to conduct official performance tests on experimental airplanes, engines, aircraft accessories, and equipment; to maintain the flying records of all aircraft operating at the division; and to perform all maintenance of these craft. The section administered the activities of the Office of the Flight Surgeon at Wright Field and operated the Air Corps Engineering School until 1930, when the school transferred to the jurisdiction of the chief of the Materiel Division. Section personnel also prepared and prosecuted all patent applications initiated by Materiel Division personnel, and supervised the compilation and dissemination of technical information generated at the field. There were 269 employees assigned to the Administration Section in fiscal year 1927 to perform this wide range of responsibilities.[49]

Among the section's more interesting enterprises were those of its Flying and Technical Data branches. Of particular importance were the on-base activities carried out under the various civil and public works projects during the Depression.

Flying Branch

The Flying Branch conducted all authorized flight testing of experimental airplanes, engines, aircraft accessories, and miscellaneous equipment. This responsibility also included ferrying new airplanes from contractors' plants to the Materiel Division. During August 1929, the Flying Branch moved from temporary hangars at the Fairfield Air Depot to new hangars on Wright Field. Improved calibration and storage of flight test instruments were among the most important features of the new facilities.

From its new location, the Flying Branch supported a variety of missions. Branch pilots flew night missions to test airplane landing lights and flares. Important projects also supported the aerial photography work at Wright Field. During the winter of 1929, for example, Flying Branch pilots flew a Keystone LB-5A light bomber to Fargo, North Dakota, to photograph and bomb an ice jam.

In 1929, and again in 1931, the Flying Branch provided support for the Air Corps maneuvers staged at Wright Field. During the maneuvers all test and incidental flying was suspended, and all test pilots were detailed for special duty. Mechanics and laborers assigned to Wright Field were diverted from normal work and spent thousands of hours supporting the maneuvers.

The Flying Branch contributed many hours of public relations work for Wright Field by performing special flying exhibitions. These exhibitions stimulated great public interest in aeronautics, and in some cases raised funds to establish municipal airports and support worthy relief organizations. In fiscal years 1932 and 1933, for example, the exhibition itinerary included appearances at the All American Races in Miami, Florida; the christening ceremony for the U.S. Navy dirigible *Akron* at Akron, Ohio; the George Washington Bicentennial Military Tournament and the Progress Exposition in Chicago; the Ohio State Fair at Columbus; the National Air Races in Cleveland; and the inauguration ceremonies for President Franklin D. Roosevelt in Washington, D.C.[50]

Technical Data Branch

The Technical Data Branch had primary responsibility for the Materiel Division's publicity, public relations, and photographic services. Its major functions,

The Wright Field aircraft operations center, Hangar 3

Wright Field test pilots in the early 1930s included (left to right): Captain V. Strahm, Captain Reuben C. Moffat, Lieutenant Ployer P. Hill, and Lieutenant Irvin A. Woodring.

SARAH CLARK

When the United States entered World War I in 1917, a young business school graduate, Sarah Clark of Fort Wayne, Indiana, applied for a Civil Service position at McCook Field. When asked on her employment application what position she was most qualified to fill, she responded "executive." All executive positions must have been filled because the civilian organization responsible for acquiring badly needed military aircraft for the Army Air Service hired her as a "Production Expert" instead. The Production Engineering Department reorganized into the Army Signal Corps' Airplane Engineering Division at McCook Field, and Miss Clark became chief of Central Files, only nine months after entering federal service. She remained in that job until her retirement in 1956.

Prior to U.S. entry into World War I, the Army Adjutant General's Office, charged with the task of standardizing Army correspondence and other records, adapted the Dewey Decimal System of library book classification to create a Central Decimal Filing System for Army records. Miss Clark implemented that system within Engineering Division's Central Files at McCook and then spent the rest of her career expanding and improving the system.

In 1927, Miss Clark and the Central Files moved to the Materiel Division's new home at Wright Field. She managed a staff of analysts and clerks, who collected, indexed, filed, and preserved the research, development, test, and procurement records created by managers, engineers, scientists, test pilots, and acquisition personnel at McCook Field, Wright Field, and Wright-Patterson Air Force Base. Sarah Clark ran an efficient organization, where speed and accuracy remained paramount. Young pilots stopping by to talk with file clerks soon caught the notice of Miss Clark and they did not linger.

Central Files, Wright Field, 1936

During Sarah Clark's 39-year career, the Air Service became the Air Corps, then the Army Air Forces, and finally the U.S. Air Force. As the service expanded throughout the decades, the volume of files, records, and reports stored in Central File organizations Air Force-wide grew tremendously, particularly during the World War II military buildup. In 1955, Sarah Clark had 63,000 cubic feet of files. At that time, the Air Force eliminated the Central File system and implemented a new system of records management. Offices began reviewing files yearly and sending them offsite for storage. Old files (dating back to 1917 at Wright Field) were offered to the National Archives and Records Service (today the National Archives and Records Administration [NARA]). Sarah Clark supervised the packing of nearly 40-years worth of files in preparation for transfer to the National Archives. She ensured they were systematically boxed, with detailed item-level inventory lists prepared for each box. Then she retired.

Today, the part of the collection of most interest to researchers includes the Research and Development Case Files, which have come to be known as the Sarah Clark collection. These are dispersed to various NARA storage areas, with the largest block residing in College Park, Maryland. Historians and archivists prize this unique collection of documents that trace the evolution of aviation technology and the early days of aeronautical research and development at McCook and Wright fields.

Sources: Records of the United States Air Force Commands, Activities, and Organizations (Record Group 342), online at http://www.nara.gov/guide/top; Mabel E. Deutrich, "History of the Decimal Filing System in the War Department," National Archives Seminar [paper] on Record Keeping Practices, September 14, 1956, National Archives Library, College Park, Maryland. Illustration by Jill Josupeit.

The reading room of the Technical Data Branch library, Building 12, Area B

however, were to collect and review all available foreign and domestic aeronautical publications and disseminate the information to Materiel Division personnel. The branch was responsible for accurate translation of applicable foreign aeronautical research, as well as detailed review of current English-language aeronautical journals, books, and reports.

In 1929, an Information Unit was created to review all aeronautical information, both foreign and domestic, published in current engineering magazines, technical reports, and the like. After technical evaluation, this information was disseminated on a daily basis to Materiel Division personnel by means of a typewritten, hectographed review entitled the *Technical News Service*. In later years, this service was provided by the *Technical Data Digest*, a semi-monthly review of aeronautical periodicals and literature received by the Technical Data Branch. The *Digest* received considerable commendation from Air Corps personnel as the best means of maintaining contact with aeronautical developments throughout the world and it was eventually republished by special permission of the Air Corps' chief on a regular basis in the *Journal of the Institute of Aeronautical Sciences*. To further assist Wright Field military and civilian engineers in keeping abreast of current developments, the Information Unit frequently showed movies on aeronautical subjects in the Building 11 auditorium.

The Technical Data Branch also made efforts to update and upgrade the technical public, as well. It updated and regularly republished the *Air Corps Handbook of Instructions for Airplane Designers*. Its staff generated technical orders and bulletins along with all manner of articles for the public press, lectures, motion pictures, and exhibits depicting the technological advances being made at Wright Field. Exhibits of Air Corps equipment were staged at various state fairs and aviation shows. The "Tech Data" Branch also prepared special articles on aeronautical subjects for publication by the Office, Chief of the Air Corps.

In November 1938, the new Training Film Field Unit No. 2 was established to produce historical and technical films for the Air Corps. The first sound film, *Wings of Peace*, told the story of the 1938 flight of six Air Corps B-17s to South America. When sound was added to a number of early silent films, *Wings of the Army* and *Flying Cadets* were among the first projects. Three regular employees visited Hollywood motion picture studios to learn the latest methods and equipment for sound film production. This resulted in increased Air Corps capacity to photograph its own maneuvers, tactical concentrations, and other activities, and to produce films for release as newsreels or use in official Air Corps productions. In March 1941, the film unit's name was changed to Signal Corps Training Film Production Laboratory, Wright Field Branch. It continued to operate throughout World War II under the technical control of the chief signal officer and the administrative control of the Materiel Division.[51]

Public Works Projects

The Materiel Division worked in harmony with national relief programs and was able to employ a large number of personnel at Wright Field under the auspices of various public and civil works projects. Funds provided under these programs helped the Materiel Division to accomplish tasks that otherwise might have gone unfunded because of the severe budgetary restraints imposed on the Wright Field experimental and research programs.

Manpower available under the Works Progress Administration (WPA) was used for several Wright Field projects during the 1930s. One of the more interesting of these involved the Materials Branch of the Engineering Section. Building 16, occupied partly by the Materials Branch, was originally constructed as a one-story building with no basement. Its wooden floor was supported by concrete pillars resting on underground footers. WPA crews assumed the arduous task of digging out a basement under the entire building. The digging was done by hand (one section at a time), and steel girders erected. Concrete floor and wall sections were then poured. The completion of this project late in 1939 came just in time to support World War II mobilization and the attendant need for more space.[52]

In fiscal year 1935, the public works program funded over $500,000 in improvements to Wright Field. These public contract projects, under supervision of the Constructing Quartermaster, included construction of a new static test building and the large Technical Data building (Building 12, Area B), the latter of which became home to the Army Aeronautical Museum.[53]

Annual reports of the Materiel Division showed that in fiscal year 1937, and again in fiscal year 1938, $76,000 in projects was allotted to Wright Field by the Works Progress Administration. A total of $119,579 in projects was performed in fiscal year 1939 under supervision of the chief of Maintenance, primarily in repairs and improvements to buildings, grounds, and public utilities. In fiscal year 1940, WPA funding for work at Wright Field exceeded $221,000. In lesser proportion, a certain amount of work at the field was accomplished under Civil Works Administration projects, also under direct supervision of the chief of Maintenance.

In a separate and special project area, selected professional and technical WPA workers were assigned to support the Army Aeronautical Museum. Their accomplishments included construction of an Air Corps exhibit for the 1939 New York World's Fair, including a scale model of Wright Field, a scale model of the Wright Brothers Memorial at Kitty Hawk, North Carolina, and three special glass cases for displaying 1/16-scale models of Army airplanes. Other exhibits were furnished by the Army Aeronautical Museum during fiscal year 1939 to the Golden Gate International Exposition in San Francisco; the Aero-Medical Association of the United States in Dayton; the National Air Races in Cleveland; the Pacific International Livestock Exposition in Portland, Oregon; and the Second Annual Peninsula Charity Fair at Langley Field, Virginia.[54]

(Top) Building 12 on Wright Field was an art deco masterpiece when completed in 1935. It housed the Technical Data Branch offices and the Army Aeronautical Museum. (Below)The lobby featured a green marble floor, wood paneling, and rotunda. The stylized, aluminum, "pilot-wing" clock was flanked by busts of Orville and Wilbur Wright.

Field Service Section

The Field Service Section, formerly known as the Property, Maintenance, and Cost Compilation Section, exercised control over the Air Corps' depot system. Originally established in 1921, the section was administered separately until it became part of the newly created Materiel Division in October 1926. As part of the Materiel Division, the Field Service Section managed all supply and maintenance operations at Air Corps depots. In 1927, there were six depots, located at Fairfield, Ohio; Little Rock, Arkansas; Middletown, Pennsylvania; Rockwell, California; San Antonio, Texas; and Scott Field, Illinois.

Although the Field Service Section underwent several reorganizations between 1927 and 1941, when it was absorbed by the Provisional Air Corps Maintenance Command, its chief functions of supply and maintenance remained basically the same. The section supervised the issue, storage, maintenance, salvage, and disposal of all Air Corps property under the jurisdiction of the Materiel Division. It also worked to standardize Air Corps supply methods and was responsible for the annual preparation of cost estimates, programs, schedules, and reports. Annual engineering supply conferences held at Materiel Division headquarters provided a forum for discussing pertinent issues connected with the supply field.

Field Service Section personnel maintained detailed records on each item of depot materiel, including everything from airplanes and engines to goggles and cameras. Field Service records tracked the quantities of materials available, their location, condition, current performance, periods of serviceable use, and total life. Rates of consumption and replacement requirements were tracked also, as were disposal processes when Air Corps property became unserviceable.

In another facet of the Field Service Section mission, policies were set for the periodic repair and overhaul of Air Corps airplanes and engines. This included significant standardization of engineering methods, tools, and equipment at field and repair depots.

Technical orders, catalogs, and Air Corps circulars were published by the Field Service Section on a regular basis to keep depot personnel informed of the latest instructions on maintenance, assembly, and operation of Air Corps equipment. Manufacturers' handbooks were procured and distributed when available and suitable, so that information would get to the field as quickly as possible. In some instances, aircraft and equipment manufacturers produced instructional handbooks to accompany catalogs of parts that conformed to specifications prepared by the Materiel Division.

Thousands of visitors attended the Wright Field celebration of the 30th anniversary of the Army Air Corps in August 1939. The celebration commemorated the anniversary of the delivery of the first military airplane to the Signal Corps by Wilbur and Orville Wright in 1909.

Industrial War Plans Section

Prior to World War I, military tradition called for stockpiling supplies and equipment of all kinds against future war contingencies. Logisticians realized in the aftermath of World War I that accumulating and storing war reserves was expensive. More importantly, progress was so rapid, especially in the Air Service, that equipment placed in reserve soon became obsolete. Air Service pilots were sorely aware of the limitations this imposed, as they had been forced to "make do" with obsolete World War I DeHavilland aircraft and Liberty engines for more than a decade until the huge stockpiles were depleted.

The Industrial War Plans Section was charged with making an effective transition from the time-honored concept of stockpiling war reserves to more modern concepts of planning for the national defense. The transition involved preparation of plans for the orderly movement of supplies from factories to the front lines, computation on a month-to-month basis of the amounts that would be needed under wartime conditions, and ensuring standardization of war-essential equipment. The War Plans Section also located suitable sources of supply across the country and assisted targeted factories in the preparation of plans for conversion from peacetime pursuits to wartime production once an emergency situation was declared. A healthy industrial complex, capable of rapid mobilization, was recognized as the best war reserve the nation could have.[55] As observed by Major James A. Mars, head of the Industrial War Plans Division in 1925, "Industry cannot win a war, but it can easily lose it."[56]

For purposes of Air Corps procurement planning, the United States was divided into six districts, with an Air Corps officer assigned to each. The officer had responsibility for locating sources of equipment, surveying factories that were reported as suitable, and securing needed information about the industrial establishments in his district. Each district representative had a civilian advisor, usually a prominent businessman from the district, appointed directly by the chief of the Air Corps to aid and support the procurement planning work.

A separate Procurement Plan was prepared for each article of Air Corps equipment. Negotiations were conducted with individual factories and schedules were proposed for production of specific equipment. Power, labor, and transportation requirements were also figured, including any expansion or special tool designs that might be needed.

A Unit Plan was prepared for each Air Corps procurement district. This plan became part of the overall Air Corps Industrial War Plan. The assistant secretary of war coordinated this plan with those received from the other branches of the Army to ensure that no one district was overloaded and that distribution of the production load would be relatively equitable in an emergency.

Another significant job of the Industrial War Plans Section was to develop substitutes for strategic materials not readily available within the country. Many of these projects were coordinated with the work being done by the Materials Branch of the Engineering Section in developing, for example, synthetic rubber, substitutes for tin, and American-made optical glass.

Since virtually all of the military supplies and equipment used in the Air Corps came from outside sources, the concept of war planning became closely allied with the development of commercial aviation. If the aeronautical industry did not prosper, the efficiency of industrial war plans would be severely restricted; a prospering industry guaranteed the government a larger number of potential sources of Air Corps materiel. To keep the aeronautical industry alive and healthy in the late 1920s, steady growth in commercial aviation was essential.

During the Depression of the 1930s, this cause-and-effect relationship became even more clearly defined. Government orders, in many instances, were the only means by which aircraft manufacturers were able to maintain minimum operations. Even so, new production facilities had to be secured on a regular basis to replace sources that went out of business. Had an emergency arisen, many manufacturers would have had to sustain wholesale refitting of their production organizations before proceeding with an Air Corps emergency program.

Furthermore, planners judged that despite counting all the aircraft manufacturers in the country and assuming full-time operation of all plants, the facilities would still be inadequate to meet emergency requirements. Other sources of production, including facilities that did not normally supply Air Corps needs, had to be located. Efforts were directed toward placing schedules with automotive manufacturers who possessed equipment capable of conversion for the manufacture of aircraft, aircraft engines, and related equipment. It was not until the end of the decade that industrial planners realized it was not realistic to deal with manufacturers outside the aircraft industry as prime contractors for wartime requirements. The aircraft industry was unanimous in considering that the auto industry was not a potential source of production. The auto industry likewise concluded that airplane production was not a fertile field, due to its lack of trained personnel and equipment peculiar to the aircraft industry.[57]

The 1924 War Department General Mobilization Plan was replaced in 1933 with an Industrial Mobilization Plan, a joint effort by the Army and the Navy. This necessitated recomputation of all requirements and the revision of all existing procurement plans. Since many articles required by the Air Corps in an emergency were the same as, or similar to, those required by the Bureau of Aeronautics in the Navy Department, intensive efforts were made to eliminate conflicts in the use of production facilities and to foster cooperation between the two services for procurement of common items.[58] A 1936 revision to the Industrial Mobilization Plan shifted overall supervision of industrial planning from the Office, Assistant Secretary of War, to joint Army and Navy agencies. This heavily influenced the trend of Air Corps procurement planning. As Naval aviation grew, Air Corps industrial planning increasingly shifted to a joint Army-Navy viewpoint and finally reached a point when Navy aviation took equal share with the Army in production resources.[59]

The War Department Industrial Mobilization Plan was discontinued during fiscal year 1937 and replaced by a new War Department Protective Mobilization Plan that reflected policy changes made in the mid-1930s. Substantial reorganization of the Industrial War Plans Section again took place. Its name changed from "Industrial War Plans" to "Industrial Planning" to obviate the deleterious effects the word *war* had upon some components of the industry."[60]

In 1939, the Materiel Division consolidated procurement planning districts and inspection districts to further decentralize planning activities and reduce overhead expenses. The procurement planning offices located in Cleveland, Chicago, and Detroit were closed, and the personnel transferred to the former central inspection district headquarters located at Wright Field. The Buffalo office remained as a sub-office of the consolidated Central District.[61]

Despite the valuable work performed by members of the Industrial Planning Section, the industrial war planners of the late 1930s failed to envision the scope of the war that was to come. The science of industrial war planning had progressed dramatically from concepts that prevailed prior to World War I, but pre-World War II planners still held unrealistic ideas about the requirements that another global conflict would demand and the ability of the American industrial complex to meet those needs.

WRIGHT FIELD AND WORLD WAR II

Hitler's *Luftwaffe* and panzer divisions invaded Poland on September 1, 1939. Great Britain and France declared war on Germany two days later. A second world war had begun. Within nine months the Germans held Norway, the Netherlands, and Belgium. In June 1940, the defeat of the British on the shores of Dunkirk led to the fall of France. The overwhelming strength of the German *Luftwaffe* demonstrated conclusively that, for the first time, air power would be a deciding factor in war.

The first step toward American rearmament occurred with passage of the Naval Expansion Act in May 1938, which called for a 3,000-airplane program. On April 3, 1939, Congress gave similar support to the Air Corps by authorizing $300 million for the creation of a force of 5,500 military airplanes. Chief of the Air Corps Major General Henry H. Arnold was assured of open-ended appropriations and mandated to build the best air force money could buy.

Major General Henry H. Arnold (second from left), Army Air Corps chief, greets General Motors Corporation executives (left to right) Charles F. Kettering, William S. Knudsen, and E. V. Rippenville upon their arrival at Wright Field on August 20, 1940, to tour the Materiel Division laboratories and hangars.

THE AVIATION HERITAGE OF THE INDIANAPOLIS MOTOR SPEEDWAY

The Indianapolis Motor Speedway has a colorful aviation heritage, and it should come as no surprise that four past winners of the Indianapolis 500—Bobby Unser, Rodger Ward, Sam Hanks, and Ralph DePalma—served with the United States Air Force or its precursors. The famous speedway's relationship with aviation began in 1909 when Carl Fisher, the speedway's builder, invited the Aero Club of America to hold its first national balloon race at his new track. A year later Orville and Wilbur Wright appeared at the speedway with members of their Wright Exhibition Company in the first official aviation meet ever held in the United States. An aviation repair depot was established at the speedway before World War I and it continued to operate until late 1920, when it was moved to the Fairfield Air Depot (later a part of Patterson Field, Dayton, Ohio).

In 1911 Eddie Rickenbacker competed in the first Indianapolis 500 race; a few years later the famous racer became a famous fighter pilot in World War I. In 1915 Ralph DePalma won the Indianapolis 500 and three years later was taking pilot training at McCook Field. Rodger Ward went from being a P-38 fighter pilot in World War II to becoming a two-time winner of the Indy 500. Sam Hanks, the 1957 record-breaking winner of the Indy 500, was stationed at Wright Field from 1943 to 1945 as an Army Air Forces flight engineer in the Engine Procurement Division. The experience that B-29 flight engineer Herbie Porter acquired from working with turbochargers during World War II assisted him later as an Indy Speedway mechanic when he helped develop a turbocharger for racecar engines, a groundbreaking feature used on the engine of every automobile raced at the Indy 500 for over 30 years. Former propulsion personnel from Wright-Patterson Air Force Base served as crew members and crew chiefs at the Indianapolis 500, where their expertise in turbine engines was greatly valued.

Sources: "Aviation at Indianapolis Motor Speedway," *Indiana Historian* (Indiana Historical Bureau), online at http://www.statelib.lib.in.us/www/ihb/tiharch-jun98.html; Dick Ralstin's Racing Home Page, online at http://home.flash.net/~dralstin/stories/RodgerWard.htm; "Eddie Rickenbacker," from International Motorsports Hall of Fame, online at http://www.motorsportshalloffame.com/halloffame/1992/Eddie_Rickenbacker_main.htm; Donald Davidson, telephone conversations on June 18, 2002 and July 15, 2002; Dick Ralstin, email to Robin Smith dated May 9, 2002; Alice Hanks, telephone conversation with Robin Smith on July 22, 2002; "Speedway has ties to Air Force," *Skywrighter*, August 10, 2001, p 11; "The 500-Mile Adventure," *Rare Sportsfilms, Inc.*, online at http://www.raresportsfilms.com/1957indian.html; "1957 Belond Exhaust Special," online at http://www.indycals.com/Museum/winners/1957.html.

Former Army Air Forces flight engineer Sam Hanks stands by the car he drove to first place in the 1957 Indianapolis 500. The number 9 Belond Exhaust Special, pictured here at the Indianapolis Motor Speedway Museum, was built and owned by George Salih, and had a unique engine configuration which lowered the car's center of gravity. Hanks broke the Indy speed record by almost five mph. (*Alice Hanks*)

Wilbur and Orville Wright at Indianapolis in 1910 with their teammates Frank Coffyn, Ralph Johnston, and Walter Brookins, preparing for the airplane competition at the Indianapolis Motor Speedway. Brookins set a new world record for altitude while flying at the Speedway. (*Special Collections and Archives, Wright State University*)

One of the many airplanes that took to the skies over the Indianapolis Motor Speedway from June 13 to June 18, 1910, as pilots from all over the nation attempted to break boundaries of speed, altitude, and distance. (*Special Collections and Archives, Wright State University*)

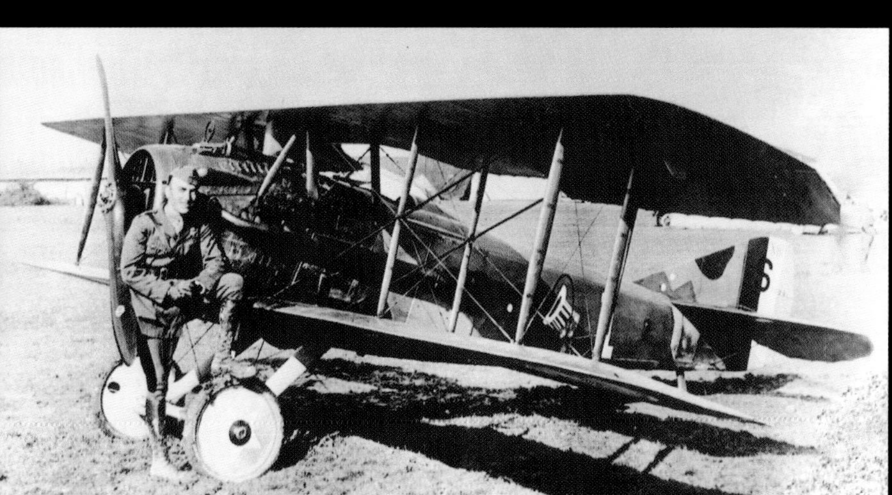

Before becoming America's Ace of Aces in World War I, Eddie Rickenbacker was a champion racecar driver. In 1927 he bought the Indianapolis Motor Speedway. (*National Archives and Records Administration*)

After winning the Indianapolis 500 in 1915, Ralph DePalma took pilot instruction at McCook Field during World War I. (*Ludvigsen Library*)

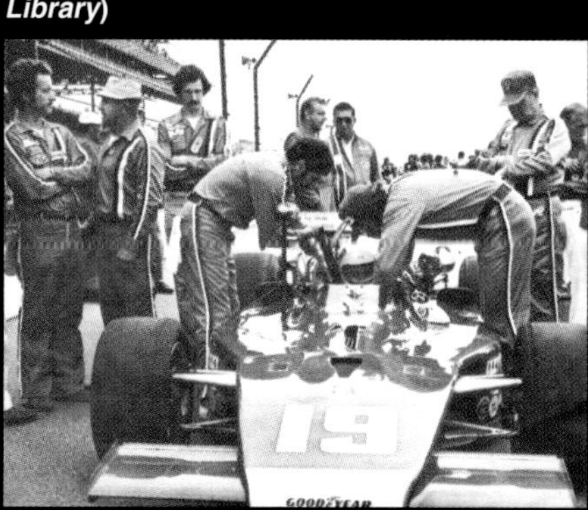

Wright-Patterson mechanic John Morrow (second from left) worked as an assistant crew chief at the Indy 500 for Mel and Don Kenyon. *(John Morrow)*

After serving as a P-38 fighter pilot in World War II, Rodger Ward won the Indianapolis 500 in 1959 and 1962. (*Dick Ralstin*)

Sam and Alice Hanks pose proudly by the car that Sam drove to victory in the 1957 Indianapolis 500. Sam and Alice met at Wright Field during World War II and were married in 1947. (*Alice Hanks*)

On June 26, 1939, the Army Chief of Staff Major General George C. Marshall, approved the First Aviation Objective, in which an Air Corps composed of 54 combat groups and 4,000 combat airplanes was to be constituted by April 1942. Even as it set about structuring this force, Arnold's staff was preparing blueprints for an even larger one. The Second Aviation Objective was approved by the War Department in March 1941 and provided for a force of 84 combat groups, 7,800 combat airplanes, and 400,000 personnel by mid-1942.

A reorganization, which became effective June 20, 1941, established the Army Air Forces (AAF) with the Air Corps as a subordinate element. General Arnold, as head of the new AAF, was made responsible to the Army chief of staff and given responsibility for establishing policies and plans for all Army aviation activities.

In July 1941, President Franklin D. Roosevelt asked the secretaries of war and navy to prepare estimates of production requirements necessary "to defeat our potential enemies." The resulting report was submitted to President Roosevelt in September. For a multi-theater war, the plan estimated that the AAF would need 239 combat groups and 108 separate squadrons, 63,467 airplanes of all types, and 2,164,916 men. This assessment proved to be uncannily accurate: at its peak, the Army Air Forces had 243 combat groups, nearly 80,000 airplanes, and 2,400,000 men.[62]

The logistics support for this wartime force originated at Wright and Patterson fields. By June 1943, nearly 50,000 men and women, military and civilian, worked at the two fields, laboring day and night to provide the materiel support for an Allied victory.[63]

Expansion And Reorganization Of The Materiel Division

The outbreak of World War II in 1939 provided a crucial test for the Materiel Division. During the past 12 years, the division had managed its experimental engineering and procurement functions with the limited appropriations characteristic of peacetime. It had spent a considerable percentage of its restricted budget on maintenance of the existing air force; therefore, relatively little remained for new experimentation programs. The crisis of 1939 demanded the immediate expansion of both activities to levels far beyond any previously considered.

The Materiel Division's work was central to the rearmament process. Before plans for an accelerated airplane program could proceed, they had to clear the various offices and laboratories within the division. Thus, the Materiel Division expanded all phases of its activities many months before the rest of the nation. By the end of 1939, it had increased its activities to a pace and a degree not required of the rest of the nation until after the attack on Pearl Harbor.

Wright and Patterson Field executives often conferred on matters of mutual concern. Shown here are (left to right): Colonel Merrick G. Estabrook, Patterson Field commander; Lieutenant Colonel Oliver P. Echols, Materiel Division technical executive; and Lieutenant Colonel Lester T. Miller, Materiel Division administrative executive.

The extent of this expansion may be judged by the magnitude of the increase in procurement. In July 1938, the Materiel Division expected to administer less than $80 million in appropriations during the next 12 months. President Roosevelt's Message to Congress on January 12, 1939, however, outlined a vastly expanded National Defense Program. The $300 million congressional authorization for 5,500 Air Corps airplanes was granted in April. By the end of June, the Materiel Division had awarded contracts worth more than $110 million in airplanes and equipment. During the fiscal year that began July 1, 1939, Congress appropriated more than $240 million for expenditures within the sphere of the Materiel Division.[64]

Major changes were required within the Materiel Division to accommodate the Air Corps' expansion program. The organization had to be enlarged and realigned to sustain the procurement of airplanes in production quantities and, at the same time, provide facilities to sustain a large-scale program of testing and development.

A clear delineation was first made between the division's technical and administrative functions. The Office of the Executive, Materiel Division, was abolished and two new offices created in its stead: the Office of the Administrative Executive and the Office of the Technical Executive. The former was responsible for all administrative matters of a non-technical nature, while the latter handled "all technical matters involving plans, policies, and programs for all engineering, procurement, inspection, maintenance, supply, and repair activities of the Materiel Division."[65] This arrangement remained in effect until January 28, 1941, when the offices of the technical and administrative executives were once again combined into one Executive Office.

The most essential changes in the technical arena included the establishment of the Production Section (later expanded into a division) to handle engineering procurement matters, and the expansion and reorganization of the Engineering Section (later the Engineering Division). The chief functions of the latter were, as the name implies, the research, testing, and development necessary to secure the safest and most effective airplanes and equipment possible.

The Procurement Section underwent additional change as it absorbed much of the field force of the procurement planning activity from the Industrial War Plans Section, as mentioned earlier. The three procurement districts (Eastern, Western, and Central) remained basically intact and operated under the direct supervision of the chief of the Materiel Division.

These changes marked the beginning of much larger reorganizations throughout the Air Corps. On October 2, 1939, the Office of the Chief of the Materiel Division was relocated from Wright Field to Washington, D.C., and established in the Office, Chief of the Air Corps. Brigadier General George H. Brett, division chief at the time, took with him a small staff of officers and specially trained civilian employees. His job was to advise the Air Corps' chief on materiel and supply matters and to eliminate the bottleneck within the Supply Division that resulted from the rapid pace of the Air Corps' expansion program.

Although division headquarters had moved to Washington, the mission and daily functions at Wright Field remained the same. Lieutenant Colonel Oliver P. Echols (later major general), the assistant Materiel Division chief, directed division activities at Wright Field and in the field procurement districts and individual air depots.

In late 1940, the Air Corps proposed to separate the function of logistics from the Materiel Division and organize it as a separate command. After approval of this action in the spring of 1941, the Provisional Air Corps Maintenance Command came into existence on March 15 of that year. This provisional command, however, remained under the direction of the Materiel Division, with headquarters at Wright Field. It was composed of its headquarters, the Field Service Section, the 50th Transport Wing, six major Air Corps depots (four inherited from the Field Service Section, plus two new depots at Ogden, Utah, and Mobile, Alabama), and a number of sub-depots located at various Air Corps bases. On April 29, 1941, the Provisional Maintenance Command was permanently established as the Air Corps Maintenance Command, though it remained under the guidance of the Materiel Division for some time. Colonel Henry J. F. Miller (later brigadier general) was designated commanding officer, with assigned headquarters at Patterson Field. Maintenance Command headquarters remained at Patterson for only two months and then returned to Wright Field on June 19.

The Maintenance Command became the nucleus of the Air Service Command (ASC), established on October 17, 1941, with headquarters in Washington, D.C.

Troops and spectators assembled to greet President Franklin Delano Roosevelt, October 1940.

Major George W. Goddard (left) demonstrated his aerial photography capabilities to President Franklin D. Roosevelt during the latter's visit to Wright Field on October 11, 1940. Orville Wright and former Ohio Governor James M. Cox are beside the president.

The formation of ASC marked the full separation of the logistics function from the Materiel Division. All logistics activities and installations (including the Field Service Section) were removed from the jurisdiction of the Materiel Division and transferred to the new, independent Air Service Command. In December 1942, ASC headquarters moved to newly constructed quarters at Patterson Field (now Gillmore Hall, Building 262, Area A).

The Materiel Division was also elevated to command status on March 9, 1942. Materiel Command headquarters remained in Washington, and on March 16, the materiel organization at Wright Field was redesignated the Materiel Center. The commanding general of the Materiel Command and his advisory, technical, and executive staffs in Washington determined all matters of policy, then referred them to the Materiel Center at Wright Field for execution. The Materiel Center functioned, in other words, as the operating end of the Materiel Command.

On April 1, 1943, Materiel Command headquarters moved from Washington to Wright Field and absorbed the Materiel Center.[66] The headquarters functions were housed in new buildings constructed for that purpose (Buildings 14 and 15, Area B).

The logistics and engineering procurement functions of the Army's air arm were now officially separated into two different organizations: the Materiel Command and the Air Service Command. This arrangement remained in effect until the summer of 1944, when the two commands again merged into a single organization known as the AAF Air Technical Service Command.

Building 16B, constructed in 1943 to provide wartime laboratory space, was similar in style to Building 11. This building was destroyed by fire in 1975; Building 46 stands on the site today.

Preparing The Physical Plant

The reaction at Wright Field to the devastating news of Pearl Harbor was immediate and spirited. It characterized the attitude of Materiel Division personnel throughout the ensuing months of the war. Upon receipt of the news that rocked the nation, key military and civilian personnel at Wright Field spontaneously reported to their duty posts to volunteer for any extra service they might be able to render. Military members, many of whom dressed in civilian clothes for daily work, showed up first thing Monday morning, December 8, in full military dress.

The physical protection of the field remained uppermost in the minds of base officials and plans were formulated at once to provide adequate protective measures. On December 8, 1941, a Mobile Plant Protection Force, consisting of military personnel, was established under the direct jurisdiction of the Wright Field commander and assigned space in Hangar 3 at Wright Field. It was to act as a reserve force to supplement the civilian guard already on duty and to assist in the protection of property and interests against "enemy action, mob violence, or domestic insurrection, including sabotage, espionage, incendiarism, or acts pertaining to any of these."[67] The plans for this new unit included the assignment of a detachment commander who received his orders from the Air Plant Protection Branch, and the assignment of such officer personnel from the Materiel Division as the commanding officer directed. Working 24-hour shifts, personnel were "armed with side arms and machine guns mounted on vehicles."[68]

Buildings 14 and 15, Area B, under construction in 1942 as headquarters for the Materiel Command

A critical component in Wright Field's wartime expansion was the acquisition of additional land. The physical size of the field doubled as the government purchased several surrounding farms by the flightline and area on the hilltop. The acquisitions included land along Kauffman Avenue that became Woodland Hills and a portion of the real estate that Wright State University later owned. A tract at the corner of Kauffman Avenue and present-day Colonel Glenn Highway was used to construct wartime housing and became known as Area D when Patterson and Wright fields merged in 1948.

The flying field was being upgraded and would soon be able to fully support wartime activities. Wright Field's grass runways could not safely accommodate the giant aircraft under development. In fact, the Dayton airport was often used for testing because it had superior—concrete—runways. The expansion of Wright Field's flightline also became necessary to accommodate testing of larger planes. In the spring of 1941, Materiel Division engineers had decided to pave the runways at Wright Field in anticipation of a testing program on the experimental Douglas B-19 heavy bomber, which had a gross weight of 140,000 pounds.

The Army Corps of Engineers agreed to take on the runway project, and Colonel James B. Newman, Jr., came from the Cincinnati district office to collaborate with Wright Field civil engineers. Together, they drew up construction specifications for the new runway complex. Bids let in April attracted contractors from across the country. Selection of the Price Brothers Company of Dayton as the chief contractor occurred in May, and actual construction began in early June.

10 SPORTS SECTION — Local News — DAYTON SUNDAY JOURNAL-HERALD, JUNE 7, 1942. — Local News

"MR. BIG" Of The Skies

B-19 In a Nutshell

Weight—82 tons (fully loaded) . . . Wing spread—212 feet . . . Fuselage length—132 feet . . . Range—7,750 miles . . . Speed—in excess of 200 miles an hour—Fuel capacity—11,000 gallons . . . Top of rudder—towers 42 ft. 9 in. above ground . . . Bomb capacity—18 tons . . . Main landing wheels—8 feet in diameter . . . Motors—four 2,000-horsepower Wright Duplex-Cyclones . . . Propellers—17-foot Hamilton standards.

"MR. BIG" of the skies—that's the Army's B-19, the world's largest flying laboratory, which now is in the air over Dayton and Wright and Patterson Fields almost daily. Everything on the B-19 is mammoth as these new pictures, taken at Wright Field, demonstrate. The B-19 has a 132-foot fuselage, a wing spread of 212 feet (above). It's tail assembly includes a rudder (left) whose top towers 42 feet, 9 inches above the ground. (Staff photos by Keen)

GIANT LANDING wheels, eight feet in diameter, fold into huge wells (above). An idea of sizes on the B-19 may be obtained by comparison with the average size man in the picture. Below is the business-like nose of the bomber, bristling with armament.

TO OBTAIN an unusual closeup of the giant bomber, Staff Photographer Keen climbed out on one of the B-19's big wings (above). Mechanics have easy access to the plane's four motors while the ship is in flight. Passageways connect the motors with the fuselage.

COL. HOWARD G. BUNKER (left) and Lt. Col. Ernest K. Warburton (right) have been flying the B-19 on its Wright Field tests.

CREW of the B-19, most of whom have been up every time the bomber has been flown, includes, left to right: James Funderburk, Eugene Richards, Walter Rader, Stanley Potts, crew chief and flight engineer, James Stevens and Elwood Eakes.

THE CAMERA had a tough time getting all of the B-19 in the picture below. The ship measures 212 feet from wing tip to wing tip.

The "Eagle" Spreads Its Wings To Help Liberate Democratic Peoples

When "Mr. Big," the Douglas XB-19 four-engine experimental bomber, landed at Wright Field for extensive testing in June 1942, the *Dayton Journal-Herald* gave the airplane top photographic coverage.

The grass flying field was relatively flat and had served the experimental flying program for light aircraft for over a decade. In the paving process, however, more than one million cubic yards of earth were moved to grade the field to specified elevations and create contours to ensure proper drainage. O'Connell and Company, an earth-moving contractor from Huntington, West Virginia, accomplished the grading. Price Brothers then supplied and installed the 5,000 feet of 108-inch, reinforced, concrete culvert pipe needed to drain rainwater from the field, across the highway, and into the Mad River at Harshmanville.

The mild winter of 1941 allowed runway construction to continue throughout the fall and into the new year. The Hinton and Smalley Company of Celina, Ohio, did the actual paving, using standard Ohio highway specifications for lack of more pertinent guidelines. Areas graded and ready to receive paving, as well as runway sections completed each day, were covered with burlap, overlaid with a foot of straw, and topped with tarpaulins at night to take advantage of the natural heat generated by the concrete as it cured. When complete, each of the two new runways measured 150 feet in width. The east-west runway (09/27) was the longest at 7,147.7 feet and was laid out to take advantage of the prevailing winds. The northwest-southeast runway (16/34) was 5,569.3 feet in length. Both runways were completed by mid-February 1942, although fine grading and seeding of the surrounding ground were not finished until June.[69]

Nearly halfway through the construction process, it was learned through captured enemy intelligence that the Germans were planning to build runways along the coast of France implementing a new technique—inclining the runways slightly to shorten takeoff and landing distances. Materiel Division officials quickly decided to undertake similar construction at Wright Field to test the validity of the concept. Consequently, the Price Brothers Company contract was expanded to include construction of an inclined runway just east of the new runway complex. The accelerated runway had a 10 percent grade and was completed shortly after the two main runways. (After extensive testing, it was concluded that the concept for the accelerated runway was not practical, and use of the runway was discontinued. The third major runway at Wright Field, the northeast-southwest runway which runs by the present site of the United States Air Force Museum, was 6,478.5 feet in length and was completed two years later.)

The most critical problem for the commanding officer at Wright Field in the early months of America's involvement in the war was dealing with a chronic shortage of space. The emergency brought continuing increases in functions and personnel assigned to the field. The Wright Field leadership had been seeking approval for additional construction for nearly two years, to no avail. In 1940, Colonel Echols sought approval for a badly needed addition to the administration building (Building 11, Area B). His report to Washington pointed out that all available space was already being used and urged that further construction be undertaken immediately: "There is not a single activity at this station which is not terrifically overcrowded and becoming more so daily. Efficiency and morale is [sic] suffering because of these conditions."[70]

Little relief came during fiscal year 1940. Major construction during the year was confined to a substation, transformers, and a high-speed wind tunnel for the Aircraft Laboratory; a lab building and a dynamometer building for the Power Plant Laboratory; and general expansion of post utilities.[71] Construction in 1942 included several temporary and a few permanent structures that added 711,271 square feet of floor space, but the demand for space continued to outstrip the rate of construction.[72] It was not until 1943 that the physical plant was sufficiently expanded to accommodate the functions assigned to the field.

Wright Field flightline, showing the first paved runway (identified as 16/34), completed during the winter of 1941. The construction of hangars and the Armament Laboratory's 200-yard gun range are visible in the center right of the photograph. The large XB-19, with its 212-foot wingspan, is parked in front of the hangars.

Overall, the lack of funds and not of foresight on the part of Wright Field administrators was fundamentally responsible for the delay in construction. Requests for new buildings were routinely deferred because funds were not available currently, but would be added to future budgets.

A number of ingenious measures were taken to provide temporary relief of the overcrowded conditions. Two auto-parking sheds were remodeled late in 1941 and converted into offices. A third floor of temporary frame construction (later known as the "Penthouse") was added to the administration building (Building 11) in February 1942. The former Steele High School building in downtown Dayton was leased to accommodate the Industrial Planning Section of the Production Division. The post garage was transformed into an office building in April 1942 and occupied by personnel of the Production Division. Desks, chairs, typewriters, file cabinets, and other office equipment placed in the corridors of all buildings accommodated a large number of new wartime employees. Rotating eight-hour shifts were adopted so that equipment intended for the use of one person served three. These arrangements sometimes contributed to an impression that employees were wasting government time and occasionally gave rise to criticism in the local public press.[73]

Contributing to the general confusion and crowded conditions was a steadily increasing number of contractors' representatives and other personnel visiting the field. In August 1942, there was an average of 500 visitors per day, with a peak of 603 in one day. By December, the daily average had increased to 700.

Continuing space problems also curtailed a number of less essential activities for the duration of the war. Courses for the 1939-1940 term at the Air Corps Engineering School, which had been operating since 1926 under the direction of the Materiel Division chief, were suspended by order of the secretary of war, and the school was later closed indefinitely.[74] The Army Aeronautical Museum was closed to all casual visitors on June 1, 1940. Shortly after, the exhibits were removed from the

A B-50D taxies up the accelerated runway in 1953.

museum and placed in storage, and the Civilian Personnel Section of Wright Field occupied the vacated space.[75] The museum remained closed until August 1954, when it reopened in new quarters at Patterson Field (Building 89, Area C).

The rapid expansion of activities at both Wright and Patterson fields, as well as the expansion of industrial plants in Dayton and the vicinity, put a great strain on housing facilities for base personnel. Local, state, and federal authorities negotiated for the erection of many new houses. A large percentage of the facilities built with federal funds were allocated for the use of Wright Field employees and their families. The Employees' Service Unit of the Civilian Personnel Section at Wright Field received applications for these new homes and assigned them on the basis of need. In addition, many patriotic families in the Dayton area graciously offered to open their private homes to newcomers.[76]

By 1943, the national emergency was more directly under control, and the situation began to ease at Wright Field. A vast construction and improvement program was approved that included an extensive network of roads and streets, and the completion of numerous new buildings. During the year, approximately 140 buildings and major building additions were transferred to the Wright Field commander by the Army Corps of Engineers. Foremost among these were two large administration buildings (Buildings 14 and 15, Area B) to house the Materiel Command, 21 civilian housing units, a jet-thrust propulsion laboratory, an equipment laboratory, a post exchange, and a large number of barracks and mess halls.[77]

While at Wright Field, Colonel Oliver Patterson Echols was assistant chief of the Materiel Division. Echols rose to the rank of major general in February 1942.

Materiel Command complex at Wright Field, shortly after the end of World War II, including Buildings 14 and 15, 11 and 11A, 16 and 16B

The Army Aeronautical Museum, forerunner of the United States Air Force Museum, originally opened in 1923 to showcase the technological developments at McCook Field (such as tachometers and statoscopes, displayed above). In 1927, the museum moved to Wright Field, and in 1935 it was located in specially designed Building 12 constructed through the Works Progress Administration (below). During World War II, the building was converted to offices, and the museum collections went into storage for 14 years.

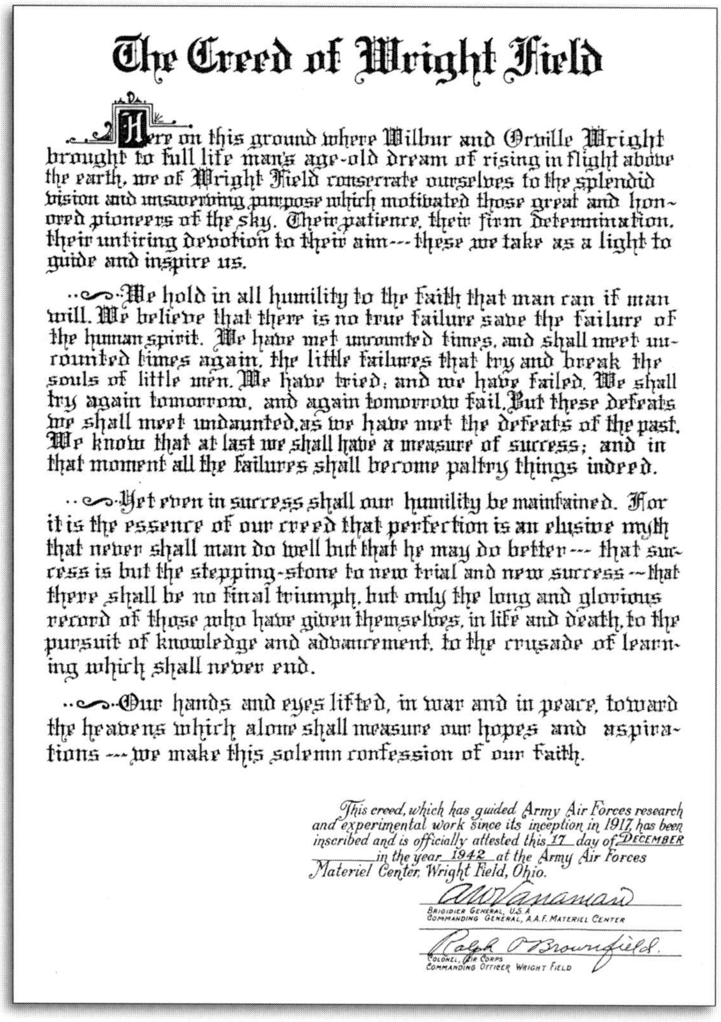

The Creed of Wright Field

Here on this ground where Wilbur and Orville Wright brought to full life man's age-old dream of rising in flight above the earth, we of Wright Field consecrate ourselves to the splendid vision and unswerving purpose which motivated those great and honored pioneers of the sky. Their patience, their firm determination, their untiring devotion to their aim--- these we take as a light to guide and inspire us.

We hold in all humility to the faith that man can if man will. We believe that there is no true failure save the failure of the human spirit. We have met uncounted times, and shall meet uncounted times again, the little failures that try and break the souls of little men. We have tried; and we have failed. We shall try again tomorrow, and again tomorrow fail. But these defeats we shall meet undaunted, as we have met the defeats of the past. We know that at last we shall have a measure of success; and in that moment all the failures shall become paltry things indeed.

Yet even in success shall our humility be maintained. For it is the essence of our creed that perfection is an elusive myth that never shall man do well but that he may do better --- that success is but the stepping-stone to new trial and new success -- that there shall be no final triumph, but only the long and glorious record of those who have given themselves, in life and death, to the pursuit of knowledge and advancement, to the crusade of learning which shall never end.

Our hands and eyes lifted, in war and in peace, toward the heavens which alone shall measure our hopes and aspirations --- we make this solemn confession of our faith.

This creed, which has guided Army Air Forces research and experimental work since its inception in 1917, has been inscribed and is officially attested this 17 day of DECEMBER in the year 1942 at the Army Air Forces Materiel Center, Wright Field, Ohio.

BRIGIDIER GENERAL, U.S.A.
COMMANDING GENERAL, A.A.F. MATERIEL CENTER

Ralph P. Brownfield.
COLONEL, AIR CORPS
COMMANDING OFFICER WRIGHT FIELD

The Wright Field Creed, 1942

By 1944, Wright Field had sustained striking alterations. From an installation of only 20 buildings in 1927, the field had grown to a military establishment of approximately 40 buildings in 1941. By the spring of 1944, Wright Field had mushroomed to some 300 buildings and a vast, modern landing field, occupying some 2,064 acres.[78]

Early in 1944, all Wright Field headquarters offices moved from the lower area of the field to the newly completed administration building (Building 125) on the hilltop. This brought all of the commanding officer's staff together for the first time. It also placed the staff in closer proximity to the troops, housed in barracks along the eastern boundary of the hill, and to other activities in which they were involved.[79]

Although the initial year of the war had presented many difficulties at Wright Field, Materiel Division personnel had proved themselves equal to the task. The all-important procurement and engineering functions had managed to survive the administrative reorganizations necessary in order to stimulate and oversee the production that would eventually turn the tide of the war. The outstanding engineering and production records achieved by Wright Field personnel stood as adequate proof of the integrity and effectiveness of the organization.

Wright Field, 1944. The hilltop area, which was largely vacant prior to World War II, was occupied by the new headquarters building and row after row of military barracks for Wright Field personnel.

MAJOR GENERAL FRANKLIN OTIS CARROLL

Brigadier General Franklin Otis Carroll

Major General Franklin Otis Carroll was a visionary leader who made significant contributions to aviation and to the American war effort in World War II. He witnessed a revolution in aircraft design, materials, performance and manufacturing, and became instrumental in guiding the Air Force's transition from reciprocating engines to jet propulsion. As the director of Wright Field's experimental engineering operations, he skillfully balanced the desires of dreamers, designers and operators.

General Carroll was born in 1893 in Washington, Indiana. After completing Officers Training Camp at Fort Sheridan, Illinois, and flight training at Kelly Field, Texas, in 1918, he was commissioned as a first lieutenant in the Aviation Section of the Signal Reserve. Throughout his 37-year military career, Carroll was assigned to McCook and Wright fields no fewer than four times. His first assignment in Dayton was in the summer of 1921, when he reported to the Air Corps Engineering Division at McCook Field, Ohio, as an engineer in the Structures and Dynamics Branch of the Airplane Section. When McCook transferred to the newly opened Wright Field, Carroll became assistant chief of the Experimental Engineering Section and two years later he was assigned chief of the Airplane Branch. Throughout World War II, he served as chief of the Experimental Engineering Section, during which time he was at the center of every major experimental and engineering project at the field. He approved the creation of the world's most advanced wind tunnels and laboratories for aeromedical research, communications, navigation and radar and oversaw the introduction of the first jet engine to Wright Field.

In October 1942, Carroll was promoted to brigadier general, and in January 1945 assumed the additional duty of commandant of the Army Air Forces Engineering School at Wright Field, which later became the Air Force Institute of Technology. He was assigned to the Air Materiel Command headquarters at Wright Field as assistant to the deputy commanding general for engineering in January 1947. In mid-1947, Carroll left Wright Field for higher headquarters, serving as director of research and development at Air Materiel Command and later as commander of the Arnold Engineering Development Center, in Tullahoma, Tennessee. General Carroll died on September 13, 1988. He was honored posthumously on June 1, 2001, when a new addition to the General Doolittle Acquisition Management Complex at Wright-Patterson Air Force Base was named after him.

Brigadier General Frank Carroll (center) with General Hap Arnold (left) at Wright Field, May 20, 1944

Sources: "Major General Franklin O. Carroll," United States Air Force Biography, online at http://www.af.mil/news/biographies/carroll_fo.html. Program, "Dedication of the Major General Franklin Otis Carroll Hall" (Wright-Patterson Air Force Base, Ohio, June 1, 2001).

Brigadier General Franklin Carroll in front of the P-59B Reluctant Robot used during drone experimentation at Wright Field, 1940s. Carroll was a guiding force in the transition from reciprocating engines to jet engines in the Army Air Forces.

Brigadier General Franklin Carroll (right) views an exhibit of the Wright Flyer with Orville Wright.

VERTICAL WIND TUNNEL

Wright Field's Vertical Wind Tunnel was constructed in 1943-1945 to study aircraft spin characteristics and parachute performance. The 75-foot-tall, cylindrical facility was equipped with a 1,000-horsepower motor to power a 16-foot-diameter fan capable of generating wind speeds up to 100 mph. Tests helped engineers determine the characteristics of aircraft least susceptible to the dangerous tailspin phenomenon, and contributed to the development of several of the early X-planes, the F-86 fighter, and the Century Series fighters. The Vertical Wind Tunnel also provided extensive information regarding parachute dynamics. Experiments to study drag, opening shock, and stability were conducted on parachutes up to six feet in diameter. Other tests conducted in the tunnel included drag and stability of missiles and re-entry bodies, rotary wing characteristics, and ejection-seat stabilization. Beginning in the mid-1980s, the United States Army used the tunnel to teach free-fall principles to its paratroopers.

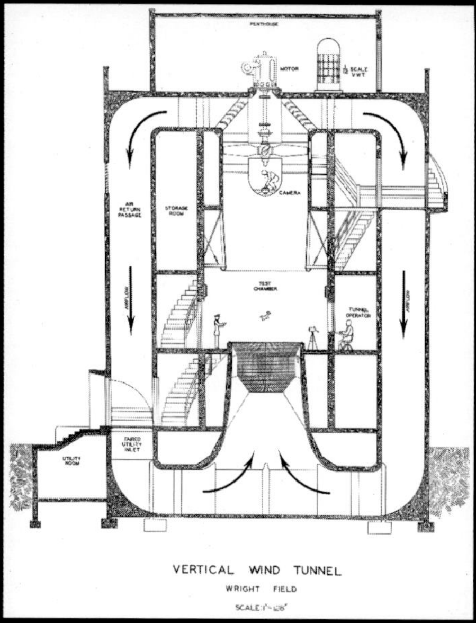

Interior diagram of the Vertical Wind Tunnel

Source: Emma J. H. Dyson, Dean A. Herrin, and Amy E. Slaton, The *Engineering of Flight: Aeronautical Engineering Facilities of Area B, Wright-Patterson Air Force Base, Ohio* (Washington, D.C., 1993), pp 141-143.

The largest and fastest free-flow, open-throat, vertical wind tunnel in the world, located on Wright Field's "Hurricane Hill." This wind tunnel, constructed in 1942, was designed especially for parachute testing. The 20-foot horizontal wind tunnel is visible in the background.

Wartime Engineering Activities At Wright Field

Two major divisions of the Materiel Command, the Engineering Division and the Production Division, conducted the primary work at Wright Field during the war. "Three years ahead of the procession," was the goal of the Engineering Division as it continuously planned newer and better airplanes and aircraft equipment for the Army Air Forces inventory. Some Wright Field engineers referred to it as the "Buck Rogers" Division because of the radically new and unorthodox designs frequently tested. Brigadier General Franklin O. Carroll headed the Engineering Division and guided this large and very important organization throughout the war years. Under his direction, neither the magnitude of production problems nor the expansion of Allied military offensives deflected the scope or intensity of Engineering Division projects. In 1943, more than 800 major research and development projects were in progress under the auspices of the Engineering Division, in laboratories filled with more than $50 million in special equipment.[80]

The wind tunnel was one of the key test processes to which scale models of new airplanes were submitted. In 1941-1942 the largest wind tunnel in the world was completed at Wright Field. Among the major programs conducted in the tunnel, with its 20-foot-diameter test chamber, were research in parachute stability and on spin characteristics of model airplanes. Models with wingspreads up to 16 feet were tested at airspeeds up to 400 mph.

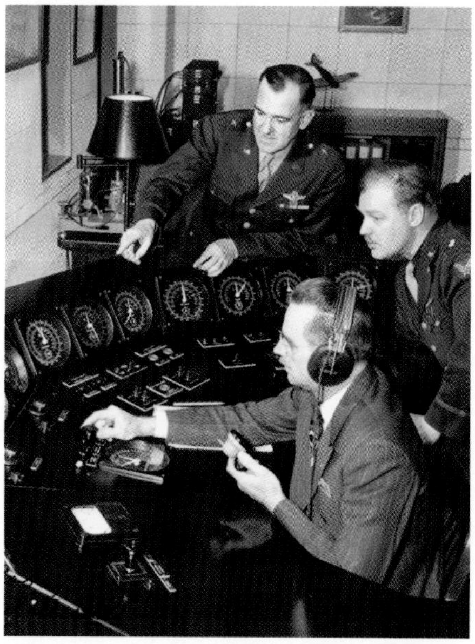
Brigadier General Franklin Carroll in the control room during a test at the 20-foot wind tunnel, February 1945

Civilian workers in the Materials Laboratory, August 29, 1945. Additionally, 46 officers and 73 enlisted persons were assigned to the lab.

These powerful airstreams were generated by a 40,000-horsepower electric motor that drove two 16-bladed fans.[81]

The Materials Laboratory of the Engineering Division was heavily involved in the development of synthetic or substitute materials for any items of AAF equipment that might be difficult to obtain in wartime. One major achievement was the development of nylon fabrics and other synthetic silk materials for use in such items as parachutes and corded tires. New cotton materials, in like fashion, were turned out as substitutes for the linen webbing used in parachute harnesses. The laboratory also formulated vital camouflage paints that provided warplanes with dull, non-reflecting protective coloration. Non-glare paints and lacquers, usually dull red or black, were also developed for use on propeller blades.

Engineering Division technicians and engineers fabricated devices for rapid servicing and maintenance of airplanes. They developed and tested huge fueling trucks, crash trucks, mobile field repair outfits, maintenance stands for mechanics, portable field-lighting equipment, portable steel mats to convert soggy fields into useable runways, and jacks for hoisting bombers so that tires or landing gear could be serviced.

Inertial brake-testing machine used to simulate landing conditions on the largest of new aircraft wheel, tire, and brake assemblies

Additional equipment used to test aircraft gear. This machine is a radial-and-side-load applicator.

Wartime Production Activities

An A-20 prepared to conduct live-fire testing on the 500-yard gun range (near Building 22, Area B), 1944

The engineering developments at Wright Field were supported by the achievements of the Production Division in building America's air armada. Skilled engineers and attorneys prepared purchasing contracts at Wright Field for thousands of warplanes and vast quantities of supplementary equipment. At aircraft production facilities in the private sector, technical experts from the Production Division supervised the details of contract administration and helped speed production schedules. (See Chapter 4 for a detailed accounting of engineering activities at Wright Field during World War II.)

Early in the war, the Production Division was headed by Brigadier General Kenneth B. Wolfe, a "most vigorous and masterful chief," who later served as chief of the B-29 Special Project Staff and as commanding general of the Materiel Command. General Wolfe assembled a strong staff of production engineers and business executives and laid a firm foundation for the production process.[82] In 1943, he was succeeded by Brigadier General Orval R. Cook, who assumed command of the Production Division for the latter part of the war.

Airplane production was a complex process that required detailed planning and elaborate scheduling. An airplane was not built in its entirety by one manufacturer; component parts were usually manufactured at different locations across the country. Parts such as engines, propellers, wheels, armament, radio equipment, and the like—as many as 4,000 different items—were procured by the government from any number of different sources and shipped to airframe manufacturers for final assembly. Thus, most of the famous airplane manufacturers, such as Douglas, Martin, and Boeing, produced only the airframe (i.e., the tail, wings, and fuselage). They then assembled the entire airplane, using parts furnished to them by the government.

The Production Division coordinated and facilitated manufacturing efforts to make certain that production schedules were met. It ensured that some 15,000 manufacturers received the necessary materials in the proper amounts at the proper time. It also aided manufacturers in expanding their current factories, constructing new ones, or in acquiring machines and tools to fulfill their contracts. Accomplishing all of this in a timely and efficient manner was a monumental task, but was essential to sustain a smooth flow of finished airplanes to Army Air Forces units on the battlefronts.

In the overall process, the work of the Production Division was coordinated closely with the Engineering Division, which provided design work, and with the Procurement Division, which supervised the actual purchase and delivery of materials. According to a 1943 employee handbook, the Procurement Division of the Materiel Command ranked as the second largest procurement organization in the armed forces. Its authorization to spend "billions of dollars for aircraft, aircraft equipment, and supplies" reflected the combined efforts of Engineering and Production.[83]

This close coordination was especially visible in the approach to problems with in-service battlefront equipment. The first American airplanes that joined the Allies in Europe, for example, had serious problems due to inadequate firepower; and they were not equipped with leak-proof fuel tanks and armor plating. These deficiencies were a natural consequence of the then-current philosophy in aircraft design, which emphasized superior flight performance over armament considerations. Wright Field observers—most of them production engineers—hurried to France and England in early 1940 to study guns and armor on the airplanes being used in combat. After consultation with Engineering Division personnel and representatives of the various manufacturers involved, the Production Division recommended in-process modifications. Balance was shifted slightly from speed and range to incorporate increased firepower and provide additional defensive plating.[84]

In these problems and in the general gearing-up of production, the crucial factor was time. Prior to the war, aircraft development was a linear process. The Army bought one experimental airplane and tested it—often to destruction. If it decided to purchase a model, it ordered small quantities, as needed. This whole process took anywhere from one to five years. As the war heightened, new models had to be produced much more quickly. The Army began making frequent exception to its linear process and ordered some new airplanes "right off the drafting boards," without requiring advance testing of a prototype. Brigadier General George C. Kenney, as assistant chief of the Materiel Division, once remarked, "One of our newest bombers was ordered built after we saw it on the back of an envelope, and 18 months later the ship was flying."[85]

This abbreviated procurement procedure was often called "off-the-shelf procurement" because production contracts were let on the basis of drawing-board plans.[86] This policy was implemented only with manufacturers who had satisfactorily built airplanes of the same general type previously, or in cases where the new design had been thoroughly proven by wind-tunnel tests and other preliminary checks.

Brigadier General Franklin Carroll (center) examines aircraft engineering drawings, February 1945.

Major General Kenneth B. Wolfe. As a brigadier general, Wolfe led the Production Division at Wright Field during the early part of World War II. In 1943, he became the driving force behind the development and deployment of the B-29 bomber, and subsequently organized and trained the 20th Bomber Command before directing the first B-29 strike against Japan. In 1944, Wolfe returned to Wright Field as commander of Materiel Command. After the war, Wolfe served at Wright Field as chief of Engineering and Procurement at Air Technical Service Command and then in 1948 as director of Procurement and Industrial Mobilization Planning.

Under the new plan, Wright Field took delivery on an early production model of the new design and "put it through the wringer" to ascertain its maximum speed, range, rate of climb, ceiling, landing and takeoff runs, and other vital data, while mass production on additional airplanes continued.[87]

The Army called this routine "accelerated tests." Although the majority of these tests were conducted at Wright Field where the Flight Section compiled the data, a special section at neighboring Patterson Field assisted in the process. At Patterson, pilots and crews were brought from various tactical squadrons to conduct the accelerated tests. They flew each production model night and day for 150 hours, simulating actual combat conditions to see how the craft performed to Army specifications. Fighters were flown at full-throttle, half-throttle—fast, slow, high, and low—through every conceivable maneuver, for the equivalent of more than a year of service for the airplane. Bombers were loaded with full crews and heavy duds to simulate the bomb loads, and flown at high altitudes for as many as 18 hours non-stop, to approximate performance under regular mission conditions.[88]

Additional accelerated tests were conducted at the Dayton Army Air Field at Vandalia, Ohio, under the jurisdiction of the Accelerated Service Test Branch.[89] The Glider Branch of the Aircraft Laboratory carried out troop-carrier glider tests at Clinton County Army Air Field near

A huge acoustical enclosure, designed by Wright Field engineers, was built over the propeller test rigs and their craneway during the latter part of the war to muffle the deafening noise produced during testing. The enclosure was completed in 1944. The octagon-shaped test enclosures on the right in the lower photograph were used for testing helicopter blades.

The completed Static Test Building (Building 65), shown here in November 1944, was tall enough and wide enough to flip over a B-36 fuselage and wing assembly in order to perform a full range of static tests.

Troop-carrying gliders such as this one were tested at the Clinton County Army Air Field near Wilmington, Ohio, in connection with work at Wright Field. The Clinton County airfield later became part of the Army Air Forces Technical Base, along with Wright and Patterson fields and the Dayton Army Air Field at Vandalia, Ohio.

Testing a radio in a Freon immersion bath in the Materials Laboratory. The liquid protected against atmospheric change and its features eliminated danger of burnouts or explosions.

Wilmington, Ohio, southeast of Dayton. Test work in electronics was done at the Commonwealth Airport at East Boston, Massachusetts. The military units that performed the tests were transferred to the Materiel Command as the Electronics Experimental Detachment.[90]

In June 1943 at Wright Field, steps were taken to supplement the data being compiled by the Flight Section through its test activities. A U.S. Equipment Unit was established in the Technical Data Laboratory that not only collected information, but also arranged for conferences between Materiel Command personnel and manufacturers' representatives returning from abroad.

It was also during 1943 that one of the outstanding test bases of the AAF became a formal military installation. The test facility at Rogers Lake, Muroc, California, was established in March 1942. On February 17, 1943, the 477th Base Headquarters and Air Base Squadron (Reduced) moved from Wright Field to Muroc. The Materiel Command Flight Test Base, which operated under the administrative control of the Materiel Command and the technical supervision of the Engineering Division, was fenced off and segregated from the remainder of the Muroc Army Air Base reservation. Its establishment satisfied the demand for a satisfactory place to test aeronautical developments that required an unusual degree of physical protection and security because of their classified status, or projects that required a large flying field due to their experimental nature. In spite of the complex administrative arrangements that accompanied the base's establishment, the Flight Test Base was recognized as one of the finest test establishments of the Materiel Command, and the 1943 evaluation program carried on at Muroc more than justified the expense and labor involved in its maintenance.[91]

Aero Medical Research Laboratory (Building 29, Area B), shortly after completion in 1942

THE END OF THE WAR AND BEYOND

By the end of 1943, it became apparent that the wartime arrangement of separating logistics and procurement into two different organizations had its drawbacks. The Materiel Command, with headquarters at Wright Field, and the Air Service Command, with headquarters at Patterson Field, supervised functions that, although entirely different in theory, often overlapped in actuality. The Air Service Command was concerned with the maintenance and distribution of supplies, while the Materiel Command conducted research and development and managed the aircraft procurement program. In practice, however, it was not always easy to distinguish between their respective responsibilities. Jurisdictional entanglements over such issues as spare parts procurement, disposal of surplus property, and administration of air cargo service contracts invariably led to confusion and frustration between the two commands.

Both commands actively pursued solutions to these problems. Policy and coordination committees considered broad policy matters; officers of both commands performed reciprocal tours; and regulations and directives were issued in an attempt to resolve conflicts and improve working relations. Eventually, time and experimentation demonstrated that the most efficient method of correcting the difficulties was to eliminate the separation factor entirely.

On August 31, 1944, the Materiel Command and the Air Service Command were discontinued and their functions merged into a single organization known as the Air Technical Service Command (ATSC). Lieutenant General William S. Knudsen, former president of the General Motors Corporation, was designated the first director of the new command, with Major General Bennett E. Meyers as his deputy. General Knudsen requested that his new title as head of ATSC be "director," rather than "commanding general," to emphasize the business aspect of the new command's operations.[92]

ATSC headquarters was located in Building 262 at Patterson Field. From there, the Air Technical Service Command directed both the logistical and engineering operations of the Army Air Forces through the end of the war and beyond. This restructuring made ATSC responsible

ANN BAUMGARTNER CARL

Ann Baumgartner stands on the wing of the AT-6 she flew during WASP training at Avenger Field, Sweetwater, Texas. *(The Woman's Collection, Texas Woman's University Library)*

Young Ann Baumgartner was sitting in the front row when Amelia Earhart came to her school one day to talk about the adventure of flying, and with her inspiring words, Baumgartner's future as a pioneer aviator was sealed. Baumgartner earned her pilot's license in 1940 while working in the public relations department of Eastern Airlines, and a year later started flying search-and-rescue missions for the Civil Air Patrol. She interviewed with Jackie Cochran in late 1942 about the possibility of joining the Women Airforce Service Pilots (WASP) and was accepted into the third class of the Women's Flying Training Detachment (WFTD), but graduated with the fifth class of the WFTD due to a case of measles. While on a temporary tour of duty at Wright Field, Baumgartner discovered that was the place to be for pilots who were interested in flying planes of all kinds, and she asked for a permanent assignment to Wright Field. Her request was granted, and in March 1944 Baumgartner was assigned as an assistant operations officer in the Fighter Test Section at Wright Field. She was soon checking out such aircraft as the P-47 Thunderbolt, the British Mosquito, and the German Ju-88. While briefly assigned to the Bomber Test Section, she had the opportunity to garner pilot, copilot, and pilot observer time in the B-17, B-24, and B-29 bombers. On October 14, 1944, Baumgartner became the first woman to fly a turbojet-powered plane when she flew the Bell YP-59A, a feat that undoubtedly would have made Amelia Earhart very proud.

Sources: "Ann Baumgartner Carl on: Her Interest in Flying," Fly Girls, *American Experience*, PBS, online at http://www.pbs.org/wgbh/amex/flygirls/filmmore/reference/interview/carl01.html; *Women Pilots in WWII, WASP Class 43-W-5*, United States Air Force Museum, online at http://www.wpafb.af.mil/museum/history/wasp/wasp26.htm.

V-E Day cartoon on the front page of *The Wright Flyer* newspaper illustrated that the war was not yet won and encouraged Wright Field workers to stick to their jobs.

for functions on two different, but adjacent, installations and made Wright Field subordinate to the new ATSC headquarters at Patterson Field. To overcome the psychologically divisive effect of this arrangement on the installation and give the entire headquarters a common address, the portion of Patterson Field from Huffman Dam through the Brick Quarters (including the command headquarters in Building 262) was reassigned from Patterson Field to Wright Field. To avoid confusing the two areas of Wright Field, the new acquisition was designated "Area A" and the original Wright Field became "Area B." This trend toward combining the two bases became an increasingly practical necessity and logical eventuality that culminated several years later in the merger of Wright and Patterson fields (January 1948).[93]

V-E Day (Victory-Europe), May 8, 1945, marked the unconditional surrender of the German government to the Allies. World War II in the West officially ended at midnight, May 7-8, 1945. The news was jubilantly hailed in both areas of Wright Field. Major General Meyers, acting ATSC director, addressed Wright Field troops and employees at the Hilltop Parade Grounds in Area B. At the core of his message was the reminder that the war was not yet won and an appeal to Wright Field workers to redouble their efforts to bring about a speedy victory in the Pacific theater.[94]

The spirit of ultimate victory ran high in the closing months of the war. Commanding officers were not the sole source of this encouragement. During 1945 a number of big-name bands made appearances at Wright Field to bolster morale, among them Glen Gray and his Casa Loma Orchestra, Les Brown and his Band of Renown accompanied by the lovely young vocalist Doris Day, and the Stan Kenton Band. Prominent entertainers such as Bob Hope, Glenn Miller, Tommy Dorsey, Sammy Kaye, Les Elgart, and Woody Herman visited both Wright and Patterson fields throughout the war to entertain and encourage the troops. Lawrence Welk and his orchestra played at the opening of the Civilian Club (Building 274, Area A) on December 1, 1944.[95] The Columbia Broadcasting System (CBS) radio program "Cheers from the Camps" was broadcast from the old steel hangar on Patterson Field (Building 145, Area C) and was heartily welcomed by men from both fields.[96]

Wright Field paused briefly on August 1, 1945, to celebrate the 38th anniversary of the Army Air Forces (first created as the Aeronautical Division of the Army Signal Corps in 1907). To mark the occasion, and for the benefit of some 150,000 visitors, a massive display of AAF power was exhibited on the flightline. It included not only the airplanes that had gained prominence during the war, but also the technical developments that made them possible. Civilian personnel were excused from duty at noon to attend the open house. The high spot of the afternoon was the review of 10,000 Wright Field troops on the Hilltop Parade Grounds by Major General Hugh J. Knerr, who had assumed command of ATSC on July 1. At his side were Orville Wright and Edward Ward. Mr. Ward, of Dayton, was the first enlisted man in the Aeronautical Division.

Captured enemy airplanes and equipment were placed on exhibition by the traveling "Shot From the Sky" show. Included in the displays were captured Japanese airplanes and a German Junkers that was flown from Munich in time for the celebration.[97] Beginning at 3:00 p.m., the public was treated to a spectacular air show. The star performer of the show was the dazzling P-80 Shooting Star, the AAF's first jet-propelled fighter, revealed publicly in flight for the first time. (Within 143 days of the request to build an airplane around a jet engine, a special team of Lockheed engineers and workmen, headed by Chief

Research Engineer Clarence "Kelly" Johnson, had designed, built, and delivered the first model P-80 for ATSC experimental flight test.)

V-J Day (Victory-Japan) came August 15, 1945, when Japanese forces laid down their arms. The official surrender to the Allies was September 2, 1945, aboard the USS *Missouri* in Tokyo Bay. When Wright Field received word that the Japanese had capitulated, the installation reacted with "bombastic glee." An account in the Wright Field enlisted newspaper, *The Post Script*, exclaimed:[98]

> Barrack after barrack rocked and trembled as shouts of pent-up emotion burst from the throats of enlisted personnel. Soldiers thumped each other on the back, shook hands, jumped about the shredded newspapers, bulletins (from bulletin boards) and bits of stationery. They poured out from the barracks, shouting the good news to each other and headed for the orderly rooms. . . .On the post the merriment hit an all-time high: the NCO Club was a mad-house of lively military personnel, the bowling alley PX rocked to all-out celebration. Headquarters Area was a scene of similar festivities.

NIPPON QUITS! WAR IS PAST THE RISING SUN HAS SET AT LAST

The WRIGHT FLYER

BUY WAR BONDS — TO HAVE AND TO HOLD

Headquarters, Air Technical Service Command, Wright Field, Dayton, Ohio — V-J Edition

V-J DAY Issue

Force Reduction Plan Announced

Total Victory has been achieved. The question now uppermost in the minds of most employees is "what will happen to my job?" This is not an easy question to answer. Although it is assumed that a relatively large post-war installation will be maintained at Headquarters, ATSC, it is believed that, as the result of the defeat of Japan, there will shortly be some considerable reductions in force. The exact extent of such reductions, the types of positions affected, etc., cannot possibly be determined at this time. However, as soon as definite information is received from higher authority, all employees will be promptly informed.

The rules governing reduction in force have been set up by the Civil Service Commission and have been designed so that the best qualified employees will be retained. These rules will be fairly applied at Headquarters, ATSC. Presented below for your information is a series of

may have different titles) in which interchange of personnel is feasible. For example, all Clerk-Typists, CAF-2 of this Headquarters will compete with one another. Clerk-Typists, CAF-3 will not compete with Clerk-Typists, CAF-2. However, Clerk-Typists, CAF-2 may compete with Teletype Operators, CAF-2 inasmuch as interchange of positions is feasible within a reasonable period of training time.

Employees of Wright Field will not compete with Fairfield ATSC employees. Graded employees and ungraded employees will not compete with one another.

The persons separated are those holding positions like the ones abolished who stand lowest on the "retention register."

Q—What is a "retention register?"

A—A retention register is a listing of employees grouped according

The Wright Flyer **published a special issue on V-J Day. After victory over Japan, the top story was reduction in force.**

One of the most spectacular events at Wright Field in the months following the end of the war was the staging of a huge Army Air Forces Fair. More than a million visitors from across the United States and from 26 foreign countries were attracted to Wright Field beginning Saturday, October 13, 1945. The fair was originally intended as a local, weekend event. Public response was overwhelming, however, and more than 500,000 people flocked to Wright Field in the opening two days. ATSC officials quickly decided to extend the event for an additional week.

The fair displayed technological advances in aviation made during the war; showed captured German and Japanese weapons; and presented the AAF story to the American people. Over $150 million worth of equipment, much of which had

An open house for Wright Field personnel during World War II attracted a large crowd.

In 1945, Colonel Harold E. Watson was assigned by General Henry H. Arnold to acquire two of every German aircraft and transport them to Wright Field for technical analysis. Watson later commanded the Air Technical Intelligence Center, predecessor of the National Air Intelligence Center (NAIC).

German Junkers 290 flown directly to Wright Field by Colonel Harold E. Watson

German ME-163B on display at the AAF Fair. Captured German and Japanese airplanes added a special aura of excitement to the fair.

German Bachem BP-20 Natter rocket-propelled interceptor

been highly classified during the war, was exhibited. Cameras were welcome and photographers rushed to shoot airplanes and equipment that only a week before had been strictly "hush-hush." Weapons that had been only mental pictures for many became not only visible, but touchable. "From behind locked doors and out of guarded test chambers [came] the latest in electronics, radar, jet propulsion, rockets, satellite devices and secret projects that for years [had] been mentioned only by code names."[99]

Captured German aircraft placed on display brought the enemy's most dreaded airplanes and missiles to life for the public. A Junkers 290 with *Alles Kaputt* (All is Finished) emblazoned on its side, was flown directly to the fair from Germany by Colonel Harold E. Watson. Also on display were the German V-2 rocket; the Messerschmitt 262—the world's first operational, turbojet fighter-bomber; the Messerschmitt 163B Komet rocket-propelled interceptor; the Arado 234B twin-jet, 500-mph reconnaissance aircraft; and a Bachem BP-20 Natter. (The Natter was a catapult-launched, rocket-propelled interceptor that would split in two and parachute to earth after completing its mission, thus enabling expensive components to be recovered and reused.)

Japanese spoils of war placed on display included the Mitsubishi ZEKE 52 (Zero) fighter, famed for outmaneuvering many an American fighter in the Pacific. Also on display was *Thumper*, one of the B-29s to fly over Tokyo.

Virtually every type of AAF aircraft, including experimental models, was available for viewing. In the words of General Knerr, ATSC had, in effect, turned its laboratories "inside out to show our visitors the wonders of modern science that went into the creation of the world's greatest air force."[100]

Thumper, one of the B-29s to fly over Tokyo

George Churchill Kenney (shown here when a general), a 1921 graduate of the Engineering School at McCook Field, came to Wright Field in 1939 as chief of the Production Engineering Section. Between January 1941 and February 1942, he served as assistant chief of the Materiel Division with the rank of brigadier general. Kenney later became the first commander of Strategic Air Command (1946). He retired in 1951 after a 34-year military career.

Visitors to the 1945 Wright Field Air Fair included (left to right) Major General Benjamin W. Chidlaw, Colonel Edward A. Deeds, Orville Wright, and Brigadier General Laurence Craigie.

Distinguished visitors to the Air Fair included top-ranking officers of the War Department and the AAF, members of Congress, state and municipal officials, leading industrialists, and of course, with the event being held in Dayton, aviation pioneer Orville Wright. On Sunday, October 21, the fair honored General George C. Kenney, commander of the Far East Air Forces at the time of the Japanese surrender.

So enthusiastic was public response to the fair that a selection of the exhibits was later developed by ATSC into a traveling show. The 4140th Army Air Forces Base Unit (Research and Development Exhibition) was formed to organize and handle the road show.[101] The traveling display proved a popular concept and was continued; the 4140th became the predecessor of the Orientation Group, United States Air Force (AFOG), headquartered for many years at Wright-Patterson Air Force Base. (AFOG later moved to Gentile Air Force Station, Dayton, Ohio, where it remained until its inactivation in 1992.)

The National Air Intelligence Center (NAIC) was another Wright-Patterson Air Force Base organization that traced its roots to World War II. During the war, the Technical Data Laboratory at Wright Field (successor to the Technical Data Branch of the Administration Section) was responsible for evaluating foreign documents, aircraft, and related equipment. The Technical Data Laboratory also prepared performance characteristics reports on various German and Japanese aircraft and weapons, distributed them to the combat forces of all services, and introduced the assignment of nicknames for Japanese aircraft. This latter procedure standardized aircraft identification: feminine names such as BETTY and NELL were used for bombers, and masculine names such as FRANK, ZEKE, and NATE were used for fighters and observation airplanes.

With the formation of the ATSC, the Technical Data Laboratory changed its name. Under the new T-system organizational concept, the name became simply T-2 Intelligence. T-2 Intelligence continued to play a major role in the organization and exploitation of captured materiel, manpower, and documents.[102] One such documentation effort began in the waning days of the war and burgeoned into a major program operated out of T-2 at Wright Field. Prior to the Allied victory, the Army Air Forces assumed prime responsibility for seeking out and impounding *Luftwaffe*

The Hangar 4 complex, built in 1944, housed the Modification Hangar and Flight Research Laboratory. It was isolated at the end of the flightline to protect the classified work on experimental equipment that was performed here. Captured enemy aircraft were brought to Wright Field to be secretly examined and tested in these hangar bays. These hangars are currently used for storage and restoration by the United States Air Force Museum.

"Lineup of Foreign Aircraft at Wright Field and Crew," October 7, 1944

THE NATIONAL AIR INTELLIGENCE CENTER (NAIC)

During World War I, the United States realized it lagged behind Europe in aircraft technology and implemented a program to study the aircraft of both friendly and hostile nations. In 1917, the Foreign Data Section of the Aircraft Engineering Department at McCook Field was formed to collect and analyze aircraft technologies from foreign nations and determine their potential for use in American systems. By 1919, the office maintained a collection of 347 foreign aircraft, 2,000 engines, and 5,000 foreign technical reports for study and use by American engineers. Over the next 75 years, the unit underwent a number of name and organizational changes, including but not limited to: Technical Publications and Library Department (1918); Technical Data Section (1919); Technical Data Branch (1927); T-2 Intelligence (1945), under Air Materiel Command; Air Technical Intelligence Center (1951), under Air Staff's Director of Intelligence; Aerospace Technical Intelligence Center (1959); Foreign Technology Division (1961), under Air Force Systems Command; and NAIC (1993), currently under Air Combat Command. Throughout these numerous changes, however, the organization's mission remained the same—the collection, analysis, and dissemination of foreign technical data to American researchers.

One of the notable contributions of the organization was its role in Project Lusty near the end of World War II. T-2 Intelligence was responsible for the project, through which it obtained German research documents and aircraft, such as the Me-262 jet fighter and the V-1 and V-2 rockets, and transferred them to the United States for analysis. Its personnel also recruited German scientists to work in American research and development programs. In the Cold War, the unit's role extended to Soviet space technologies, and its personnel pioneered intelligence analysis methods with computers. During the Vietnam War, the Foreign Technology Division contributed significant data regarding countermeasures against surface-to-air attacks.

The NAIC, with headquarters at Wright-Patterson Air Force Base, is the Air Force's only scientific and technical intelligence production center, and it continues to provide information on foreign aerospace systems, forces, and threats, as well as predictions about other nations' future technological programs. Its work contributes significantly to the Air Force's ability to maintain its leading role in aerospace technology.

Sources: Robert Young, "The National Air Intelligence Center's Legacy;" William B. Stacy, "Foreign Technology Division," in Lois E. Walker and Shelby E. Wickam, *From Huffman Prairie to the Moon: The History of Wright-Patterson Air Force Base* (Dayton, Ohio, 1983), pp 435-437.

National Air Intelligence Center, 2001

documents, for locating German scientists and technicians, and for securing the records of German engineering developments. As Allied armies pushed the Germans from their strongholds, Army Air Forces intelligence teams and similar U.S. Navy and British organizations followed close behind, "liberating" ton upon ton of German aeronautical research materials.

Under Project Lusty, all of these documents were flown to an Air Documents Research Center organized in London for processing. Initial sorting and classification of 1,500 tons of this material was accomplished at a rate of some 10 tons per day, until the bulk had been reduced to 250 tons. In September of 1945, an Air Documents Research Office was established at Wright Field under the commanding general of ATSC. In November 1945, operations of the Air Documents Research Center in London were moved intact to Wright Field, with all personnel and selected equipment, and placed under T-2 Intelligence.[103]

Work started in December 1945 on some 55,000 documents, representing the cream of German aeronautical research and development. Nearly 400 civil service employees, and over 100 officers and enlisted personnel of the Army Air Forces and the Navy Bureau of Aeronautics, were involved in cataloging the documents, drawing abstracts and indexes, and scheduling the documents for translation. The goal was to organize the German documents in such a manner that they would form the nucleus of a huge catalog, embracing the entire science of aeronautics. It was hoped the project would save hundreds of millions of dollars over a period of time, and hundreds of thousands of valuable man hours, by avoiding duplication and wasted efforts.

Project Lusty included the collection of foreign equipment as well as documents. Late model German aircraft and engines were flown to Wright Field and other airfields for study. T-2 personnel also participated in a Technical Air Intelligence unit formed in October 1944 and attached to the Far East Air Forces. Its mission was to take possession of all captured Japanese aircraft and equipment in the Pacific theater.

When the Air Technical Service Command became the Air Materiel Command (AMC) in 1946, the Air Documents Division (ADD), as the Air Documents Research Office was then called, proceeded uninterrupted with its work. The Wright Field Technical Library was a section of this division. (Organized

PROJECT LUSTY
TESTS ON CAPTURED GERMAN AIRCRAFT

As World War II approached its end in the European theater, the United States launched a bold technical intelligence mission to bring captured German aircraft to America for testing. Colonel Harold E. Watson, who later commanded the Air Technical Intelligence Center, hand-picked American pilots, who received just enough training to be able to fly German aircraft out of the crumbling Third Reich. Fearing that Allied forces would destroy many of the captured aircraft, "Watson's Whizzers" initially flew many of the planes to France until they could be shipped to the United States. The Whizzers piloted some of Germany's most advanced models such as the Me-262 and Ar-234 jet-powered aircraft.

American officials hoped to gain as much technical information as possible about the German jets to aid U.S. designers currently developing their own jet aircraft. Air technical intelligence issued "black lists" of enemy equipment they hoped to acquire for study. The project's name, Project Lusty, was derived from "Luftwaffe Secret Technology."

The plan called for the aircraft to be brought to Wright Field for testing. As aircraft began arriving, officials decided to conduct much of the work at Freeman Field, near Seymour, Indiana. Eventually, engineers at Middletown Air Depot, Pennsylvania, also tested many of the Japanese aircraft captured in the Pacific. American technicians performed flight and structural integrity testing on the captured aircraft and analyzed their power plants and the manufacturing techniques employed. In addition to conducting some of the testing, Wright Field's Technical Data Laboratory prepared performance characteristics reports on the foreign aircraft, rockets, and helicopters. The laboratory also acquired tons of German equipment and aeronautical research materials. The mass of material eventually occupied six buildings, part of a hangar, and a large outdoor lot at Wright Field. Personnel in the shops at Patterson Field also tested some aircraft components.

Colonel Watson and a crew flew the largest aircraft, a four-engine Ju-290, to Wright Field after its capture outside of Munich, Germany. The plane, dubbed "Alles Kaputt" carried an extra "crewmember" named "PFC Schnapps," a German dachshund. Translated, the plane's name meant "All is Finished." Watson and his crew were unaware that the Germans had placed explosive charges under the aircraft's main fuel tanks—but they failed to explode! Approximately one million people viewed this plane and other enemy aircraft and systems on display at the Army Air Forces Fair at Wright Field in October 1945.

With the establishment of T-2 Intelligence, a forerunner of the Air Force's National Air Intelligence Center (NAIC), in July 1945, the Army Air Forces increasingly integrated intelligence information within the engineering community. Project Lusty also included the translation, cataloging, indexing, and microfilming of thousands of German technical documents related to aerodynamics and aircraft design. The knowledge gained from the captured aircraft, equipment, and documentation literally revolutionized American industry. After testing the German jets, aircraft experts learned the advantages of using swept wings for aircraft flying near the speed of sound. Consequently, U.S. designers quickly adopted this feature for the new generation of American fighter aircraft.

Sources: Photographs and reports in "Foreign Aircraft" files, Box 5873, Aeronautical Systems Center History Office Archive; Bruce Ashcroft & Rob Young, *A Brief History of Air Force Scientific and Technical Intelligence*, NAIC History Office; Phil Scott, "Watson's Whizzers," *Air & Space* 12 (October-November 1997):4, pp 66-73.

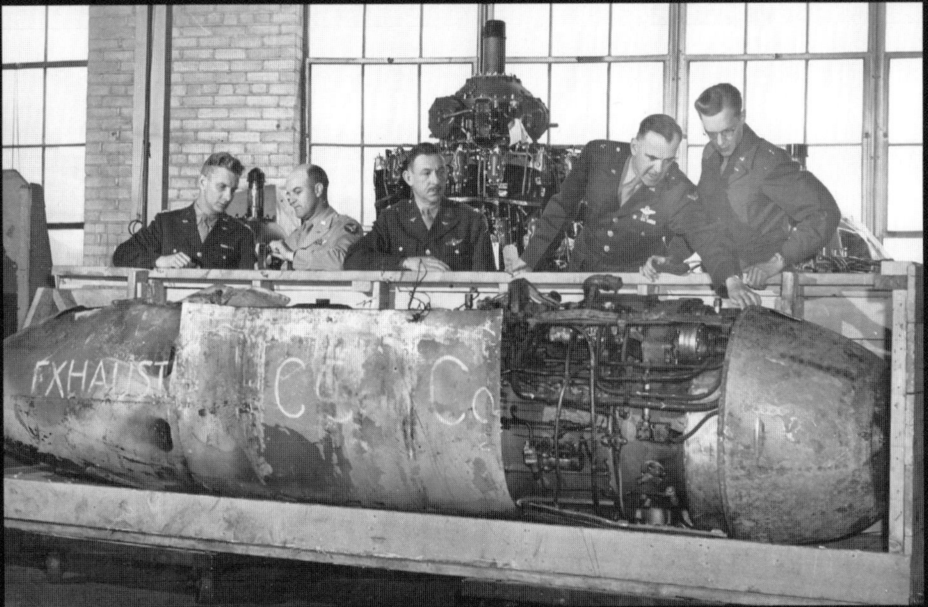

A Jumo 004 German jet engine, from an Arado 234 twin-engine fighter plane, arrives at the Power Plant Laboratory, Engineering Division, Air Technical Service Command (ATSC), and is immediately inspected by top-ranking jet propulsion experts. They are, left to right, Lieutenant Colonel F. P. Nay, assistant chief, Research Branch; Colonel J. M. Hayward, chief, Technical Data Laboratory; Colonel D. J. Keirn, acting chief, Power Plant Laboratory; Brigadier General Franklin O. Carroll, chief, Engineering Division, ATSC; and Captain W. C. Harradine, Air Technical Intelligence courier, who brought the engine from Germany. The photo was taken at Wright Field, Dayton, Ohio, April 30, 1945.

originally at McCook Field in 1919, the library moved to Wright Field in 1927 as a component of the Technical Data Branch. For many years it was housed in the Army Aeronautical Museum, Building 12, Area B.)

The German documents program, originally scheduled for completion by the end of 1948, finished 14 months ahead of schedule in November 1947. When completed, this effort represented one of the outstanding events in the history of documentation, as an entire nation's aeronautical research and development literature was indexed, abstracted, and microfilmed. A master card index of the cataloged materials was maintained at Wright Field, while smaller indexes were maintained by qualified government, scientific, and industrial organizations throughout the United States. By August 1947, over 10 million cards and hundreds of thousands of copies of documents had been distributed to the holders of these indexes and to more than 2,500 government agencies and contractors. One useful result of this exploitation of German documents was the publication of a dictionary containing over 110,000 German aeronautical terms related to new technological areas.[104]

Building 8 was constructed in 1943 to house Wright Field Operations and the Flight Test Division. The control tower remained in use until flying operations at Wright Field ended in 1976.

Northeast view of the Wright Field flightline from the control tower, May 1943

Another significant achievement of the Air Documents Division was the initiation of a Standard Aeronautical Index. Accomplished under joint contract to the Army Air Forces and the Navy by the Institute of Aeronautical Sciences, this index was considered at the time to be the most radical innovation in the history of classification and was accepted as an authoritative source by major organizations concerned with the indexing and dissemination of aeronautical literature.

Paving the way for the future, that portion of the German documents program involved in pure intelligence work was broken out in August 1947 to form a separate department of AMC known as the Technical Intelligence Department. This organization, a direct antecedent of Air Combat Command's National Air Intelligence Center headquartered at Wright-Patterson Air Force Base, concerned itself with the larger task of collecting, processing, and evaluating data pertaining to foreign military and industrial capabilities, and matters relating to foreign military technological advancements.

As Wright Field settled into a postwar routine, many activities curtailed for the duration of the war were reestablished. Chief among these was the Army Air Forces Engineering School. With a mission expanded to include "Maintenance Engineering" and "Air Logistics," the Army Air Forces Institute of Technology (AAFIT) was authorized at Wright Field on December 15, 1945. The Institute of Technology was to operate under the jurisdiction of the Air Technical Service Command. Lieutenant General Nathan F. Twining, the ATSC commander, appointed a resident committee of ATSC officers to prepare an operating plan for the proposed institute. General Twining formally dedicated the institute on September 3, 1946.[105] The first classes were opened that same month. AAFIT, the antecedent of today's prestigious Air Force Institute of Technology (AFIT), became part of Air University, Maxwell Air Force Base, Alabama, on April 1, 1950, although the school's principal operations remained at Wright-Patterson.

On December 15, 1945, Wright Field (home of the Air Technical Service Command) and Patterson Field (home of the Fairfield Air Technical Service Command) were consolidated along with two smaller installations, for administrative purposes, into an umbrella organization entitled the Army Air Forces Technical Base. The other installations affected by this merger

Components of the AAF Technical Base were Wright Field and Patterson Field, the Dayton Army Air Field, Vandalia, Ohio (above), and the Clinton County Army Air Field, Wilmington, Ohio (below).

were the Dayton Army Air Field at Vandalia, Ohio, and the Clinton County Army Air Field at Wilmington, Ohio. Brigadier General Joseph T. Morris, the Wright Field commander, was appointed commanding general of the new Technical Base and charged with providing operational support for the primary elements of the Technical Base, Wright and Patterson fields, as well as the Clinton County and Vandalia airfields. (The latter two organizations were subsequently separated from the Technical Base in 1946.) On December 9, 1947, consequent to the establishment of the U.S. Air Force as a separate service, the AAF Technical Base, Dayton, Ohio, was redesignated the Air Force Technical Base. One month later, on January 13, 1948, the name was finalized to its present form when the installation was redesignated Wright-Patterson Air Force Base.

LOGISTICS AND RESEARCH IN THE POSTWAR PERIOD

The Air Materiel Command was tasked with two major functions in the postwar period: demobilization and ongoing research and development. Directing these efforts was Lieutenant General Nathan F. Twining, the AMC commander from March 1946 to October 1947.

First on AMC's agenda was the overwhelming task of postwar demobilization. The highly effective wartime machinery that had provided the logistical support for victory had to be shifted into reverse. Gorged supply pipelines connecting the United States to points around the world had to be cleared. Stations had to be inactivated and vast quantities of materials withdrawn from distant battle areas. Domestically, wartime industries had to be reoriented without major dislocations to the economy. With the sudden surrender of Japan, work had stopped on some 31,000 military aircraft. At AMC headquarters and throughout the various procurement districts, procurement, supply, and adjustment personnel worked at top speed to shut off contracts, curtail all forms of Army Air Forces manufacture, and facilitate the conversion to civilian production.[106]

Meanwhile, millions of dollars of surplus supplies had to be disposed of or identified and warehoused. Materiel and physical property had to be readied for turnover to the War Assets Administration. Airplanes and equipment had to be "cocooned" or otherwise prepared for storage as war reserve. From a wartime peak of 80,000 aircraft, for example, by mid-1947 the active inventory shrank to only 12,000 airplanes.[107]

Simultaneously, reductions in manpower occurred at all echelons. From a wartime peak of almost 2.5 million uniformed personnel, the AAF diminished to little more than 300,000 military members by

Lieutenant General Nathan F. Twining, commanding general of the Air Technical Service Command. Twining was later the first Air Force general to serve as chairman of the Joint Chiefs of Staff.

Panorama of Wright Field at the zenith of its growth, July 1945

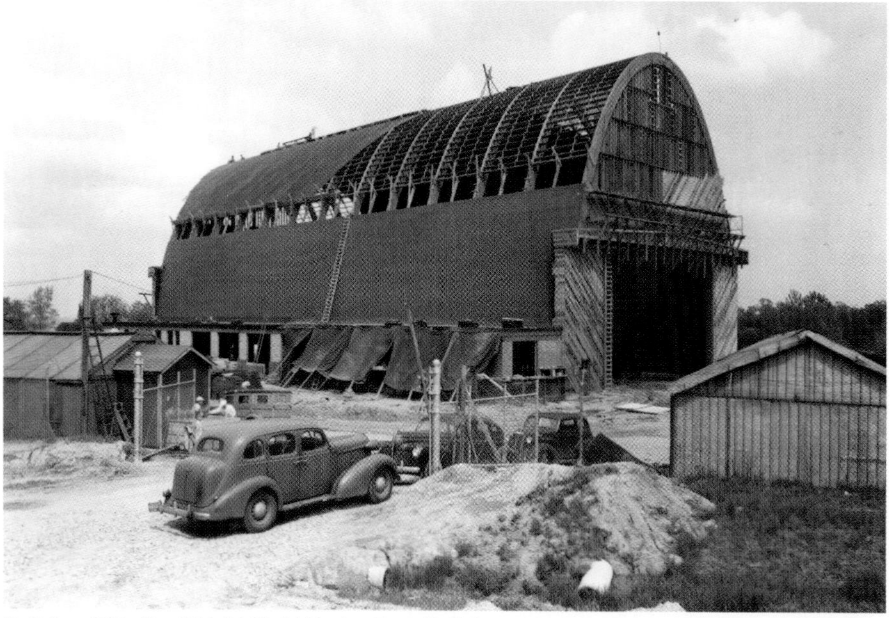

Building 821, the Wright Field Radar Test Building, was constructed in 1947. Nicknamed "The Cathedral," the building was often misidentified as a dirigible hangar. When originally constructed, the building was made entirely of wood, including the use of wooden pegs rather than metal nails.

mid-1947. This drastic reduction also challenged AMC as it struggled to adjust to the needs of the peacetime Air Force.

The second major responsibility given the Air Materiel Command was aeronautical research and development. Throughout most of World War II, this responsibility had belonged to the Materiel Command. With the creation of the Air Technical Service Command in 1944, however, research and development had become an adjunct of the logistics function. Under ATSC, the Engineering Division was essentially a collection of laboratories. During 1945 there were 14 in total—nine aeronautical laboratories and five electronics laboratories. The aeronautical laboratories were all located at Wright Field and were concerned with the development of airplane components and special categories of aeronautical equipment, including armament. Four of the five electronics labs were also at Wright Field, while the fifth, the Watson Laboratories, was located at Eatontown, New Jersey. The electronics labs at Wright Field worked with airborne

A special tower constructed to test aircraft ejection seats. Sergeant Lawrence Lambert of Wright Field became the first person in the United States to exit an airplane in flight by means of an ejection seat on August 17, 1946.

electronic equipment, while Watson Labs was responsible for the development of ground electronics equipment, both communication and radar.[108]

Other installations and liaison offices operated by ATSC, and later AMC, were closely linked to the research work conducted at Wright Field. Ladd Field, Fairbanks, Alaska, housed a testing detachment concerned with the winterization testing of all items of equipment, from ground equipment to complete aircraft. The Muroc Flight Test Base in California was used for flight testing of experimental airplanes. A pilotless aircraft and guided missile testing range was located at Wendover, Utah. A testing station at Dover, Delaware, worked under the Armament Laboratory in testing rockets and rocket installation on airplanes. Eglin Field, Florida, also provided excellent range facilities for the testing of armament equipment. At Boca Raton Army Air Field in Florida, a Watson Laboratories substation developed and tested radar bombing equipment.[109]

An additional association was maintained with the Cambridge Field Station in Massachusetts, established as an AAF installation in June 1946. It absorbed personnel and facilities of the former Radiation Laboratory of the Massachusetts Institute of Technology and the Radio Research Laboratory of Harvard University.[110]

DEVELOPMENT OF HIGH SPEED ESCAPE METHODS

The manual bail-out method of escaping an airplane, made possible by the development of the first practical, free-fall parachute at McCook Field in 1919, served well through the 1930s. However, as fighter aircraft became faster it became apparent that the pilot needed assistance in getting out of the aircraft. At the end of World War II, using German ejection seats as a baseline, the Air Force began developing an ejection seat and catapult system at Wright Field, utilizing the combined resources and talents of the Equipment, Aircraft, and Aeromedical laboratories.

An F-15 version of the ACES II ejection seat during a zero altitude/zero speed test of the seat

On October 11, 1945, the first (but unsuccessful) attempt at ejection-seat firing in the United States occurred. Flight tests of the seat and catapult system continued at Wright Field from a modified P-61 Black Widow. Later flight tests conducted at Muroc Field (later Edwards Air Force Base), California, used the same aircraft with test dummies strapped into the seat, giving rise to the nickname "Jack-in-the-Box." Following the tests at Muroc, the aircraft returned to Wright Field for use in the first attempt at a live ejection. On August 17, 1946, Sergeant Lawrence Lambert became the first person in the United States to be successfully ejected from an aircraft. Lambert, who was a test jumper in the Wright Field Equipment Laboratory Parachute Branch, won the 1946 Cheney Award for the mission. Three years later, on May 31, 1949, Captain Vincent Mazza of the Wright Field Aero Medical Research Laboratory made the first ejection seat escape from a jet aircraft, a modified TF-80C, over San Pablo Bay, California.

Improvements in ejection seats continued in the 1950s and 1960s but, unlike the early postwar development, most of the actual design and testing was done by contractors. In the mid-1970s the Aeronautical Systems Division's Life Support Systems Program Office managed the development of a new, standardized ejection seat called the Advanced Concept Ejection Seat II (ACES II). The ACES II ejection seat evolved from a McDonnell Douglas design that won an Air Force competition for a new standardized seat. Versions of the ACES II seat were used in most Air Force front-line aircraft including the A-10, F-15, F-16, F-22, F-117, B-1 and B-2. The ACES II provided an increased survival rate for aircrew members with a significant performance improvement over its predecessors.

Sergeant Lawrence Lambert (center, facing camera) after landing in a field by the town of Osborn (now Fairborn), Ohio, following the first live ejection in the United States, August 17, 1946

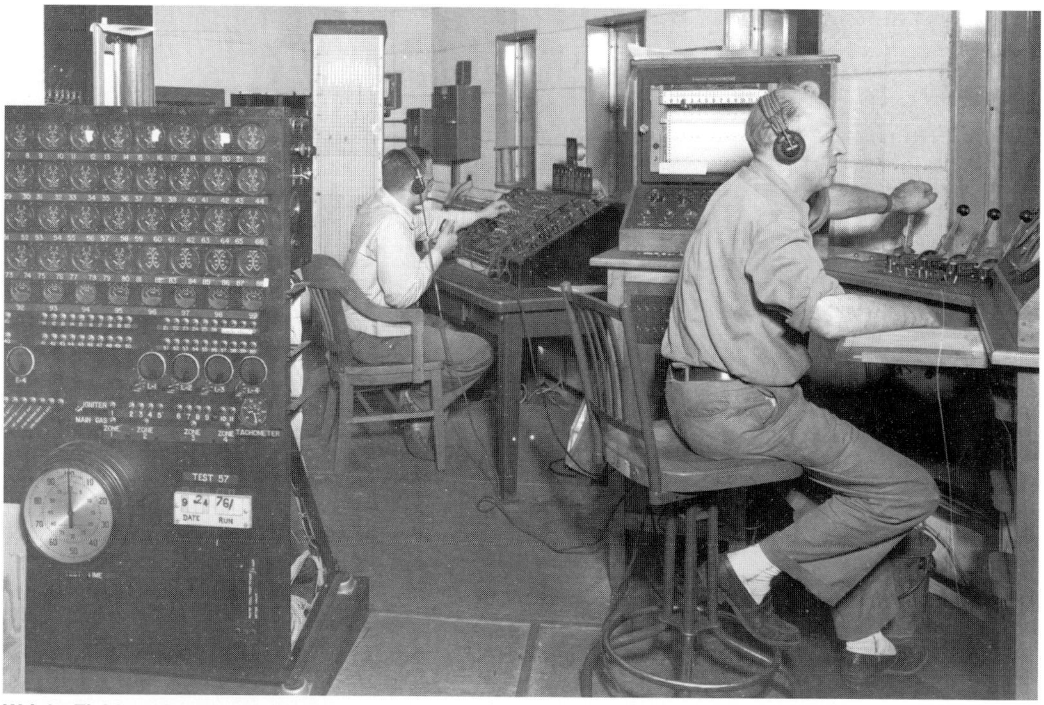

Wright Field engineers operate test chamber controls during testing of an early jet engine.

Technicians perform adjustments following the cold weather test of a J34 turbojet engine. The bell mouth at the right of the picture is the air intake for the engine.

During the summer of 1946, three major events highlighted activities at Wright Field. On June 3, 1946, Lieutenant Henry A. Johnson set a world speed record of 426.97 mph in a Lockheed jet-engine P-80 over a 1,000-kilometer course (without payload). On the same day, Wright Field Captain James M. Little established another world record by flying a B-29 over a 2,000-kilometer course between Dayton and St. Louis at an average speed of 361 mph. Captain Little's skill narrowly averted a crash ending to his flight as he was forced to land on one engine.[111] On August 17, 1946, Sergeant Lawrence Lambert of Wright Field became the first person in the United States to exit an airplane in flight by means of an ejection seat. While his P-61 airplane was traveling 302 mph at an attitude of 7,800 feet, Sergeant Lambert successfully activated a pilot ejector seat developed at Wright Field.[112]

In December 1946, AMC used Kirtland Army Air Field, Albuquerque, New Mexico, to provide flight services for the Manhattan District at Sandia and Los Alamos in atomic bomb testing.[113] In addition to its own facilities, AAF research and development drew on the facilities of outside agencies, especially the principal organization for basic aeronautical research at the time, the National Advisory Committee for Aeronautics. Close liaison and coordination also was maintained with agencies of the Navy and the Army Technical Services. AMC made a strong effort to use the knowledge and facilities of non-profit scientific institutions, universities, and colleges, and the aircraft industry itself. Among the most important of these outside agencies involved in AAF research were the Jet Propulsion Laboratory at the California Institute of Technology in Pasadena, California; the Applied Physics Laboratory at Johns Hopkins University; the Aberdeen Proving Ground in Aberdeen, Maryland; the Bureau of Aeronautics of the Naval Research Laboratory; and the Office of Naval Research.[114]

Research and development programs during World War II had been in the hands of the National Defense Research Council (NDRC) and private industry. In the years following the war, however, with the NDRC disbanded and contracts with private industry cancelled, the Air Materiel Command initiated more and more of its own research programs and slowly assumed responsibility for a greater proportion of research and development efforts, until research became a major part of the logistics mission. By 1947, AMC was actively engaged in more than 2,000 research projects.[115]

Important changes were made in the focus of research after the war, as AMC developed new channels of technological advancement. During the war, for example, the Engineering Division had concentrated on aeronautical weapons of war, with emphasis on perfecting and producing those items that had been in an advanced state of development prior to 1942. In the months following V-J Day, the Engineering Division turned its attention from the airplanes and weapons of World War II to the development of concepts for the future, such as jet-propelled aircraft and guided missiles. Emphasis also shifted from development of individual items to a coordinated systems approach. Modification and improvement of existing models, therefore, assumed a lesser role, as the overall focus turned to the development of entire new systems and models.[116]

Under Project Overcast, and later Project Paperclip, prominent German scientists were brought to work at Wright Field. By the end of World War II, the Germans had spent nearly a decade in developing rockets such as the V-1 and V-2. They contributed valuable experience at Wright Field to such modern-day projects as the perfection of rockets and gliders, ramjets, heavy presses, and ribbon parachutes, as well as the farsighted design of rocket refueling bases that would serve as orbiting space stations some 4,000 miles from the earth. By December 1946, the War Department estimated that the background and experience contributed by German scientists to U.S. efforts had already saved more than $750 million in basic research.[117]

Wright Field personnel were involved in a variety of special accomplishments during 1947. Important strides were made in developing gyro-computing sights for the guns, bombs, and rockets mounted on fighter aircraft. On February 10, 1947, Major E. M. Cassell set an unofficial world helicopter altitude record of 19,167 feet in a Sikorsky R-5A. On August 8, 1947, Adolf L. Berger received the Thurman H. Bane Award for his work in developing new, high-temperature ceramic coatings for use in aircraft engines. On September 22, a Wright Field C-54 landed in London after completing the first robot-controlled flight across the Atlantic Ocean. On October 14, Captain Charles Yeager flew faster than the speed of sound in the Bell XS-1, a feat based on a plan originated at Wright Field, where much of the theory and testing had been accomplished.[118] The stage was set for even greater discoveries and developments as Wright Field boldly entered the aerospace age.

When Wright Field and Patterson Field merged to create Wright-Patterson Air Force Base on January 13, 1948, the new installation inherited a long and proud heritage. In retrospect, the kaleidoscope of activities at Wright Field had achieved a spectrum and brilliance that even the most optimistic of its early promoters found marvelous to behold.

The crew of President Harry S. Truman's airplane, *The Independence,* at Wright Field during a September 1947 visit to the field

BRIGADIER GENERAL "CHUCK" YEAGER

After graduating from high school in 1941, Charles E. Yeager enlisted in the Army Air Forces. After a superb performance as a double ace fighter pilot in Europe, Yeager transitioned from combat to test pilot at Wright Field. Despite the fact that he was a captain with 1,100 flying hours, Yeager did not have the formal education to qualify as a test pilot. His experience did qualify him to be an assistant maintenance officer in the Fighter Test Section, where he was required to test fly the planes after maintenance before turning them over to the test pilots. He had the opportunity to fly jet aircraft, and the first time he flew in a jet plane (the Lockheed P-80 Shooting Star) he said he was as "happy as a squirrel hunter who had bagged a mountain lion," although he admitted that flying a jet was "like trying to learn how to ride a race horse after riding only on elephants." Known for his boldness and deeds of derring-do, Yeager once flew the jet-propelled Bell P-59 down the main street of his hometown of Hamlin, West Virginia. He often engaged test pilots in "dogfights," where his cool, aggressive flying skill gained the confidence of Colonel Albert G. Boyd, then chief of the Flight Test Division. Seeing Yeager's potential, Colonel Boyd sent him to test pilot school for intensive training in the data-gathering and reporting methods necessary for determining specific limits of aircraft. After Yeager graduated, Colonel Boyd named him as principal test pilot for the Bell XS-1, the craft destined to make Chuck Yeager the first man to break the sound barrier on October 14, 1947.

Captain Charles E. Yeager (*United States Air Force Museum*)

Sources: ASC History Office, *Birthplace, Home, and Future of Aerospace*, (Wright-Patterson Air Force Base, Ohio, 1999), p 45; General Chuck Yeager and Leo Janos, *Yeager: An Autobiography*, (New York, 1985), pp 83-85.

During 1945, Captain Yeager served as assistant maintenance officer in the Fighter Test Section of the Flight Test Division at Wright Field. (*United States Air Force Museum*)

Captain Chuck Yeager broke the sound barrier on October 14, 1947, in a Bell XS-1.

FORGING AN AIR FORCE—FLIGHT VEHICLE AND AERONAUTICAL MATERIEL, 1917-1951

Dayton witnessed the refinement of controlled, powered flight through the dedicated efforts of the Wright brothers in 1904-1905 on Huffman Prairie. From 1917 to 1926, Dayton enthusiastically supported Air Service efforts at McCook Field to develop the muscles and sinews of military aviation. With the establishment of Wright Field in 1927, Dayton and the nation witnessed the opening of an even greater era in the development of American air power. Military and civilian Air Corps scientists, aeronautical engineers, craftsmen, and pilots assigned to Wright Field during the 1930s and 1940s expanded the science of aeronautics beyond all earlier horizons. Their contributions helped carry America to victory in World War II and guided the country to the threshold of the aerospace age.

McCook Field in north Dayton, 1918

MCCOOK FIELD 1917-1918

During World War I, the experimental facility at McCook Field developed "almost overnight [into] the single most influential agency in the early years of American air power."[1] On November 22, 1917, the chief signal officer in Washington, D.C., described McCook's wartime mission: technical and experimental work would concentrate on the correlated areas of airplane and airplane engine development, on aerial cameras installed on experimental aircraft, and on "work pertaining to the synchronization of machine guns." McCook's companion in aircraft experimentation, testing, and development, Langley Field, Virginia, was given responsibility for "all matters pertaining to instruction and experimentation in bombing, photography, radio and telegraphy." Langley also was identified as the center of foreign aircraft demonstration, although several types of foreign aircraft were later assembled and flown at McCook Field as well.[2]

Fokker D-7, one of many foreign aircraft brought to McCook Field for test and evaluation

McCook Field opened officially on December 4, 1917, as the arena of the Airplane Engineering Department, a major element of the Signal Corps Equipment Division. The Airplane Engineering Department concentrated on advanced design and engineering. Its responsibilities included exhaustive tests on experimental aircraft and those standard production types being modified into advanced models, and on related accessories. Once aircraft and accessories were developed, the designs, models, and engineering information were passed to the Production Engineering Department, which released the information to manufacturers. The Production Engineering Department also conducted stringent tests on the airplanes and accessories as they neared and entered production.[3]

The focal point of airplane engineering was the McCook Field Experimental Factory, an amalgamation of the former Plane Design and Engine Design sections. The factory's components were the wood, metal, assembly, and dope shops. All the work performed in these shops was of experimental nature and included nearly all phases of airplane and engine manufacture and modification. Prominent products of the Experimental Factory included the

Drafting room at McCook Field where engineering drawings for most of America's early military airplanes were produced

USAC-1 combat aircraft, the USD-9A bomber, the USXB-1 and USXB-2 bombers, and the LUSAC-11.

The McCook Field Machine Shop produced experimental engines ranging in size and horsepower from small, single-cylinder test machines to the 12-cylinder Liberty engine. The famous Nelson machine gun control system was also developed in the Machine Shop.

The Aeronautical Research Department, organized in November 1917, was the service center for other McCook Field functions. Stress testing was the department's original mission. A few weeks after operations began, the department formed a close partnership with the Massachusetts Institute of Technology (MIT) aerodynamics laboratory in its stress-testing research. Together they designed the methods and procedures that became standard in the field. An airplane (less engine and accessories) was subjected to stress analysis of its various components by placing sandbags of different sizes, configurations, and weights on the surfaces of wings, tails, and various sections of fuselages. These procedures determined the ultimate strengths of materials and structural design.

The Aeronautical Research Department also conducted flight tests and materials tests. A special experimental airplane (never numbered or identified) was configured as a flying aerodynamic laboratory. Another section of the Aeronautical Research Department was dedicated to materials testing, including studies of fittings, struts, spars, and similar parts. An area of special interest was the testing of various types and designs of ribs.

Development of flight instrumentation went hand in hand with aircraft development. These McCook Field engineers and members of the Flight Test Branch worked closely together to develop some of the world's earliest altimeters, tachometers, airspeed indicators, flight compasses, and navigational aids.

TECHNICAL PUBLICATIONS AND LIBRARY DEPARTMENT

An achievement of inestimable value was the accumulation, organization, and publication of aircraft engineering knowledge gained at McCook and other early experimental facilities. In the spring of 1918, a Technical Publications and Library Department was organized at McCook Field as a service agency for collecting and disseminating technical information. Originally the department was charged with obtaining and maintaining technical data and information for use by engineers working at McCook. By the end of 1918, however, the department was reorganized to form the McCook Field Aeronautical Reference Library, one of the most impressive collections in the country. In November 1918, the library reported holdings of 700 technical reference books, 200 pamphlets, and 42 aeronautical and technical magazine subscriptions.

Particular emphasis was placed on publishing the experimental findings of engineers at McCook. The first publication of the Reference Library was a monthly entitled "Bulletin of the Experimental Department, Airplane Engineering Division," which gained national recognition for its valuable contribution to aeronautical literature.

Similarly impressive was the series of Technical Orders published by the Technical Data Branch of the Technical Section, located in the Air Service Building in Dayton, beginning in September 1918. These "tech" orders dealt directly with defects in aviation materiel, proper correction of defects, and other technical information of general interest to engineers working in the field. Also published at a later date was an Information Circular dealing with aviation equipment, and a series of Aircraft Technical Notes giving instructions in processes and techniques used by mechanics, as well as information for specific experiments and tests.

The McCook Field Reference Library provided the foundation for what became the prestigious Wright Field Technical Library. The Air Force Research Laboratory inherited the collection in 1997 and elected to transfer much of it to the Air Force Institute of Technology Library as an economy measure.

Sources: Captain H. H. Blee, *History of Organization and Activities of Airplane Engineering Division, Bureau of Aircraft Production*, August 15, 1919, p 84; Walter D. House, "Warbird Tech Data," American Aviation Historical Society *Journal* 26 (Fall 1981), pp 206, 208.

Bookplate used by the McCook Field Aeronautical Reference Library

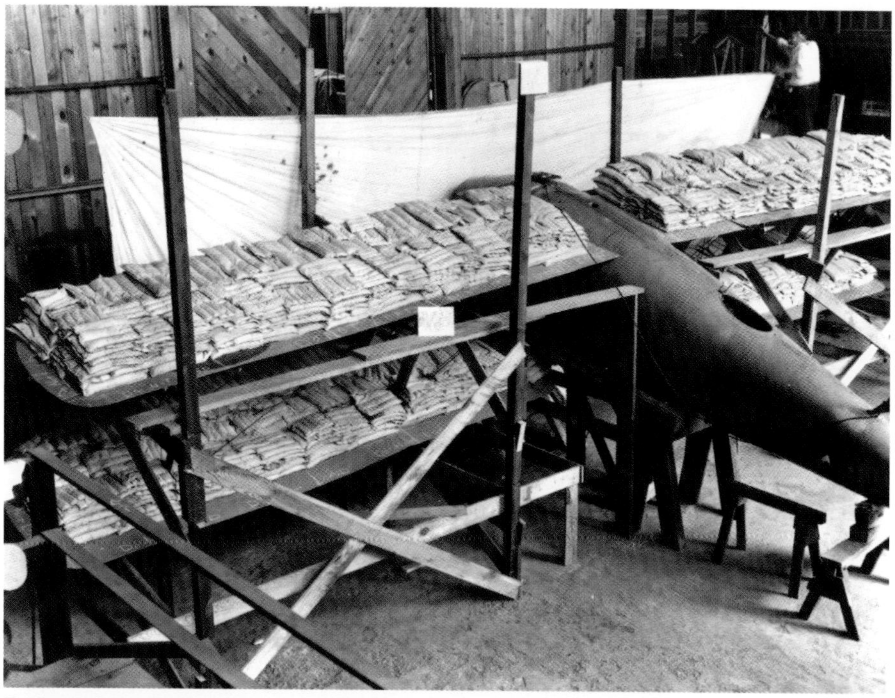

Early static testing performed by the Aeronautical Research Department. Stress-testing of airplane components was conducted by loading sandbags of different sizes, configurations, and weights onto the surfaces of the wings, tail, and various sections of the fuselage.

The Wood Shop fabricated fuselage and wing structures.

The Mechanical Research Department at McCook received special note for its development of the Loomis cooling system. This significant improvement over previous systems "fulfilled all the rigid requirements for service planes used over the battlefront," and was named after Mr. Allen Loomis, head of the Mechanical Research Department and an "experimental engineer of wide experience in the automotive industry."[4] The new system featured an expansion tank that surrounded the honeycomb cooling element and formed an integral part of the nose radiator, thus replacing the usual shell. A second improvement was an injector in the water connection between the radiator and the circulating pump. The latter drew water from the bottom of the expansion tank and injected it into the circulation system, thereby keeping a constant volume of water in motion.

The Chemical and Physical Material laboratories conducted ongoing tests and experiments on various engine fuels, lubricating oils, metals, and metal alloys. Special examinations and studies also were conducted on a multitude of materials associated with work in the other laboratories at McCook.

Laboratories of the Engine Assembly and Testing Department performed tests of all types on aviation engines and accessories, including radiators, gasoline assemblies, and heating and lighting systems. The department tested experimental engines and accessories, standard production engines sent to McCook either for calibration or for installation in experimental model airplanes, and routine overhauling and testing of machines at McCook. In particular, the Engine Testing Department contributed significantly to the increased power and general efficiency of the powerful Liberty engine.

The Propeller Department developed propellers for various experimental, standard, and training aircraft. This included all Air Service and numerous Navy machines. The department also researched a wide range of propeller problems by means of full-flight and destructive whirl tests. Some of the most notable experiments involved tipping propeller blades with copper, brass, pigskin, linen, and other materials as protection against abrasion. Other work was done on propeller thrust and torque meters used in full-flight testing and propeller construction. A variable-pitch propeller that showed "interesting possibilities" was tested thoroughly in 1918 but not widely used.

A crucial problem confronting the Armament Department, headed by Mr. A. L. Nelson, was how to control/synchronize the fire of a fixed machine gun through the propeller arc of an airplane without shattering the blades. Under Nelson's leadership, a "single shot" trigger mechanism was developed for the Marlin, Vickers, and Browning .30-caliber fixed (mounted) guns. The previous system, called the Constantinesco, operated on "a pressure-wave principle, transmitting the timing impulses from the engine to the gun through a tube containing a column of oil under high pressure." The Nelson control system sent the timing impulses "by means of a positive mechanical connection between the engine and the gun, thus eliminating the lag inherent in a system that operated on the pressure-wave principle."[5]

Thoroughly tested at McCook and Wilbur Wright fields, the Nelson gun control system proved its superiority over earlier devices. The Nelson was more accurate and could be used with both twin-bladed and four-bladed propellers over a wide speed range. The new system confined the shots within a narrow arc and, when used with the single-shot trigger mechanism, eliminated stray shots entirely.

Wooden propellers constructed in the Propeller Shop were formed from wood laminations glued to the desired thickness then shaped, carved, and finished to exact specifications. Experiments were also made on propellers manufactured from duralumin and Bakelite Micarta.

The Engine Assembly Shop in 1918 was equipped with 12 engine stands for overhauls and repairs.

Assembly hangar, where final assembling of fuselages, wings, and accessories took place. Airplane in the foreground is a Vought VE-7 advanced trainer.

Airplane Engine Developments

Even before McCook existed, many of the military and civilian mechanical and electrical engineers who would become the nucleus of the McCook Field staff—especially those with considerable experience in the automotive industry—were in the vanguard of the nation's military aviation effort. They provided outstanding service in designing one of America's most significant contributions to Allied air power—the Liberty engine—and in preparing it and another stalwart, the British DeHavilland DH-4 biplane, for mass production in American factories.

A few weeks after the United States entered World War I, the Aircraft Production Board decided that one of America's most expedient contributions to victory would be the large-scale production of a high-powered airplane engine. No other country was producing any single engine in large quantities; in late 1916 and early 1917, Great Britain experimented with 37 different service engines while France tested 46 types. No country was better suited to the mass production of airplanes and engines than the United States, with its well-developed automotive industry. It remained only to develop a single, suitable design.

By June 4, 1917, an American engine design was approved and given the appropriate name of Liberty. The first Liberty engine was completed late that month and tested, appropriately, on July 4. It was an eight-cylinder, 200-horsepower model, and was shortly joined in production by more powerful 12-cylinder, 300-horsepower versions. Further refinement eventually increased the horsepower of the 12-cylinder Liberty to 440 horsepower. By the end of the war, six American automobile manufacturers had produced about 15,600 Liberty engines and another 60,000 were on order by the United States and its Allies for use on a wide range of aircraft.[6]

Throughout the war, McCook Field remained heavily involved in testing and improving airplane engines and accessories. In an October 21, 1918, status report, Colonel Jesse G. Vincent, chief engineer at McCook, listed "no less than 46 current experimental projects" which concentrated heavily on aircraft engines. These included the improved Liberty eight-cylinder and design of the single-cylinder and two-cylinder Liberty test engines for laboratory experimentation.

The Liberty Airplane

Much of the success of Allied air power in the latter months of World War I stemmed from the marriage of the Liberty engine with the British DeHavilland DH-4 two-place biplane. This aircraft was the only foreign machine produced in quantity in the United States. In fact, only one American airplane was built on a similar scale—the Curtiss Corporation's JN-4D Jenny primary trainer.

The DH-4 was an all-wood machine, designed originally for the dual functions of observation work and light bombing. The airplane's original power plant was a British Rolls-Royce engine. The DeHavilland's basic specifications were: wingspan 42 feet 6 inches, length 30 feet 6 inches, gross weight 3,557 pounds, speed 128 mph, and range 400 miles.[7] Its operational combat armament when serving with American squadrons in France consisted of twin .303-caliber Lewis aerial machine guns mounted on the rim of the rear cockpit and two Marlin machine guns mounted on the fuselage in front of the pilot, the latter of which fired through the propeller arc. The airplane could carry up to 200 pounds of bombs. The 50- or 100-pound

The Liberty 12-cylinder engine was America's greatest engineering contribution to World War I. (*United States Air Force Museum*)

Liberty 12-cylinder engine mounted on a torque stand (*United States Air Force Museum*)

Curtiss JN-4D (foreground) in the main hangar at McCook, March 1918

DH-4 variations remained in the Air Corps' active inventory through 1931. This civilian model was reconfigured to fly mail.

Completed DH-4 fuselages await final assembly of the wings and tails at the Dayton Wright Airplane Company.

The 1,000th DH-4 rolled off the assembly line at Dayton Wright in July 1918.

bombs attached in racks beneath the lower wing.

A sample DH-4 airframe arrived in the United States on August 15, 1917. It was rushed in the original shipping crates by rail to McCook Field. Over the next two months the machine underwent "extensive detail redesign" to accommodate American production methods, and was fitted with the new 12-cylinder, 400-horsepower, Liberty engine specifically designed for it. It was a good marriage and the modified English bride was renamed the "Liberty Airplane."[8] On October 18, 1917, the Dayton Wright Airplane Company received an initial order for 250 redesigned DH-4s equipped with Liberty engines. The first production model was test flown at McCook Field on October 29.

The first American model DH-4 reached France in May 1918. In the course of testing and using the airplane, serious questions arose concerning its combat reliability and performance. American Air Service pilots in the United States and in France were uneasy drivers of the machine. After considerable—and often heated—discussions in Washington, a board of veteran military and civilian aeronautical engineers and pilots convened at McCook Field from April 24 to May 2, 1918, to examine and evaluate the American version of the DH-4. Many significant mechanical problems were found in both the engine and the fuselage. Tragically, on May 2, an assembly-line model used as a test aircraft spun into the ground at Wilbur Wright Field from 300 feet, killing Lieutenant Colonel Henry J. Damm and Major Oscar Brindley. Brindley, with 2,000 flying hours, was considered one of the most highly skilled pilots in the Air Service. Based on the board's evaluations and tests, the major mechanical and structural shortcomings were corrected before large numbers of DH-4s reached American squadrons in France.

By the end of November 1918, American manufacturers had produced more than 4,500 Liberty airplanes (DH-4s); Dayton Wright had constructed 3,106 of them.[9] War's end in Europe, however, did not mean the end of the ubiquitous DH-4. Through a long list of changes from the DH-4A to the DH-4M, the airplane remained in the Air Corps' active inventory through 1931.[10]

New Airplane Designs

Although the DH-4 was America's major contribution to the war effort in Europe, other significant projects were also under way at McCook Field. Modification and production of the most combat-effective British, French, and Italian warplanes were immediate priorities. As the war progressed, however, increased military needs and a keen sense of national pride led McCook Field engineers to apply their efforts toward developing original American designs as well.

Immediately following the amalgamation of the Plane Design and Engine Design sections at McCook on October 13, 1917, design work began on the USAC-1 (U.S. Army, Combat-1) two-seat biplane. The model for the USAC-1 was the British Bristol Fighter. The American version had a plywood fuselage and a "rather fancy empennage" (defined as "the rear part of an airplane, comprising the stabilizer, elevator, vertical fin, and rudder").[11] The USAC-1 weighed about 3,500 pounds and was powered by a high-compression, straight, spur-geared Liberty 12 engine. The airplane carried five .30-caliber machine guns. Two of the three flexible weapons were mounted on the gunner's (rear) cockpit. The third flexible gun was positioned to fire through the bottom of the fuselage (thus antedating by several generations of airplanes the ball turret of the B-17 Flying Fortress bomber). Two fixed machine guns were mounted on the nose of the fuselage in front of the pilot's cockpit for firing through the propeller arc. About 2,400 separate engineering drawings were made before the prototype was

Modified USD-9A in which Lieutenant Harold R. Harris made the world's first, pressurized, high-altitude flight in 1921

Lieutenant Harold R. Harris (*Mrs. Darlene Gerhardt*)

Artist's inboard profile of the USD-9A, a reconnaissance version of the DH-9 redesigned and standardized at McCook Field in 1918 (*United States Air Force Museum*)

Overhead view of the USD-9A (*United States Air Force Museum*)

built. Preliminary drawings were begun for the USAC-2, an experimental model of similar design, but with a streamlined veneer fuselage. The prototype USAC-1's performance was adequate, but only a little better than either the British DH-4 observation-bomber or the Bristol Fighter. Production was not approved. Nevertheless, the USAC-1 left a valuable legacy in that it firmly established an engineering discipline at McCook that permitted the rapid development of other aircraft.

In March 1918, work commenced on redesigning and standardizing the DeHavilland DH-9 (a later model of the DH-4) for production. The McCook Field version, named the USD-9, was equipped with the high-compression, Liberty 12A engine. As design work progressed, some significant variances were made from the original airframe, including omission of the bomb-carrying compartment in the fuselage and increased fuel capacity. The latest mechanical improvements, such as the Nelson gun control system, the Loomis cooling system, and the McCook gasoline system, also were incorporated into the modified aircraft.

Flexibility of design permitted the airplane to be flown as a day bomber, night bomber, or as a reconnaissance aircraft. The reconnaissance version, follow-on model USD-9A, had a gross weight of 4,520 pounds and a top speed of 124 mph.[12] It carried two parallel, flexible-turret, .30-caliber Lewis aerial machine guns on the rim of the rear cockpit. A fixed, .30-caliber Browning gun mounted on the right side of the fuselage fired through the propeller arc. The weapon had two sights. One was a ring on the gun, *per se*. The second was an Aldis sight on the left side of the pilot's windshield. A control mounted directly on the "camshaft driving member" of the Liberty engine timed the gun's firing through the propeller. According to one authority, this was not the "ultimate synchronizer," but it was reliable and adaptable to all aircraft.[13] After modification of the wing structure, the USD-9A was scheduled for mass production. This was the first aircraft for which a complete set of construction drawings was created. Approximately 3,000 were published for the parts and assemblies, exclusive of the engine and standard appurtenances such as machine guns and mountings.[14]

Plans called for the Curtiss Aeroplane and Motor Corporation of Buffalo, New York, to manufacture 4,000 USD-9A's. The order was cancelled, however, when Allied victories in France during the summer of 1918 forecast Germany's ultimate defeat. Fragmentary records indicated that engineers at McCook, not Curtiss, manufactured at least four USD-9A airplanes.

Meanwhile, in April 1918, work commenced on redesigning the British Bristol two-place biplane fighter to accommodate the eight-cylinder, 300-horsepower, Hispano-Suiza engine. This aircraft, renamed the USB-1, was intended for contract manufacture, and thus about 2,500 production drawings were made of parts and assemblies. A short time later, work started on two experimental models of the USB-1; these were designated the USXB-1 and USXB-2 (X denoting experimental). The first model incorporated a "carefully stream-lined [sic] three-ply veneer fuselage and steel landing gear" but made use of all USB-1 "flying surfaces." The USXB-1 carried two flexible, .30-caliber machine guns on the rear cockpit, and two .30-caliber fixed guns mounted forward and fired through the propeller arc. The USXB-2 was very similar, except that it was powered by the Liberty eight-cylinder engine.[15]

By late summer, with the approaching end of hostilities, plans for mass production of the USB-1 were halted. In an early November reversal, however, firm orders were placed for the manufacture of three airplanes of this type.[16]

In the Experimental Non-Production category, McCook Field engineers worked on two American airplanes and one Italian aircraft. In mid-June 1918, the Airplane Engineering Department, in coordination with a contractor, initiated redesign and standardization of the Vought VE-7, two-seat, biplane advanced trainer. This Lewis and Vought Corporation product was an experimental airplane equipped with a 180-horsepower Hispano-Suiza engine.[17] It was followed by the VE-8 model, four of which were ordered by the Air Service for testing at McCook Field. The VE-8 was basically wood, and in the final analysis was not a satisfactory performer. Pilots claimed that it was "sluggish on controls and handled like a heavy DeHavilland 4 two-seater." Ground crews complained of "excessively difficult maintenance problems." Of the four VE-8s ordered, only two were delivered to McCook. One was static tested and the other was flight tested. No further orders were placed for the aircraft.[18]

The Pomilio FVL-8 was another airplane whose future terminated with the end of the war. The F designated fighter and the VL-8 identified the small V-8, 290-horsepower, Liberty engine designed for fighters. The aircraft bore the name of Octavio Pomilio, a noted aircraft designer and manufacturer on loan to McCook by the Italian government. The airplane had a length of 21 feet 8 inches, a wingspan of 26 feet 8 inches, and a wing area of 264 square feet. The airplane's gross weight totaled 2,284 pounds. It used a four-bladed propeller and had a maximum speed of 135 mph. The fuselage was built of plywood over oval formers and the wood-frame wings were covered with clear, doped fabric. McCook Field shops built only one of six scheduled prototypes.

Antioch College and University of Cincinnati students work on a Vought VE-7 advanced trainer under the tutelage of their McCook Field instructor.

Italian Pomilio FVL-8 with four-bladed propeller (*United States Air Force Museum*)

Martin MB-1 flown at the 1924 Dayton Air Races at Wilbur Wright Field by Lieutenant D. M. Myers. Myers won the Dayton Chamber of Commerce trophy when he attained a speed of 109 mph in 10 laps over a 15-mile course.

Perhaps the most important American-designed airplane to emerge from World War I was the Glenn Martin bomber, the GMB-1. This big, twin-engine biplane, designed for both day and night bombardment, was credited with establishing "an aviation dynasty . . . [which] shaped U.S. bomber strategy, tradition and history." The GMB-1 "sired a long line of follow-on aircraft . . . influential on world aerial and naval policy. It was the right plane at the right time, built by the right company."[19] The GMB-1 made its maiden flight at Cleveland, Ohio, on August 17, 1918. On September 2, the aircraft flew to McCook Field. The next day, McCook Field pilots and engineers began a series of thorough acceptance tests on the GMB-1 at Wilbur Wright Field. On October 22, the Glenn L. Martin Airplane Company of Cleveland received a War Department order for 50 bombers.[20]

Given the urgency of wartime testing, probably little if any thought was given to the fact that America's largest airplane was flying over the birthplace of military aviation. The bomber's almost 72-foot wingspan was nearly three times the length of Orville Wright's initial flight of 25 feet at Huffman Prairie. Each of the two powerful, 12-cylinder, Liberty engines on the GMB-1 generated nearly 25 times the horsepower of the tiny 18-horsepower engine that pushed the Wright's fragile biplane eight feet into the air on the initial launch over Huffman Prairie in 1904. The GMB-1 had an impressive profile and strength: wingspan 71 feet 5 inches, wing area 1,070 square feet, length 46 feet 10 inches, height 14 feet 7 inches. The aircraft was powered by two 12-cylinder, 420-horsepower, Liberty engines to a top speed of 99.8 mph at an optimum altitude of 6,500 feet. The bomber carried a crew of four: pilot, observer, and two gunners. Armament consisted of five .30-caliber Lewis machine guns. Maximum bomb load was one ton, with ordnance carried both within and beneath the fuselage.[21]

The Martin bomber was manufactured too late for combat service in Europe. Instead the Allies' successful bombers were the French Breguet and British DH-4 biplanes and the heavier, twin-engine, British Handley-Page and Italian Caproni bombers.[22] After the war ended, the order for GMB-1s was reduced from 50 to four. The airplane's immediate successor was the GMB-2—more specifically identified as the MB-2, which played a major role in the development of the Air Service immediately after World War I.

The Packard-LePere LUSAC-11 was the only American-built, two-place, biplane fighter to go overseas in late 1918, although it never flew against enemy forces. French Army Captain G. LePere, who was on loan by his government to the Air Service at McCook Field, designed the airplane, and the Packard Motor Car Company manufactured it. The first model was manufactured in the summer of 1918 and trial flights occurred August 13-16. The airplane was a "strikingly handsome" machine somewhat similar in appearance to the British Bristol Fighter. It had an overall wingspan of 41 feet 7 inches, a length of 25 feet 3 inches, and a height of 9 feet 6 inches. The power plant was a 12-cylinder Liberty engine generating 425 horsepower; top speed was 136 mph. Armament consisted of two forward-firing, .30-caliber Marlin machine guns and two .30-caliber Lewis guns fired by the observer from the rear cockpit.

Twenty-seven of this model were built. According to one aviation writer, the LUSAC-11 program put the Army "firmly into aeronautical research and development" and constituted "a major step forward in the development of American flight test methods and research."[23]

Martin M12P 12-passenger transport (second adaptation of the MB-1)

Italian Caproni Ca42 triplane bomber (*United States Air Force Museum*)

MCCOOK FIELD 1919-1926

At the end of World War I, the impact of military demobilization and curtailed operating budgets slowed the tempo of activities at McCook Field, but did not diminish the mission itself. Much of the momentum of late 1918 carried over into the earlier part of the new year. On November 11, 1918, McCook had a workforce of 58 officers, 267 enlisted men, and 1,915 civilian employees. By January 1, 1920, the number had shrunk to 286 military and 1,061 civilians. Between that date and 1926, the workforce averaged about 50 officers and from 1,100 to 1,500 civilians.[24] Over its remaining years, McCook served as the bellwether of American aviation. In 10 short years, the visionary engineers, scientists, artisans, and pilots of McCook Field established traditions of excellence that stand to this day.

Packard-LePere LUSAC-11. This airplane (tail number P53) was used as a test bed for the Hart controllable-pitch propeller (not shown). It also was flown by Lieutenant Rudolph "Shorty" Schroeder in setting new solo and two-man world altitude records in 1919 and 1920. (*Dr. Jerry Meyer*)

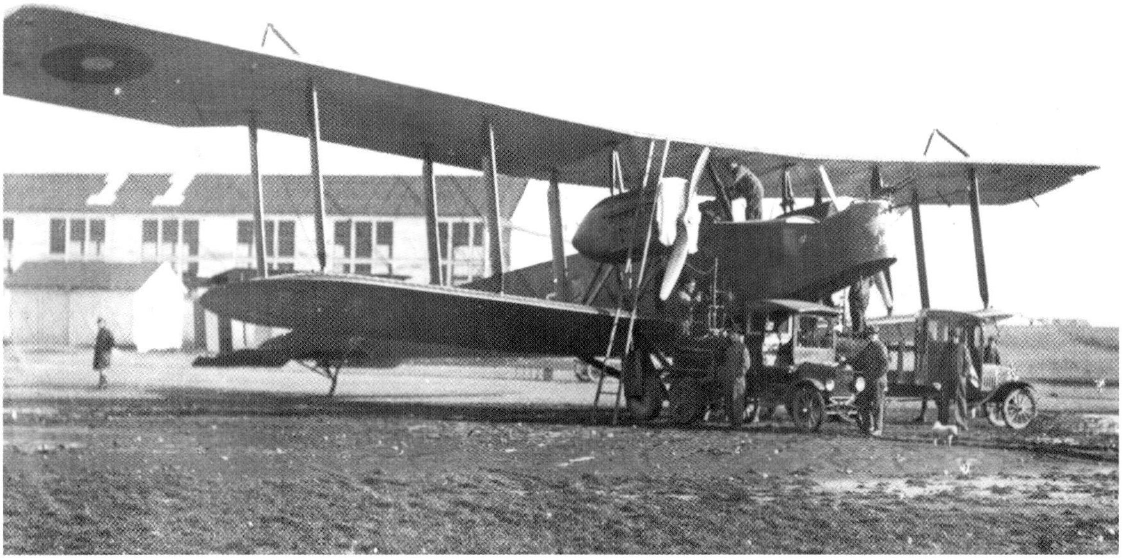

British Handley-Page O/400 twin-engine bomber (*United States Air Force Museum*)

French Breguet 14 with distinctive experimental wing camouflaging (*United States Air Force Museum*)

McCook Field engineers pursued a variety of interesting personal projects in their off-duty hours. One such project was a human-propelled, multi-winged vehicle called the Cycleplane. The aircraft was designed and built by Dr. W. Frederick Gerhardt, with the assistance of fellow workers in the Flight Test Section at McCook, and financed by private funds. Preliminary construction was completed in secrecy in a barn loft. Engineering Division officials then permitted Dr. Gerhardt to use the McCook helicopter hangar for final assembly of the unusual vehicle and to house it during tests.

The Cycleplane had seven vertically mounted wings. Inside, the operator powered the aircraft by pedaling a bicycle gear attached to the propeller. An automobile towed the Cycleplane into the air, glider-fashion, after which Dr. Gerhardt was able to maintain steady, level flight for brief periods. Aeronautical engineers considered this to be the first instance in which a man accomplished the feat of free flight by his own power.

The Cycleplane and its inventor, Dr. W. Frederick Gerhardt

The multi winged Cycleplane stayed aloft solely by the propulsive power of the pilot, July 1923.

Jewelers in the McCook Field Instrument Laboratory perform intricate adjustments and repairs on airplane instrumentation.

The torque stands housed in this building were used to test engines under conditions resembling those encountered in actual flight. Three double observation rooms separated the three torque stands and enabled engineers to monitor and measure engine performance.

The reduction in personnel resulted from sharply reduced appropriations. For fiscal year 1920 (which began July 1, 1919), the Engineering Division at McCook operated with less than $6 million of the total Air Service allocation of $25 million. This was a pittance compared to 1917-1918, when McCook's "patriotic, involved, intelligent young men . . . had more damn money than they knew what to do with."[25] The fiscal drought continued, with appropriations evaporating from $5 million in 1921 to $3 million in 1924. The active inventory followed suit, decreasing from 1,970 airplanes in 1923 to 289 machines in 1926.[26]

For years, a large percentage of the inventory consisted of World War I aircraft. At the end of hostilities, the Air Service had more than 3,400 DeHavilland DH-4s and nearly 12,000 Liberty engines on hand, as well as several Handley-Page and Caproni heavy bombers. At first nearly all replacement airplanes and equipment were drawn from these stocks, and the Engineering Division was forced to modify existing models rather than develop new aircraft and engines. Of far greater concern was the operational danger of the wartime stocks. During 1920 alone, 150 war-weary airplanes crashed, causing a high rate of casualties.[27]

When the Engineering Division asked for 50 Martin M-1 bombers for experimental purposes, Chief of the Air Service Major General Charles T. Menoher denied the request. He pointed out that the Air Service had British Handley-Page bombers in the active inventory that could be used for experimentation. An exasperated Colonel Thurman H. Bane, Engineering Division and McCook Field commander, was not pleased. He described the British bomber as "an antiquated old bus," a "flying barge" that did not handle like an airplane, and claimed that "the best thing which could happen for us would be for a fire to occur and burn them all." He clearly preferred the Martin bomber, proclaiming it as "probably the greatest development of the war."[28]

Despite the unsettled ambiance and restrictive funding of the immediate postwar period, McCook's engineers and pilots did make significant progress in many areas. As one author has commented, "Ironically, the lean years . . . produced the greatest achievements at McCook Field, for during the mid-1920s the scientists and engineers of the Engineering Division had little to work with but their own genius."[29]

During 1919, the Engineering Division devoted its efforts to the design, development, and test of airplanes, engines, and associated equipment:[30]

> The Airplane Section of the Engineering Organization worked on various types of pursuit and bombardment aircraft, for both day and night operations and powered by both liquid and air-cooled engines. The Power Plant Section devoted its efforts to developments for Liberty, Hispano-Suiza, and new liquid-cooled and air-cooled engines, superchargers, testing rigs, cooling systems, and fuel systems. The Equipment Section concentrated on such aspects as parachutes, leakproof tanks, flotation gear, modification of DH-4s for photography, a gyro compass, a portable field engine cranker, a pressure fire extinguisher, and a central electric power plant. Approximately 48 different types of tests were run on aircraft, engine, and equipment materials by the Material Section, while the Armament Section worked on developments for various types of machine guns, flexible mounts, armament installations, synchronizing devices, aircraft cannon, and bombs and bombing equipment.

Lieutenants John A. Macready and Albert W. Stevens took this aerial photograph of the city of Dayton on May 2, 1924, from a height of more than 31,500 feet. This was the first photograph taken at such a high altitude and it also covered the greatest area (19 square miles) ever in a single exposure. The flight established an unofficial world's record for the highest altitude attained by a two-man crew.

In fact, until McCook Field closed in 1927, these were the dominant areas of development in the field of aviation engineering.

The Flight Test Section at McCook conducted flight tests of all aircraft and equipment. Among the most exciting tests conducted during 1919 were those performed on a LePere fighter with a Moss supercharger. Altogether, 1,276 test flights and 3,550 incidental flights were conducted by McCook Field test pilots during 1919 alone.

Heavier-Than-Air Developments

In the immediate postwar period, the Air Service classified all aircraft—both domestic and foreign—into five main categories: pursuit, attack, bombardment, observation, and training. These five main categories were further divided into 15 types. There was also a "miscellaneous" grouping that encompassed such machines as racers and rotary wings.[31] Engineering activities at McCook Field were involved with nearly all of these types, as well as with lighter-than-air developments, in the years from 1919 to 1926.

Type	Description	Type Symbol
I.	Single-seat Pursuit—Water-cooled engine	PW
II.	Single-seat Pursuit—Night attack	PN
III.	Single-seat Pursuit—Air-cooled engine	PA
IV.	Single-seat Pursuit—Ground attack	PG
V.	Two-seat Pursuit	TP
VI.	Two- or multi-seat Ground Attack	GA
VII.	Two-seat Infantry Liaison	IL
VIII.	Two-seat Night Observation	NO
IX.	Two- or multi-seat Army and Coast Artillery Observation and surveillance	AO
X.	Two-seat Corps Observation	CO
XI.	Two- or multi-seat Day Bombardment	DB
XII.	Two- or multi-seat Night Bombardment—Short distance	NBS
XIII.	Multi-seat Night Bombardment—Long distance	NBL
XIV.	Training—Air-cooled engine	TA
XV.	Training—Water-cooled engine	TW
XVI.	Miscellaneous	—

Parachute Branch at McCook Field, responsible for the design, development, and improvement of all Air Service parachutes. (Inset) Guy Ball demonstrates the original seat-pack parachute developed because existing airplanes could not accommodate back-packs. This type of parachute was used by Lieutenant Harold R. Harris in the first emergency jump from a disabled airplane in 1922.

Air Service Engineering School classroom at McCook Field in the early 1920s. Engineering students worked side-by-side with McCook scientists to gain hands-on experience in such areas as the early design of superchargers for aircraft engines (on blackboard above and at right).

FLIGHT TEST SECTION

The Flight Test Section was the most exciting and glamorous unit of the Engineering Division. Test pilots pushed, pulled, and in all other ways punished and pounded airplanes, especially experimental models, to demonstrate their strengths and uncover their weaknesses. This activity was the literal "proof of the pudding." (Most of the records and accomplishments were attributed to McCook Field since the pilots were members of the Engineering Division at McCook. The actual scene, however, was often Wilbur Wright Field. As a case in point, the XNBL-1 Barling bomber's size prohibited it from using McCook; it lived and died at Wilbur Wright Field.)

Major Rudolph "Shorty" Schroeder* and Lieutenant Harold R. Harris were two of the most distinguished chiefs of the Flight Test Section. Another McCook Field test pilot who achieved international fame was Lieutenant James H. "Jimmy" Doolittle.

One of Major Schroeder's most daring exploits was an altitude record of 33,113 feet, set February 27, 1920, over McCook in an open cockpit LePere biplane. At that altitude the temperature was –67° F. Schroeder nearly lost his life on the record flight due to an oxygen shortage and carbon monoxide poisoning from the exhaust gases.

Lieutenant Harris, who became a brigadier general in World War II, set 10 world and 15 American records for speed, distance, altitude, and endurance. Lieutenant Doolittle, who rose to the rank of lieutenant general in 1944, also established many outstanding records during his career. These included the September 4, 1922, first transcontinental crossing of the United States, east-west, in a single day. This exploit earned him the Distinguished Flying Cross. He won both the Schneider Trophy speed race and the Mackay Trophy in 1925 while assigned to McCook.

Often the price of progress was paid in blood, pain, and death. From January 22, 1919, through May 25, 1936, 17 military and civilian pilots and crewmembers of the Engineering Division died in airplane crashes. The "Roll of Honor" included:

Lieutenant Frank Banks	January 22, 1919
Captain W. F. Jones and George Buzane	July 14, 1919
Sergeant Strong B. Madan	October 4, 1920
W. W. Stryker, Thomas H. Harriman, Allan B. MacFarland, Robert H. Hanson, Charles N. Schulenberg, William O'Laughlin	February 21, 1922**
Lieutenant F. W. Neidermeyer	March 13, 1922
Lieutenant L. P. Moriarty and William P. Stonebraker	August 14, 1922
Lieutenant Theodore S. VanVechten	April 8, 1924
Robert Anderson	May 13, 1924
Lieutenant Alexander Pearson, Jr.	September 2, 1924
Lieutenant Eugene H. Barksdale	August 11, 1926

* Major Schroeder was nicknamed "Shorty" because of his stature: 6 feet 4 inches and 155 pounds.

** Killed in the crash of the airship *Roma* near Norfolk, Virginia.

McCook Field personnel, 1919. Major Rudolph "Shorty" Schroeder is the tallest man in the photograph. (*United States Air Force Museum*)

TEST FLYING AT MCCOOK FIELD, 1919

HEADQUARTERS TECHNICAL DIVISION
BUREAU OF AIRCRAFT PRODUCTION

SPECIAL MEMORANDUM NO. 27

1. Test flights have priority over all other flying. All test flights will be under the direction of Major Schroeder. He will designate the pilot to fly the test, the time at which the test will be flown, and he will give all instructions covering the flying of the test. The Planes & Engines Maintenance Department will furnish the machine and the crew.

2. Pilot will inspect machine before taking it up.

3. Pilots will make sure that they thoroughly understand the operation of all controls, especially the motor controls, before taking off.

4. Be certain that the air pressure, the oil pressure, and the temperature are right before leaving the ground.

5. Taxy machines slowly, well away from the hangars before taking off in order not to blow a cloud of dust and dirt into the hangars.

6. Take full advantage of the wind and the size of the field in getting away.

7. Never leave the ground with a missing motor or if anything else is wrong.

8. Pilots will remain within gliding distance of McCook Field at all times. There is no excuse for forced landings outside the field.

9. Whenever possible land into the wind.

10. No stunting will be done below 1,000 feet.

11. Report any trouble that may develop during flight, or anything else that is wrong with motor or machine, no matter how slight, to the crew chief immediately upon landing.

12. Owing to the small number of machines available and the large number of Officers desiring flights, no machines will be flown to Wilbur Wright Field or to other outside fields, except on important official business that can not be handled otherwise. This rule will be strictly observed.

13. Certain parts of the field have recently been graded and seeded. These spots are soft in wet weather. In order not to cut up the field, avoid these spots when field is in a muddy condition.

14. Whenever the field is muddy and the wind is from the right direction, take off and land on the runway.

15. All flying, except important tests that cannot be delayed will stop at 4:00 P.M. from Monday to Friday, and at 11:00 A.M. on Saturday, and all machines will be at the hangars by that time.

16. Except on test flights, flying will be limited to one hour per day per man.

Dayton, Ohio, February 5, 1919

T. H. BANE
Colonel, A.S.A.
Chief of Division

By
DELOS C. EMMONS
Lieutenant Colonel, A.S.A.
Business & Military
Executive

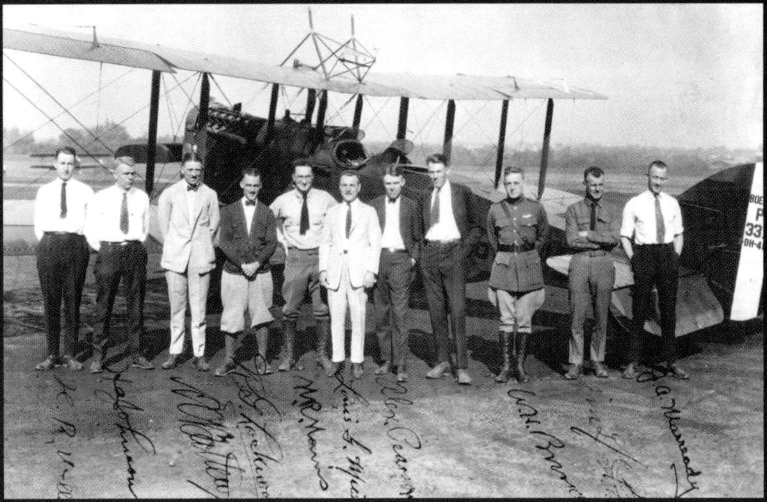

Flight Test Section, McCook Field, 1924. The only man who did not autograph the photograph was Lieutenant Eugene "Hoy" Barksdale, who died in the line of duty on August 11, 1926. (*United States Air Force Museum, Eugene Barksdale Collection*)

Flight Test Section, McCook Field, 1925. The section's mascots, the Quacking Duck and the Flying Jackass, were placed on the desks of braggarts and those who pulled boners. (*United States Air Force Museum, Eugene Barksdale Collection*)

Lieutenant Wendell H. "Brook" Brookley displays the Test Section's Oilcan and Dumbbell trophies. (*Mrs. Darlene Gerhardt*)

1924 Curtiss model PW-8 Hawk pursuit assigned to the 17th Pursuit Squadron

Engineering Division TP-1 pursuit (*United States Air Force Museum*)

British Bristol Fighter (*United States Air Force Museum*)

Cox-Klemin TW-2 trainer with water-cooled engine (*United States Air Force Museum*)

The Engineering Division armor-plated GAX-1, designed and manufactured at McCook, was the Air Service's only twin-engine triplane. (*United States Air Force Museum*)

Fokker CO-4 Corps Observation (*United States Air Force Museum*)

British Avro 504K trainer (*United States Air Force Museum*)

Curtiss NBS-1

Boeing MB-3A pursuit with water-cooled engine assigned to the 94th Pursuit Squadron. The MB-3A was an improved version of the Thomas-Morse MB-3.

Airplanes of Type I (PW) were designed to destroy enemy aircraft within a specified region and/or to protect friendly airplanes such as bombers, ground attack, and reconnaissance-observation. These single-seat pursuits had water-cooled engines and were "high speed, quickly maneuverable [airplanes] . . . carrying machine guns [either .30- or .50-caliber] synchronized to fire through the rotating propeller." Models of this type accepted by the Engineering Division were the Orenco D-1, the Curtiss PW-8 Hawk, and the Thomas-Morse MB-3 (as well as improved MB-3A's built by Boeing).

Type II (PN) single-seat aircraft were intended for night operations, but no airplanes produced during World War I were placed in this classification. Day pursuit aircraft were used in a limited amount of after-sundown operations. In 1920, at Engineering Division request, Curtiss built a single-place, externally braced biplane for this purpose. Three models were delivered to the Engineering Division for testing and evaluation.

Type III (PA) airplanes featured air-cooled engines, but otherwise shared the purpose and nearly the same characteristics as the Type I (PW) pursuits. One example of this type was the PA-1, designed by the Loening Aeronautical Company. The PA-1 was a "thick-wing" externally braced biplane with a 350-horsepower Wright radial engine.

The Type IV (PG) airplane was designed as a "high-speed, armored, single-seater biplane" primarily for attacking enemy ground forces and enemy airplanes. The Aeromarine Plane and Motor Corporation built such a machine for the Engineering Division for testing and evaluation purposes. It was an externally braced biplane powered by a 300-horsepower Wright K engine.

Within the Type V (TP) two-seat, biplane-pursuit category the best known example was the British-designed Bristol Fighter. Although the Engineering Division evaluated the respective merits of the Curtiss Wasp biplane and triplane, the LePere two-place biplane, the Loening two-place monoplane, and the Thomas-Morse two-seat MB-1 monoplane and MB-2 biplane, none was ever mass produced.

Type VI (GA) was a heavily armored, ground-attack airplane designed to provide sustained aerial support of ground forces under enemy fire. The first pilot model GA was the LePere triplane. Using that model's general specifications and characteristics, the Engineering Division designed and manufactured the GAX-1, the Air Service's only twin-engine triplane. It was impressive, with an overall wingspan of 65 feet 6 inches, a length of 35 feet 6 inches, and a height of about 14 feet. The GAX-1 used two 400-horsepower Liberty engines and was specifically equipped for on-the-deck strafing. One ton of quarter-inch armor shielded the crew and engines. In lieu of bulletproof glass, "revolving slotted armor-plate discs" gave the gunners protection against enemy fighter action. The airplane carried eight .30-caliber Lewis machine guns and a 37-mm Baldwin cannon. The weapons fired from the armor-plated nose that protruded beyond the wings.[32]

Type VII (IL) was a two-seat infantry liaison biplane. The best known machine in this category was the armored German Junkers biplane. The Air Service counterpart was the Orenco IL-1, a two-place, externally braced biplane with a 400-horsepower, 12-cylinder, Liberty engine.

Type VIII (NO) aircraft were two-seat biplanes used for night observation. The Engineering Division did not develop a specific airplane for this purpose since most two-seat Corps Observation (CO) biplanes could be modified for night work as required.

Type IX (AO) machines were two- or three-place biplanes used for Coast Artillery observation and reconnaissance. The Air Service did not employ this type of airplane although "this field [had] some very interesting possibilities" and was considered worth studying.[33]

Type X (CO) was the Corps Observation airplane. This category included several familiar names, i.e., the DeHavilland DH-4, British Salmson, and French Breguet. McCook's XB-1A, which was similar to the Bristol and equipped with a 300-horsepower Wright engine, was manufactured by the Dayton Wright Airplane Company under contract with the Air Service. Several of these airplanes were delivered to pursuit squadrons in the field. Later developments in the area of Corps Observation aviation included the Engineering Division's CO-1, CO-2 (only one model was built for static testing), and CO-5; the Fokker CO-4; and the Gallaudet CO-1. McCook's CO-1, CO-2, and the Gallaudet CO-1 were high-wing, metal monoplanes with enclosed cabins. The other aircraft were two-place, open cockpit biplanes. The monoplanes were internally braced; structural members were steel and the covering was made entirely of duralumin.[34]

Type XI (DB) aircraft were two- or multi-seat, day bombardment machines. The best known of this series was the Engineering Division's first product, the USD-9A (discussed earlier). In late 1923, the Gallaudet DB-1 was tested. It was a two-place, open cockpit, low-wing monoplane. Its 700-horsepower engine was an Engineering Division-developed W-1-A. The "W" engine, designed and developed entirely in-house, consisted of 18 cylinders mounted in a "W" formation, six cylinders in a row. It developed 700 horsepower at 1,700 rpm and weighed 1,720 pounds.

Type XII (NBS) two- or multi-seat, night bombardment, short-distance machines included the famous World War I British Handley-Page and Italian Caproni bombers. These airplanes formed the nucleus of the Allied heavy bombardment squadrons in Europe. Also in this category was the American Glenn Martin bomber (GMB-1) completed in August 1918 but never sent overseas.

Type XIII (NBL) multi-seat, night bombardment, long distance. The two best known foreign aircraft in this category were the British Super-Handley-Page and the German Zeppelin Giant bombers that were operational during World War I. The most famous American machine of this type—and one of the milestones in the history of Wright-Patterson Air Force Base—was the NBL-1 six-engine triplane designed in 1920 by Walter Barling.

Type XIV (TA) trainer, air-cooled engine. The best known foreign aircraft of this type were the British Avro, the Thomas-Morse S-4C, and the French Nieuport 23. Four trainers (all two-place biplanes) in this category were evaluated at McCook.

Type XV (TW) trainer, water-cooled engine. TWs were close kin to their counterparts with air-cooled engines, i.e., the TA classification. The best known of the TWs was the famous Curtiss JN-4D Jenny biplane that saw considerable service at Wilbur Wright Field and at other Signal Corps aviation schools. The Airplane Engineering Division at McCook Field tested and evaluated four TWs during the early 1920s: the Engineering Division TW-1 biplane, the Cox-Klemin TW-2 biplane, the Dayton Wright TW-3 biplane, and the Fokker TW-4 high-wing monoplane.

Type XVI was a miscellaneous category. Though the airplanes had no particular letter designation, this classification held some of the most famous airplanes associated with the Engineering Division and/

Alfred V. Verville, aviation pioneer and aircraft designer. Verville worked at McCook Field between 1918 and 1925 before establishing his own company, the Verville Aircraft Company. He continued to support military aviation until his death in 1970. (*Dr. Squire L. Brown*)

or McCook Field (including the smallest, the largest and several "first-evers"). In 1922, among the four aircraft in this classification was the Dayton Wright PS-1 (Pursuit Special), a rigidly braced, high-wing monoplane constructed around the 200-horsepower, Lawrance J-1, radial, air-cooled engine.

By the mid-1920s, the categories of airplanes had been reduced from 16 to five: P for pursuit, B for bomber (with variations such as LB for light bomber and HB for heavy bomber), C for cargo, O for observation, and T for trainer. The symbol "-1" (dash one) indicated the first model in the category. The X prefix indicated the experimental status of a design. In 1929, the Y prefix was added to designate service test status.

By 1924, the Engineering Division at McCook had ceased all aircraft construction and concerned itself solely with monitoring airplane design and aircraft produced by private manufacturers. Although the Air Service devoted almost one quarter of its 1924 appropriations to research and development, the total budget amounted to only $3 million. According to one source, "this period of postwar retrenchment [continued] until the budget for research reached its lowest ebb in 1927."[35]

Of the many aircraft associated with McCook Field in the early 1920s, several models drew considerable attention to the work being accomplished by McCook Field engineers. Four in particular stand out as all-time favorites in the history of aviation.

The Sperry Messenger

Rightfully known as the smallest airplane at McCook Field, the Sperry M-1 Messenger was a single-seat, externally braced biplane designed by Alfred V. Verville, a civilian employee of the division. The airplane was designed specifically for liaison operations and manufactured by the Lawrence Sperry Aircraft Company. The machine was less than 18 feet in length and 7 feet in height, with an overall wingspan of 20 feet. Its motor was a 60-horsepower, three-cylinder, Lawrance radial engine. The 862-pound Messenger could carry a useful load of 239 pounds at a top speed of 96.7 mph. It could climb to 6,500 feet in 21 minutes. Service ceiling was 13,400 feet and absolute ceiling was 15,600 feet.[36] The Air Service ordered 42 Messengers. Some were fitted with "skids and special jettisonable landing gear for specialized missions." Others were used to test various airfoil sections.

One of the intended uses of this versatile airplane was that of a "dispatch rider of the sky." To play this role, a "trapeze hook-up arrangement" was mounted on the upper wing. In several demonstrations the tiny bird made both hook-ups and drop-offs from beneath the cabin of an Air Service airship. Such a complete maneuver was one of the highlights of the October 1924 International Air Races at Wilbur Wright Field.

Sperry Messenger suspended from the gondola of a TC-7 airship

The Sperry Messenger single-place biplane was the smallest airplane ever designed at McCook. The airplane, built to Engineering Division specifications by the Lawrence Sperry Aircraft Corporation, was designed to carry written messages and orders between front lines and higher headquarters. Using the "trapeze hook-up arrangement" on the upper wing, the Messenger hung suspended from the gondolas of the Air Service's airships.

The Barling Bomber

Dramatically overshadowing the tiny 862-pound Sperry Messenger was the largest airplane associated with McCook, the 42,000-pound XNBL-1 Barling bomber. About the only thing the two aircraft had in common was maximum flying speed: with its single three-cylinder engine, the Messenger biplane flitted at 96.7 mph; the six-engine triplane lumbered along at a top speed of 95.5 mph.

Historians have attributed the bomber to Brigadier General William Mitchell, the colorful, farsighted assistant chief of the Air Service. He recruited Walter J. Barling, Jr., of England as an aircraft designer for the Engineering Division. Shortly after Barling arrived in the United States in late 1919, General Mitchell asked him to design and build an airplane of sufficient size to carry enough bombs to sink a battleship during a sustained attack. On May 15, 1920, the Engineering Division sought bids on the construction of a triplane bomber based on statistics and modified sketches made by Barling.

Several weeks later, the Witteman-Lewis Company of Hasbrouck Heights, New Jersey, received a contract to build two of the six-engine triplanes at a total cost of $375,000. At General Mitchell's insistence, the Air Service named Barling as the chief engineer in charge of the project—with salary and expenses paid by the aircraft manufacturer. Only six fields were large enough to accommodate the huge aircraft: Hasbrouck Heights, New Jersey (near the manufacturer); Mitchel Field, Long Island, New York; Langley Field, Virginia; Ellington and Kelly fields, Texas; and Wilbur Wright Field. The latter was selected because of its proximity to McCook Field. Plans called for the airplane's components to be shipped by rail to Wilbur Wright Field for assembly and testing.

By the time the project ended in 1923, the costs had risen from the original $375,000 for two bombers to over $525,000 for just one prototype. The manufacturer had to absorb the costly overrun. (This cost was never recovered; the second triplane was never built; and a few months after delivery of the Barling the aircraft company closed its doors.) Ninety-four days after work began on assembling the bomber at Wilbur Wright Field, the aerial leviathan was ready for its initial flight on August 22, 1923.

A TRIO OF HEAVIES

	Barling Bomber (1923)	B-36 (1947)	B-52B (1952)
Wingspan	120 feet	230 feet	185 feet
Length	65 feet	162 feet, 1 inch	156 feet, 6 inches
Wing area	4,017 square feet	4,772 square feet	4,000 square feet
Empty weight	27,132 pounds	145,000 pounds	164,000 pounds
Gross weight	42,569 pounds	358,000 pounds	420,000 pounds
Top speed	95.5 mph	435 mph	546 mph

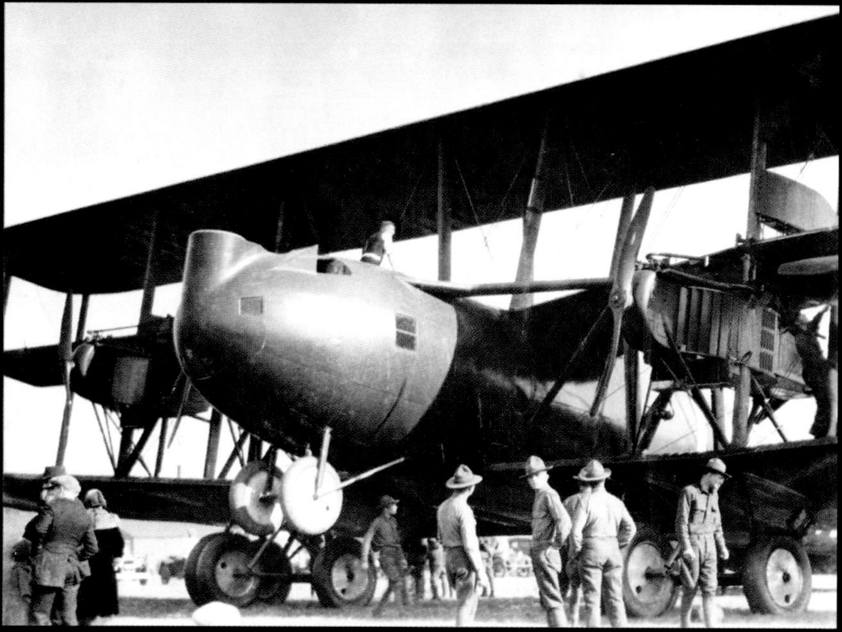

The Barling bomber

Walter H. Barling
— Designer
THE BARLING BOMBER — WORLD'S LARGEST AIRPLANE

XNBL-1 Barling bomber, designed at McCook Field by Walter J. Barling, Jr., and assembled at Wilbur Wright Field

The XNBL-1 was not, technically, a triplane. More correctly it was a two-and-one-half wing aircraft, since the middle wing was shorter and narrower than the other two and had no control surfaces (the upper and lower wings had ailerons). The tail structure, which looked "more like a box kite than an airplane," had vertical fins. According to one description:[37]

> The top and bottom wings had a chord of 13 ft. 6 in. and each had an area of approximately 2,000 sq. ft. There were 575 sq. ft. in the stabilizer and elevator surfaces, which had an 8-ft. chord, and 250 sq. ft. in the fins and rudders.

Barling bomber in flight over Wilbur Wright Field. The huge bomber set several world records. On October 25, 1923, it achieved an altitude of 6,722 feet carrying a 4,409-pound load. Two days later, it reached 5,344 feet altitude with a load weighing more than 6,600 pounds. It maintained this altitude for 1 hour 19 minutes 11.8 seconds.

The wingspan was 120 feet; fuselage length was 65 feet; and height 28 feet. Power came from six 420-horsepower, 12-cylinder, water-cooled, Liberty engines. Two tractor engines and one pusher engine were situated on each side of the fuselage. The Engineering Division had no choice but to use engines from wartime stocks. The engines were greatly underpowered for the job. They barely produced the power required to lift and propel the heavy aircraft, leaving the bomber only a one-engine reserve. One authority pointed out, "if two engines had to shut down, the plane had to land—as quickly as possible."[38] That factor restricted the machine's practical operational range to the Midwest, between the Mississippi River and the Appalachian mountains.

The Barling carried seven .30-caliber Lewis machine guns operated from five positions, thereby covering "practically the whole field" of incoming hostile fire. Bomb racks beneath the gasoline tanks could carry any of the bombs in the Air Service inventory, including the giant 2,000- and 4,000-pound bombs developed for use against battleships. "Trap doors" in the bottom of the fuselage permitted bomb drops.

With Lieutenant Harold R. Harris (later brigadier general), chief of the McCook Field Flight Test Branch, and Lieutenant Muir Fairchild (later general) in the cockpit, the XNBL-1 made its maiden flight of 28 minutes in the afternoon of August 22, 1923, at Wilbur Wright Field. Also aboard were the bomber's "father," Walter J. Barling, and McCook Field civilian employees Douglas Culver as flight engineer and Daniel Comansea as crew chief. After a takeoff roll of 320 yards in 13 seconds (thereby astounding the spectators), the huge bomber took flight. During its initial flight the airplane climbed to 2,000 feet.

In October 1923, the giant bomber set four very significant world records, thereby firmly establishing the concept of the heavy bomber. The Barling bomber also made a number of exhibition flights during its career. Perhaps the most spectacular occurred on September 14, 1924, when it accompanied the Douglas World Flight Cruisers on their inbound flight from Columbus, Ohio, to McCook Field. The bomber's last flight of record was made May 7, 1925.

The Barling bomber sits inside the hangar being constructed specifically to house it.

XNBL-1 Barling bomber at Wilbur Wright Field, 1926 *(Bob Cavanagh)*

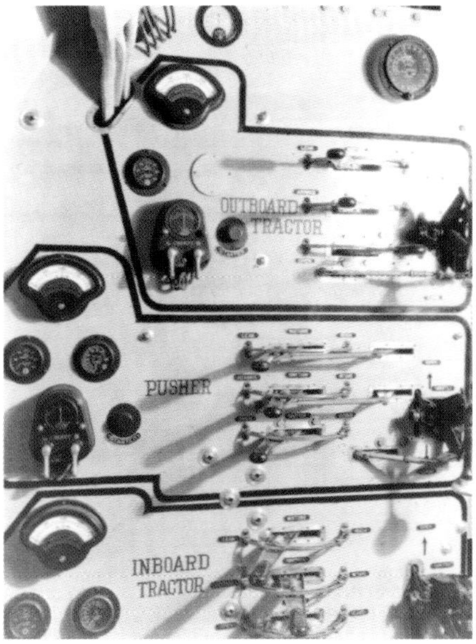

A portion of the complex instrument panel of the Barling bomber

Despite criticism that the bomber failed to reach its popular expectations, the airplane was not a total waste of money and effort. In retrospect, according to General Henry H. Arnold in his autobiography, *Global Mission,* the Barling resolved many technical problems. "Records from wind-tunnel tests, theoretical analyses of details of assemblies and newly devised parts on paper are all right, but there are times when the full-scale article must be built to get the pattern for the future." He pointed out that "if we look at it without bias certainly [the Barling] had influence on the development of B-17s . . . and B-29s."[39]

The Barling's inability to cross the Appalachian mountains with any degree of safety, plus costly overruns and the unforeseen expense of $700,000 to construct a special hangar, curtailed any additional funding for the project. In 1927, the machine was dismantled and stored at Fairfield Air Depot. Shortly after Major Henry H. Arnold became depot commander in 1929, he submitted a Report of Survey to the Office of the Chief of the Air Corps, seeking permission to salvage parts of the bomber and to burn the rest. Because of residual congressional interest in the airplane, permission was denied. Undaunted, Major Arnold then submitted a similar Report of Survey on the "XNBL-1"—carefully omitting a reference to the Barling bomber by name. Higher headquarters approved this request, and the machine was destroyed in 1930.[40]

The Fokker T-2

A significant milestone for both military and civil air transportation was the construction, at Engineering Division direction, of an internally braced, high-wing monoplane powered by a 420-horsepower, 12-cylinder, Liberty engine. This aircraft, the Air Service Fokker T-2 transport, was a product of the Netherlands Aircraft Company. The T-2 had a wingspan of 79 feet 8 inches, a length of 49 feet 1 inch, and a height of 11 feet 10 inches. The eight-passenger airplane had a gross weight of 10,750 pounds and a top speed of 95 mph. A slightly smaller version of the T-2 transport had an overall wingspan of 62 feet, was 42 feet long, and had a height of nine feet. It was powered by a 400-horsepower, 12-cylinder, Liberty engine.

The airplane was designed by Anthony Herman Gerard Fokker (1890-1939), a native of the Netherlands, who was one of the chief designers of German pursuits in World War I. He was noted for his triplanes and biplanes. One of the most famous was the Fokker D-7, which was called the "best single-seater" of the war by both friendly and enemy airmen. (As part of postwar reparations, a Fokker D-7 was brought to McCook Field for evaluation.)

On May 2, 1923, McCook Field test pilots Lieutenants John A. Macready and Oakley G. Kelly made the first continental nonstop flight, from Roosevelt Field, New York, to Rockwell Field, San Diego, California, in a T-2. Their airplane was modified at McCook to carry 790 gallons of gasoline in special fuel tanks in the cabin. They made the 2,520-mile odyssey in 26 hours and 50 minutes at an average speed of 94 mph. For this spectacular achievement the pilots shared in the prestigious Mackay Trophy awarded annually for aerial achievement, and each man received the Distinguished Flying Cross.[41]

Fokker T-2 transport (center), flanked by a Boeing MB-3A pursuit (left) and a Verville-Sperry monoplane racer

Lieutenants John A. Macready (left) and Oakley G. Kelly made the first continental nonstop flight May 2-3, 1923, in this Fokker T-2.

Lieutenants Macready and Kelly relax beside their airplane. (*United States Air Force Museum*)

The de Bothezat helicopter in flight with pilot and three "passengers" (*Bob and Dottie Gheen*)

Inventor Dr. George de Bothezat (left) with McCook Field commander Colonel Thurman H. Bane, the first man to fly the machine

This same type aircraft, redesignated the A-2, was modified for use as an aerial ambulance. It accommodated four litters and as many vertical seats for passengers or medical attendants. This role was soon abandoned as better types of aircraft were designed for this purpose. (McCook Field aeronautical engineer and designer Alfred V. Verville designed the first-ever aerial ambulance in 1919. The airplane, a modified DH-4A, carried two litters.)[42]

The de Bothezat Helicopter

McCook Field designers and engineers not only improved the proficiency and effectiveness of reciprocating, fixed-wing airplanes of one-, two-, and three-wing construction, but they also experimented with rotorcraft, which later became known as helicopters. In 1921, Dr. George de Bothezat, a distinguished Russian émigré, inventor and mathematician, designed the first rotorcraft constructed at McCook Field for the Engineering Division. The aircraft weighed 3,550 pounds and cost about $200,000 to build. It was described as having:[43]

> Four six-bladed rotors mounted at the ends of beams 65 feet, 7 3/8 inches (20 meters) in length, forming a cross and intersecting in all directions. The rotor axes were not parallel but slightly

inclined inwards so that if prolonged they would have met at a point directly above the centre of gravity. Besides the rotors with variable-pitch blades, the helicopter had two horizontal propellers called "steering airscrews" as well as two small airscrews placed above the gearbox and acting as regulators for the 220 [horsepower] engine. The power plant was a LeRhone engine.

The initial flight occurred on December 18, 1922, with Colonel Thurman Bane, McCook Field commander, at the controls. The machine reached an altitude of six feet and hovered for 1 minute 42 seconds, then "drifted along with the wind for three hundred feet or more." On the following January 23, the aircraft lifted two persons to a height of four feet, and on April 17, 1923, lifted five people off the ground. Although the helicopter demonstrated a high degree of inherent stability and completed a successful series of sustained flights, "the Air Service rapidly lost interest in it."[44]

Lighter-Than-Air Developments

Brigadier General William Mitchell, assistant chief of the Air Service, was a staunch champion of the Army's airship operations. He envisioned huge airships as transports for carrying troops and supplies long distances, as gun platforms for destroying enemy airplanes, and as air bases in the clouds "on to which heavier-than-air pursuit planes could hook, refuel, then disengage for heavier-than-air operations" such as controlling air superiority and close support of ground troops.

In 1919, a Joint Army-Navy Board decision virtually ended the Air Service lighter-than-air fleet by giving the Navy exclusive operation of rigid airships. The Air Service was relegated to flying the smaller, less effective (and far less dramatic) semi-rigids, non-rigids, and blimps. A rigid airship consisted of "a weather-resistant fabric envelope stretched tautly around a giant metal framework containing gas-filled cells to impart lift." The non-rigid airship, or blimp, relied almost entirely on internal gas pressure to maintain the vehicle's shape. "A rubberized, gas-tight streamlined envelope which was stressed internally with cross cables and fabric curtains" was inflated with either hydrogen or helium. Beneath the envelope was a control car, similar to an airplane fuselage, which housed the airship's crew, engines, and control surfaces. The Air Service lighter-than-air inventory also included free and captive balloons of World War I heritage.

In March 1922, the Balloon and Airship Section from Omaha, Nebraska, was transferred and attached to the Engineering Division and acted in an advisory capacity on balloon and airship matters. The aeronauts advised McCook designers and engineers on such matters as improved inflation equipment, better equipment for mooring and handling balloon envelopes, development of motorized observation balloons, use of helium gas in balloons, and airship mechanical devices.[45] Testing activities of the Balloon and Airship Section, especially those involving flying, took place mainly at Wilbur Wright Field, which had considerably more space and less interference with airplane flying. A 72-foot-high Terry mast was installed at Wilbur Wright Field especially to accommodate the TC-5 training airship.

Special emphasis was placed on devising equipment for balloons, such as portable gas plants, generators, and compressor units for use on motor trucks and railroad equipment. Blimps required special engines, propellers, fabrics, gases, and

An Air Service non-rigid dirigible lands at McCook Field after flying from its home base at Scott Field, Illinois. These "blimps" were used for observation/reconnaissance missions. As late as 1923, the Air Service tactical force included two airship and two balloon squadrons.

Barrage balloon at McCook Field, early 1920s. A DH-4 airplane is flying around the balloon. Island Park on the Stillwater River is visible in the lower left of the photograph. (*Mrs. Darlene Gerhardt*)

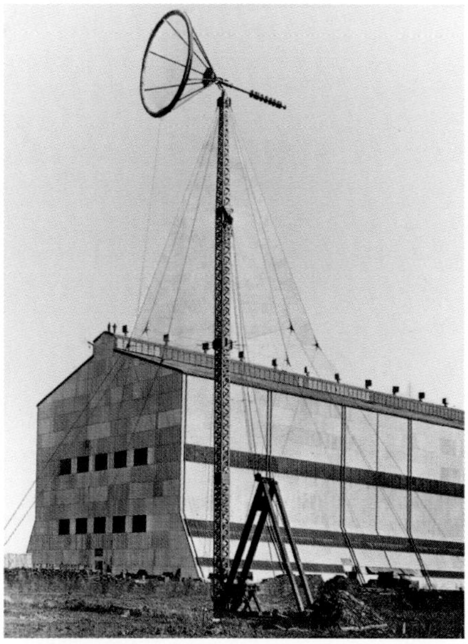

A 72-foot-high Terry mast similar to this one was installed at Wilbur Wright Field to moor dirigibles so that they could be worked on and boarded outside the hangar. (*United States Air Force Museum*)

B-1 caterpillar-type dirigible winch developed by the Balloon and Airship Section. It replaced about 150 crewmen previously needed to handle a semi-rigid airship.

valves. The Balloon and Airship Section researched improved methods of inflating and deflating envelopes and of reclaiming gas. One of the more significant improvements in ground-handling equipment was the "grab winch" similar in design to a Caterpillar tractor. The machine replaced about 150 crewmen previously needed to handle a semi-rigid airship.

The section built a free balloon that could ascend to 50,000 feet to obtain meteorological data. In place of the usual open wicker basket beneath the gondola, there was a dual cylinder of airtight construction with weather instruments mounted on the outside. This allowed the balloon pilot within the cylinder to observe weather phenomena without suffering the effects of high altitude.[46]

Air Service airships averaged top speeds of 65 mph and service ceilings of about 11,000 feet. The largest airship purchased was the semi-rigid *Roma,* an Italian-made vehicle of 1,200,000-cubic-feet gas capacity, powered by six 400-horsepower Ansalno engines. The aircraft was 410 feet in length and 82 feet in diameter. It had a cruising speed of 68 mph and a 5,300-mile cruising range. It ordinarily carried a crew

Although much of the work at McCook centered on heavier-than-air machines, considerable attention was devoted to improving lighter-than-air, non-rigid dirigibles and spherical balloons. This 35,000-cubic-foot balloon is one-fifth inflated in a test of its fabric.

of 12, although there were 45 men aboard when it crashed and burned near Norfolk, Virginia, on February 21, 1922. Among the 34 killed were six McCook Field employees. Disaster was brought closer to home on June 6, 1923, when the TC-1 training airship burned at Wilbur Wright Field. The three-man crew managed to escape without injury.

WRIGHT FIELD 1927-1934

State-Of-The-Art 1927

For many who attended the formal dedication of Wright Field on October 12, 1927, the main attraction was the aerial extravaganza at the adjacent Fairfield Air Depot Reservation (FADR) (formerly the Fairfield Air Intermediate Depot). In the spotlight were 22 military airplanes aligned wing tip to wing tip on static display in front of the depot's wooden hangars. Representing the Air Corps' finest that day were:[47]

DH-4M-2P Atlantic—Special Photographic
DH-4M-2S Atlantic—Special Supercharger
P-1A Curtiss—Pursuit
AT-4 Curtiss—Advanced Training, Pursuit
AT-5 Curtiss—Advanced Training, Pursuit
PW-7 Fokker—Pursuit
PW-9 Boeing—Pursuit
O-1 Curtiss—Observation
O-2A Douglas—Observation
O-2H Douglas—Observation
XO-6 Thomas-Morse—Observation (Experimental)
CO-4A Fokker—Corps Observation
XCO-5 Engineering Division—Special Altitude, Corps Observation (Experimental)
XCO-6 Engineering Division—Corps Observation (Experimental)
XCO-8 Atlantic—Corps Observation (Experimental)
XA-2 Douglas—Attack (Experimental)
XHB-1 Keystone—Bomber (Experimental)
XB-2 Curtiss—Bomber (Experimental)
C-2 Atlantic—Transport
PT-1 Consolidated—Primary Training, Steam-Cooled
XPT-3 Consolidated—Primary Training (Experimental)
VE-9 Vought—Training, Adjustable Propeller

Among the airplanes displayed for visitors were a number of models of World War I acclaim. Others were postwar models destined to earn banner headlines in military and civilian aviation in the coming years. All were outstanding examples of their respective categories of service.

The DeHavilland DH-4M-2P Special Photographic airplane and the DH-4M-2S Special Supercharger exemplified the progression from World War I to modern aviation. These were modernized versions of the venerable, British-designed, DH-4 single-engine biplane, which had been used during World War I as a bomber, a reconnaissance-observation machine, and a "battle plane" for close support of ground troops. The postwar version was constructed around a skeleton of welded steel tubing, a method developed by Anthony Fokker and made standard in the mid-1920s for all Air Corps airplanes.

Although the DeHavilland was a bit trimmer in its new togs, it remained somewhat dowdy when compared to the three fast, sleek-lined pursuits displayed at FADR. The Curtiss P-1A Hawk pursuit stood out as the most attractive—aesthetically, aerodynamically, and operationally. This was the first standard model in the family of Hawk aircraft that, in the view of distinguished pilot Brigadier General Ross C. Hoyt, dominated the Air Corps' pursuit field from 1925 to 1930.[48]

The P-1A displayed at FADR was a single-place tractor biplane. Powered by the 440-horsepower, water-cooled, Curtiss D-12 engine, its maximum speed at sea level was 170 mph. The machine could climb to 15,000 feet in 14 minutes, and had an absolute ceiling of 22,150 feet. Armament consisted of two .30-caliber, fixed, Browning machine guns firing through the propeller arc. Small bombs could be carried under the bottom wing.[49]

Sharing the spotlight on the FADR flightline were the AT-4 and AT-5 advanced trainers used in pursuit pilot training, handmaidens to the P-1 pursuit. The AT-4, a single-seat biplane,

The Curtiss P-1, shown here at Wright Field, was the first of the taper-wing Hawk series aircraft.

Curtiss AT-4 Hawk advanced trainer (*United States Air Force Museum*)

Curtiss XP-6E Hawk pursuit aircraft

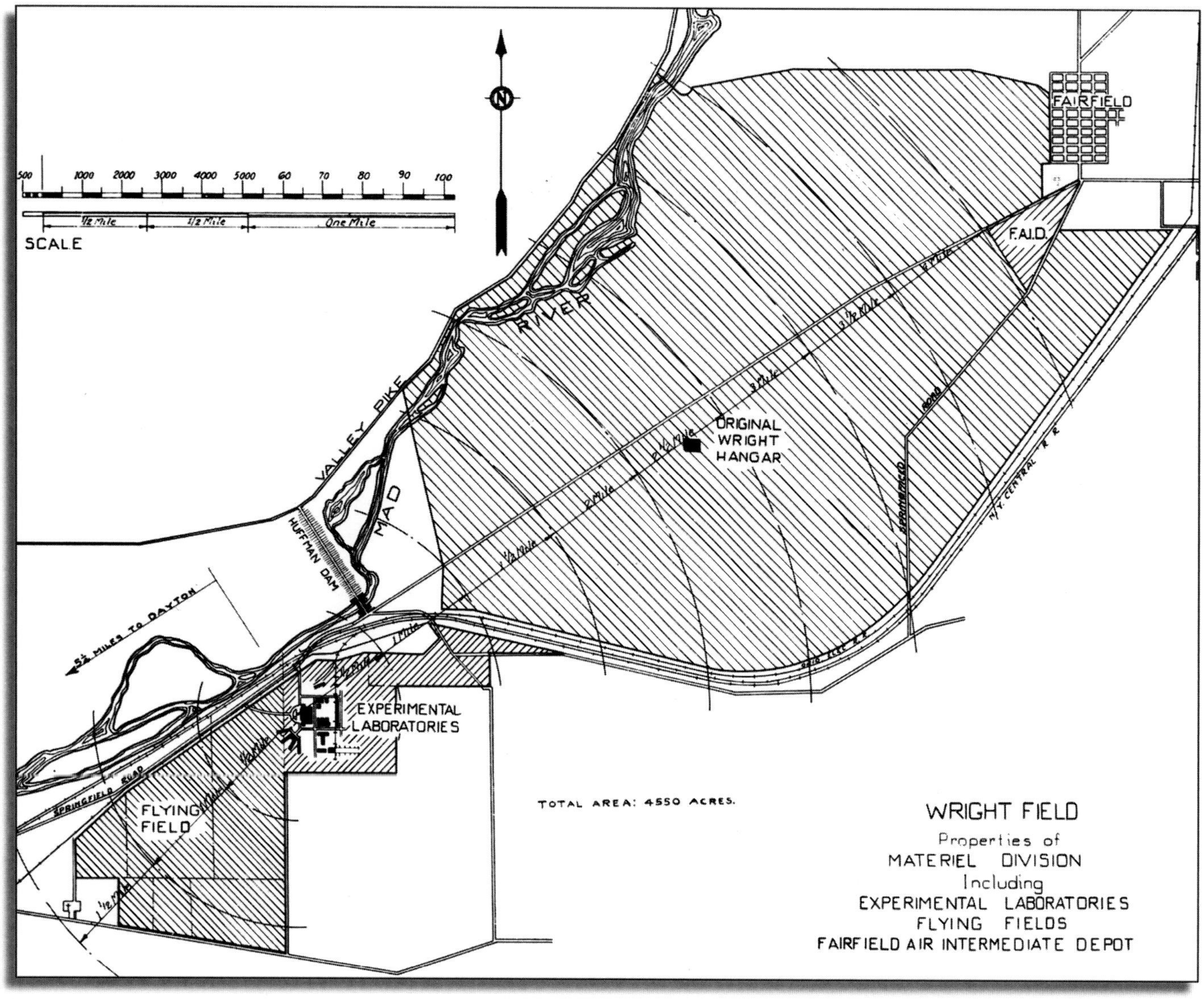

Outline of Wright Field facilities, 1927. The 4,550 acres included the Materiel Division experimental laboratories, two flying fields, and the maintenance and supply facilities of the Fairfield Air Intermediate Depot.

was the first Air Corps production trainer for pursuit pilots. Initially manufactured in 1927, the AT-4 used a water-cooled, 180-horsepower engine and had a top speed of 126 mph. It carried two .30-caliber machine guns. The companion AT-5, also produced in 1927, was equipped with a 220-horsepower engine.[50]

Two other biplane pursuits equipped with water-cooled engines were the Fokker PW-7 and the Boeing PW-9. The Fokker had been imported to Wright Field on a trial basis from the company's plant in the Netherlands. It was equipped with a 440-horsepower Curtiss D-12 engine with a top speed of 150 mph. The Boeing—last of the water-cooled engine type—also had a 440-horsepower Curtiss D-12 engine with a top speed of 155 mph. Armament on both airplanes consisted of twin .30-caliber machine guns.

Of the three pursuit airplanes exhibited on the FADR tarmac, only the Curtiss was long-lived. In 1927, two P-1 Hawks took first and second place in the Spokane, Washington, air races with respective top speeds of 201 and 189 mph. Impressed with these performances, the Materiel Division ordered eight more airplanes for further service testing at Wright Field. Continued experimentation with engines and improved streamlining during the subsequent five years produced more-powerful and faster airplanes and resulted in the P-6E Hawk pursuit aircraft.[51] In the opinion of many pursuit pilots, the P-6E was one of the most beautiful fighters ever built. In July 1931, an order for 46 of these airplanes was placed with the Curtiss Airplane Division of Curtiss-Wright. The P-6E series remained in active service until succeeded by the Boeing P-26A, the Air Corps' first all-metal monoplane, in 1934.[52]

The two categories of combat airplanes with the largest number of representatives at the Wright Field dedication were the Observation (O) and its twin, the Corps Observation (CO). The eight airplanes in these categories displayed at FADR were: the Curtiss O-1, the Douglas O-2A and O-2H, the Fokker CO-4A, the Engineering Division XCO-5 and XCO-6, the Thomas-Morse XO-6, and the Atlantic XCO-8.

The Curtiss and Douglas airplane companies were the principal suppliers of airplanes within the observation category. A development of the Curtiss O-1 was especially satisfactory for observation missions where speed and maneuverability were prime requirements. The Curtiss O-1B and the O-11B mounted Curtiss D-12 and Liberty 12A engines respectively. Both models had 38-foot wingspans, lengths of 28 feet 4 inches, and top speeds of 135 mph.[53]

The Curtiss A-3 attack aircraft on display was developed in response to the needs of tactical organizations within the

Air Corps. In the mid-1920s, emphasis was placed on developing specific attack and bombardment airplanes as temporary expedients until an "ideal service type" could be identified. The Curtiss A-3 and Douglas XA-2 were modified from standard observation to attack airplanes by adding machine guns in the wings and light bombs in the fuselage. The A-3 became the Air Corps' first production attack airplane. It was a two-seat, open cockpit biplane with a 435-horsepower Curtiss V-1150 engine. The vehicle carried six .30-caliber machine guns and 300 pounds of bombs and had a top speed of 140 mph. The Douglas XA-2 was a variation of the O-2 family of Douglas observation biplanes. The XA-2 featured a 420-horsepower Liberty V-1410 engine with a top speed of 130 mph and a range of 500 miles.[54]

The three largest airplanes on display at FADR were two bombers and a transport. In addition to size, their power and load capacity reflected a significant progression in those categories of airplanes since World War I.

The Huff-Daland (Keystone) XHB-1 Super Cyclops bomber was a single-engine biplane, an outgrowth of the company's LB-1 Pegasus light biplane bomber. (Huff-Daland Airplanes Inc. was reorganized as the Keystone Aircraft Corporation in 1927.) The Super Cyclops' wingspan reached 84 feet 7 inches, and its length was 59 feet 7 inches. It carried a four-man crew, six .30-caliber machine guns, and 4,000 pounds of bombs. Built in 1926, this machine represented the Air Corps' only single-engine heavy bomber experiment.

Just a few weeks prior to the Wright Field dedication, the newest Air Corps bomber arrived for testing and evaluation. This was the Curtiss XB-2 Condor biplane, equipped with two 600-horsepower Curtiss engines. Wingspan totaled 90 feet and length was 47 feet 5 inches. The airplane carried a five-man crew, six .30-caliber machine guns, and 4,000 pounds of bombs. Maximum speed was 128 mph and service ceiling was 15,000 feet.[55] A unique aspect of the aircraft featured gunners placed in turrets in the rear of each engine nacelle.

The Fokker C-2 trimotor transport built by the Atlantic Aircraft Corporation was the most popular airplane at the October 1927 exhibit. The Atlantic Aircraft Corporation went into business in 1924 with Anthony Fokker as the company's first president. Atlantic-Fokker, as it was sometimes known, became General

The XHB-1 Super Cyclops was an outgrowth of the Huff-Daland (Keystone) LB-1 Pegasus light biplane bomber and the XB-1 single-engine Cyclops. When the Air Corps decided that bombers should have two engines, the XB-1 was cancelled and Huff-Daland offered the twin-engine XHB-1. The gunner sat on a retractable bombing platform beneath the plane (top). The original underpowered engines were replaced, and the aircraft was redesignated XB-1B (the XB-1A was the Engineering Division's Bristol fighter).

The Curtiss XB-2 Condor, a derivative of the Martin MB-2, at McCook Field, August 1927 (above). The airplane had six guns in three positions. The man in the gunner's cockpit is identified as Mr. McDaniels (below).

Aviation Corporation, an affiliate of General Motors, in May 1930. Fokker-designed products of Atlantic and General Aviation commonly became known as Fokker airplanes. First manufactured in 1925, the Fokker C-2 was already making headlines in the world's newspapers. In its original configuration, the high-wing cabin plane had a wingspan of 63 feet 4 inches, a length of 49 feet 2 inches, and a height of 12 feet 9 inches. The original power plants were three 220-horsepower, nine-cylinder, air-cooled, Wright Whirlwind radial engines. Top and cruising speeds were 122 mph and 100 mph respectively.[56] The Fokker fuselage and wings were constructed from plywood, in contrast to the equally famous and much safer all-metal Ford trimotor transport.

A Fokker transport made the first flight over the North Pole on May 2, 1926, with Lieutenant Commander Richard E. Byrd, U.S. Navy, as navigator and Floyd Bennett as pilot. Thirteen months later, two airplanes of the same type flew across the Pacific and Atlantic oceans respectively—on the same day! Wright Field and the Dayton area had a special interest in the Pacific adventure, for that airplane (*Bird of Paradise*) was modified locally and one member of the two-man crew was assigned to the Materiel Division.

Curtiss Condors of the 11th Bombardment Squadron in formation (*Bob and Dottie Gheen*)

The Bird of Paradise

In September 1926 the Materiel Division purchased a Fokker C-2 to fulfill a special mission, the testing of experimental radio directional beacons as navigational aids. Plans called for one such beacon to be installed near San Francisco and another on the island of Maui in the Hawaiian archipelago. An airplane was to fly between Oakland, California, and Wheeler Field, Hawaii, guided solely by the beacons. If such navigational aids proved effective, both military and civilian aviation would take a collective, giant stride forward. There was also an unpublished reason for the experiment—to generate favorable publicity for the Air Corps in its struggle to secure more funds and better airplanes so it could expand its mission beyond the coastlines.

Shortly after the C-2 was accepted, it flew to FADR where Wright Field technicians installed additional fuel tanks and made other modifications to prepare it for the perilous Pacific flight. Among the experts engaged in this effort were the assistant chief of the Materials Laboratory, L. B. Hendricks; aeronautical engineer Fred Herman; navigation engineers Bradley Jones and Victor E. Showalter; radio engineers Clayton C. Shangeraw and Ford Studebaker; and airplane mechanic James Rivers.

Pilot for the historic flight was Lieutenant Lester J. Maitland, assistant executive officer to the Assistant Secretary of War for Aeronautics, Washington, D.C., and former McCook Field test pilot. The navigator was Lieutenant Albert F. Hegenberger of McCook Field.

Lieutenants Lester J. Maitland (right) and Albert F. Hegenberger, crew of the historic 1927 C-2 Hawaiian Flight

TRANSOCEANIC PIONEERS

In no subsequent year did the aviation world thrill to as many spectacular achievements as were flown in 1927. All involved extremely hazardous, nonstop transoceanic flights that tested to the maximum degree the courage and professionalism of the aviators and the mettle of their machines.

Perhaps the most famous flight, logged forever in the hearts of aviation buffs, was the May 20-21 nonstop, 3,610-mile mission of Charles A. Lindbergh from Minneola, Long Island, New York, to Paris, France, in 33 hours 29 minutes 30 seconds. His Ryan airplane, the *Spirit of St. Louis*, was a high-wing monoplane equipped with a single Wright J-5C engine.

On June 4-5, 1927, Clarence D. Chamberlain and Charles Levine flew the high-wing Bellanca single-engine monoplane *Columbia* from Roosevelt Field, New York, to the outskirts of Berlin, Germany. The nonstop 3,911-mile flight was made in 43 hours 49 minutes.

Yet a third Atlantic crossing was made June 29-July 1, 1927, when Lieutenant Commander Richard E. Byrd, U.S. Navy, and a three-man crew flew the Fokker T-2 high-wing cabin plane *America* from Roosevelt Field, New York, to Ver-Sur-Mer, France. The 3,477-mile flight was completed in 46 hours 6 minutes and established a new record for a four-man transoceanic flight.

These flights, along with the experimental navigation mission of the *Bird of Paradise*, were more than transitory banner headline achievements. These exploits made the general public permanently "air-minded," in the words of Brigadier General William E. Gillmore, chief of the Air Corps Materiel Division at Wright Field. They were also, General Gillmore observed, a "most convincing demonstration of the improved reliability of aircraft," which had been obtained only through "constant experimentation and service use" of Air Corps equipment before it was released for quantity production.

Sources: Air Force Pamphlet 190-2-2, p 25; Brigadier General W. E. Gillmore, "Review of Air Corps Developments in 1927," press release prepared by Materiel Division headquarters, Wright Field, January 31, 1928.

Charles Lindbergh visits Wright Field, June 22, 1927. Left to right: Orville Wright; Major John F. Curry, former McCook Field commander; Lindbergh; and Brigadier General William E. Gillmore; chief, Air Corps Materiel Division.

Fokker C-2 *Bird of Paradise*

The *Bird of Paradise* circles Wheeler Field before landing. The first-ever aerial crossing from the mainland to Hawaii was completed in 25 hours and 50 minutes on June 28-29, 1927.

Lieutenants Maitland and Hegenberger decorated with traditional Hawaiian leis (*United States Air Force Museum*)

Hegenberger, a former chief of the Instrument and Navigation Branch, was a pioneer in the development of aerial navigation.[57]

The intrepid airmen picked up the modified Fokker C-2, named the *Bird of Paradise*, at FADR on June 15, 1927, and headed toward California. On this "shakedown" flight, a select crew of Wright Field civilian experts closely monitored the performance of both airplane and equipment in preparation for the transoceanic flight. At Rockwell Field, San Diego, a 70-gallon auxiliary fuel tank was installed in the Fokker's already cramped fuselage.

The radio directional beacon system to be tested on the flight to Hawaii was described by Lieutenant Maitland in a contemporary article:[58]

> An electric current [is] sent through the air at a set wave length and forms an airway along which the plane travels to its destination. The airway has three parallel zones—the T, N, and A zones. The T zone is the center of the road. It is about two miles wide at its maximum. While his ship stays in the center zone the pilot gets the [Morse] code letter T through his receiving set. If he veers to the right the T changes to an A; if he swings to the left the T gives way to N. All the pilot has to do when he hears N or A is to correct his course.

The beacon also operated three lights on the aircraft instrument panel. A white light indicated the airplane was on the correct or true course; a red light indicated the airplane had strayed to the left, and a green light warned when it wandered too far to the right.

At 7:15 a.m. on June 28, the *Bird of Paradise*, with Lieutenants Maitland and Hegenberger aboard, took off from the Oakland Municipal Airport. Shortly after departure the new earth-induction compass failed, and Lieutenant Hegenberger was forced to navigate by other means. The crew's radio receiver also failed and could be used only intermittently throughout the long flight. Lieutenant Hegenberger resorted primarily to celestial navigation, making sextant observations through a port located in the top of the aircraft's fuselage. He also took drift readings and utilized basic dead reckoning techniques throughout the flight. His navigation was so accurate that the flight ended directly on target.[59]

By optimistic estimate, the *Bird of Paradise* should have touched down at Wheeler Field on Oahu about 3:00 a.m. Hawaiian Standard Time, June 29. Island residents and military people turned out by the thousands, bringing picnic baskets under their arms to welcome the fliers. After waiting for two hours, much of the crowd sadly concluded that the airplane and its crew had probably been lost at sea. Not so. Lieutenant Hegenberger had sighted the Kauai lighthouse on schedule, but then had to circle offshore for about three hours waiting for first light and clear visibility of the Wheeler runway. The airplane landed at 6:29 a.m., Hawaiian time, thus completing a 2,407-mile journey in 25 hours and 50 minutes.

The courageous aviators were feted by the military and civilian communities. "Feather capes of the Hawaiian Alii—the royalty—were presented amid appropriate ceremony at a banquet at Waikiki's plush New Royal Hawaiian Hotel."[60] The officers returned to California several days later aboard the Army transport *Maui*. Both received the Distinguished Flying Cross and were awarded the Mackay Trophy for 1927.

Early Wright Field Developments

Development of 500- and 600-horsepower engines to the point where they could be mounted in existing airplanes became a major milestone in 1928. These improved power plants included the Curtiss H-1640 hexagon, air-cooled, radial engine; the Curtiss V-1570, V-type, water-cooled engine; the Pratt & Whitney R-1960 Hornet air-cooled, radial engine; and the Wright R-1570 Cyclone and V-1640 air-cooled, radial engines.

Over the next several years, progress continued to focus on improvements in power plants and in the "aerodynamical, flying, and structural characteristics of service airplanes."[61] Three significant achievements, for example, were realized in the area of improved engines. One was the development of ring-type cowling for cooling air-cooled radial engines. This innovation increased a typical pursuit airplane's speed by 17 mph. Another gain was the first successful application of high-temperature liquid cooling to water-cooled engines, which reduced the size of the radiator by 70 percent. The third area of significant research was continued development of anti-knock aviation gasoline.

Many improvements were made in aerodynamic and structural characteristics. Drag was reduced through improved airfoil design, retractable landing gear, faired chassis, and better streamlining of cockpit enclosures, windshields, and other external portions of the airplane. Streamlining was also improved by "varying the aspect ratio of the fuselage and by adding ring cowling." Other efforts at improving the overall structure explored using wings of various sections as "high, low, and mid-wing monoplanes with single- and twin-engined installations and in some cases by using slots, flaps, and floating ailerons."[62] Development of the all-metal airplane continued "with a decided tendency toward monoplane monocoque construction because of its more efficient structural and aerodynamic qualities."[63]

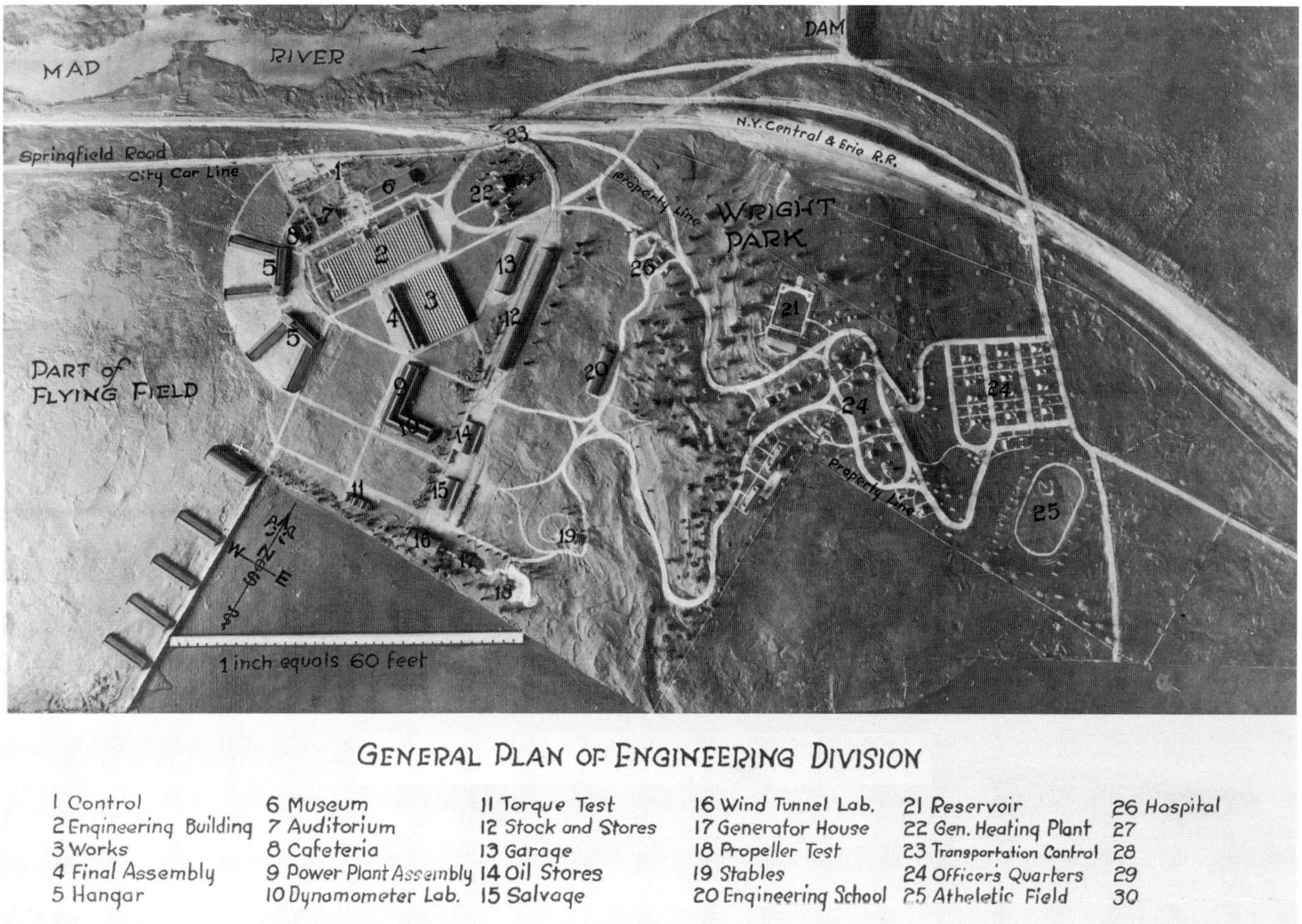

GENERAL TYPES OF AIR VEHICLES OF THE LATE 1920s AND EARLY 1930s

Class	Designation
Attack	A
Bombardment	B
Transport (cargo, ambulance, workshop)	C
Observation	O
Pursuit	P
Photographic	F*
Primary Training	PT
Basic Training	BT

* During fiscal year 1934, the designation Photographic (F) was discontinued since all photographic work was henceforth to be accomplished from observation airplanes. In a related move, the Observation category divided to include a separate classification for Observation Amphibian (OA).

The specific status of each vehicle type was defined by the use of prefixes:

Experimental Status	X
Service Test Status	Y, Y1
Obsolete Status	Z

The Curtiss D-12D engine on the A-3 Falcon, 1927 (*United States Air Force Museum*)

Curtiss A-3 Falcon, February 15, 1928

Attack Airplanes

In the attack category, the Curtiss Falcon A-3 biplane was the standard attack vehicle in the late 1920s. The Curtiss A-3A served as "limited standard," while the A-3B served as a "substitute standard" attack aircraft. Improvements in the A-3B model included Frise ailerons, oleo-type landing gear, and simplified, wing-gun installations. By 1930, the A-3B had become the standard attack type.

During fiscal year 1930, the Materiel Division purchased two additional airplanes for evaluation purposes, a Fokker XA-7 and a Curtiss XA-8. Both were single-engine, two-place, low-wing monoplanes of all-metal, monocoque construction. Monocoque was defined as a fuselage structure in which "the stressed outer skin (of metal or plywood) carries all or a major portion of the torsional and bending stresses."

The Fokker XA-7 was equipped with a 600-horsepower, Prestone-cooled, Curtiss G1V-1570 engine. Prestone was a commercial name for ethylene glycol. The XA-7 had a cantilever-type wing, carried 400 pounds of bombs, and was armed with four fixed, M-2, .30-caliber machine guns (two in each lower wing firing outside the propeller disc) and one flexible machine gun mounted on the rear cockpit. The Curtiss XA-8 had a direct-drive, Prestone-cooled, V-1570 engine and a multiple-spar, cantilever wing with external bracing, slots, and flaps. Armament was identical to the XA-7.

By the beginning of fiscal year 1932, the XA-8 had progressed to the point where a service test contract was let for 13 aircraft of this type. (The XA-7 was not produced in quantity.) Three A-8 Shrikes were delivered by the end of the year. The Shrike had a wingspan of 44 feet and a length of 32 feet 6 inches. It was powered with a 600-horsepower Curtiss V-1570 Conqueror engine with a top speed of 196 mph. The Shrike featured two enclosed cockpits "fully convertible for the pilot and semi-convertible for the gunner."[64]

Subsequent improvements in the Curtiss A-8 design led to the development of the Curtiss A-10, with a Pratt & Whitney R-1690 engine, and the Curtiss A-12, powered by an R-1820-21 air-cooled engine. The Air Corps purchased 46 model A-12 Shrikes during fiscal year 1933.

Materiel Division engineers also monitored developments in attack/pursuit aircraft made by the Consolidated Aircraft Corporation, such as the four A-11 airplanes produced for the Air Corps during the early 1930s. The A-11, which also carried P-30 and PB-2 designations, was an all-metal, low-wing monoplane with an unbraced, cantilever wing; enclosed cockpit; and retractable landing gear. The power plant was a liquid-cooled, 675-horsepower, V-1570 engine with turbosupercharger and a top speed of 225 mph. The two-seat airplane carried five guns and 300 pounds of bombs.[65]

Curtiss XA-8 all-metal monoplane (*United States Air Force Museum*)

Flexible machine gun mounted on the rear cockpit of the XA-8 (*United States Air Force Museum*)

PB-2A of the 33rd Pursuit Squadron, 8th Pursuit Group, during the West Coast Maneuvers of 1937 over Muroc Dry Lake in California. This aircraft sustained damage to its right gear, wing, and fuel tank during a full squadron takeoff. After gaining altitude, the group commander and crew successfully bailed out. (*United States Air Force Museum*)

Keystone LB-6 (serial number 29-12), May 1930. Oil on the wings and tail was from the plane's Cyclone R-1750 engines.

Dynamic test of the Keystone B-3A landing gear. The airplane structure is in position for a six-inch drop. (*United States Air Force Museum*)

Bombardment Airplanes

Steady progress occurred in the development of bombardment airplanes during the 1930s. The procurement of the Boeing B-9 and the Martin B-10 in the early years of the decade represented important steps in the design of true bombardment aircraft and presaged the development of the bombers that would play a deciding role in World War II.

During 1928, six prototype bombers were tested at Wright Field. Two were authorized for limited production: the Curtiss B-2 Condor and the Keystone XLB-6. Both were twin-engine biplanes; the B-2 had two 600-horsepower Curtiss V-1570 engines and the Keystone featured two 525-horsepower Wright R-1750 power plants.

By fiscal year 1930, the Keystone B-3A biplane, powered with twin 525-horsepower, direct-drive, Pratt & Whitney R-1690-A engines, had become the standard Air Corps bomber. It had a single rudder, unlike the prototype LB-6 series that had dual rudders. The B-3A had a span of 74 feet 9 inches, and a length of 48 feet 10 inches. It carried a four-man crew, three guns, and 2,500 pounds of bombs. Its top speed was 114 mph.

During fiscal year 1930, the Air Corps began pushing for development of a twin-engine, monoplane bomber "suitable for fast day-and-night missions." Materiel Division specifications called for a machine equipped with Prestone-cooled V-1570 engines, capable of carrying 1,250 pounds of bombs, with a service ceiling of 18,000 feet and a top speed of 170 mph.

Five manufacturers submitted either prototypes or designs for the new bomber. Ford submitted the XB-906, similar in design to the company's C-4A transport. The XB-906 was powered with three SR-1340-D supercharged engines and carried a ton of bombs on a rack within the fuselage.

Boeing submitted the XB-901, an all-metal, low-wing monoplane powered with two 600-horsepower Pratt & Whitney R-1860 engines, featuring retractable landing gear and external bomb racks beneath the fuselage. The aircraft had a four-man crew and could carry 2,000 pounds of bombs.

The Fokker XB-8 bomber candidate was similar to the Fokker XO-27, a model previously submitted as an observation airplane. The XB-8 had two 600-horsepower, Prestone-cooled, V-1570 engines and could carry 1,100 pounds of bombs on a rack installed in the fuselage.

Keystone Aircraft designed the XB-908, a low-wing, all-metal monoplane with two G1V-1570 geared engines and retractable landing gear. The bomber could carry a five-man crew and a ton of bombs.

Douglas submitted the XB-7 (originally designated XO-36), which had two 600-horsepower, Prestone-cooled, Curtiss V-1570 geared engines and externally mounted bomb racks below the fuselage.[66]

Boeing's XB-901 survived the rigorous competition to become the B-9 bomber. When it reached the production and acquisition stages in 1932, it represented a new concept in aerodynamic design. The mid-wing, all-metal monoplane had a span of 76 feet 10 inches, a length of 52 feet, and a height of 12 feet. Its twin Pratt & Whitney R-1860-11 engines gave the aircraft a top speed of 188 mph with a ceiling of 20,750 feet and range of 540 miles. Despite a 14,320-pound gross weight, the bomber was comparable in speed to contemporary pursuit airplanes. Although the B-9 had open cockpits in tandem for the four crewmembers, it had the "big bomber" look and raised the hopes of airmen who believed in strategic bombardment.[67]

Boeing B-9 bomber and Boeing P-26 pursuit. Note the Wright Field "spearhead" insignia painted on the fuselage of each airplane. (*United States Air Force Museum*)

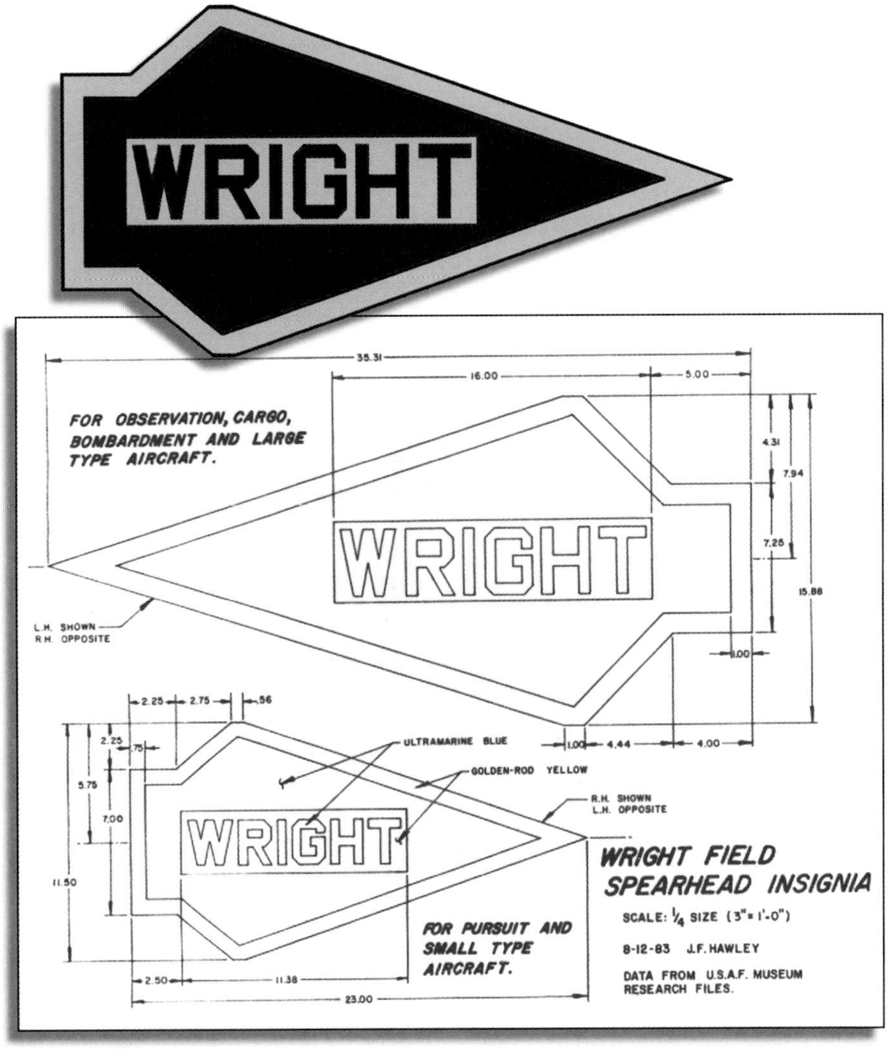

The Wright Field "spearhead" insignia is believed to have been designed by Major Hugh Knerr (later general) and authorized for use on Wright Field aircraft no later than January 1931. The spearhead "pointed the way forward." The emblem also became the model for a standard Materiel Division aircraft insignia for Air Corps air depots. In 1942, Technical Order 01-1-21 directed that the spearhead be replaced by the emblem of the Air Service Command, an internal gear wheel overlaid with a four-bladed propeller. Despite the order, the spearhead emblem continued in use at several depots as late as December 1953.

Douglas XB-7 experimental light bomber

Martin B-10B at Wright Field, December 1936

Airmen of the 9th Bomb Squadron load a bomb onto a Martin B-12 bomber

The Douglas XB-7 later found acceptance as an experimental light bomber, and seven were ordered for service testing. It became the first twin-engine monoplane bomber in Air Corps history, with a wingspan of 65 feet 3 inches, a length of 46 feet 7 inches, and a top speed of 182 mph. The vehicle had retractable landing gear and carried a four-man crew, two guns, and 1,200 pounds of bombs.[68]

During fiscal year 1933, the Martin Company produced the B-907, a mid-wing light bomber featuring a full, stressed-skin, box cantilever wing developed originally by the Materiel Division. After initial flight tests, during which the airplane achieved a top speed of 196 mph, the B-907 returned to the manufacturer for modifications. Significant changes included a slight increase in wing area, the use of wing fillets, reworking of the rudder, alteration of the engine nacelles, and the installation of new twin 775-horsepower Wright 1820 engines. A front gun

Alaskan Flight personnel at Bolling Field, July 19, 1934. Their 8,290-mile, round-trip odyssey to Fairbanks, Alaska, and return lasted 33 days and involved extensive mapping of airways in and out of Alaska. (*United States Air Force Museum*)

B-12 in flight

turret was installed also, and the airplane's bomb racks were relocated inside the fuselage. One authority indirectly attributed much of the Martin machine's success to the advanced wing designed by Major Carl F. Greene, an expert on structural design assigned to the Materiel Division at Wright Field.

Upon return to Wright Field the airplane was redesignated the XB-907A (XB-10) and tested as a heavy bomber. According to the official report, "the modifications produced the desired results and the airplane attained a high speed of 207 miles per hour at 4,000 feet altitude and a service ceiling of 21,000 feet."[69] According to a second account, when the airplane returned for testing in October 1932, it was nicknamed the "Flying Whale." Its top speed of 207 mph made "all other bombers then in the Army obsolete," including the Boeing B-9 and the Keystone series.[70]

After reviewing the bomber's performance and evaluation reports, the Headquarters Air Corps Bombardment Group (Office, Chief of Air Corps) recommended the purchase of "additional airplanes of this type to be designated the YB-10 and the YB-12." Both established historical "firsts" although the B-10 gained wider and lasting fame. Their respective specifications were:

	B-10	B-12
Wingspan	70 feet 6 inches	70 feet 6 inches
Length	44 feet 9 inches	45 feet 3 inches
Engines	Two 775-horsepower Wright Cyclone R-1820-33	Two 775-horsepower Pratt & Whitney R-1690-11

The B-10 had a gross weight of 16,400 pounds and a maximum speed of 212 mph, with a ceiling of 24,200 feet and range of 1,240 miles. The bomber carried a four-man crew, three guns, and 2,260 pounds of bombs. It was the first twin-engine, all-metal, mid-wing monoplane bomber produced in quantity. Salient features included an enclosed cockpit, a power-operated turret, retractable landing gear, newly designed engine cowling, and the famous Norden bombsight.[71]

The B-12 varied only slightly from the B-10. It had the distinction of being the Air Corps' first coastal-defense, "float-fitted," long-range bomber. Like the B-10, it had retractable landing gear and carried a four-man crew, three guns, and 2,260 pounds of bombs. Top speed was 215 mph.[72]

The Air Corps ordered 119 B-10s and 32 B-12s during the 1933-1936 period, at an individual cost of $55,000, the largest procurement of bomber aircraft since World War I. The Martin B-10 remained in the Air Corps' active inventory until the Douglas B-18 and Boeing B-17 arrived in the late 1930s. China and the Netherlands flew export models of the B-10 against Japanese targets prior to and during the early months of World War II.

After the first months of operation, the Air Corps became so confident of the B-10's reliability and durability that Lieutenant Colonel Henry H. Arnold led a flight of 10 bombers on an 8,290-mile round trip between Bolling Field, D.C., and Fairbanks, Alaska. His mission was to test the concept of reinforcing outlying possessions by air. Arnold and his crew carried out an unprecedented survey during the month-long flight, mapping airways in and out of Alaska from Siberia and across the Arctic Circle. This historic Alaskan journey occurred between July 19 and August 20, 1934. The northbound flight required 25 hours and 30 minutes; the return took 26 hours. For this spectacular flight, Colonel Arnold received the Distinguished Flying Cross, and the Mackay Trophy on behalf of the crews.[73]

GENERAL HENRY "HAP" ARNOLD

Lieutenant Henry Arnold took flying lessons at the Wright School of Aviation at Simms Station in 1911, and the Wright brothers taught him not only the mechanics of flight, but also to believe that nothing was impossible. It was an attitude that Arnold said shaped the future of the United States Air Force, and that molded Arnold's illustrious Air Force career. Arnold set a world altitude record a year after receiving his pilot's license, and he won two Mackay trophies for daring flights he made in 1912 and 1934. During World War I, Arnold operated 30 training schools as assistant director of the Office of Military Aeronautics. In the summer of 1929, Arnold became commander of the Fairfield Air Depot and head of the Field Service Section of the Materiel Division. A year later he became the executive officer to the chief of the Materiel Division at Wright Field. While stationed in the Dayton area, he often had Orville Wright as a guest for Sunday dinner.

In 1938, Arnold assumed command of the Air Corps, and on the eve of World War II, he became the chief of the Army Air Forces. In April 1941, Arnold went to England and saw the Gloster E.28/39, a British plane with a jet propulsion engine. He took immediate action to ensure that the United States would not be left behind in the jet age; 18 months later the United States had its first jet plane, the Bell XP-59A. In 1943, Arnold became a four-star general and was made commander of all the flying services. Arnold's leadership before and during the war contributed significantly to the development of America's air power, and for this reason he received a very rare fifth star on December 15, 1944.

Arnold retired in 1946, but three years later Congress gave him the title of "General of the Air Force," a distinction shared by no other person in U.S. military history. Arnold passed away at age 63 at his home near Sonoma, California, in 1950.

Sources: Laura Romesburg, *Henry Harley ("Hap") Arnold*, (Wright-Patterson Air Force Base; July 19, 1994); United States Air Force Link Biographies, *General Henry H. Arnold*, online at http://www.af.mil/news/biographies/arnold_hh.html; James O. Young, "Riding England's Coattails: The Army Air Forces and the Turbojet Revolution," *Technology and the Air Force: A Retrospective Assessment*, edited by Jacob Neufeld, Geroge M. Watson, Jr., and David Chenoweth (Washington, D.C., 1997), pp 9, 16, 22.

Transport Airplanes

During the early years at Wright Field, the "standard" airplane in the cargo or transport category was the Atlantic C-2 (*Bird of Paradise* model). It was later joined by the C-2A, an improved version featuring an increased wing area, an additional 90-gallon fuel tank, and "a more ideal ambulance arrangement."[74]

In the early 1930s, transport developments aimed generally toward a new ideal: a single-engine monoplane that could operate more economically than the multi-engine models. Materiel Division engineers and test pilots evaluated new transport aircraft in the early part of the decade as a number of manufacturers vied for acceptance. Among the early airplanes tested were the Ford C-3A, C-4 and C-4A; the Atlantic C-5; the Sikorsky C-6 and C-6A (the Air Corps' first amphibian cargo transport); the Atlantic C-7 and C-7A; and the Ford C-9. These were all twin-engine or trimotor models. The Atlantic-Fokker trimotor F-10A cargo monoplane was specially modified, redesignated as the C-5, and assigned to the Assistant Secretary of War for Aeronautics, F. Trubee Davison. Only one model was manufactured.[75]

The Fairchild XC-8 was one of the first single-engine transports tested. It was modified so that in addition to its transport/passenger capacity, it could be used as a special photographic airplane (F-1, UC-96). It was equipped with a 410-horsepower Pratt & Whitney Wasp R-1340 engine. The airplane accommodated a three-man crew and seven passengers at a top speed of 140 mph.

During fiscal year 1931, General Aviation Corporation (formerly Atlantic-Fokker) sold 20 Y1C-14 single-engine airplanes to the Air Corps for service tests. The Y1C-14 was a parasol-type monoplane with a conventional, fabric-covered, steel-tube fuselage and a plywood-covered cantilever wing. The high-wing cabin plane accommodated a pilot, six passengers, and 215 pounds of baggage.[76]

One Y1C-14 was converted into an ambulance and redesignated the YC-15. The remainder were designated C-14 and performed credibly in the transport service organized by the Materiel Division during fiscal year 1932. The new service flew both freight and passengers throughout the division's air depot control area (including Fairfield Air Depot on Patterson Field).[77]

Douglas Y1C-21 Dolphin amphibian transport, 1933

The Air Corps' first amphibian cargo transport, the Sikorsky C-6A

Curtiss YC-30 Condor transport (*United States Air Force Museum*)

Bellanca Y1C-27 Airbus

During fiscal year 1932, the American Airplane and Engine Corporation (Fairchild) provided four models of its Y1C-24 Pilgrim for service tests. The Pilgrim was a single-engine, high-wing monoplane that accommodated a pilot, eight passengers, and 131 pounds of baggage. Without seats, the airplane could transport airplane engines or two standard litters for medical evacuation.[78]

The Bellanca Company's Y1C-27 Airbus was an additional entry in the transport airplane competition. It was a high-wing monoplane of somewhat unusual construction in that the external wing bracing, the landing gear, and the fuselage served as additional lifting surfaces. Another unusual feature was its "fancy pants," or housing for its non-retractable landing gear struts. The airplane mounted a single, geared, Pratt & Whitney Hornet engine and normally accommodated a two-man crew, 10 passengers, and 142 pounds of baggage.[79] During 1933, 10 C-27s were delivered to various Materiel Division depots for service tests.

Within the special, high-speed transport category, eight airplanes were placed in service testing in the early 1930s. Consolidated provided one C-11A and three Y1C-22 Fleetster high-wing monoplanes with monocoque fuselages and wood cantilever wings. Lockheed submitted two entries, the Y1C-12 Vega and the Y1C-17 Speed Vega powered by single Pratt & Whitney R-1340 engines. Northrop manufactured three YC-19 Alphas, low-wing monoplanes equipped with 450-horsepower Pratt & Whitney R-1340 engines.[80]

In fiscal year 1933, the major development in high-speed transport was the purchase of two Curtiss-Wright C-30 Condors. The C-30 was a twin-engine biplane powered by two Wright R-1820 engines. The C-30 could carry 15 passengers and 4,000 pounds of cargo at a top speed of 130 mph. (This same type of airplane was used by Rear Admiral Richard E. Byrd, U.S. Navy, on his second Antarctic expedition in October 1933.)

In the amphibian transport field, in-service aircraft in the early 1930s included the Sikorsky C-6A with twin R-1340 engines, the Douglas Y1C-21 Dolphin, and the Douglas Y1C-26A, also called Dolphin. The Y1C-21 was a twin-engine, high-wing monoplane with a 60-foot wingspan and a length of 43 feet 10 inches. It

This Fokker C-14 made the world's first entirely automatic landing at Patterson Field, August 1937.

carried seven persons, including the pilot, and had a top speed of 140 mph. The aircraft were dispersed among Army bases in the Panama Canal Zone, Hawaii, and the Philippine Islands. The Douglas Y1C-26A was built on similar lines, but had a longer flying range and could carry one additional passenger. It was purchased for newly organized coastal patrol and frontier defense. Two other Dolphins procured in 1933 were designated C-29s and were equipped with Pratt & Whitney R-1340 engines.

Observation Airplanes

In the closing years of the 1920s, the Air Corps observation airplane category included observation, corps observation, and amphibian type aircraft. The observation type inventory was dominated by the Curtiss O-1 Falcon family (especially the O-1B and O-1G models) and the Douglas O-2 family (particularly the O-2C, O-2H, and O-2K models). The Loening OA-2 became the standard amphibian aircraft in the observation class.

The Thomas-Morse O-19 series, developed in 1928 and 1929, became the first successful, all-metal observation biplane. A total of 175 O-19s were produced for the Air Corps.[81] The Douglas O-25 series was introduced in 1929. It was followed in 1930 by development of the Douglas O-38 series. Models of both families became standard Air Corps types in the early 1930s, particularly the O-25A, the O-25C, the O-38, the O-38B, and the O-38E.[82]

To meet the need for long-range missions with maximum reliability, development of the Fokker YO-27 was encour-

Douglas O-38 observation biplane at Wright Field

Curtiss O-1 Falcon observation airplane fitted with wing ballast tanks (*United States Air Force Museum*)

aged. The YO-27 and the Y1O-27 became the first monoplane observation airplanes in the Air Corps. Both were twin-engine, high-wing aircraft with retractable landing gear. The wing featured veneer-covered, wood construction with watertight bulkheads for flotation. The fuselage was of conventional, steel-tube construction, fabric covered, with an efficient, convertible enclosure for the pilot's cockpit. Six YO-27s and six Y1O-27s were delivered to the Materiel Division during 1931 and 1932 for service tests.

Five Douglas YO-35 high-wing monoplanes were scheduled for service testing in 1933. This aircraft had an externally braced gull wing, part-metal monocoque fuselage, and twin 600-horsepower G1V-1570-E engines.[83]

On order in 1933 were two single-engine-type observation aircraft, the Douglas O-31 and the Curtiss YO-40A. The O-31 was an all-metal, butterfly-wing monoplane, with a wingspan of 45 feet 8 inches, and a length of 33 feet 10 inches. It was a two-seater with enclosed cockpits, a 600-horsepower Curtiss V-1570 engine, two guns, a sliding canopy, and a top speed of 190 mph. The Curtiss YO-40A was of "sesquiplane" construction, and used the Wright Cyclone SR-1820-E supercharged radial engine. A sesquiplane was a biplane having one wing of less than half the area of the other.

At the end of fiscal year 1933 the standard Corps Observation airplanes were the Curtiss O-39 Falcon; Douglas O-25C and O-38E/F, and the Thomas-Morse O-19E. Seventeen earlier models produced by these three manufacturers were classified as limited standard types.

Pursuit Airplanes

In 1929, the Curtiss P-1C Hawk and the Boeing PW-9D were the standard pursuit biplanes. Both used the Curtiss D-12E engine, though future plans were to replace it with faster Curtiss V-1570 and H-1640 power plants. Also being standardized was the Boeing P-12B, a versatile airplane used by the airmail service of the U.S. Post Office and also by the Navy (as the F4B-1). In pursuit configuration, this single-engine biplane was equipped with a 525-horsepower engine and two mounted guns; it carried 232 pounds of bombs and had a top speed of 166 mph.

In search of a pursuit airplane capable of reaching 225 mph at 15,000 feet of altitude, the Materiel Division contracted

Curtiss O-39 Falcon assigned to the 94th Observation Group (*United States Air Force Museum*)

Thomas-Morse O-19B (*United States Air Force Museum*)

Douglas O-31 observation monoplane (*United States Air Force Museum*)

Douglas O-25A, bearing the Wright Field "spearhead" insignia (*United States Air Force Museum*)

Close-up of a Curtiss P-1C pursuit (*United States Air Force Museum*)

Synchronized gun installation on the Curtiss P-1 (*United States Air Force Museum*)

Curtiss XP-10 experimental pursuit

with the Boeing Airplane Company to produce the XP-9, and with the Curtiss Aeroplane and Motor Corporation to produce the XP-10. The Boeing XP-9 was a monoplane equipped with a single, 600-horsepower, Curtiss V-1570 engine. The Curtiss XP-10 was a biplane with the same engine.

To answer the need for a two-seat pursuit, the Berliner-Joyce Aircraft Corporation received a contract for the XP-16, a biplane equipped with a 600-horsepower Curtiss V-1570 supercharged engine. The production model of the P-16, the first two-seat pursuit biplane since 1924, rolled out in 1932.

By 1930-1931, the Boeing P-12C/E models had joined the Curtiss P-1C Hawk family as standard-service pursuit airplanes. Many aircraft historians consider the P-12 single-place biplane one of the most successful fighters in the long line of Air Corps fighter aircraft. It had a wingspan of 30 feet, a length of 20 feet 5 inches, and a gross weight of 2,536 pounds. Its engine was a 450-horsepower Pratt & Whitney R-1340-7 air-cooled radial with a top speed of 171 mph.[84] The P-12 was the first production-built pursuit with an all-metal monocoque fuselage.

The P-12 series had a long life, serving with front-line squadrons from 1929 to 1936. Boeing manufactured 366 of this series, including 110 E models. According to the Secretary of the Air Force Office of Information:[85]

> During the 1930's this plane was flown by more young officers who were to become renowned and successful generals than any other aircraft. Lessons learned flying this aircraft were applied in combat during World War II. The prewar era of biplanes, helmets, and goggles was probably most typified by this fine little pursuit.

During fiscal year 1932, a new airplane in the light pursuit category, the Boeing Y1P-26, seemed most promising. It was a semi-low wing, wire-braced monoplane of all-metal construction, built around the SR-1340-G supercharged engine. The Y1P-26 had a high speed of 227 mph at altitudes of 6,000 to 10,000 feet.[86] After extensive tests, a contract was placed with Boeing for 136 of the airplanes, designated P-26A's.

The P-26A became popularly known as the "Peashooter." Once in production, it had the distinction of being "for the first time in several years the only standard pursuit airplane in the Air Corps." (Thc P-6, P-12, and P-16 had been reclassified as limited standard.) The A model included many improvements over the experimental aircraft, such as a tapered wing, internal aileron control, flush rivets on all exterior surfaces, a redesigned landing gear with single fork strut, improved cowling, air-oil oleo gear, and friction dampers on the wing brace wires in place of the anti-vibration "birds" originally installed.[87] One spokesman described the P-26A as representing the "first major attempt by the Air Corps to modernize its fighter force, departing from designs based on outdated fabric-covered biplanes." The durable fighter became the oldest pursuit in World War II when it operated valiantly against the technically superior Japanese Zero fighter in the Philippine Islands during the early days of the war.

During fiscal year 1933, the Materiel Division tested two Y1P-25 experimental pursuits manufactured by Consolidated. The Y1P-25 was a two-place monoplane with an internally braced low wing. It was equipped with a 600-horsepower, geared, Curtiss V-1570 engine; one model was supercharged. During tests each model displayed remarkable performance at its

Boeing P-12 pursuits in flight. The P-12 was the first production-built American pursuit with an all-metal monocoque fuselage.

Consolidated P-30 monoplane pursuit (*United States Air Force Museum*)

P-12E during and after restoration at the United States Air Force Museum (*United States Air Force Museum*)

Boeing P-26 Peashooter

The Fairchild F-1A high-wing monoplane was the Air Corps' sole photographic type during the 1930s.

appropriate altitude, i.e., high performance at low altitude for the non-supercharged model and high performance at high altitude for the supercharged model. Unfortunately, both airplanes crashed and burned at Wright Field before the testing cycle ended. As a follow-on, the Materiel Division ordered from Consolidated four airplanes of improved design that were designated P-30s when completed.[88]

Photographic Airplanes

In February 1930, a board of Materiel Division officers recommended the development of a high-wing, single-engine cabin monoplane for photographic work. It would have to display "good stability directionally, longitudinally, and laterally" and operate at 16,000 feet. Other requirements were "controllability at all speeds, good visibility, and ample cabin space for camera installation and operation."[89]

A long series of comprehensive tests and careful evaluations were made of the 12 competitors. The Fairchild 71 monoplane was selected and procured as the F-1, becoming the Air Corps' first officially designated photographic airplane. The high-wing monoplane had a wingspan of 50 feet and a length of 33 feet. Powered by a 410-horsepower engine, the airplane had a three-man crew and flew at a top speed of 131 mph.[90] For the following 10 years it was the Air Corps' sole photographic type.

Training Airplanes

The two classifications within the training category during the late 1920s and early 1930s were PT, for Primary Trainer, and BT, for Basic Trainer.

The Consolidated PT-3 Trusty, a modification of the PT-1, became the standard primary trainer in 1928. (In use since 1924, the PT-1 had been the first trainer ordered in quantity since the Curtiss JN-4 Jenny.) The PT-3, and later the PT-3A, were standard biplanes with tandem open seats and single, 225-horsepower, Wright J-5 engines. The PT-1 and the PT-3 were the mainstays of the Air Corps' fleet of primary trainers until introduction of the Stearman PT-13 in 1936.[91]

In the basic trainer category, the Douglas BT-2C biplane was the "standard service" basic trainer. The BT-2C was powered by a 450-horsepower Pratt & Whitney R-1340 engine and had a top speed of 135 mph. Earlier models (BT-1 through BT-2B) were classified as "limited standard." The BT-1 was the last aircraft in the Air Corps' active inventory to be equipped with a World War I-era, 420-horsepower, Liberty engine and had a top speed of 132 mph.

Early in 1929, the Materiel Division considered buying a light commercial airplane for use as a military primary trainer. By the close of the fiscal year, 28 commercial trainers had been inspected. A contract was awarded to Consolidated Fleet for 15 airplanes (10 YPT-6s and five YPT-6A's) for further service tests.

To satisfy the needs of the Pilot Training Center at Brooks Field, Texas, specifications for an intermediate type of airplane were issued to the industry in January 1930. Six manufacturers submitted

Consolidated PT-3A Trusty primary trainer (*United States Air Force Museum*)

Douglas BT-2B basic trainer on the Wright Field compass rose (*United States Air Force Museum*)

Consolidated Y1PT-11 primary trainer (*United States Air Force Museum*)

airplanes. These were the Consolidated XPT-933, the Inland XPT-930, the New Standard XPT-931, the Spartan XPT-913, the Stearman XPT-912, and the Verville XPT-914.

The Materiel Division officers appointed to evaluate these airplanes found the Stearman, Verville, and Consolidated entries satisfactory for service test; four of each model were then purchased. Redesignated, the Stearman YPT-9 and the Verville YPT-10A aircraft were delivered to the training center at Brooks Field in March 1931, and the Consolidated Y1PT-11s in May. The popular Stearman PT-9 Cloudboy, when equipped with a 200-horsepower engine, served as a primary trainer; with a 300-horsepower engine it was a basic trainer.

The Materiel Division also sought a biplane that could serve as both a primary and as a basic trainer, affording considerable economies both in initial and operating costs, and simplifying the training process. The Stearman XBT-915, similar to the YPT-9, came close to satisfying both needs and was brought to Wright Field for initial testing during fiscal year 1931. The XBT-915 was fitted with a 300-horsepower Wasp Junior engine and additional fuel capacity, and sent to the Pilot Training Center at Brooks Field for further evaluation.

During fiscal year 1932, Consolidated joined the competition for the combined-function trainer. The Consolidated XBT-937 biplane, equipped with a 300-horsepower Pratt & Whitney R-985 engine, was accepted. The XBT-937 also served as the prototype for the Y1PT-12 primary trainer.[92]

THE "JULES VERNE" DEPARTMENT

Jules Verne gave the world science fiction in the form of fan-astic voyages around the moon, to the center of the earth, and to he ocean's depths. More importantly, he endorsed the use of echnology to advance civilization to its full potential. Verne served as a pioneer of aviation and was fascinated by Americans and their inclination toward scientific development. In the months before America's entry into World War II, officials at the Army's aeronautical laboratories at Wright Field, Ohio, used Verne's fa-miliar name to inspire new inventions in the world of aeronau-ics.

According to a contemporary newspaper account, the Jules Verne Department "thinks nothing of testing, sober-faced, the most weird airplane designs." The Army established the unique esting department to evaluate ideas from its own engineers, oth-ers in the aircraft industry, and literally from every-day citizens off the street. Anticipating the United States' impending entry nto World War II, many citizens expressed a genuine desire to help the nation's preparedness effort by proposing some far-fetched ideas. One gentleman recommended "try a bomb with a case made of Lucite and filled with nitroglycerin or some other transparent explosive." Another individual proposed using a swing for aircraft to take off, instead of a runway. Still another suggested building an airplane with two sets of wings, one be-hind the other like a dragonfly.

Other ideas included a "fuelless" motor equipped with a hand pump propelled by a gasoline engine; a machine soldiers could fly as easily as driving a car and hover over a target like a hum-mingbird; an aerial torpedo self-propelled as a rocket; a "flying wing" type of plane; and visual aids for seeing at night. In the tradition of Jules Verne, the last two ideas have become reality with the B-2 stealth bomber (and its 1940s predecessor the XB-35) and night-vision goggles. Many letters sent to Wright Field be-gan with statements such as "Dear Sir, I have a screwy idea," or this idea "may not be worth the paper it is written on." One inventor stressed, "I intend this to be used for the benefit of the U.S. Government…at no cost" while others voiced a need fo funds to carry out their ideas: "I am unemployed and penniless."

The office was apparently established in the first half of 194 but could not keep up with the tremendous flow of ideas, sug-gestions, and inventions, so the president established the Na-tional Inventors Council in Washington, D.C. Consequently, by the middle of that same year, the Jules Verne Department re-verted to testing only those ideas referred to it by the council Although its existence was brief, the Jules Verne Departmen provided a valuable service to the nation by linking the inspira-tion of modern day Jules Vernes with the technology of the times to help prepare America for World War II.

Sources: Reference file of letters received by Jules Verne Department in 1941, ASC History Office; Peter Haining, *The Jules Verne Companion* (New York 1978).

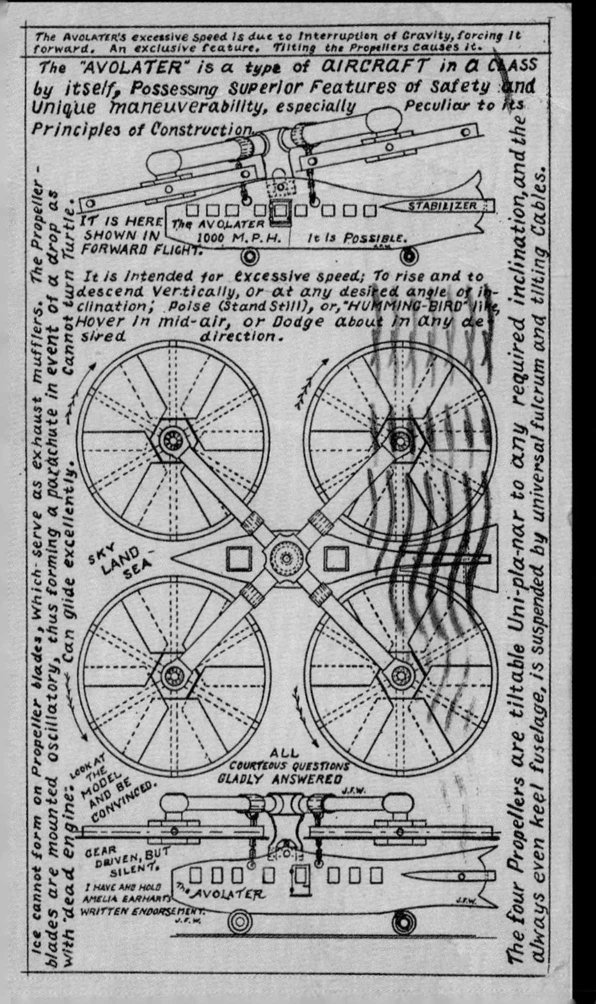

copy

June 16, 1941.

Maj. R. C. Wilson,

Dear Sir:

I have just read about the weird ideas for airplanes. It was very interesting to say theleast.

I have always wanted to see an airplane with two sets of wings, directly in back of each other, with flaps. Yes, just like a dragon fly. You know how they fly. But of course, use the standard tail on the airplane.

The wings must be place so that if one was shot off, it wouldn't nose-dive.

I have been just waiting since I first saw an airplane, look like the one above. It can be done. (P.S. Please try it.)

Yours truly,

Arthur A. Jacques

copy

WRIGHT FIELD CONTRIBUTIONS TO WORLD WAR II 1935-1945

By fiscal year 1935, the Materiel Division had begun working on plans and designs which would, less than a decade later, drastically change world history and introduce a new age of air power. According to Air Force historians Wesley Craven and James Cate, the Army Air Forces fought World War II with aircraft that were all either in the production stage or under development before December 7, 1941.[93] The time lag between approved design and the acceptance of production models usually ranged from three to five years. This meant that the Army Air Forces' (AAF) first-line tactical and non-tactical fleets between 1941 and early 1944 had their origins in the mid-1930s—1935 in the case of the Boeing B-17 Flying Fortress.

These, and the considerably more sophisticated and destructive airplanes of the latter years of the war, were the products of the dynamic development triad of pilot, engineer-scientist, and manufacturer, represented nowhere better in America than at Wright Field. Together, they met the ultimate challenge to produce machines capable of forcing the enemy into surrender.

Specific developments in military aviation from 1935 forward continued the trend toward diversification, expansion, and modernization of aircraft design begun in the early 1930s. In 1935, the Air Corps increased its aircraft classifications from eight to 12:[94]

Attack	A
Autogiro	G
Bombardment	B
Bombardment, Long Range	BLR
Observation, Corps and Army	O
Observation, Long Range	OLR
Observation, Amphibian	OA
Pursuit, Monoplace	P
Pursuit, Biplace	PB
Transport, Cargo	C
Training, Primary	PT
Training, Basic	BT

The work at Wright Field contributed to the war effort in each of these categories. One historian summarized this effort:[95]

> They don't build airplanes at Wright Field. They don't teach men to fly them. But they dictate the size and shape and number of every plane we use for military purposes. They buy it, follow it into production. They test it to see if it meets with required standards. And they do the same thing with every piece of equipment that pertains to military aviation.

It was air power that ultimately determined the course of World War II, in both the European and Pacific theaters. All eyes were upon Wright Field, the "nerve center of air power," as the airplanes responsible for Allied victories were conceived and put into production.

Throat of the 20-foot wind tunnel at Wright Field, constructed in 1941-1942. Model aircraft with wingspans up to 16 feet were tested at airspeeds up to 400 mph in this tunnel during the war years.

Wright Field, June 1946. The orange aircraft on the right is the X-1, before its record-breaking flight. Its B-29 mothership is on the X-1's left side.

Interior of the power building for the Wright Field 20-foot wind tunnel. The giant 40,000-horsepower motor for the tunnel (into which this rotor and stator are being installed) drove two carefully synchronized 16-bladed fans.

The Douglas A-20 Havoc, developed at Wright Field, became the foremost attack airplane of World War II.

Principal Developments

Attack Airplanes

The Douglas A-20 Havoc was the foremost attack airplane developed at Wright Field for use in World War II. Developed from the Douglas DB-7B bomber, the A-20 was the Air Corps' first combat airplane to have a tricycle landing gear. The high-wing monoplane was powered by twin 1,600-horsepower Wright R-2600 engines, carried a three-man crew, and was equipped with seven .50-caliber machine guns. The airplane carried 2,600 pounds of bombs internally and another 1,400 pounds under the wings. Maximum and cruising speeds were 350 mph and 230 mph respectively. Range was 675 miles and service ceiling was 28,175 feet. When A-20 production stopped in 1944, more than 7,000 Havocs (models A through K) had been manufactured for the United States and its allies.

The A-20 was normally used as a low-level attack bomber. It fought in the Pacific, Middle East, Russian, and European theaters, as well as in North Africa, where it became instrumental in defeating the German Afrika Korps during the desert campaign. On July 4, 1942, six A-20s of the 15th Bombardment Squadron made the first American daylight bombing raid over Europe. The targets were four German airfields in the Netherlands. Final statistics from the European theater indicated that A-20 Havocs flew 39,500 sorties, dropped 57 million pounds of bombs, and shot down 12 enemy aircraft.[96] Later in the war, A-20s equipped with radar and additional nose guns were redesignated P-70s and used as night fighters until the Northrop P-61 Black Widow became operational in 1944.

Autogiros and Helicopters

According to Materiel Division reports, the Air Corps recognized "a definite military requirement for autogiros" by fiscal year 1935. An autogiro was an aircraft having a conventional propeller for forward motion and a horizontal rotor, rotated by airflow, for lift. These versatile machines were intended particularly for missions involving observation, reconnaissance, and photography. Once requirements were established, the Air Corps contracted for one autogiro from the Kellett

Aircraft Corporation and a similar machine from the Pitcairn Autogiro Company for testing at Wright Field.[97] These early rotary aircraft were precursors of the AAF helicopters used so effectively during World War II.

The Kellett gyroplane was designated YG-1. It had a span of 40 feet and a length of 28 feet; the fuselage contained two open, tandem seats. The machine had a top speed of 125 mph. It was powered by a single 225-horsepower engine but had no tail rotor. The commercial (and original) version was designated the KD-1 (K for Kellett, D for direct control). The pylon containing the aircraft's rotor was in front of the forward seat to provide free access to both front and rear cockpits. The YG-1 version at Wright Field "was tested for all types of missions [and] also given comparative tests against balloons for artillery fire control, night missions with flares to illuminate moving targets, etc."[98]

The Pitcairn autogiro, designated the YG-2, had two open seats in tandem, and was powered by a single 400-horsepower Wright R-975 engine.

In 1941, the G designation for Autogiro was replaced by the R for Rotating Wing. Two surviving Kellett YG-1 gyroplanes were redesignated the XR-2 and XR-3. In 1942, seven XR-25s were delivered as YO-60 observation aircraft, the first autogiros to carry an O designation.[99]

The Vought-Sikorsky R-4, developed in 1942, became the first full-production helicopter for the American military forces. The Air Rescue Service successfully used the R-4 and its successors, the R-5 and R-6, in World War II.

Pitcairn YG-2 autogiro with a Wright R-975 Whirlwind engine (*United States Air Force Museum*)

Kellett YG-1B autogiro

Orville Wright (right) with helicopter pioneer Igor Sikorsky at Wright Field

Bombardment Airplanes

The long-range bomber program at Wright Field is an epic in the annals of military aircraft procurement. In the years preceding World War II, the Air Corps' struggle to produce effective medium- and long-range bombers significantly shaped activities at Wright Field and brought both victory and tragedy to the facility. In July 1933, following several months of detailed study, the Materiel Division theorized it possible to build an airplane capable of carrying 2,000 pounds of bombs a distance of 5,000 miles at a speed of 200 mph. Six months later, the Air Corps submitted to the War Department a detailed proposal ("Project A") to manufacture such an airplane. On December 19, 1933, the War

Boeing's XB-15 long-range heavy bomber originated as Project A at Wright Field in 1933.

Department General Staff gave tentative approval to the concept and on February 12, 1934, a $609,300 Air Corps budget was approved "in principle" for long-range bomber development.

On May 12, 1934, the Army chief of staff authorized negotiation of contracts for preliminary design work with the Boeing and Martin corporations. Preliminary contracts were completed in late June 1934.[100] This program culminated in the 1937 production of the gigantic, four-engine Boeing XB-15. Although the airplane proved too large for the power plants then available, the engineering knowledge gained from the XB-15 provided great benefit in the design of the B-17, and later the B-29.

During 1934, the Materiel Division began efforts to develop a medium-range bomber. Army Circular Proposal 35-356, containing design specifications for such a bomber, was distributed to the industry. General requirements called for a multi-engine machine capable of carrying 2,000 pounds of bombs for 2,000 miles at over 200 mph. Three manufacturers submitted designs: Bellanca, Douglas, and Boeing. The first two firms planned twin-engine airplanes. Boeing, however, taking advantage of the ambiguous term "multi-engine," submitted a design for a four-engine bomber—and won the competition. The contract called for Boeing to deliver a prototype airplane for testing within one year of receiving the contract.

Boeing's speculation was not a shot in the dark, but was based on the company's signed contract of June 28, 1934, with the Air Corps for design of the experimental XB-15. In addition, Boeing had a design in process for a four-engine civilian transport (Model 300) that matched the general specifications contained in the Army circular. On July 28, 1935, the Boeing four-engine, mid-wing monoplane, designated company Model 299, made its maiden flight at Boeing Field near Seattle. According to a contemporary account:[101]

> It was a beautifully designed, streamlined, gleaming giant of a plane. The wings spread to more than a hundred and three feet; the cylindrical fuselage stretched almost sixty-nine feet from turret to tail. Immediately striking was the array of four giant Pratt & Whitney engines [750-horsepower R-1690] protruding from the wing, each with a three-bladed, eleven and a half foot in diameter, propeller. In the nose, a complex of plastic and steel stripping, was a gun position—another bulged from the rear of the cabin, yet another underneath the fuselage and two more on either side of the fuselage. These five gun emplacements won the 299 the name of Flying Fortress. So did the size, as has been suggested.

According to another account, a Seattle newspaperman, on seeing the Model 299 for the first time, exclaimed, "Why, it's a Flying Fortress."

After a month-long series of test flights at the factory, Model 299 took off on August 20 for even more strenuous competitive tests by Materiel Division experts at Wright Field. The 299 vied for acceptance with the Douglas Aircraft DB-1 (similar to the DC-2) and the Martin Company 146 (an updated version of the B-12). Areas of competition included speed, endurance, time-to-climb, service ceiling, structure and design, power plant, armament and equipment installation, maintenance, landing characteristics, and utility as a type. Boeing Model 299 far surpassed all of the Army specifications for speed, range, and load-carrying. On its maiden cross-country flight, the sleek bomber set records, covering the 2,100 miles from Boeing Field to Wright Field nonstop in nine hours at an average speed of 232 mph, flying at an average altitude of 12,000 feet.

At Wright Field, disaster struck. On the morning of October 30, 1935, the Boeing bomber was to undergo a flight test in view of Air Corps military and civilian experts

Military and civilian experts present for official flight test of the Boeing 299 at Wright Field. Left to right: Mr. C. B. Benton of Boeing, Mr. Mark Koogier, Captain Stanley M. Umstead, Mr. Roy Grooms, Major Y. D. Corkille, Mr. E. K. Lasswell, and Lieutenant Leonard F. Harman. Mr. Benton was on board the 299 when it crashed; Lieutenant Harman was badly burned in heroic rescue efforts. (*United States Air Force Museum*)

Four-engine Model 299 bomber at the Boeing plant near Seattle, Washington (*United States Air Force Museum*)

The Model 299 arrives at Wright Field to undergo competitive tests, August 20, 1935. (*United States Air Force Museum*)

THE WEATHER: Partly cloudy and slightly warmer tonight; Thursday partly cloudy and warmer

DAYTON DAILY NEWS

ONLY AFTERNOON PAPER IN DAYTON RECEIVING ASSOCIATED PRESS NEWS AND WIREPHOTO SERVICE

THE WIREPHOTO PAPER HOME EDITION

VOL. LIX. NO. 69. DAYTON, OHIO, WEDNESDAY, OCTOBER 30, 1935 PRICE THREE CENTS

1 DEAD, 4 HURT AS HALF MILLION-DOLLAR BOEING BOMBER CRASHES IN FLAMES AFTER ITS TAKEOFF AT WRIGHT FIELD

Quick Action of Two Officers Prevents Loss of Several Lives

Lurch of Bomber Warns Lieuts, Harman and Giovannoli Who Rush to the Rescue

A sickening lurch that ended in a turn of 180 degrees warned Lieuts. L. F. Harman and R. K. Giovannoli that the huge Boeing bomber was going to crash and they sprinted towards the spot where they knew it would fall even before the left wing dropped and the plane smashed into the ground.

To the quick action of these two officers several members of the crew owe their lives. A second after the crash, flames enveloped the plane, trapping those of the five members of the crew who had not leaped at the moment of impact.

Lieuts. Harman and Giovannoli had watched the takeoff. They reached the plane as the flames soared and danger of an explosion mounted. They threw their coats over their heads and their arms over their faces and leaped through the flames and clambered into the wreckage.

First one and then another of the crew they dragged through the blaze to safety. Just how many or who, no one knows. One, maybe two, had leaped at the moment or a split second, before the crash and escaped the worst of the flames.

When the ambulance kept at the field for such emergencies, bumped across the terrain to the wreckage, all of the crew had been pulled to safety. But in those few seconds before Harman and Giovannoli risked their lives to rescue their friends, the gasoline and oil-fed flames had taken their toll. Some of the crew were unconscious, the others with hands, arms and bodies burned, were unable to talk because of pain and shock.

Both Harman and Giovannoli were burned, but neither seriously. They were treated at the field hospital and then removed to Miami Valley hospital and kept for observation. Both suffered first and second degree burns.

WRECKAGE AND FIGURES IN CRASH AND RESCUE

MAJ. PLOYER HILL, AIR BRANCH CHIEF, FATALLY INJURED

BULLETIN

Maj. Ployer P. Hill died of injuries received in the crash of the Boeing bomber, at Miami Valley hospital at 12:45 p. m.

THE DEAD

Maj. Ployer P. Hill, chief of Wright Field flying branch.

THE INJURED

Lieut. Donald L. Putt, flying branch, Wright Field.

Leslie Tower, Seattle, Boeing pilot.

John Cutting, test observer, Wright Field equipment branch.

Mark H. Koogler, flying branch, Wright Field.

The half-million-dollar flying fortress built by the Boeing Aircraft Corp. for the army air corps, crashed in flames at Wright Field about 9:30 a. m. Wednesday, with more or less serious injury to five occupants.

The crash occurred just after the huge all-metal, four-motor bomber left the ground on an experimental test flight with aircorps officers, civilians, and Leslie

The crash of the Model 299 on October 30, 1935, killed Wright Field Chief Test Pilot Major Ployer P. Hill and resulted in the death of Boeing Chief Test Pilot Leslie Tower. (*United States Air Force Museum*)

and representatives of the three competing airplane manufacturers. Major Ployer P. "Pete" Hill, chief of the Wright Field Flight Testing Section, was the pilot. In the copilot's seat was Lieutenant Donald Putt, the project test pilot. Behind them stood Boeing's Chief Test Pilot Leslie Tower, the first man to fly the 299 when it rolled from the hangar in July 1935. Also aboard were the Pratt & Whitney representative, Henry Igo, and C. B. Benton of Boeing.

The 299 warmed up and taxied down the field. The four engines roared as the airplane began the takeoff run, smoothly lifted from the ground and began to climb. Then the great airplane stalled, turned on one wing, plunged to the ground, and burst into flames.

Lieutenant Putt and company representatives Igo and Benton staggered from the burning fuselage. Spectators sped to the crash. Lieutenant Robert K. Giovannoli jumped onto the burning wing and "in spite of the fierce heat, reached the copilot's window . . . forced it open, thrust head and shoulders into the smoke-filled cockpit . . . and struggled to work [Leslie] Tower's body through the window."[102]

Major Hill was trapped, however, his foot caught under the rudder. Lieutenants Leonard F. "Jake" Harman and Giovannoli struggled with a penknife to cut the shoe off his foot and ease him through the window of the cockpit. Then, badly burned, they made their own exit.[103] Major Hill never regained consciousness and died the same day in the base hospital. Tower, according to one historian, "blamed himself for the disaster and [although not seriously injured] died a few days later because he no longer wished to live."[104] (On December 1, 1939, the Army Air Depot at Ogden, Utah, was named Hill Field in honor of Major Hill.)

A thorough investigation of the wreckage and a review of actions prior to the fatal plunge of the 299 disclosed that neither Major Hill nor Lieutenant Putt "nor any of the others remembered to disengage the mechanism that locked the elevators and rudder while the plane was parked, a simple matter of pulling a short lever."[105] Ironically, it was this locking of elevators when the airplane was on the ground that was considered to be one of the best innovations of the Model 299. In fact, the horizontal tail surfaces of the 299 were so large that "if the elevators were not secured while the plane was on the ground a strong wind could damage them."[106] Prior to taxiing the airplane, the pilot was supposed to unlock the tail surfaces by releasing a spring lock in the cockpit.

The result of this tragedy was the establishment of a standard operating procedure that is used today for all airplanes—the preflight checklist. The checklist for the B-17 (successor to the 299) was developed by the 2nd Bombardment Group, Langley Field, Virginia. Indirect proof of the value of the procedure was the fact that the group's fleet of B-17s flew more than 9,000 hours totaling 1,800,000 miles during a two-year period without serious mishap.[107]

The loss of Model 299 almost—but not entirely—eliminated Boeing from further contention. The initial Air Corps contract went to Douglas, for 82 low-wing, twin-engine B-18 medium bombers. This order was soon increased to 133 airplanes with deliveries beginning in October 1936.[108] The Air Corps ultimately purchased 350 of these bombers.

The Douglas B-18 Bolo was an outgrowth of the renowned Douglas DC-3. The all-metal bomber had a wingspan of 90 feet, a length of 56 feet 9 inches, and a height of 15 feet 1 inch. It was powered by two 1,000-horsepower Wright R-1820-1 engines. It carried a six-man crew, three machine guns, and 6,500 pounds of bombs on racks within the fuselage. A radar-equipped version of the B-18 was used in the early months of World War II for antisubmarine patrol off the eastern coast of the United States and around the Caribbean Sea. Other models of the aircraft were used for bombardier training.[109]

B-18 Bolo specially modified for photographic work. Standing with their standard and experimental aerial photographic gear are (left to right): Ed Woodford; Robert Feicht; Major George W. Goddard, father of modern military reconnaissance; and Roy Whitacre. (*United States Air Force Museum*)

Douglas B-18 Bolo bomber in flight

Despite the acceptable performance of the B-18, the decided superiority in all aspects of the Model 299 could not be ignored. Because of the "exceedingly interesting possibilities" of the Boeing bomber, the Air Corps contracted for the delivery of 13 airplanes under the designation YB-17 for service tests. Later, a fourteenth bomber was ordered specifically for static testing. The YB-17 differed from the Model 299 in only one respect: it had 850-horsepower Wright 1820 engines, while the 299 had 750-horsepower Pratt & Whitney power plants.[110]

Ten four-engine Boeing Y1B-17 Flying Fortress bombers were delivered to the Air Corps in early 1937 and began a yearlong period of service testing. At the conclusion, the Materiel Division analysis stated "the exceedingly interesting military possibilities of this type reported last year have been well demonstrated."[111] The Materiel Division chief in his fiscal year 1938 report to the chief of the Air Corps observed that "the success of the B-17 airplane in service indicated clearly the soundness of the basic principles underlying current procurement procedure." In the opinion of Major General Henry H. "Hap" Arnold, Air Corps chief, the B-17 Flying Fortress proved to have "only one predecessor of equal importance in air history . . . [the] Wright brothers' first 'military aircraft' in which Lieutenant Thomas Selfridge was killed."[112]

Another truly significant date in military aviation history was October 15, 1937, when "Project A" reached fruition with the launching of Boeing's long-range bomber, the huge, four-engine XB-15. Designed in 1934 as mentioned earlier, this progenitor of the B-17 and forerunner of the B-29 had a wingspan of 149 feet (45 feet more than the B-17), and a length of 87 feet 11 inches (13 feet longer than the B-17). The XB-15 weighed 37,609 pounds empty. It carried a 10-man crew, six guns, and 12,000 pounds of bombs. Fully loaded, however, the aircraft strained its four 1,000-horsepower Pratt & Whitney radial engines to capacity, limiting it to a top speed of only 197 mph (in contrast to a top speed of 310 mph for the B-17G).[113]

The Flying Fortress and the XB-15 became shining stars in the Air Corps firmament during the late 1930s. One of the most spectacular achievements was the goodwill flight of six B-17s assigned to the 2nd Bombardment Group, Langley Field, to South America and return in 1938. The flight departed Miami, Florida, on February 17 and landed at Buenos Aires, Argentina, the following day. The bombers returned to Langley on February 29. The southbound flight required 33 hours and 30 minutes total flying time; the return flight was made in 33 hours and 35 minutes. This flight, acclaimed as "the most important one since . . . Arnold led a mission of Martin B-10 bombers from Washington to Alaska and return in the summer of 1934," clearly demonstrated the Flying Fortress' range and dependability.[114]

The XB-15's best known flight was an emergency airlift from Langley Field to Chile in February 1939, carrying 3,250 pounds of medical supplies for earthquake victims. Total flying time for the 10,000-mile round trip was 29 hours 53 minutes, with refueling stops in Panama and Peru. Generating smaller headlines in newspapers, but of far greater significance to heavy airplane research and development, were two world's records for altitude and payload set by the XB-15 at Wright Field. On July 30, 1939, the giant bomber lifted 22,046 pounds to 8,228 feet and 31,164 pounds to 6,561.6 feet.[115]

During World War II, the B-17 became known as "the plane that carried the war to the enemy's homeland." Following attacks on Pearl Harbor and the Philippines in 1941, B-17s flying from Del Monte Field became the first American aircraft

Douglas-built B-17G at the Long Beach plant

Douglas-built B-17F in production at the Long Beach plant, October 1942

B-17 in flight over Wright Field

in offensive action as they attacked Japanese ships off the coast of Luzon. They showed that Japan had, indeed, "awakened a sleeping Giant." In the summer of 1942, B-17s flew softening-up raids in the Solomon Islands prior to the American invasion of Guadalcanal that marked the beginning of the Allied offensive in the Southwest Pacific. Forts assigned to the 12th Air Force participated in the defeat of Germany's crack Afrika Korps in October 1942. B-17s flew the first raids over occupied France and made the first raid on Germany in early 1943. By the end of the war in Europe, B-17s had claimed 6,660 enemy aircraft and participated in the devastating attacks on the German industrial complex by dropping 640,000 tons of bombs on enemy targets.

Crew of an XB-15 assigned to the 2nd Bombardment Group, Langley Field, during the February 1939 emergency airlift of medical supplies to earthquake victims in South America (*United States Air Force Museum*)

Although overshadowed by the accomplishments of the Flying Fortress and other four-engine bombers, the XB-15—called "Old Grandpappy" by Boeing engineers—did see limited "stateside" service during World War II, carrying passengers and oversize cargo between air bases within the continental United States.

Even as the B-15, the B-17, and the B-18 entered the inventory, the Materiel Division continued to seek better machines. During fiscal year 1939, for example, North American delivered one XB-21 twin-engine bomber. More importantly, Consolidated Aircraft received a contract to produce seven B-24 four-engine Liberator bombers for delivery in 1940.

The B-24 represented one of the earliest products of President Franklin D. Roosevelt's intervention in behalf of air power. In January 1939, Air Corps Chief Major General Henry H. Arnold asked Consolidated to manufacture a four-engine bomber with a 3,000-mile range and a top speed above 300 mph, capable of a ceiling of 35,000 feet. "Drawing heavily upon experience with the B-15 and B-17," Consolidated produced the prototype by December 1939.[116]

The Liberator had a wingspan of 110 feet, a length of 66 feet 4 inches; and a height of 17 feet 11 inches. It used four

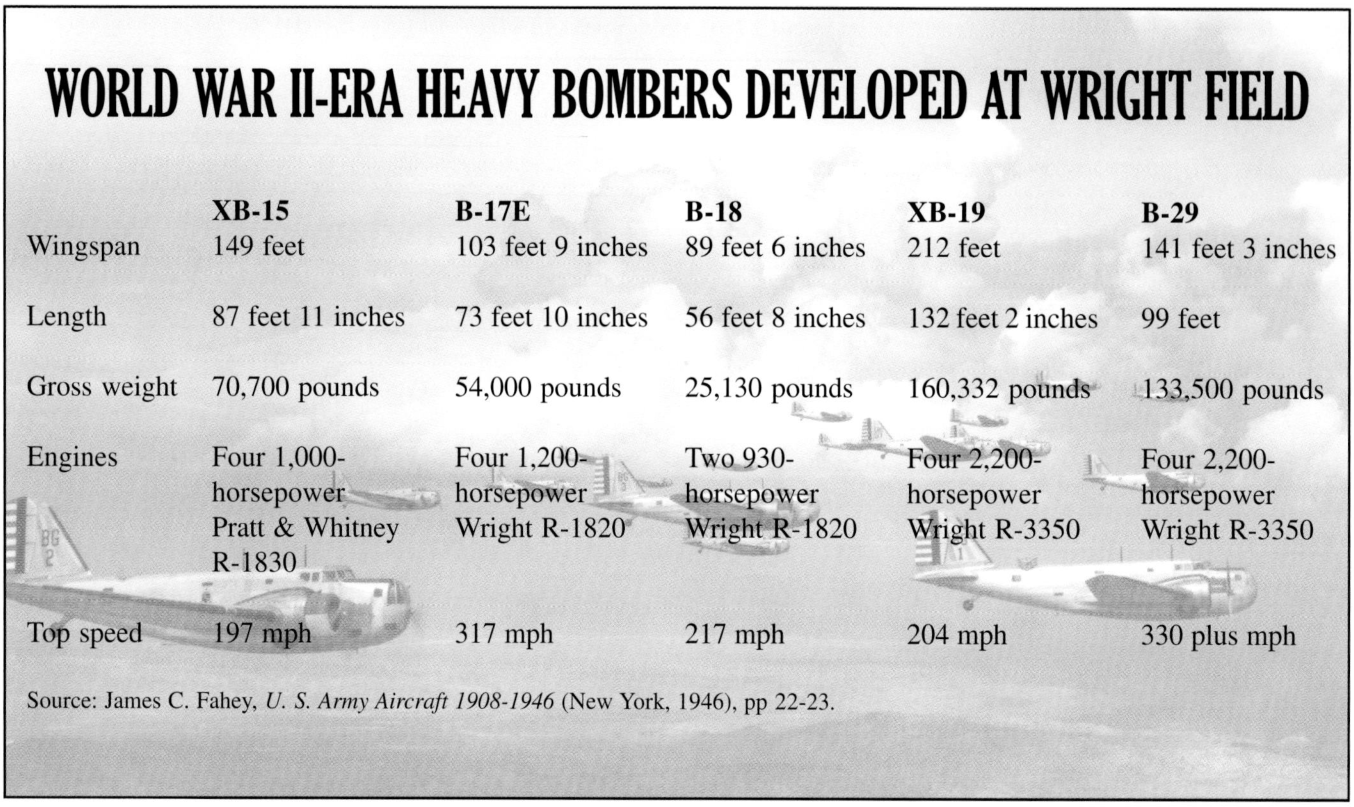

WORLD WAR II-ERA HEAVY BOMBERS DEVELOPED AT WRIGHT FIELD

	XB-15	B-17E	B-18	XB-19	B-29
Wingspan	149 feet	103 feet 9 inches	89 feet 6 inches	212 feet	141 feet 3 inches
Length	87 feet 11 inches	73 feet 10 inches	56 feet 8 inches	132 feet 2 inches	99 feet
Gross weight	70,700 pounds	54,000 pounds	25,130 pounds	160,332 pounds	133,500 pounds
Engines	Four 1,000-horsepower Pratt & Whitney R-1830	Four 1,200-horsepower Wright R-1820	Two 930-horsepower Wright R-1820	Four 2,200-horsepower Wright R-3350	Four 2,200-horsepower Wright R-3350
Top speed	197 mph	317 mph	217 mph	204 mph	330 plus mph

Source: James C. Fahey, *U. S. Army Aircraft 1908-1946* (New York, 1946), pp 22-23.

1,200-horsepower Pratt & Whitney R-1830 engines. The bomber carried a 10-man crew. Early models had three .50-caliber and four .30-caliber machine guns and carried 8,800 pounds of bombs.

The bomber went into mass production in 1941 and experienced many modifications before production stopped near the end of World War II. More than 18,000 B-24s were manufactured, more than any other World War II combat airplane. The three models most widely used in combat operations were the D, H, and J series. Major additions to the early vehicles included turbosuperchargers, more protective armor, power-operated gun turrets, 10 .50-caliber machine guns, and an increased bomb load of 12,800 pounds.

The B-24 Liberator operated in every combat theater, especially in the Mediterranean and the Pacific. Insufficient armor and armament limited B-24 operations in the European theater, since the aircraft was more vulnerable to German fighters than was the "rugged and steady" B-17. In 1959, a Liberator that had flown combat missions from North Africa with the 512th Bomb Squadron during 1943-1944 was put on permanent display at the United States Air Force Museum.[117]

Two medium bombers ordered in fiscal year 1940 that gained battlefield fame were the North American B-25 Mitchell and the Martin B-26 Marauder. Both were twin-engine, all-metal, mid-wing monoplanes. Each carried a six-man crew. Other similarities were:[118]

	B-25B Mitchell	B-26G Marauder
Wingspan	67 feet 7 inches	71 feet
Length	52 feet 11 inches	58 feet 3 inches
Height	15 feet 9 inches	19 feet 10 inches
Gross weight	28,460 pounds	38,200 pounds
Engines	Two 1,700-horsepower Wright R-2600-9	Two 2,000-horsepower Wright R-2800-43
Top speed	300 mph	283 mph
Range	1,350 miles	1,000 miles

The B-25 roared into history on April 18, 1942, as Lieutenant Colonel James H. Doolittle led a flight of 16 bombers on a low-level attack of Tokyo, Japan. The B-25s were launched from the deck of the U.S. Navy aircraft carrier the USS *Hornet*. American, Australian, British, Chinese, Dutch, and Russian crews flew the Mitchell in every combat arena of World War II.

The B-26 Marauder entered combat in the Southwest Pacific theater during the spring of 1942, but saw more extensive use in Europe and the Mediterranean. Aside from the United States, six nations flew the Marauder. Single models of both the B-25 and the B-26 are on display at the United States Air Force Museum.[119]

On June 21, 1941, the maiden flight of the Douglas XB-19 Hemisphere Defender culminated "seven years of engineering challenges." The low-wing, four-engine bomber had originated in October 1935 as "Project D," the "ultra-long range bomber" intended to succeed the Boeing XB-17. Air Corps intent to develop a long-range bomber, however, dated from "Project A" in 1934, which led to the XB-15.

The XB-19 was enormous, with a wingspan of 212 feet, a length of 132 feet 2 inches, an empty weight of 84,431 pounds, and a gross weight of more than 140,000 pounds. The bomber had an 11-man crew and carried 12 guns (two 37-mm cannon, six .30-caliber machine guns, and four .50-caliber machine guns). It carried 16,000 pounds of bombs internally and an additional 20,000 pounds on exterior racks.

The behemoth was originally equipped with four 2,200-horsepower, 18-cylinder, Wright R-3350-5 Cyclones. These power plants were insufficient for the demand and could pull the bomber through the air at a top speed of only 204 mph. In 1943, these engines were replaced with four 2,600-horsepower, liquid-cooled, Allison V-3420-11 engines, but even these increased top speed to only 265 mph (XB-19A). The bomber was still too slow to escape most enemy fighters. In the final analysis, the B-19, "like the B-15, served only to test, and thus to advance, the engineering knowledge that went into the construction of other and more successful planes," such as the four-engine B-29 and B-50, and the 10-engine B-36.[120] During 1942 and 1943, the XB-19A became a frequent visitor to Wright Field, where its various components were tested.

On June 15, 1944, the first bombs fell on the Imperial Iron and Steel Works at Yawata, the "Pittsburgh of Japan" located on Kyushu Island. The airplanes that carried out the mission were the culmination of a Wright Field program that began September 6, 1940. On that date, contracts were let to Boeing Aircraft and Consolidated Aircraft for one experimental model each of a "super bomber." Boeing developed the XB-29; Consolidated designed the XB-32. Both airplanes flew two years later, but only the B-29 Superfortress went into mass production.

The project officer for the "very heavy bomber" program was Captain Donald L. Putt, Materiel Command aeronautical engineer and test pilot who had survived the fiery crash of Boeing Model 299 at Wright Field in 1935. Perhaps few military airplanes and sustained programs ever received as much Wright Field attention and effort as did the B-29. It became one of the largest wartime projects at the field, involving scores of Wright Field scientists, engineers, and pilots.

The aircraft's specifications and its stellar performance in combat justified the B-29's classification as a Very Heavy Bomber (VHB) or Very Long Range (VLR) bomber. The B-29 Superfortress had several unique features: it was the AAF's first pressurized-cabin bomber; it had a central fire control system; and it

B-17 *My Oklahoma Gal* at Patterson Field for reconditioning by Fairfield Air Service Command repair crews. Decorations on the fuselage translate to 203 missions, six Japanese aircraft downed, eight Japanese ships sunk, and five Purple Hearts awarded to crew members. (*United States Air Force Museum*)

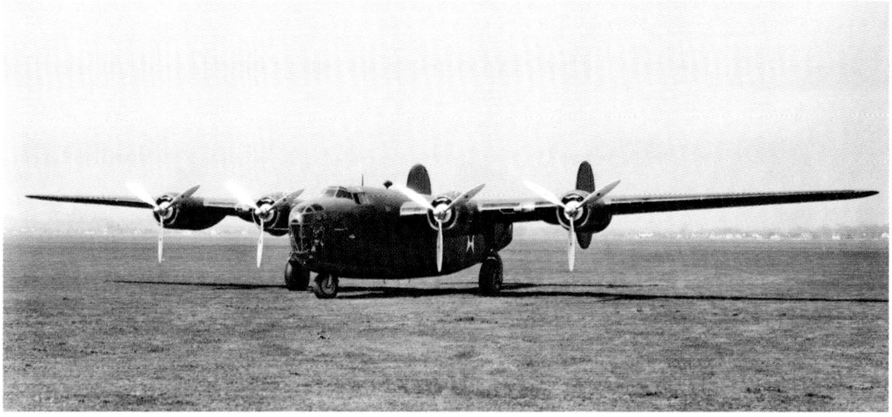

Consolidated-Vultee XB-24 Liberator bomber at Wright Field, April 1943

XB-19 at the Douglas facility

Lieutenant Colonel James H. Doolittle, Rear Admiral Marc A. Mitscher, and the Tokyo "Doolittle Raiders" aboard the USS *Hornet*, April 1942

North American B-25 Mitchell bomber

Martin B-26 Marauder bomber being stripped of camouflage paint at Building 13, Fairfield Air Service Command, Patterson Field

Douglas XB-19 making a low pass over Springfield Street adjacent to Wright Field

was equipped with a complex radar system for both offensive and defensive use. The bomber's maximum fuel load of 9,548 gallons gave it a range exceeding 5,000 miles. By the end of World War II, three manufacturers (Boeing, Bell, and Glenn L. Martin) had produced 3,960 Superfortresses. Most were configured as bombers, but 18 were converted to F-13 photographic-reconnaissance vehicles.

The huge bomber hastened the end of World War II by dropping two atomic bombs, the first and only such weapons used in warfare, on Japan. The first uranium device exploded over Hiroshima, Japan, at 9:15 a.m. on August 6, 1945. The second weapon, a plutonium bomb, was dropped over Nagasaki on August 9. In summary, "the technological breakthroughs of this plane [B-29], coupled with the simultaneous development of the atom bomb, ushered in a new era in warfare and strategic air power."[121]

Unlike the B-29, the Consolidated-Vultee B-32 Dominator bomber program was crippled by lengthy technical difficulties. The first production airplane was not service tested until August 1944, and only 13 were accepted by the end of that year. The B-32 had a wingspan of 135 feet and was 83 feet in length. The four 2,200-horsepower engines were Wright R-3350 power plants. The airplane carried 8,000 pounds of bombs and 5,460 gallons of fuel. Cruising and top speeds were 290 mph and 357 mph. The aircraft had a maximum range of 4,200 miles and a ceiling of 30,000 feet.

Total production by the end of August 1945 was 118 bombers, but only 15 saw combat in the Pacific theater during the closing days of World War II. The production contract was cancelled in October 1945, and the existing airplanes were declared surplus.[122]

War correspondents witness a press preview of the first Consolidated-Vultee B-32 Dominators to reach the overseas war zone at Clark Field, Philippines. (*United States Air Force Museum*)

Boeing B-29 Superfortress (*United States Air Force Museum*)

WRIGHT FIELD AND THE MANHATTAN PROJECT

Wright Field engineers made an important contribution to the success of America's World War II atomic bomb program—the Manhattan Project—by providing the flight test team's first full-scale delivery system. That product was a B-29 bomber specially modified to carry the experimental atomic bomb casings, or "drop shapes," evaluated by the Manhattan Project in 1943 and 1944. By studying the aerodynamic performance of those shapes, Manhattan Project researchers greatly improved the designs needed for accurate, assured bomb delivery in combat.

The *Enola Gay (United States Air Force Museum)*

In 1940, Dr Albert Einstein, the world-famous physicist, persuaded President Franklin D. Roosevelt to fund an atomic bomb research program. Secret government studies identified two unique materials with the potential to make a practical atomic bomb: uranium, a naturally occurring radioactive element, and plutonium, a more active man-made substance created by 'cooking' uranium in a nuclear reactor. Six months after the United States entered the war, the Army Corps of Engineers established the Manhattan Engineering District (MED), with the sole mission to oversee the design and production of atomic bombs.

The crew of *Bock's Car (United States Air Force Museum)*

By the fall of 1943, MED scientists envisioned two possible weapon configurations using plutonium. One used a cannon to join two small pieces of plutonium into one critical mass; the idea was that the pieces should stay together long enough to produce a nuclear detonation before the pent-up propellant blew the cannon and its contents to bits. But joining the two pieces quickly enough was difficult, and reaching the needed muzzle velocity meant using a gun barrel at least 17 feet long. The other assembly method, implosion, was even harder: a sub-critical plutonium ball was surrounded with a sphere of explosive charges about five feet in diameter. If all the charges could be set off at exactly the right time, their converging shockwaves would crush the ball into a dense, critical mass. But in addition to being unwieldy, both bomb configurations would be very heavy—MED estimates ranged upwards of five tons—and only one Army Air Forces (AAF) bomber was capable of delivering either weapon—the Boeing B-29 Superfortress.

On November 29, 1943, AAF and MED representatives met at Wright Field in the strictest secrecy to arrange for the modification of a small number of B-29s to carry atomic bombs, beginning with a single aircraft to test weapon drop shapes. Security was paramount, and they devised a simple, but plausible cover story: British Prime Minister Winston Churchill (the "Fat Man") would tour U.S. defense plants with President Roosevelt (the "Thin Man") in a specially modified ("Silver-plated") B-29 (the "Pullman"). The codename was shortened to Silverplate, and within Air Materiel Command channels it bore the classified program designation of MX-469.

On November 30, 1943, the AAF took delivery of the fifty-ninth Superfortress (serial number 42-6259) built at Boeing's new factory near Wichita, Kansas. In Wright Field's modification shop, skilled technicians removed the fuselage skin between the two existing bomb bays to make one long opening, replaced the four 12-foot bomb bay doors with two 27-foot doors, and fitted the forward section of the rear bay with a special bomb rack for the proposed Thin Man plutonium gun. The shape's 17-foot length easily cleared the underside of the B-29's main spar box, but there was little room to spare for its bulbous, two-foot-diameter nose when the doors were closed. The modifications took just over two months, consuming more than 6,000 man-hours, and the first modified B-29 arrived at Muroc Field, California, in late February 1944.

During flight tests in March, the Thin Man performed well, but the Fat Man proved unstable; its tail design needed refinement. The aircraft was damaged during one test, and while it was being repaired MED scientists concluded that the plutonium gun concept was unworkable. They decided instead to use uranium in the same configuration, but with a shorter gun barrel. The result was called "Little Boy," and its 10-foot length easily fit within a standard B-29 bomb bay.

The modified bomber returned to test work in June 1944, and it was soon joined by additional B-29s provided by the Martin Modification Center in Omaha, Nebraska. Martin also produced the operational Silverplate B-29s assigned to the AAF's 509th Composite Group, including the *Enola Gay*, which dropped a Little Boy atomic bomb on Hiroshima, Japan, on August 6, 1945, and *Bock's Car*, which leveled Nagasaki, Japan, with a Fat Man three days later. As for 42-6259, it served in various flight test and ground training roles until mid-1948, when the airplane was declared surplus and broken up for salvage.

Transport Airplanes

Air Corps' active inventory in the transport category in 1935 totaled only 61 airplanes. By the end of the fiscal year, however, the Materiel Division was evaluating bids from four airplane manufacturers who had responded to a new Air Corps circular proposal. Among those airplanes proposed were the first members of the famous Douglas DC family, which later dominated the transport field in the World War II years and beyond. DC stood for Douglas Commercial. Famous models of the DC family included the DC-2, DC-3, and DC-4.

The Douglas C-32 was the first Air Corps cargo transport from the DC series. Produced in 1936, the C-32 was a redesignated DC-2, a twin-engine, low-wing personnel transport. It had a crew of two and accommodations for 14 passengers or a cargo load of 4,000 pounds.[123] Included on the same contract with the C-32 was the C-33. At a top speed of 205 mph, the C-33 was the first Air Corps transport to exceed 200 mph. The C-33 was also a DC-2, but with more powerful engines and the addition of a large door in the fuselage for handling bulky freight. The C-33 became a familiar airplane at Patterson Field in the years prior to World War II. Local organizations equipped with the C-33 were the 1st Transport Squadron (1936-1939), the 5th Transport Squadron (1939-1942), and the 9th Transport Squadron (1940-1941).[124]

In 1937, the Lockheed XC-35 became the world's first cargo transport to have a pressurized cabin. For its development, the Air Corps was awarded the 1937 Collier Trophy for aircraft achievement. The twin-engine, low-wing Y1C-36 Lockheed Electra became the follow-on model to the XC-35. The airplane had a wingspan of 55 feet and a length of 38 feet 7 inches. It carried a two-man crew and eight passengers at a top speed of 205 mph. Three Electras were purchased for use by command and staff personnel during fiscal year 1937.

The acquisition of the Y1C-36 indicated a Materiel Division tendency toward procuring transport airplanes off-the-shelf from contemporary commercial aircraft sources, thus avoiding the significant costs involved in modifying civilian aircraft to meet military requirements.[125] Twenty-six twin-finned C-36s (later designated UC-36, Utility Cargo) were delivered to the Air Corps in 1942.

Douglas C-32 cargo transport

Instrument board of the Douglas C-33. Included on the same contract as the C-32, the C-33 was also a DC-2, but had different engines and a large cargo door. (*United States Air Force Museum*)

Lockheed Y1C-36 Electra

Curtiss C-46 Commando. Pursuit in the background is a Curtiss P-40. (*United States Air Force Museum*)

C-46 being loaded for a flight "over the Hump" from India to China (*United States Air Force Museum*)

A procurement order was placed during fiscal year 1939 for three single-engine Beechcraft Traveler YC-43 light-transport biplanes. This model was referred to as the "Staggerwing" because of the negative or backward stagger of the top wing from the lower wing. The airplane was later redesignated as the UC-43, and 207 production models were ordered in 1942.

Of more prominence during fiscal year 1939 was the acquisition of 11 Beechcraft Expediter C-45 twin-engine cabin planes. Affectionately dubbed the "Bugsmasher" by pilots, the C-45 was a low-wing monoplane with a twin-fin tail section and conventional, three-wheeled retractable landing gear. Engines were two 450-horsepower Pratt & Whitney R-985s. Maximum and cruising speeds were 215 mph and 150 mph respectively. The airplane accommodated two crewmen and six passengers. In 1943, the C-45 was redesignated the UC-45 and became, according to many, the most popular light cargo transport of World War II.

The Curtiss C-46 Commando, which came into the active inventory in July 1942, was another twin-engine transport that earned a permanent niche in military aviation history. The twin-engine, low-wing monoplane had a wingspan of 108 feet and a length of 76 feet 4 inches. Maximum weight was 50,675 pounds. Power plants consisted of two 2,000-horsepower Pratt & Whitney R-2800s. Maximum and cruising speeds respectively were 245 mph and 175 mph. The airplane could carry 50 troops, 33 litters, or 16,000 pounds of freight. The C-46 Commando gained its greatest fame by flying war materials to American, British, and Chinese forces over the Himalaya mountain range—"the Hump," between India and China during 1943-1944 after Japanese forces interdicted the Burma Road. In addition to trans-

C-46 Commandos were also used to tow gliders filled with paratroopers. In this 1950 photograph, a C-46E is towing a Waco CG-15 glider with an experimental rigid tow bar. (*United States Air Force Museum*)

Douglas C-47 Skytrain

porting cargo, the airplane also towed gliders filled with paratroopers. Altogether, the AAF accepted 3,144 C-46s during the war. In 1972, a C-46D was placed on permanent display at the United States Air Force Museum.

One of the most legendary airplanes of either civilian or military aviation was the militarized Douglas DC-3 low-wing monoplane known as the C-47 Skytrain. When the DC-3 first rolled off the production line in 1936, it was a luxurious airplane designed to carry passengers (the claim was 14 berths or 21 seats). The vehicle had a wingspan of 95 feet 6 inches, a length of 63 feet 9 inches, and used two 750-horsepower Pratt & Whitney power plants. The passenger liner weighed 24,000 pounds and cruised between 165 and 180 mph. Within a few months after it was introduced commercially the airplane began carrying about 95 percent of all passenger traffic.[126]

In fiscal year 1940, the Materiel Division ordered modified DC-3s to meet military needs. Designated the C-47, the airplane entered the active inventory in 1942. Thousands of Americans in uniform during World War II came to know the airplane as the "Gooney Bird," the epitome of reliability. The AAF purchased 10,000 DC-3 type airplanes. This amount was nearly half of all transport aircraft procured between 1940 and 1945.[127] The DC-3, with slightly different modifications, was also designated C-48, C-49, C-50, C-51, C-52, and C-53.

In the early part of World War II, the C-47 was flown by the 5th, 9th, 11th, and 13th Transport Squadrons at Patterson Field. Gooney Birds continued to fly actively at Wright-Patterson Air Force Base as late as December 1968. According to one author, the DC-3/C-47 series was "the most famous transport family ever built." Serving in over 40 countries, these airplanes flew more miles, hauled more freight, and carried more passengers in their day than any other aircraft.[128]

Another transport that came off the 1942 production lines to gain a reputation for sterling performance and reliability was the Douglas C-54 Skymaster, the first four-engine cargo transport in AAF history. This military variation of the DC-4 had a wingspan of 117 feet 6 inches, and a length of 93 feet 11 inches. The Skymaster could accommodate 50 passengers, 26 stretchers, or 14,000 pounds of cargo at a top speed of 285 mph. More than 1,000 of these airplanes entered the AAF inventory before the end of World War II. The C-54 served on long hauls such as the "Hump" route between India and China. The airplane also made over 100,000 transoceanic flights.[129]

C-47 cabin with seats installed for transporting troops (*United States Air Force Museum*)

Douglas C-54 Skymasters on the Patterson Field flightline

Consolidated C-87, a modified version of the B-24 Liberator bomber

The AAF's primary, long-range heavy cargo transport during the war, however, was the C-87, a modified version of the B-24 Liberator four-engine bomber. Introduced in 1942, the heavy transport had a five-man crew, accommodations for 25 seats or 10 berths, and a capacity for 12,000 pounds of cargo. The airplane could reach a top speed of 305 mph with a range of 2,900 miles. Much of the C-87's work was hauling large quantities of aviation fuel "over the Hump" into China.

Observation Airplanes

In 1935, the Materiel Division awarded Douglas a contract for the delivery of 71 (later increased to 90) O-46A single-engine monoplanes. This observation aircraft had a wingspan of 45 feet 9 inches, a length of 34 feet 10 inches, and was powered by a 725-horsepower Pratt & Whitney R-1535 engine. The airplane carried two crewmembers in an enclosed cockpit with a sliding canopy. Its armament consisted of two .30-caliber Browning machine guns (one mounted in the wing and another that was flexible). Maximum and cruising speeds were 200 mph and 171 mph respectively; range was 635 miles and ceiling was 24,500 feet.

The O-46A was the last of a long line of distinguished Douglas observation airplanes. It was designed to operate from established bases behind "fairly static battlelines" as existed in World War I. In 1939, at the outbreak of World War II, the Air Corps decided that this newest observation airplane was too slow and too heavy to outrun and outmaneuver enemy pursuit aircraft. It also weighed too much to operate from small, wet, unprepared landing strips and was too large to conceal beneath trees. Although at least 11 O-46A's were sent overseas, the remainder of the inventory was used primarily in training and in utility roles such as photography. The only remaining O-46A was restored by the Department of Aviation Technology, Purdue University, Indiana, and placed on display at the United States Air Force Museum in 1975.[130]

In fiscal year 1937, the Materiel Division placed an order with North American Aviation for 109 O-47A three-place, single-engine monoplanes. The first machine was delivered in April 1938 and the remainder was scheduled for fiscal year 1939. The O-47A represented a marked advance in corps and division observation aircraft. In addition to the high-speed characteristics required for observation, the airplane was well suited for photographic missions and was "an outstanding weapon for direct support of ground forces."[131] It had a wingspan of 46 feet 4 inches, and a length of 33 feet 3 inches. It was powered by a 975-horsepower engine and carried a three-man crew and two machine guns. It could achieve a top speed of 223 mph.[132]

In fiscal year 1939, the Materiel Division ordered 74 North American O-47B airplanes. The O-47B was similar to the O-47A but was fitted with a 1,060-horsepower engine and an extra 50-gallon fuel tank. The O-47B also had a single-lens aerial camera.[133]

In contrast to the armed, high-powered O-47 series, the Air Corps ordered 74 Stinson O-49 (later the Vultee L-1) high-wing cabin planes, equipped with a single 295-horsepower Lycoming R-680 engine, for observation and liaison work. Maximum and cruising speeds respectively on the O-49 were 129 mph and 109 mph with a range of 280 miles. Maximum altitude was 18,000 feet. The 3,325-pound airplane had a two-man crew and carried no

Douglas O-46 observation aircraft designed to carry sophisticated photographic equipment (*United States Air Force Museum*)

armament. The O-49 featured full-span automatic slots on the leading edge of the wing and pilot-operated slotted flaps on the trailing edge. This configuration resulted in low takeoff and landing speeds, allowing the airplane to use short fields or landing strips. The versatile O-49 was used both in the continental United States and overseas in diverse roles such as towing training gliders, artillery spotting, liaison missions, emergency rescue and ambulance airlift, transporting supplies, and special espionage flights deep in enemy territory. On occasion, the aircraft was used to drop light bombs.

Other observation aircraft procured during World War II included the Curtiss O-52 Owl and the Taylorcraft O-57 Grasshopper. The Owl was an all-metal, high-wing monoplane powered by a 600-horsepower Pratt & Whitney R-1340 engine. The O-52 was never used in combat, but helped to fill the need for trainers in the early years of the war. The O-57 Grasshopper was a light, unarmed cabin plane designed for liaison duty in support of front-line ground troops. In 1942, all O-57s were redesignated L-2 (Liaison) Grasshoppers.[134]

North American O-47 observation aircraft with Wright Field insignia

Stinson O-49 observation (later the Vultee L-1 Vigilant)

Observation work performed from a Curtiss Owl assigned to the 119th Observation Squadron, New Jersey National Guard (*United States Air Force Museum*)

AIRPLANES ON HAND IN THE AAF BY MAJOR TYPE, JULY 1939-AUGUST 1945

Year—As of June 30

AIRPLANE TYPE	1940	1941	1942	1943	1944	(Aug. 31) 1945
Very Heavy Bombers				2	445	2,865
Heavy Bombers	54	120	846	4,421	11,720	11,065
Medium Bombers	478	611	1,047	4,242	5,427	5,384
Light Bombers	166	292	696	1,689	2,914	3,079
Fighters	477	1,018	2,950	8,010	15,644	16,799
Reconnaissance	414	415	468	486	1,056	1,971
Transports	127	144	824	4,268	9,433	9,561
Trainers	1,243	4,124	12,610	22,849	27,907	9,558
Communications	7	53	1,732	3,051	4,211	3,433
Total	2,966	6,777	21,173	49,018	78,757	63,715

Source: ATC Pamphlet 190-1, *History of the United States Air Force* (Randolph AFB, Texas, 1961), pp VII-4.

Pursuit Airplanes

Just as bombers underwent rapid development in the 1930s, pursuit airplanes also changed significantly. In the mid-1930s, the Air Corps began to establish requirements for single-place pursuits that could double as interceptors and "multi-place fighter types." The P-series airplanes developed into the dynamic and effective fighters of World War II renown. After May 1942, airplanes previously identified as pursuits, interceptors, or fighters were officially designated "fighters"; however, the P prefix continued throughout World War II.

During fiscal year 1936, the Seversky Aircraft Corporation was chosen over Northrop and Curtiss to produce a single-place, all-metal pursuit airplane. The P-35 was the last Seversky airplane accepted by the Air Corps before the company became Republic Aircraft in 1939. (The latter, in turn, merged with Fairchild in 1965.) A procurement contract was signed for 77 P-35 airplanes with deliveries starting in 1937. The low-wing, cantilever, all-metal monoplane was the Air Corps' first pursuit with an enclosed cockpit and retractable landing gear. The P-35 had a wingspan of 36 feet, a length of 25 feet 2 inches, and a height of 9 feet 9 inches. One .50-caliber and one .30-caliber machine gun was mounted the the fuselage. Its power plant was a 950-horsepower Pratt & Whitney R-1830; respective maximum and cruising speeds were 281 mph and 260 mph. The P-35 had a service ceiling of 31,400 feet and a range of 950 miles.[135]

The Japanese Navy ordered 20 of a two-seater version of the P-35 in 1938. This was the only American-built airplane used by the Japanese during World War II. Sweden also placed an order for 60 improved P-35s, but the Air Corps preempted the order in 1940. This improved model, designated the P-35A, had a 1,200-horsepower engine, carried four guns, 350 pounds of bombs, and had a maximum speed of 320 mph. The A models were assigned to the 17th and 20th Pursuit Squadrons in the Philippine Islands and all were lost in action during the early weeks of World War II. The only surviving P-35 was later restored and placed on display at the United States Air Force Museum.

The Curtiss Aeroplane Division of the Curtiss-Wright Corporation won the 1937-1938 competition to produce the single-seat fighter known as the P-36 Hawk, an all-metal, low-wing monoplane. The P-36, which evolved from the Hawk Model 75, was distinguished as a pioneer in wing-mounted machine guns (two .30-caliber) and had a top speed of just over 300 mph. Range was 825 miles and service ceiling was 33,000 feet. Eventually the Air Corps/Army Air Forces acquired a total of 210 P-36A pursuits. English and French air forces flew the Hawk 75A against German fighters in 1939 and 1940. In 1941, the AAF transferred 39 P-36A's to Wheeler Field, Hawaii. During

Seversky P-35 pursuit (*United States Air Force Museum*)

the Japanese attack on Pearl Harbor, December 7, 1941, two P-36A's from the 46th Pursuit Squadron at Wheeler Field shot down two enemy aircraft.

Another famous pursuit aircraft to emerge from Wright Field on the eve of World War II was the Curtiss-Wright single-engine, low-wing, P-40 Warhawk (also dubbed the Hawk, Tomahawk, and Kittyhawk by other nations). The airplane had a semi-monocoque fuselage and hydraulically operated, retractable landing gear. The P-40B carried two fixed, synchronized, .30-caliber machine guns in each wing, plus six bombs. Subsequent models increased armament to six .50-caliber guns and 700 pounds of bombs. The P-40 wingspan measured 37 feet 4 inches; length was 31 feet 9 inches. Thc single engine was a 1,040-horsepower Allison V-1710-33; maximum and cruising speeds were 362 mph and 235 mph respectively. Range was 950 miles with a service ceiling of 32,750 feet. The manufacturer received an order for 524 P-40s for delivery during fiscal year 1940. By the time production stopped in 1944, 13,738 of these pursuits had come off the production lines.

The P-40, with its nose painted to resemble a shark's snout, gained fame with the Flying Tigers of the U.S. 14th Air Force in China in 1942-1943. During an eight-month period, American pilots in P-40s shot down 286 Japanese airplanes while suffering only eight losses. The Warhawk flew on nearly every fighting front in World War II. Dozens of P-40s were shipped to Russia and 27 other Allied nations.[136]

Making its initial flight at Wright Field in April 1939 was another pursuit destined for combat fame in practically every arena in World War II, the Bell P-39 Airacobra. A single-engine, low-wing monoplane, the P-39 had a wingspan of 34 feet, and a length of 30 feet 2 inches. Its power plant was a 1,200-horsepower Allison V-1710 mounted behind the cockpit; the propeller shaft passed between the pilot's feet. Top speed was 385 mph. The airplane had a 37-mm gun mounted in the nose and four .50-caliber machine guns in the wings.

The Airacobra was especially prominent in the Southwest Pacific and Mediterranean theaters. Not equipped with a turbosupercharger, the airplane achieved its best performance below 17,000 feet of altitude, making it an effective ground support weapon. Because of this characteristic, the Soviet Union ordered 4,773 of this type airplane under the lend-lease program. This figure represented nearly half of the 9,558 P-39s manufactured by the time production ceased in August 1944.[137]

Lockheed's P-38 Lightning, described in contemporary reports as a "high-flying twin-engine fighter of outstanding qualities," was another pursuit airplane evaluated at Wright Field about the same time as the P-39. It was a strikingly beautiful airplane with a distinctive, short center fuselage and twin booms, which housed the two 1,425-horsepower engines, superchargers, radiators, and landing gear. One of the Lightning's outstanding characteristics derived from its opposite rotating propellers, which eliminated torque and gave it superior maneuverability. The airplane's wingspan totaled 52 feet; length was 37 feet 10 inches. The Lightning's gross weight was 15,340 pounds; maximum speed was 390 mph. Armament consisted of one 20-mm cannon and four .50-caliber machine guns. It could carry 10 5-inch rockets or 4,000 pounds of bombs. Without bombs and with a maximum fuel

COSTS OF REPRESENTATIVE AIRCRAFT, WORLD WAR II

AIRPLANE	COST
Very Heavy Bombers	
B-29	$509,465
Heavy Bombers	
B-17	187,742
B-24	215,516
Medium Bombers	
B-25	116,752
B-26	192,427
Light Bombers	
A-20	100,800
A-26	175,892
Fighters	
P-38	97,147
P-39	50,666
P-40	44,892
P-47	83,001
P-51	50,985
Reconnaissance	
OA-10	207,541
Transports	
C-43	27,332
C-45	48,830
C-46	221,550
C-47	85,035
C-54	259,816
Trainers	
PT-13, PT-17, PT-27	9,896
PT-19, PT-23, PT-26	15,052
BT-13, BT-15	23,068
AT-6	22,952
AT-7, AT-11	68,441
Communications	
L-4	2,701
L-5	8,323

Source: ATC Pamphlet 190-1, *History of the United States Air Force* (Randolph AFB, Texas, 1961), pp VII-4.

Curtiss P-36 Hawk pursuit (*United States Air Force Museum*)

Curtiss XP-40 Warhawk, October 1938

Bell XP-39 Airacobra (*United States Air Force Museum*)

Lockheed XP-38 Lightning on Wright Field (*United States Air Force Museum*)

load, the airplane was an outstanding, long-range, fighter escort vehicle, with an operational range of 1,500 miles.

Analysis of the January 1939 tests on the P-38 coincided with the presidential thrust to expand airplane production, and the Materiel Division ordered 13 service test models from Lockheed for delivery in fiscal year 1940. In September 1939, Lockheed received a firm order for 607 Lightnings. Between that date and the cessation of production in August 1945, 9,923 P-38s were built. Confidence in the P-38 proved to be completely justified—the Lightning set an enviable combat record that few other fighters could match and none could surpass. It was credited with shooting down more Japanese airplanes than any other fighter in the Pacific. The P-38's "rapid roll, ability to dive at extremely high speeds, and concentrated firepower made it a formidable adversary." The airplane flew a variety of missions with ease: bomber escort, level bombing, dive bombing, ground strafing, and photographic. German Luftwaffe pilots in North Africa called the P-38 "the forked-tail devil."[138]

In 1942, Republic Aviation's production line began turning out another of America's leading fighter airplanes. The P-47 Thunderbolt earned a reputation for being "the roughest, toughest fighter of the war, with the ability to take a tremendous amount of punishment." The airplane was affectionately and more commonly called the "Jug" (for "Juggernaut"). A direct descendant of the tiny Seversky P-35 manufactured in 1935, the P-47 had a wingspan of 40 feet 9 inches. Its length was 36 feet 1 inch, and height was 14 feet 2 inches. The single 2,000-horsepower Pratt & Whitney R-2800 engine "put the-P-47 ahead in this category of all single-engine fighters of the AAF and gave it rank with any other contemporary, single-engine fighter in the world." Armament varied from six to eight .50-caliber machine guns and six 5-inch rockets with a 2,000-pound bomb load, or 10 rockets without bombs. Gross weight was 14,500 pounds.

The Thunderbolt started out with a top speed of 425 mph, but subsequent improvements to the engine increased the top and cruising speeds respectively to 460 mph and 260 mph. In 1943, the airplane had a range of 500 miles as a fighter-bomber and 1,000 miles as an escort fighter for heavy bombers. Additional fuel capability with external tanks increased the respective ranges to 800 and 2,000 miles—deep into Germany. Equipped with a turbosupercharger, the P-47's service ceiling was 42,000 feet. On April 8, 1943, the Thunderbolt made its initial sweep over western Europe. By the end of World War II this powerful fighter had flown 546,000 sorties (mainly in the European and Mediterranean theaters), had destroyed 11,874 enemy airplanes, 9,000 locomotives, and 160,000 railroad cars and equipment.[139]

The North American Aviation P-51 Mustang, developed from a British request in 1940 for a machine similar to the P-40 Kittyhawk pursuit, was arguably the best all-around, American-built fighter of World War II. The Royal Air Force (RAF) used the airplane for close ground support missions and quickly labeled it "the best American fighter" of its day. The P-51A was a single-engine, low-wing monoplane with an Allison V-1710 engine. The P-51B rolled off the North American production line in 1943. It had a wingspan of 37 feet, a length of 32 feet 3 inches, and a height of 13 feet 8 inches. Maximum weight was 8,400 pounds. The aircraft's power plant was a 1,380-horsepower British Rolls-Royce Merlin V-1650 (built by American Packard). Armament consisted of six .50-caliber machine guns and 10 5-inch rockets, or 2,000 pounds of bombs (without rockets). The Mustang's maximum and cruising speeds were 437 mph and 275 mph respectively, and its service ceiling was 31,350 feet. Drop fuel tanks gave the airplane a range of 1,000 miles and permitted its use as an escort for heavy bombers from England to Germany, and for B-29s from Iwo Jima to Japan in 1945.

The first AAF P-51 entered combat in Europe in December 1943. By the end of the war, Mustangs had destroyed 4,950 German airplanes in the air. Between 1942 and 1945 the AAF ordered 14,855 Mustangs (including A-36A dive bomber and F-6 photo-reconnaissance variations). Of the total procured, 7,956 were P-51D models. In 1957, a P-51, the last propeller-driven U.S. Air Force fighter assigned to a tactical unit, was transferred from the West Virginia Air National Guard to the United States Air Force Museum for permanent display.[140]

In late 1943, Northrop Aircraft Corporation began manufacturing the first AAF airplane specifically designed for service as a night fighter. The P-61 Black Widow was a coal-black, twin-engine monoplane with a twin fuselage and a twin tail. The P-61 resembled the P-38, but was larger and considerably more powerful with its two 2,000-horsepower Pratt & Whitney R-2800 engines. In size and weight, the

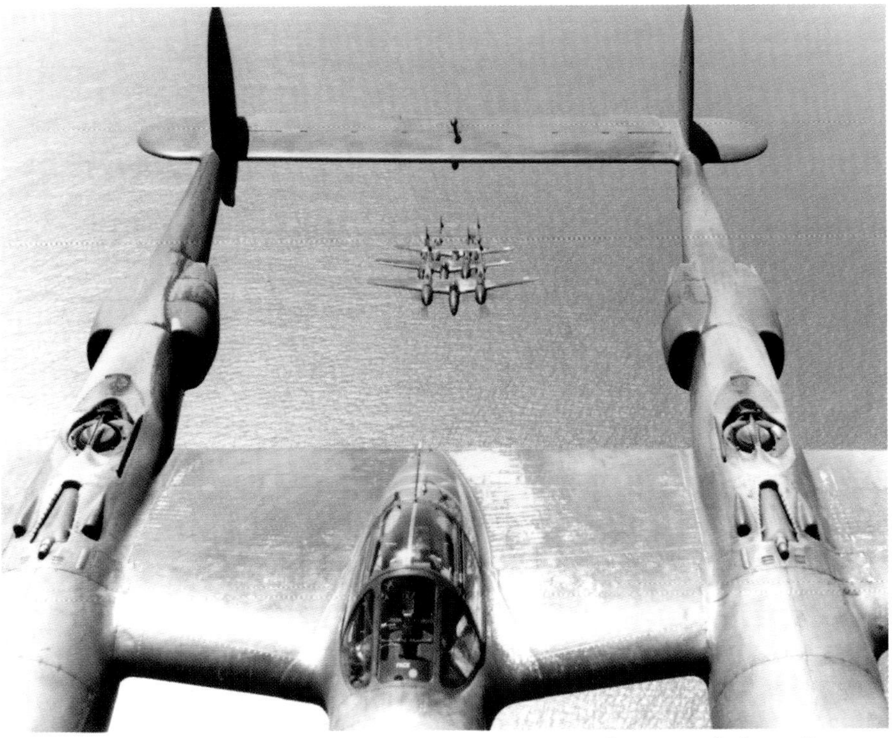

The P-38 Lightning was credited with shooting down more Japanese airplanes than any other Army Air Forces fighter in the Pacific theater. (*United States Air Force Museum*)

Republic XP-47H Thunderbolt, an advanced configuration tested at Wright Field

North American XP-51 Mustang (*United States Air Force Museum*)

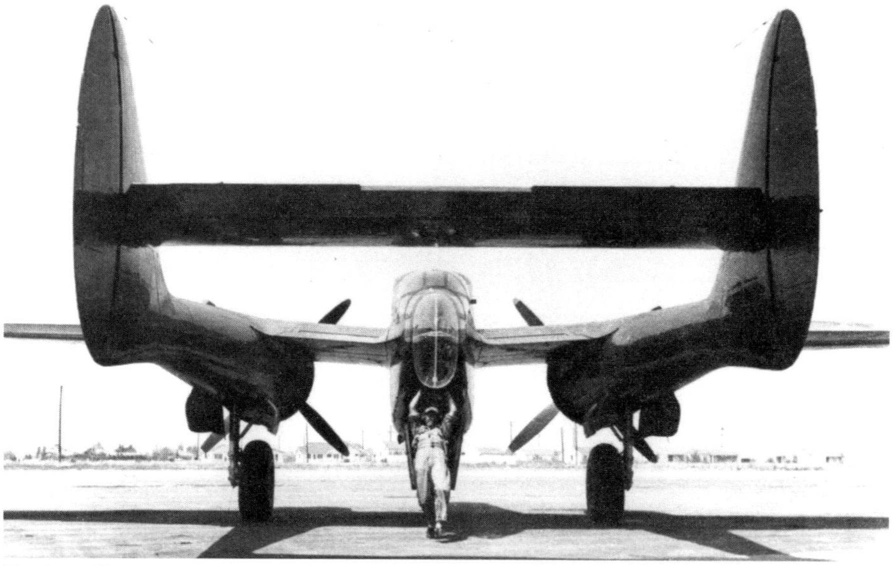

Northrop P-61 Black Widow night fighter with twin fuselage and twin tail (*United States Air Force Museum*)

Black Widow was nearer to a medium bomber than a fighter.

The P-61 wingspan measured 66 feet; its length was 49 feet 7 inches; and its maximum weight totaled 38,000 pounds. The airplane carried a pilot, radar operator, and gunner, and was crammed with radar and electronic equipment, much of it stored in its elongated nose. The airplane used both airborne and ground radar in locating and tracking targets. The P-61 located enemy aircraft in total darkness, using sophisticated equipment to guide it into proper attack position. Armament consisted of four .50-caliber machine guns in the upper turret, four 20-mm cannon in the belly, and 6,400 pounds of bombs.

An internal fuel capacity of 640 gallons supplemented by two or four wing tanks holding either 165 or 310 gallons of gasoline gave the airplane an ultimate combat range of 1,200 miles and a ferrying range of nearly double that figure. Maximum speed was 360 mph with a service ceiling of 33,100 feet.

About 700 P-61s were manufactured during 1944-1945 and were used in both the European and Pacific theaters. Thirty-six others were produced in 1946 as F-15A unarmed, photo-reconnaissance airplanes. Although the P-61 was twice the weight of the P-47 and three times the weight of the P-51, the Black Widow "proved to be highly maneuverable—more so than any other AAF fighter."[141]

Training Airplanes

Following the progress of bombers and pursuits, the Air Corps made major improvements in training-type airplanes. Three classes of airplanes composed this category: primary trainers (PT), basic trainers (BT), and advanced trainers (AT).

A circular proposal for primary trainers during fiscal year 1935 elicited bids from the Stearman Aircraft, Consolidated Aircraft, and St. Louis Aircraft companies. Stearman (later Stearman-Boeing) received a contract for 25 PT-13 Kaydet primary trainers, with delivery starting in March 1936. This popular biplane had two open cockpits, a wingspan of 32 feet 2 inches, and a length of 24 feet 8 inches. Gross weight was 2,571 pounds. The original model was powered by a 220-horsepower Lycoming R-680 engine. Maximum and cruising speeds were 125 mph and 104 mph, respectively. The same airplane was designated the PT-17 when equipped with a Continental engine, and the PT-18 with a Jacobs engine. A later version, the Boeing PT-27, had a cockpit canopy and was built entirely for export to the Allies.

The favorite monoplane primary trainer of the war period was the Fairchild Cornell series, including the PT-19, the PT-23, and the PT-26. These had 175- to 220-horsepower engines and top speeds to 130 mph.

Yet another popular monoplane trainer was the Ryan series of Recruits, the PT-20, PT-21, and PT-22. These were low-wing, all-metal airplanes with tandem open seats, 125- to 160-horsepower engines, and top speeds of 130 to 140 mph.[142] A new concept proposed for the basic trainer category was that of a low-wing monoplane to serve as a transition between the low-speed primary training type and the high-speed advanced trainer. It would carry "as many

North American BT-9B basic trainer at Wright Field

[of the] special instruments, controls, and devices found on modern high performance service aircraft as practical."[143] These would include "complete instrument flying-and-landing equipment, complete radio installation, flaps or other high lift devices, controllable pitch propellers, and a retractable alighting [sic] gear." Accordingly, Circular Proposal 35-15 published these requirements to airplane manufacturers during fiscal year 1935. Bids were received from Seversky, Douglas, Consolidated, Chance-Vought, and General Aviation. Seversky won the competition with its model SEV-3XAR, designated the BT-8, and received a contract for 35 trainers. The BT-8 was the first low-wing, monoplane basic trainer with an enclosed cockpit. It had a wingspan of 36 feet, a length of 24 feet 4 inches, and a height of 9 feet 9 inches. It had a 400-horsepower Pratt & Whitney R-985 engine and a top speed of 175 mph.

In fiscal year 1936, North American Aviation received a contract for 82 BT-9 basic trainers. This low-wing monoplane was the Air Corps' first combat trainer. The machine had a wingspan of 42 feet and a length of 27 feet 7 inches. It was powered by a 400-horsepower Wright R-975 engine. The airplane had an enclosed cockpit, carried two .30-caliber machine guns and a camera. Top speed was 172 mph.[144]

The next year, North American received a contract for 117 BT-9B's. Later procurement included 33 machines for the Organized Reserve Corps and 40 for the Naval Bureau of Aeronautics (which the Navy designated NJ-1). During World War II, basic training for both the AAF and the Navy was largely dominated by the Vultee BT-13 and BT-15 Valiant trainers. These were single-engine monoplanes with 450-horsepower engines, retractable landing gear, and top speeds of 185 mph.[145]

In the advanced trainer category, North American received a sizeable procurement order in fiscal year 1939 for 92 BC-1A trainers. This single-engine, low-wing monoplane subsequently became famous as the AT-6 Texan advanced trainer. Nearly all AAF advanced, single-engine training was conducted in the AT-6, as was a considerable amount of Navy advanced training. The AT-6 had a wingspan of 42 feet, a length of 29 feet, and a height of 11 feet 1 inch. The power plant was a 600-horsepower Pratt & Whitney R-1340 engine. The airplane's respective maximum and cruising speeds were 210 mph and 145 mph, with a range of 870 miles and a service ceiling of 24,750 feet. Between late

Fairchild PT-19 Cornell

The PT-13A Kaydet primary trainer evolved from Stearman's privately financed X70 prototype, shown here. The Air Corps eventually purchased nearly 5,000 of the two-seat biplane trainers and its successors (the PT-17, PT-18, and PT-27).

Ryan PT-20A Recruit

North American T-6F Texan advanced trainer at Wright Field for tests of cross-wind landing gear, May 1950

Curtiss AT-9 Fledgling ("Jeep")

Beechcraft AT-7 Navigator (*United States Air Force Museum*)

1938 and 1945, North American produced 15,495 Texans. Of these, 10,057 were sold to the Army as AT-6s. Others went to the Navy as SNJs, and still others were sold to 30 Allied nations.[146]

Several outstanding multi-engine advanced trainers were developed during this period for training bomber pilots and aircrews. One of these was the Beechcraft AT-10 Wichita, an all-wood, four-seat, low-wing monoplane with two 295-horsepower Lycoming R-680 engines and a top speed of 190 mph. Another multi-engine advanced trainer was the Cessna AT-17 Bobcat, a four-seater with twin 245-horsepower Jacobs R-775 engines and a top speed of 195 mph. A third was the Curtiss AT-9 Jeep, a four-seater with 295-horsepower engines and top speed of 197 mph. Later in the war, the North American AT-24 Mitchell, converted from the versatile B-25 bomber, became the most popular transition and aircrew trainer.[147]

Rounding out the advanced trainer category were the aircraft used for training navigators and bombardiers, the Beechcraft AT-7 Navigator and the AT-11 Kansan. Nearly all of the 45,000 bombardiers and 50,000 navigators trained during the war were taught in these aircraft. The AT-11 was configured with a transparent nose, a bomb bay, internal bomb racks, and two .30-caliber machine guns. The AT-11A was retrofitted with astrodomes placed in the ceiling of the fuselage.[148]

POSTWAR CONTRIBUTIONS TO AVIATION 1946-1951

In 1944, the Materiel Command at Wright Field merged with the Air Service Command at Patterson Field to form the Air Technical Service Command (ATSC). This wartime merger of research, procurement, and logistics was perpetuated when ATSC was redesignated the Air Materiel Command (AMC) in March 1946. In the postwar period from 1946 to 1950, AMC supervised research, development, and procurement efforts at Wright Field and, after January 1948, at the consolidated Wright-Patterson Air Force Base. With the creation of the Air Research and Development Command (ARDC) in 1950, Air Force airplane research and development again became a separate command, and thus entered a new era. Throughout these organizational changes, the Dayton installation continued to make significant contributions to military aviation through the development of specific aircraft.

As World War II ended, the AAF inventory included such veterans as the B-17, P-38, P-39, P-47, P-51, C-46, and C-47, as well as the newly developed P-61 Black Widow, C-54 Skymaster, and B-29 Superfortress. These airplanes would continue to play prominent roles in the AAF and the U.S. Air Force. Additional aircraft soon entered the inventory, including the P-82, C-82, C-118, and B-50. Even newer aircraft, such as the B-35 and B-36, that would bridge the transition between the reciprocating engine generation and the jet age, were in development.

Beechcraft AT-11 on a bombing training mission. The bombadier student and instructor ready the bomb site in the nose of the plane.

One of two North American XP-82A Twin Mustangs built. The P-82 designation was changed to F-82 in 1948.

Fairchild C-82A Packet with experimental belt landing gear at Patterson Field

Fairchild C-119A Flying Boxcar, the only A model built

The North American P-82 Twin Mustang became the last AAF propeller-driven fighter acquired in quantity, and was also the last aircraft to carry the designation P for pursuit. (Starting in 1948, all such airplanes carried the new designation of F for fighter, including many of the existing World War II pursuits.) The P-82 was a twin P-51 Mustang, i.e., two P-51 airframes wedded at the wing to form a twin-engine, twin-tail, twin-cockpit airplane. The wingspan was 51 feet 3 inches; length was 38 feet 1 inch. Maximum weight was 24,600 pounds. Armament consisted of six .50-caliber machine guns, 25 5-inch rockets, and 4,000 pounds of bombs. The two engines, one in each airframe, were 1,380-horsepower Packard V-1650s. Maximum speed was 482 mph. Range was 2,200 miles and service ceiling was 39,000 feet. The P-82 was developed to carry a pilot and copilot/navigator on long-range bombing missions. Although the first production airplane arrived in late 1945, it was not until the following year that these radar-equipped airplanes were produced in quantity.

The Fairchild C-82 Packet, a twin-engine, twin-boom, twin-fin, high-wing monoplane, was designed as a troop carrier and cargo transport. It came off the production line in late 1945 after hostilities ended. Wingspan of the C-82 was 106 feet; length was 75 feet 10 inches. The airplane had 42 seats, a top speed of 223 mph, and carried 11,500 pounds of cargo.[149] In 1947, a C-82 modification appeared with a longer wingspan (109 feet 4 inches), an extended fuselage (85 feet), and an increased top speed (280 mph). It was designated the Fairchild C-119 Flying Boxcar. The C-119 retained the "twin" configuration of the C-82, and had a five-man crew, 62 seats, and a cargo capacity of 20,000 pounds.

The Douglas C-118 Liftmaster was another cargo airplane designed in late World War II and procured by the Air Materiel Command in 1947. A stretched version of the C-54 Skymaster, the Liftmaster had the same wingspan (117 feet 6 inches) but was about 12 feet longer (105 feet 7 inches). Assigned to the Military Air Transport Service (MATS) as a transoceanic personnel and cargo carrier, the C-118 had accommodations for 76 seats or 60 litters and 27,000 pounds of cargo. It had a 4,910-mile range and a top speed of 370 mph, nearly 100 mph faster than the C-54.[150]

The versatility of the B-29 Superfortress had not been fully realized when World War II ended. This magnificent machine had been modified for use as the F-13 photographic-reconnaissance vehicle, but two far more significant modifications were programmed. The first—and perhaps most significant—was the 75-percent modification that resulted in the B-50 Superfortress (initially designated the B-29D). This follow-on aircraft had more powerful engines, a taller rudder, a new wing structure, and hydraulic nose-wheel steering. Respective specifications of the two versions of the Superfortress were:

	B-29	**B-50**
Wingspan	141 feet 3 inches	141 feet 3 inches
Length	99 feet	99 feet
Gross weight	124,000 pounds	168,408 pounds
Engines	Four 2,000-horsepower Wright R-3350-23	Four 3,500-horsepower Pratt & Whitney R-4360-35
Top Speed	385 mph	385 mph
Range	3,250 miles	4,650 miles
Ceiling	31,850 feet	37,000 feet

The B-50 Superfortress had at least two claims to fame. It was the last propeller-driven bomber delivered to the Air Force. It also became the first airplane to fly nonstop around the world. The B-50A *Lucky Lady II* departed Carswell Air Force Base, Texas, on February 26, 1949, and completed a 23,452-mile nonstop circumnavigation of the world in 94 hours, 1 minute. The bomber was air-refueled four times: over the Azores in the mid-Atlantic, Saudi Arabia in the Middle East, the Philippine Islands in Southeast Asia, and Hawaii in the central Pacific.[151]

KB-29 tankers provided air-to-air refueling of the *Lucky Lady II*. The KB-29 represented the second major modification of the B-29, basically a stretched version. The KB-29 entered the active inventory in 1948 with the same wingspan as the bomber (141 feet 3 inches), but was about 21 feet longer (120 feet 1 inch). In the tanker, ordnance and weapons gave way to huge fuel cells. The KB-29 initially used a gravity-flow system of fuel transfer. Two years later, Boeing developed the more versatile flying boom in the tail of the tanker, a "telescoping aluminum tube that could be used up, down, or to either side," a precursor of modern refueling systems.[152]

AMC's aeronautical and logistical experts at Wright Field also played prominent roles in the development of the B-36 Peacemaker intercontinental bomber, the largest combat airplane to reach full production status without ever flying a combat mission, and in the concurrent development of the YB-35 Flying Wing. The concept of the intercontinental bomber germinated with the XB-15 and B-19 programs in the 1930s. On April 11, 1941, the Air Corps returned to the concept and invited manufacturers to submit preliminary designs for a very heavy, long-range bomber. On May 3, Consolidated responded with a proposal for "a high-wing, single-tail, pressure-cabin bomber with a range of 10,000 miles carrying a 10,000-pound bomb load."

Boeing B-50A Superfortress, second production airplane

Northrop submitted a daring design for an all-wing bomber "without the drag-producing fuselage and tail assembly of conventional craft."

In October 1941, the Army Air Forces awarded a contract to Consolidated for two of its experimental, six-engine bombers, designated the XB-36, for delivery within 36 months. The following month, Northrop received a contract to produce an experimental model of its airplane, designated the XB-35. In June 1943, General Henry H. Arnold, the AAF commander, requested procurement of 100 B-36s. In August 1944, the secretary of war approved the contract, at an estimated cost of $154,250,000. Wartime conditions, however, hampered development of both the XB-36 and the XB-35, and neither aircraft was completed before the end of the war.

Northrop's XB-35 became the first of the "very, very heavy bombers" (VVHB) to fly, taking off from the company's plant in Hawthorne, California, in June 1946. The aircraft had a wingspan of 172 feet and a length of 53 feet. Four Pratt & Whitney R-4360 engines propelled the airplane to a top speed of 391 mph. With an 18,000-gallon fuel capacity, the XB-35 had a range of 10,000 miles, sufficient to fly nonstop across the Atlantic and return. Bomb load was 41,200 pounds, and armament consisted of 20 .50-caliber machine guns.

After limited production, the XB-35 project was abandoned because of serious problems with reduction gear arrangements and propeller governors. However, on June 1, 1945, Northrop received a contract to modify two YB-35s into jet-powered YB-49 Flying Wing aircraft. These delta-designed airplanes were equipped with eight Allison J35-A-5 turbojet engines with 4,000 pounds of thrust each. Within two months after taking to the air in October 1947, both YB-49s were destroyed in crashes and plans for a reconnaissance version were abandoned shortly thereafter.[153]

Meanwhile, the first XB-36 Peacemaker (manufactured by Consolidated-Vultee) made its maiden flight August 8, 1946, at Fort Worth, Texas; the first production model B-36 flew a year later. The XB-36 featured "a graceful tubular fuselage" 163 feet in length. At the rudder it stood 46

The B-50A Superfortress *Lucky Lady II* was the first airplane to complete a nonstop circumnavigation of the world, departing February 26, 1949. (*United States Air Force Museum*)

YB-49 flying wing, December 1948

Northrop's YB-49 jet-powered flying wing in flight

Aerial view of Northrop's four-engine B-35 flying wings at Northrop's plant

NB-36H NUCLEAR REACTOR TESTS

Following World War II, America's scientists envisioned many potential uses for atomic energy. In addition to ideas for nuclear-powered ships, locomotives, and automobiles, some innovative thinkers envisioned aircraft powered by the atom. Beginning in 1946, the United States government spent approximately $1 billion over the next decade trying to develop the latter of these through the Air Force's Nuclear Energy for the Propulsion of Aircraft (NEPA) and the Aircraft Nuclear Propulsion (ANP) programs.

Growing Cold War tensions and reports of Soviet technical advancements, both real and imagined, provided impetus for the NEPA and ANP programs. In 1950, the Joint Chiefs of Staff endorsed the need for a nuclear-powered aircraft and some officials advocated developing a long-range, nuclear-powered bomber. Planners envisioned that a nuclear-powered bomber would provide long-range capability without sacrificing speed, high-altitude capability, and evasion of defensive measures. The Air Force had reservations about the utility of nuclear aircraft and anticipated their use only for selected missions where chemical-powered systems would be unsuitable.

The Air Force awarded a contract to General Electric, effective March 21, 1951, to develop a nuclear turbojet engine, and the Atomic Energy Commission (AEC) selected the same company to develop a nuclear reactor for use with the engine. Originally, project officials planned to create a new aircraft, the X-6, to test the feasibility of nuclear-powered flight. Plans called for the X-6 to take off using its chemical-fueled engines and then switch to nuclear power supplied by an onboard reactor. Aircraft designers estimated the nuclear propulsion system would weigh approximately 165,000 pounds. Although intending to build two X-6 aircraft, the Air Force scrapped this plan after the initial design stage. Instead, Wright Field's Engineering Division recommended using an existing airframe—the huge B-36 bomber. Following this recommendation, the Air Force decided to modify a single B-36 because it was the only aircraft capable of carrying the weight necessary for the tests.

The Convair Division of General Dynamics Corporation in Fort Worth, Texas, extensively modified B-36H, serial number 51-5712, for use as the Nuclear Test Aircraft (NTA). The modifications included a totally redesigned nose section capable of supporting a 12-ton crew shield and a windshield containing 9- to 11-inch-thick transparencies. Technicians also modified the fuselage to carry nine water-filled shield tanks and other instruments necessary for the tests. Officially, the NTA carried the designation NB-36H and Convair nicknamed the plane "Crusader."

In November 1952, Wright Field officials inspected a mock-up of the aircraft's nose section and accepted the configuration for use. Convair conducted 47 radiation monitoring test flights over uninhabited areas with the NB-36H test bed between September 1955 and March 1957. The one-megawatt reactor, weighing approximately 35,000 pounds, was mounted in the aircraft's bomb bay to test shielding suitability, radiation effects on aircraft materials and components, and other aspects of nuclear flight operations. The nuclear reactor never powered the NB-36H. Instead, it flew on the power of its six propeller and four turbojet engines. During these flights the reactor was "made critical" to generate nuclear power. The lead and rubber shield completely surrounded the crew compartment and a closed-circuit television system provided the crew with views of the reactor and other areas of the aircraft.

Collectively, both NEPA and ANP encountered management and administrative problems throughout their existence, especially because of changes in direction dictated by world events and the focus of U.S. leaders. The Air Force managed its role in the program through a weapon system project office consisting of personnel from Air Research and Development Command (ARDC) and Air Materiel Command (AMC) at Wright Field. Difficulties multiplied when international tensions forced a change in focus for the program. Most significantly, U.S. officials felt compelled to sacrifice performance for speed. Originally designed as a 15-year research and testing effort, NEPA was dissolved in May 1951 and replaced by ANP. The program continued to make progress, but in early 1953 presidential advisors questioned the military worth of nuclear-powered aircraft. Although the program survived this change in direction, the administration significantly reduced funding and terminated the X-6 test bed. However, the program continued to receive approximately $150 million annually.

Following the flight tests, work continued on the project in various ways until President Kennedy's administration officially terminated ANP in the spring of 1961. Program officials considered the flight tests highly successful and the technology base produced by NEPA and ANP created the most extensive data collection on the subject of nuclear-powered flight anywhere in the world. Crusader, the NB-36H that served the program so well as the NTA, was dismantled and sold for scrap. To date, the nation has not revisited the effort to develop a nuclear-powered aircraft.

The NB-36H, a modified B-36 bomber, completed 47 radiation-monitoring tests between 1955-1957. The plane itself was not powered by its onboard nuclear reactor.

Sources: Robert L. Perry, *History of the Nuclear Engineering Test Facility* (unpublished final draft), Aeronautical Systems Division, Historical Division, Information Office n.d.; Jay Miller, *The X-Planes* (Arlington, TX, 1988), pp 68-73; Marcelle Size Knaack, *Post-World War II Bombers* (Washington, D.C., 1988), pp 43-48.

Convair B-36B Peacemaker with insignia red arctic markings on the outer wings and rear fuselage (*Mrs. Darlene Gerhardt*)

Fuselage and wing of the first B-36A in the Wright Field Static Test facility (Building 65, Area B), being turned upside down in order to conduct positive angle of attack structural tests (*Bob Cavanagh*)

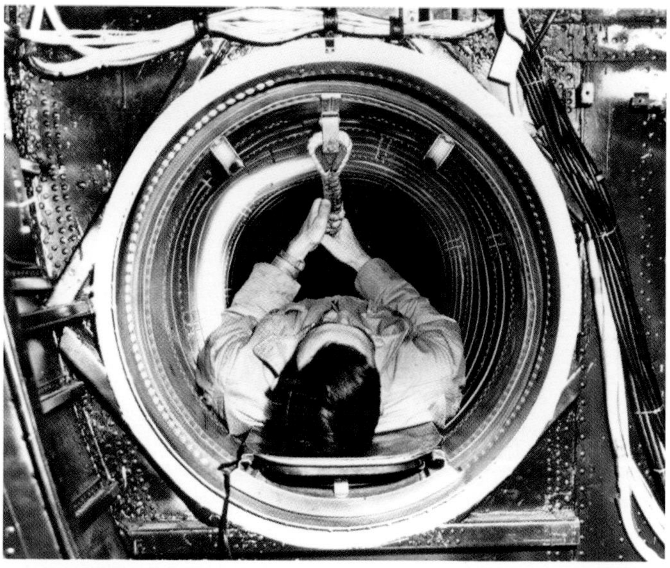

The giant XB-36 was so large that a special tunnel, two feet in diameter and 85 feet long (shown here), was designed to allow crew members to move from the front of the airplane to the aft cabin while in flight. This crew member is lying on a four-wheeled scooter and moves by pulling on an overhead cable. (*United States Air Force Museum*)

feet 10 inches tall. The wing had a span of 230 feet and a total area of 4,772 square feet. The high-wing monoplane was powered with six Pratt & Whitney R-4360-25 Wasp Major engines that delivered 3,000 horsepower to each of the 19-foot pusher propellers. The bomber's gross weight was 260,000 pounds. Integral fuel tanks in the wing spar held 19,197 gallons. Top speed was 346 mph with a range of 10,000 miles.

An improved B model flew July 8, 1948. The D model, which came out in 1949, was even further improved by adding four General Electric J-47-GE-19 jet engines, each having a thrust of 5,200 pounds.

The J model, last of the B-36 line, was the most powerful of all, with six 3,800-horsepower Pratt & Whitney R-4360s and four General Electric J47s with 5,200 pounds of thrust each. Maximum speed on the J model was given as 435 mph, with a range of 10,000 miles and a service ceiling of 45,700 feet. By the time production ended in August 1954, more than 380 B-36s had been manufactured.

The Army Air Forces entered the age of jet-engine aircraft in October 1942, with the maiden flight of the Bell Aircraft Company XP-59A Airacomet at Rogers Dry Lake, California (now a part of Edwards Air Force Base). Four Wright Field engineers played key roles in the project. Major Donald J. Keirn (later brigadier general) of the Power Plant Laboratory had studied jet airplane engines and airframes in England prior to America's involvement in the war. Major Ralph P. Swofford (later lieutenant general) of the Fighter Project Office assumed responsibility for developing the airframe of the XP-59. Choosing the location of the flight test site was the responsibility of Major General Benjamin W. Chidlaw (later lieutenant general), chief of the Materiel Command Engineering Branch. He and Major Swofford selected Rogers Dry Lake for two key reasons: it permitted the long takeoff roll required by jet aircraft (based on RAF experience) and it met the requirement for absolute secrecy. Lieutenant Colonel Laurence C. Craigie (later lieutenant general), chief of the Aircraft Projects Branch at Wright Field, became the first AAF jet pilot when he flew the Airacomet on October 2, 1942. (Bell's chief test pilot Bob Stanley had made the first jet flight in American history in the XP-59A the day before.)

The XP-59A was a "shoulder-wing single-seat monoplane." It had a wingspan of 45 feet 6 inches, and a length of 38 feet 2 inches. Its power plants were twin General Electric I-A jet engines, giving the airplane a top speed of 415 mph at 30,000 feet. Combat range with 1,000 pounds of weapons was 525 miles. The first production models of the P-59A Airacomet were delivered to the 412th Fighter Group, 4th Air Force, at March Field, California, in August 1944. The 412th became America's first, all-jet unit.[154] Bell manufactured a total of 66 P-59A and P-59B Airacomets.

The last B-36J rolls off the Convair production line at Fort Worth, 1954.

At Wright Field in October 1944, Women Airforce Service Pilot (WASP) Ann Baumgartner became the first woman to operate a turbojet airplane when she flew the XP-59A for 30 minutes. (The first woman pilot in the world to fly a jet was Hannah Reitsch of Germany who flew the rocket-powered Messerschmitt Me 163 in 1943.)[155]

The P-59 Airacomet never flew in combat, but it served a valuable role as the precursor of more advanced jet aircraft, such as the P-80. In May 1943, the Materiel Command asked Lockheed to manufacture an experimental airframe to be powered by a British jet engine. Lockheed began work prior to actual signing of the contract for the XP-80 in October 1943, and the airplane made its first test flight January 8, 1944, at Rogers Dry Lake. By that time, a modified version of the XP-80 was already in development (the XP-80A), using a considerably more powerful American engine, the General Electric I-40 (later named the J33). The first XP-80A Shooting Star, with the improved power plant, made its maiden flight in June 1944. The P-80A had a wingspan of 39 feet and a length of 34 feet 10 inches. Gross weight was 13,780 pounds.

The F-80C was the first Shooting Star to carry the F (fighter) designation. Its single engine was an Allison J33 with water-cooled injection that developed 5,400 pounds of thrust. Armament consisted of six .50-caliber machine guns and eight 5-inch rockets or 2,000 pounds of bombs. Maximum and cruising speeds were 580 mph and 437 mph respectively. Of 1,731 Shooting Stars produced, 798 were C models. The Shooting Star was used extensively as a fighter-bomber during the Korean War, especially for low-level rocket, bomb, and napalm strikes against ground targets. On November 8, 1950, an F-80C shot down a Russian-built MiG fighter in the world's first all-jet fighter air battle.[156]

A series of postwar changes in command structure gave fresh impetus to engineering research at Wright Field. Culminating these realignments was the establishment of the Wright Air Development Center (WADC) on April 2, 1951, in the Wright

AN ENCOUNTER BETWEEN THE JET ENGINE INVENTORS

As a student at the Royal Air Force College in Cranwell, England, in 1928, Frank Whittle wrote a prize-winning thesis proposing the use of a gas turbine engine as a means of jet propulsion. At that time, however, light metals sturdy enough to survive the high temperatures and stresses of such a powerful engine did not exist. Whittle sought the backing of the Air Ministry for research and development in order to make his jet engine a reality, but the Air Ministry refused to get involved because Whittle's idea seemed too far-fetched. Neither did private industry show any interest. Undaunted, Whittle patented his idea—thus making it available for the entire world to see in 1932. At the time, few people realized the military ramifications of a jet-propelled plane.

Meanwhile, Dr. Hans von Ohain in Germany worked on his own version of a jet engine. Unlike Whittle, von Ohain was able to get industry support (from the Heinkel-Hirth Company) for the research, development, and experimentation necessary to build a jet engine. In 1937, after the Nazis rose to power, von Ohain built the first working model of an aircraft turbine engine. Soon afterwards he built an engine powered by liquid hydrocarbon fuels, and on August 27, 1939, that engine turned Heinkel's He-178 aircraft into the world's first jet plane. When high-ranking Luftwaffe officials looked up into the sky and witnessed the jet power of the He-178, they were not impressed. Like the British Air Ministry officials, they were slow to comprehend what the invention of the jet engine meant to the future of aviation.

Back in Britain, Frank Whittle started his own promising jet research business, and when it looked as if war might be brewing in Europe, the Air Ministry in Great Britain began showing interest in the Whittle engine. Whittle finally gained the backing he needed to make his plans for a jet plane a reality. During a visit to England in April 1941, Army Air Corps Chief Major General Henry "Hap" Arnold learned of Whittle's jet engine and determined that America should have a jet engine of its own. After the first flight of a British plane with a W.1 turbojet engine on May 15, 1941, three of Whittle's colleagues traveled to the United States to assist the Americans in building a jet engine. On October 1, 1942, the Bell XP-59A thundered into the sky as America's first jet plane. A year later the British were flying Gloster's Meteor, their own prototype of a dual jet engine fighter.

After the war, Hans von Ohain enjoyed a long career with the United States government, working 32 years at Wright-Patterson Air Force Base. As a researcher and chief scientist in the Aerospace Research Laboratories, and later as the chief scientist of the Aero Propulsion Laboratory, von Ohain used his talents to maintain the high level of cutting-edge propulsion research and development for which the base is still known. In May of 1978, Frank Whittle met with his German counterpart in a panel discussion on the stage of the United Sates Air Force Museum, Wright-Patterson Air Force Base. Many of the base's scientists were inspired by the stories the two men told about the technical and bureaucratic problems they had to overcome in order to do what many said could not be done.

Source: *An Encounter Between the Jet Engine Inventors: Sir Frank Whittle and Dr. Hans von Ohain, 3-4 May 1978, Wright-Patterson Air Force Base, Ohio,* (Wright-Patterson AFB, 1978).

On May 3-4, 1978, two inventors of the jet engine—Sir Frank Whittle (far left) and Dr. Hans von Ohain (far right)—met with scientists at Wright-Patterson Air Force Base to discuss the trials and tribulations each had to endure in his quest to build the world's first jet engine.

Field portion (Area B) of Wright-Patterson Air Force Base. (Wright and Patterson Fields had been administratively merged in 1945 and redesignated Wright-Patterson Air Force Base on January 13, 1948.) WADC was one of the 10 research and development centers organized under the Air Research and Development Command (ARDC). ARDC headquarters was also located in the Wright Field area of Wright-Patterson Air Force Base until June 1951, when the function moved to Baltimore, Maryland. The center comprised four elements broken out from the Air Materiel Command: the Engineering Division, the Flight Test Division, the All-Weather Flying Division, and the Office of Air Research.

Wright Field's "golden era," however, was drawing to a close. Since the time of McCook Field, every Air Force airplane designed and constructed, tested and evaluated, could call Wright Field its "home." By 1951, Wright Field's testing program had largely been assumed by the Proving Ground at Eglin Air Force Base, Florida, and the new facilities at Edwards Air Force Base, California. Design and procurement systems entered a new, more sophisticated age. Under WADC, the procurement process underwent continuous development and refinement in an effort to meet the demands of an ever-advancing technology.

In 1944 and 1945, two P-59s were used for drone experimentation. (Inset) The P-59B Reluctant Robot (serial number 44-22633) was a pilotless drone controlled by YP-59 Mystic Mistress (serial number 42-108783), shown above on the Wright Field flightline. (*William T. Larkins*)

The Women Airforce Service Pilots (WASPs) were a special category of civil service employees—experienced female pilots who performed auxiliary flying services for the Army Air Forces. Between September 1942 and December 1944, 1,074 women served as WASPs, some of them at Wright and Patterson fields. Their flight duties ranged from ferrying airplanes and towing antiaircraft targets and aerial gunnery sleeves to engineering flight testing and simulated strafing. They flew 60 million miles of operational flights and more than nine million miles of ferrying operations. Thirty-seven were killed in the line of duty.

Lockheed P-80A Shooting Star at Wright Field, 1946 (*William T. Larkins*)

THE LITTLE GREEN MEN IN HANGAR 18 AT WRIGHT FIELD

In the modern mythology of the Unidentified Flying Object (UFO) phenomenon, it is believed that in mid-1947 the remains of a crashed flying saucer and its occupants were moved from Roswell, New Mexico, to Hangar 18 at Wright Field for investigation and scientific research. Although Wright Field never had a Hangar 18, UFO enthusiasts believe that the storage place in question is actually a former hangar located near the Building 18 Propulsion Laboratory complex at Wright-Patterson Air Force Base. Believers in extraterrestrials claim that the United States government has covered up the so-called "Roswell Incident" for fear of causing a national panic. Unfortunately for believers in the paranormal, flying saucers and little green men have nothing to do with what was actually found at Roswell.

After World War II, the United States knew that the Soviet Union had the capability to build an atomic bomb, and it was imperative that the American government know exactly when the USSR's first atomic explosion occurred. Therefore, through Project Mogul, researchers from New York University were hired to construct devices that could detect the changes that take place in the earth's atmosphere upon detonation of an atomic bomb. The devices were attached to the long trains of weather balloons (similar to the tails of kites) and launched into the sky from Alamogordo Army Air Field (now Holloman Air Force Base), New Mexico, in June and early July of 1947. The airfield was located 100 miles west of Roswell. The tracking devices attached to a balloon identified as "Flight 4" stopped transmitting after it took off on June 4, 1947, and the balloon was never heard from again.

On June 14, 1947, W. W. Brazel and his son Vemon discovered some unusual debris on their ranch near Roswell. Later Brazel heard stories that some people in the area had been seeing strange flying discs in the sky. Thinking that perhaps the remains he had found had come from one of the flying discs, he contacted the local sheriff who, in turn, contacted Roswell Army Air Field (later Walker Air Force Base). The Air Force believed that because Flight 4 was built from the same materials that Brazel reported—rubber, balsa sticks, pastel-colored tape with flowery designs, tinfoil, paper with eyelets, and a large amount of scotch tape—it must have been the remains of the lost balloon. As for the little aliens who purportedly were found onboard the UFO, the earliest accounts of the Roswell Incident make no mention of them; they are a later addition to an ever-growing myth.

It is understandable that the United States government was concerned about the reaction of the American people to the news that the Soviet Union had the power to wage atomic war. When the press questioned military officials about the debris found at Roswell the public was truthfully told that the debris was from a weather balloon, but the top-secret details of its mission were not revealed.

From 1947 to 1969, the U.S. Air Force investigated 12,618 sightings of Unidentified Flying Objects. This massive investigation was called Project Blue Book and it was headquartered at the Air Technical Intelligence Center (which later became the National Air Intelligence Center) at Wright-Patterson Air Force Base. This is probably how Wright-Patterson made its way into UFO folklore as a storage area for flying saucers and aliens. The Roswell Incident was not even mentioned in Project Blue Book because it was not considered a possible UFO case until the supermarket tabloid *The National Enquirer* described it as being one in 1978—over 30 years after rancher Brazel found the very low-tech debris on his ranch.

In 1994, the Air Force declassified information on Project Mogul and made it available to the public. The Project Mogul explanation of the Roswell Incident is not as exciting as the story of a crashed UFO with aliens onboard, which undoubtedly explains why Project Mogul has received little attention in the media. There is also no doubt that some people will continue to believe in the myths of Roswell and Hangar 18, regardless of the facts.

Sources: Fact Sheet, U. S. Air Force, "Unidentified Flying Objects and Air Force Project Blue Book," June 2000, online at http://www.af.mil/news/factsheets/Unidentified_Flying_Objects_a.html; Colonel Richard L. Weaver, "Report of Air Force Research Regarding the 'Roswell Incident,'" July 1994, online at http://www.af.mil/lib/roswell.html; Alien Clipart by 13-year-old Tom Brown, online at http://www.awesomeclipartforkids.com/, used with permission.

PIONEERING AIR FORCE ACQUISITION— A WORK IN PROGRESS

In the broadest sense, the Air Force acquisition process refers to every aspect of obtaining weapons. This process includes the research, development, test and evaluation, procurement, logistics planning, and initial deployment of aerospace vehicles, weapons, and support equipment. In this chapter, the acquisition process refers primarily to the institutions, regulations, and policies that concern the development and procurement of airplanes, missiles, and related aerospace equipment. Although this chapter adopts an overall Air Force perspective, for much of the previous century the evolution of acquisition policy, procedures, and institutions occurred as a result of a dynamic synergism between the Air Force's principal acquisition center near Dayton, Ohio, and headquarters in Washington, D.C. It is, therefore, appropriate that much of the chapter concerns the organizations, policies, and programs that evolved at McCook Field, Wright Field, and Wright-Patterson Air Force Base.

ACQUISITION UNDER THE SIGNAL CORPS

The history of Air Force acquisition begins with the establishment of the Aeronautical Division in the U.S. Army Signal Corps in 1907.[1] The division was established at the behest of President Theodore Roosevelt, who had been informed about the Wright brothers and their attempts to

Wright Field, 1980s

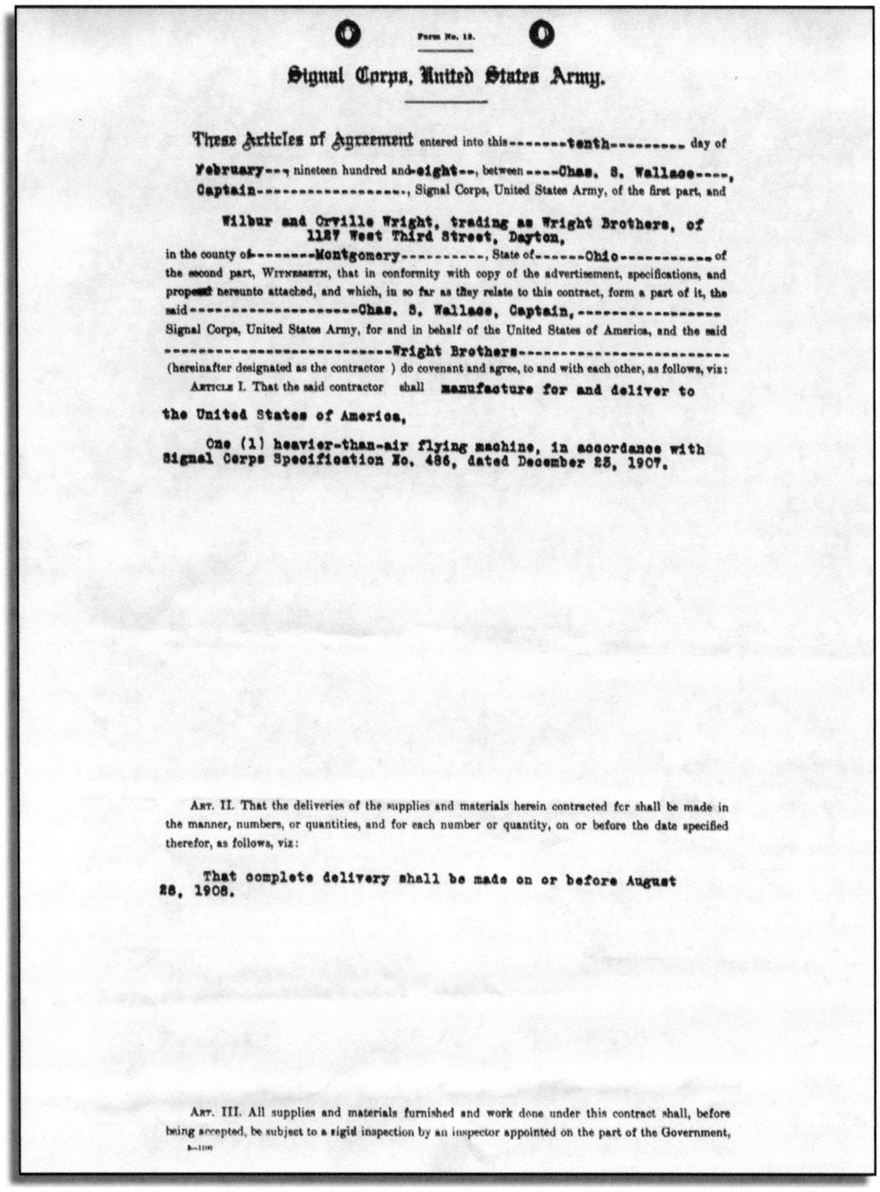

Form No. 18.

Signal Corps, United States Army.

These Articles of Agreement entered into this--------tenth--------- day of February---, nineteen hundred and-eight--, between----Chas. S. Wallace----, Captain------------------, Signal Corps, United States Army, of the first part, and

Wilbur and Orville Wright, trading as Wright Brothers, of 1127 West Third Street, Dayton,

in the county of--------Montgomery----------, State of------Ohio----------- of the second part, Witnesseth, that in conformity with copy of the advertisement, specifications, and proposal hereunto attached, and which, in so far as they relate to this contract, form a part of it, the said--------------------Chas. S. Wallace, Captain,----------------- Signal Corps, United States Army, for and in behalf of the United States of America, and the said --------------------------Wright Brothers------------------------ (hereinafter designated as the contractor) do covenant and agree, to and with each other, as follows, viz:

Article I. That the said contractor shall manufacture for and deliver to the United States of America,

One (1) heavier-than-air flying machine, in accordance with Signal Corps Specification No. 486, dated December 23, 1907.

Art. II. That the deliveries of the supplies and materials herein contracted for shall be made in the manner, numbers, or quantities, and for each number or quantity, on or before the date specified therefor, as follows, viz:

That complete delivery shall be made on or before August 28, 1908.

Art. III. All supplies and materials furnished and work done under this contract shall, before being accepted, be subject to a rigid inspection by an inspector appointed on the part of the Government,

Signal Corps contract with the Wright brothers for the delivery of one heavier-than-air flying machine, February 10, 1908

interest the government in their flying machine.[2] The division was manned by a handful of Signal Corps officers, whose interest and experience in aeronautics was confined to balloons—the Corps' specialty since the Civil War—and, for those with advanced views, dirigibles.

By 1908, the division and the Wright brothers had entered negotiations about the terms under which the government should conduct a flight trial of the brothers' invention. This demonstration occurred in September 1909 at Fort Myer, Virginia, just outside Washington, D.C. The Wrights' machine surpassed the Army's performance specification, allowing them to collect a bonus. Subsequently, the Signal Corps accepted delivery of a Wright A Flyer, the world's first military airplane.[3]

In 1914, the Aeronautical Division was subsumed by the Signal Corps' Aviation Section, which was established and funded by Congress.[4] The Aviation Section continued the practice of the Aeronautical Division of approaching inventors and nascent airplane companies for designs of aircraft with potential military application, primarily as trainers and observation platforms for Army field operations.[5] The section's engineering staff was divided into two offices, for Plane Design and for Engine Design. In charge was a chief engineer, usually a recent engineering graduate, such as Grover Loening[6] and Donald Douglas.[7] Both went on, after a short stint with the government, to jobs in industry, finally establishing their own airplane companies. The Aviation Section, however, lacked in-house facilities for testing and evaluation.[8] This activity was left to industry or, in some cases, to university laboratories that possessed propeller testing or wind-tunnel facilities. Generally, airplanes were simply flight tested, as was the Wrights' machine, before acceptance.

SETTING UP SHOP

American entry into World War I, in April 1917, precipitated the need to build a combat-worthy air arm virtually overnight. The Army established an Equipment Division in the Aviation Section to oversee airplane development and production.[9] During the summer of 1917, the Equipment Division established an Airplane Engineering Department and a Production Engineering Department.[10] In the autumn of 1917, both departments were relocated from Washington, D.C., to Dayton, Ohio. The Airplane Engineering Department was ensconced at newly built McCook Field, just north of downtown Dayton.[11] The Production Engineering Department, initially housed in several office buildings in Dayton's downtown, transferred to McCook before war's end.[12] Procurement authority resided, throughout the war and for several years thereafter, in the Supply Division, located in Washington, D.C.[13]

These arrangements were reorganized several times during and shortly after the war. In May 1918, responsibility for airplane development was taken from the Signal Corps when the promised number of airplanes failed to materialize quickly enough, and was turned over to the Bureau of Aircraft Production (BAP). This body, together with the Division of Military Aeronautics (DMA) which developed requirements, constituted the U.S. Army Air Service.[14]

Under the new regime, the Airplane Engineering Department and the Production Engineering Department were redesignated *divisions*. In the spring of 1919 (the war ended in an armistice on November 11, 1918), the Airplane Engineering Division was renamed: first the Technical Division, and then the Engineering Division.[15] The Engineering Division was divided into several technical sections: the Airplane Section, the Power Plant Section, the Equipment Section, the Armament Section, the Materials Section, and (after 1920) the Lighter-than-Air Section.[16] The Engineering Division also absorbed the Production Engineering Division, greatly reduced in size and business activity with the end of the war.[17]

World War I proved an important milestone in the history of U.S. military aircraft acquisition. The war demonstrated the futility of developing a large and capable aerial force without some form of in-house agency to advise and assist both the government and industry. To be effective, this agency needed a critical mass of expert personnel and technical facilities to conduct its mission of test and evaluation of the airplanes and equipment produced by industry. This expertise was provided by McCook Field.

However, the war also demonstrated the need to closely coordinate the activities of the agency's several technical disciplines and to determine when an airplane or type of equipment was ready for advancing from its experimental engineering phase to production. In the end, the Army produced 11,754 airplanes during World War I, nearly all modifications of proven European warplanes. Had the war lasted another six months, the first American aircraft would have been produced in quantity for operational deployment.[18]

The postwar period presented the Air Service's acquisition corps at McCook Field with numerous challenges. The first challenge was a severe depression in the American aircraft industry, caused by the precipitate cancellation of contracts after the armistice and the dumping of wartime airplanes and equipment.[19] Initially, the depression staunched the flow of engineering talent from the Engineering Division to industry. However, it also caused industry to complain of the "brain trust" at McCook amid fears that the Army intended to establish the field as an arsenal for airplane design and production. By 1924, industry convinced Chief of the Air Service Major General Mason Patrick to prohibit the Engineering Division from performing any further in-house prototyping and fabrication of experimental aircraft.[20] At the same time, McCook Field began to lose some of its experts to industry and academe, as the division's manpower budget contracted. This was not, of course, all bad, for many companies acquired a chief engineer who had worked at McCook and was familiar with the Engineering Division's methods, objectives, and requirements.

In 1926, the president and Congress enacted a number of measures that affected aircraft acquisition well into the 1930s, some to the eve of World War II. In July 1926, Congress authorized creation of the Air Corps to supersede the Air Service.[21] Under the Air Corps, in October 1926, a Materiel Division was created to supersede and subsume the Engineering Division at McCook Field. The Materiel Division combined the Engineering Division's experimental engineering and production engineering activities with supply and maintenance. Most significantly, the new division was invested with procurement authority for Air Corps aircraft and other

Wing fabrication at the Dayton Wright Airplane Company, Dayton, Ohio

Early production of military bombers

In 1926, the Materiel Division at McCook Field combined experimental engineering with procurement and supply.

Aircraft Branch in Building 16, Wright Field, September 1932

materiel, a function that hitherto had resided in the Supply Division, Washington, D.C.[22] Congress further authorized the inauguration of a five-year aircraft production program for the Army and Navy, in a move to modernize the services and financially help the still ailing aircraft industry.[23]

In 1927, the Materiel Division moved to the outskirts of town, to newly opened Wright Field built on land donated by the citizens of Dayton. Unlike McCook's wooden buildings, Wright Field's were built of concrete, brick, glass, and steel, and included a number of unique experimental facilities.

The challenge for the Materiel Division in the late 1920s and early 1930s was how to sustain aircraft development and procurement during a period of international economic stagnation and deflation. In fact, the Division aided and abetted a *revolution* in aircraft design, materials, and manufacturing throughout the period.

In October 1929, share values plummeted on the New York Stock Exchange heralding the Great Depression of the 1930s.[24] In 1931, the five-year aircraft production program ended for the Army and Navy and was not renewed.[25] At Wright Field, the hiring of new engineers, which had resumed in the late 1920s, once more slowed to a trickle and the experimental budget stagnated until the eve of World War II.[26] However, engineers had little reason to leave the Materiel Division for industry, which was itself depressed with little relief in sight.[27]

One of the greatest hindrances to the acquisition of innovative aircraft and equipment during this period was the aircraft procurement legislation and practice of the 1920s. After World War I, industry was accused of profiteering from wartime cost-plus-percentage contracts. Congress, therefore, enacted legislation mandating fixed-price contracts.[28] Such contracts, however, had other drawbacks, allowing little incentive for financial or technological risk-taking.

Furthermore, the Air Corps divided contracting for experimental development from contracting for production. Wright Field issued performance specifications for a new airplane and conducted a competition among contractor entries for an experimental prototype. However, the winning contractor did not necessarily receive the follow-on production contract, since the Air Corps bought the rights to the prototype design and then conducted a *second* competition for producing the item. This approach could be financially disastrous for firms that had invested substantial sums for an advanced prototype only to lose out on the more lucrative production run. The process did not provide much incentive for innovation and proved particularly harsh to smaller firms.[29]

Yet, during the late 1920s and throughout the 1930s, substantial, even revolutionary, advances were made in American commercial and military aircraft design and manufacture. One result was the all-metal, stressed-skin, cantilevered, low-wing monoplane. Many advances came from men of foresight and genius within the aircraft industry.[30] However, many also originated in work conducted in-house and in cooperation with industry by the Materiel Division at Wright Field.

One of the most significant programs conducted by the Materiel Division's Airplane Branch was a series of experimental wings, the largest being all metal and measuring 55 feet. The success of this in-house program bolstered confidence in Wright Field's engineers to encourage industry in the direction of all-metal aircraft for the Air Corps.[31] The result was a series of airplanes delivered to Wright Field, beginning in 1930: most notably the B-9, B-10, and B-17.

Another program undertaken by Wright Field in the mid-1930s was for an aircraft with a pressurized cabin that would be capable of sustained flight at high altitudes. Wright Field designed, fabricated, and tested a non-flying prototype of the cabin and then contracted with Lockheed for a flying model.[32] The XC-35, which resulted from this collaboration, won the Collier Trophy in 1937. This technical breakthrough almost immediately benefited both commercial and military aviation and led to development of the B-29 during World War II.[33]

Throughout the 1920s and 1930s, Wright Field pursued a method of aircraft development that proceeded serially from experimental vehicle to prototype to operational vehicle. The process began when the Air Corps informed the Materiel Division of new operational requirements that might necessitate the development of a new airplane model. The Design Unit of the Materiel Division's Airplane Branch drafted a preliminary design, on the basis of which the division issued a performance specification to industry. Interested companies then submitted a design and wind-tunnel model to the Materiel Division that

Wright Field in May 1931 during aircraft demonstration maneuvers

was scrutinized and tested. Any design flaws detected were communicated to the contractor for correction. The contractor then submitted one or several full-scale, flyable models of the new airplane to the division for approval. The division subjected them to a rigorous set of dynamic and static structural tests on the ground, as well as a series of flight tests. On the basis of the test results, the Materiel Division selected the model it wished to develop for production. If this testing uncovered defects, a second series of ground and flight tests was conducted on the model chosen for prototype development. Once the vehicle had passed these tests, the Air Corps purchased the design and competed it for a production contract.

As a result of this approach to aircraft development, the Air Corps at any one time had many different experimental aircraft and operational prototype models undergoing test and evaluation. Meanwhile, production tended to be quite limited.[34] At the end of the 1930s, the Air Corps had only 800 first-line combat aircraft in its inventory.[35]

World War II changed all this.

CRUCIBLE OF WAR

Fighting broke out in Europe in September 1939 when Germany invaded Poland. As in World War I, both Britain and France approached the United States' aircraft industry to help provide war materiel, including aircraft, engines, and supporting equipment. The Materiel Division also began hiring large numbers of engineers and began to expand its physical plant and experimental facilities. In May 1940, President Franklin D. Roosevelt challenged America's aircraft manufacturers to produce 50,000 aircraft immediately and 50,000 per year thereafter.[36] The call for a massive increase in aircraft production ended the Materiel Division's slow and meticulous airplane development cycle of the previous two decades. Instead, Air Corps Chief of Staff Major General Henry H. "Hap" Arnold immediately ordered the freezing of all aircraft designs in the interests of standardization and mass production.[37]

Wright Field engineers spread out among the nation's aircraft, engine, and automobile manufacturing plants taking notes and dispensing advice—and direction—for the forthcoming production runs. For example, a year before his famous raid on Tokyo in January 1942, Colonel James Harold "Jimmy" Doolittle led one such Wright Field team to industry plants in the Midwest.[38]

In 1942 the Army Air Forces staged a mock assault on Wright Field. Present at the exercise were General George C. Marshall, U.S. Army chief of staff; Lieutenant General Frank M. Andrews, commanding general of the Caribbean Area; Lieutenant General Henry H. Arnold, commanding general of the Army Air Forces; and Major General Oliver P. Echols, commanding general of the Materiel Command.

Organizational changes quickly reflected this wartime acceleration in aviation activity. The most visible change was the redesignation of the Air Corps as the Army Air Forces (AAF) in June 1940, with General Arnold appointed commanding general. In October 1939, the Air Corps had transferred the office of chief of the Materiel Division to Washington, D.C., although the division's research, development, and procurement personnel remained at Wright Field.[39] In 1942, the Materiel Division became the Materiel Command. The command's operational elements at Wright Field were designated the Materiel Center.[40] In 1943, the command's headquarters returned to Wright Field.[41] Meanwhile, in April 1941, the Army broke out the logistics functions from the Materiel Division as the Air Corps Maintenance Command, subsequently renamed the Air Service Command. The command's headquarters, initially located in Washington, D.C., transferred in December 1942 to Patterson Field, adjacent to Wright Field.[42] In July 1944, the AAF combined the Materiel Command and the Air Service Command to form the Air Technical Service Command (ATSC), with headquarters at Patterson Field.[43]

These elements of the AAF were part of a broader national and inter-allied network of agencies and authorities directing aircraft acquisition. The War Production Board, at the apex of this structure, was created in 1942 to mobilize and allocate industrial resources.[44] Beneath the War Production Board was the Joint Aircraft Committee comprised of representatives from the U.S. Navy, the AAF, and Britain. The committee determined overall priorities in aircraft production and issues of

THE ARSENAL OF DEMOCRACY IN WORLD WAR II

3-17 Flying Fortresses are assembled at the Boeing Aircraft fac-
ory. (*United States Air Force Museum*)

Curtiss C-46s in production (*United States Air Force Museum*)

3-29s on the Boeing assembly line
United States Air Force Museum)

Curtiss P-40 Warhawks (on right) in production (*United States Air Force Museum*)

GOVERNMENT-OWNED, CONTRACTOR-OPERATED FACILITIES

With the growing instability in Europe and Asia during the 1930s, President Franklin D. Roosevelt advocated a rearmamen program for the United States. The federal government took unprecedented steps to prepare the nation for war and to support its Allies' war needs. To meet production goals for war materiel, the government authorized the construction or expansion of more than 350 production and modification facilities, including 290 for airframes, aircraft engines, and aircraft components. Although buil with federal money, a large majority of these plants were run by companies with government contracts, giving rise to the acronym GOCO, or Government-Owned, Contractor-Operated facilities.

Following World War II, production at government-owned plants was cut back drastically. While the military services recognized the importance of maintaining some facilities for readiness purposes, the government could not afford to keep all the plants in operation during peacetime. Over the years, the government sought to sell the plants to the contractors operating them. Mos contractors declined to purchase the plants they used for economic reasons. Many of the aircraft plants remained in the government's inventory (some idle and some with reduced operations) for numerous years before they were disposed. The gradual disposa process reduced the number of GOCOs the Air Force managed from 80 plants in 1958, to 50 in 1968, and to 35 in 1973. By 1987 that number dropped to 13 and included plants in Tulsa, Oklahoma; Fort Worth, Texas; Marietta, Georgia; San Diego, California Evendale, Ohio; Binghamton, New York; Palmdale, California; Tucson, Arizona; Johnson City, New York; Sacramento, California Brigham City, Utah; Columbus, Ohio; and Waterton, Colorado.

Management of the plants originally fell to Air Materiel Command, and through its long line of successors, the task eventually came to the Aeronautical Systems Center (ASC) of the Air Force Materiel Command. Throughout the 1990s, ASC's Acquisition Environmental Management Directorate not only arranged for leases, sales, or transfers of most of the plants, but also oversaw environmental compliance, remediation and pollution prevention programs at the facilities. After years of use, ground water pollution problems at many of the plants surfaced. Several of the plants were placed on the Environmental Protection Agency's National Priorities List of contaminated sites, also referred to as the "Superfund" list, and the Environmental Management Directorate oversaw efforts to build water treatment plants and provide other remedial actions to "clean up" the sites.

By 2000, the Air Force maintained only four GOCO plants: Plant 4 in Fort Worth (operated by Lockheed); Plant 6 in Marietta (Lockheed); Plant 42 in Palmdale (Northrop, Lockheed, and Rockwell); and Plant 44 in Tucson (Raytheon Missile Systems). Over a period of 55 years, these four plants had significant roles in the production of the B-24, B-29, B-36, B-47, B-58, B-1B, and B-2 bombers; the F-94, F-104, F-111, F-5, F-117, F-16, and F-22 fighters, the C-130, C-141, and C-5 transports; and the Falcon Walleye, Advanced Medium Range Air-to-Air Missile (AMRAAM), and Maverick missiles.

Sources: Philip Shiman, *Forging the Sword: Defense Production During the Cold War* (Washington, D.C., 1997), pp 6-7, 15-16, 39, 55; History of Aeronautical Systems Division, January – December 1987, pp 66-68; History of Aeronautical Systems Center, October 1993 – September 1994, pp 87-88; Karen J. Weitze *Evolution of Air Force R&D and Logistics Installations During the Cold War: Command Lineage, Scientific Achievement, and Major Tenant Missions*, Vol. II (DRAFT) (Wright-Patterson Air Force Base, 2001), pp 487-505.

Air Force Plant 42, Palmdale, California

standardization between the Allies and the services. Alongside the Joint Aircraft Committee was the Aircraft Production Board, which coordinated American production and oversaw decisions of the committee for the United States.[45]

The pressure to mass produce and field airplanes and supporting equipment often required modifications to correct errors or to add newly developed equipment, like radar sets. Such retrofitting was inevitable when many airplane models were being purchased while still on the drawing board. These modification efforts—which almost amounted to a subsidiary industry—were handled in several ways. Initially, the AAF's depots, and even field maintenance operations, were forced to add the modifications while performing routine repair work. In time, the AAF constructed a series of huge modification centers around the nation to perform modifications and upgrades to aircraft after they had left the production line but before they were deployed for operations.[46] Wright Field's own modification shops accomplished highly specialized modifications, like those done to the B-29 to carry the atomic bomb. During the war, the shops moved from their original location adjacent to the final assembly building (Building 31) to a vast, one-story facility (Building 5) built in conjunction with a large new flight test hangar along the field's recently laid concrete flightline. Smaller "zone shops" were collocated with the laboratories they supported.[47] Before the war ended, the government and the manufacturers introduced the system of building aircraft in production lots or "blocks." Each block incorporated the latest improvements and modifications to the standard model or represented a specialized use, such as surveillance, for airplanes within that block.[48]

During the war, changes also occurred in such key areas of acquisition as contracting, development engineering, and business practices. To stimulate technical innovation in industry, the government replaced its prewar, fixed-price contracts with cost-plus-fixed-fee contracts, with the fee pegged at a maximum seven percent. In addition, the government provided manufacturers advance payments for aircraft and materiel not yet delivered.[49] Also in the interest of accelerating and encouraging innovation, the government turned over to industry much of the research, development, test, and evaluation (RDT&E) activity that had been closely orchestrated and performed by the prewar Materiel Division.[50] This change did not mean that the Wright Field operation ceased performing these functions entirely. Indeed, the field's laboratories were busier than ever; however, despite a three-to-tenfold increase in personnel—depending on the laboratory—and a quadrupling of the field's facilities infrastructure, the Wright Field operation was simply overwhelmed with projects. The changes signaled a new era, one that continued after the war and characterized the airplane industry and Wright Field operation into the twenty-first century.

To help industry manage the costly expansion of production capacity, the government also constructed a number of government-owned, contractor-operated production plants around the country.[51] The government retained ownership of these facilities even after the war. The AAF also made a conscious attempt to upgrade its business practices and to recruit and retain procurement and production personnel. Retention of experienced personnel was not easy, due to higher paying jobs available in industry. On the other hand, many of the AAF's officers brought prewar business experience to the war effort, most notably ATSC Commander Lieutenant General William S. Knudson, who, before donning a uniform, had been president of General Motors.[52]

The emphasis on production at the beginning of the war did not cause the AAF to ignore research and development. Indeed, the AAF was fortunate in having a technically-minded commander in General Arnold. Arnold, who had served in the Air Service's Division of Military Aeronautics during World War I, had become intimately familiar with the workings of McCook and Wright fields during the interwar years and was determined to keep its technical expertise on the cutting edge.[53] As early as 1939, General Arnold initiated work on a vast new wind-tunnel complex at Wright Field on the advice of his chief scientific advisor, Dr. Theodore von Karman of the California Institute of Technology.[54] In 1941, Arnold, on a visit to Great Britain's aeronautical laboratories, became acquainted with the Whittle gas turbine engine and secured British permission to send a model to Wright Field. This acquisition inaugurated America's jet engine research at Wright Field.[55] Early in the war, Arnold also directed the Wright Field laboratories to explore plastics and composite materials as substitutes for strategic metals.[56] All such projects soon radiated from Wright Field to the nation's industry and academic research centers in a series of contracts.

By 1943, with the nation's aircraft production running full throttle, Arnold gave the Wright Field laboratories approval to turn their attention to R&D projects for the postwar AAF. In the same spirit, as Allied advances in Europe resulted in the capture of Axis research and development facilities and technical experts, Arnold had von Karman form a group to study both Allied and enemy R&D accomplishments in Europe in order to formulate a set of recommendations for the postwar AAF.[57] In December 1945, von Karman's team, formally called the AAF Scientific Advisory Group (forerunner of the Air Force Scientific Advisory Board), submitted its report, entitled *Toward New Horizons*, which outlined contemporary and future scientific research in over 30 technical areas.[58]

By the end of World War II, the nation's aircraft manufacturers had produced over 300,000 aircraft, exceeding President Roosevelt's goal.[59] Perhaps more important for the future, however, was the impetus the war afforded to such areas as gas turbine engines, ballistic missiles, and radar. The war had left the United States the world's leader in aircraft production and technology. The war also left the nation with an immense aircraft production infrastructure and hundreds of thousands of skilled technical experts and production workers as well as thousands of government personnel—procurement specialists, legal experts, engineers, inspectors—experienced in every stage of an increasingly complex acquisition process.

Demobilization following World War II had a number of effects—both positive and negative—on research, development, production, and procurement of modern aircraft and support equipment. As with the end of World War I, the end of World War II brought about the abrupt cancellation of aircraft orders and the layoff of thousands of skilled engineers and workers from airplane plants across the country. A postwar surge in orders for commercial aviation products proved short-lived.[60] The government sector suffered immediate and drastic cuts. Thousands of engineers and procurement officers in uniform were discharged. Many civilian engineers and other specialists also lost their government positions. At Wright Field, the laboratories took substantial manpower cuts. The Materials Laboratory, for example, was reduced to 1939 levels within a year.[61] All this took place at a time when the world was in the midst of a technology revolution in propulsion, a revolution that promised in a few years to transform the

AAF's aircraft inventory, tactics, and even doctrine.

The dichotomy between available means and potential ends disrupted the orderly transition to peacetime activity for the AAF's materiel acquisition authorities. Despite the decommissioning of more than 60 percent of its wartime active inventory of 80,000 planes, the AAF was still hard put to fund the repair and maintenance of the remaining 30,000, let alone fund new production or pursue even low-level R&D projects.[62] The few spectacularly successful projects during these years, such as the X-1 aircraft, which broke the sound barrier on October 14, 1947, only whetted the appetite of those advocates of advanced R&D who were impatient with the AAF's logistical and procurement priorities.

ORGANIZING COLD WAR WEAPONS DEVELOPMENT

These concerns were soon reflected in a debate over how the acquisition process should be organized. This debate intensified after the Air Force gained its independence from the Army in September 1947. The wartime Air Technical Service Command (ATSC) was superseded in 1946 by the Air Materiel Command (AMC). In 1947, AMC reorganized the internal structure inherited from ATSC. ATSC's five technical divisions were consolidated into three large directorates: Research and Development, Supply and Maintenance, and Procurement and Industrial War Plans.[63]

Meanwhile, pressures were building to create a separate command for research and development. In 1949, the Air Force undertook two studies of this issue, one conducted by the Air Force Scientific Advisory Board (SAB), the other by Air University at Maxwell Air Force Base, Alabama. The SAB study, chaired by Dr. Louis N. Ridenour of the Massachusetts Institute of Technology (MIT), was generally referred to as the Ridenour Report. The second, led by Major General Orvil Anderson, was known as the Anderson Study. Both the Ridenour Report and the Anderson Study concluded that the Air Force needed to devote more of its resources to R&D and that the best way to accomplish this was to establish a separate command for this purpose.[64] In January 1950, Vice Chief of Staff of the Air Force General Muir S. Fairchild, agreed and directed the creation of the new command.[65]

Formation of the Research and Development Command was announced in February 1950. In September, it was redesignated the Air Research and Development Command (ARDC), and on April 2, 1951, the new command was activated.[66] ARDC was initially headquartered at Wright Field, but moved to Baltimore, Maryland, in June 1951.[67]

The new command assumed responsibility for AMC's RDT&E activities. These elements included laboratory and engineering facilities at Griffiss Air Force Base (AFB), New York; Hanscom Field, Massachusetts; and Wright-Patterson AFB, Ohio. In addition, there were test ranges and facilities at Edwards AFB, California; Eglin AFB, Florida; and Wright-Patterson. Among the newer facilities was the vast

Major General Frederick R. Dent, Jr., first commander of WADC

Major General Albert Boyd (right), commander of WADC (1952-1955), at the inspection of a MiG-15 at Kadena Air Base, Okinawa, October 1953

LIEUTENANT GENERALS ORVAL R. COOK AND LAURENCE C. CRAIGIE

Two names closely associated with the early evolution of post-World War II weapon system acquisition were Cook and Craigie.

Orval Ray Cook was born in West Union, Indiana, in 1898. He was commissioned a second lieutenant in the Air Service in 1922 and completed his flying training at Brooks Field in Texas. He first arrived at Wright Field in 1929 to attend the Air Corps Engineering School and upon graduation was assigned to the Aircraft Branch at Materiel Division headquarters. After pursuing further education, he returned to Wright Field in the early 1940s and became the chief of the Production Division in 1942. In 1949, he was appointed director of Procurement and Industrial Mobilization Planning at Air Materiel Command, Wright-Patterson Air Force Base. He then became deputy chief of staff for Materiel at Air Force headquarters.

Laurence Cardee Craigie was born in Concord, New Hampshire, in 1902. Commissioned a second lieutenant in the Air Service in 1923, Craigie also finished his flight training at Brooks Field. After graduating from the Air Corps Engineering School, Craigie became the assistant chief of the Engineering Section at Wright Field in 1937. By 1941, he was chief of the Aircraft Projects Branch there. Craigie became the first military pilot to fly a jet aircraft when he flew the XP-59 on its first flight at Muroc Dry Lake (now Edwards Air Force Base), California, in 1942. In 1945, Craigie became the chief of the Engineering Division at Wright Field. After commanding the U.S. Air Force Institute of Technology, Craigie became vice commander of the Far East Air Forces in Tokyo and from there went on to become deputy chief of staff for Development.

It was during their tenures as deputy chief of staff (DCS)/Materiel and DCS/Development that Lieutenant Generals Cook and Craigie collaborated on the Cook-Craigie Plan. The two men outlined several management concepts that aimed to reduce the amount of time between development and procurement. They first advocated the concept of a weapon system, which included not only the development of an air vehicle itself, but also development of its related airborne and ground equipment, construction of facilities, and training of personnel necessary to make it a combat weapon. Also part of the plan was the resurrection of the World War II idea of concurrent research, development, testing, production, and deployment, as opposed to the step-by-step prototype process normally followed in the 1920s and 1930s. As part of concurrency, the Air Force initially contracted for a small number of production aircraft for testing purposes. This committed the Air Force to production early in the development process, but in return the service received test articles made with production tooling, which provided them with test results more directly comparable to operational capabilities. The Cook-Craigie plan became the basis for acquisition for the F-102 interceptor and the B-58 supersonic bomber in the 1950s. Other parts of the plan were not as successfully implemented because of the increasing complexity of aircraft designs.

Sources: Lawrence R. Benson, *Acquisition Management in the United States Air Force and its Predecessors* (Washington, D.C., 1997), pp 24-26; United States Air Force, official biographies for Lieutenant Generals Orval Ray Cook and Laurence Cardee Craigie.

Orval R. Cook (pictured here when a major general)

Laurence C. Craigie (pictured here when a major general)

complex of wind tunnels, engine test cells, and ballistics ranges under development near Tullahoma, Tennessee, that was designated the Arnold Engineering Development Center (AEDC), in honor of General Arnold, in 1951.[68]

ARDC's largest field unit was the Wright Air Development Center (WADC), located at Wright-Patterson Air Force Base. Formation of the center, initially called the Air Development Force (Provisional), was announced in March 1951 and activated in April. In May, it was redesignated WADC.[69] The center initially comprised the elements of AMC's R&D directorate at Wright Field, including the 12 laboratories of the former Engineering Division, the Flight Test Division, the All-Weather Flying Division, and laboratory elements of the Office of Air Research.[70]

The mission of ARDC applied only to the R&D elements in the acquisition process. Procurement and production as well as supply and maintenance (logistics) remained the responsibility of AMC. Indeed, throughout the existence of the two commands, this division of the acquisition process proved problematical. A major bone of contention was determining when a project had progressed to the point where all or most of its engineering development had been accomplished and it was ready for production. In other words, when was ARDC to transfer primary responsibility for the project to AMC?[71]

This problem, in fact, predated the establishment of ARDC. During World War II, separate project offices, for research and development and for procurement and production, had evolved within the Materiel Command.[72] The first attempt to coordinate these in a joint project office (JPO) was for the B-29 long-range bomber. Subsequently, a number of such joint offices were established for major aircraft and missile projects.[73] When ARDC was established this arrangement was institutionalized. Thus, between WADC and AMC there were established a number of joint project offices, soon renamed weapon system project offices (WSPOs), that included personnel from both commands.[74]

During the developmental stages of a weapon system, WADC's program managers and engineers had primary responsibility. At the point when the system was ready to transition to production, the WADC component in the WSPO was scaled down and the AMC component scaled up and assumed responsibility for producing, deploying, and maintaining the new system.[75] However, in practice, the development and production process seldom was so clear cut. Invariably residual developmental tasks bedeviled a system in production. Additionally, WADC's laboratories retained responsibility for in-service engineering, i.e., R&D support of depot maintenance of fielded systems.

Lieutenant General Bernard A. Schriever, commander of ARDC, visits Major General Stanley T. Wray, commander of WADC, 1959.

The term "weapon system" itself was a new entry in the Air Force's acquisition lexicon. It reflected an integrated *systems* approach to air vehicle development that recognized the necessity for the various subsystems and components comprising modern airplanes and missiles to work in concert. The systems concept grew out of the wartime experience of the Materiel Command's airplane project managers, especially those responsible for the development of large, complex aircraft like the B-29 and B-36, and continued with projects like the B-47 and B-52.[76] From the very beginning of a project, managers had to anticipate and plan for all aspects of development, production, and deployment requirements as an integrated whole. This was particularly important on large, complex aircraft and missiles for which all components' and subsystems' development schedules had to be carefully integrated.

The real test of the joint project office and the weapon systems concept came in the early 1950s with the onset of the Cold War. The Korean War (1950-1953) forced a hurried rebuilding of the Air Force's acquisition manpower and infrastructure.[77] Thereafter, the Cold War between the United States and the Soviet Union increased the urgency of acquiring advanced aircraft and missile systems.

Since World War II, Wright Field had been the Air Force's principal center for the development of missiles and other "pilotless aircraft." The most important effort was the development of intercontinental ballistic missiles (ICBMs) capable of delivering nuclear warheads to an enemy's home territory within minutes of launch.[78]

The executive leadership of WADC in 1959 included: (front row, left to right) Colonel D. Diehl, Mr. J. E. Keto, Colonel W. Grohs, and Colonel H. Huglin; (second row, left to right) Mr. L. Hallman, Dr. F. W. Berner, Mr. R. Nordlund, and Mr. E. Phillips; and (third row, left to right) Dr. L. Wood, Mr. L. J. Charnock, Mr. W. T. Harding, Mr. C. Bryan, and Mr. E. Kotcher.

Adding urgency to the Air Force's ballistic missile program was the Soviet Union's breaking of America's postwar nuclear monopoly and its accelerated development of ICBMs.

Several challenges caused Wright Field to experience difficulties in developing ICBMs in what the Air Force considered an expeditious manner. First was the novelty and difficulty of the various technologies that went into producing an operationally reliable ICBM, especially guidance and propulsion technologies.[79] Second was the very newness of the systems approach to weapon system development. Throughout the 1950s, AMC, ARDC, and WADC experimented with several different organizational arrangements and what would later be termed "process improvements" for developing missiles and aircraft.

One of the most ambitious attempts to accelerate weapon system development was the revival of *concurrency*. Concurrency had evolved during World War II from the need to begin production of aircraft before they could be prototyped and vetted through ground and flight testing. Concurrency thus abandoned the prewar model of aircraft development.[80] Concurrency often required considerable modification to aircraft once they left the assembly line, either to add some latest piece of equipment or to make a design correction or needed repair.

The introduction of the systems approach to aircraft development during and after World War II led senior acquisition officers to think that a degree of concurrency might help accelerate development of aircraft and missile programs. Among these officers were Lieutenant Generals Laurence C. Craigie and Orval R. Cook, both of the Air Staff: the former was the Deputy Chief of Staff (DCS) for Development; the latter, the DCS for Materiel. What came to be called the "Cook-Craigie" plan called for the prime aircraft contractor to start production tooling early in the development of a new air vehicle. The initial production models would then be flight tested and any corrections would be made to subsequent production lots (in the form of modifications), as occurred during World War II.[81]

One of the first attempts at concurrency, General Dynamics' F-102 Delta Dart, ran into a number of serious development problems, however, suggesting shortcomings in the concurrency approach.[82] Ultimately, it took more than improved weapon systems planning and early production tooling to make concurrency work—or any other form of accelerated acquisition. It required a major shake-up in the organizations used by the Air Force to develop and procure its weapon systems. This shake-up began in 1954.

In that year, ARDC transferred ballistic missile development from WADC to a new organization called the Western Development Division (WDD) that it established specifically for this purpose.[83] Put in charge of WDD was Major General Bernard A. Schriever. Schriever was a former Wright Field test pilot and a protégé of former WADC and ARDC commander General Donald L. Putt, who had earlier spearheaded the move for an independent R&D command.[84] Over the next five years, Schriever's organization successfully developed and began deployment of the nation's first operational ICBM, the Atlas. This success was accomplished by applying the principles of systems acquisition and, to a substantial degree, concurrent development.[85] However, WDD's success could also arguably be attributed to its internal organization and *modus operandi*. What made WDD different from WADC, above all, was its employment of a contract organization, the Ramo-Wooldridge Corporation, to supply *dedicated engineering support* at each stage in the ICBM's development process.[86]

In contrast with the Western Development Division, WADC had inherited the 12-laboratory organization of AMC's Engineering Division. There were basically two kinds of laboratories at Wright Field: those that directly supported development of weapon system components (airframe, landing gear, canopies, control systems, engines, fuels, lubricants, electronics, and miscellaneous equipment), and laboratories whose focus was more research oriented, such as materials and basic research. Each of the laboratories in various ways provided engineering support to the airplane and missile project offices. Sometimes a laboratory engineer would be assigned several projects at a time in support of several different project offices. In addition, he would ordinarily have his own research projects in support of his assigned laboratory's research and development programs. Finally, the same engineer might be called upon to solve a service problem with an operational system documented by an unsatisfactory report (UR) from the field.[87]

This system worked well enough during the prewar period, when airplane development had been a simpler affair. The system even worked reasonably well during the war, when the Wright Field laboratories had swelled to unprecedented size. But it worked much less well in the postwar period, when demobilization hit laboratory manpower especially hard. Postwar manpower cutbacks were not entirely made good, moreover, even as weapon system development began to accelerate in the early 1950s. Neither the laboratories' focus on component development nor the way engineers were assigned to support the project offices suited an accelerated systems approach to aircraft and missile development. However, all this was about to change.

General Bernard A. Schriever, commander of AFSC, and Major General Robert G. Ruegg, commander of ASD (1962-1964), at Wright-Patterson Air Force Base, October 1963

FORGING AN ACQUISITION COMMAND

In 1959, having successfully developed the nation's first ICBMs, General Schriever became commander of ARDC. He assumed command determined to reform the weapon system development process—indeed the entire Air Force acquisition process. General Schriever immediately convened a committee of senior colonels, chaired by ARDC's Assistant for Test and Operations Colonel Jewell C. "Bill" Maxwell, to review and make recommendations for restructuring ARDC's laboratory and engineering activities. On the Maxwell Committee was WADC's Director of Laboratories Colonel Fred J. Ascani.[88]

Based on the Maxwell Committee's recommendations and General Schriever's direction, Colonel Ascani conducted a complete reorganization of Wright Field's laboratory and engineering establishment. At the end of this process, which occurred during the last six months of 1959, the laboratories, as they had existed and operated for nearly 40 years, ceased to exist.[89] The result was unveiled in December 1959 as the Wright Air Development Division (WADD), which superseded WADC. The new organization consisted of three line directorates: Systems Management, Advanced Systems Technology, and Systems Engineering.[90]

The directorates of Advanced Systems Technology and Systems Engineering represented the truly innovative aspect of General Schriever's reforms based on his experience as ICBM program director.[91] The two directorates had literally divided between them the manpower of the 12 Wright Field laboratories, about half going to systems engineering, the other half to advanced systems technology. They also divided up the mission of the former laboratories.[92] The laboratories' applied research mission went to Advanced Systems Technology. The directorate comprised three divisions for Aero-Mechanics (Propulsion and Flight Dynamics), Avionics, and Materials.[93]

The mission of direct dedicated engineering support of the project offices went to Systems Engineering. Here was the decisive innovation of General Schriever's reorganization, for systems engineering replicated in all essentials the engineering development function of WDD's support contractor, Ramo-Wooldridge. The difference in this case was that WADD's Directorate of Systems Engineering consisted of government engineers, both military and civilian.[94]

The formation of WADD was only the first step in the wide-ranging reform of the Air Force acquisition process championed by General Schriever. Another major reform realigned R&D with procurement and production in one command. The idea of combining R&D with procurement and production also reflected General Schriever's experience in directing ICBM development, when he had experienced firsthand the frustration that system program managers had with the functional split between AMC and ARDC.[95]

Indeed, in May 1959, as Schriever was empanelling the Maxwell Committee, the Air Force formed a Weapons Systems

GENERAL BERNARD A. SCHRIEVER

For nearly a dozen years, from 1954 to 1966, General Bernard A. Schriever spearheaded Air Force acquisition reform. From the day when he took over the Air Force's development of ballistic missiles to the day when he retired as commander of the Air Force Systems Command—an organization largely of his own creation—Schriever represented the best and brightest of a generation of Air Force officers conversant in the complexities of science, engineering, and business management. Schriever added to these qualities a *nonpareil* political savvy and an apostolic pedigree going back to Hap Arnold, Theodore von Karman, Donald Putt, and young, enthusiastic instructors like Ezra Kotcher in the Air Corps Engineering School at Wright Field.

Little of this could have been foreseen when Bernard Adolph Schriever was born in Bremen, Germany, in 1910. Only weeks before the United States declared war on the Reich, in April 1917, Schriever was taken by provident parents to America, where the family settled in Texas. In 1923, at age 13, Schriever became a naturalized American citizen. In 1931, he graduated from Texas A&M with a bachelor of science degree. A year's reserve appointment with the Army field artillery persuaded him to enter flight training at Randolph Field, Texas. He earned his wings and commission as second lieutenant in the Army Air Corps Reserve in 1933. After Air Corps assignments in California and the Panama Canal Zone and a piloting stint with Northwest Airlines, Schriever received a regular commission with the Army Air Corps in 1938, with assignments in California and at Wright Field, Ohio. At Wright Field, Schriever, like Doolittle and others before him, served as a test pilot and attended the Air Corps Engineering School.

After Pearl Harbor, Schriever applied for combat duty, but was sent by the Air Force instead to Stanford University, where he earned a master's degree in mechanical engineering (aeronautical), in 1942. In June, he was assigned to the 19th Bomb Group in the Southwest Pacific, where he participated in seven campaigns, while building a reputation for efficiency as a logistician.

Following the war, Schriever quickly advanced to the front ranks of those advocating a more aggressive Air Force approach to research, development, and materiel procurement. He began as chief of the Air Force's Scientific Liaison Section at Air Force headquarters. In 1949 he entered the National War College. After graduation the following year, he served as the Air Force's assistant for Development Planning and joined those favoring an independent command for R&D.

In 1954 Schriever became assistant to the commander of the Air Research and Development Command and the following month became commander of the Western Development Division with a mandate to develop and build the nation's first intercontinental ballistic missile system. Schriever's experience at WDD (later renamed the Ballistic Missile Division) lent him insight on how to accelerate the weapon system development cycle and convinced him of the need to unite weapons research, development, and procurement in one command.

Assuming command of ARDC in 1959, Schriever quickly convened a committee of senior colonels to reform the Air Force's laboratory and engineering organization and *modus operandi*. He also began politicking for a transfer of weapons procurement authority from the Air Materiel Command to ARDC. In 1961, the Air Force agreed, creating the Air Force Systems Command (AFSC) to develop and acquire weapon systems, and the Air Force Logistics Command for their logistical support.

As AFSC commander, General Schriever, in 1963, convened the largest and most comprehensive study of future Air Force technologies and systems requirements and possibilities ever held. Called *Project Forecast*, the study comprised several hundred representatives from academe, industry, and government product divisions and research centers. *Project Forecast*'s final report numbered over 30 volumes. By the time he retired, in 1966, General Schriever saw a number of the study's forecasted systems leave the drawing board and enter the nation's service.

Sources: Lawrence R. Benson, *Acquisition Management in the United States Air Force and its Predecessors* (Washington, D.C., 1997), pp 27-28, 31; Walter J. Boyne, "The Man Who Built the Missiles," AIR FORCE Magazine Online 83 (October 2000), viewed online April 29, 2002, at http://www.afa.org/magazine/Oct2000/1000bennie.html; Biography File, ASC/HO archives.

General Bernard A. Schriever, commander of ARDC (1959-1961) and AFSC (1961-1966)

Lieutenant General James H. "Jimmy" Doolittle (U.S. Air Force, ret.) with Major General Charles H. Terhune, ASD commander (1964-1967)

Management Study to review the acquisition cycle and concurrency. The study group examined whether to recombine AMC and ARDC or to transfer procurement authority to ARDC, as favored by General Schriever. Neither proposal was approved by Air Force Chief of Staff General Thomas D. White.[96]

The issue remained unresolved for another year and a half while General Schriever discretely lobbied for the transfer of procurement authority to ARDC. Finally, when the Kennedy administration (1961-1963) offered the Air Force the military space mission on condition that it fundamentally reform its acquisition processes, Secretary of the Air Force Eugene M. Zuckert adopted Schriever's recommendations.[97] The result was the formation of two new commands in April 1961: the Air Force Systems Command (AFSC) that combined ARDC's R&D mission with AMC's procurement and production responsibilities and the Air Force Logistics Command (AFLC) that retained AMC's supply and maintenance mission.[98]

AFSC comprised six product divisions that combined the R&D and procurement responsibilities of ARDC and AMC. AFSC's product divisions included the Armament Division, Eglin AFB, Florida; the Electronic Systems Division, Hanscom AFB, Massachusetts; the Space and Missile Division, Los Angeles Air Force Station, California; the Ballistic Missile Division, Norton AFB, California; and the Aerospace Medical Division, Brooks AFB, Texas. At Wright-Patterson AFB, WADD merged with AMC's Aeronautical Systems Center (ASC) to form the Aeronautical Systems Division (ASD).[99] Finally, AFSC also inherited all of ARDC's laboratories, test centers, and ranges.[100]

ASD retained the three-directorate model of WADD, redesignating the directorates *deputates*.[101] At the heart of ASD were the weapon system project offices, which during the transition period had been renamed system program offices (SPOs). The operation of the SPOs was spelled out in the 375-series regulations adopted by the Air Force in August 1960.[102] The 375-series regulations superseded AFR 20-10, which had been formulated in the early 1950s as the first attempt to spell out the role of the project office in supervising the prime contractor of a weapon system and monitoring all stages of a weapon system's development, production, deployment, and retirement from the inventory.[103] The 375-series regulations strengthened the authority and extended the responsibilities of the program office, and defined a new "hand-off" point of a system between the systems command and the logistics command. This was called the point of *program management responsibility transfer* (PMRT) and occurred sometime after a weapon system was well into production and was entering deployment.[104]

Reorganization of the new command was further refined the next year. Advocates of science and engineering on the Air Staff and in the office of the Air Force Chief Scientist prevailed upon AFSC headquarters to establish a new division in 1962, called the Research and Technology Division (RTD).[105] The new division, headquartered at Bolling Air Force Base, D.C., included all AFSC laboratories and engineering organizations.[106] At Wright Field, this restructuring transferred ASD's Deputy for Technology (the laboratories) and the Deputy for Systems Engineering to RTD. The laboratories were themselves consolidated into four Air Force constituted units: Flight Dynamics, Aero Propulsion, Avionics, and Materials.[107] Systems Engineering was renamed the Systems Engineering Group (SEG).[108] All these organizations, however, remained at Wright Field and continued to work closely in support of ASD.

In 1967, the Air Force abolished RTD, and placed the laboratories under AFSC's Directorate of Laboratories, a new staff office. The Systems Engineering Group rejoined ASD, where it was divided into the Deputy for Engineering (ASD/EN) and the Deputy for Development Planning (ASD/XR).[109]

General Schriever's reform program also included the convening of a study group called *Project Forecast. Project Forecast* was the most ambitious postwar science, technology, and systems forecasting enterprise since *Toward New Horizons*, commissioned by General Arnold, in 1944. *Project Forecast* included nearly 500 participants from the Air Force, other federal agencies, 26 institutions of higher learning, 70 corporations, and 10 non-profit organizations. Its final report comprised more than 30 volumes and included recommendations for both technology and systems development for the following 10 to 25 years.[110]

REFORMING THE ACQUISITION PROCESS

In addition to providing impetus for establishing the new acquisition command, the administration of President Kennedy inaugurated a number of other acquisition process reforms. Secretary of Defense Robert S. McNamara introduced a number of measures to improve the efficiency and cost effectiveness of military acquisition. His reforms included improved program management, better tracking and control of program costs, and elimination, where possible, of unnecessary weapon system duplication between the services.[111]

The most enduring of Secretary McNamara's reforms was introduction of the Planning, Programming, and Budgeting System (PPBS). At the heart of the PPBS was the attempt to link the planning of future defense programs with cost-benefit analysis to outline a realistic Five-Year Defense Program (FYDP) across the Department of Defense. Hitherto, the Air Force and other services had submitted their budgetary requirements for new weapons to the Department of Defense (DOD) with little regard to their overall impact on the president's budget.[112] The increasing expense of systems development and the alleged duplication between the services in some weapon procurements caused an ever-increasing portion of the national budget to be devoted to defense programs.[113]

To reduce duplication of programs between the services, McNamara advocated more *commonality* in weapon systems development, particularly in the development of aircraft by the Air Force and Navy.

McNamara also attempted to reform specifically how major aircraft systems

LIEUTENANT GENERAL JAMES T. STEWART

General Stewart was Aeronautical Systems Division's (ASD) leader for six crucial years beginning in 1970 when the systems that won the Cold War and Desert Storm were under development. In fact, most of those systems were still in the active inventory a quarter century later. ASD's first three-star commander, Stewart was a charismatic leader who successfully focused his efforts on three fronts: systems acquisition, organizational change, and workforce morale.

Following service in World War II as a B-17 pilot, Stewart devoted his career to understanding how the system acquisition process worked, and should work. During his tenure at ASD, he managed many of the Air Force's most successful programs: the F-15 air superiority fighter, the F-16 air combat fighter, the A-10 close air support aircraft, the B-1A supersonic strategic bomber, the C-5A cargo transport, the AGM-69 Short Range Attack Missile (SRAM), the AGM-65 Maverick air-to-surface missile, and the F-5E international fighter. He also oversaw the development of the Advanced Medium Short Takeoff and Landing Transport (AMST)—the YC-14 and YC-15—in addition to remotely piloted vehicles and electronic warfare systems. During his tenure, ASD entered into partnership with the Defense Advanced Research Projects Agency (DARPA) for the incorporation of stealth technology into flight vehicles.

Lieutenant General James T. Stewart, commander of ASD (1970-1976)

General Stewart advocated advanced prototyping ("fly before buy") to systems acquisition, and established a Prototype Program Office at ASD to manage 15 prototype programs, including the Lightweight Fighter (F-16), the A-10, and the Advanced Short Takeoff and Landing (STOL) transport. In 1973 he established a Simulator Systems Program Office, thereby consolidating the management of ASD's aircraft ground simulator development and acquisition programs. During his tenure, the 4950th Test Wing was established from elements of ASD's Flight Test Directorate and in 1975 was reorganized under Project Have Car.

General Stewart knew that the acquisition process was only as good as the people who implemented it, so he placed a high priority on workforce recruitment, training and morale. He saw a direct link between ASD's success and the welfare of its civilian and military workforce. General Stewart strove to make employees aware of the importance of their work and how their collective effort contributed to the defense of the nation. He believed that hard work and dedication to the job should be augmented by casual social events that boosted morale, promoted teamwork, and strengthened the ASD community. His tenure was filled with festivals, celebrations and parties where workers could relax and have fun outside of the office. In 1971, he inaugurated the annual Stewart Open golf tournament at Wright-Patterson to promote goodwill and charity contributions to the Air Force Museum Foundation, Inc. and the Air Force Association Wright B Flyer Fund.

He took care of his existing workforce and augmented it with the last great hiring surge of the twentieth century. Young engineers with leadership skills in addition to technical expertise were recruited from colleges and universities across the nation. He also was the first ASD commander to institute an Equal Employment Opportunity program to diversify the workforce.

General Stewart retired on August 31, 1976, as one of the most successful and respected commanders in ASD history. General Stewart died on September 3, 1990. The Air Force subsequently conferred on him the Eugene M. Zuckert Award, its highest management honor. The numerous trees he planted throughout Area B serve as living memorials to his legacy and, in 1994, the Aeronautical Systems Center named the first building of its new Acquisition Management Complex the Lieutenant General James T. Stewart Hall. The memorialization plaque reads:

> Lieutenant General James T. Stewart:
> A man for systems, a man for people, a man for the time

Source: Program, "Dedication of the General James H. Doolittle Acquisition Management Complex and the Lieutenant General James T. Stewart Hall," September 16, 1994.

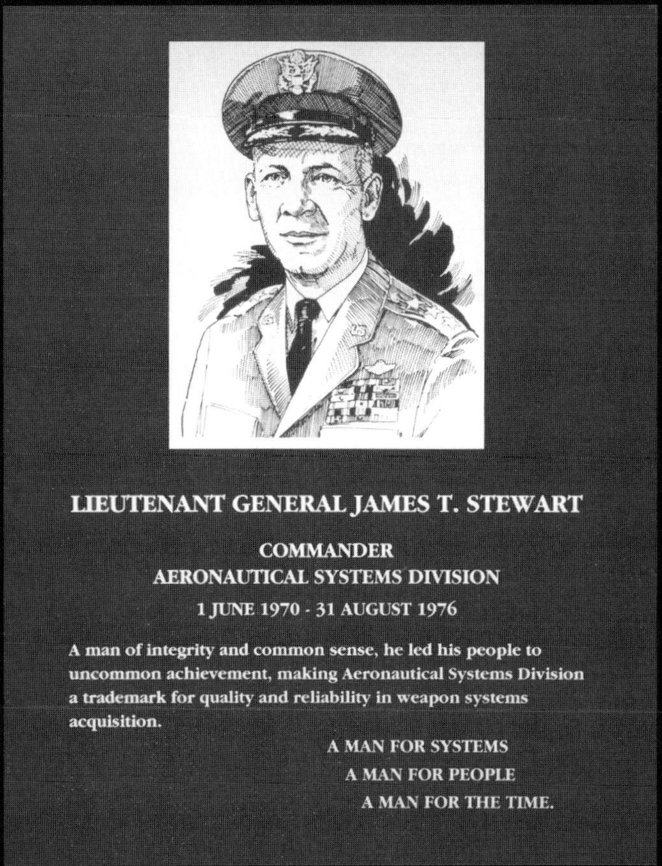
LIEUTENANT GENERAL JAMES T. STEWART
COMMANDER
AERONAUTICAL SYSTEMS DIVISION
1 JUNE 1970 - 31 AUGUST 1976
A man of integrity and common sense, he led his people to uncommon achievement, making Aeronautical Systems Division a trademark for quality and reliability in weapon systems acquisition.
A MAN FOR SYSTEMS
A MAN FOR PEOPLE
A MAN FOR THE TIME.
Lieutenant General James T. Stewart Hall dedication plaque

were developed and procured. In the past, competing aircraft manufacturers bid on development contracts that represented about 20 percent of a program's total cost, with production accounting for the remaining 80 percent. In part, this cost breakdown reflected the division of responsibilities between ARDC and AMC since ARDC focused primarily on the development phase. However, with AFSC now responsible for both development and production, a *total package procurement* (TPP) approach became more feasible. Under TPP, aircraft manufacturers had to compete on the basis of estimating the total cost of the program, i.e., both development and production phases.[114]

PPBS is largely the basis of today's acquisition planning and budgeting process. However, McNamara's efforts to achieve commonality in aircraft development and his attempt to impose TPP on the acquisition process were considerably less successful.

The first big test of the commonality principle was the Tactical Fighter Experimental (TFX) program, conducted jointly by the Air Force and Navy. Very early in the program, the Air Force's and Navy's operational requirements forced incompatible design compromises. In the end, the Navy pulled out of the program, and the Air Force forged ahead with what became the F-111.[115]

The TPP approach to aircraft acquisition, on the other hand, proved even less successful and acceptable. TPP early ran into trouble in the development of the C-5A heavy airlift aircraft. The C-5 was considered a relatively low-risk venture using largely proven technology. The winning contractor, the Lockheed Corporation, believing that the C-5 constituted primarily a scale-up of its earlier C-141 airlifter, made a relatively low bid for rights to develop and produce the aircraft. Lockheed's estimates proved far too low in light of the technical difficulties encountered on the program. Changes in the original design also compromised the schedule. The overall program ended with a 100 percent cost overrun. Consequently, the Air Force acquired 40 fewer than the 120 airplanes it had originally intended to purchase.[116] ASD had no more success applying the principles of TPP to the acquisition of the AGM-69 Short Range Attack Missile (SRAM).[117]

In addition to proposing dramatic changes in how the Air Force organized and conducted its acquisition business, the Pentagon, under Secretary McNamara, also made significant changes in the types of weapons the Air Force acquired. In 1961, ASD's three largest SPOs were for development of the X-20A Dyna-Soar, the GAM-87 Skybolt missile, and the XB-70 supersonic bomber. All were cancelled by McNamara or maintained in experimental status, such as the XB-70 Valkyrie; indeed, the X-20 never got off the ground.

These changes signaled, among other things, a major redirection in defense policy by the Kennedy and Johnson (1963-1969) administrations. First, the vulnerability of high-flying aircraft to surface-to-air missiles (SAMs) had been dramatically demonstrated by the shooting down, in 1959, of a U-2 aircraft over the Soviet Union, calling into question the Air Force's ability to penetrate enemy defenses at high altitude. Second, the reliance on nuclear weaponry during the 1950s had tied the hands of national leaders in responding to threats of conventional warfare. The United States decided to rebuild its conventional forces to provide a flexible response deterrent. Finally, U.S. involvement in Vietnam had demonstrated the inadequacy of conventional aircraft developed during the 1950s with strategic rather than tactical purposes in mind.[118]

Lieutenant General Thomas H. McMullen, ASD commander (1982-1986), with Ivonette Wright Miller and Horace Wright, niece and nephew of Wilbur and Orville Wright

The clearest change in direction as the 1960s came to a close was in the development of fighter aircraft. The F-100, F-101, and F-105 aircraft developed in the 1950s largely as adjuncts to the strategic bomber force were less suitable in the tactical fighter role assigned to them over Vietnam. Initially, the Air Force modified the Navy's F-4 Phantom for tactical purposes. However, before the end of the 1960s, ASD had begun to develop a number of wholly new fighter aircraft, such as the F-15 and F-16, and attack aircraft, such as the A-10, all of which were deployed in the 1970s and which characterized Air Force tactical airpower into the twenty-first century.[119]

Acquisition reforms continued under the Nixon administration (1969-1974), but along a different trajectory. Deputy Secretary of Defense David Packard spearheaded these reforms. Packard was concerned that cost overruns and performance

GENER AL LAWRENCE A. SKANTZE

General Lawrence A. Skantze, who became one of the most outspoken and prescient commentators on Air Force acquisition began his military career at sea. Skantze, who was born in the Bronx, New York, in 1928, enlisted in the Navy after graduating from high school. After serving as radio operator with the Atlantic Fleet, young Larry Skantze won a competitive appointment to the U.S Naval Academy, Annapolis, Maryland. In 1952, he graduated with a bachelor of science degree in engineering and a commission as second lieutenant in the U.S. Air Force. After receiving his pilot wings in 1953, Skantze served with the 90th Bombardment Squadron in South Korea and then as aide to the commanding general of the 14th Air Force at Robins Air Force Base, Georgia.

Skantze's R&D and acquisition career began when he studied nuclear engineering at the Air Force Institute of Technology, 1957-1959. His first R&D assignment was as project engineer on the nuclear-powered airplane (NB-36) program, sponsored by the Air Force and the Atomic Energy Commission. This was followed by a series of staff assignments, from 1961-1965, with Air Force headquarters and the Office of Secretary of the Air Force. In 1966, he graduated from the Armed Forces Staff College and served for the following three and a half years, as the director of system engineering and advanced planning for the Air Force's Manned Orbiting Laboratory at the Space and Missile Systems Organization, Los Angeles, California.

Following a short stint, from 1969 to 1971, on the staff of Air Force Systems Command (AFSC), Skantze became deputy for the AGM-69A Short Range Attack Missile (SRAM) at the Aeronautical Systems Division (ASD), Wright-Patterson Air Force Base. In 1973, he was appointed deputy for the E-3A Airborne Warning and Control System (AWACS), Hanscom Field (later Hanscom Air Force Base), Massachusetts, and in 1977, he returned to the AFSC headquarters staff as deputy chief of staff for systems.

In 1979, Skantze became commander of ASD, where he served until 1982, when he was appointed deputy chief of staff for research, development, and acquisition at Air Force headquarters, Washington, D.C. In 1983, he became vice chief of staff of the U.S. Air Force. In 1984, he was appointed commander of AFSC.

As AFSC commander, General Skantze convened *Project Forecast II*. Modeled on *Project Forecast* some 20 years earlier, *Project Forecast II* sought to propose innovative weapon system concepts based on the latest scientific trends. *Project Forecast II* was conducted from August 1985 to March 1986. The final report, published in June 1986, addressed more than 70 systems and supporting technologies.

General Skantze retired from active duty in 1987. In retirement, he remained an outspoken advocate of research and development in the acquisition of weapon systems and of the systems command concept in organizing this activity.

Sources: Air Force Institute of Technology Alumni Homepage, online at http://www.afit-aog.org/ag.html; History of the Aeronautical Systems Division, October 1978-September 1979, pp 81-82; "General Lawrence A. Skantze," United States Air Force Biography, online at http://www.af.mil/news/biographies/skantze_la.html

Lawrence A. Skantze, shown here when a lieutenant general and commander of ASD (1979-1982). He was promoted subsequently to full general and appointed commander of AFSC (1984-1987).

Lieutenant General Skantze with Lieutenant General James H. "Jimmy" Doolittle (U.S. Air Force, ret.) and Major General Robert A. Rushworth, ASD vice commander and former X-15 pilot.

Lieutenant General John M. Loh, ASD commander (1988-1990), introduced the Total Quality Management process to ASD.

problems plagued many major weapon systems across the Department of Defense despite the numerous measures adopted by his predecessors. Packard's solution was, essentially, to de-emphasize concurrency in favor of competitive prototyping for major systems. In the case of aircraft, the approach resulted in competitive "fly-offs" between the prototypes of rival contractors, a procedure dubbed "fly before buy."[120] Among the fly-off competitions conducted by ASD during the 1970s were those for the Lightweight Fighter (YF-16 and YF-17), the A-X Close Air Support aircraft (YA-9 and YA-10), and the short takeoff and landing (STOL) transport (YC-14 and YC-15).[121]

Superficially, prototyping seemed to be a return to the aircraft development process of the pre-World War II period. However, Packard's reform program was more in line with the policies of his immediate predecessors. Packard's program included more realistic cost estimating, more precisely defined operational requirements, and technical risk analyses. In order to provide improved top-level vigilance and control over major programs, Packard introduced the Defense Systems Acquisition Review Council (DSARC) to monitor the status of programs and to make recommendations to the secretary of defense at each major stage or "milestone" in a system's development.[122]

Additionally, in July 1970, a Blue Ribbon Panel appointed by President Nixon called for the establishment of independent operational test and evaluation (OT&E) organizations to validate the readiness of major weapon systems for production. Secretary Packard adopted this reform. These processes were institutionalized in 1974 with the establishment of the Air Force Test and Evaluation Center (AFTEC) at Kirtland Air Force Base, New Mexico. In 1983 AFTEC was renamed the Air Force Operational Test and Evaluation Center (AFOTEC).[123]

Before the end of the 1970s, however, this decentralized management began to be reversed by an increase in program reviews at different levels of the defense establishment. This trend began in 1976 with the publication by the Office of Management and Budget (OMB) of circulars A-102 and A-109 that addressed problems with cost estimating and program instability as well as inadequate threat analyses and excessive technological risk in major programs.[124] DOD thereupon expanded the DSARC process, and the Air Force established a corresponding Air Force Systems Acquisition Review Council (AFSARC) to conduct its own internal reviews. Meanwhile, AFSC also increased the number of review panels to track the programs of its product divisions, placing particular emphasis on controlling costs and encouraging competition among contractors.[125]

The reassertion of more centralized control of the acquisition process continued under Secretary of Defense Harold Brown, during the Carter administration (1977-1981). The Carter administration also attempted to control defense program costs and to critically examine, in this light, the mix of weaponry available to the Air Force and the other services. One result was the decision, in 1977, to cancel the B-1A program in favor of using relatively inexpensive cruise missiles to perform the low-altitude penetration mission. Both programs were managed by ASD. Indeed, cancellation of the B-1A was partly attributable to ASD's success in developing and integrating guided and cruise missile technology and systems.[126]

However, world events soon imposed on the Carter Pentagon the perceived need to begin increasing defense expenditures, a trend that continued—dramatically—under the Reagan administration (1981-1987).[127]

The Reagan administration's increased defense spending significantly affected the acquisition process. First, it funded the largest peacetime expansion of the military in American history, an expansion that translated into a number of new weapon systems, including revival of the B-1 bomber program as the B-1B. Second, it inaugurated a series of reforms of the acquisition process that carried into the twenty-first century. Increased defense funding extended through the first five years of the Reagan administration. A large proportion of this funding went for the acquisition of advanced weapons primarily in response to gains in the sophistication and number of Soviet weapons over the previous decade.[128] Air Force programs managed by ASD benefiting from the Reagan defense build-up included, in addition to the B-1B, the acquisition of 50 additional C-5 aircraft, called the C-5B; the F-117 stealth fighter-bomber; upgrades to the F-15 and F-16; the B-2 stealth

THE DEFENSE BUILD-UP OF THE 1980s

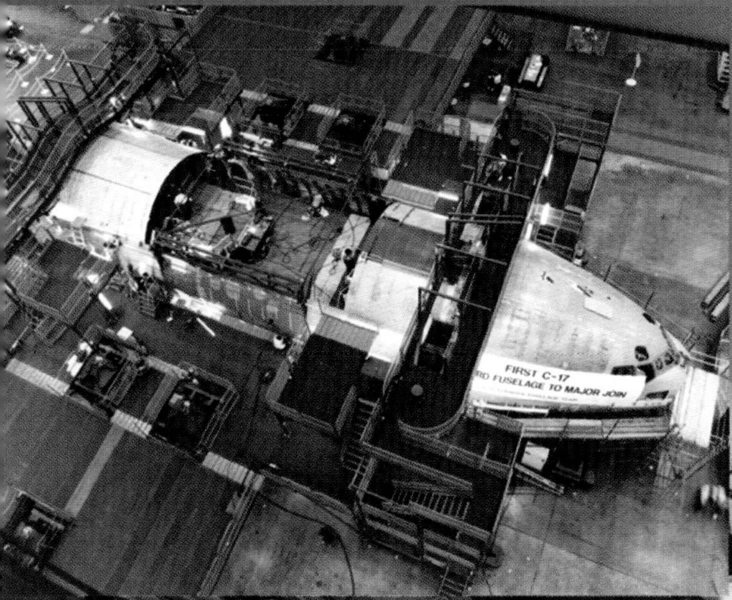

(Clockwise from upper left) the first C-17 nears major join; B-1B in production; B-1B production (interior view); a production line that never ends—the F-16; Advanced Cruise Missile in production

bomber; acceleration of work on the Advanced Tactical Fighter (ATF), leading to the F-22; the MC-130H Combat Talon II aircraft; and the AC-130U gunship—to name just a few.

Deputy Secretary of Defense Frank C. Carlucci directed the first major reform of the acquisition process under the Reagan administration. Carlucci's study was published in April 1981, three months after Reagan's inauguration.[129] The "Carlucci Initiatives," known formally as the Defense Acquisition Improvement Program (DAIP), consisted of 32 proposals intended to decentralize and streamline the acquisition process. Among the proposals were those advocating multi-year procurement, increased competition in contracting, stable budgets and more realistic budgeting, and a return to fixed-price contracts to help control escalating program costs.[130] AFSC immediately set about implementing those initiatives applicable to the acquisition of Air Force systems.[131]

The revived B-1B program was viewed by the administration, moreover, as a test case, particularly of decentralized management with accountability to higher echelons. Unfortunately, the program almost immediately ran into problems that attracted congressional attention and increased management oversight, not only of the B-1B but also of other Air Force and DOD acquisition programs.[132]

Problems with weapon system development, such as the B-1B program, as well as the alleged overpricing of spare parts, caused Congress and the administration to push for further reforms.[133] In 1986, Congress passed and the president signed the Goldwater-Nichols Department of Defense Reorganization Act (PL 99-433p). The Goldwater-Nichols legislation strengthened the chairman of the Joint Chiefs of Staff and the unified commands. The law also sought to reduce the size of the defense acquisition establishment by streamlining and eliminating layers of management, including the military acquisition staffs, and consolidating their functions in the civilian-run secretariats.[134]

Even more far-reaching reforms and restructuring of the DOD and Air Force acquisition establishment and processes were initiated by a commission created by President Reagan and chaired by former Under Secretary of Defense David Packard. The "Packard Commission," officially called the Blue Ribbon Commission on Defense Management, convened in 1985 and released its final report the following year.[135]

Among the report's recommendations was a streamlined acquisition structure with clear lines of communication and authority from top to bottom. The report recommended a corporate structure similar to many large private companies. The apex of defense acquisition management was to be a Defense Acquisition Executive (DAE), analogous to the Chief Executive Officer (CEO) of a corporation; Service Acquisition Executives (SAEs) to act as subsidiary CEOs; Program Executive Officers (PEOs) to oversee related major programs; and finally, Program Managers (PMs) to execute individual programs. Program managers reported directly to the appropriate PEO.[136] On April 1, 1986, President Reagan issued National Security Decision Directive 219, directing the implementation of many of the Packard Commission's key recommendations.[137]

The directive established an Under Secretary of Defense for Acquisition to act as the DAE and directed each of the services to establish an SAE.[138] At the PEO level, the Packard reforms had the greatest impact on the services' traditional acquisition structure and processes, particularly those of the Air Force.

Initially, the Air Force sought to comply with the Packard Commission's corporate model by naming each of AFSC's product division commanders as a PEO, responsible for the programs of his division. The AFSC commander, in turn, was to serve as PEO for all major programs that cut across the product divisions.[139] However, in 1989, the Bush administration (1989-1993) reexamined acquisition issues during a comprehensive Defense Management Review (DMR), chaired by Secretary of Defense Richard B. Cheney. The DMR report, issued in July 1989, strongly affirmed the recommendations of both the Goldwater-Nichols legislation and the Packard Commission.[140]

In 1990, Secretary of the Air Force Donald Rice directed full implementation of the Packard Commission's acquisition recommendations. On February 15, 1990, the Air Force transferred PEO authority from AFSC's product division commanders to the Pentagon, where half a dozen offices were established for PEOs managing strategic systems; tactical strike systems; tactical airlift systems; space systems; command, control, and communication systems; and information support systems. Thereafter, the program managers of major systems were to report directly to their respective PEOs, bypassing the product division commanders. The product division commanders were, meanwhile, to assume responsibility for smaller systems as Designated Acquisition Commanders (DACs). Both AFSC headquarters and the product divisions, laboratories, test centers, and ranges were responsible for managing and providing research, engineering, test, and evaluation support to all programs.[141]

RECREATING MATERIEL COMMAND

Among the major initiatives of the DMR was reduction of administrative overhead, bureaucratic duplication, and personnel in consonance with reductions throughout the defense establishment following the end of the Cold War. In November 1990, Defense Management Review Decision (DMRD) 943 proposed the disestablishment of AFSC, much of whose management responsibility had shifted to the PEOs, and the transfer of its remaining elements to AFLC.[142]

This proposal resurrected, in a sense, the former Air Materiel Command. Indeed, the resurrection of AMC had been under discussion for some time before DMRD 943 was issued. One could go back to the mid-1970s for evidence that dismemberment of the Air Materiel Command had caused acquisition problems. Creation of ARDC in 1951 had raised the issue of transferring the management of weapon systems between ARDC and AMC at the point of production. Similarly, creation of AFSC

Lieutenant General Thomas R. Ferguson, Jr., ASD commander (1990-1992). Under Ferguson's management, ASD received the Quality Improvement Prototype Award from the Federal Quality Institute in 1992.

and AFLC in 1961 had produced uncertainty and friction over the handing off of systems at the point of deployment and sustainment.

Perhaps even more critical for AFLC's logisticians than program management transfer, however, was the degree to which systems in planning and development under AFSC incorporated adequate provision for their reliability, maintainability, and supportability, the so-called "ilities." In order to maintain more oversight of this process, in 1976, the Air Staff created the Acquisition Logistics Division (ALD) at Wright-Patterson Air Force Base.[143] This "half-way house" between the two commands was strengthened when AFSC and AFLC agreed to restructure ALD as the Air Force Acquisition Logistics Center (ALC), which began operations in July 1984. Unlike ALD, ALC was *jointly* manned by personnel from the two commands and represented the first move toward consolidation.[144] Although ALD and ALC addressed and ameliorated many of the misunderstandings and problems between AFLC and AFSC regarding the "ilities" and the PMRT of systems, they did not go far enough in the view of many senior personnel within the logistics community and the operational commands.

The early 1990s, was a period of massive restructuring and consolidation within the Air Force. In 1991 the Air Force inactivated its two venerable warhorses of the Cold War, the Strategic Air Command (SAC) and the Tactical Air Command (TAC), to form the Air Combat Command (ACC). Likewise, the Military Airlift Command (MAC) was restructured as the Air Mobility Command (AMC). Despite some initial resistance and hesitation, in January 1991, at the direction of Secretary of the Air Force Rice, the commanders of AFSC and AFLC began in earnest to discuss the circumstances and timing of consolidating their two commands.

In April 1991, a provisional headquarters for the Air Force Materiel Command (AFMC) was established in the AFLC headquarters building at Wright-Patterson Air Force Base (Patterson Field). A "double liquidation" of the two commands and a "merger of their assets" in a new corporate body were accomplished on July 1, 1992.[145] Concomitant with the planning and establishment of AFMC was the restructuring of AFSC's product divisions, including ASD.

At the time of the formation of AFMC, ASD was at the apogee of its organizational size and geographical reach. In 1982, AFSC had once more realigned the laboratories at Wright Field under the product division. For the first time since 1963, the product division commander had direct control over the transition of technology from the laboratories to the program offices.[146] Then in 1990, AFSC disestablished its Munitions Systems Division (MSD) at Eglin Air Force Base, Florida, and realigned its programs under ASD, including the Armament Laboratory, which became part of ASD's Wright Laboratory.[147] With the formation of AFMC, moreover, the span of control of the ASD commander became even greater, as he assumed responsibility for operating both Wright-Patterson Air Force Base and the Wright-Patterson Medical Center.[148]

Under the new command, ASD also changed its name to the Aeronautical Systems Center (ASC). Likewise, the other product divisions were renamed centers. While this recalled the systems centers under AMC in the late 1950s, there was, in fact, no genuine parallel. Those centers had been responsible primarily for procurement matters, while the AFSC product divisions were responsible not only for the management and procurement of systems but also for science and engineering activities. These latter activities remained a core responsibility of the systems centers under AFMC.

Like the other product centers in AFMC, ASC confronted a number of interrelated challenges during the decade of the 1990s. The most significant challenge confronting the Air Force was the inexorable shrinking of the defense establishment with the end of the Cold War (1989). This "downsizing" began in the mid-1980s and accelerated in the early 1990s. This contraction determined virtually all other actions throughout the decade. ASC and the rest of the command were mandated annual cuts in manpower authorizations, both

Generals Charles C. McDonald (left) and Ronald T. Yates (right), commanders of Air Force Systems Command and Air Force Logistics Command, respectively, during the 1992 double liquidation that resulted in the formation of the Air Force Materiel Command (AFMC). General Yates became the first AFMC commander.

FOREIGN MILITARY SALES

The Foreign Military Sales Program managed government-to-government purchases of weapons and other defense materiel, services, and military training. A foreign military wishing to buy United States military weapons conducted its business through the Department of Defense. Historically, the F-16 was the U. S. Air Force's best-selling aircraft, with more than 4,000 delivered to 19 nations. Some of these aircraft were produced on assembly lines in Belgium, the Netherlands, Turkey, and Korea. The F-5, developed originally as an international fighter, was the second largest seller, with more than 2,600 sold. Other aircraft sold to foreign nations included the C-47, C-118, C-119, C-130, A-37, A-7, T-33, T-37, T-38, F-4, F-111, and F-15.

Once an Air Force weapon system was sold to a foreign nation, the Air Force Security Assistance Center (AFSAC) located at Wright-Patterson Air Force Base managed the sustainment support. In 1999, AFSAC supported more than 9,000 aircraft of 170 different models in use in 80 foreign nations, including Argentina, Australia, Canada, Denmark, Greece, Israel, Poland, Spain, Thailand, and the United Kingdom.

Sources: History of Aeronautical Systems Center, October 1993 – September 1994, pp 171-178; History of Aeronautical Systems Center, October 1994 – September 1995, pp 176-177; Air Force Security Assistance Center Web Site.

More than 2,600 F-5s were produced for service with the air forces of 26 countries, including the United States. These two F-5s were produced for Saudi Arabia in 1976.

The first F-16 delivered to the Republic of Indonesia, on an acceptance flight over Texas

Lieutenant General James A. Fain (center), ASC commander (1993-1994). During his 16-month tenure, Fain oversaw the extensive drawdown of acquisition personnel.

military and civilian, to accord with a declining Air Force budget. During previous periods of defense downsizing—after World War II, after the Korean War, and after Vietnam— substantial reductions-in-force (RIFs) had affected the military. Such RIFs tended to undermine both morale and the conduct of programs and projects in the laboratories and program offices. Moreover, those individuals most affected were usually younger employees, who had insufficient seniority to hold onto their positions. RIFs thus caused both hardships to these employees and their families and also confronted the Air Force with future potential leadership and experience "gaps."

In an effort to avoid as much disruption to both morale and program management as possible, the AFMC and ASC leadership during the 1990s attempted to ameliorate the impact of RIFs by freezing the hiring of new employees and by encouraging early retirements of eligible workers. Overall, this policy was successful. In the long term, however, it created problems by endangering continuity in the command and product centers. The loss of senior employees often meant the loss of valuable experience. Meanwhile, the continuing freeze on hiring new employees meant that the command and product centers were foregoing a generation of future workers and leaders.

Hand in hand with defense downsizing were attempts to improve business practices. Even prior to large-scale outsourcing of non-core functions, AFMC and ASC had begun experimenting with more efficient business practices. This activity actually began in the late 1980s under AFSC and ASD with the adoption of quality processes in acquisition management under a national program called Total Quality Management (TQM). One of the most important elements that TQM imparted to Air Force acquisition was its emphasis on teamwork. Under TQM, teaming was a highly structured process whose purpose was, for any given problem, to encourage ideas and input from all experts relevant to its solution.[149]

In the early 1990s, the teaming principal was recast as Integrated Product Development (IPD). The purpose of IPD was to integrate, from the very beginning of product development, all financial, procurement, engineering, and management expertise necessary for a project's success. IPD did this through integrated product teams (IPTs). Soon IPTs were established at every stage of product development. Some of the most effective IPTs coordinated the insertion of advanced technology from the laboratories into weapon systems under development and were called technology planning IPTs (TPIPTs).

The Air Force also sought to improve its acquisition practices by issuing a series of guidelines, called "lightning bolts," directed to specific acquisition and logistics processes.[150] Two sets of lightning bolts were promulgated during the 1990s. The first 11 lightning bolts were issued in 1995 and 1996 and addressed such issues as work force reduction and giving more responsibility to contractors. A second set was issued in 1999. Many of these guidelines issued by the Air Force acquisition executive, in fact, represented "lessons learned" by ASC and other product and logistics centers within AFMC.

In addition to honing its business practices and processes, AFMC and ASC also continued to restructure the various organizations within the acquisition process. One of the most momentous changes during the decade was the creation of a single Air Force Research Laboratory (AFRL) in 1997. As a result, the Air Force's four "super laboratories" were inactivated and their technical directorates reorganized and transferred from the product center commanders to the commander of AFRL. Among the reasons for the reorganization was the opportunity to consolidate staffing to reduce manpower authorizations and to have the Air Force's laboratory units more easily serve the entire Air Force and not just their assigned product center. Under AFRL, AFMC's laboratory community also received a stronger voice in a command preoccupied with logistical and procurement concerns, sometimes to the detriment of science and technology (S&T).[151]

Within ASC, important organizational changes also occurred, in addition to the inactivation of Wright Laboratory and the reassignment of its directorates to AFRL. Throughout the decade, the center worked to clarify the role of the product center, the center commander, and the system program office (SPO) in relation to the Air Force's PEO management of major systems, to the operation of AFMC, and to the expanded mission of ASC itself.

The Air Force's oversight of major weapon systems by PEOs in the Pentagon left the product center commander responsible for providing logistical support to the major programs while directly overseeing the management of smaller programs in his role as the designated acquisition commander (DAC).

The product center commander's role was further restricted under the Integrated Weapon System Management (IWSM) process instituted by AFMC upon its establishment in 1992. What IWSM sought to do was solve the problems surrounding the transfer of program management responsibility when two separate commands existed for logistics and acquisition. IWSM designated a single manager for each program. Those programs in development at ASC, for instance, were managed, as before, by a SPO director. The director became responsible for both acquisition activity at ASC and for any logistical planning and preparation at the depot (air logistics center, ALC) that would eventually service the fielded system. Not only was the director responsible for "cradle-to-grave" planning and management, but he also had ownership of the

PEACE PEARL PROGRAM

Following decades of virtual hostility toward one another, relations between the People's Republic of China and the United States gradually began to thaw during the 1970s and 1980s. Several factors led to this change including President Richard M. Nixon's visit to China in 1972, negotiations during the Jimmy Carter administration, granting of "most-favored nation status" to China, and President Ronald Reagan's visit in 1984. This created a climate conducive to improved relations between the two superpowers. The Chinese faced an increasing threat from the Union of Soviet Socialist Republics, who had amassed a significant military force along the Sino-Soviet border. Consequently, the Chinese made overtures to the United States for technological assistance in developing subsystems for their new F-8II interceptor aircraft.

Assistance such as this fell within the realm of the Foreign Military Sales program and the United States had to tread lightly and take existing agreements with friendly nations into consideration. The United States especially did not want to damage its alliance with Taiwan. The American government also remained concerned about China's ability to protect the security of any technologies provided to them under the program. However, the possibility of building "an enduring military relationship" with the Chinese as a way of countering and balancing the Soviet threat in East Asia outweighed these concerns.

Representatives from both countries had outlined the program by 1984 and the Aeronautical Systems Division (ASD) was aware of the proposed sale early in that year. Responsible for overseeing the program, ASD would develop, test, and acquire the system(s) needed. This would be accomplished through the Foreign Military Sales program by an American contractor. In May 1984, a Chinese delegation came to the United States and visited military, industrial, and government organizations, including Wright-Patterson Air Force Base. During 1986, ASD continued the contractor selection process and received the mock-up of an F-8II from China. Officials from ASD arranged for the mock-up, which arrived in a bamboo crate, to be stored in Hangar 255. Late in the year the Chinese established a liaison office at ASD and in January 1987, ASD hosted a Peace Pearl Configuration/Training Conference. In May 1987, Secretary of the Air Force Edward C. Aldridge, Jr., visited ASD to inspect the mock-up and learn about Peace Pearl.

After three contractors submitted proposals, ASD awarded the contract to the Grumman Aerospace Corporation. Program officials anticipated more bids, but approximately 15 other companies had dropped out of the competition for various reasons. As Grumman undertook the contract, frequent roadblocks hindered the company's ability to provide the services required. The persistent lack of technical data on the new Chinese fighter and frequent design changes severely limited the company's ability to do its job. Despite this, work progressed and the Air Force arranged for two F-8II aircraft to be brought to the United States in January 1989. To accomplish this, ASD sent several engineers to China with an American airfield survey team to help the Chinese prepare their aircraft for shipment. The team evaluated the airfield's capability to handle a giant C-5B Galaxy and advised Chinese officials how to effectively pack and protect the aircraft and related equipment to make the best use of the transport plane's cargo capacity. The airlifter successfully transported the F-8IIs, disassembled into three pieces, to the United States.

Just as Peace Pearl appeared to be well on the way to successful completion, a major world event stopped all progress dead in its tracks. In June 1989, Chinese forces committed an act of repression that again changed U.S. foreign policy toward the communist country. The Tiananmen Square incident, where Chinese soldiers fired on civilian demonstrators, caused President George H. W. Bush to suspend all foreign military sales to the People's Republic of China in retaliation for the human rights violations. Consequently, the Air Force denied access to Chinese personnel at Peace Pearl work areas at Grumman and Wright-Patterson. The Chinese reacted to the president's sanctions by temporarily halting payments to the program trust fund.

Grumman had performed ground tests on the aircraft and was approximately five months away from beginning flight testing when the Chinese abruptly announced they were terminating Peace Pearl. Chinese officials claimed the suspension had caused unacceptable cost increases. Initially, the United States declined to return the two F-8IIs to China because of the existing presidential suspension, but this was lifted in February 1992 and the aircraft were returned by ship.

Despite vast cultural and technological differences, Peace Pearl was well on the road to success when China terminated the program. This is unfortunate because Peace Pearl could have led to more cooperative ventures between the two nations. Regrettably, several factors slowed the progress of Peace Pearl and led to cost overruns. China's inherent secrecy impaired Grumman's ability to do its job, and the lack of a standardized aircraft design frustrated those working on the system. Still, those involved with the program fondly remember the personal relationships they developed with the Chinese as they worked through cultural barriers.

People's Republic of China and United States officials with the F-8II "Peace Pearl" aircraft

Sources: History of Aeronautical Systems Division, Janurary-December 1986, Vol I, pp 177-179; Dr Bruce R. Wolf, *Peace Pearl* (U-FOUO), Aeronautical Systems Center, c.a. 1991; personal communication, Ms. Virginia Brown, Peace Pearl program, w/J. Ciborski, ASC/HO, March 8, 2002.

Lieutenant General Richard M. and Mrs. Cornelia Scofield. General Scofield spent much of his career in the "black" world. He was assigned to the F-117 program in 1981 and served as director of the B-2 program from 1984 to 1991. As ASC commander (1994-1996), he was the Air Force Gray Eagle, the aviator with the longest rated service still on active duty.

resources at ASC and the ALC. Subsequently, once a program matured to the point where management by an ALC was appropriate, however, an ALC director would be appointed to manage the entire program, including the personnel and other assets necessary for its support by ASC.[152]

The IWSM arrangement thus provided a "single face to the user" and "seamless management" of programs. However, it caused a number of practical problems for the local management of the affected programs at ASC. Traditionally, many ASC programs were grouped into so-called "basket SPOs." Basket SPOs reflected the fact that there had never been enough management, engineering, comptroller, or contract personnel to fully service every program, particularly the plethora of smaller ones. Instead, the basket SPOs and their directors determined how their limited resources would be distributed to the smaller programs, using various criteria for prioritizing their support. The basket SPO directors, therefore, wielded considerable influence over the various programs within their organizations. The IWSM system, by distributing authority for programs great and small around the command, compromised the role of the basket SPO directors and the function of those organizations.

By the mid-1990s, ASC attempted to redefine the basket SPO as purely a "support" organization, one more in keeping with the overall principles of IWSM. Accordingly, ASC replaced its basket SPO organizations with Mission Area Groups (MAGs) and Product Support Offices (PSOs). However, this arrangement quickly reverted to the system of basket SPOs when Lieutenant General Robert F. Raggio became the ASC commander in 1998.

General Raggio also wrestled with the problem of defining the place of the program acquisition offices as a whole within ASC. Since its formation in 1992, ASC was composed of various elements: air base wing, medical center, test wing (until 1994), and laboratory (until 1997). Each element was an Air Force constituted unit—all, that is, except the functional and program offices that lay at the heart of the center's acquisition mission. Initially, the functional and program offices were collectively designated the Systems Acquisition Mission Unit (SAMU). However, outside the product center they had no official standing within the Air Force. In 1996 consideration was given to constituting them formally as an "acquisition wing," at least in part to assist in the career development of military officers assigned to the SPOs. Wing status would also give the acquisition elements of the center standing equal to the other "pillars," as these units were called. Upon becoming commander, General Raggio designated the acquisition elements of the center as the *Acquisition Force*. Moreover, he rejected the pillar analogy that included acquisition as one among three equal partners in the center. Instead, he regarded acquisition as essentially the *raison d'être* of ASC, with all other elements providing support to the essential mission.

The late 1990s also saw other changes in both ASC and AFMC. Perhaps the most notable was an intensified business orientation of the command and its product centers, including ASC. In 1998, the AFMC commander, General George Babbitt, introduced the *business area* paradigm for organizing and reporting the command's acquisition and other activities. At ASC, for instance, activities were divided into business areas for Product Support, Installations and Support, Information Management, Medical, and Center. The Center commander acted as CEO with each business area headed by a chief operating officer (COO) who presided over a "corporate board" consisting of the directors of the principal organizations under its aegis. Thus, the Product Support Business Area—which paralleled the Acquisition Force—included the chiefs of finance (comptroller), systems management, systems engineering, plans and programs, human resources, and the local directors of several of the larger SPOs. (In 1999, the business areas were redesignated *mission areas* but remained unchanged in organization and purpose.)[153] General Babbitt also introduced "activity based costing and management" (ABC/M) to AFMC and its product centers. Activity based costing aimed at injecting into the acquisition process commercial business methods of accounting for the marginal value of every dollar spent on each activity in order to determine cost effectiveness.[154]

The twentieth century closed with a number of additional reorganizations affecting ASC. In 1998, ASC formed, in accordance with command policy, a Plans and Programs Directorate (ASC/XP) among its functional organizations. Under ASC, XP was to serve as a corporate planning agency to integrate the center's business strategy, financial planning, and customer service and accountability responsibilities.[155] As a result of establishing the directorate, however, ASC disestablished several other organizations including its Development Planning Directorate (ASC/XR). Development Planning, a vital part of the product center since the late 1960s, included cost-estimating functions dating to the 1950s and preliminary systems design dating to the 1920s. ASC also established a Human Resources Directorate in 1998 to develop and coordinate the center's numerous manpower and personnel programs for both military and civilian personnel. In large part, that directorate's mission revolved around "reshaping" and re-educating the workforce for the challenges of the new century.[156]

Finally, in 1998, ASC transferred management of munitions systems to a new Air Armament Center (AAC), headquartered at Eglin Air Force Base, Florida. At the same time, ASC acquired management of so-called "human systems" with the disestablishment of the Human Systems Center (HSC), Brooks Air Force Base, Texas, which was reorganized as the 311th Human Systems Wing (HSW) and assigned to ASC.[157] The latter reorganization represented the first time since the end of the 1950s that the development of human (aeromedical) systems had been directed from Wright Field. In order to forge closer cooperation between the product center and the laboratory, ASC and AFRL established an Advanced Technology Council (ATC). ASC and AFRL jointly sponsored an annual National Aerospace Systems and Technology Conference

THE AIR FORCE IN THE SPACE AGE

What is the role of the United States Air Force in the space age? The Air Force was once part of the United States Army until the need for a separate and independent military branch devoted to aviation was recognized. Should there be a new branch of the U.S. armed forces dedicated to outer space, a branch that is independent of the Air Force?

This was one of the issues addressed by the Commission to Assess United States National Security Space Management and Organization. The commission was headed by Donald H. Rumsfeld before he was chosen to become President George W. Bush's secretary of defense. On May 8, 2001, the commission announced its recommendations: the Air Force should be the "Executive Agent for Space within the Department of Defense;" the undersecretary of the Air Force should become the Space Acquisition Executive and director of the National Reconnaissance Office; and the Space and Missile Systems Center should change its alignment from Air Force Materiel Command to Air Force Space Command.

The report declared that it was no longer just a matter of time before the United States would face threats from space. Enemies of the United States had the capability to wreak havoc from beyond the earth's atmosphere. Especially at risk were American satellites that were crucial to government and business communications. One of the goals of the report was to prevent a space version of the attack on Pearl Harbor; since the terrorist events in the United States on September 11, 2001, the urgency of eternal vigilance—on the ground, in the air, and in space—had dramatically escalated. The Space Commission's report thus proved an impetus for the creation of new Air Force doctrines and plans for national and global security.

Sources: "The Honorable Donald Rumsfeld: Secretary of Defense," DefenseLINK, U.S. Department of Defense, online at http://www.defenselink.mil/specials/ secdef_histories/; "Report of the Commission to Assess United States National Security Space Management and Organization," online at http://www.defenselink.mil/pubs/space20010111.html.

Donald H. Rumsfeld chaired the Commission to Assess United States National Security Space Management and Organization before becoming the twenty-first secretary of defense. As secretary of defense (2001-), it became his responsibility to address the recommendations of the commission's report. (Department of Defense)

(NASTC), beginning in June 2000.[158] Finally, AFMC, in cooperation with ASC and other product centers, undertook to explore ways to reinvigorate the Air Force's development planning using a command-wide approach.[159]

At the outset of the new century, Air Force acquisition was once more undergoing significant change. This change was part of a far broader "revolution in military affairs" that had gained momentum throughout the previous decade. This revolution began with Operation Desert Storm (1991) and continued through Operation Enduring Freedom, undertaken in response to the terrorist attack upon the United States homeland on September 11, 2001.

The hallmark of this revolution was the decisive factor of air power in each and every conflict waged—in the Persian Gulf, the Balkan peninsula, and Afghanistan. While decisive, air power did not operate alone. Its effectiveness was dependent in large measure on space platforms, primarily communication satellites, which together with precision guided munitions launched from manned and unmanned aerial vehicles assured the surgical application of overwhelming destructive force to the battle area. The aerial vehicle was thus an integral part of a "system of systems" network that linked space, air, and ground. The challenge for the Air Force acquisition community was to develop air and space platforms that would function in flawless synergy with one another.

A complicating factor was the diverse challenges confronting the Air Force warfighter in each contingency and operation of the post-Cold War era. No two conflicts were alike, and none came close to the apocalyptic dimensions of a superpower collision for which the United States had planned and equipped its armed forces for nearly half a century. Thus, an additional challenge confronting the Air Force acquisition community was to modernize, upgrade, and re-equip an inventory of legacy platforms designed for a different kind of conflict from those confronting the United States following the end of the Cold War. Among the areas of modernization, most pressing were electronics, avionics, and information technology.

Under the banner "transformation," the Air Force, at the beginning of the twenty-first century, introduced a number of concepts and processes to refine and reform acquisition practices to better meet the equipment and materiel needs of the warfighter.[160]

Lieutenant General Robert F. Raggio, commander of ASC (1998-2001), reaffirmed ASC's acquisition mission as the center's primary activity.

Lieutenant General Richard V. Reynolds, ASC commander (2001-), led ASC into an era of transformation.

One of the most important new acquisition concepts was *enterprise management*. Enterprise management recognized, above all, the "system of systems" operational environment. Under enterprise management, individual weapon systems were developed with an eye to their integration and interaction with other related systems across the warfighting enterprise. Enterprise management was organized into four *enterprise zones*. These zones were the Aeronautical Enterprise, the Command and Control (C2) Enterprise, the Armament Enterprise, and the Space Enterprise. Each product center commander served as an *enterprise commander* and was responsible for all programs within his respective enterprise zone, whether these were located at his product center or other product centers and logistics centers. The purpose of this cross-cutting responsibility among product and logistics centers was to give the operational warfighter a single focal point whenever equipment problems arose in the field. The Aeronautical Enterprise, for instance, centered on the programs located within ASC at Wright-Patterson Air Force Base. However, this enterprise zone also included aeronautics-related programs located at the three other product centers and the logistics centers.

Another key concept during the new era of military transformation was that of *evolutionary acquisition*. Evolutionary acquisition recognized two facts of the post-Cold War Air Force. First was the necessity of fielding weapon systems as quickly as possible in response to operational requirements. Second was the uncertainty of future requirements. Thus, under evolutionary acquisition the development community fielded a system with certain *core capabilities*, but designed the system so that additional capabilities could be added, in modular, incremental fashion, as needed. In fact, evolutionary acquisition was not a new idea. In principle, it underlay the block system of upgrading aircraft, first developed during World War II, and best exemplified in the history of F-16 development.

What was different from earlier weapon system development cycles, however, was the accelerated pace of change. Nowhere was change faster than in the software and electronics industries, and it was there that still another refinement in the acquisition process, called *spiral development*, emerged. Spiral development sought to promote constant interaction among the user, tester, and development communities *within each stage* in the development of a new weapon system or upgrade in capability. Not surprisingly, spiral development was first adopted within AFMC by the Electronic Systems Center (ESC), Hanscom Air Force Base, Massachusetts. By 2002, it had been embraced by all other AFMC product centers, most notably by ASC.

RETROSPECT AND PROSPECT

For almost a century ASC and its predecessor organizations, in cooperation with higher echelons in the Air Force and the national defense establishment, have carried on a tradition of excellence in acquiring the most advanced aerospace systems to maintain America's command of air and space. This activity has represented an investment in peace and prosperity that far exceeds the sums expended on aircraft and spacecraft and their related subsystems, armament, and equipment.

Less obviously, perhaps, the Air Force's acquisition process has made indirect contributions to the civilian economy and to America's competitive edge in world commerce. These contributions date to McCook Field, which experimented with crop dusting over agricultural acreage near Troy, Ohio, in the early 1920s. During the 1920s and 1930s, the Air Corps sponsored development of piston engines, advanced airframe designs, new fuels and lubricants, and assorted aeronautical equipment that made flight faster and safer for both military personnel and civilians.

The Air Force's underwriting of jet engine technology and large bomber aircraft during and following World War II accelerated the adoption of jet airliners by the commercial airlines and made the United States the world leader in gas turbine engine technology and sales. Likewise the Air Force underwrote the development of advanced manufacturing equipment and processes and the development of microelectronics.

As a new millennium commences, the Air Force continues to develop and acquire superior aerospace products. It also continues to reengineer the various processes by which these products are developed, procured, and sustained. Like so much in the history of aerospace development, it is a pioneering endeavor . . . and a work in progress.

THE ACQUISITION CORPS IN A HOME OF ITS OWN

The General James H. Doolittle Acquisition Complex

In the beginning . . . project officers for new airplanes and equipment worked in or near the laboratories at Wright Field. Thes ɔfficers might have one or two civilian engineers and a typist as support personnel. One or two desks, a filing cabinet, and a hat rac night suffice their "office" needs. As airplane projects became more complex beginning in World War II, project offices of some imes 20 to 100 or more personnel were formed to manage the various procurement items on, say, a B-29 or B-36. Findin contiguous space for so many people became a problem. Initially, the solution was to move project offices into buildings originall ntended for laboratory work, as the labs transferred to larger and more sophisticated facilities. Building 16, the original laborator building at Wright Field, built in 1926, became (and remains) a favorite locale for project offices and later system program office (SPOs). Indeed, the basement area of 16, hollowed out by hand during the Great Depression by Civilian Conservation Corp workers, became the home of the most advanced "stealth" programs during the depths of the Cold War. Likewise Building 17, onc home to the Aircraft Radio Laboratory, provided the initial quarters for the C-17 SPO and the original Wright Field laundry an garage facilities housed the National Aerospace Plane (NASP) program in the late 1980s.

Such facilities were often woefully inadequate in providing office and conference space for some of the Air Force's most sensitiv and expensive programs. In the late 1980s, Aeronautical Systems Division (ASD) commander Lieutenant General William E Thurman proposed bringing ASD's acquisition corps, at last, into the twentieth century. At a time when the Air Force was increas ngly espousing "business values" it seemed appropriate that ASD's engineering and acquisition workforce should operate in build ngs built to modern business (and security) standards. General Thurman called his vision "ASD Tomorrow." The vision consiste of one vast complex originally billed as being "larger than the Dayton Mall."

Congress initially balked at the proposed cost and financing. However, by the early 1990s, a more modest, incremental approac to the basic concept had won sufficient support for a groundbreaking in 1992 and the dedication of the first building, named in hono of late ASD Commander Lieutenant General James T. Stewart, in 1994. This structure houses the Reconnaissance SPO and othe programs requiring an especially secure environment.

In 1996, two additional buildings were completed and dedicated: Frederick T. Rall Hall and Lieutenant General Kenneth B Wolfe Hall. Rall Hall, named for ASD's chief engineer from 1969 to 1989, houses the "home office" of Aeronautical System Center's (ASC) Engineering Directorate. Wolfe Hall, named for the B-29 project officer and commander of the Air Materie Command, houses the C-17 SPO. The fourth structure completed houses the B-1 and B-2 SPOs and is named for Major Genera William L. "Billy" Mitchell, an early advocate of strategic bombing and an independent Air Force. The most recent addition to the complex was begun in 2001 and is to house the Aerospace Control/Strike Mission Group that includes the Air Combat, F-22, F-117 and F-16 SPOs.

When completed, the new acquisition complex will provide a state-of-the-art office environment befitting ASC's commitment to excellence in the acquisition of aerospace weapon systems.

Sources: History of the Aeronautical Systems Division, January – December 1990; program, "Dedication of the Lieutenant General Kenneth B. Wolfe Hall Major General William L. Mitchell Hall, and the Frederick T. Rall, Jr., Hall," April 1997; point paper, "Acquisition Management Complex," November 13, 2001

ASD Commander Lieutenant General William E. Thurman (1986-1988), envisioned a new acquisition complex at Wright-Patterson Air Force Base. His concept of ASD Tomorrow became reality in 1994 with the dedication of Lieutenant General James T. Stewart Hall the first of several new buildings in the General James H. Doolittle Acquisition Manage-

FROM AIR POWER TO AEROSPACE DOMINANCE—AEROSPACE SYSTEMS DEVELOPMENT, 1951-2003

A number of factors influenced the acquisition of new weapon systems over the past 50 years. Possibly most important, U. S. foreign policy and the existence of real or potential threats drove military acquisition. Dr. Richard P. Hallion, noted Air Force and aviation historian, stated that acquisition also was driven by replacement requirements.[1] In turn, replacement requirements were influenced by technological advances, as seen in the turbojet engine revolution of the 1950s and the stealth revolution of the 1980s and 1990s. The influence of all these factors combined was illustrated in the acquisition of major Air Force weapon systems throughout the second half of the twentieth century and into the twenty-first century. Although the Air Force conducted a number of requirements studies, beginning in 1945 with Theodore von Karman's *Toward New Horizons*, followed by *Project Forecast* (1963), *Project Forecast II* (1985), and *New World Vistas* (1995), forecasting did not always accurately predict the needs of the military in the rapidly changing political atmosphere of the world. Despite some deficiencies during critical eras (particularly the late 1960s in Southeast Asia), the Air Force remained a leader in military weapon systems and provided its forces with powerful and lethal weapons of air power.

KC-10 Extender refuels a B-2 Spirit at sunset.

WHERE DOES THE SPIRIT COME FROM?

Why was the stealth bomber designated the B-2? Who gave it the name Spirit? For many years the Aeronautical Systems Center named Department of Defense aircraft, but that responsibility later transferred to the Logistics Information Support Branch of the Air Force Materiel Command in Battle Creek, Michigan. The branch assigns all aerospace vehicles, including those from the National Aeronautics and Space Administration and the Defense Advanced Research Projects Agency, their initial Mission Design Series (MDS) designators. An MDS designator represents a specific category of vehicle for operations, support, and documentation purposes (for example, the "B" in B-2 stands for bomber, and the "2" differentiates it from other bombers). Designator requests are processed and approved by the Directorate of Plans and Programs, Program Integration Division, at Air Force headquarters. Popular names (such as Spirit) originate in the branch and are approved by the public affairs offices of AFMC and the secretary of the Air Force. The names are designed to characterize aerospace vehicle missions and aid communications and media references.

Sources: Designating and Naming Defense Military Aerospace Vehicles – Air Force Joint Instruction 16-401, online at http://afpubs.hq.af.mil; John Bauer, Air Force Materiel Command, Logistics Information Support, email to Robin Smith, ASC History Office, January 30, 2002.

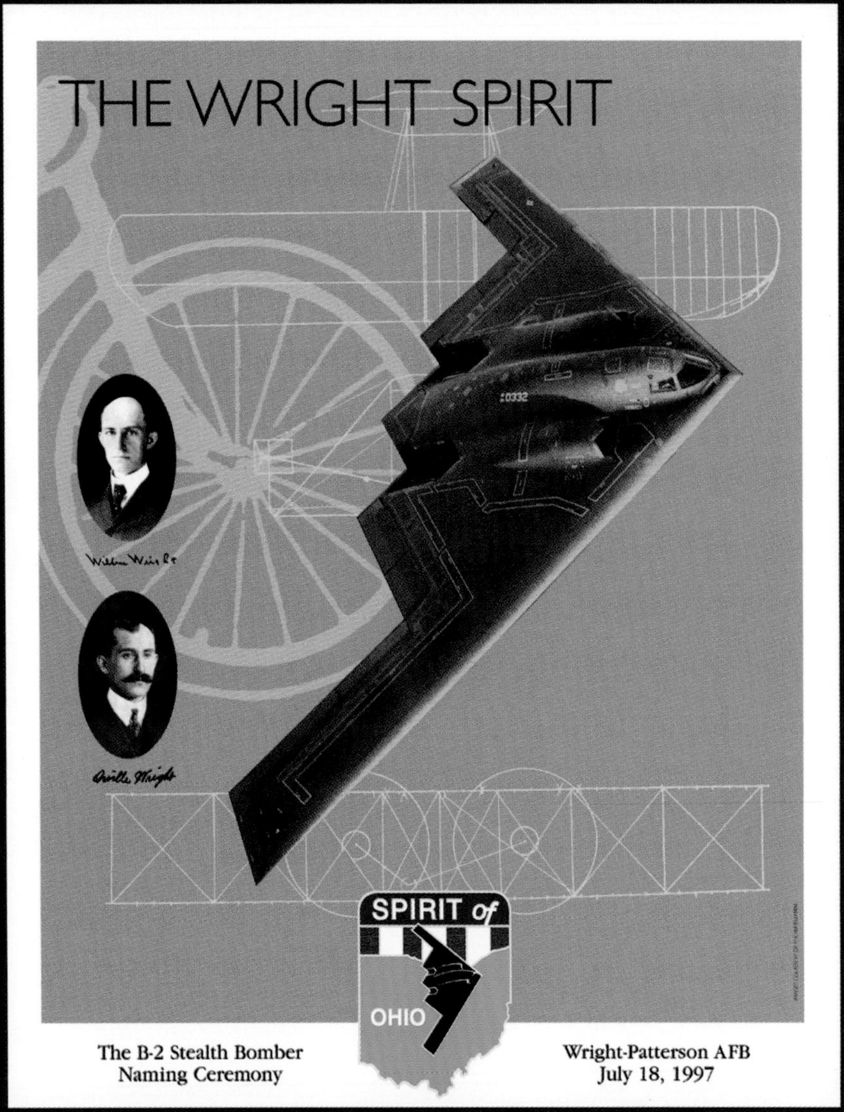

In the 1950s, the nation was still recovering from the events of World War II. The destructiveness of the atomic bomb was fresh in the minds of the American public, as well as the rest of the world. The United States' new global commitments led to increasingly tense relations with the Soviet Union. At that time, the anticipated threat was an enemy's bomber-delivered nuclear attack on the continental United States. The United States pursued a strategy of nuclear deterrence backed by the promise of swift and equally destructive retaliation if attacked. Such a policy led to an emphasis on the development of atomic weapons, strategic bombers (B-36, B-50, B-47, B-52), and fighter-interceptors (F-86D, F-94, F-89, F-102A, and F-106) in the late 1940s and 1950s. With the emphasis on strategic systems, tactical and logistical aircraft received lower priority, but later in the decade the Air Force did field a tactical bomber (B-57), two tactical fighters (F-100 and F-104), and several new transports (C-123 and C-130), including one (the C-133) large enough to accommodate intercontinental ballistic missiles (ICBMs).

In addition to the political climate, the number of new aircraft programs in the 1950s was driven by the jet-engine revolution of the 1940s. The new engine technology, coupled with associated developments such as the swept wing, delta wing, advanced adhesive bonding, high-strength materials, and expanding applications of radar led to a total revamping of the nation's aerial weapons throughout the 1950s. The Air Force began replacing most of its propeller-driven aircraft with faster, more versatile jets. The attainment of supersonic speeds fueled the quest for even faster aircraft, which culminated in the experimental XB-70 that could fly at Mach 3.

By the early 1960s, the nation's increasing reliance on ICBMs and advances in radar technology (which made it virtually impossible for invading aircraft to escape detection) plus the shift to a national policy of flexible response, all contributed to a decreased need for manned bombers. Many were phased out of the inventory at this time, and the XB-70 program was terminated. By the late 1960s, with increasing American involvement in Southeast Asia, the flaws of the acquisition policies of the past 15 years became truly notable. Aircraft developed for the atomic role were unsuited to the limited war being fought in Vietnam. The lack of attention to tactical aircraft in the previous decade

Doing more with less: With a payload capability of approximately 20 tons and a high-altitude range of 6,000 miles, one B-2 stealth bomber (right) carried the destructive power that once took scores of bombers, such as the B-17s (left), to deliver. The B-2 possessed the capability to destroy as many as 16 targets on a single pass. General Robert L. Fogleman, former Air Force chief of staff, described its evolutionary effect on strategic bombing: "We are beginning to change our thinking from how many aircraft it takes to destroy one target, to how many targets we can destroy with one aircraft."

left the Air Force vulnerable against more advanced enemy fighters. Consequently, the nuclear-capable aircraft (such as the B-52) were modified to carry conventional weapons, and the Air Force embarked on a number of programs to replace its over-specialized Century Series fighters with multi-mission aircraft (F-111, F-4, and A-7). Several new programs proved successful, such as the use of attack gunships and reconnaissance drones. Fortunately, attention to the nation's deficient airlift capability early in the 1960s had led to the fielding of two new transports (C-141 and C-5) prior to the end of the war. The Air Force's space program also accelerated in this period.

The number of new program starts and the number of different aircraft types procured in the 1960s and later decades decreased dramatically compared to acquisition in previous decades. For example, in the 1950s the Air Force had at least eight ongoing bomber studies, and of these, five eventually were produced in quantity. Between 1960 and 1990, only three bomber programs reached the development stage, and only two of those, the B-1 and the B-2, became operational. Fighter and transport aircraft, helicopters, and even missile programs, experienced a similar trend. The primary reason for the decrease in new programs was the rising cost of research and development in the 1960s. The increased cost of developing new aircraft also led to scrutiny of past acquisition methods and the push for multi-service aircraft. The Air Force often found it more cost-effective to upgrade and install new avionics in existing airframes worthy of further exploitation.

The 1970s was a difficult period due to the unpopularity of the military and defense expenditures with the American public, a legacy of the Vietnam War. Still, the Air Force recognized the need to modernize its force, and the *Project Forecast* study of 1963 provided guidance for the development and acquisition of new systems for the 1970s. Focusing particularly on deficiencies highlighted during the Vietnam and Yom Kippur wars, the Air Force developed an air-superiority fighter (F-15) with advanced air-to-air missiles. Expanding applications of electronic warfare technology led to the development of the EF-111 and improved Wild Weasels (F-4G). An aircraft was acquired specifically for close air support missions (A-10), and numerous air-to-ground missile programs (AGM-65 Maverick, the AGM-69A Short Range Attack Missile [SRAM], and the AGM-86B Air-Launched Cruise Missile [ALCM]) began. The short-lived Advanced Manned Strategic Aircraft (AMSA, B-1A) program also began in this period only to be cancelled in favor of accelerated development of cruise missiles. A new refueling tanker (KC-10A) was introduced, and a multi-mission fighter program (F-16) began. Finally, the Air Force's poor performance in night missions led to efforts to make aircraft safer and more lethal at night.

The 1980s proved to be a reversal of the scaled-back defense expenditures of the 1970s. The Reagan administration planned to rebuild the demoralized military. As a result, strategic and tactical systems were upgraded, new models of existing aircraft were acquired, and new aircraft types were developed. The B-52 was modified to carry the ALCM; the B-1 program was reinstated (as the B-1B); and a contract for the development of the Advanced Technology Bomber (a program begun in 1978, later the B-2) was issued. Stealth programs of the previous decade were accelerated, leading to the F-117 fighter and the AGM-129A Advanced Cruise Missile (ACM). The tactical force was modernized with the Low-Altitude Navigation and Targeting Infrared system for Night (LANTIRN), Advanced Medium-Range Air-to-Air Missiles (AMRAAMs), and the newly launched Advanced Tactical Fighter program (later the F-22). Another major advance of this period was fly-by-wire flight control, first used on the F-16 fighter. The C-X program developed into the C-17, a short takeoff and landing transport. Finally, the Ground-Launched Cruise Missile (GLCM) program began as a bargaining chip in arms limitations talks with the Soviet Union.

With the end of the Cold War in 1989, national policy shifted from a global focus on containment of Communist expansion to a focus on regional threats. Secretary of the Air Force Donald Rice issued

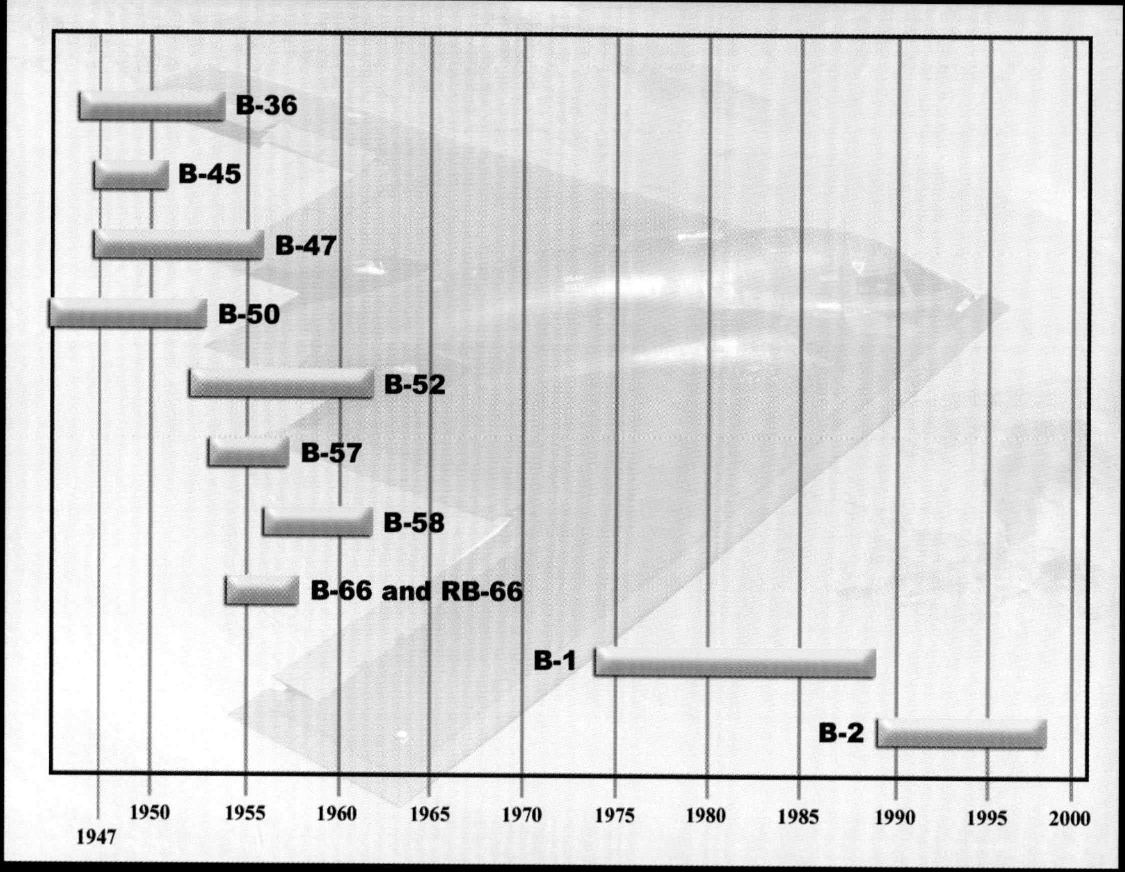

Shown are the dates of research, development, and acquisition for bomber aircraft, measuring from first flight of a prototype to the end of production.

his White Paper called *Global Reach—Global Power,* which emphasized the inherent strengths of an Air Force with speed, range, flexibility, precision, and lethality.[2] The Air Force transformed itself into a more efficient and powerful force with fewer but more lethal aircraft. Aging aircraft, such as the B-52, were modernized, and nuclear-deterrence aircraft, like the B-1B, were modified to carry conventional weapons. Upgrades included the addition of Joint Direct Attack Munitions (JDAMs) for near-precision attacks on ground targets. In the 1990s, development of the F/A-22 fighter and the multiservice Joint Strike Fighter promised U. S. dominance of the skies well into the twenty-first century.

As previous chapters have shown, Wright Field was the birthplace of aeronautical technology since the early twentieth century. In the past 50 years, Aeronautical Systems Center (ASC) and its antecedents evolved into an organization devoted to acquisition and management of the development programs related to new weapon systems and modification and modernization of systems in service. (See Chapter 5: Pioneering Air Force Acquisition for organizational changes and acquisition methods.) Still, despite organization and name changes through the years, the basic mission at ASC remained the same: to keep the Air Force and air power in the forefront of technology and to provide the most flexible systems to ensure that the Air Force always maintained air superiority and, ultimately, aerospace dominance in any conflict. In 1961, the Aeronautical Systems Division (the forerunner of ASC) described its role in this way: "Its projects of yesterday are the weapons systems that protect the security of America today...the projects of today will become tomorrow's aircraft and space vehicles...and the accomplishments of the past and the present set the pace for the technical superiority of the future."[3] As the Air Force entered the new century, ASC continued to provide the Air Force with the most powerful weapon systems in the world.

BOMBER AIRCRAFT

In the decade following World War II, the Air Force began a modernization program focused primarily on the conversion to jet aircraft. The Air Force believed propeller-driven aircraft were quickly becoming obsolete with the advances in jet engine technology. A number of new bombers, most designed in the mid-1940s, made their appearance shortly after the Korean War ended in 1953, including manned tactical bombers (B-57 and B-66) and strategic bombers (B-47, B-52, and the supersonic B-58). Initial development focused on speed, altitude performance, and the ability to carry and drop thermonuclear weapons, while later modifications added more extensive and versatile electronics systems, low-level bombing capability, and equipment to carry air-to-ground missiles.

In the 1960s, the quest for faster speeds resulted in an extensive development program for the unconventional XB-70

Lieutenant Colonel Henry E. "Pete" Warden was chief of the Bombardment Branch in the Engineering Division (Air Materiel Command) during the immediate postwar period. During his five-year tenure at Wright Field (1945 to 1950), Lieutenant Colonel Warden was instrumental in the development of several infant strategic-bombing aircraft programs (the B-47, B-52, and B-58) that formed the backbone of the United States' manned bomber fleet throughout the early Cold War.

The first of two Boeing XB-47 Stratojet prototypes. This one had six General Electric J35 engines.

Boeing XB-52 Stratofortress made its first flight in October 1952.

bomber. As events related to the Cold War resulted in an increased reliance on ICBMs and antiballistic missiles (ABMs), the need for manned bombers decreased. It was this trend that led to the cancellation of the XB-70 program in the mid-1960s. In order to remain a leader of technology, however, the Air Force replaced the XB-70 with the Advanced Manned Strategic Aircraft (AMSA) program, which eventually became operational as the B-1B bomber in the 1980s. Finally, the stealthy B-2 became operational in 1993.

In 1950 the Air Force's primary bomber aircraft included the intercontinental Convair B-36 Peacemaker and the shorter-range Boeing B-50 Superfortress, the last of the propeller-driven bombers. Both became operational in the late 1940s, and both were designed to carry atomic weapons. Although the B-36, in particular, served as a symbol of American air power in the early Cold War, by the end of the 1950s, the two bombers had been replaced by new jet aircraft.[4]

The B-50's replacement, Boeing's B-47A Stratojet, was initiated in 1944 for photographic reconnaissance and medium bomber missions. The aircraft's design included a swept-wing configuration with six externally mounted General Electric J35 axial flow jet engines (later replaced with J47s). The prototype aircraft made its first flight in 1947, and production contracts for the B-47A were let in the fall of 1948 before development was completed.[5] The Air Force hoped to have its first strategic jet bomber operational in Korea by mid-1951, but production problems and program modifications pushed the operational date to late 1952. Later testing of the production model revealed several deficiencies requiring extensive production line and in-service modifications. Because the aircraft was so complex, the testing program for the Stratojet became the "largest ever performed by the Air Force on a single airplane" up to that time.[6]

The B model of the Stratojet became operational in the fall of 1952 and, by 1956, replaced Strategic Air Command's (SAC) B-50s. The next variant, the B-47E, became operational in 1953. A new feature of the B-47E was reinforced landing gear that permitted heavier takeoff weights. This improvement allowed for larger fuel capacity, which in turn extended the range of the bomber. In 1956, 150 B-47E's were modified for low-level, high-speed bombing, a tactic up to this time performed only by fighter-bombers such as the F-84 Thunderjet.[7] Between 1957 and 1966, the Air Force's first swept-wing jet bomber was phased out as SAC acquired the more

PROJECT BRASS RING

In 1950, the Air Force began looking at delivery methods for the hydrogen bomb then in development (Project Caucasian). Because the bomb was so lethal, the carrier and its crew were likely to be destroyed during delivery. Furthermore, the target date for completion was only two and one-half years, ruling out development of a completely new weapon system. For these reasons, the Air Force studied the feasibility of modifying one of its production aircraft to deliver the package while keeping the crew out of danger. The B-47 Stratojet was chosen over the B-36 and B-49 because of its dependability, low cost, low vulnerability to enemy attack, and its near-production schedule. The Air Force initiated Project Brass Ring in the spring of 1950 with Boeing Airplane Company as the prime contractor. The project was put on an expedited schedule and given a "Special Project" designation that essentially waived normal test and training regulations. Potential configurations had the Stratojet as either a manned carrier (until the last refueling operation, after which the crew would eject over friendly territory) or a drone ("mothered" to the target by another B-47 director aircraft).

Boeing was contracted to deliver three B-47B directors and two B-47B carriers, and Sperry Gyroscope Company was subcontracted to develop the stellar inertial, auto-navigator guidance system for the unmanned B-47B. By 1953, three aircraft (two carriers and one director) had been delivered. In March 1953, a Brass Ring-modified Stratojet made its first flight, including "an automatic takeoff, climb and cruise with air maneuvers and landing remotely controlled from the ground director station." Subsequent flight tests of the three aircraft totaled 117 hours and by the spring of 1953 the project was 75 percent complete. Despite the $5.9 million spent on the project, the Air Force cancelled Brass Ring in April 1953, when it was determined that a manned B-36, although more vulnerable to enemy defenses, could more accurately deliver a parachute-equipped hydrogen bomb.

Source: "RDB Project Card: Special Carrier (MX-1457) (Nickname: Brass Ring) Termination Report," August 23, 1954, in Brass Ring Termination Report File, Box 3197: AC/B-47, Box 1, ASC History Office Archive. See Delmer J. Trester, *History of Project Brass Ring*, Vol. I: Text (Wright Air Development Center, 1953).

Boeing B-47B (serial number 51-2163), converted for use as a drone director under Project Brass Ring

modern B-52. In the late 1960s, Wright-Patterson's Flight Dynamics Laboratory used one B-47E as a test bed for the new flight control system later incorporated in the Air Force's first fly-by-wire aircraft, the F-16 fighter.[8]

The Boeing B-52 Stratofortress program originally began in 1946, but did not see progress until 1948. After a number of near cancellations, the outbreak of the Korean War ensured the production of the B-52. The prototype of the long-range, swept-wing jet bomber first flew in April 1952, and the B-52B, powered by eight Pratt & Whitney J57 turbojets, became operational in the summer of 1955. The B-52 was built to conduct high-altitude bombing and to carry thermonuclear weapons, one of which it dropped during a test over the Bikini Atoll in 1956. Along with the B-36, the Stratofortress was one of the primary elements of the nation's strategic defense during the early Cold War. In addition to high-altitude bombing, in the early 1960s the aircraft also was modified for low-level flight in light of the Soviet Union's increasingly accurate air defense against high-altitude aircraft.

The B-52 had few substantial problems. Instead, in more than 16 years of tests, development, and production, each model series was an improvement (advanced electronics equipment, more powerful engines, and increased armament capability) over the last. Beginning in 1960, the Stratofortress went through extensive testing for structural fatigue, and Hi-Stress modifications throughout the decade extended the aircraft's life. Big Four modifications prepared the bomber for low-altitude missions. Additional modifications on the D and F models, operational in 1956 and 1958, respectively, allowed them to carry heftier bomb loads for service in Southeast Asia. The B-52F's, the first to arrive in Vietnam, were fitted with equipment that allowed them to carry 24 750-pound bombs externally, double their original capacity. The B-52F's were soon replaced with B-52D's with reconfigured bomb bays that increased their bomb-load capacity to 60,000 pounds, 22,000 pounds more than the B-52F's.[9] Many of these earlier B-52

B-52H Stratofortress carrying AGM-129A Advanced Cruise Missiles

Prototype XB-58 Hustler with detachable pod mounted beneath the fuselage

models were phased out in the 1970s as part of a reduction of the U. S. strategic bomber force.

SAC began considering replacements for the B-52 as early as 1954, but a suitable alternative did not materialize. Notably, after flying the first production B-52 in 1954, Major General Albert Boyd, commander of Wright Air Development Center (WADC), reportedly called it the finest airplane yet built, and 10 years later, a life-expectancy study of the B-52 determined that "with funds for appropriate modification, there was [sic] no finite limits on B-52 service life."[10] The accuracy of these statements was proven as Stratofortresses (H models) built prior to 1965 continued to serve the Air Force into the twenty-first century. The B-52H, in particular, proved to be a versatile platform for ALCMs and SRAMs. Powered by eight TF33 turbofans, the last model had improved performance, range, and fuel consumption. The Stratofortress continued to perform decades beyond expectations, making significant contributions to Operations Desert Storm in 1991 and Enduring Freedom in 2001. It was projected to continue flying until 2030 or later.

The most unconventional strategic bomber program of the 1950s was Convair's B-58 Hustler, the first U. S. supersonic strategic bomber. The program began with a design competition between Boeing's XB-59 and Convair's XB-58, the latter of which was chosen by the Air Force in 1952.[11] The state-of-the-art winning design incorporated many unproven characteristics, including a delta-wing configuration. Other radical departures were its small size (made possible by the external

On March 13, 1957, a B-36F Peacemaker delivered a B-58 Hustler to Wright Air Development Center for structural testing. The B-58 was suspended under the bomb bay of the B-36 for the flight from Carswell Air Force Base, Texas. The propellers from two of the inboard engines had to be removed to accommodate the Hustler and the landing gear remained down during the entire flight.

B-58 being moved into Building 65 for structural testing at Wright Air Development Center, 1957

The flight crew of the XB-58 (left to right): Captain Robert S. Ballard, 3rd station operator; Major Andrew Z. Doka, 2nd station operator; and Major Joe B. Thomson, pilot

location of a detachable bomb pod), and the honeycomb sandwich structure of its wings (which counteracted the extremely hot temperatures experienced at supersonic speed). The design of the B-58, along with its sister programs—the F-102A/F-106 interceptors—also incorporated the Jones-Whitcomb "area rule" theory, which resulted in the "coke-bottle" fuselage: an extended fuselage that narrowed at the leading edge of the wing and expanded again near the tail. This wasp-waist shape allowed the aircraft to pass more easily through the shock waves experienced at the speed of sound.

Because of design modifications and SAC's objections to the airplane's short range and its inability to perform specific missions, the status of the B-58 remained in flux throughout the early 1950s. Retention of the program owed much to the persistence of the WADC commander, General Boyd, who argued that the unconventional technical characteristics of the aircraft needed to be explored to determine their feasibility and practicality for Air Force missions. In 1954, the Air Force reduced the program to research and development only, and then reinstated it for full-scale production the following year. The first prototype flew in 1956. During the intense testing program, the YB-58 showed spectacular performance in speed and altitude, exceeding Mach 2 (1,300 mph) and surpassing 50,000 feet altitude.[12] The Hustler became operational in 1961 and during its life span, broke 12 world speed records and won every major aviation award.[13] In this respect, the developmental risk the Air Force took with the B-58 program paid off. In addition to the aircraft's unique structural characteristics, the B-58 became the first aircraft to pro-

Glenn L. Martin's XB-51 was a response to the Army Air Forces' requirement for a light bomber in 1945. The bomber made its first flight in 1949, becoming the Air Force's first high-speed, jet-propelled, ground support bomber. Only two XB-51s were accepted before the program was cancelled because the airplane could not meet range requirements.

Martin B-57B Canberra. The forward fuselage was redesigned from the original British design to seat the pilot and navigator-bombardier in tandem. This aircraft is now on display at the United States Air Force Museum.

vide each crewmember with an individual, pressurized, escape capsule for emergency use at even the highest speed and altitudes.[14] By 1962, the Air Force had acquired 116 of the unconventional bomber, including test vehicles.

As the enemy developed increasingly accurate air-defense weapons for use against high-altitude aircraft, the Air Force found that the B-58 bomber no longer fulfilled its requirements. Primarily, the Hustler was not suitable for low-level bombing and suffered severe structural fatigue when flying at low altitudes. Although planning a B-58B low-level strike version, the Air Force cancelled the program in 1959, opting instead for the B-52. The B-58 was phased out of the Air Force inventory by 1970.[15]

In 1950, the only tactical bomber the Air Force had in service was the Douglas B-26 Invader. With the outbreak of war in Korea, the Air Force looked for a replacement for the propeller-driven light bomber with a goal of quickly deploying it to the Far East. The English Electric Company's Canberra, Britain's first jet bomber, fit the Air Force requirements for a rugged, all-weather, tactical bomber with night capabilities. The Air Force chose the aircraft over four other possibilities, including the in-service North American B-45 Tornado, considered too heavy for tactical bomber missions, and the Glenn L. Martin Company's experimental XB-51, which could not meet range requirements. The Air Force recognized Martin as the best candidate to oversee the design conversion and domestic production of the aircraft, designated as the B-57. From the beginning, design faults, engine malfunctions, and production problems delayed operational deployment of the aircraft. The RB-57A reconnaissance version entered service in mid-1954, followed by the B-57B bomber variant later that year. The RB-57D and F models, operational in 1956 and 1964, had new larger wings (1,505 square feet compared to 960 square feet) that enabled them to fly well above 50,000 feet.[16]

In comparison to the B-26, the B-57, powered by two Wright J65 engines, could fly twice as fast at a service ceiling twice as high. The B-57B featured a tandem cockpit, in which the navigator-bombardier sat behind the pilot. This arrangement provided better visibility and more space for electronic components. Fifteen B-57B's (redesignated B-57G's) were modified to a night-strike configuration for use in Southeast Asia. These aircraft had additional armor plating, new ejection seats, and self-sealing fuel tanks mounted in the fuselage. They also were fitted with televisions designed to operate in the absence of light. These low-light-level televisions, with the aid of forward-looking radar and infrared sensors, displayed a video presentation of the terrain for the pilot. Although the radar proved deficient, the configuration of the G model was considered an important step forward in the development of a self-contained, night-and-all-weather system.

Douglas B-66B Destroyer

Prototype of the FB-111A

The B-57B remained in the active Air Force inventory until the early 1970s, when most transferred to the Air National Guard.[17]

The Douglas B-66 Destroyer, an adaptation of the Navy's A3D-1 Sky Warrior, was the second tactical bomber developed and acquired during the 1950s. Originally planned as a replacement for the B-57, the B-66 was to fulfill Tactical Air Command's (TAC) high-speed, low-altitude bombing needs. The Air Force wanted a quick modification of the Navy version, but changing the A3D-1 to a land-based aircraft with a low-flying mission proved difficult. The reconnaissance version, the RB-66A, made its first flight in 1954 with disappointing results due to engineering flaws. The operational B-66B bomber entered service with TAC in 1956, but only 72 aircraft were accepted—half the number originally ordered. Subsequent flight tests, however, proved that the aircraft was especially suited for low-level flying. Initial phase-out of the B-66 began in 1963 except for specially equipped B/RB-66B's used for electronic warfare (see reconnaissance aircraft section below).[18]

The B-66 was the last manned bomber the Air Force acquired in quantity for more than two decades. Production of the B-52 and B-58 both ended in the fall of 1962 and the Air Force did not acquire its next new bomber until the B-1B in the late 1980s. In the interim, the Office of the Secretary of Defense issued a requirement for a strategic bomber version of the F-111 fighter, designated the FB-111, to replace the B-47 and the B-52 (models C through F) until the B-1 became available. With a longer fuselage, longer wings, stronger undercarriage, and bigger fuel tanks, the FB-111 weighed almost 30,000 pounds more than the F-111A. It also incorporated more advanced avionics (the Mark IIB) and the capability to carry the SRAM. The FB-111 became operational in 1969 and served the Air Force for over 20 years before being withdrawn in 1991. During that time, it won numerous awards, including consecutive top honors in SAC's bombing and navigation competition.[19]

Also during the lag in bomber acquisition, the Air Force considered several new designs, only one of which made it to development. This aircraft, the North American XB-70 Valkyrie, was the result of a mid-1950s Air Force requirement for a strategic penetrating bomber to replace the B-52. The Air Force desired an all-weather bomber that could attain a maximum service ceiling of at least 60,000 feet, produce short bursts of supersonic speed, carry 25,000 pounds of high-yield nuclear weapons, and travel 4,000 nautical miles without being refueled. Initially, six companies received study contracts for the proposed, chemically powered, intercontinental bomber, and in 1955, Boeing and North American Aviation were given follow-on contracts. The two companies submitted new designs, both indicating that the mission could best be accomplished with an all-supersonic-cruise air vehicle (instead of subsonic cruise and supersonic dash). In 1958, North American Aviation was chosen to continue the program, identified as Weapon System 110A. Their design proposed an aircraft that, using high-energy (boron) fuels, would fly at Mach 3.[20]

North American drew from its experience with several other programs including the F-100 fighter, the X-15 high-speed rocket plane, the surface-to-surface Navaho missile, and the XB-70's sister program—the F-108 fighter (cancelled in 1959). The ambitious program required a breakthrough in several elements of state-of-the-art technology (high-energy fuels, folding wing tips) in a very short period of time. The majority of the airframe (including the wings, the underbody, and the rear two-thirds of the aircraft) was made of brazed stainless steel honeycomb sandwich, which provided the aircraft with superior strength and insulation against high temperatures at supersonic speeds. The forward part of the upper fuselage (around the cockpit) was constructed of titanium alloys. The XB-70 also incorporated the compression lift theory, which featured a flat-topped vehicle with delta wings shaped to follow the shock waves formed by its pointed body. The

PROJECT SMART

The Supersonic Military Air Research Track (SMART) was constructed on the top of Hurricane Mesa in southwestern Utah between 1954 and 1957 by Coleman Engineering of Los Angeles. On July 25, 1957, the Aircraft Laboratory at Wright Air Development Center (WADC) officially opened the SMART track with an operating budget of more than $3.7 million. Coleman operated and maintained the facility (renamed the Hurricane Supersonic Research Site in November 1957) for WADC.

The 12,000-foot-long track, consisting of two standard-gage railroad rails, was built atop a flat mesa, and it terminated at a 1,500-foot-high cliff. The facility was used as a test site for ejection systems in supersonic aircraft (particularly the B-58, F-104, F-105, and F-106). Specially designed test sleds carrying photographic and electronic equipment (either strapped to dummies or directly to the sled) were catapulted from the track over the cliff, and during their descent, operational behavior and related physiological aspects of high-speed flight were measured and documented.

The B-58 ejection capsule built by Stanley Aviation was possibly the track's greatest success story. Throughout 1960, aerodynamic, reliability, and parachute problems were associated with the design-flawed capsule, and installation schedules had slipped considerably. The track was scheduled for closure in June 1961, but through a special contract with Convair, Coleman Engineering allowed the aircraft manufacturer to continue its tests of the B-58's pilot capsule through November. A number of tests were conducted to determine the cause of stability issues, and Convair and Stanley concluded that the problem stemmed first from parachute design and second from the ejection angle. Major hardware redesign and selection of a new parachute led to 10 consecutive successful capsule ejections. The capsule ejection system was evaluated as superior to open ejection seats, particularly at low speeds and altitudes and at speeds greater than 600 knots.

In addition to tests of ejection seats, WADC laboratories and private contractors used the track for tests related to the track's own water-brake system and liquid propulsion for the rocket sleds. Some additional tests conducted by WADC included the Defensive Anti-Missile Sub-System (DAMS), a type of countermeasure for bombers that could disable interceptor missiles with a dispersion of pellets (Weapons Guidance Laboratory, 1958), and an applied research program to determine the structural integrity and operational behavior of large-diameter parachutes at low supersonic speeds (Flight Accessories Laboratory, 1960). In December 1961, the Air Force sold the track and transferred its sled tests to Edwards Air Force Base, California. Contractors continued to operate the track (known as the Hurricane Mesa Test Track) into the twenty-first century.

Sources: History of WADC, July-December 1957, pp 32-34; History of WADC, January-December 1958, p 223; History of Wright Air Development Division, January-June 1960, Volume III, pp III-62-III-63 and Volume IV: Technology, p IV-85; History of Aeronautical Systems Division, April-December 1961, Volume II, pp II-119-II-128; *User's Manual, United States Air Force Smart Track* (Los Angeles: Coleman Engineering, undated), in ASC History Office Archive.

A view of the SMART Track from the air *(Coleman Engineering)*

A sled test in progress on the SMART Track *(Coleman Engineering)*

North American XB-70 Valkyrie

XB-70 with a T-38A escort

wing tips folded downward, providing the aircraft with increased stability and the necessary high pressure under the wing for a favorable lift/drag ratio.[21]

The aircraft originally was designed to use General Electric's J93-GE-5 engines that burned high-energy fuels. Curtailment of the fuel program led to a modification of the aircraft to accept J93 engines that burned the much-improved, conventional JP-6 fuel. The aircraft also incorporated an innovative bombing-navigation system that used stellar inertial guidance and the ASQ-28 (V) digital computer.[22]

President Dwight D. Eisenhower believed the future of strategic retaliation lay in ICBMs and did not appreciate the necessity of an unconventional bomber. In 1960, the program was reduced to a single prototype with no subsystems. President John F. Kennedy, who entered office in 1961, first reinstated the program, and then reduced it to two prototypes. The XB-70A made its first flight in September 1964, and the second prototype flew the following year. In May 1966, the XB-70A flew for more than 30 minutes at Mach 3. In 1967, NASA took over program management of the prototypes.[23] Although it never reached production, the XB-70 contributed a number of technological innovations later used in commercial industry, particularly the joint French and British Concorde, which began supersonic passenger transport in 1976.

The B-1A bomber program (initially referred to as the Advanced Manned Strategic Aircraft or AMSA) was born in the same atmosphere that killed the XB-70. Kennedy's Secretary of Defense Robert McNamara believed that ballistic missiles alone would perform the United States' strategic mission better than manned bombers. Nevertheless, he realized that ongoing research and development of subsystems and components would keep the nation at the forefront of aeronautical technology. The AMSA program was funded for research between 1963 and 1968. With the election of Richard M. Nixon as president in 1968, the AMSA received the support it needed for development, and the following year it was redesignated the B-1A, a Mach 2, manned, low-level, precision strike system. In 1970, North American Rockwell (later Rockwell International) was selected as prime contractor for the new weapon system. Benefiting from North American's experience with the XB-70, the B-1A made its first flight in 1974.[24]

By the mid-1970s, progress on the Boeing AGM-86 ALCM threatened the B-1A program, as it was determined that a B-52 could deliver the missile from far outside enemy defenses at less cost than a penetration bomber. Consequently, in 1977, President Jimmy Carter cancelled the B-1A program. Ironically, in 1981 newly elected President Ronald Reagan reinstated the program as the B-1B with the intent of using it as a carrier for the ALCM until the more stealthy B-2 bomber became operational.[25] Following a first flight in 1984, the B-1B Lancer became operational in 1986, and the Air Force accepted 100 of the bombers by 1988. They provided the air leg of the modernized Triad of strategic forces (which also included land-based ICBMs and submarine-launched ballistic missiles or SLBMs).

The in-service B-1B differed from the original B-1A design in many ways. Foremost, the B-1B carried cruise missiles, a critical element to its reinstatement in the 1980s. It could penetrate at lower altitudes (at subsonic speeds) and had longer range. Using new stealth technology, the Lancer had a reduced radar cross-section (RCS), and it carried a larger payload, including external stores. Other notable features of the B-1B included variable-geometry swept wings (also used on the F-111), a body shape that blended into the wings, and four General Electric F101 engines mounted under the inboard wing near the aircraft's center of gravity. The blended wing-body concept reduced drag and enhanced lift, while the engines' locations provided the aircraft with added stability for low-altitude flying. The "swing" wings could be fully retracted or extended in flight, allowing the aircraft to take off from shorter runways. With its aerial refueling capability, the B-1B carried twice the bomb load over the same intercontinental

Prototype of the Rockwell B-1B Lancer

Secretary of Defense Donald Rumsfeld (left) and Major General Abner B. Martin, B-1 program director, following a flight in the B-1A bomber, April 17, 1976.

B-1B undergoes icing tests in the McKinley Climatic Laboratory at Eglin Air Force Base, Florida, 1987. The tests included temperatures ranging from –65° F to 165° F.

distances as the B-52.[26] The B-1B also had a tail-warning system that alerted its pilot to enemy aircraft approaching from the rear.

In the 1990s, with the end of the Cold War, the Air Force transformed the mission of the B-1B from one of nuclear strategic deterrence to one of conventional warfare. The long-term Conventional Mission Upgrade Program (CMUP) included the addition of the Joint Direct Attack Munitions (JDAM), which gave the aircraft the ability to perform near-precision attacks on ground targets and increased weapons flexibility, allowing it to carry three different weapons simultaneously. On December 17, 1998, 95 years to the day of the Wright brothers first flight, the B-1B had its combat debut in Operation Desert Fox, striking Iraqi targets. The following year, the aircraft also took part in Operation Allied Force strikes against Yugoslav military targets in Kosovo.[27] In the fall of 2001, the Lancer conducted bombing missions over Afghanistan during Operation Enduring Freedom. In the first two months of the operation (October-November 2001), B-1B's dropped nearly four million pounds of weapons.

In 1993, the Air Force added another bomber to the air leg of the strategic forces Triad: Northrop's B-2 Spirit, also known as the "stealth" bomber. The B-2 program began in 1978 when the Air Force awarded a concept formulation contract to Lockheed for a stealthy, medium tactical bomber for high-altitude penetration. The following year, a design competition for the Advanced Strategic Penetrating Aircraft (ASPA) pitted the Lockheed and Rockwell team against the team of Northrop, Boeing, and Ling-Temco-Vought (LTV). The Air Force first awarded Northrop a concept definition contract, and in 1981 an additional contract to build 132 B-2s, then known as the Advanced Technology Bomber (ATB).[28] The aircraft was redesigned in 1983 to enable low-level penetration in response to improved Soviet air defenses against high-altitude aircraft. The new bomber, designed primarily by computers, incorporated flying-wing and stealth (low-observable) technology.[29]

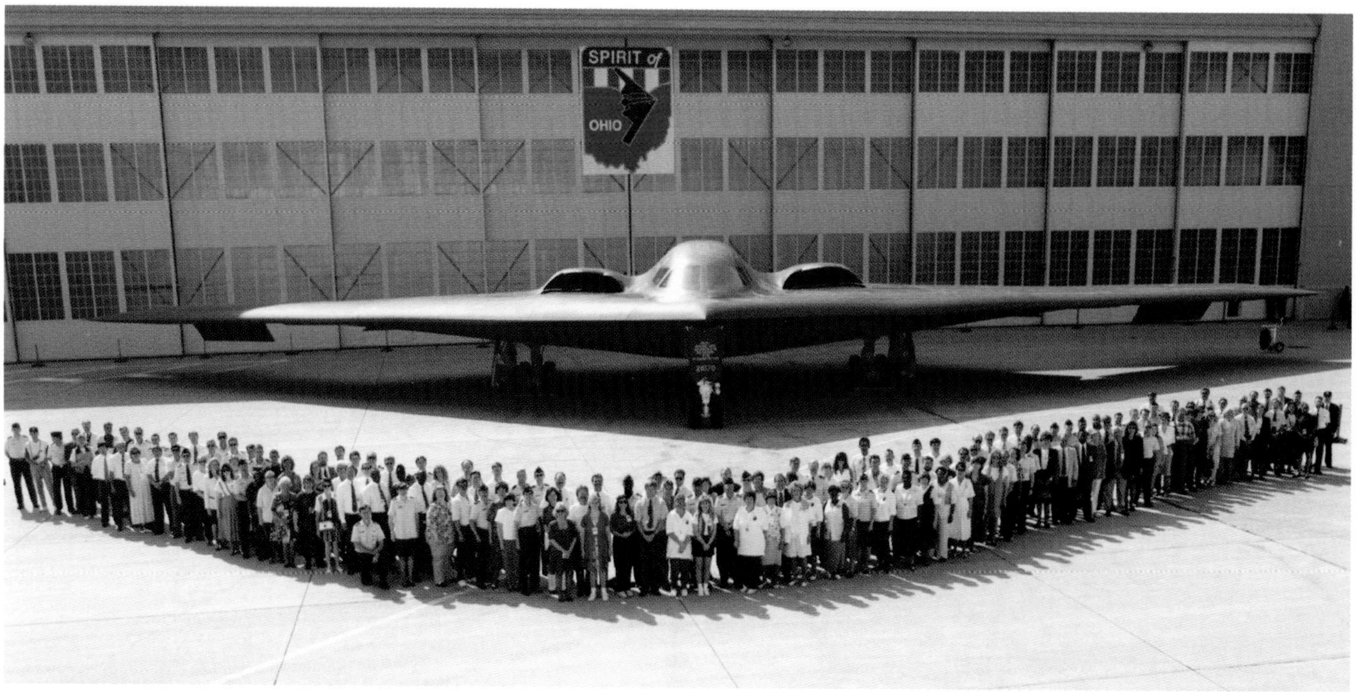

The B-2 System Program Office staff at Wright-Patterson Air Force Base gather at an official naming ceremony for the "Spirit of Ohio," July 18, 1997. The fifth production B-2 (serial number 82-1070) was used for climatic testing and earned the additional nickname "Fire and Ice."

Northrop B-2 Spirit

Colonel Richard M. Scofield (shown here when a lieutenant general) served as program manager for Project Senior Trend from 1981 until 1989 when he was selected to be program manager for the Advanced Technology Bomber (later the B-2).

The ATB, renamed the B-2 in 1988, completed its first test flight in 1989. Like the B-1B, the B-2 had a tumultuous production history. In 1990, the need for the new nuclear bomber was reevaluated in light of diminishing tension between the United States and the Soviet Union. President George H. W. Bush's Secretary of Defense Dick Cheney reduced the program from 132 to 75 B-2s, and further reductions were considered throughout the early 1990s. By 1992, the purchase of only 21 aircraft (15 production and six test articles retrofitted to production configuration) was finalized. The first B-2, named the Spirit of Missouri, was delivered for operational service in late 1993.[30]

The B-2, manned by two crewmembers, was powered by four non-afterburning General Electric F118 turbofan engines. The bomber incorporated an innovative, quadruple-redundant, digital flight control system (fly-by-wire); an electronic warfare system; low-probability-of-intercept radar; and a targeting system guided by the Global Positioning System (GPS). It had a 40,000-pound payload and used a GPS-aided munitions system that allowed it to bomb multiple targets during one pass.[31] In March 1999, the B-2 had its combat debut in the Republic of Yugoslavia during Operation Allied Force. The B-2s participated in 49 sorties during the operation, and the JDAMs released on assigned targets resulted in an 80 percent destruction rate.[32] Six B-2s also took part in Operation Enduring Freedom in the fall of 2001, flying 44-hour missions from their home at Whiteman Air Force Base, Missouri, to Afghanistan and back, the longest bombing missions ever flown.

FIGHTER AIRCRAFT

As with the bomber programs, the 1950s marked several transitions in Air Force fighter programs. Propeller-driven fighters, such as the F-51 and F-82, were phased out in favor of faster jet fighters. The Air Force's first successful jet fighter, the F-80, became operational in 1946.[33] In 1947, the F-84 entered operational service, and the F-86 followed two years later. Modifications of these early jet aircraft designs dominated the fighter program for the next decade as budget pressures of the late 1940s forced the Air Force to improve existing aircraft instead of contracting for new designs.

This situation changed drastically by 1950, spurred in part by the Soviet Union's test of its first atomic bomb in 1949. A flurry of new fighter designs, known popularly as the Century Series (due to their numerical designations), marked a new focus on defensive aircraft both to protect the nation's strategic bomber force and to intercept enemy bombers intent upon attacking the continental United States. The resultant operational aircraft included the F-102 interceptor (originally referred to as the 1954 Ultimate Interceptor), which evolved into the F-106; the F-101 strategic fighter, a long-range penetration escort designed to accompany and protect attacking bombers; the F-100 and the F-104 day fighters; and the F-105 fighter-bomber.[34] Dominant trends in the early fighter programs of the 1950s included attainment of supersonic speeds, all-weather capabilities, and extended range.

The multitude of fighter aircraft designs of the 1950s (and earlier decades) gave way to fewer development programs in later years. In the early 1960s, several new models of aircraft already in service became operational, including the F-105D and F-105F fighter-bombers and the F-106B fighter-interceptor. The F-4 and small numbers of the F-5, designs of the mid-1950s, also entered service in the early 1960s as a multi-purpose fighter and lightweight fighter/trainer, respectively. Later in the decade, the Air Force added the F-111 tactical fighter, and in the 1970s, the F-15 air-superiority fighter and F-16 multi-role fighter made their first flights. The 1980s ushered in the stealth era as the F-117 entered service. In the 1990s, development of the F/A-22 air-superiority fighter and the multi-service Joint Strike Fighter (JSF) ensured U. S. dominance of the skies well into the twenty-first century. Major advances of these later fighter aircraft programs were attributed to the development of low-observable technology and fly-by-wire flight control.

Upon entering the second half of the twentieth century, the Air Force had three jet fighters in its inventory: the F-80 (see Chapter 4: Forging an Air Force), the F-84B, and the new F-86A. The Republic F-84 Thunderjet, the jet successor to the P-47 Thunderbolt of World War II fame, was the Air Force's first postwar fighter in production. It was designed in 1944 as a mid-wing day fighter with a top speed of 600 mph and a radius of 705 miles. The XP-84 made its first flight in 1946, and the F-84B became operational in 1947.[35] Later models followed in 1948 (C model) and 1949 (D/E models). Tests

FIFTY-FIVE YEARS OF AIR FORCE ACQUISITION: FIGHTER AIRCRAFT

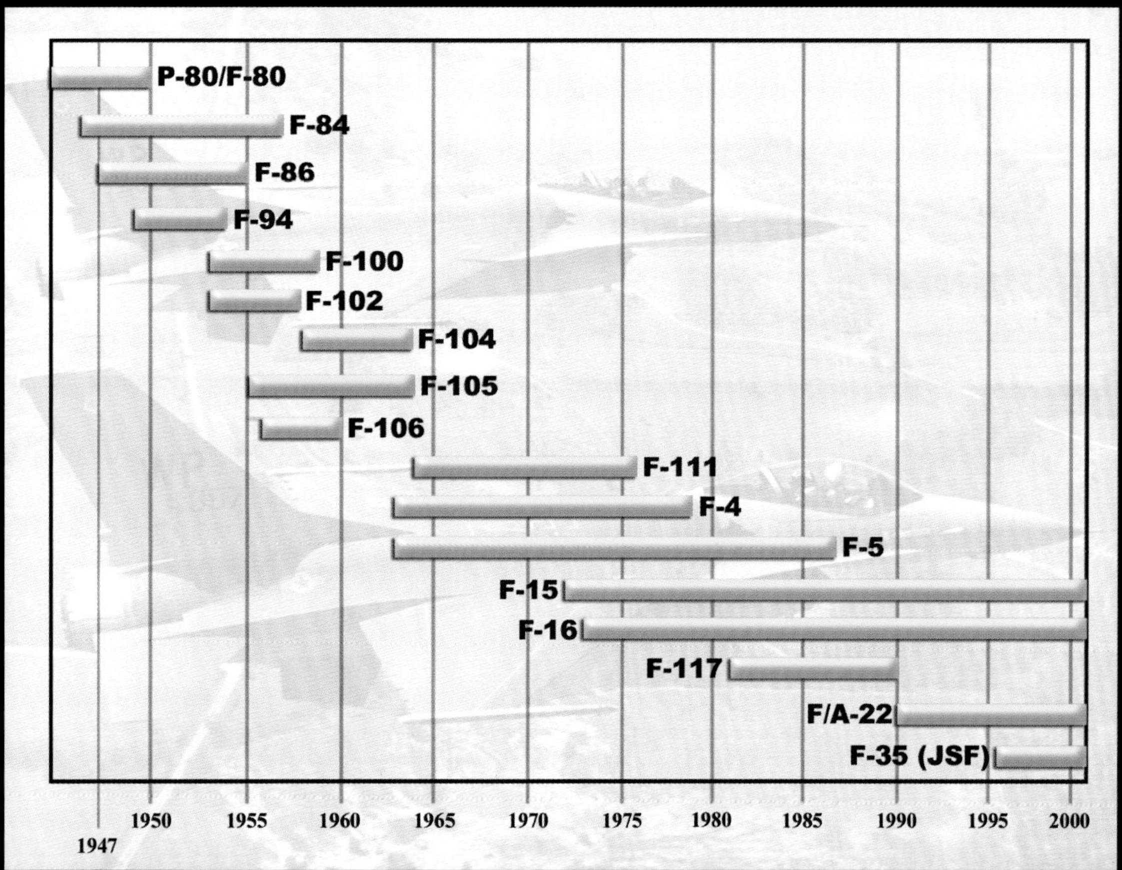

Shown are the dates of research, development, and acquisition for selected fighter aircraft, measuring from first flight of a prototype to the end of production.

Republic YP-84 Thunderjet, one of three prototypes, at Wright Field, 1946

F-84F Thunderstreak with swept wings

at Wright-Patterson Air Force Base indicated that the Thunderjet exceeded the performance of the F-80 in range, acceleration, load-carrying ability, high-altitude climb, and level-flight speed. The F-84G entered service in 1951 as the first nuclear-weapon-capable, single-seat fighter-bomber and the first fighter with aerial refueling equipment installed on the production line. It was also the last subsonic fighter-bomber to enter the Air Force inventory.[36]

Many early F-84 models were phased out beginning in 1952. Development of the aircraft continued, however, with the F-84F Thunderstreak (originally the YF-96A), with a swept wing and tail instead of the straight wing-tail combination on the basic F-84. It also had a Wright J65 turbojet engine with 7,220-pound thrust output, giving the F model more speed than the F-86H, the fastest American jet at that time. Overall, the F-84F, which became operational in January 1954, was a far superior aircraft to its predecessor F-84 models. It remained in service until replaced by the F-100 Super Sabre in the mid to late 1950s.[37]

The North American F-86 Sabre was the third jet fighter to enter the inventory in quantity. Development began in 1945 when the Army Air Forces issued a requirement for a variant of the North American XFJ-1 (a planned Navy jet fighter) as a medium-range, day fighter/fighter escort/dive bomber. To meet the requirement for a top speed of 600 mph, the contractor incorporated swept wings into the XP-86, which made its first flight in 1947. The F-86A became operational as the Air Force's first supersonic fighter in early 1949 and was deployed to Korea in late 1950 for air-superiority battles against the Soviet-built MiG-15. The A models soon were replaced with E and F models, the latter enhanced as a fighter-bomber specifically for use in Korea. They had higher thrust engines, droppable fuel tanks, and "6-3" solid-wing leading edges. The new

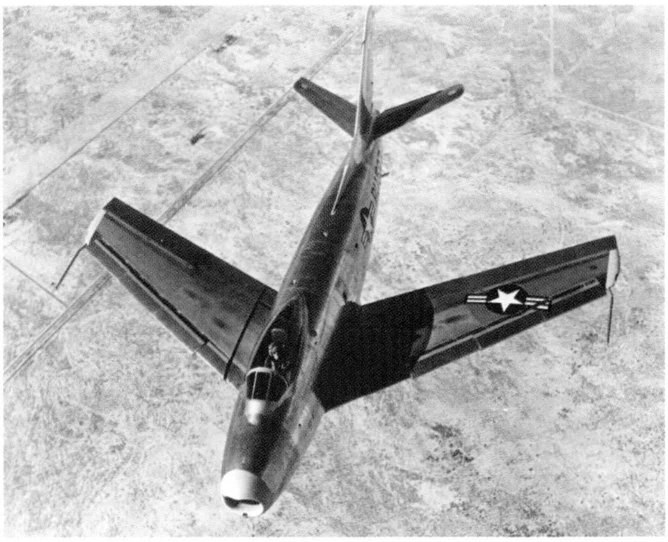

North American XP-86 Sabre, first of three prototypes

F-86A of the Wright Air Development Center's All-Weather Flying Center undergoing major inspection, 1951

During the Korean War, Wright Air Development Center engineers designed the "6-3" wing to make the performance of the F-86 fighter more comparable to the Soviet-built MiG-15 flown by the Chinese. Based on a suggestion from combat returnee Colonel John Meyer, the sealed leading edge slats on the wings of the F-86F (shown here) led to an appreciable increase in speed. The "6-3" designation described the extension of the wing chord by six inches at the base of the wing and three inches at the wing tip. The new wing was easily identifiable by the fence on the forward edge. (United States Air Force Museum)

wing appreciably increased the plane's speed and rate of climb, making it more equal to the MiG-15. Official WADC histories called this "undoubtedly one of the most spectacularly successful undertakings of its kind in Air Force history."[38]

The F-86A/E/F models phased out of the Air Force inventory by 1954. Development of the aircraft continued, however, with the F-86D all-weather interceptor (originally referred to as the XF-95), which entered operational service in 1953, and the F-86H day fighter/fighter-bomber, operational in late 1954. The single-seat D model was virtually a new design with a new fuselage, an afterburner, stronger wings, and an enlarged vertical tail. The most significant feature of the F-86D was the Hughes E-4 fire control system that guided the fighter to a target on a collision intercept course at night and in poor weather. It was also the first single-seat fighter armed with rockets (the 2.75-inch Folding Fin Aircraft Rocket also known as Mighty Mouse) instead of machine guns. The Air Force began replacing the D models with F-101s and F-102s and the H model with F-100s in the mid to late 1950s.[39]

The Northrop F-89 Scorpion, another fighter design of the mid-1940s to enter production in the early 1950s, was planned as an all-weather ground attack fighter with secondary missions of interception and penetration. After undergoing its first flight in 1948, the Scorpion entered service as the F-89B and F-89C interceptors in 1951 and 1952, respectively. The next model, the F-89D, armed with High Velocity Aircraft Rockets (HVARs), became operational in 1954. Subsequent F-89J's, essentially converted D models, were the first fighters to carry nuclear armament (two MB-1 Genie rockets) in addition to four Falcon air-to-air missiles. The J model became operational in 1957. Although flown by Air National Guard units well into the late 1960s, most Scorpions were phased out of active Air Force units by 1960.[40]

The Lockheed F-94 Starfire was the last World War II-era fighter design to be procured in quantity. The Air Force acquired the all-weather jet interceptor, composed of 75 percent F-80C parts, because it was more readily available than the F-89. The F-94A made its first flight in July 1949 and entered operational service in May 1950. Powered by an Allison J33 engine, it was the first production aircraft with an afterburner for added power during climb and dash operations. The F-94B entered service in the spring of 1951 with gyroscopic instruments for more accurate landings in poor weather, a high-pressure oxygen system, and larger wing-tip fuel tanks (mounted on the outer edge of the wing tip instead of being attached under the wing tip).[41]

Despite deficiencies with its engine and fuel system, the F-94 proved less troublesome than the more complex F-89 Scorpion. Still, the fate of the F-94 was evident almost immediately upon acceptance. WADC's commander, Major General Boyd, described the F-94 as a "second-rate airplane" and "not worthy of any sustained

Northrop XP-89 Scorpion with wing-tip fuel tanks

Lockheed's F-94C Starfire could fire 24 rockets from its nose. The rocket doors are open in this photograph.

improvement effort."[42] Although development work continued on the F-94 through the early part of 1952, most Starfires were phased out of the Air Force inventory beginning in mid-1954. The final model, the F-94C (originally referred to as YF-97) with a redesigned wing and tail plane and more powerful engines, was phased out in 1959.[43]

The first Century Series fighter was the North American F-100 Sabre-45 (later called the Super Sabre). The Air Force considered it an improvement of the latest F-86 design and ordered immediate production in 1952 as a day fighter to complement the high-end, all-weather F-102 interceptor. The F-100 was more than an updated F-86, however. The new aircraft incorporated a 45-degree-angle swept wing, a larger fuselage, new armament (the 20-mm T-160 cannon in place of the .50-caliber machine guns), and a new engine (Pratt & Whitney's J57 turbojet rated at 14,800 pounds of thrust) with afterburner. The first flight of the YF-100A took place in May 1953, and in a later flight test, the aircraft exceeded the speed of sound.[44]

The F-100A aircraft, the world's first operational supersonic (in level flight) fighter,[45] joined Air Force squadrons in the fall of 1954. The later model F-100C fighter-bomber (operational in 1955) had external and internal tanks for additional fuel and proved to be particularly suited for low-altitude bombing. The Super Sabre also went through a D and F model series. The D model fighter-bomber could be equipped with Bullpup air-to-ground missiles, and F-100F's armed with Shrike missiles were used for Wild Weasel defense suppression missions during the Vietnam conflict. The Air Force acquired twice as many F-100s than the next most prolific Century Series fighter (the F-102). All models of the F-100 were phased out of the active forces by 1972 but continued to fly with Air National Guard units until the end of the decade.[46]

In 1946, the Air Force sponsored a prototype flyoff for a long-range jet fighter-escort. The immaturity of available jet engines made this competition challenging for potential aircraft designers. Flight tests of three competitors, Lockheed's XF-90, North American's XF-93 (evolved from the F-86), and McDonnell's XF-88, proved the inadequacy of all three designs. The XF-88 had great potential and warranted further development. The XF-88 program was cancelled in 1950 due to lack of funding, but it was restarted in early 1951 in response to Korean combat experiences proving the need for a long-range bomber escort. The result was the swept-wing F-101 Voodoo which made its first flight in 1954 and became operational in 1957 as a replacement for the F-84. The C model followed later in 1957 and the B model interceptor (originally called the F-109), capable of carrying the MB-1 Genie nuclear rocket, entered service in 1959. The F-101 had two J57 engines, four 20-mm T-160 cannon, and built-in aerial refueling equipment. The most notable feature of the F-101 was an unrefueled range of 1,900 miles, a marked improvement over its contemporaries. Escort fighters became obsolete with the development of supersonic bombers, and by 1971, all F-101A's had been phased out.[47]

The Convair F-102 Delta Dagger, the world's first supersonic, all-weather jet interceptor, preceded the F-101 into operational service by one year.[48] The F-102 became the first Air Force delta-wing aircraft scheduled for large-scale production.[49] Contracted for in the summer of 1951 as the "1954 Ultimate Interceptor," the F-102 was designed to use the British J67 Olympus turbojet engine (built by Wright) and the Hughes MX-1179 "electronic brain" package to integrate fire control, flight control, navigation, and communications. In order to achieve supersonic speeds, Convair engineers incorporated the "coke-bottle" fuselage, a similar configuration to the one Convair later used on the supersonic B-58 bomber. In 1952, many of the F-102's components, including the J67 engine, were still in development, and the Air Force pushed ahead with limited production using less powerful but available J57 engines and simplified electronics equipment.[50] The Delta Dagger entered service in April 1956. As early as 1961, however, phase-out began as the F-102 was replaced with its direct descendent—the F-106 (originally designated the F-102B).[51]

As the second production step of the "1954 Ultimate Interceptor," the all-weather Convair F-106 Delta Dart incorporated the MX-1179 "electronic brain" (later referred to as the MA-1 Automatic Weapon Control System) originally planned for the F-102 and a more powerful Pratt & Whitney J75 engine. The prototype F-106 made its first flight in 1956. Subsequent Air Force flight tests pushed the speed of the prototype to Mach 1.9 at an altitude of 57,000 feet. The F-106A barely escaped budget reductions of the late 1950s and entered operational service, albeit in reduced numbers, in 1959. The F-106B, with a tandem, two-seat cockpit and redesigned fuselage fuel tank area, entered operational service the following year. All production F-106 aircraft underwent extensive modifications and modernization (improved ejection seats, navigation equipment, external wing supersonic fuel tanks, and aerial refueling capability for long-range ferrying), allowing them to remain in service until 1988.[52]

Development of the Lockheed F-104 Starfighter, an advanced day fighter scheduled to replace the F-100, began in 1952 but did not make significant progress until mid-1954. The F-104 had a thin, straight wing attached to a long, slender fuselage and a high, all-maneuvering tail. Powered by a General Electric J79 engine, the aircraft reached a top speed of Mach 1.83, and in 1955, a YF-104A became the first production aircraft to fly faster than Mach 2.[53] This aircraft, called a "minimum concept weapon," was meant to perform air-superiority missions at less expense, with less weight, and with less complexity than its contemporaries. When it became operational in 1958, however, it entered service as an interceptor with Air Defense Command. The F-104s were too small to carry the data-link equipment for the Semi-Automatic Ground Environment (SAGE) air defense control system, which led to their phase-out in 1960. Temporarily reactivated in the early 1960s for the Berlin and Cuban Missile crises, the early model F-104s were phased out again by 1969. The F-104C fighter-bomber, powered by higher-thrust J79 engines and sporting a new fire control system, was retired by 1967 after a short stint in Southeast Asia. They were replaced by F-4D's.[54]

The single-seat, single-engine Republic F-105 Thunderchief began development in 1951 as an air-superiority fighter and an atomic-bomb carrier to replace the F-84F Thunderstreak. The F-105 fighter-bomber had a unique internal bomb bay that could carry either a nuclear bomb or additional fuel. The aircraft also was equipped with a 20-mm T-171D Gatling-type cannon. The F-105B entered service in 1958; the D model followed in 1961 and the F in 1963. The D and F models participated in tactical air strikes in Southeast Asia beginning in 1965, and the aircraft underwent a number of special modifications for their combat role, including the addition of armor plates, backup flight control systems, pods for electronic countermeasures on the wings, and new gun sights. In 1973, the F-105s were phased out and replaced with F-4D's.[55]

By the late 1950s, the Soviet Union's increasing inventory of ICBMs lessened the threat of a bomber-delivered attack on the continental United States. In the event of a bomber offensive, the Air Force felt its fighter force, made up of the new

PROJECT FICON

In 1951, the Air Force awarded a contract to Convair for Project Ficon (Fighter Conveyor), a range extension program in which a fighter aircraft was carried by and air-launched from a mother bomber. The concept had first been attempted in 1948 using the XF-85 Goblin as a parasite on the B-29, and the feasibility of the Ficon concept using an RF-84F and an RB-36 had been proven in wind-tunnel tests in 1951 and 1952. Similarly, flight tests using a straight wing F-84E had been successful. In May 1953, flight tests using the RF-84F indicated that the swept-wing version was more stable than the straight wing. The Air Force authorized modification of 10 B-36 carriers (redesignated GRB-36D) in mid-1953 and production work on the RF-84F's was expected to begin shortly thereafter. Strategic Air Command was scheduled to have an operational Ficon squadron by the end of 1955. By late 1954, problems with the first modified B-36 carrier, the trapeze mechanism that carried the parasite half in and half under the bomb bay of the B-36, and engine deficiencies with the RF-84 delayed the program substantially. Flight tests were finally under way in 1955 with promising results. The structural integrity of the trapeze had been proven, and air pickups of the parasite were perfected. By March 1956, however, the program was phased out as aerial refueling had proven to be a cost-effective and efficient means of range extension.

Sources: History of Wright Air Development Center, 1 January – 30 June 1954, Vol. III, p 298; History of Wright Air Development Center, 1 July – 31 December 1954, Vol. II, pp 237-239; History of Wright Air Development Center, 1 January – 30 June 1955, Vol. II, p 241; "GRB-36 Aircraft (FICON), Revision of Test Requirements," Memorandum to File, March 15, 1956, in GB-36 file, Box 3195: Aircraft/Bombers/B-36, Box 1, ASC History Office Archive.

GRB-36D bomber with its parasite fighter, a YRF-84F. The fighter has just completed its recovery maneuver.

CENTURY SERIES FIGHTERS

Two North American F-100A Super Sabres. The one on the left is the same configuration as the prototype YF-100A. It has a taller fin and rudder designed to overcome control difficulties. The first 70 aircraft, including the one on the right, had shorter fins and rudders but were later retrofitted to the original prototype design.

One of four YF-102A's, with the wasp-waist fuselage

Republic YF-105A Thunderchief all-weather fighter-bomber

First production McDonnell F-101A Voodoo, August 17, 1954

Avionics equipment for the F-105B included seven "robot" units to handle navigation, bombing and fire control, radar search, and automatic identification. A specially developed computer regulated the jet's "breathing by sensitively handling the rush of air through the inlet air ducts."

Lockheed XF-104 prototype

Convair F-106A Delta Dart, the second production step of the 1954 Ultimate Interceptor

Century Series fighters, could intercept and destroy the existing Soviet bombers. Consequently, research and development funds were shifted to advanced missile programs, and the Air Force concentrated on modernizing its fighter fleet with upgraded weapons and avionics.[56] The Air Force's next production fighters to emerge were the F-4 and F-5 in the early 1960s, followed closely by the F-111 in the late 1960s.

The McDonnell F-4C Phantom II entered the Air Force inventory as a quick solution to a requirement for a tactical fighter.[57] An example of "commonality," as insisted upon by President Kennedy's Secretary of Defense Robert McNamara due to budget restrictions of the era, the F-4C was an Air Force version of the Navy's F4H-1 (later redesignated F-4B) supersonic, long-range interceptor developed in the mid-1950s. The F-4C, originally referred to as the F-110A, was the first Air Force production model, and it quickly became known as the "leading all-around combat aircraft of the entire 1960s."[58] The Air Force variant had few changes over the Navy's version, with the exception of boom refueling equipment, larger wheels, and different avionics. The tactical fighter could carry Sparrow, Bullpup, Shrike, Genie, Falcon, and Sidewinder missiles; napalm; and conventional and nuclear bombs. In fact, the F-4 could carry three times the bomb load of a World War II-era B-17.

The F-4C, powered by two General Electric J79 engines, entered operational service in late 1963, and the F-4D became operational in 1966. These were closely followed by the E model sporting the General Electric Vulcan 20-mm armament system, an improved fire control system, more powerful J79 engines, and armor plating. The F-4's experiences in Vietnam led to a newly designed wing (with thicker skin, fatigue straps, and large hydraulic slats that extended automatically in violent high-g turning maneuvers) to accommodate heavy combat loads.[59] The F-4G, the last variant of the Phantom, was originally designed as a "Wild Weasel" configuration for Vietnam to suppress and destroy enemy antiaircraft artillery batteries and surface-to-air missile launch sites.[60] The F-4G's were used during Operation Desert Storm in the early 1990s and remained active with Air National Guard units until replaced with F-16s in 1995.[61]

The F-5 Freedom Fighter was designed by Northrop in 1955 as a lightweight, inexpensive, high-performance fighter. The Air Force first acquired the N-156T

McDonnell F-4E Phantom II

This F-4B, armed with AIM-9 Sidewinder air-to-air missiles, is one of two that the Navy loaned to the Air Force. The Air Force originally referred to the F-4 as the F-110. *(Department of Defense Still Media Depository)*

YF-5A on its first flight, 1959. The single-seat fighter version of the T-38 trainer was originally called the N-156F.

WILD WEASELS

During the conflict in Southeast Asia, the Air Force lost a number of aircraft to enemy surface-to-air missiles (SAMs) because it lacked the equipment to counter such radar-controlled weapons. The Air Force needed an escort aircraft to locate enemy SAM sites and suppress or destroy them before they could harm bombers and fighters en route to their targets. A subsequent increase in electronic warfare research led to the fielding of a number of aircraft, called Wild Weasels, that quickly became critical to operations in Southeast Asia. These aircraft used the electromagnetic energy emitted from hostile radar sites to locate and home-in on the enemy's deadly air defense weapons.

The original Wild Weasels (Wild Weasel I) were F-100F's, which participated in hunter-killer strike missions with F-105s beginning in 1965. The F-100F's were specially equipped with radar homing and warning systems and rockets that marked the locations of missile sites to be destroyed by the following strike forces. These aircraft also carried the Navy's radar-seeking AGM-45 Shrike missiles. The F-100F's were replaced by faster F-105F and F-105G Wild Weasels (Wild Weasel III) in 1966 and 1967. These were originally armed with the Shrike missiles and later the Navy's AGM-78 Standard anti-radiation missiles (ARMs) to locate and then destroy enemy radar sites. The F-105 Wild Weasels flew in hunter-killer teams with F-105D's and F-4 Phantoms or as strike-force escorts for B-52 bombers. In 1969, the F-105s were supplemented with F-4C's armed with CBU-52 cluster bombs (Wild Weasel IV) to detect and destroy missile launch sites.

In 1975, the Air Force introduced the latest model of Wild Weasel, the F-4G Phantom II. The Air Force modified 116 F-4E's into the Wild Weasel V configuration by removing the cannon and replacing it with AN/APR-38 electronic warfare equipment. The two-seat F-4G's carried AGM-88 High Speed Anti-Radiation Missiles (HARMs). For self-protection, they also could be armed with Shrike, AGM-65 Maverick, AIM-7 Sparrow, and AIM-9 Sidewinder missiles. F-4G's with updated AN/APR-47 equipment performed admirably during Operation Desert Storm. They flew over 2,500 sorties and suppressed or destroyed most of Iraq's air defenses early in the war. The F-4G Wild Weasels stayed in the inventory until 1996 and were essentially the last Wild Weasels. That role was subsequently filled by the single-seat F-16 Viper equipped with the HARM targeting system.

Sources: Marcelle Size Knaack, *Post-World War II Fighters*, (Washington D.C., 1986) pp 130-131, 202, 267, 274; Wayne Thompson, *To Hanoi and Back: The United States Air Force and North Vietnam, 1966-1973* (Washington, D.C., 2000), pp 36, 205, 231; "Wild Weasel," viewed online December 5, 2001, at http://www.boeing.com/defense-space/military/f4/wildweasel.htm; "McDonnell Douglas F-4G 'Wild Weasel'" viewed online December 5, 2001, at http://www.wpafb.af.mil/museum/research/fighter/f4g.htm.

F-4D (serial number 66-7635), the first Wild Weasel test aircraft

version as the T-38 trainer in 1961. Parallel development of the single-seat fighter version (N-156F), with two General Electric J85 engines, resulted in the prototype's first flight in May 1963. Most F-5A's and F-5B's (two-seat fighter) were acquired for foreign sales or for the United States' NATO allies under the Military Assistance Program (MAP). The F-5C was combat tested in Vietnam during 1965-1966, but the Air Force decided not to acquire large numbers of this fighter version. Instead, it procured a number of trainers to train allied pilots under MAP. The F-5E Tiger II international air-superiority fighter, which entered service in 1973, was slightly bigger and more powerful than its predecessors but maintained much of their simplicity. This aircraft was also largely purchased by allies of the United States.[62]

Concurrent with the development of the F-4C, the Air Force acquired the General Dynamics F-111 Aardvark,[63] which made its first flight in 1964 and became operational in 1967 as a follow-on to the F-105 fighter-bomber. The aircraft began as the Tactical Fighter Experimental (TFX) program, a requirement for an aircraft with maximum commonality (like the F-4) for use by the Air Force and Navy. The aircraft's multiple roles included close air support, air defense, and interdiction. The final F-111A design incorporated variable-sweep wings, tracing its roots to the Bell X-5 research plane and the Navy's experimental Grumman XF10F-1. With the wings extended straight out, the aircraft was capable of taking off from short, unimproved landing strips and could fly at low speeds. With the wings swept back, the F-111 could exceed Mach 2.5 at high altitudes.[64]

The Air Force acquired several models of the F-111, including the E model in 1969, the D and F models in 1971, and the strategic bomber version (the FB-111) in 1969. While the E model closely resembled the F-111A, the D model had improved avionics equipment (the Mark II) and more powerful Pratt & Whitney TF30 turbofan engines. The F model, a stripped-down D model due to production and financial problems with the Mark II avionics system, had a more powerful version of the TF30 engine and improved landing gear, and later was modified to carry the Pave Tack electronic tracking system. All three models carried the Sidewinder air-to-air missile. Using the first terrain-following radar (TFR), the aircraft could fly at night at high speeds and low altitudes to escape enemy radar and missiles. Because of the superior accu-

Rollout of the first production F-111A fighter, 1963

racy of the bombing radar, six F-111A's were sent to Vietnam just five months after becoming operational. Half of these aircraft were lost within one month of operation (one to malfunction of the tail servo actuator and two to pilot error and poor mounting of the M-61 gun) and were withdrawn from the conflict. Structurally modified F-111A's returned in 1972 and flew numerous, poor-weather strike missions over North Vietnam.[65] In addition to combat service in Vietnam, the F-111s (F models) participated in El Dorado Canyon operations against terrorists in Libya (1986) and in over 2,500 missions in Operation Desert Storm (1991). The last F-111s left the active Air Force inventory in 1996 after 30 years of service.[66]

Secretary of Defense Robert McNamara speaks at the rollout of the F-111, the result of the TFX program.

The problems associated with multi-role aircraft, particularly in light of combat experiences in Southeast Asia, led to a drive within the Air Force to acquire single-mission fighters. In the 1960s, controversy stirred over whether the new fighter should be specialized for air superiority or close air support. The Air Force believed it needed a specialized air-superiority fighter to close the gap between its existing fighters and the Soviet Union's new interceptors and antiaircraft missiles. The secretary of defense believed that dogfights, such as those during World War II and Korea, were a thing of the past and that missiles would fill that role in the future. The F-15 program began as the Advanced Tactical Fighter Experimental (F-X) concept, stressing maneuverability over speed, to replace the F-4 in the next decade. The original design provided a multi-role aircraft to fill both non-nuclear air-to-air and air-to-ground missions. Three events provided the support the Air Force needed to acquire the F-15 as an air-

First McDonnell Douglas F-15A Eagle

Brigadier General Benjamin N. Bellis (far left), deputy for the F-15 program, discusses the F-15 model with (left to right) Secretary of the Air Force Robert Seamans; General James Ferguson, commander of Air Force Systems Command; and Lieutenant General James Stewart, commander of Aeronautical Systems Division.

superiority weapon: the loss of two F-105s to supposedly obsolete MiG-17s in Southeast Asia, the Soviet Union's unveiling of its new generation fighters (the MiG-25 Foxbat and the MiG-23 Flogger), and the Air Force's obligation to acquire the Navy's A-7 for close air support (see Attack Aircraft below).[67]

In 1969, a design competition culminated in McDonnell Douglas being chosen as prime airframe contractor over the Fairchild Hiller Corporation and the North American-Rockwell Corporation.[68] The F-15A Eagle made its first flight in 1972, and when it became operational in 1975, it was the Air Force's first air-superiority fighter since the F-86 that had served so admirably in the Korean War. The single-seat aircraft featured two Pratt & Whitney F100 turbofan engines. With the high thrust-to-weight ratio of the engine and low wing-loading, the aircraft had superior maneuverability and acceleration and could handle tight turns without losing airspeed. The avionics carried in the Eagle included a head-up display (which projected flight information on the windshield at the pilot's eye level), an inertial navigation system, ultrahigh-frequency communications, an internal electronic warfare system, and pulse-Doppler radar, the latter of which provided the F-15 with "beyond-visual-range" combat capability. In addition to an internal 20-mm cannon, the F-15 could carry a combination of three different weapons: Sparrow air-to-air missiles, advanced medium range air-to-air missiles (AMRAAMs), and/or Sidewinder missiles.[69]

The A model was followed by the C (single-place) and D (two-place) models in 1979. The F-15C had increased fuel capacity through its two specially designed, low-drag conformal fuel tanks that attached to the sides of the angular, air-intake ducts. The aircraft also had radar capable of picking individual targets out of a cluster. A multi-mission variant, the F-15E Strike Eagle, first reached operational units in 1988 for all-weather deep interdiction and air-to-air combat. It had two cockpits (one for the pilot and one for the weapons system officer), improved fire control and weapons delivery equipment, conformal fuel tanks, LANTIRN (Low Altitude Navigation and Targeting Infrared system for Night), and TEWS (Tactical Electronic Warfare System) to perform night, all-weather missions at low altitudes. For interdiction missions, it could carry over 24,000 pounds of ordnance, including laser-guided bombs, cluster munitions, and conventional "dumb" bombs.[70]

The F-15s first saw combat service for the U. S. Air Force during Operation Desert Storm in 1991. (In 1981, Israeli Air Force's F-15s participated in Israel's attack on the Osirak nuclear power plant in Iraq, marking the first actual combat use of the fighter.) During air-to-air combat missions, they maintained a 26:0 kill ratio against enemy fighters. The LANTIRN-equipped F-15E's were used successfully for night missions against enemy Scud missile launch sites and antiaircraft artillery batteries. The Eagles also supported a variety of other military missions, including Operation Southern Watch in the no-fly zone over southern Iraq, NATO-sponsored operations in Bosnia, and Operation Provide Comfort in Turkey.[71] In the fall of 2001, they were used in the war against terrorism in Afghanistan (Operation Enduring Freedom).

The F-16 program began in the early 1970s when the Air Force announced its requirement for a low-cost, Lightweight Fighter (LWF) to augment the F-15. In 1972, the Air Force awarded contracts to General Dynamics[72] and Northrop to produce prototypes of their designs: the YF-16 and the YF-17 (later developed into the Navy's F/A-18), respectively, both of which made their first flights in 1974. In

McDonnell Douglas F-15C with conformal fuel tanks removed

Three F-15E Strike Eagles being prepared for bombing missions into Afghanistan as part of Operation Enduring Freedom, November 2001

LANTIRN

The cover of darkness hindered the missions of fighter pilots since World War I. That cover was penetrated by Aeronautical Systems Division (ASD) in the 1980s when it developed and produced LANTIRN, the Low-Altitude Navigation and Targeting Infrared system for Night. Working with the Martin Marietta Corporation (later Lockheed Martin Inc.), ASD began research and development on LANTIRN in September 1980, and the manufacturer delivered the first system on March 31, 1987.

LANTIRN integrated the functions of a navigation pod and a targeting pod. The navigation pod used terrain-following radar (TFR) and a forward-looking infrared (FLIR) sensor to allow pilots to fly in the night below the level of radar detection; the targeting pod used information provided by the navigation pod's sensors to detect, track, select, and lock-on to targets. Both pods were mounted on pylons underneath an aircraft's wing or fuselage.

During Operation Desert Storm, a team from ASD's LANTIRN System Program Office (SPO) traveled to the Persian Gulf to supervise LANTIRN's operation. F-15E's, flying over dark desert terrain with the assistance of LANTIRN, were able to detect and destroy Iraq's menacing Scud missile launchers, while LANTIRN-armed F-16C/D's flew successful missions against other Iraqi targets. Impressed by LANTIRN's capabilities, the U.S. Navy began equipping its F-14s with LANTIRN in 1996, a move that has been called one of the "biggest advances" ever made to the F-14 because it transformed the Tomcat from an escort plane to a long-range, precision-attack night fighter. LANTIRN became an essential accessory for the planes of many of the world's air forces.

Sources: Fact Sheet, U.S. Air Force, "LANTIRN," June 29, 2001; "LANTIRN," *Martin Marietta Electronics & Missiles*, July 1994; Henry Narducci, *A Century of Growth: The Evolution of Wright-Patterson Air Force Base* (Wright-Patterson Air Force Base, 1999); William B. Scott, "Lantirn Gives Tomcat Night Attack Role," *Aviation Week and Space Technology*, June 10, 1996, pp 40-43.

LANTIRN pods mounted on an F-16 fighter

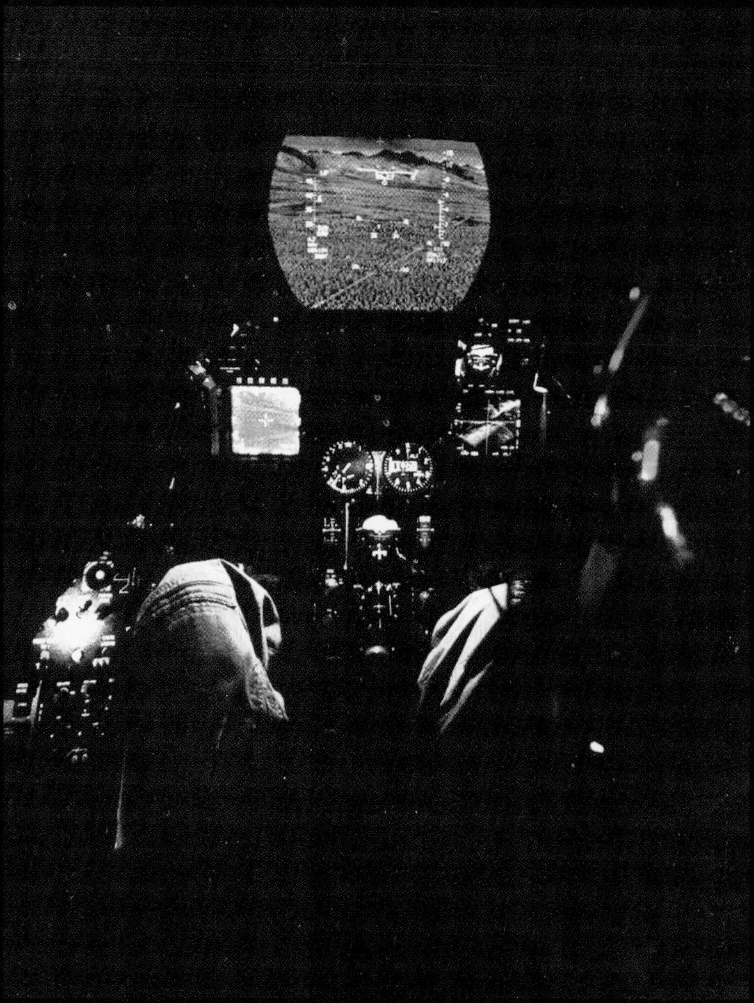

Visual display produced by LANTIRN as compared to the complete darkness outside the cockpit

YF-16, winner of the Lightweight Fighter competition

Brigadier General Richard K. Saxer (left), deputy for the F-16 System Program Office, and Major General James A. Abrahamson, deputy for Tactical Systems, with Lieutenant General Lawrence A. Skantze (right), commander of ASD, at Wright-Patterson Air Force Base, 1980

1975, the Air Force awarded a contract to General Dynamics to develop the multi-role F-16 Fighting Falcon as an air-combat fighter with ground attack capabilities. The first production F-16s, including the single-seat F-16A and the two-seat F-16B operational trainer, were delivered to the Air Force in 1978. The single-seat C and two-seat D models followed in 1984. By 2000, the Fighting Falcon had become the most numerous fighter in the Air Force inventory, with more than 2,200 procured. In addition to Air Force use, the F-16 became one of the most popular export fighters, with more than 4,000 delivered to 19 nations. The first Foreign Military Sales F-16s were delivered to the European Air Forces in 1979.

The initial production program for the F-16 involved five equal partners, including manufacturers in the United States, Belgium, Denmark, the Netherlands, and Norway, with the latter four expressing interest in the F-16s as a replacement for their F-104G's. This was the first time European companies produced major airframe and engine components for the U. S. Air Force.[73] The F-16 program evolved into the world's largest and most successful, international co-production program, involving industries in 13 countries and final assembly lines in five countries.

The Fighting Falcon incorporated many advanced technologies, which gave it unmatched maneuverability and mission per-

First of two YF-16 prototypes in final assembly at the General Dynamics Fort Worth plant. Alongside the aircraft is the Pratt & Whitney (P&W) F100 engine, one of two advanced engines developed during the "Great Engine War." When problems with the prototype F100 engine led to contractual disagreements with Pratt & Whitney, the Air Force contracted with General Electric (GE) for the F101 engine as a standby, demonstrated technology. In 1984, the Air Force awarded a split-buy contract, with 75 percent to GE and 25 percent to P&W. The competition forced P&W to make necessary improvements to the F100 engine, and both engines (the GE F101 renamed the F110) were used on F-15 and F-16 fighters, providing the Air Force with unparalleled performance into the twenty-first century.

formance, particularly in close-in air combat, or "dogfights." These technologies included fly-by-wire flight control; relaxed static stability; blended wing-body cross section; variable camber wing; "high-g" cockpit with a bubble canopy, reclined ejection seats and hands-on/head-out philosophy mechanizations; and highly integrated digital fire control avionics.[74] Through production block and model changes, major retrofit programs, or software updates, the F-16 evolved from a day-only air-to-air fighter to a fully capable multi-role fighter. Its combat capabilities included beyond-visual-range intercept, day/night precision strike, suppression of enemy defenses ("Wild Weasel"), photographic reconnaissance, maritime interdiction, close air support, and forward air controller (airborne). The aircraft was powered by either the Pratt & Whitney F100 engine or the General Electric F110 turbofan engine.[75]

The F-16 saw combat during Operation Desert Storm in 1991. During that conflict, the Fighting Falcons flew more missions than any other aircraft. These missions included deep interdiction against Iraqi airfields and military production facilities and suppression of Scud missile

F-16s of the U.S. Air Force Thunderbirds

Two Lockheed F-117 Nighthawks

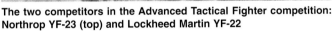

The two competitors in the Advanced Tactical Fighter competition: Northrop YF-23 (top) and Lockheed Martin YF-22

YF-22 Raptor, winner of the ATF competition

launch sites. In 1995, the aircraft received the "Sure Strike" precision targeting system for operations in Bosnia, and in 1998, the F-16s were fitted with the Night-Vision Imaging System (NVIS), a development program accelerated in response to the Bosnia missions.[76] In the fall of 2001, as part of Operation Noble Eagle, F-16s patrolled the skies over major American cities following the September 2001 terrorist attacks on New York City and Washington, D.C. In a non-combat role, the F-16 also was flown in air shows by the U.S. Air Force Thunderbirds for more than 20 years and was used as a test bed for advanced technologies (the Advanced Fighter Technology Integration [AFTI]/F-16).

The Lockheed F-117 Nighthawk (also known as the stealth fighter) culminated from joint Air Force and Defense Advanced Research Projects Agency (DARPA) design studies in the mid-1970s for an aircraft with low radar cross-section to defeat increasingly effective Soviet air defense radar systems. For this aircraft to perform its ground attack mission against vital targets without being seen on radar or heard, it had to forgo the supersonic speeds that had become a hallmark of new fighters since the 1950s. Under the code name Have Blue, Lockheed's Skunk Works facility in California was given a contract to develop two prototypes known as Experimental Survivable Testbeds (XSTs); the data from flight tests were then used to design the F-117's unique, multi-faceted airframe. The first prototype of the operational F-117, powered by two General Electric F404 turbofan engines, made its first flight in 1981 and 10 of the aircraft entered operational service in total secrecy two years later. The F-117 precision attack aircraft was a single-seat, semi-flying wing configuration with a V-shaped tail. It incorporated fly-by-wire technology, aerial refueling capability, and an environmental control system. The internal weapons bays could carry precision guided munitions (GBU-27s), air-to-air missiles (Sidewinders and Mavericks), and High Speed Anti-Radiation Missiles (HARMs).[77]

In 1988, the Air Force revealed the existence of the stealth fighter, and two years later, finally allowed the public to see the

X-32A, Boeing's entry in the Joint Strike Fighter competition, on its first flight, September 2000

Lockheed Martin X-35A, winner of the Joint Strike Fighter competition, on its first flight

aircraft. Shortly thereafter, the F-117A played a significant role in Operation Desert Storm as the only aircraft authorized for missions over the heavily defended parts of Baghdad. Using the laser-guided GBU-27, the aircraft boasted 95 percent accuracy during precision strike missions, and no F-117s were hit or lost to enemy fire throughout the conflict. Over the years, the aircraft underwent a number of improvement programs, including a weapon system computational subsystem upgrade (1984-1992); a new graphite/thermoplastic composite tail fin (1986-1992); a four-dimensional flight management system comprised of a revised cockpit, improved autopilot, auto throttle, and pilot-activated attitude recovery system (1988-2001); and a new Infrared Acquisition and Designation System (IRADS) and inertial navigation system supplemented with a GPS unit.[78]

The Lockheed Martin F/A-22 began as part of the Air Force's requirement for an Advanced Tactical Fighter (ATF) in 1981. Planned as a twenty-first century replacement for the F-15, the ATF was envisioned as an all-weather, supersonic, stealthy air-superiority fighter with superior maneuverability, survivability, and maintainability. The concept development investigation phase concluded in 1984, and the prototype competition, similar to the prototype program for the Lightweight Fighter that resulted in the F-16, began in 1986 with the Lockheed, Boeing, and General Dynamics team competing against the Northrop and McDonnell Douglas team. These two contractor teams submitted the YF-22 and YF-23 designs, respectively. General Electric's YF120 turbofan and Pratt & Whitney's F119 turbofan competed for the Joint Advanced Fighter Engine (JAFE) contract. The YF-23 made its first flight in August 1990, and the YF-22 first flew in September 1990.[79] Although both prototypes performed successfully during flight tests, in 1991 the Air Force chose the YF-22 and the Pratt & Whitney F119 engine combination for their higher capabilities and lower cost.[80]

The Air Force approved the final design of the F-22 Raptor (similar to the F-15 with a two-fin tail, angular air intake ducts on either side of the nose, and a bubble canopy) in 1995. The new fighter was designed for air-to-air combat and air-to-ground strikes. A first look/first kill sensor suite allowed the F-22 to identify and shoot an enemy aircraft before being detected on enemy radar. With more thrust than contemporary engines, the F119 engines allowed the F-22 to cruise at supersonic speeds without using afterburner, thus increasing the aircraft's speed and range. The F-22 carried AMRAAMs and Sidewinders, and for air-to-ground missions, it carried internally two 1,000-pound Joint Direct Attack Munitions (JDAMs).[81] Low Rate Initial Production for the first 10 F/A-22s began in the fall of 2001 with operational status scheduled for 2005.[82]

Another aircraft planned for operational service in the early twenty-first century was the Joint Strike Fighter, a multi-service aircraft for use by the Air Force, Navy, and Marine Corps. The multi-purpose, supersonic, stealth aircraft was planned to replace several in-service aircraft, including the Air Force's F-16 and A-10. Contractor teams led by Boeing and Lockheed Martin each developed flying concept demonstrators: the X-32 and X-35, respectively. These prototypes made their first flights in 2000. In October 2001, Lockheed Martin was awarded the contract for the Joint Strike Fighter, referred to thereafter as the F-35. Three variants of the F-35 were planned: a conventional takeoff and landing version for the Air Force, a carrier-deck compatible version for the Navy, and a short takeoff and landing version for the Marine Corps. The Air Force planned to purchase more than 1,700 of its variant and field them beginning in 2008.[83]

ATTACK AIRCRAFT

The first Air Force-developed attack aircraft of the post-World War II era was the Cessna A-37A Dragonfly, essentially a "beefed-up, modified" T-37 jet trainer.[84] The Air Force contracted for a

Cessna A-37A Dragonfly, a T-37B Tweet trainer rebuilt as an attack aircraft with a 7.62-mm mini-gun in the nose and eight under-wing pylons

LTV A-7D Corsair II armed with conventional bombs

prototype of the A-37 in 1963, and in 1967 it sent 25 A-37A's to Southeast Asia for combat evaluations. The A-37s logged more than 10,000 combat sorties in less than a year. Armed with conventional weapons, the attack aircraft conducted close air support for ground forces, armed escort for Army helicopters, armed reconnaissance, forward air control, and counterinsurgency operations. The Air Force acquired a total of 39 A-37A's and, in 1968, introduced the A-37B to service. The B models were new production airframes with aerial refueling equipment, more powerful General Electric J85 turbojet engines, and improved fire control systems. In addition to a 7.62-mm mini-gun mounted in the forward fuselage, the B model Dragonfly carried a variety of conventional weapons on eight under-wing pylons.[85]

As a result of experiences in Vietnam, the Air Force recognized its need for specialized aircraft to replace the multi-purpose fighters in the inventory, such as the F-111 and F-4. To fulfill the close air support role, a prototype competition for an attack aircraft, the A-X program, was initiated. As an interim close air support aircraft, the Air Force compared an improved version of the F-5 to the Navy's A-7 Corsair II.[86] The Air Force decided to purchase the A-7D variant of the Corsair, a subsonic, swept-wing aircraft with the 20-mm Vulcan cannon, additional armor plating, and aerial refueling equipment. In addition to close air support, the single-place aircraft was configured with all-weather bombing radar for long-range strike and deep interdiction missions. It had six under-wing pylons for carrying 15,000 pounds of weapons, including air-to-air missiles, air-to-ground missiles, general-purpose bombs, rockets, or gun pods. Strike cameras were mounted in the rear fuselage for bomb damage assessment. The Ling-Temco-Vought (LTV) A-7D production model made its first flight in 1968 and became operational later that year.[87]

YA-7F prototype fighter made its first flight on November 29, 1989. The aircraft is a modified A-7D with a lengthened fuselage, additional fuel and avionics, and an airframe-mounted accessory drive unit.

Meanwhile, the A-X program focused on two attack aircraft prototypes: the Northrop YA-9A and the Fairchild-Republic YA-10. In late 1970, the Air Force awarded the two companies contracts to develop prototype aircraft for a flyoff competition.

In the early 1970s, enhanced capabilities in computer-aided design, computation of complex mathematical codes, materials, and manufacturing processes provided a fertile ground for the exploration of new and innovative aerodynamic concepts. The Defense Advanced Research Projects Agency (DARPA) and the U.S. Air Force first demonstrated the ability to design and fabricate a Very Low Observable (VLO) air vehicle using these capabilities during concept demonstrations for the next generation of Remotely Piloted Vehicles (RPVs) at the conclusion of the Vietnam War. Both DARPA and the Air Force understood the technological and tactical potential of "stealth," which quickly went "black," i.e., Special Access Required. A program office was established in the Pentagon under the cover of the Air Force Reconnaissance Office to study potential applications for the technology and to manage funding for these studies and DARPA's technology efforts.

In the mid-1970s, DARPA pursued stealth technology development using the contracting and engineering expertise of the Aeronautical Systems Division (ASD), now the Aeronautical Systems Center (ASC), at Wright-Patterson Air Force Base. A small compartment, led by Lieutenant Colonel Jack Twigg, was carved out of the RPV System Program Office (SPO) to support DARPA. Mr. Bill Elsner was technical director/chief engineer and Mr. Herbert H. (Skip) Hickey was the flight systems engineer.

In 1975, DARPA and the Air Force conducted limited competition among several aerospace companies to develop and test two VLO prototype aircraft before awarding the contract to Lockheed's Advanced Development Projects (ADP), also known as the Skunk Works, in early 1976. Designated Have Blue, the program's first vehicle flew in December 1977 to explore the flying qualities of its unusual faceted design. The second vehicle was used to demonstrate and verify VLO characteristics. While all program objectives were met, both prototypes were lost in accidents, with no loss of life, during the test program.

Lieutenant Colonel Twigg and his small team at ASD managed the Have Blue contract in utmost secrecy. Most work was done at the contractor's plant in Burbank, California, or the test range at Nellis Air Force Base in Nevada. In early 1978, ASD provided technical support to the Air Force program office in the Pentagon for the study of potential stealth applications under the Senior High program. A small group of ASD engineers, including Skip Hickey, worked directly with the Air Staff program team (consisting

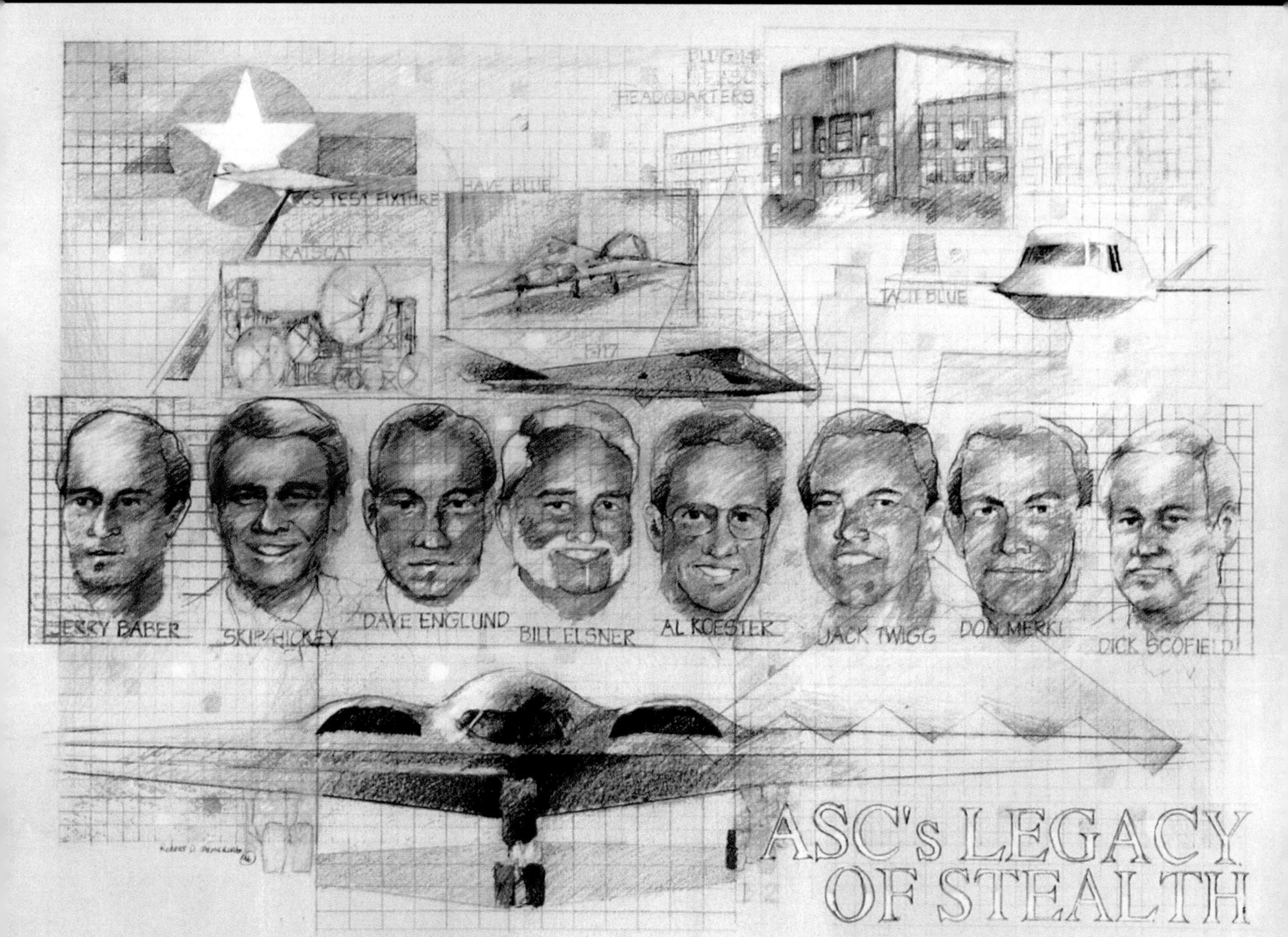

The illustration "ASC's Legacy of Stealth," by Robert D. Memering, depicts key programs, places, and the Pioneers of Stealth that brought a tantalizing idea from the laboratory to the runway: Colonel Jerry Baber, Mr. Skip Hickey, Brigadier General Dave Englund, Mr. Bill Elsner, and Colonel Jack Twigg—the founding fathers; Colonel Allen Koester, Colonel Don Merkl, and Lieutenant General Dick Scofield. Their extraordinary efforts led to innovative designs for fighter aircraft, bomber aircraft, and missiles with unprecedented capabilities.

of Lieutenant Colonels Ken Staten, Joe Ralston, Bob Swarts and Jerry Baber) to oversee the studies being conducted by the Skunk Works. These studies ultimately led to full-scale development of the F-117 fighter, the B-2 bomber, and the Advanced Cruise Missile.

By mid-1978, an internal debate within the Air Force arose as to whether stealth development programs should be managed by the Air Staff or Air Force Systems Command, of which ASD was a part. To posture ASD for eventual management of these programs, ASD Commander Lieutenant General George Sylvester tasked Colonel Dave Englund from the F-15 SPO to lead the low-observables programs under ASD's Deputy for Development Planning. Colonel Englund brought with him Colonel Don Merkl from the F-16 SPO and Lieutenant Colonel Allen Koester from F-15 Special Projects as his two principal program directors along with Lieutenant Colonel Twigg, who continued to manage Have Blue and Senior High. As the programs transitioned to ASD during the first half of 1979, Lieutenant Colonel Baber of the Air Staff team joined the office as director of contracting. Colonel Merkl became the first F-117 program director and Lieutenant Colonel Koester, ultimately, became the first program director for the Advanced Cruise Missile.

In July 1978, the Air Force, DARPA and the Northrop Corporation teamed up to develop Tacit Blue to explore the feasibility of a different design approach to low observables. Only one highly secret flight vehicle was constructed, but one was all that was needed to validate the technology. Tacit Blue differed dramatically in appearance from the multi-faceted Have Blue, and its smooth, bulbous appearance earned it a nickname of "The Whale." The extremely successful test program, which began in February 1982, was completed in 1985 after 135 flights. Tacit Blue then was placed on display at the United States Air Force Museum.

Enormous databases were developed to store and process all information amassed throughout the years of research and testing the Have Blue and Tacit Blue aircraft. At a secret Radar Scattering Range near Alamogordo, New Mexico, beyond visual range of a curious press and public and under the cover of darkness, test articles were hoisted onto a large Radar Cross-Section Test Fixture and subjected to every conceivable test to determine the optimum design and combination of materials needed to provide the highest possible degree of stealth capability to operational vehicles.

The successes of Have Blue and Tacit Blue as VLO demonstrators provided the basis for a spirited competition between Lockheed and Northrop for a stealth bomber. In late 1982, ASD awarded Northrop a contract to build the B-2. Colonel Richard Scofield, who had joined the ASD team in 1981 as the second F-117 program director, became the B-2 Spirit program director, a duty he held until 1991.

Hundreds of Air Force and thousands of contractor employees labored in extreme secrecy to turn the theories of low-observable technology into actual air vehicles capable of flying virtually undetected inside enemy territory to deliver lethal blows or observe enemy actions. As details of the amazing development of low-observable technology and systems at ASD (ASC) are slowly emerging, the world is finally learning about the incredible research and development effort by these pioneers of stealth.

Bill Elsner was chief engineer and head of ASD's Remotely Piloted Vehicle/Special Projects Office in 1975. The office assisted the Air Force and DARPA in development of the Experimental Survivable Testbed (XST) demonstrator vehicle which later became Project Have Blue and led to development of the F-117A Nighthawk.

The first aircraft developed by Lockheed under the Have Blue program made its initial flight in late 1977 to test the flying characteristics of the faceted airframe design. A second Have Blue prototype was used to test the very-low-observable characteristics. In 1978, Northrop was awarded a contract to develop a third VLO prototype, this one a smooth and bulbous design, referred to as Tacit Blue (inset). The information gained during these two programs was applied to other flight programs, and eventually culminated in the production of the Northrop B-2 bomber and the Lockheed F-117 fighter.

Colonel Dave Englund was the first program manager for the ASD Low Observable Project Office after management authority was transferred from the Pentagon to ASD in 1979.

One of two Northrop YA-9A prototypes in the A-X competition, 1973

Fairchild-Republic YA-10A, winner of the A-X competition, during its first flight in 1972

A-10A Thunderbolt II with Pave Penny laser-tracking pod mounted on a pylon under the fuselage. The multi-barrel GAU-8/A cannon is visible under the nose.

Northrop worked with Avco Corporation for development of a suitable engine, and Fairchild worked with General Electric. The Air Force also contracted with General Electric and Philco-Ford Corporation to develop a 30-mm gun system, the GAU-8/A, for the aircraft. The two prototypes both flew for the first time in May 1972. After seven months of flight testing, the Air Force chose the Fairchild model with two General Electric TF34 turbofan engines for production. General Electric also received a contract to produce their gun system.[88]

In 1977, the A-10A Thunderbolt II became operational as the first Air Force aircraft designed specifically for close air support. The Thunderbolt incorporated a head-up display; the multi-barrel, forward-firing GAU-8/A cannon in the nose; and five pylons under each wing that carried general-purpose bombs, incendiary bombs, flares, cluster bombs, Maverick air-to-ground missiles, Sidewinder missiles, or laser-guided bombs. The AN/AAS-35 Pave Penny laser-tracking pod (developed by Martin Marietta) was carried under the fuselage. During Operation Desert Storm, the A-10's ability to carry heavy weapon loads and to loiter for long periods of time proved indispensable for United States and allied support of Kuwait.[89]

GUNSHIPS

During the Vietnam War, a need arose for an aircraft that could supplement fighters, specifically for interdiction and close air support of ground troops. The aircraft needed to fly at low altitudes and at low speeds, have an extensive range, and be large enough to carry flares, spotlights, sensor equipment, and extra ammunition. The solution was a side-firing gunship that circled enemy strongholds and targets while firing large quantities of ammunition from internally mounted guns. Transport aircraft filled the requirements of speed, altitude, range, and load-carrying capacity. The first gunship, the AC-47, was developed in-house through the cooperative efforts of the Aeronautical Systems Division (ASD) and the Avionics Laboratory. The Limited War Office at ASD handled all modifications for the gunship. The AC-47 (popularly, but unofficially, known as "Puff the Magic Dragon" or "Spooky") was combat tested in Southeast Asia in 1964 using three .30-caliber machine guns; the guns were later changed to three 7.62-mm mini-guns. The underside of the aircraft was painted black and the top was camouflaged for night reconnaissance and escort missions. In 1969, as American units in Vietnam received newer gunships (AC-119s and AC-130s), the AC-47s were turned over to the South Vietnamese Air Force.[90]

The gunship version of the C-119 Flying Boxcar arrived in Southeast Asia in December 1968. The AC-119G Shadow was equipped with four 7.62-mm mini-guns, advanced sighting systems, flare launchers, and armor protection. The later K models, referred to as Stingers, had the added firepower of two 20-mm cannon, and two J85 auxiliary turbojets provided improved performance, increased payload capability, and reduced takeoff distances. Both models transferred to the South Vietnamese after the United States withdrew from the conflict.[91]

The AC-130 gunship began combat evaluations in Southeast Asia in 1967, more than a year prior to the AC-119G. The A model included four 20-mm Vulcan cannon and four 7.62-mm multi-barreled guns; searchlights; and forward-looking, infrared, target-acquisition equipment. These were upgraded to Surprise Package configuration with the addition of two 40-mm guns and a digital fire control computer. The AC-130E provided even more ammunition, heavier armor, and advanced electronics. Following the war, all remaining AC-130s were upgraded to the H configuration, referred to as Spectres. This modification included a combination of one 105-mm howitzer, two 20-mm cannon, and two 7.62-mm mini-guns, and an avionics upgrade with new sensors, forward-looking infrared target tracking, low-light-level television, and aerial refueling capability.[92]

AC-47 gunship at Pleiku Air Base, South Vietnam, 1967

Placement of the machine guns in the AC-47 gunship

A few of the key personnel in the development of the first AC-47 gunship included Staff Sergeant Estell P. Bunch (far left), who developed the original gunsight; Captain Ronald W. Terry (later lieutenant colonel, third from left), who flew 52 missions in the AC-47 over Vietnam and later headed the AC-130 Gunship System Program Office at ASD; and Lieutenant Edwin Sasaki (fifth from left) of the Aerospace Medical Research Laboratory.

The most recent model, the AC-130U Spooky, was an upgraded H model. Modifications began on the 12 aircraft in 1990. New equipment included combined inertial/Global Positioning System navigation, head-up display, triple armor protection, and poor-weather attack radar. With new fire control radar, the guns could be trained on the target, relaxing the need for absolute precision flying, and two targets could be fired upon simultaneously. The gunships' mission also expanded to include surveillance, search and rescue, escort, and armed reconnaissance.[93] Beginning in the fall of 2001, the AC-130

C-119 transformed into the AC-119 gunship

Crew of the prototype AC-130A, (serial number 54-1626) return to Wright-Patterson Air Force Base following combat tests in Vietnam. This gunship was nicknamed "Vulcan Special."

First AC-130U Spooky gunship

FIFTY-FIVE YEARS OF AIR FORCE ACQUISITION: CARGO AIRCRAFT

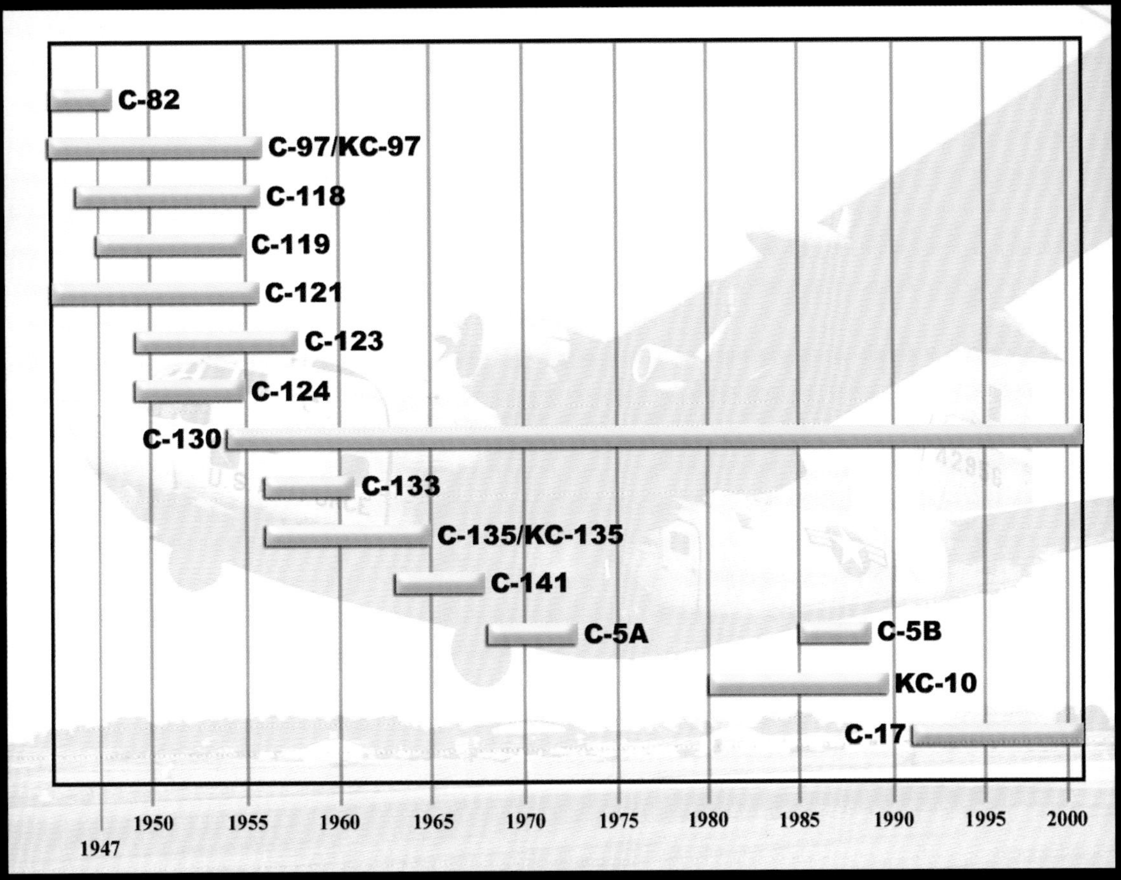

Shown are the dates of research, development, and acquisition for selected cargo aircraft, measuring from first flight of a prototype to the end of production.

gunships conducted operations over Afghanistan as part of Operation Enduring Freedom.

TRANSPORT AIRCRAFT

As the primary mission of cargo aircraft, the United States' ability to rapidly deploy and sustain its troops and equipment was essential to national security and the defense of its allies. The Air Force acquired new transports to meet forecasted requirements and to modernize and upgrade its airlift capabilities. The Air Force also acquired transport-type aircraft for use as tankers, special operations aircraft, gunships, and operational support aircraft. Developments over the past 50 years included greater payload, longer range, faster speeds, and shorter takeoff and landing distances, as well as advances in aeromedical accommodations and aerial refueling.

Upon entering the second half of the twentieth century, the Air Force inventory contained such war veterans as the Curtiss C-46 Commando (operational in 1942) and the Douglas C-54 Skymaster (1943), as well as the Douglas C-47 Skytrain (1941), and the Fairchild C-82 Packet (1944). Postwar developments included the Boeing C-97 Stratofreighter (1947), the Douglas C-118A Liftmaster (originally used as a presidential aircraft—Truman's *Independence*, 1947) the Fairchild C-119 Flying Boxcar (an improved C-82, 1949), and the Lockheed C-121 Constellation (1948). The Douglas C-124 Globemaster II, an improved C-74, was added to the inventory in 1950.[94] In the 1950s, the Air Force also acquired the Lockheed C-130 Hercules, the Douglas C-133 Cargomaster, and the Boeing KC-135 Stratotanker

YC-97 in front of Hangar 4, Wright-Patterson Air Force Base ***(Peter M. Bowers)***

Fairchild's XC-119A, a modified XC-82B

Douglas YC-124 Globemaster II was a C-74 with a redesigned fuselage and clam-style nose loading doors.

YC-123H equipped with two General Electric J85 jet engines in under-wing pods and modifications for use on rough fields. Auxiliary jet engines were also added to the C-123K's (modified C-123B's).

refueling aircraft. Like bomber and fighter programs, the 1950s were a period of heightened procurement, primarily illustrating the shift from piston engines to turboprops and turbojets.

Despite the acquisition of a number of new transports following World War II, the importance of military mobility was overshadowed by the United States' Cold War deterrence policy. Limited and conventional wars, such as that fought in Korea, were thought to be a thing of the past. Consequently, the Air Force focused on the acquisition of atomic weapons, guided missiles, intercontinental ballistic missiles, and strategic bombers. With the introduction of Flexible Response in the late 1950s, quick and easy mobility of the nation's armed forces, particularly strategic airlift, became critical to military plans. Airlift exercises during the early 1960s proved that existing transports were too slow, too old, too small, and too few to provide adequate airlift capability. The result of these deficiencies was funding for three new transport aircraft: the Lockheed C-141 Starlifter for quick cargo and passenger transport, the Lockheed C-5 Galaxy for movement of outsize cargo, and the McDonnell Douglas C-9A for aeromedical evacuation.[95]

After the C-5 became operational, 15 years elapsed before the Air Force again increased its airlift capacity with the production of the C-5B (1985), and another 10 years before its newest transport, the McDonnell Douglas C-17 Globemaster III became operational (1995). In the interim, the McDonnell Douglas KC-10A Extender refueling tanker (a converted DC-10) became operational to complement the KC-135 tankers that had been in service since the mid-1950s.

The two newest transports of the early 1950s were the C-119 and the C-124. The Fairchild C-119 Flying Boxcar was developed from the World War II-era Fairchild C-82 Packet, which had been disappointing in performance and reliability. Over several years' time, Fairchild strengthened the new aircraft structurally and upgraded its engines and propellers. By 1947, the C-119A was ready for its first flight, and two years later the C-119B entered operational service. Powered by two Pratt & Whitney R-4360 engines, the aircraft had a maximum load capability of 30,000 pounds and could transport 62 paratroops or 35 patient litters. According to official Air Force press releases, it was the "first truly operational cargo-troop carrier aircraft designed in the 'shoulder wing' configuration to provide a low-slung fuselage for loading ease."[96]

The redesign of the Douglas C-74 Globemaster was initiated in 1947, but the new Douglas C-124 Globemaster II did not make its first flight until April 1950. The huge aircraft could carry a maximum load of 74,000 pounds, including 200 troops or 136 patient litters. Its primary advantage was its combat radius of 1,000 miles, allowing it to transport cargo or troops to a remote base and return without refueling. The new aircraft had four R-4360 engines, cabin heat, clam-style nose loading doors, hydraulically operated ramps, and an electrically operated elevator. The C-124s remained in service until the mid-1970s when they were replaced by C-141s.[97]

The Fairchild C-123B Provider began as a Chase Aircraft Company glider design (the XG-20) of the late 1940s. Chase designed the glider for conversion to a piston-engine-powered assault transport; the first prototype (the XC-123) flew in 1949. The Kaiser-Frazier Corporation acquired a majority interest in Chase in 1953, but shortly thereafter experienced financial difficulties leading to the cancellation of its production contract with the Air Force. After obtaining a number of bids, the Air Force renegotiated the contract with Fairchild. The first Fairchild C-123B flew in 1954, and the production aircraft entered service the following year. The twin-engine (Pratt & Whitney R-2800s) transport could accommodate 61 troops, 50 patient litters, or 23,000 pounds of cargo, and carried fuel in jettisonable, external fuel tanks. The J and K models, the latter serving in Vietnam, were fitted with two auxiliary turbojets (on the wing tips on the J and in under-wing pods on the K) for emergency power augmentation.[98]

The two Lockheed YC-130 prototypes

Interior of the C-130 Hercules accommodated more than 90 troops.

Prior to 1955, the transport aircraft in the Air Force inventory were all powered by piston engines. The two transports that became operational during the late 1950s incorporated turboprop engines. The first of these, Lockheed's medium assault C-130 Hercules powered by four Allison T56 engines, was the first turboprop production aircraft in the United States. It was designed in the early 1950s, and later models of this aircraft remained in service into the twenty-first century. The prototype YC-130 made its first flight in 1954 and production C-130s entered service two years later. Designed for passenger and cargo transport, the tactical Hercules was a high, straight-wing configuration and its retractable tricycle landing gear allowed it to land and take off from short and/or rough airfields. The aircraft had an upswept rear fuselage with the floor serving as the loading ramp, and it sat low to the ground for ease in loading. The original C-130A could accommodate 92 passengers, 70 litters, or 36,000 pounds of cargo, but later models had increased payload capabilities, as well as increased range through larger, internal fuel tanks and external, under-wing tanks.[99]

The Hercules went through a number of model series and was configured for a variety of Air Force missions, including: gunship (AC-130A/E/U), drone carrier (DC-130A/E), satellite tracker and recovery (JC-130A), photo reconnaissance and mapping (RC-130A/B), weather reconnaissance (WC-130B/E), special operations (MC-130E/H Combat Talon), electronic surveillance (EC-130H Compass Call), and refueling tanker (KC-130H). Additionally, several C-130B's and E's were modified for Coast Guard search-and-rescue missions, and C-130D's were equipped with landing skis for operations in Antarctica. The C-130H was originally produced in large quantities for export, but

C-130E Hercules with Aeronautical Systems Division markings on tail

the Air Force quickly sent this model overseas after Iraq invaded Kuwait in 1990. The C-130J entered production in 1997, replacing the older E and H models. The J model constituted the first major upgrade to the aircraft since it entered service in the 1950s. Using four Allison AE2100D3 turboprops, it could climb faster and higher, was faster in level flight, and had increased range.[100]

Several C-130s were modified for special operations duties. The MC-130E Combat Talon and the MC-130H Combat Talon II had the capability of dropping special operations forces and supplies with great accuracy day and night and in all types of weather. Improved features included aerial refueling equipment, terrain-following/terrain-avoidance radar, inertial and Global Positioning System navigation, and high-speed aerial delivery systems. The MC-130E's first deployed in 1966 and participated in numerous combat missions in Southeast Asia. Before being replaced by MC-130H's in active Air Force units in 1991, they were used during Operation Urgent Fury in Grenada, Operation Just Cause in Panama, and in Operation Desert Storm in Iraq. The MC-130P Combat Shadow was used for clandestine or low-visibility missions, aerial refueling of helicopters, and night airdrops of special operations teams.[101]

Following closely behind the C-130, the second turboprop transport to enter the inventory was the large C-133 designed to carry the nation's ICBMs. Planned to supplant the C-124s, the Cargomaster carried twice the payload (133,000 pounds versus 74,000 pounds) of the Globemaster II. The first production C-133A made its initial flight in 1956 and entered service the following year. The C-133, powered by four Pratt & Whitney T34 turboprop engines, was the largest, propeller-driven, production cargo aircraft ever acquired by the Air Force. Loading doors were at the rear, with later production A models and all B models designed with clam-style doors, thereby lengthening the cargo hold by three feet to allow the Titan ICBM to be carried without disassembly. The Cargomasters served as the Air Force's heavy strategic freighter until replaced by the C-5s in the early 1970s.[102]

The C-141A was the first jet aircraft designed specifically for use as a military transport. The Starlifter made its first flight in 1963 and entered operational service in 1964. The aircraft had high, swept-back wings, four Pratt & Whitney TF33

Special operations forces board an MC-130 Combat Talon en route home from Grenada following Operation Urgent Fury in 1983.

turbofan engines in under-wing pods, an all-weather landing system, and rear loading doors. With a maximum cruising speed of nearly 500 mph, it could deliver four times as much cargo in the same amount of time as a C-124. Using a changeable cargo compartment (floor rollers to smooth floor to sidewall seats), the C-141 could transport 164 troops or 123 fully equipped paratroopers, 80 patient litters, or 68,000 pounds of cargo. By 1965, Starlifters made daily flights to transport cargo, troops, or aeromedical patients between the United States and Southeast Asia.[103]

The C-141B program began in the early 1970s as a solution to the United States' difficulties during the Yom Kippur War in Israel. During operations to supply Israel, the Air Force's attempts to land at American overseas bases for refueling were repeatedly rejected by European allies. In need of a transport to carry outsize cargo and with capability for aerial refueling, Lockheed proposed lengthening the fuselage of the C-141A by cutting it and adding two more central fuselage sections. This program increased the length of the Starlifter by 23 feet and its capacity by one-third. Lockheed also added aerial refueling equipment. The prototype YC-141B made its first flight in 1977, and the first production aircraft entered service in 1980.[104]

The C-141's advantage of speed was undercut by the Air Force's need to transport outsize cargo over long distances. Consequently, in the early 1960s, the Air Force issued a Request For Proposals under the C-X program for a large transport to replace the C-133. The requirements were altered and cancelled several times before being reissued in 1963 as the CX-HLS (Cargo, Experimental-Heavy Logistics System). This program culminated in the Lockheed C-5A Galaxy, a feat directly attributable to the development of advanced, high-bypass-ratio turbofan engines (the General Electric TF39). The aircraft was nearly as long as a football field, weighed over 750,000 pounds, and could carry up to 265,000 pounds of cargo, including all military equipment (tanks, trucks, helicopters, ICBM missiles). Despite its large size, crews maintained that it was easy to handle, and it could travel over 3,200 miles without refueling. Its cargo compartment was accessible from either end of the aircraft, and although designed primarily for freight, it also could carry up to 270 troops. Its avionics package allowed it to fly at low altitudes and to perform airdrops with great accuracy at night and in poor weather. The first Galaxy flew in 1968, and it became operational in 1970.[105]

First production Douglas C-133A Cargomaster

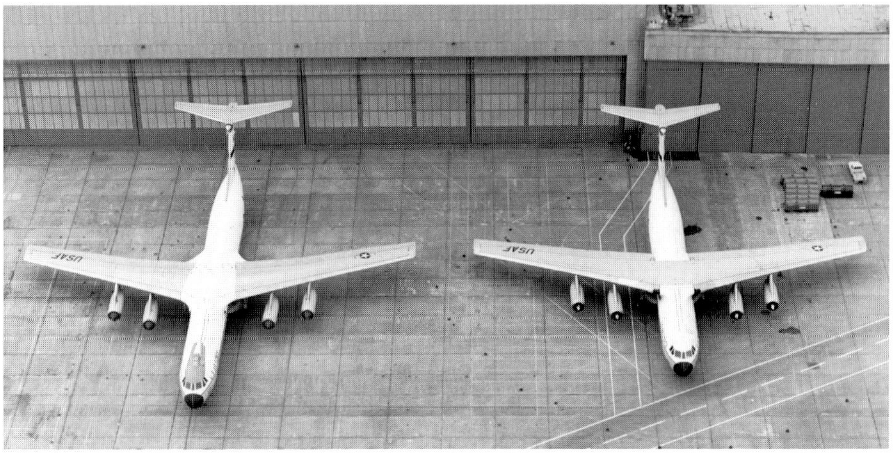
A "stretched" C-141B alongside the smaller C-141A. The C-141B had 30 percent more cargo capacity than the earlier model.

The C-5A was developed and produced under a "total package procurement" plan through which the Air Force let one contract to cover both development and production. In the final analysis, the plan was a failure, with cost overruns and delinquent deliveries leading the Air Force to limit its purchase to 81 aircraft instead of 120, but at a price two times higher. Furthermore, the original C-5 wing was poorly designed and required an expensive retrofit that, when finally completed in 1987, extended the service life of the aircraft to 30,000 hours (over the 8,000 hours estimated for the original wings). In the mid-1980s, the C-5B program incorporated more powerful engines and all modifications made in the C-5A's for improved maintainability and reliability. This new model, of which the Air Force acquired 50, made its first flight in 1985 and became operational the following year. In 1998, the Air Force scheduled an avionics modernization program and engine replacement on all C-5s in the inventory.[106]

The Air Force also acquired the McDonnell Douglas C-9A Nightingale in the 1960s. This medium-range, twin-engine jet transport was acquired in 1968 for aeromedical evacuation. An off-the-shelf version of the commercial DC-9 (Series 30), it had a convertible interior to accommodate up to 40 patient litters. The C-9C

An Army XM-1 battle tank is loaded onto a C-5A at Wright-Patterson Air Force Base, 1980.

General James Ferguson, commander of Air Force Systems Command, and Major General Harry E. Goldsworthy, commander of Aeronautical Systems Division, during an inspection of the C-5 transport at the Lockheed plant

Colonel Guy M. Townsend, director of the C-5A program, 1965

Four C-5A Galaxies. In the left background is the much smaller C-141.

Rollout of the C-5A at Lockheed's Marietta, Georgia, facility, 1968. A Lockheed Jetstar is in the foreground, emphasizing the immense size of the Air Force transport.

Servicemen board a C-5 for a 10-hour flight test. The tail of the giant transport is 65 feet tall.

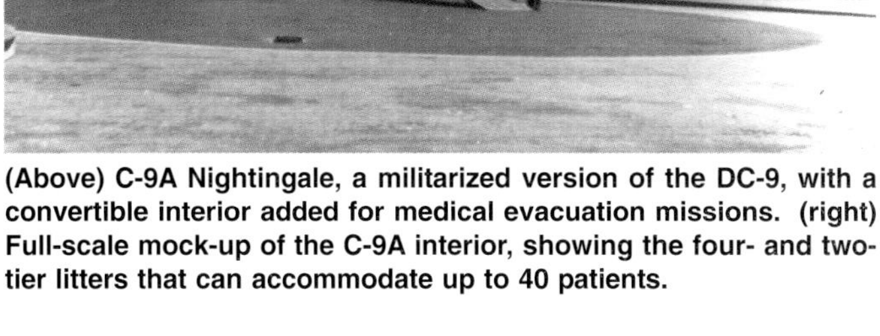

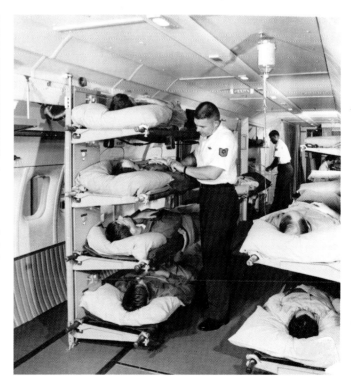

(Above) C-9A Nightingale, a militarized version of the DC-9, with a convertible interior added for medical evacuation missions. (right) Full-scale mock-up of the C-9A interior, showing the four- and two-tier litters that can accommodate up to 40 patients.

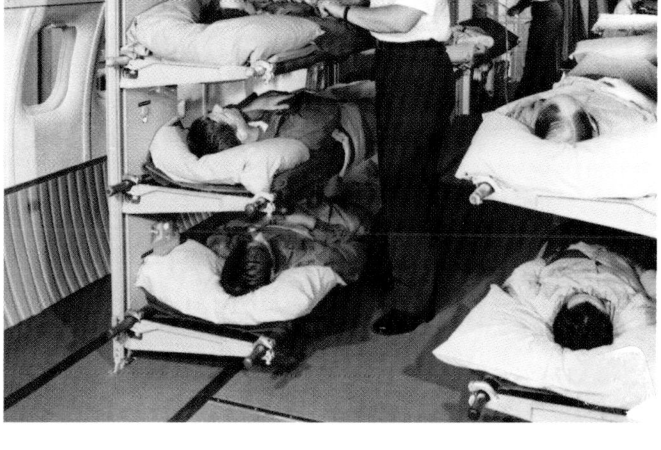

CHARACTERISTICS OF POST-1950 TRANSPORTS

	Maximum Cargo Payload (pounds)	Useable Cargo Compartment (cubic feet)	Accommodations
C-47D	17,900	Unknown	27 Troops/24 Litters
C-119B	30,000	3,150	62 Troops/35 Litters
C-124A	65,000	10,000	200 Troops/127 Litters
C-123B	23,000	2,420	60 Troops/50 Litters
C-130A	37,000	3,700	92 Troops/70 Litters
C-133A	115,000	13,000	Cargo Only
C-141A	63,000	6,500	154 Troops/80 Litters
C-141B	74,000	8,900	209 Troops/108 Litters
C-5A	265,000	34,700	270 Troops in Cargo Compartment plus 75 in Upper Level
C-17	172,000	20,900	102 Troops

Source: U. S. Air Force Standard Aircraft Characteristic Charts and Characteristic Summaries for individual aircraft located in Aeronautical Systems Center History Office Archive.

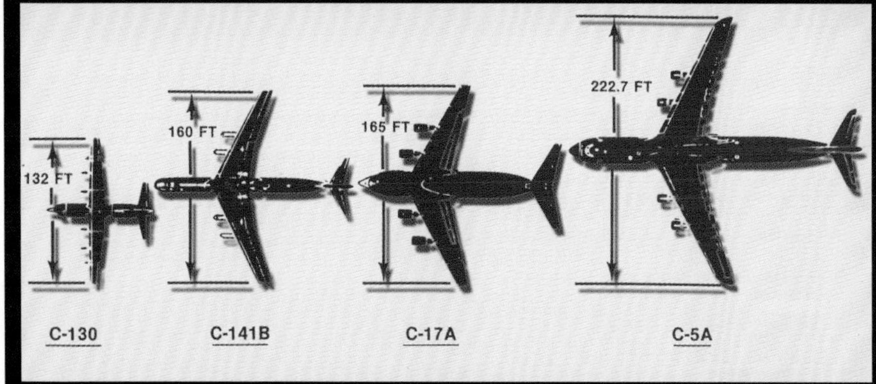

AMST contenders, the Boeing YC-14 (right) and the McDonnell Douglas YC-15, at Wright-Patterson Air Force Base en route to the 1977 Paris Air Show

variant for distinguished-visitor transport also was ordered in 1973.[107]

Following the disastrous C-5 total package procurement program, the Air Force reverted to a "fly before buy" philosophy that resulted in a number of prototype competitions in the 1970s (see the Lightweight Fighter and Advanced Tactical Fighter competitions in the Fighter Aircraft section of this chapter). The Advanced Medium Short Takeoff and Landing Transport (AMST) competition began in 1972 to provide a C-130 replacement for intra-theater airlift. Boeing and McDonnell Douglas were chosen from nine competing companies to develop prototype aircraft for a demonstration of advanced short takeoff and landing (STOL) technology and a determination of its military usefulness. The Air Force set performance goals that included routine use of a 2,000-foot airfield and a minimum mission radius of 400 nautical miles carrying a 27,000-pound payload. The results of the program were the Boeing YC-14 and the McDonnell Douglas YC-15.

The YC-14 had a small, supercritical high wing over which were mounted two turbofan engines that provided powered lift through the "upper surface blowing" concept. The location of the engines also provided the aircraft with efficient thrust reversal, low infrared radar signature, and reduced noise. Cargo capacity was 27,000 pounds during STOL operations, 81,000 pounds during conventional operations, or 150 troops. The YC-15 was powered by four turbofan engines mounted on pylons under high, straight wings. The location of the engines resulted in high-velocity airflow under the leading edge of the wings (an advanced, externally blown flap system) and triple inboard spoilers acted as direct-lift controls and speed brakes for STOL operations. The aircraft could accommodate 150 troops or approximately 62,000 pounds of cargo.[108] The prototypes made their first flights in 1976 and 1975, respectively. By 1979, however, budget cuts and rising costs resulted in cancellation of the program. The aircraft were sent to storage near Tucson, Arizona.[109]

Although the Air Force did not acquire either of the prototypes in the AMST competition, the requirement for an intra-theater transport to deliver outsize cargo in combat areas still existed. In fact, the same day that the AMST program was cancelled, the Air Force established the C-X competition, a program geared toward acquisition of an aircraft that could land on unprepared surfaces. In 1980, McDonnell Douglas received a contract for research and development of a transport that combined the cargo capacity of the C-5 with the short landing abilities of the C-130. The Air Force did not commit to purchasing the transport at that time and instead considered the feasibility of using the C-X's prime competitor, an upgraded C-5, for the role. However, although the C-5's 28-wheel landing gear was supposed to allow it to land on rough or hastily prepared fields, subsequent testing showed that the giant transport had to be restricted to paved runways to prevent damage to engines, tires, landing gear, and flaps. After comprehensive analysis of the two aircraft in 1985, the Air Force gave McDonnell Douglas an additional contract for development of the C-17A.[110]

The C-17 made its first flight in 1991 and began operational service in 1995. McDonnell Douglas used much of its earlier YC-15 AMST design for the C-17, including the externally blown flap system to generate additional lift and decrease landing speeds. The Globemaster III was powered by four Pratt & Whitney F117 turbofan engines and carried a maximum payload of 172,000 pounds over 2,400 miles. It alternately accommodated 102 paratroopers and their equipment. It was the Air Force's first transport with digital fly-by-wire technology and head-up display. The C-17 had its operational debut during Operation Vigilant Warrior, supplying American forces in Saudi Arabia who were preparing for a possible second attack against Iraq. C-17 transports also participated in a number of humanitarian relief efforts and in the deployment of peacekeeping troops to the Balkans. A C-17 also transported "Keiko" the movie-star killer whale from an aquarium in Oregon to his home waters near Iceland.[111] In December 2001, C-17s reached a milestone after dropping over two million pre-packaged meals to refugees in Afghanistan as part of Operation Enduring Freedom.

In addition to these large-scale production transports, in the 1990s the Air Force acquired a small fleet of 10 Alenia C-27A Spartans. The C-27A intra-theater transport, capable of transporting 34 troops or 10,200 pounds, made its first flight in 1991. The aircraft also had STOL capability. It served mainly in Panama, providing airlift capability for loads too large for helicopters and too small for the C-130. Spartans participated in Joint Task Force exercises, hurricane relief missions, medical evacuations, and counter-drug missions in South and Central America until being retired in 1999.[112]

C-17 Globemaster III, 1992

General Colin Powell, chairman of the Joint Chiefs of Staff, speaks to C-17 workers during a visit to the McDonnell Douglas plant, March 23, 1992. David Swain, C-17 program manager, is seated to Powell's right.

Keiko is lifted by crane out of his tank and placed in the custom-built shipping container that will hold him for his trip from Oregon to Iceland aboard an Air Force C-17 Globemaster III, September 1998.

The shipping container holding Keiko, the 10,000-pound killer whale who starred in the "Free Willy" movies, is loaded onto the C-17 for the nine-hour journey to Iceland.

C-27A Spartan

Another transport program in the Air Force was the Joint Services Vertical Lift Aircraft (or JVX for Joint VTOL Experimental), known as the V-22 Osprey. The program began in the early 1980s for an advanced rotary wing aircraft that could fill a variety of missions, such as special operations, assault transport, and search and rescue. Program management was placed within the Navy with the Air Force as a partner. Following a 1982 design competition, the Bell-Boeing tiltrotor design based on Bell's XV-15 (first flown in 1977) was chosen. The V-22, powered by two Allison T406 engines, could take off vertically via 38-foot diameter, three-bladed rotors mounted on each of its wing tips. Once airborne, the engine nacelles rotated forward and powered the aircraft like a conventional turboprop. The aircraft was made of composite materials, incorporated fly-by-wire technology, folded up for storage, and carried 24 troops. Low Rate Initial Production was authorized in 1997, and the first lot of MV-22s went to the Marines. In 2000, the Air Force received its first CV-22 for operational testing at Edwards Air Force Base, California. The Air Force planned to acquire the CV-22 for nighttime special operations and search-and-rescue missions performed by its MH-60G and MH-53J helicopters.[113]

First flight of the Bell-Boeing V-22 Osprey in Arlington, Texas, March 19, 1989

SUPERSONIC TRANSPORT

In the late 1950s and early 1960s, a worldwide race to launch the first supersonic transport (SST) got under way. Heading the race were France and Britain, who joined financial support and expertise in their Concorde program. To maintain national prestige, the United States also began a government-funded supersonic transport program, marking the first time Congress had approved financial support to a commercial aviation venture. Because of past and ongoing experience with supersonic flight, both the Air Force and the National Aeronautics and Space Administration (NASA) joined with the Federal Aviation Administration (FAA) to manage the development program. The Air Force's role in the program was managed by the Aeronautical Systems Division, which provided administrative and technical support and shared research data from ongoing supersonic aircraft development programs, such as the XB-70 and the YF-12A. The Air Force maintained that it had no plans to acquire the SST itself and its participation was primarily to help hasten the progress of development.

Originally planning for an operational date of 1968 (later pushed to 1974), the FAA-NASA-DOD team let contracts to Boeing and Lockheed for design studies of the SST in 1964. General Electric and Pratt & Whitney were given contracts to develop suitable engines for the aircraft that would fly at three times the speed of sound for more than 3,000 nautical miles. By the mid-1960s, however, the program was facing insurmountable problems, including rising costs, budget cuts, and concerns over air and noise pollution. The potentially damaging sonic booms of such an aircraft flying over populated areas led citizens to form coalitions against SST development. Given these obstacles, in 1971 President Richard Nixon terminated the program. The joint France-Britain venture resulted in the Concorde's first flight in 1969, one year after the Russian Tupolev 144, based largely on stolen Concorde research data, first flew.

Source: Mark A. Lorell, Alison Saunders, and Hugh P. Levaux, *Bomber R&D Since 1945: The Role of Experience* (RAND, Santa Monica, 1995), pp 41-42; Various periodical articles and press releases regarding the SST, on file in Aeronautical Systems Center History Office Archive.

YF-12A landing at Wright Field upon its delivery to the United States Air Force Museum, 1979. The Air Force provided research data from the YF-12 program, forerunner of the SR-71, for development of the supersonic transport in the 1960s.

Tankers

Range extension became an important area of technological development during the Korean War when Air Force aircraft operated out of air bases in Japan. The distance to North Korea left fighters and bombers with less than a half hour of combat flying time before they had to return to base. Although the feasibility of aerial refueling had been demonstrated as early as 1923, practical methods for the aerial delivery of fuel were not adopted until the late 1940s and early 1950s. The earliest refueling tankers were conversions of existing transports and bombers, such as the KB-29 and the KC-97. The Boeing KC-97E became operational in 1951 as the primary tanker of the early 1950s. Equipped with the flying boom, the tanker had a transfer fuel capacity of roughly 8,400 gallons. The F model, sporting more powerful engines, entered service in 1952. The G model, with under-wing fuel tanks, could be used as either a tanker or transport without modification.

Refueling jet bombers with the propeller-driven KC-97 was difficult because the tanker could not fly as fast or as high as the new bombers. Consequently, in the late 1950s, the KC-97s were replaced with Boeing KC-135 Stratotankers.[114] The KC-135 was Boeing's Model 367-80, which also formed the basis for Boeing's 707s and 717s. The new jet tanker-transport had swept wings, four Pratt & Whitney J57 turbojet engines mounted in pods under the wings, and fuel tanks located in the wings. It carried approximately 124,000 pounds (over 20,000 gallons) of transfer fuel, and boom refueling

Boom aerial refueling equipment on the KC-97

The last KC-97G produced (right) and the first KC-135A

KC-135A refuels a KC-135R equipped with new turbofan engines.

First KC-10A equipped with wing-mounted, aerial refueling pods during tests at Yuma, Arizona, 1989

equipment was installed in the lower fuselage. The boom equipment later was fitted with a drogue kit so the tanker could refuel any Air Force or Navy aircraft. The aircraft also carried 80 passengers or 83,000 pounds of cargo on a deck above the refueling compartment. The KC-135A made its first flight in 1956 and entered the Air Force inventory the following year. Most of the A models were modified into KC-135R's with new CFM International CFM56 engines or KC-135E's (Air National Guard and Air Force Reserve aircraft) with Pratt & Whitney TF33 engines, both of which allowed for quieter, more cost-efficient and fuel-efficient transport. Additionally, EC-135C's were acquired as flying command posts, RC-135s for reconnaissance, and OC-135s as unarmed observation platforms under the 1989 Open Skies Treaty.[115] KC-135 tankers supported operations in the Vietnam War, the El Dorado Canyon strikes against Libya, Operation Just Cause in Panama, the Gulf War, and in Afghanistan as part of Operation Enduring Freedom.

In the 1970s, simultaneous with the AMST competition for a STOL-capable transport, the Air Force initiated procurement of an Advanced Tanker Cargo Aircraft (ATCA)—the McDonnell Douglas KC-10A Extender. The basis of the KC-10 was the company's DC-10 (Series 30CF), which first flew in 1973. In 1977, the Air Force chose the DC-10 over Boeing's 747 for production. Air Force modifications required installation of additional fuel cells in the lower fuselage, boom equipment, an improved cargo-handling system, and military avionics. The first Extender flew in 1980 and entered service less than a year later. After 1987, all production KC-10A's were refitted with two under-wing, hose-and-drogue refueling systems, making them the first three-point jet tankers in the inventory. The advanced boom in the KC-10A had a higher rate of transfer than the older boom in the KC-135 and operated with digital fly-by-wire technology. The KC-10 also carried more than two times as much fuel as the older tanker, with an ability to offload approximately 390,000 pounds (roughly 63,000 gallons) of fuel.[116]

AERIAL REFUELING

The feasibility of aerial refueling had been demonstrated in the early 1920s, and research in this field was conducted at Wright Field over the years. In August 1923, Lieutenants Lowell H. Smith and John P. Richter were able to fly their DH-4 for more than 37 hours by refueling in the air from another DH-4. In 1929, Major Carl Spaatz and his crew set a world's record for endurance, with the assistance of aerial refueling from two Douglas C-1s allowing their Fokker C-2 to stay aloft for 151 hours. Advancements in the delivery method in the late 1940s and early 1950s led to the operational use of aerial refueling during the Korean War, a major milestone in increasing the amount of time fighters could remain in the combat zone. Prior to 1950, the "flying boom," a remote-controlled, rigid, telescopic boom containing a tube through which fuel flowed, was the primary method of aerial fuel transfer. In mid-September 1950, another system called the "probe-and-drogue," developed in Great Britain, quickly became indispensable to the Air Force.

In the mid-1950s, the Power Plant Laboratory at Wright Air Development Center (WADC) conducted an in-house program for the Boom to Drogue Adaptor that would allow all Strategic Air Command boom-equipped tankers to refuel Tactical Air Command's drogue-equipped fighters. Flight tests in 1956 using the KB-29P and KC-97G tankers and F-100 fighters and B-66B bombers as receivers were successful, and a future program to provide the KC-135 with the adaptor was recommended. The program was cancelled after the Air Force determined no firm requirement existed for the system.

Another WADC project for aerial refueling was referred to as the "Buddy Mission." Because the best tanker for any aircraft was one that had the same flight characteristics, studies began to determine the feasibility of using fighters to refuel other fighters. The Aircraft Laboratory began flight tests for the buddy refueling system on the F-100 in 1956, and the F-105 system was scheduled for 1958. Funding problems delayed the program until other aerial refueling systems were further along in development.

Sources: Historical Office, Air Force Materiel Command, *Case History of Air-to-Air Refueling*, March 1949, in Air Refueling File, Box 8081: Subsystems/ Refueling Box 1, ASC History Office Archive; "Boom to Drogue Adaptors, KC-135," Memorandums to File, December 17, 1956 and March 12, 1957, in Air Refueling File, Box 8081: Subsystems/ Refueling Box 1, ASC History Office Archive; H.R. Shows and Capt. D.I. Hackney, *Staff Study of the Aerial Refueling Program*, (Wright Air Development Center, May 1957), Box 8081: Subsystems/ Refueling Box 1, ASC History Office Archive.

A KC-135A tanker refuels an F-101 with the probe-and-drogue/boom adaptor.

Using the probe-and-drogue method, an F-100D refuels an F-100C during a "Buddy" mission.

VC-25A presidential aircraft

Operational Support Aircraft

In addition to cargo and troop transports, the Air Force maintained a fleet of operational support aircraft (OSA) for passenger transport, pilot training, medical evacuation, and small cargo airlift during peacetime. These aircraft also transported military officials to remote locations during wartime. Many of the aircraft in the OSA fleet were off-the-shelf variants of commercial, propeller-driven and jet passenger aircraft. OSAs acquired by the Air Force over the years included the Boeing C-137 (a modified 707), the Lockheed C-140 Jetstar, the C-12F Beech Super King Air, the C-20 Gulfstream III, the C-21A Learjet, the C-22 (a Boeing 727-100), the C-25 (a Boeing 747-200B), the C-32A (a Boeing 757-200),[117] the C-37A Gulfstream V, and the C-38A (Israel Aircraft Industries-built Astra SPX business jet). Additionally, the North American CT-39 and Boeing CT-43A were passenger-transport versions of Air Force trainer aircraft. These aircraft were upgraded with military navigation, communications, and flight-information equipment as well as other off-the-shelf items as they were developed for use on commercial airplanes.

The most famous of the OSA fleet was the Boeing VC-25A (a 747-200B), also known as "Air Force One" when transporting the president, which replaced the VC-137 previously used for presidential transport since 1962. The Air Force acquired two VC-25s in 1990. The aircraft, powered by four turbofans, had an unrefueled range of nearly 7,000 miles. With over 4,000 square feet of interior floor space, it carried up to 80 passengers and 23 crewmembers, in addition to accommodating the presidential office, stateroom, and lavatory; two galleys; and an emergency medical facility.[118]

HELICOPTERS

The first practical, rotarywing aircraft developed in the United States was the Sikorsky Model VS-300, designed by Russian-born Igor Sikorsky in the late 1930s. In 1941, the Army ordered a similar model of the Sikorsky helicopter and by late 1944, the R-4 was serving in the Pacific theater for observation, medical evacuation, and crew transport. Having proved their worth during World War II, rotarywing aircraft continued to develop at an accelerated pace throughout the 1940s and 1950s. Three helicopters were in Air Force service in 1951: the Sikorsky H-5 Dragonfly, the Bell H-13 (later designated the Sioux), and the Sikorsky H-19 (later the Chickasaw).

In the early 1950s, research and development programs for helicopters involved four types—liaison, utility and rescue, cargo, and heavy lift. Wright Air Development Center was involved in at least 10 helicopter programs in 1951, many for the Army. Although the Air Force acquired experimental and prototype versions of several helicopters, it procured only two in quantity. The Air Force ordered the twin-rotor Piasecki/Vertol H-21 Work Horse equipped with "omniphibious" landing gear for arctic rescue missions on snow, ice, water, marsh, or land. The Hiller H-23 Raven, designed to carry two enclosed patient litters externally, was acquired for medical evacuation. In addition to Air Force

PRESIDENTIAL AIRCRAFT

Every president, beginning with Franklin D. Roosevelt, had an official aircraft to transport him to official functions all over the world. Aeronautical Systems Center and its predecessors managed these aircraft programs. The first official presidential aircraft was the Douglas C-54C *Sacred Cow* used by President Roosevelt. The aircraft had a specially designed elevator behind the passenger cabin for Roosevelt's use. The president made his only flight in the *Sacred Cow* in February 1945, when he traveled to Yalta for a conference with Winston Churchill and Joseph Stalin to plan for the occupation of Nazi Germany. The *Sacred Cow* also was used by Roosevelt's successor, President Harry S. Truman, who signed the National Security Act of 1947 on board, thereby establishing the U. S. Air Force as an independent service. Beginning in 1947, Truman flew on the VC-118 *Independence*, named for his hometown in Missouri. In 1954, the *Independence* was replaced by President Dwight D. Eisenhower's aircraft, the VC-121E *Columbine III*.

In 1962, a VC-137C, tail number 26000, became the presidential aircraft, and was used by Presidents John F. Kennedy, Lyndon Johnson, and Richard Nixon. It was the first jet (Boeing model 707-320) designed exclusively for presidential use and the first presidential aircraft to use the radio call sign "Air Force One" when the president was on board. Following his assassination, Kennedy's body was flown to Washington, D.C., and Johnson took the oath of office on board the 26000. The aircraft, officially named *The Spirit of '76* in 1971 to honor the upcoming bicentennial, was replaced by another VC-137C, tail number 27000, in 1972. The 27000, also nicknamed *The Spirit of '76*, served as the primary aircraft for Presidents Nixon, Gerald Ford, Jimmy Carter, Ronald Reagan, and George H. W. Bush. In 1990, the Air Force unveiled the newest presidential aircraft, the VC-25A (a modified Boeing 747-200B). It has since served Presidents George H. W. Bush, Bill Clinton, and George W. Bush.

President Franklin D. Roosevelt's aircraft, the VC-54C *Sacred Cow*

VC-137C, tail number 26000, illustrating the distinctive paint scheme commissioned at the request of President John F. Kennedy and still used on presidential aircraft today

Two of 18 Piasecki YH-21 helicopters acquired by the Air Force for service testing

UH-1F Huey, the Air Force variant of the Army's UH-1B

HH-43B Huskie picks up an airborne fire-fighting kit. The spherical container held enough water and liquid foam to make 850 gallons of expanded foam that could be discharged in less than 50 seconds.

acquisitions, the Army ordered the H-21 (which it named the Shawnee) for troop and cargo transport, and both the Army and Navy placed orders for the H-23.[119]

Most of the early 1950s programs were replaced with other helicopter programs later in the decade.[120] Of these, however, only the Bell H-40 (later known as the HU-1, still later as the UH-1 Iroquois, and unofficially as the Huey) and the Kaman H-43 served extensively with the Air Force. The H-40 program began as an Army competition for a helicopter suitable for aeromedical evacuation of front-line casualties and for instrument training. The Huey was a lightweight, single-rotor aircraft powered by a Lycoming T53 turbine engine. The aircraft could reach speeds of 140 mph, and could run on JP-4 fuel, automotive fuel, or kerosene. It carried five passengers in addition to the pilot, stretchers or an 800-pound payload of freight, and it had an optional external rack for carrying air-to-ground rockets and missiles. The HU-1A made its first flight in 1956 and was delivered (as the UH-1A) to the Army in 1959.[121] Subsequent models of the UH-1, including the UH-1B/D's, had more powerful engines, improved rotor systems, and larger passenger capacity. These also were equipped with machine guns for close air support of ground troops in Vietnam.[122] The UH-1B was used by more air forces worldwide and was built in greater numbers than any other military aircraft since World War II.

The Air Force acquired the UH-1F in the early 1960s for missile-site-support duties. This model was based on the UH-1B, but had a General Electric T58 shaft-turbine engine, accommodations for a pilot and 10 passengers, and larger cargo-carrying capacity. Many of the UH-1F's were replaced by UH-1N's in 1970. This latter model featured accommodations for up to 13 passengers, six litters, or bulk cargo. It was powered by two Pratt & Whitney T400 turboshaft engines, making it safer and more capable than the single engine UH-1F. The UH-1N provided support for missions such as airlift of emergency response teams, security surveillance, space shuttle landing support, and search and rescue. The Air Force also maintained a small fleet of HH-1H Iroquois helicopters for distinguished-visitor transport and support of missile sites and ranges. These single-engine Hueys became operational in the early 1970s and featured longer fuselages and more powerful engines than the original Huey.[123]

Sikorsky CH-3C

The Kaman H-43 Huskie (later the HH-43) program began as a modified HOK-1, a test bed for the experimental Lycoming XT53 shaft-turbine engine used on the H-40. It made its first flight in 1956, and the Air Force subsequently ordered production model H-43B's. The engine of the production model, mounted above the cabin, freed up more cabin space and provided a larger payload capacity for up to 10 passengers or two stretchers. The Air Force ordered the HH-43B (and updated B models redesignated as HH-43F's) for local crash rescue operations at its installations around the world. Although considered inadequate for operations in Southeast Asia, three Huskie units were deployed there in 1964 for use until a replacement (the CH-3) could be acquired. These helicopters actually proved indispensable for deep-jungle rescues. The HH-43 was replaced in the Air Force inventory by the HH-1H in the 1970s.[124]

The Air Force began only two new helicopter programs in the 1960s—the Sikorsky CH-3 and the Sikorsky H-53—both in response to inadequacies noted in Southeast Asia rescue operations. The CH-3, the Air Force variant of the Sikorsky S-61 (also known as the Navy's SH-3 Sea King anti-submarine helicopter), made its first flight as the HSS-2 in 1959. The CH-3C twin-engine, amphibious transport fulfilled the Air Force's need for a long-range helicopter to perform drone recovery and search-and-rescue missions. Powered by two turbine engines and a five-blade main rotor, the CH-3C reached a maximum speed of 165 mph and a range of over 800 miles using auxiliary fuel tanks. The cabin accommodated 25 passengers, 15 patient litters, or 5,000 pounds of cargo, and the helicopter had an additional external cargo sling for a 10,000-pound payload. Following its first flight in 1963, deliveries to the Air Force started in 1964.[125]

CH-3E deliveries to the Air Force began in 1966, and all CH-3C's were upgraded to the new configuration with uprated engines and defensive armament. The HH-3E rescue helicopter, popularly known as the "Jolly Green Giant," served extensively in Southeast Asia. This variant had armor protection; jettisonable, self-sealing fuel tanks; probe aerial refueling equipment; defensive armament; and a rescue hoist. In addition to admirable service in Vietnam, two HH-3E's made the first transatlantic helicopter flight in 1967, a feat that required nine aerial refuelings in 31 hours.[126]

The Air Force added the Sikorsky H-53 heavy-lift helicopter to the inventory for search-and-rescue operations. This helicopter had General Electric T64-3 shaft-turbine engines, but was otherwise similar to the HH-3E (described above). Although the CH-53, a heavy assault variant for the Marines, made its first flight in 1964, the Air Force's HH-53B model did not fly until 1967. The HH-53B was the first helicopter in the Air Force inventory able to make poor-weather rescues. The technology that allowed it to perform these missions originally had been developed for the AC-130 gunship. The HH-53 was large enough to carry two Jeeps or one 105-mm howitzer.[127]

In the early 1970s, a team of engineers in the Aeronautical Systems Division modified eight HH-53s to the Pave Low configuration for all-weather and night operations over all terrain. The Pave Low had advanced search and navigation equipment with its infrared scanner and radar systems linked to an airborne computer.

MH-53H Pave Low III helicopter

Staff of ASD's Deputy for Systems' Specialized Systems Program Office gather in front of the Pave Low III prototype helicopter it managed during modification.

Prototype of the HH-60A Night Hawk search-and-rescue helicopter, at the International Business Machine Corporation's facility in Owego, New York, 1985

The prototype made its first flight at Wright-Patterson Air Force Base in 1975, and in 1979 the Air Force accepted deliveries of its first MH-53H Pave Low III helicopters. These aircraft, along with all HH-53B/C models, were further upgraded to the MH-53J configuration in the mid-1980s. The J model was the largest and most powerful helicopter in the Air Force and the most technologically advanced in the world. The 1980s upgrade included the addition of inertial navigation systems, forward-looking infrared radar, and Doppler navigation equipment. The MH-53J Pave Low "Enhanced," and the later MH-53M with superior defensive capabilities, performed low-level, long-range operations into enemy territory to drop, extract, and resupply special operations forces. They participated in missions in Panama, Iraq, the Balkans, and Afghanistan.[128]

The last helicopter added to the Air Force inventory was the HH-60 Blackhawk, which made its first flight in 1974. The H-60 was Sikorsky's entry into an Army competition for a Utility Tactical Transport Aircraft System (UTTAS) in the early 1970s. Following a flyoff competition, it was chosen over Boeing/Vertol's YUH-61A in 1976. By the late 1970s, the Blackhawk became the Army's primary combat assault helicopter. The Air Force acquired the UH-60D variant in the early 1980s through the H-X program for an interim search-and-rescue aircraft. Its first Blackhawks were in the standard Army configuration, with the addition of rescue hoists, de-icing systems, and air-transportability (folding rotor blades) kits.[129]

The first H-60 built specifically for the Air Force was the HH-60A Night Hawk, a combat search-and-rescue craft designed to perform unescorted, low-level, day or night missions. The Night Hawk's large cabin was used for aeromedical evacuation without modification or for reconnaissance, command-and-control, and troop-resupply missions. Its advanced avionics included terrain-following/terrain-avoidance radar, forward-looking infrared radar, and inertial navigation equipment (with provisions for the Global Positioning System). It also had auxiliary, internal and external fuel tanks; aerial refueling equipment; and defensive armament. These HH-60A's were later brought up to the HH/MH-60G Pave Hawk configuration, adding an integrated Doppler/inertial/Global Positioning navigation system and the Pave Low III forward-looking infrared radar. Pave Hawk also had two 7.62-mm machine guns mounted in the doors and an external stores support system that carried up to 16 Hellfire missiles. The helicopters performed search-and-rescue missions during Operations Desert Storm and Allied Force and airlifted relief supplies to flood victims in Mozambique, Africa, during Operation Atlas Response.[130]

TRAINING SYSTEMS

The Air Force long recognized that a well-trained force was critical to effective and efficient operations. To support that need, a variety of systems for flight training, including aircraft trainers and ground-based simulators, were procured. The Cessna T-37 twin-engine jets, popularly known as Tweets, were the first trainers acquired in the post-1950 period. The aircraft made its first flight in 1955 and became operational in 1956. The B models, each with two CAE J69 turbojets, entered service in 1959. The T-37s served as the Air Force's primary jet trainers, preparing students for advanced flight training tracks with the T-38s and other more sophisticated trainers. In 1989, the entire fleet of Tweets was upgraded or modified in a program designed to increase the aircrafts' structural life into the next century. Twelve years later, however, the Air Force began replacing the T-37B's with the new T-6A Joint Primary Aircraft Training System (JPATS, see below).[131]

Northrop T-38 Talons were the first operational, supersonic jet trainers, parallel versions of the popular F-5 fighters produced primarily for foreign sales. The T-38 made its first flight in 1959 and entered service in 1961. Talons were continuously produced until 1972. The aircraft provided advanced flight training and introduced pilots to supersonic flight techniques, aerobatics, formation flight, night and instrument flight, and cross-country navigation. The AT-38B's carried external armament and weapons delivery equipment, and were used to train students for the newer fighter aircraft in the Air Force inventory, such as the F-15 and F-16. Beginning in 1997, ASC assisted the San Antonio Air Logistics Center's T-38 System Program Directorate with major upgrades to the remaining 500 Talons.

One of three XT-37 Tweet prototypes

YT-38 Talon jet trainer prototype on its first test flight in 1960

T-1A Jayhawk prototype. The first production T-1A was added to the inventory in 1992.

The T-3A Firefly was dropped from the inventory following a number of training accidents.

With an improved wing design, upgraded General Electric J85 turbojet engines, and new, state-of-the-art, digital avionics packages, the life of the supersonic jet trainers was extended for another 40 years of service. The upgraded aircraft were redesignated T-38C's; the first was delivered in July 1998.[132]

In addition to the Tweets and Talons, the Air Force acquired a small fleet of Boeing T-43 airborne navigation trainers and three Fairchild T-46A Next Generation Trainers (NGTs) in the 1970s and 1980s, respectively. The nineteenth and final T-43 was delivered to the Air Force in 1974. Development of the T-46 began in 1982, and the aircraft made its first flight in 1985. The Air Force accepted the last of these trainers (pre-production aircraft) in 1987.[133]

The T-37s and T-38s served as the most common Air Force trainers for over 30 years, but both had outdated equipment that, prior to upgrades, failed to adequately prepare pilots for flight in the Air Force's newer jet aircraft. In 1989, a Department of Defense Trainer Aircraft Master Plan recommended a comprehensive upgrade of primary pilot training technologies to replace those of the older aircraft. Consequently, during the 1990s, ASC initiated and managed the acquisition of three new trainer aircraft and the avionics upgrade of the T-38s mentioned previously. In 1992, the first of the new trainers, the T-1A Jayhawk (the Tanker-Transport Training System [TTTS]), entered the inventory. Jayhawks were procured for Specialized Undergraduate Pilot Training (SUPT) for student pilots in the airlift and tanker aircraft track. These trainers were the culmination of a 1990 contract issued to the team of McDonnell Douglas Training Systems, Beech Aircraft Corporation, and Quintron Corporation for an off-the-shelf version of the Beech 400A. In 1998, bomber-bound pilots also began training in the T-1s. The three-seat Jayhawks had two Pratt & Whitney JT15D turbofan engines, single-point pressure refueling, and increased bird-strike protection on the windshields and leading edges for sustained, low-level operations.[134]

Between 1994 and 1996, the Air Force also accepted 113 Slingsby T-3A Firefly aircraft for use in its Pilot Selection and Classification System (enhanced flight screening) program. The new trainers were bought off-the-shelf from the British manufacturer and modified in the United States with more powerful Textron-Lycoming AEIO-540-D4A5 piston engines. The propeller-driven T-3A's flew over 60 mph faster the Cessna T-41s used for the screening program since the 1960s, and they could perform acrobatic and other basic military-style maneuvers. Pilot candidates at the Air Force Academy were trained in Fireflies and evaluated for aptitude before moving forward to undergraduate pilot training with the T-37s. In 1997, after a number of engine stoppages and three fatal crashes in as many years, the Air Force grounded the fleet of Fireflies and proposed millions of dollars worth of modifications. In the meantime, the Air Force Academy turned its introductory flight training program over to civilian flight schools. In 1999, the Air Force permanently grounded the fleet of T-3A's.[135]

In June 1995, the Air Force announced the selection of the Beech PC-9 Mk II aircraft for the Joint Primary Aircraft Training System (JPATS) program. In 2000, the JPATS began replacing the Air Force's T-37B primary trainers and the Navy's T-34C trainers previously used for entry-level flight training. The turboprop-powered T-6A Texan IIs manufactured by Raytheon Aircraft Company included ejection seats, improved bird-strike protection, electronic flight instrumentation and digital cockpit display, and pressurized cockpits. The name was chosen to honor the Air Force's popular T-6 Texans of the 1940s and 1950s. The first production JPATS aircraft made its initial flight in July 1998, and the Air Force received its first operational T-6A in 2000. Training officially began in November 2001. To meet both Air Force and Navy requirements, 740 aircraft were planned for production through the year 2014, along with the accompanying JPATS Ground-Based Training System manufactured by Flight Safety Services Corporation.[136]

T-6A Texan II, the JPATs aircraft

Simulators

Reduced aircraft inventories, tight budgets, and restricted airspace for training put new emphasis on training through simulators with unprecedented realism. The Air Force procured these types of training systems for all in-service aircraft, as well as specialized simulators for particular tasks. A prime example was the computerized cockpit of the KC-135R with state-of-the-art avionics, radar, monitoring and control systems, gravity/fuel-level advisory systems, and computer-generated scenery, all of which provided realistic aerial refueling training. Trainee pilots began using this simulator in the 1980s. Another simulator procured in the 1990s provided training in the techniques and operation of the LANTIRN system. As in-service aircraft were upgraded with new avionics and equipment, flight simulators were similarly equipped to ensure trainees received proper instruction in up-to-date capabilities. The B-52 Weapon Systems Trainers (WST), for example, were enhanced in 1985 with new radar, upgraded offensive avionics packages, and new center-of-gravity/fuel-level advisory systems.[137]

In addition to procuring flight and maintenance simulators for individual weapon systems, Aeronautical Systems Center also served as focal point for the new Distributed Mission Training (DMT) initiative, in which the Air Force purchased hourly training services instead of hardware. A program begun in 1997, DMT networked geographically dispersed aircraft simulators into a real-time synthetic environment for team training. The system allowed up to four aircraft simulators flying together in a Mission Training Center (MTC) on one base to connect, via communications links, to a MTC at another base anywhere in the world. The system became fully operational in May 2000 with two F-15 MTCs offering 360-degree, wrap-around visual systems for increased realism during simulated combat maneuvers and debrief capabilities for post-training review. Similar systems for the F-16, A-10, in-service transports and tankers, and the E-3 Airborne Warning and Control System (AWACS) were planned, as well as a link between the Air Force's F-16 and the Navy's F-18 training simulators for joint training experience. Simulators did not replace actual flight training, but through the use of DMT, Air Force pilots rehearsed actual flying missions and thus increased their combat readiness more affordably and safely.[138]

Computerized cockpit of the KC-135R simulator with state-of-the-art avionics, radar, monitoring and control systems, and gravity/fuel-level advisory systems

Martin RB-57D with "flying test patterns." The aircraft was used by the Reconnaissance Laboratory at Aeronautical Systems Division to improve military reconnaissance techniques, 1963. Test flights were conducted at Holloman Air Force Base, New Mexico.

Two mechanics load the nose camera onto an RF-101 tactical reconnaissance aircraft, late 1950s.

MANNED RECONNAISSANCE AIRCRAFT

Military aerial reconnaissance was pioneered in a balloon during the Civil War and then was later adapted to aircraft and more recently to spacecraft. Although the methods of aerial reconnaissance were known as early as the mid-nineteenth century, it was not until World War I that it became an important part of military strategy. In fact, reconnaissance constituted the original military use for aircraft. The field matured during World War II and, during the Korean War, reconnaissance squadrons outperformed and broke all existing records, nearly doubling and, in a few cases, tripling the monthly number of sorties performed by World War II units. As the value of aerial imagery was repeatedly proven in peacetime and in war, photographic equipment evolved to keep pace with the aircraft in which it was carried. Hand-held cameras were replaced by fixed cameras, and the parachute method of photograph delivery to the battlefront was replaced by electronic data links. Camera shutter speed became increasingly faster and focal lengths longer. Night photographic methods and illuminants were developed. Finally, a multitude of sensors were developed that allowed surveillance aircraft to acquire not only photographic coverage, but also to gather electronic and communications intelligence. Reconnaissance technologies continued to evolve, but remained a key part of tactical and strategic operations. Since the Vietnam War and even more so following successful applications in Operation Desert Storm, the military services pursued programs for unmanned aerial vehicles to perform aerial reconnaissance and long-dwell surveillance missions (see below).

As early as 1951, engineers at WADC realized that the complexity of reconnaissance aircraft had surpassed that of the bomber.[139] The growing importance of reconnaissance in the 1950s was evidenced by the fact that for nearly every bomber program, a reconnaissance variant of that bomber was developed once the design of the original aircraft was proven.[140] In fact, many of the aircraft used for reconnaissance up to that time, such as the RB-26, RB-29, RB-45C, RF-51D, and RF-80A used in Korea, were redesigned from their original missions to that of photographic reconnaissance. In the 1950s, the Air Force recognized the need for a mixed force of tactical and strategic reconnaissance aircraft that could fly at high and low speed at a variety of altitudes. The result was a small fleet of aircraft that included the RB-47 for electronic reconnaissance, the RB-57 high-altitude photographic aircraft, the RB-66 low-altitude reconnaissance aircraft, the RF-101 variant of the tactical fighter, and the all-weather RF-4C. In some cases, such as the B-66, the aircraft proved more successful in the reconnaissance role than in its original mission.

The RB-66 was the reconnaissance variant of the Douglas B-66 Destroyer, a high-speed, low-altitude bomber derived from the Navy's A3D-1 Sky Warrior. The RB-66A made its first flight in 1954 with disappointing results, but many of the engineering flaws were fixed before the subsequent RB-66B became operational in January 1956, three months prior to the bomber version. The RB-66C ferret version, operational in 1956, used electronic intelligence (ELINT) to locate and jam enemy radar. The RB-66 closely resembled the bomber variant, with the addition of night photographic equipment, electronic reconnaissance equipment, and electronic countermeasures. The aircraft, however, was trouble-riddled from the beginning and was not able to fulfill its night photography and all-weather roles adequately. Phase-out was scheduled as early as the mid-1960s, but the Vietnam conflict kept the RB-66s active for several more years.[141]

By 1966, many RB-66s were replaced with RF-4C's, and others were reconfigured to the EB-66 variant for electronic warfare. These latter aircraft had been extensively modified with enhanced electronic warfare capabilities for clandestine missions, and continued to serve throughout the 1960s in the Vietnam War. In fact, the EB-66B/C/E served as the Air Force's only dedicated electronic warfare platform until phased out in the mid-1970s. A replacement was not found until the EF-111A Raven became operational in 1982.[142]

The RF-101A tactical reconnaissance variant of the F-101 Voodoo fighter-bomber made its first flight in 1954 and became operational three years later, replacing the RF-84F. It was the world's first supersonic, photographic reconnaissance aircraft. Differences from the fighter included lighter weight, a longer nose for photographic equipment, and the addition of a 75-gallon fuel tank built into each wing. The RF-101A's also retained the bombing capability of the Voodoo fighter-

RF-4C parked in a revetment at Nakhon Phanom Air Base, Thailand, 1975. The aircraft has centerline and under-wing fuel tanks, and inboard on the left wing is an AN/ALQ-119 electronic countermeasures pod.

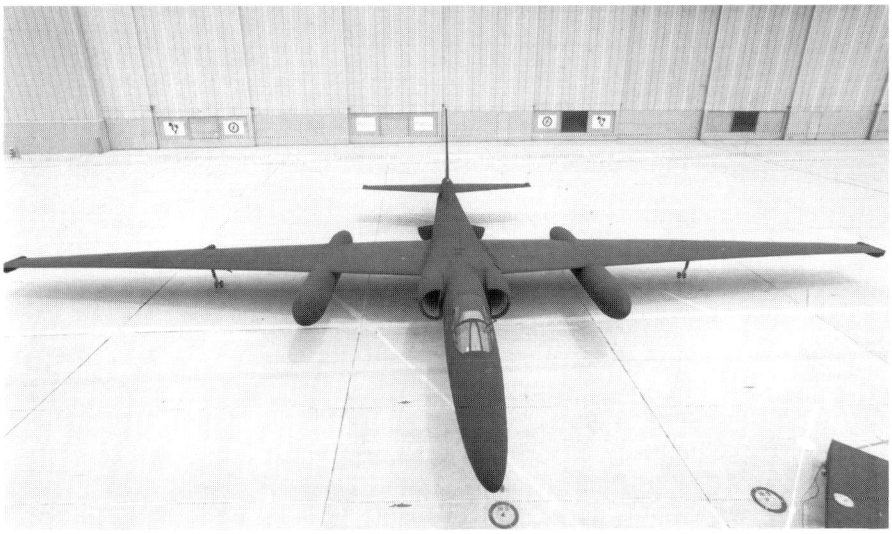

Rollout of the new TR-1 (later redesignated the U-2R), July 1981

EF-111A Raven with the ALQ-99 jamming system. Research in electronic warfare alternatives was accelerated after the loss of several aircraft to enemy air defense weapons in North Vietnam. In 1975, the Air Force contracted with Grumman to modify two F-111A's into electronic warfare platforms to detect and block enemy radars. Modifications included the addition of a radome under the fuselage to house the jamming equipment antennae, a pod on the vertical stabilizer for receiving antennae, and the installation of 8,000 pounds of electronic jamming equipment. Between 1981 and 1985, the Air Force received 42 Ravens and kept them in service until 1998 when F-16C's took over the mission.

This SR-71 Blackbird established six world altitude and speed records on July 27, 1976.

bombers. The A models were followed immediately by RF-101C's with strengthened airframes, and some had the capability to deliver nuclear weapons. In the 1960s, RF-101C's were equipped with flash cartridge pods for limited night missions and buddy refueling equipment. Addition of a new camera in the mid-1960s allowed the aircraft to fly more successful low-altitude photographic missions. The RF-101s were the only Voodoos to participate in the conflict in Southeast Asia, serving as pathfinders for F-100 fighter-bombers and providing post strike damage assessments. By the late-1960s, however, they were supplemented and then replaced by the new RF-4C's.[143]

The all-weather RF-4C program began in 1962. Compared to the F-4C Phantom fighter, the reconnaissance variant had a longer nose to house advanced reconnaissance equipment, including optical, infrared, and electronic sensors, forward-looking radar, and side-looking radar. The first flight of the production aircraft occurred in May 1964, and the RF-4C became operational four months later. Shortly thereafter, a small fleet deployed to Southeast Asia. The Air Force acquired nearly 500 of these aircraft, which had high- and low-altitude, day-and-night photographic capability and electronic reconnaissance equipment. It was the first reconnaissance aircraft to have a high-frequency communications system, allowing communication beyond line-of-sight. In the early 1970s, the RF-4C's were modernized with new radar homing and warning systems and new side-looking radar. These aircraft remained in service until retired in the mid-1990s. At this time, the Air Force added reconnaissance pods to some Air National Guard F-16s to provide a temporary surveillance capability until future requirements could be determined. As discussed below, the future of reconnaissance was foreshadowed by a growing trend toward unmanned aerial vehicles.[144]

As previously mentioned, tactical reconnaissance aircraft of the early 1950s were variants of proven bomber and fighter designs or were operational aircraft modified with special reconnaissance pods. At the same time, however, the heightening mistrust between the United States and the Soviet Union served as a catalyst for the development of a dedicated strategic reconnaissance aircraft. The requirement for long-range, high-altitude, strategic reconnaissance was fulfilled first by the U-2 aircraft, a joint effort led by the Air Force, Central Intelligence Agency (CIA), and Lockheed.

The U-2 (U for utility), powered by a single Pratt & Whitney J75 turbojet engine, made its first flight in 1955. The aircraft's lightweight construction allowed it to carry the fuel it needed for mission ranges up to 4,000 miles. It could fly at a ceiling above 70,000 feet, and because the cabin was only pressurized up to 29,000 feet to save on weight, the pilot wore a full pressure suit and helmet and breathed pure oxygen when flying above that altitude.[145]

Although the U-2 became operational in 1956, the Air Force kept the aircraft secret until May 1960 when the U-2 flown by Lockheed pilot Francis Gary Powers (flying a CIA mission) was shot down over the Soviet Union by Russian surface-to-air missiles. Despite its vulnerability, the U-2 continued in use for weather and electronic reconnaissance (albeit not directly over denied territory), high-altitude research, air sampling, and tracking and recovery of space capsules. Additionally, it served during the Cuban Missile Crisis (being the aircraft that discovered Soviet missiles in Cuba), in Vietnam, and during the 1967 Arab-Israeli conflict.[146]

The newest model of the U-2 was the all-weather tactical variant originally referred to as the TR-1, which made its first flight in 1981. It participated in reconnaissance missions during Operation Desert Storm and, using the Advanced Synthetic Aperture Radar (ASARS) and its data-link system, it transmitted sensory data to ground stations and fighter aircraft in near real-time. In the late 1990s, all U-2s (including the TR-1) in the Air Force fleet were redesignated U-2R's. After a comprehensive re-engining with lighter weight, more fuel-efficient General Electric F118 engines, the aircraft were subsequently redesignated U-2S/ST's. These also were fitted with upgraded sensors and the Global Positioning System.[147]

From its earliest operational use, the U-2 was particularly vulnerable to attack by air-to-air and surface-to-air missiles due to its low speed. Consequently, in 1957 the Air Force, the CIA, and the Navy issued general requirements for a new strategic reconnaissance aircraft to Lockheed and Convair. The result of the competition was the highly sophisticated Lockheed A-12 with 15 ultimately produced. These aircraft participated in the CIA's secret Black Shield reconnaissance missions over North Vietnam in 1967 and 1968. The Air Force acquired the two-seat version of the A-12, the SR-71 Blackbird (originally called the A-11), which could fly at Mach 3 at an altitude of over 85,000 feet, making it the highest-flying and fastest operational aircraft in the world. In addition to drawing on the basic aerodynamic concepts of the A-12, the SR-71 profited from the YF-12 high-altitude interceptor, which made its first flight in 1963. The Air Force cancelled the YF-12 fighter program in 1967 but continued with the development of the SR-71.[148]

The fundamental elements of stealth were beginning to be understood enough to incorporate them into aircraft designs, and the SR-71 was the first aircraft designed specifically with a reduced radar cross-section. The aircraft was also unique in that it was flown primarily by a preprogrammed computer, leaving the pilot responsible only for takeoff, landing, and emergency flight. Over 90 percent of the SR-71 was constructed of a specially developed titanium alloy, allowing it to withstand extreme temperatures experienced at Mach 3 speeds. Although the cabin could be pressurized, the crew wore full pressure suits (like those worn by astronauts on space shuttle missions) in case of emergencies at high altitudes. In addition to the easily changeable reconnaissance sensors in the needle-shaped nose, the aircraft had four compartments in the fuselage that housed panoramic, long-range, and infrared cameras, ELINT sensors, and side-looking radars. Later modifications allowed the aircraft to carry both the ASARS to gather visual imagery and the Electromagnetic Reconnaissance System (EMR) to collect ELINT signals. Its sensors could survey over 100,000 square miles of the Earth's surface every hour and provide peripheral photographic coverage of hostile territory while remaining in international airspace.[149]

RC-135W Rivet Joint electronic warfare aircraft. RC-135s were identifiable by the extended nose and the large fairings on either side of the forward fuselage. The fairings, or cheeks, housed antennae and receivers.

The SR-71, powered by two Pratt & Whitney J58 turbojets, made its first flight in 1964 and became operational two years later. In 1968, it took over the Black Shield missions previously flown by the A-12 in Vietnam and participated in various reconnaissance missions worldwide over the next two decades. Although retired in 1990, two SR-71s returned to active duty in 1995, with an added tactical role, before being retired once again in late 1997.[150]

In addition to photographic reconnaissance, the Air Force employed ELINT reconnaissance in war and peace. Many of the ELINT aircraft also served as airborne command posts, and others provided jamming support for fighter and bomber missions. In Southeast Asia, EC-121 Constellations served as early warning aircraft by alerting fighter pilots to the presence of enemy jets and warning ground forces of impending air strikes. RC-130A's were used to fulfill the need for cartographic mapping missions.[151]

Another aircraft served in a number of reconnaissance missions for the Air Force—the C-135. The OC-135B served as an observation aircraft in support of the Open Skies Treaty of 1989, which allowed participating countries to perform short-notice, unrestricted, aerial intelligence gathering about the military forces and activities of other countries. Aeronautical Systems Center's 4950th Test Wing modified the first Open Skies observation platform, a WC-135B, to include infrared line scanners, ASARS, video scanning sensors, and four cameras mounted in the rear of the aircraft. The first OC-135B was deployed in 1993.[152]

Since the 1960s, other variants of the RC-135 were specially configured to serve in different reconnaissance roles. Each aircraft was unique in the types of equipment carried. These included Cobra Ball (tracked rival ballistic missile tests), Combat Sent (ELINT), Cobra Eye (telemetry intelligence [TELINT]), Rivet Amber (ELINT), Rivet Ball (ELINT), Rivet Brass (TELINT), Rivet Card (signals intelligence [SIGINT]), and the 16 aircraft that made up the Rivet Joint fleet. The RC-135 Rivet Joint was a high-altitude, long-range, SIGINT aircraft. Utilizing an extensive antennae array, the aircraft provided real-time battle management information to command centers. The first Rivet Joint deployed in 1973 and the last C-135 modified for the Rivet Joint mission was delivered in 2000. These aircraft participated in missions in the Middle East, Haiti, and Bosnia. In 2001 the fleet underwent modernization with the addition of more powerful engines, strengthened landing gear, and flight control augmentation systems.[153]

UNMANNED AERIAL VEHICLES

Although the concept of unmanned (or uninhabited) aerial vehicles (UAVs) originated prior to World War I, they became increasingly popular as airborne targets for antiaircraft artillery training following World War II. The Air Force originally used them as targets for training fighter aircraft crews. By the mid to late 1950s, utility for various other missions, such as reconnaissance or strike, was being studied. UAVs were alternately referred to as drones and remotely piloted vehicles (RPVs). Guided and cruise missiles also fall within the UAV category, but these are discussed separately in a later section.[154]

SELECTED EARLY U. S. AIR FORCE R&D PROGRAMS FOR UAVS

MANAGED BY AERONAUTICAL SYSTEMS CENTER AND ITS PREDECESSORS

PROGRAM NAME	DATES	VEHICLES INVOLVED	PROGRAM DESCRIPTION
Red Wagon	1960	Ryan's Q-2C Firebee (BQM-34A)	Flight test demonstration of target drone adapted for unmanned, remotely piloted, photographic surveillance missions.
Combat Dawn	1967-1971	AQM-34Q (uprated AQM-34N) and AQM-34R	High-altitude photographic reconnaissance RPV modified for real-time ELINT and COMINT operations.
Have Lemon and Have Lime	1970-1971	BGM-34A	Studied the feasibility of using RPVs for defense suppression, delivery of air-to-ground guided weapons such as Maverick. Later evolved into the Pave Nickel program for the Advanced Location Strike System (ALSS) and the Precision Location Strike System (PLSS).
Compass Dwell	1971-1972	E-Systems' L450F (XQM-93) and Martin Marietta's Model 845A	Evaluation of quiet, high-altitude, long-range RPVs for COMINT. The XQM-93 flew for more than 21 hours (a record at that time).
Mini-RPVs	1972-1976	Models built by McDonnell Douglas, Philco-Ford (Praeire and Calere), Lockheed (Aequare), Northrop (NV-135), and ESystems (E-45/Axillary)	Programs alternately known as Very Low Cost Expendable Harassment Vehicle (VLCEHV) and LOCUST. Designs for a low-altitude battlefield RPV for surveillance, target laser designation, weapons delivery, and ELINT gathering, all-weather, day-and-night operations, low-observables technology.
Constant Angel	1972-1978	Beech Aircraft Model 1089 VSTT and Northrop's MQM-74C	High-subsonic, tactical, expendable drone system (TEDS), pre-programmed RPVs act either as decoys with active and passive ECM or as pre-strike jamming vehicles for one-way electronic warfare missions.
Project Teleplane	1974-1975	XQM-103 (a modified AQM-34)	Technology demonstration vehicle built by U. S. Air Force's Flight Dynamics Laboratory (FDL) at Wright-Patterson Air Force Base, included a television camera in the nose and a video relay for ground controllers.
Advanced RPV (ARPV)	1975-1977	Study contracts given to Boeing, Rockwell International, and Northrop	Multi-mission RPV for reconnaissance, electronic warfare, and strike missions, slated as a successor to the BGM-34C for the 1980s. Included a drone control system for simultaneous control of up to 20 vehicles.
N/A	1975-1986	XBQM-106	Designed and built by the FDL as a technology demonstrator for later mini-RPV programs, validated the loiter–decoy concept later used in LOCUST program, airframe built of cast foam.
LOCUST	1978-1984	XBQM-106	Originally a joint development program between U. S. Air Force and West Germany for a ground-launched, pre-programmed vehicle to perform loiter-decoy or radar strike missions.
Pave Tiger	1982-1984	Boeing YQM-121 (variant of the BRAVE-200 Model)	Expansion of company-funded research which began in 1979, U. S. Air Force development contract called for a ground-launched, pre-programmed, expendable mini-RPV to attack high-priority ground targets in non-nuclear theaters. Terminated before flight tests but later reinstated as the Seek Spinner program.
Seek Spinner	1986-1989	Boeing YQM-121	Reinstatement of Pave Tiger, terminated in favor of Tacit Rainbow.

Sources: William Wagner, *Lightning Bugs and other Reconnaissance Drones* (Fallbrook, California, 1982); William Wagner and William P. Sloan, *Fireflies and Other UAVs* (Arlington, Texas, 1992); Stefan Geisenheyner, "Air Force of Tomorrow," *Aerospace International* 8 (2) July-August 1972, pp 2-11; *Jane's All the World's Aircraft*, 1973-1974, pp 520-522, 529-530; *Jane's All the World's Aircraft*, 1975-1976, pp. 544, 551, 559; *Jane's All the World's Aircraft*, 1981-1982, p. 670; *Jane's All the World's Aircraft*, 1983-1984, p. 724; various official press releases in Box: Drones/RPVs, PA Files and in File: Seek Spinner, Box 3316, in ASC History Office Archive.

Northrop's Advanced RPV preliminary design quarter-scale model

Mini-RPV developed by Teledyne Ryan, 1974

XBQM-106 designed and built by engineers at the Flight Dynamics Laboratory, Wright-Patterson Air Force Base

Seek Spinner sits on rails, ready to launch, 1990.

BQM-34A Firebee jet target drone launches from a fixed ground station in the early 1960s.

Four BQM-34A Firebee drones loaded on the under-wing pylons of a DC-130A

Targets

The most common UAV of the 1950s was Ryan Aeronautical's Q-2 Firebee jet target; the C model became known as the BQM-34A for tri-service use in the early 1960s. The Q-2C, an RPV powered by a single turbojet engine, made its first flight in 1951. It was guided either by radio or radar from a ground or airborne station, and had a short range (60,000 feet or roughly 12 miles). It could be launched from a modified aircraft or from a fixed ground or naval carrier station with the assistance of a jet-assisted takeoff bottle. The targets carried an electronic scoring system that transmitted the distances of near-misses to a ground control station. Using an automatically deployed parachute, undamaged Firebees could safely land and be recovered and reused for subsequent missions. The BQM-34E/F models, called Firebee IIs, served as supersonic, sub-scale targets for the faster fighter aircraft of the 1970s. Numerous other models of the Firebee and its derivatives were developed over the years to fulfill a number of missions (see below).[155]

In 1975, the Air Force procured a small number of Beech MQM-107A Streakers, sub-scale drones for instructor training, research and development, and a variety of evaluation programs. The variable-speed drone was either preprogrammed for flight or controlled from the ground. The Air Force also acquired both the D and E models through the mid-1990s.[156]

Cockpit of a QF-80 drone used as a target for training missions

In the 1980s, Teledyne Ryan developed the AQM-81A Firebolt High Altitude High Speed Target (HAHST). This UAV was powered by a hybrid rocket engine and was designed to fly at 100,000 feet at speeds up to Mach 4. An automatic navigator could be preprogrammed or it could be controlled from the ground by a radio link. Flight tests of the air-launched vehicle took place in 1983, but two years later the Air Force cancelled the program before a production decision was made.[157]

With the exception of the Firebee and Streaker, the Air Force did not acquire many specially designed target drones. Instead, some operational aircraft were converted to drone status by replacing all unnecessary equipment (like gunsights) with lead weights and retaining only basic flight instruments and life-support equipment. Over the last 50 years, these target drones included the QB-47E, the QF-80A/C, the QF-104A, the QF-102A, the QF-100D/F, the QF-106, and the QF-4. These aircraft could be flown either manned (primarily only during ground-controller training) or unmanned (during missile evaluations and firing practice). The sole exception was the PQM-102, the Air Force's first fighter converted completely to an unmanned configuration in the 1970s.[158]

In addition to these aircraft, in the mid-1960s, some Bomarc surface-to-air missiles were modified to serve as targets with the installation of a multiple-airborne-target tracking system, a Doppler electronic scoring system, radar reflectors, and an emergency destruction device. Because the Bomarcs exceeded Mach 2 and altitudes above 55,000 feet, they made adequate targets for fighter-interceptor crews.[159]

Reconnaissance

The obvious advantage of not putting human crews at risk in high-threat areas fueled the Air Force's studies of alternate uses for UAVs. Their use for photographic reconnaissance was first investigated in the mid-1950s using Ryan's Firebee. The program lay dormant, however, as the Air Force considered the practicality of pursuing both the SR-71 and the drone program simultaneously. With the Powers U-2 incident in 1960, the program received a much-needed boost. Throughout the 1960s, several target drones, derivatives of the original Firebee such as the AQM-34 Lightning Bug, were developed for use during photographic reconnaissance missions over Vietnam.

The AQM-34 was the nation's first operational, unmanned, photographic reconnaissance vehicle. It was fielded, beginning in 1964, in several different models, including the N/P models for high-altitude photographic missions, the G model for chaff dispensing and electronic countermeasures, the K for night photography, and the L/M models for low-altitude missions. By the end of the war, Lightning Bugs also had been modified for ELINT, communications intelligence (COMINT, the Q model), and psychological warfare missions (leaflet dropping, the H model). Between 1964 and 1975, AQM-34 drones in Vietnam participated in more than 3,400 sorties flown by the U. S. Air Force's 100th Strategic Reconnaissance Wing. These RPVs also participated in a number of experimental reconnaissance programs until their retirement in 1975.[160]

The AQM series was designed specifically for air-launch from a modified DC-130, which also tracked the drone during flight. The drones were recovered by CH-3 helicopters via a parachute system after completion of their missions. The high-altitude variant had a wingspan double the length of the BQM-34 and a maximum range of nearly 1,500 miles. It was guided by a self-contained, preprogrammed, Doppler radar and carried a camera with a 24-inch focal length. In order to access the photographic intelligence, these drones had to be recovered and the film processed. The low-altitude variant had a range of

AQM-34 drone recovered by a CH-3 helicopter

AQM-34 Combat Angel, low-altitude, photographic reconnaissance drone. Measures taken to reduce the aircraft's radar cross-section included taped seams, special paint, and an inlet screen.

approximately 750 miles and was guided either by the Doppler system or a remote control from a ground or airborne station. It carried an analog camera with a three-inch focal length and a video link that could transmit imagery to a receiver 150 miles distant.[161]

Another successful variant of the AQM series, the AQM-34H/J models, were part of an Air Force program dubbed Combat Angel. These drones provided medium-altitude, tactical electronic warfare (chaff dispensing). Later modifications added wing-mounted, active ECM jamming equipment and zero-length, ground-launch capability. All Combat Angel vehicles were subsequently modified to a standardized V model. The program drones became operational with Tactical Air Command's only operational drone squadron in 1968 and were used until 1976.[162]

Throughout the Vietnam War and immediately following it, several additional UAV programs were launched. In an era of rising weapon system costs and declining defense budgets, the Air Force viewed unmanned vehicles as a cost-effective way to accomplish some aspects of its mission. Unlike the Lightning Bug and Combat Angel, most of the Air Force's early UAV programs were cancelled before the vehicles reached production. The AQM-91A Compass Arrow was an example. In 1966, a contract was issued to Teledyne Ryan for a UAV to perform high-altitude, long-range, photographic reconnaissance in a hostile environment. Building on the technology of the Firebee, Compass Arrow had low radar reflectivity and emitted low infrared radiation to prevent detection by enemy radar. Launched from a DC-130E, the drone had a 2,000-mile range, and in-flight guidance was provided through a preprogrammed, internal, Doppler/inertial navigation system. It carried an optical bar panoramic camera with a 24-inch focal length. Following completion of its mission, it was recovered by helicopter via the multi-parachute Mid-Air Retrieval System (MARS), but was additionally equipped with impact bags to cushion ground or water landings. The program was cancelled in 1971 before the UAV became operational.[163]

In the early 1970s, the Air Force initiated the Compass Cope program, a technology demonstration involving both Boeing and Teledyne Ryan for a high-altitude SIGINT vehicle to replace the RB-57. The program was alternately known as the HALE (High Altitude Long Endurance) RPV. Ryan's entry was the YQM-98A, a slightly larger AQM-91A designed for longer-range missions. It had conventional tricycle landing gear for runway takeoff and landing. The Air Force, however, chose the Boeing design, the YQM-94A, which made its first flight in 1973. Like Ryan's version, the YQM-94A could take off and land on a runway. Boeing's Compass Cope had a self-contained guidance system, a television camera, and electronic data links, and was powered by a single jet engine mounted on top of the fuselage. Although a contract to build three prototypes was issued, the program never reached production and was terminated in 1977.[164]

Full-scale mock-up of Boeing's YQM-94A Compass Cope, 1977, shortly before program termination

The Air Force retired all of its AQM series of RPVs in 1979, and despite a number of promising programs, none of the UAVs in research and development during the 1970s and 1980s became operational. The Air Force's interest was rekindled in the 1990s following the Navy, Army, and Marine Corps' successful utilization of reconnaissance drones in Desert Storm. The Air Force's manned reconnaissance fleet, primarily the U-2, was aging, and the SR-71 had proven costly to maintain, leading to its retirement in 1990. Although plans to modernize the U-2 were under way, the Air Force considered UAVs to supplement the plane's mission.

To prevent duplication by the services, most of the 1990s programs were initiated by the Defense Airborne Reconnaissance Office in the Department of Defense (DOD) and were subsequently turned over to the military services for management. In the Air Force, these programs became the responsibility of the Reconnaissance Aircraft Systems Group and the Joint Endurance Unmanned Aerial Vehicle Systems Program Office at ASC. The acquisition philosophy was termed the Advanced Concept Technology Demonstration (ACTD), which focused on quick-paced development in order to get mature technologies into the field more rapidly than traditional acquisition practices. By using already-proven technologies, the development and ensuing demonstrations designed to ensure mission utility of proposed systems were completed within two to three years as opposed to the normal 10-year timeframe.[165]

RQ-1A Predator

The first reconnaissance UAV the Air Force acquired in almost 30 years was the RQ-1A Predator, a derivative of an off-the-shelf, medium-altitude, endurance drone (the GNAT 750) built by General Atomics Aeronautical Systems for the CIA's use in Bosnia. Following the first successful,

RQ-4A Global Hawk at Edwards Air Force Base, California

DOD-sponsored ACTD initiated in 1994, Predator entered the Air Force inventory in 1996. The system was used for short-range tactical reconnaissance, surveillance, and target acquisition over Bosnia and Kosovo, and Predators armed with Hellfire missiles participated in Operation Enduring Freedom in Afghanistan. The propeller-driven UAV transmitted imagery via satellites to ground stations in real-time. It could loiter for up to 40 hours at altitudes up to 25,000 feet and had a radius of 500 nautical miles. A fully operable system consisted of four vehicles, a ground control station, and a satellite communications link terminal. A pilot flew the air vehicle remotely from a ground-based cockpit console linked to a forward-looking TV camera in the Predator.[166]

In 1994, to supplement the mission of the Predator, the DOD initiated another ACTD to acquire a UAV to fulfill high-altitude endurance (HAE) missions. The result of this program was the Tier III Minus DarkStar, developed by Lockheed Martin/Boeing, and the Tier II Plus Global Hawk, developed by Teledyne Ryan (now a part of Northrop Grumman). Both systems were to be compatible with a common ground station. Although now defunct, the RQ-3A DarkStar could fly at altitudes over 45,000 feet, had a range of 500 nautical miles, and had low-observable technology to make it nearly undetectable by hostile radars. The high-survivability vehicle was designed to loiter over high-threat areas for more than eight hours and was guided primarily by a self-contained system that utilized the Global Positioning System. The turbofan-powered prototype made its first flight in March 1996 but crashed on its second flight. A second prototype flew successfully in 1998, but the following year, the Air Force cancelled the program because the aircraft lacked aerodynamic stability and did not demonstrate sufficient military utility.[167]

The RQ-4A Global Hawk is a long-range, high-altitude vehicle that can loiter above 65,000 feet for over 24 hours, with a range of 3,000 nautical miles. It provides strategic and tactical reconnaissance over large areas and carries electro-optical and infrared sensors and synthetic aperture radar, all linked to a ground station via a worldwide satellite communications system. The jet-propelled prototype, roughly the size of the U-2, made its first flight in 1998 and was recommended for production in the fall of 2000. The UAV augments the manned reconnaissance aircraft in the Air Force inventory.[168] Global Hawk, along with the battle-proven Predator, flew its first combat mission in the fall of 2001 during Operation Enduring Freedom, the United States' war against terrorism.

Unmanned Combat Aerial Vehicles (UCAVs)

In the 1970s, the desire to prevent risks to human pilots led the Air Force to begin serious studies of the use of UAVs in combat missions. Specifically, these multi-mission aircraft would perform strikes against radar and missile sites, in addition to conducting reconnaissance, surveillance, and electronic countermeasures flights. The decade was ripe with new programs, such as mini-RPVs, Advanced RPVs (ARPVs), and expendable drones (Tactical Expendable Drone System or TEDS). Only one tactical UAV program, the BGM-34, became operational, however.

The first operational American UCAV was the BGM series of the Ryan Firebee. This program began in 1971 with the turbojet-powered BGM-34A/B. The A model was a rebuilt Firebee that carried Maverick missiles under its wings. It had the honor of being the first RPV to launch a missile for a direct hit on a target. The all-weather B model included infrared systems for detecting enemy missile launch sites. It also carried television-guided Mavericks under its wings. The last model of the series, the BGM-34C, made its first flight in 1976. The BGM-34C could either be launched from a DC-130H or from a mobile ground launcher. Its main missions were to fly forward of manned strike air-

BGM-34A armed with a Maverick missile, loaded on the under-wing pylon of a DC-130E, 1972

craft and either dispense chaff and otherwise jam enemy missile site radars or locate and lock on targets for following strike aircraft to bomb. Pods under the wings carried electronic countermeasures equipment, and a television camera mounted in the nose assisted ground controllers in locating targets. The Firebee could carry a 500-pound HOBO, two MK-81 or MK-82 bombs, or Maverick and Shrike missiles under the wings. Unlike the previous models, the BGM-34C's were not produced in quantity and, by 1980, further development of the BGM series was abandoned.[169]

The multitude of projects explored in the 1970s and 1980s, combined with technological advances in computers, sensors, flight controls, lightweight materials, and communications packages, made application of UAVs in the combat role more feasible in the post-twentieth century.[170] The Air Force and DARPA collaborated on a UCAV Advanced Technology Demonstration (ATD) with Boeing's X-45, scheduled to become operational by 2007. The proposed UCAV was similar to a light bomber and could perform both suppression of enemy air defenses (SEAD) and deep strike missions. The Air Force also studied the feasibility of weaponizing existing UAVs and successfully linked the Predator with the Army's Hellfire missile.[171]

MISSILES

Air-to-Air Missiles

In the early Cold War, the defense of the United States against enemy bomber aircraft carrying atomic bombs was considered the highest priority mission for the Air Force. Consequently, the Air Force placed air-to-air missiles (AAMs) at the top of its research and development priorities. AAMs were designed to allow air-superiority fighter aircraft to fire upon enemy aircraft at distances greater than one mile. They typically were guided either by locking on an enemy aircraft's radar signature or by an infrared system that sought the thermal energy signature of the target aircraft. They were armed with fragmentation warheads and proximity fuses, allowing them to detonate within lethal range of a target. The detonation could damage or destroy a target without striking a direct hit.[172]

ADM-20 QUAIL

The Quail decoy program began in the mid-1950s when the Air Force chose McDonnell to begin development of an air-launched decoy to pull enemy fire away from strategic bombers, particularly the B-52. Successful flight tests in 1957 and 1958 led to a production contract for the GAM-72 (later redesignated the ADM-20) Quail decoy. The Quail was a tailless, delta-wing vehicle that simulated its carrier bomber aircraft in operational performance and radar image. It carried both chaff and electronic countermeasures equipment. The Quail was preprogrammed to follow a 55-minute flight pattern complete with changes in speed and direction. The ADM-20A became operational in 1961. The B-52 could carry up to eight of the decoys in its bomb bay, and the B-47 could carry four. In 1962, the Air Force initiated the ADM-20B, with a modified flight control system to permit high or low mission capability. The A models were subsequently brought up to the B configuration. McDonnell produced more than 600 ADM-20s. Quails served the Air Force for 10 years before being retired in 1972 due to increased sophistication of enemy radar. At that time, the Air Force was testing other decoy programs, such as the Subsonic Cruise Armed Decoy (SCAD) and the Propelled Decoy. Later aircraft, such as the F-16, B-1B, and the Navy's F/A-18, carried the Navy-developed ALE-50 Towed Decoy System, which was literally towed behind the carrier aircraft.

Sources: History of Wright Air Development Center, January – June 1960, Vol. II: Space Systems and Strategic Systems, p II-79; History of Aeronautical Systems Division, April – December 1961, Vol. II, p II-64; News Release, Aeronautical Systems Division, Untitled, November 25, 1969, in Subsonic Cruise Armed Decoy file, Box 3316: Systems/Drones, 1972-98; News Release, Aeronautical Systems Division, "Propelled Decoy Successfully Flight Tested," November 7, 1974, in Propelled Decoy Successfully Flight Tested file, Box 3316: Systems/Drones, 1972-98, ASC History Office Archive.

ADM-20 Quail decoy in front of its carrier aircraft, a B-52G

AIM-4 Falcon

AIR-2A Genie air-to-air rocket in front of its carrier, the F-106A Delta Dart

The AIM-4 Falcon (originally GAR-1) manufactured by Hughes Aircraft Company was initially contracted for in 1947 as the XF-98 pilotless interceptor. This small missile powered by a single, solid-propellant rocket motor had a maximum speed of 1,500 mph and a range of seven miles. It was designed for use against subsonic targets flying between 5,000 and 40,000 feet altitude. On January 24, 1952, a ground-launched Falcon hit a QB-17 drone at a distance of one and one-half miles, marking the first time in Air Force history that a guided missile intercepted and hit an airborne target. The Falcon missile became the world's first operational, air-to-air guided weapon in 1955, and between 1954 and 1963, the Air Force accepted approximately 48,000 Falcons to arm its F-89H/J's, F-101B's, F-102A's, F-106A/B's, and F-4C/D/E's. The higher performance AIM-4F/G models carried on the F-106 were introduced in 1960 and provided increased protection from enemy countermeasures. With one exception, all Falcon variants carried conventional, high-explosive warheads. The AIM-26 (originally GAR-11), designed specifically for the F-102A, was the only variant fitted with a low-yield nuclear warhead and could be guided to a specific target. Falcons continued in service until 1988, at which time they retired along with their sole remaining carrier aircraft, the F-106 interceptor.[173]

The Douglas AIR-2A Genie (originally MB-1 and also known as Ding Dong) was produced between 1957 and 1962 for use with the Air Force's F-89J, F-101B, and F-106A fighters. This air-to-air, unguided rocket made its first flight in 1956, and in 1957, a Genie launched from an F-89J marked the first firing and detonation of a nuclear air-to-air weapon. The Genies were larger and heavier than their Falcon counterparts and had a maximum speed of 1,800 mph and a range of six miles. These weapons remained in service until 1986.[174]

Following Genie and Falcon, the Air Force relaxed priorities on AAMs and instead turned to Navy-developed systems to meet its needs during the 1970s. These included both the radar-guided Raytheon AIM-7 Sparrow and the infrared-guided AIM-9 Sidewinder programs initiated by the Navy in 1946 and 1949, respectively. The Navy originally designed the F-4 to carry four Sparrows in semi-recessed wells, and the Air Force armed its own F-4C/D/E's with Sparrows, Falcons, or Sidewinders. The AIM-7F became operational as the primary armament on the F-15 Eagle, and a later model, the

F-16B fires an AIM-7 Sparrow missile, February 23, 1989.

F-16 Fighting Falcon fires an AIM-9P4 Sidewinder missile at an MQM-107 target drone at White Sands Missile Range, New Mexico, 1988. *(Defense Visual Information Center)*

TACIT RAINBOW

In the 1980s, the Air Force studied several alternatives for suppressing enemy air defenses. One of these programs was Tacit Rainbow (AGM-136A), a low-cost tactical weapon that was part UAV and part missile. After being launched from a B-52, the jet-powered vehicle guided itself to a target based on information preloaded into its onboard computer. It loitered over an enemy target area until it identified active radar. If the radar was turned off, the missile continued to loiter until it again detected the transmissions. Once it locked onto a radar emission, the missile, armed with a 40-pound fragmentation warhead, attacked the target.

The Tacit Rainbow program began in 1982 and was managed by the Joint Tactical Autonomous Weapons System Program Office at Aeronautical Systems Division. The vehicle underwent flight testing between 1986 and 1987, but due to cost overruns, the program was cancelled in 1991 prior to production.

Sources: History of Aeronautical Systems Division, January – December 1986, Vol. I, p 162; History of Aeronautical Systems Division, January – December 1987, Vol. I, p 155; History of Aeronautical Systems Division, January – December 1989, Vol. I, p 212.

Tacit Rainbow missile awaits loading on a B-52G during flight test and evaluation, 1987.

F-16 firing an AIM-120 AMRAAM, 1990s

AIM-7M, entered service in 1982 for use on both the F-15 and the F-16 Fighting Falcon. This latter model, with a monopulse seeker that provided improved guidance even in extreme electronic countermeasures environments, proved particularly successful during Operation Desert Storm. The AIM-9B Sidewinder (designed and developed by the Naval Ordnance Laboratory and manufactured by Philco-Raytheon) first became operational in the late 1950s on Air Force F-100C/D's, and then later was used on F-104s, F-111A/E/D's, and F-4E's. The later E model was used on the F-4C/D with considerable success during the Vietnam conflict, and the most recent models, including the AIM-9J/L/M/P armed the F-15 Eagle and F-16 Fighting Falcon throughout the 1980s and 1990s. In 2000, only the AIM-9M was in service on these two Air Force fighters.[175]

In the late 1970s, the Air Force and Navy undertook a joint program for the AIM-120 Advanced Medium-Range Air-to-Air Missile (AMRAAM). In 1981, the Air Force chose Hughes Aircraft Company to develop the new missile to arm its newest fighter aircraft. In 1987, Hughes and Raytheon each were given production contracts for AMRAAM, and in 1992, the first F-16 unit became fully operational with the missile. The high-speed, all-weather AMRAAM was developed for increased success against low-altitude and beyond-visual-range targets as a replacement for the Sparrow. After launch from its carrier aircraft, the "launch-and-leave" missile was guided to its target by its own active radar, freeing the pilot to leave the area before being detected by the enemy. Several AMRAAMs could be aimed and fired at multiple targets simultaneously, and they had a 30-mile range. In 2000, the AIM-120A/B/C models were in service on the Air Force's F-15s and F-16s, and the missile was also compatible with the newly developed F-22. The U.S. Navy, as well as the military forces of Great Britain, Germany, Norway, and Sweden, also used AMRAAM.[176]

Air-to-Ground Missiles

The earliest air-to-ground missiles (AGMs) were essentially glide bombs modified with rocket propulsion. Because they were unguided, they were highly inaccurate, but they did considerable damage wherever they hit. For many years, the Air Force used the Navy-developed 5-inch High Velocity Air Rocket (HVAR), the Tiny Tim unguided rocket, and the 2.75-inch Folding Fin Air Rocket (FFAR). The vulnerability of strategic bombers to enemy surface-to-air missile sites during target over-flights made the development of more accurate, longer-range AGMs a priority of the Air Force in the early Cold War. As their technology advanced, their role expanded to include close air support of ground forces, anti-tank attacks, and missions against a variety of stationary strategic targets. Unlike AAMs launched only from fighter aircraft, AGMs were launched from both fighters and bombers. They located their targets either by infrared homing or semi-active radar homing systems. Later developments in guidance included low-light-level television seekers and laser designation.[177]

The Bell Aircraft Corporation's Rascal (XB-63, and later the XGAM-63) was one of the first AGM programs sponsored by the Air Force. The liquid-fueled missile had a speed of Mach 2.5 and was guided by an inertial navigation system. This supersonic missile was an outgrowth of the small-scale Shrike (X-9) test vehicle and was designed to have a 100-mile range. The Rascal made its first flight on September 30, 1952, and flight tests continued at Holloman Air Force Base, New Mexico, until 1957. The program was cancelled in 1958 to provide funding and support for the more promising Hound Dog program.[178]

Development of the North American AGM-28 Hound Dog (originally the GAM-77) began in 1956 as a crash program initiated by the Air Force Council. The nuclear-tipped, jet-propelled cruise missile was designed to protect the B-52 strategic bomber during atomic bomb delivery missions. The B-52G was designed to carry two Hound Dogs on under-wing pylons and all previous models of the bombers were retrofitted with the pylons. The AGM-28 was guided by an inertial navigation system and had a range of between 200 (low altitude and subsonic speeds) and 500 miles (high altitude and supersonic speeds). The Hound Dog became operational in 1961 and served until the mid-1970s when they were replaced by the Short Range Attack Missile (SRAM, see below).[179]

AGM-28 Hound Dog

AGM-48A Skybolt mated to a B-52 under-wing pylon

In the late 1950s, the Air Force sponsored a study called Project Bold Orion, which determined the feasibility of air-launching a ballistic missile from a strategic bomber. Promising results led the Air Force to let a contract to Douglas to develop an air-to-ground ballistic missile to arm the B-52H. This missile came to be the AGM-48A Skybolt (originally the GAM-87), and attracted the interest of the British Royal Air Force as well. Beginning in 1960, the missile was developed and tested extensively before being cancelled in 1962 for cost overruns and successive failures during flight tests.[180]

In the early 1960s, the Air Force acquired two Navy-developed missiles, the AGM-45 Shrike and the AGM-12 Bullpup, to arm its fighter-bomber aircraft. The Navy had the Martin Bullpup in operation since 1959, and the Air Force made its adaptation of the AGM for the F-100D/F operational by 1960, with a follow-on for the F-105D/F by 1961. In the later 1960s,

AGM-12 Bullpup on an F-100

the F-4C also could carry four Bullpups on wing stations.[181] The missile's mission was "to provide for a highly accurate, visual delivery by tactical fighter bombers, of interchangeable high explosive and small yield nuclear warheads against tactical targets."[182] The AGM-12B (originally GAM-83A) was developed with a high-explosive warhead and the AGM-12D (GAM-83B) with a small yield nuclear warhead. Bullpup missiles were used in Southeast Asia with mixed results and were replaced by the AGM-65 Maverick in the mid-1970s.[183] In early 1962, the Air Force also considered development of an anti-radar version of the Bullpup, but the program was cancelled later the same year in favor of the Navy's AGM-45 Shrike. This missile was developed in the late 1950s by Texas Instruments and was the first operational missile designed specifically to destroy radar sites. The Air Force armed its

F-4 carrying Maverick missiles on the left pylon and a Walleye glide bomb without fins on the right pylon

First production AGM-65A Maverick, 1972

AGM-69 SRAM launched from a B-52H

F-105F's and G's and the F-4 Wild Weasels with the Shrike.[184]

In 1965, as a replacement for the AGMs in service, the Air Force began the Tactical Missile Program, which culminated in the AGM-65 Maverick. As recommended by *Project Forecast*, the specific operational requirement (SOR) for the program called for a tactical AGM to act as a "round of ammunition" for contemporary fighters. The missile would be able to carry both non-nuclear and low-yield nuclear warheads, have clear-day capability (with night use added later), an automatic electro-optical homing system, and "launch-and-leave" technology. Three different missiles were planned for three types of targets: a large missile for large hard targets (e.g., bridges); a small lightweight missile for small hard targets (e.g., tanks); and a medium-size missile for intermediate targets (e.g., bunkers). To prevent duplication of effort between the services, the Air Force chose the Navy's AGM-62A Walleye, an unpowered glide bomb, as the large missile. The other two missiles became known as the ZAGM-64A Cobra and the ZAGM-65A Maverick, respectively. The following year, the program narrowed to just the Walleye and Maverick, which became operational in 1967 and 1972, respectively. During the Vietnam War, F-4D's were armed with the Walleye, the Air Force's first "launch-and-leave" missile. The missile had a television camera in its nose that pilots used to lock on to targets.[185]

Hughes and North American Aviation competed for the development contract for the Maverick, and the Air Force chose Hughes in 1968. The AGM-65A originally was planned to be operational in 1970 for use on the F-111A/D, the F-4C/D/E, and the A-7D. The A model Maverick finally became operational in 1972. The television-guided, blunt-nose missile was powered by a solid-fuel rocket motor and armed with a 125-pound conventional warhead. Improvements in later models included a narrower field of view in the seeker for more accurate lock-on to targets (B model), nighttime capability via an imaging infrared seeker (D model), and a bigger (300-pound), steel-jacketed warhead for hard targets (including armored ships, F model). A program for the Navy incorporated a laser seeker on the Maverick (E model). Over 20,000 of all Maverick models (except the C and E) were acquired by the Air Force alone, and later models (F and G) equipped nearly every American fighter and attack aircraft, including A-10 Warthogs flown in Operation Desert Storm. In 1998, the Air Force upgraded the infrared seekers on many G models with charge-coupled devices for a clearer picture, increased standoff range, and low-light capability. These new models became the AGM-65H with a shaped-charge warhead and the K with a heavyweight conventional warhead.[186]

One of the more successful missile programs of the 1960s and 1970s was originally referred to as the AGM-X-1 Missile, and later became the AGM-69A Short Range Attack Missile (SRAM). Development began in 1963 as part of the Missile X Program. A System Program Office (SPO) was created at ASD for SRAM in 1965 and the Air Force planned to acquire the missile via the total package procurement program used for the C-5 transport and the Maverick AGM. The supersonic ballistic missile had a 50-nautical-mile range, carried a nuclear warhead, and was extremely accurate by contemporary standards. Its all-weather capability and all-inertial guidance system made it applicable to strategic bomber

AGM-129 Advanced Cruise Missile (ACM) after launch

Airmen attach a pylon-load of six AGM-86 ALCMs to the wing of a B-52G bomber at Griffiss Air Force Base, New York.

aircraft performing day and night missions. SRAM's primary purpose was to destroy enemy surfacc-to-air missile sites, thus increasing the survivability of the attacking aircraft.[187]

In 1966, the Air Force chose Boeing to produce the SRAM. Tests the following year proved the SRAM's accuracy and reliability and the Air Force accepted delivery of the first production SRAMs in 1972 for the B-52G/H bombers and the FB-111A fighter-bomber. In the mid-1970s, an improved follow-on AGM-69B was planned but cancelled along with the B-1A bomber program in 1977. However, when the B-1B became operational in 1986, it was equipped with an eight-round rotary launcher in each of its three bomb bays, allowing it to carry up to 24 of the AGM-69A missiles. Development of the AGM-131A SRAM II began in 1983 as a replacement for the original SRAM on the B-52H, FB-111A, B-1B, and the advanced technology bomber (later known as the B-2). This improved strategic SRAM had increased range, better accuracy, and higher reliability. A nuclear tactical variant referred to as the AGM-131B or SRAM-T, also was planned for use on the F-15E, F-111, and F-16. After eight years of development and testing, the SRAM II and the SRAM-T were cancelled in 1991, primarily because of contractor failures to meet critical milestones. The original SRAMs were phased out beginning in 1990.[188]

By the 1970s, the Air Force grew increasingly interested in the use of cruise missiles for suppression of enemy air defenses. Although numerous programs were in development during the 1950s, work on cruise missiles had dwindled in favor of ballistic missiles in the following decade and, in fact, the last development work on cruise missiles was the Hound Dog, operational in 1961. The Air Force's modern cruise missile technology was based on much of the early development work with programs such as the Matador, Mace, and Snark surface-to-surface missiles (SSMs) (see below), as well as Hound Dog. Additional technology was borrowed from the remotely piloted vehicles then in development by Teledyne Ryan. Significant advancements in small, lightweight jet engines, fuels, materials, guidance systems, and lightweight nuclear warheads made smaller, more accurate cruise missiles more practical and feasible. In 1978, the deputy secretary of defense created the Joint Service Cruise Missile Program Office (JSCMPO, later JCMPO) to handle the Air-Launched Cruise Missile (ALCM), the Navy's Sea-Launched Cruise Missile (SLCM), and the Ground-Launched Cruise Missile (GLCM) (the latter is discussed below). The Navy was selected as the lead service, but the Air Force, through a project office at Wright-Patterson Air Force Base, was chosen as the lead for developing the cruise missiles' propulsion systems. The Navy maintained the lead for the guidance and navigation system. Once a production decision was made, the winning systems reverted to the management of their respective services.[189]

The Air Force's AGM-86 had begun as the Subsonic Cruise Armed Decoy (SCAD) program in 1968 as a replacement for the Quail, but was cancelled in 1973 due to unresolved conflict over the range of the decoy and whether it should be armed. In its place, the AGM-86B Air-Launched Cruise Missile (ALCM) was planned as a long-range, nuclear-warhead-equipped missile designed to destroy hardened targets from a distance of up to 700 nautical miles. Initially, the Air Force wanted the new ALCM to be compatible with the SRAM rotary launchers then

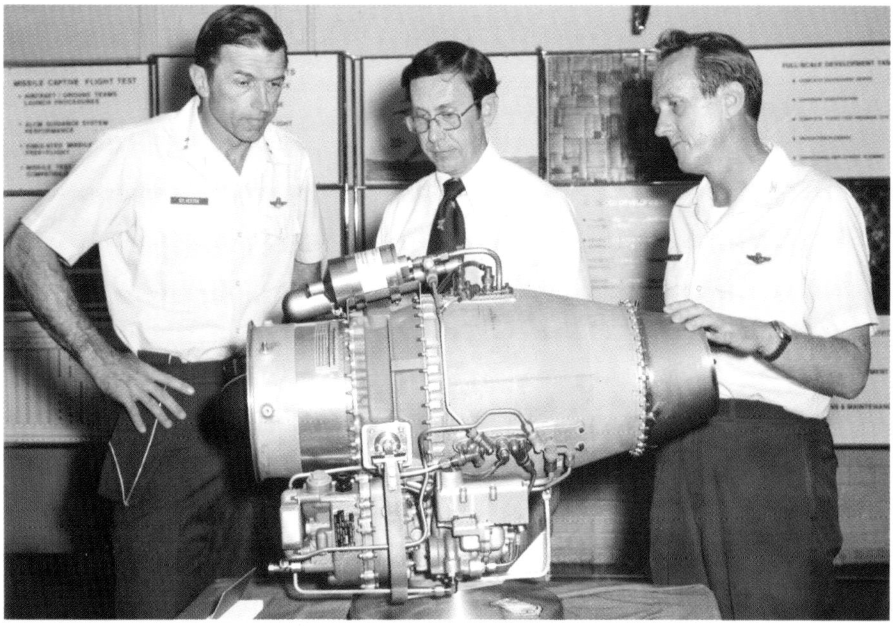

Components of the Subsonic Cruise Armed Decoy (SCAD). Major General George Sylvester, vice commander of ASD, is on the left. Sylvester became ASD commander in 1976.

Rotary launcher developed for the SRAM loaded on a B-52. Initially, the Air Force wanted the ALCM to be compatible with this launcher.

AGENA SATELLITE

When the United States' space program got under way in the early 1950s, satellite technology was a new dimension. The Air Force created a system program office at Wright-Patterson Air Force Base in 1954 with the goal of developing a military reconnaissance satellite to be launched atop the Atlas ICBM. RAND Corporation, with funding from the Air Force, had determined the technical feasibility for this system as early as 1946. It was not until 1954, however, that the Air Force issued a system requirement and initiated a design competition. Lockheed won the contract in 1956 to build what was then known as Weapon System (WS) 117L and what would later be known as Agena. The first vehicle was delivered to the Air Force in the fall of 1958, and the first launch occurred the following year from Vandenberg Air Force Base in California. At the same time, work began on an advanced B model, which was launched in late 1960. Lockheed produced 362 Agenas.

Agena was a rocket-powered spacecraft with three missions: to detect rocket launchings from land or sea, to detect nuclear detonations on Earth or in space, and to photograph Earth and transmit by radio electronically scanned images to receiving stations in the United States. As an upper-stage booster along with the Atlas or Thor, Agena launched more than 60 percent of all American payloads into space in the 1960s. It was an upper-stage booster for the launch of the Ranger, the first scientific research vehicle to land on the moon, and the Mariner, which marked the beginning of the United States' interplanetary exploration program with passes near Venus and Mars. Agenas were the first satellites to achieve circular orbit, the first to be controlled in three axes during flight, and the first to provide restart capability.

Sources: R. Cargill Hall, "The Air Force Agena: A Case Study in Early Spacecraft Technology," in *Technology and the Air Force: A Retrospective Assessment*, ed. Jacob Neufeld, George M. Watson Jr., and David Chenoweth (Washington, D.C., 1997), pp 231-243; R. Cargill Hall, "Civil-Military Relations in America's Early Space Program," in *The U.S. Air Force in Space: 1945 to the Twenty-First Century*, ed. R. Cargill Hall and Jacob Neufeld (Washington, D.C., 1998), pp 19-31; News Release, Lockheed Missiles and Space Company, Untitled, n.d., in United States Air Force, Space Systems Division, Information Kit, Box 9086: Space Related Miscellaneous Documents, ASC History Office Archive.

Special, radiation-hardened Agena satellite with modifications for the Snapshot 10-A program, which tested the feasibility of putting an orbiting nuclear reactor in space to provide an auxiliary power source for space vehicles, ca. 1965

installed in the B-52 bomber, but this limited the missile's size and thus its range. In 1979, the Air Force conducted a competitive flyoff between Boeing's AGM-86B ALCM (30 percent longer than the original ALCM) and General Dynamic's AGM-109 Tomahawk SLCM. Boeing's prototype was chosen in 1980, and the program then transferred to the Deputy for Strategic Systems at ASD.[190]

The AGM-86B ALCM was powered by a turbofan jet engine and traveled at subsonic speeds to targets via a terrain-contour-matching (TERCOM) guidance system. Once they became operational in 1982, B-52s equipped with ALCMs could attack targets from outside enemy defenses. In the late 1980s, a number of AGM-86B's were modified into AGM-86C Conventional ALCMs, or CALCMs. These missiles carried conventional warheads in place of the nuclear warheads carried by the B models and were guided by GPS-aided, inertial navigation systems. The CALCMs became operational in the late 1980s and were used with success during Operation Desert Storm. In the late 1990s, the Air Force contracted with Boeing to modify more than 300 additional nuclear ALCMs into enhanced Block 1 CALCMs (with 3,000-pound warheads) to replenish stocks depleted during missions in Bosnia and Iraq.[191]

Although further development of the AGM-86B ALCM was originally planned, the Air Force cancelled it in favor of the AGM-129A Advanced Cruise Missile (ACM). The program began as Teal Dawn at DARPA in the late 1970s, and in 1981, General Dynamics won a preliminary design competition for the new long-range, stealthy, nuclear strike missile. The Air Force took over the program in 1982 with plans to use the ACM on the B-52G/H and B-1B bombers. The newest cruise missile had greater range, accuracy, and survivability than either the ALCM or the Navy's Tomahawk. The ACM made its first flight in 1985. In 1987, production problems at General Dynamics/Convair led the Air Force to choose a second source vendor, McDonnell Douglas, to produce ACMs. Initial operating capability was achieved in 1991, shortly before President George H.W. Bush reduced the program to the acquisition of 640 missiles (down from the 1,000 planned the previous year). Budget issues further reduced this number to 520 before the program was officially closed out in 1993.[192]

The Tri-Service Standoff Attack Missile (TSSAM) program began in 1986 to provide the Air Force, Navy, and Army with a low-observable, conventional cruise missile for use against high-value fixed targets. The Air Force became lead service for the program and assigned program management responsibility to ASD's Special Projects Office. The plan was to use the Northrop Grumman-built AGM-137 missile on its B-52, B-1, and B-2 bombers and on the F-16 fighter. The stealthy, super-accurate missile was to use GPS-aided, inertial guidance en route to a target and then switch to an autonomous, precision, terminal guidance system with an imaging infrared seeker. Other variants called for dispersion of submunitions to attack area targets or armored vehicles. The Army withdrew its support of the ground-launched variant early in 1994, and by the summer of that same year, in light of flight test failures, rumors that the program would be cancelled were rampant. In December 1994, the program was terminated due to budget issues and also because the Department of Defense had determined that the level of stealth planned for the missile (a major factor in cost increases) was no longer a requirement.[193]

Following cancellation of TSSAM, both the Air Force and Navy reiterated their need for a standoff missile to weaponize fighters and bombers attacking deep interdiction targets. In 1995, the secretary of defense established a new program, the AGM-158 Joint Air to Surface Standoff Missile (JASSM), which retained a number of TSSAM characteristics. The precision cruise missile was planned for integration on the Air Force's B-52H, F-16C/D, F-15E, F-117, B-1B, B-2, and the Navy's F/A-18E/F. The guidance system for JASSM was the same as for its predecessor, but it also included a new anti-jam, GPS, null-steering antenna system for protection during mid-course guidance and a general-pattern-match, autonomous-target-recognition system for detection, tracking, and strike. Lockheed Martin was chosen in 1998 for engineering and development of the system, and the following year, management of the program transferred from ASC to the Air Armament Center at Eglin Air Force Base, Florida. Successful flight tests using prototype missiles were conducted in 1999, and full-rate production was scheduled for 2004.[194]

Surface-to-Air Missiles

With the increase in missile development during the 1940s and early 1950s, interservice rivalry also escalated as the different services came to see the role of missiles clearly within their own missions. The rivalry between the Air Force and the Army over surface-launched missiles, particularly surface-to-air types, was especially intense. The Air Force viewed them as an extension of defensive and offensive air missions, and the Army saw missiles as clearly belonging in the realm of ground missions. Ultimately, the Air Force fielded only one surface-to-air missile (SAM), the Bomarc (an acronym combining Boeing and the Michigan Aeronautical Research Center).

The Bomarc (XF-99, IM-99, later the CIM-10) was what the Air Force envisioned as an "area-defense" weapon, intended to fill the gap between its own long-range fighter-interceptors and the Army's point-defense systems (antiaircraft batteries protecting potential targets). The Bomarc had notable performance characteristics for the era: a speed of Mach 2.5, a ceiling of 80,000 feet, and a range of approximately 350 miles. It carried

IM-99B Bomarc leaves its launching pad at Cape Canaveral, Florida.

A Titan III-C being launched from Cape Kennedy, Florida, in 1967 *(Department of Defense Still Media Depository)*

TM-61 Matador at launch

TM-76B Mace launched from a Zero-Length Launcher at Holloman Air Force Base, New Mexico, for a 500-mile flight to Wendover Air Force Base, Utah

SM-62 Snark on its launcher

either a conventional or nuclear warhead and was guided electronically through the Semi-Automatic Ground Environment (SAGE) command system to the target vicinity at which time the missile's homing radar took over. The program began in 1949, and eight years later, the first Bomarc scored a direct hit against a target drone. The Bomarc A (CIM-10A) became operational in 1959, but soon began to phase out for replacement by the B model (CIM-10B), which had a longer range, a solid-fuel booster, and a pulse-Doppler radar for low-altitude targets. From its beginnings, the Bomarc competed with the Army's Nike series, particularly the Nike Hercules that became operational in 1958. Although the secretary of defense authorized procurement of both SAMs, the number of Bomarc deployment sites was consistently decreased from 40 to just 10. The SAM was removed from the inventory in 1972.[195]

Surface-to-Surface Missiles

By 1946, the Air Force had contracted for 12 surface-to-surface missile (SSM) programs, two of which (Navaho and Snark) carried over into the 1950s, and only one of which (Snark) became operational. One other mid-1940s program was cancelled in 1949 but reinstated the following year in light of the United States' involvement in the Korean War. This latter program was the Martin-built Matador (TM-61, later MGM-1), an unmanned, subsonic, turbojet-powered tactical aircraft. It was the size of a contemporary fighter and was one of the first aircraft to be fired from a zero-length launcher. It was guided by a ground-based radar operator through line-of-sight communications, limiting the missile's ultimate range capabilities. The missile's first flight occurred in 1950, and in 1954, the Matador became the Air Force's first operational missile, with deployments in West Germany, Korea, and Taiwan.[196]

The limited range of the Matador led the Air Force to try different guidance systems on the missile. The B variant of the Matador incorporated an ATRAN (Automatic Terrain Recognition and Navigation) system, which increased its range appreciably although it was still limited by the availability of radar maps. Additionally, the new system was not as easily jammed as that on the MGM-1 and it provided the missile with a low-altitude capability. This larger, more powerful version of the Matador was redesignated the Mace (TM-76A, later MGM-13A). Still later, the B model of the Mace was fitted with an inertial guidance system, which overcame the range limitations of both the Matador and the original Mace. Mace SSMs became operational in 1959 and were deployed to sites along with the Matador. Matadors were phased out beginning in 1962 and, by 1969, were replaced by the Army's Pershing missiles. Mace missiles left the inventory in the 1970s.[197]

The Snark (SM-62) air-breathing SSM program was initiated in 1946 through contract with Northrop Aircraft Inc. The nuclear-tipped cruise missile was guided by an inertial and stellar navigation system and, unfortunately, throughout its flight test program, proved to be relatively inaccurate and unreliable. Despite its shortcomings and obsolescence, the Snark was activated at Presque Isle, Maine, in early 1961. Its operational status was short-lived, as President Kennedy cancelled the program one month later to provide additional funding to the nation's ICBM programs. The Snark's supersonic counterpart was the long-range North American Navaho (XSM-64), which was in the same weight class (approximately 26,000 pounds) as most contemporary fighters. Although the program was cancelled in 1957 due to budget overruns, the Navaho incorporated some advanced technologies (materials, ramjets, guidance systems) that were later used in support of the nation's ICBM and space programs, as well as the Hound Dog air-to-ground cruise missile. In retrospect, however, it has been stated that the Air Force's ambitious requirements for these programs were beyond the state-of-the-art at that time.[198]

In the late 1950s and early 1960s, ballistic missiles proved to have advantages over cruise missiles: better accuracy, shorter flight times, better reliability, and less vulnerability to countermeasures. Originally, development of surface-to-surface ballistic missiles was conducted at the Wright Air Development Center. This included work on the United States' first ICBM, the Convair Atlas (SM-65, later CGM-16D/E/F), designed to reach anywhere in the world from inside the United States. After only five and one-half years in development, the Atlas was deployed by the Air Force, beginning in 1959, at sites throughout the western United States, Florida, and New York. Although withdrawn from service six years later, Atlas missiles nevertheless laid the foundation for the development of the nation's more successful ICBMs (such as the Titan and Minuteman).[199]

By 1954, the Air Force had moved its ballistic missile development programs to the newly formed Western Development Division, later the Ballistic Missiles Division, in Inglewood, California. (See Chapter 5: Pioneering Air Force Acquisition.) Although still involved in the development of air-to-air, air-to-ground, and surface-to-air missiles and responsible for all cruise missile work for the Air Force, Wright-Patterson Air Force Base had no further role with surface-to-surface missiles until the Ground-Launched Cruise Missile (GLCM) program began in the JSCMPO in 1978. The result was the BGM-109G Gryphon, a variant of the Navy's Tomahawk SLCM. The nuclear-tipped, subsonic GLCM had a range of over 1,500 miles, and was launched from a mobile Transporter Erector Launcher (TEL). The Gryphon made its first test flight in 1980, and five years later responsibility for the SSM transferred to ASD. The Air Force began deploying the missile to sites throughout Western Europe in late 1983, but its service life was short. In fact, from its earliest beginnings, the GLCM had been a political ploy to counter the Soviet's deployment of medium-range missiles in Eastern Europe. These missiles were banned under the conditions of the Intermediate-Range Nuclear Forces (INF) Treaty in 1987 and final withdrawal was completed in 1991.[200]

Test launch of the BGM-109 Ground-Launched Cruise Missile (GLCM) from a mobile Transporter Erector Launcher (TEL), 1980

SM-65 Atlas lifts from its pad at the Air Force Missile Test Center, Cape Canaveral, Florida, in 1959.

AIR FORCE SPACE PROGRAM

The Air Force's space program really began in 1954 with the creation of the Western Development Division (WDD) in Inglewood, California. Although missile research and development had begun during World War II, it was not until the early 1950s that associated technical and funding problems were overcome. Under the command of Major General Bernard A. Schriever, engineers with WDD, a division of the Air Research and Development Command (ARDC), were able to develop and deploy the Atlas Intercontinental Ballistic Missile (ICBM) within five and a half years. Development of the Titan ICBM, the Thor Intermediate Range Ballistic Missile (IRBM), and the Minuteman ICBM followed. By 1956, WDD, renamed the Air Force Ballistic Missile Division (AFBMD), took on a larger role with space and military satellite projects. Thor and Atlas were further developed as booster rockets to launch various payloads into orbit.

In 1961 the Kennedy administration declared the Air Force responsible for all military space development. The National Aeronautics and Space Administration (NASA) conducted research and development of civilian programs. The Air Force reorganized ARDC and created the Air Force Systems Command with two new divisions: the Ballistic Systems Division (BSD) and the Space Systems Division (SSD). BSD continued to develop the nation's ICBMs. SSD supported NASA programs by supplying Atlas and Titan boosters and launch facilities at Cape Canaveral. SSD also developed the Titan III military space launch vehicle, the Vela nuclear detection satellite, and the Initial Defense Satellite Communication System.

BSD and SSD merged in 1966 to create the Space and Missile Systems Organization (SAMSO). Under SAMSO, the Air Force developed the Defense Meteorological Satellite Program to provide accurate global weather forecasting, and the Global Positioning System used for navigation in most of the Air Force's modern aircraft. In 1979, SAMSO was inactivated and its missions were again divided into two organizations: the Ballistic Missile Office and the Space Division, still within Air Force Systems Command. Pressure for a separate organization for space operations resulted in the activation of Air Force Space Command in 1982. Research, development, and acquisition of space systems became functions of the Space and Missile Systems Center at Los Angeles Air Force Base, an organization under Space Command.

Sources: Tim Hanley, *Space and Missile Systems Organization: A Chronology, 1954-1979*; Brigadier General Earl S. Van Inwegen III, "The Air Force Develops an Operational Organization for Space," in *The U.S. Air Force in Space: 1945 to the Twenty-first Century,* ed. R. Cargill Hall and Jacob Neufeld (Washington, D.C., 1998), p 143. Space and Missile Systems Center was a part of Air Force Materiel Command until October 2001.

Test-model version of the Minuteman ICBM used to check ground support equipment, 1960

Defense Meteorological Satellite Program (DMSP) Block 5C satellite. These were launched from November 1972 until February 1976. *(Space and Missile Center History Office)*

WHETTING THE CUTTING EDGE—AEROSPACE SCIENCE AND ENGINEERING

The last hundred years have been the century of flight. Progress in flight has gone hand in hand with advances in science and technology. The Wright brothers began with what nineteenth-century theorists and experimentalists had discovered. They went on to make their own discoveries in aerodynamics, flight controls, and propulsion, including original advances in propeller theory and operation.[1] Taking up from the Wrights, European nations pressed ahead before and during World War I, fully exploiting the potential of wood and cloth biplane design and construction and experimenting with all-metal aircraft and monoplane designs. In the 1920s, both Europe and the United States made the revolutionary transition from wood to metal in aircraft structures. By the 1930s, American industry had overtaken Europe and commercialized the all-metal, stressed-skin, cantilevered, low-wing monoplane epitomized in the Boeing Monomail and 247, the Martin B-10, and the Douglas DC-3.[2] World War II ushered in the jet age with German, British, and, belatedly, American contributions. Jet propulsion ushered in revolutions in aircraft aerodynamics and design, materials, controls, and onboard electronics. The nearly simultaneous development of the first solid-state electronic devices

Aircraft during tests in the anechoic chamber. These tests focused on radio frequency signals critical to aircraft communication, navigation, and electronic jamming equipment.

The Equipment Laboratory at McCook and Wright fields engaged in research in the areas of instrumentation and navigation, parachutes and clothing, photography, and electrical, aeromedical, and miscellaneous equipment. Shown above are examples of the laboratory's products taken from an early report.

McCook Field was in every sense a "learning laboratory" for future aeronautical engineers. Pictured here is the Power Plant Section's Sam Heron (left) conducting a class in engine design.

revolutionized aviation electronics, soon dubbed "avionics." The 1950s and 1960s witnessed a further revolution in rocketry and the first significant advances into earth's exoatmosphere and beyond, popularly called "outer space." Recent decades have witnessed a revolution in electronic computation and satellite communication, much of it funded by the military and undertaken by aerospace companies. All these developments in aerospace vehicles have produced, in turn, collateral discoveries in materials (e.g., metallurgy and advanced composites), electronics (solid-state devices and digital computers), batteries and fuel cells (solar arrays), and aerospace medicine.

These discoveries and accomplishments have been achieved by close cooperation of the aircraft industry, academe, and government engineering and research centers. The latter have included the laboratories of the National Advisory Committee for Aeronautics (NACA), which in the late 1950s became the National Aeronautics and Space Administration (NASA); the laboratories of the National Bureau of Standards (NBS); the Naval Research Laboratory (NRL); and the laboratories of the U.S. Army and, subsequently, the U.S. Air Force. Of the Air Force's research and development (R&D) centers, the oldest, largest, and most diverse laboratory establishment is that in Dayton, Ohio. Historically, this science and engineering (S&E) center has been associated with research and development in aeronautics, specifically in the areas of flight dynamics, electronics, propulsion and power, materials, and aerospace medicine. Dayton's Army and Air Force S&E corps has, from the very beginning, established standards and guidelines for industry, published in numerous handbooks and other technical publications. It has provided continuity and resident knowledge during periods of industry recession and hard times. It has continually collaborated with other government centers, but in its breadth and depth of experience and technical competence and diversity of accomplishment, it has been second to none. In short, it has provided technical leadership over the past 80 years in virtually all aspects of American aerospace science and technology.

The history of this organization begins with a small group of engineers in the U.S. Army Signal Corps' Aviation Section (est. 1914), Washington, D.C. This group was headed by a chief engineer and divided into offices for Plane Design and Engine Design. The main task of this group was the technical review of airplane designs submitted by contractors to the government for procurement and production.[3] The group had no experimental facilities of its own available to test actual airplane or engine prototypes. The principal means of testing aircraft during this period was a series of flight trials, similar to those conducted for the Army's first airplane, the Wright Military Flyer, in 1909, at Fort Myer, Virginia. Offered little prospect of in-house, hands-on design or experimental work, this group experienced frequent turnover of personnel, most of whom were young engineers right out of college and looking for more challenging work in industry.

American entry into World War I, in April 1917, precipitated an aircraft production crisis. At the outset, the Army had only a handful of planes, none suitable for combat. The Army established an Equipment Division in the Aviation Section. An Aircraft Engineering Department was subsequently established under the Equipment Division to conduct experimental engineering to modify proven European airplanes and engines for American use and to assist industry in developing new model aircraft of entirely American design. In the autumn of 1917, the Airplane Engineering Department moved from Washington to Dayton, Ohio, where it was housed at newly built McCook Field, just north of Dayton's downtown. McCook provided the department's engineers with excellent experimental and test facilities, many unique in the nation. The engineering staff also increased in number from a handful to nearly 2,000 by war's end, with recruits coming from all over the country and a few also from Europe.[4]

McCook Field was established along the lines of neither an Army arsenal nor an industrial laboratory. Instead, the installation was called an "experimental field" or "engineering station." In fact, it came closest to what at the time was called an *engineering experiment station.* Such stations were originally established in association with engineering departments at predominantly land-grant colleges and universities, mostly in the Midwest. These stations allowed faculty and students to perform consultancy work on projects for industry and local and state governments. Typically, their work consisted of the *test and evaluation* of materials and structures,[5] two activities that also characterized the bulk of the work done at McCook on behalf of the Army and industry.[6]

In the early 1920s, the Signal Corps' balloon research and development activity was transferred from Omaha, Nebraska, to McCook Field, where it was constituted as the Lighter-than-Air Section of the Engineering Division. In the 1930s, this work merged with airplane research and development to form the Aircraft Laboratory at Wright Field. (Above) Blimp hovering low over McCook Field; (below) barrage balloon held captive over McCook Field.

Following the war, in 1919, the Aircraft Engineering Department was reorganized as the *Engineering Division.* The Engineering Division consisted of six technical sections: the Airplane Section, Power Plant Section, Equipment Section, Materials Section, Armament Section, and (after 1920) Lighter-than-Air Section. In 1922 the Signal Corps collocated its Aircraft Radio Laboratory at McCook. For the next two decades, the Radio Lab worked closely with the other technical sections until, during World War II, it was merged into the Engineering Division.[7]

In July 1926, the Army Air Service became the Army Air Corps. In October, the Air Corps established the *Materiel Division* at McCook. The Materiel Division combined experimental engineering with supply and procurement. The Engineering Division, in turn, was renamed the *Experimental Engineering Section,* and its technical sections were redesignated *branches.*[8]

The following year, the Materiel Division moved from McCook Field (which was razed) to larger quarters at newly built Wright Field, five miles east of Dayton. The original Wright Field complex included facilities for engine testing (dynamometer laboratory and torque stands), propeller testing (the largest propeller rig in the world), aircraft structures testing (both static and dynamic testing), landing gear testing, and aerodynamic testing (two wind tunnels). Wright Field also included a firing range for munitions testing and laboratory facilities for materials research

AERIAL PHOTOGRAPHY

BENNIE THOMAS . . . AT THE RIGHT HAND OF GODDARD

Young Bennie Thomas with his equipment

From the beginning, aerial photography was taken seriously by the engineering staff at McCook Field, as witnessed by numerous aerial photos of the field and of various in-flight experiments, such as parachute jumps. In the 1920s and 1930s, the Air Corps provided its services for an aerial survey of portions of the United States, including the Tennessee River basin and Alaska. The increasing importance of aerial photography in reconnaissance and surveillance led to the establishment of the Photography Laboratory within the Materiel Division in 1939.

Two important figures in the history of aerial photography at McCook and Wright fields were George W. Goddard and Bennie Thomas. Goddard studied aerial photography at Cornell University before being assigned to McCook Field in 1919, where he was put in charge of aerial photographic research. In the course of a career that included numerous assignments to McCook and Wright fields between deployments elsewhere, Goddard built a small research unit into the Photographic Laboratory of the 1940s and 1950s at Wright Field. Thomas, beginning as a noncommissioned officer, served under Goddard at McCook and Wright fields. With Goddard, he pioneered long-range and night photography, "instant" airborne photo-processing techniques, and aerial photographic equipment.

Goddard "stole the show" in 1940 when President Franklin Roosevelt toured Wright Field. Shortly before the president's visit, Goddard flew to New York and made an aerial survey of the Roosevelt family home at Hyde Park. Roosevelt was so taken with Goddard's display that he had little time left over to review other products of the Materiel Division's laboratories.

Sources: Biographies of George W. Goddard and Bennie Thomas in the ASC History Office Archive; *Oral History Interview: Otto Peter Morgensen, Jr., Aeronautical Engineer, Wright Field, 1936-1970*, ASC History Office, [unpublished draft].

Bennie Thomas contemplating his next aerial survey

George Goddard with one of the Engineering Division's aerial cameras

and testing. During the course of the 1930s, Wright Field added a new structures testing building, an altitude pressure chamber, and the nation's first centrifuge for aeronautical research. Plans for a 10-foot wind tunnel, to complement the 14-inch and 5-foot tunnels, were not realized before the war.[9]

From 1927 to 1939, the Materiel Division several times reorganized its experimental activity. In 1932, the Lighter-than-Air Branch merged with the Airplane Branch to form the Aircraft Branch. In the mid-1930s, the Materiel Division added a Physiological Research Laboratory in the Equipment Branch, which became the Aero Medical Research Laboratory during World War II. Then, in 1939, the Materiel Division redesignated all its technical branches *laboratories*. At the same time, it created several new laboratories, including the Propeller Laboratory and the Photography Laboratory to consolidate work in high-speed propeller development and photographic reconnaissance techniques and equipment.

World War II introduced a number of changes to Wright Field's science and engineering activities. The first change was the construction of a giant new wind-tunnel complex, beginning in 1939. This was followed by the laying of the first concrete runways for giant intercontinental bombers still in the planning stages. To conduct fatigue and other testing of the future B-36, Wright Field also built an immense, new structures test building (Building 65). Many smaller office and laboratory buildings also were constructed to accommodate the substantial increase in personnel and projects.

The number of laboratories also increased, from seven before the war to a dozen by war's end. Among the new laboratories formed during the war were the Radar Laboratory, the Aero Medical Research Laboratory (separated from the Equipment Laboratory), the Communication and Navigation Laboratory, the Electronic Components Laboratory, and the Personal Equipment Laboratory. Meanwhile, the Materiel Division also underwent several reorganizations. In 1942, the Materiel Division was redesignated the Materiel Command. In 1944, the Materiel Command was merged with the Air Service Command (logistics) to form the Air Technical Service Command (ATSC). Through these organizations, the laboratories remained part of the commands' (Experimental) Engineering Division located at Wright Field.[10]

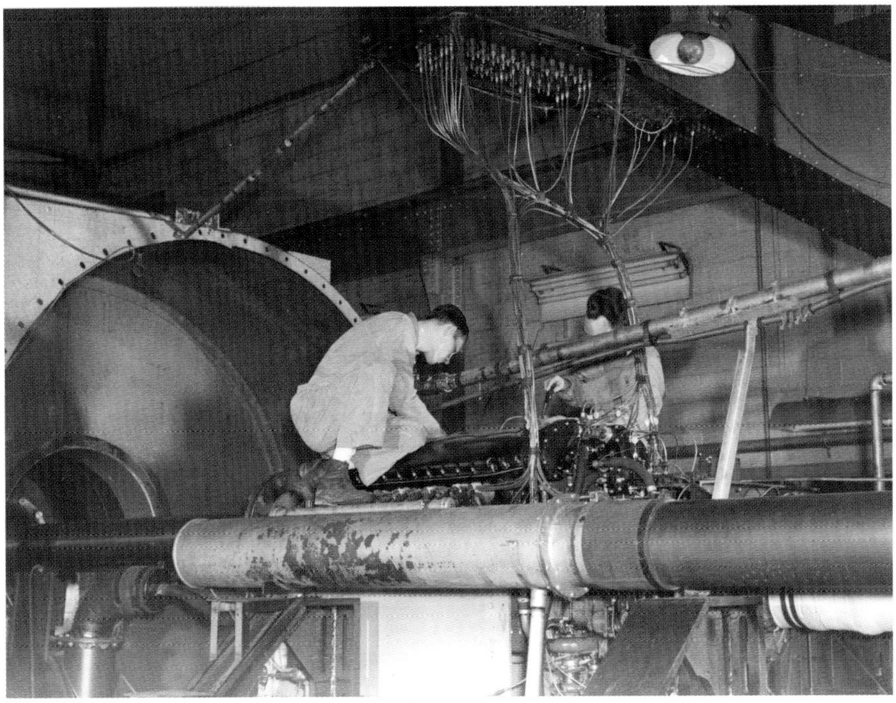

Engine shaft being examined in Wright Field's dynamometer laboratory

Whirling test of eight-blade dual propeller on one of the test rigs at Wright Field

McCook Field's 14-inch, high-speed wind tunnel (shown here) and the 5-foot tunnel were both transferred from McCook to Wright Field. Until the construction of the massive tunnel complex during World War II, the 14-inch and 5-foot tunnels were the only active wind tunnels at Wright Field. The 14-inch tunnel is today on display at the United States Air Force Museum.

WIND TUNNELS AT WRIGHT FIELD

In the early 1940s, Wright Field had both the 14-inch and 5-foot wind tunnels in operation for airplane model tests. With trends toward higher speeds and larger aircraft, what Wright Field engineers needed was a wind tunnel to accommodate larger models and facilities that could generate transonic wind speeds. The solution entailed no less than four new tunnels by the early 1950s.

Aerodynamicist Dr. Theodore von Karman consulted on the design and construction of the 20-foot wind tunnel in the late 1930s and his protégé and colleague, Dr. Frank L. Wattendorf, supervised its construction, which was completed in 1942. Able to generate 400-mph winds via two 16-bladed fans powered by a 40,000-horsepower motor, it was the largest and most powerful wind tunnel in the world at the time of its completion. It could accommodate full-scale missiles and airplane models with wingspans up to 15 feet and lengths up to 16 feet. The 20-foot tunnel was dedicated as the Massie Memorial Wind Tunnel in honor of the first chief of the Wind Tunnel Branch, Captain Louis E. Massie, who died in an airplane crash in 1940. Until it was dismantled in 1959, the 20-foot wind tunnel contributed data for numerous aircraft and components, including those used on the B-29, B-36, B-58, P-47, and P-61.

With high-subsonic speed capability, the 20-foot tunnel could not be used for tests of the supersonic aircraft being developed in the 1940s and 1950s. That role fell to the 10-foot wind tunnel, the 2-Foot Supersonic Wind Tunnel, and the 6-Inch Supersonic Wind Tunnel, that became operational in 1947, 1950, and 1951, respectively. The 10-foot tunnel was originally built to test models of high-altitude bombers and fighters, and it could simulate temperatures and pressures experienced at altitudes up to 50,000 feet. The tunnel was used more extensively, however, for transonic testing of missiles and aircraft models, including those of the B-58 bomber; the F-111, F-101, and F-102 fighters; and the Bomarc, Snark, Rascal, Matador, and Navaho missiles. Two 20,000-horsepower engines powered four 19-inch-diameter fans to generate wind speeds up to Mach 1.24. Tests conducted in the tunnel helped engineers understand and overcome many of the problems associated with aircraft crossing over from subsonic to supersonic speeds. The 10-foot tunnel was shut down in 1958.

The remaining two wind tunnels also contributed to tests concerning the effects of supersonic speeds on aircraft models. By the 1960s, the 2-foot tunnel could sustain air speeds up to Mach 5. In 1970 it was renamed the Trisonic Gasdynamics Facility when a transonic section was added to the tunnel. The Trisonic facility could handle tests of aircraft models at subsonic, transonic, and supersonic speeds by using special airflow inserts. Test results from this tunnel contributed to the development of the high-speed F-15, F-16, and F-18 fighters, as well as the X-29 forward-swept-wing experimental aircraft. The 6-inch tunnel was used for aerodynamic tests on models of supersonic aircraft. It could generate speeds up to Mach 2.5. This latter tunnel was donated to Ohio State University in 1958.

Sources: Emma J. H. Dyson, Dean A. Herrin, and Amy E. Slaton, *The Engineering of Flight: Aeronautical Engineering Facilities of Area B, Wright-Patterson Air Force Base, Ohio* (Washington, D.C., 1993), pp 120-139; Wendy Zug-Gilbert, Margaret M.M. Pickart, Douglas Dinsmore, and Conran A. Hay, *Documenting the Cold War Significance of Wright Laboratory Facilities* (1996), pp 144-148.

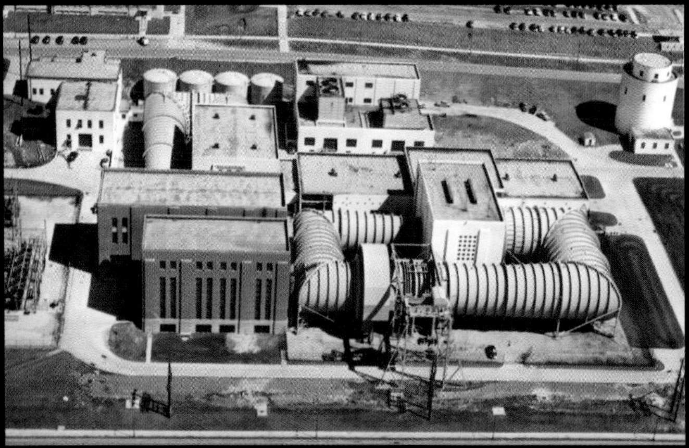

World War II wind-tunnel complex showing 20-foot tunnel (right of center)

Another view of the World War II wind-tunnel complex showing 10-foot tunnel (left of center)

The vertical wind tunnel, also built during World War II

In addition to developing long-range bomber aircraft, Wright Field also introduced the first practical helicopter in cooperation with the Sikorsky company.[11] Even more consequential was the introduction of the gas turbine engine from Britain and the development of the first American "jet" airplane, the Bell P-59A.[12] Wright Field also conducted research and development of "pilotless" aircraft including short- and long-range missiles.[13] Radar also became airborne with the introduction of the cavity magnetron from Britain, making possible smaller microwave sets. New materials, including plastics and "composites," for both major aircraft structures and more specialized uses, like radomes, were also developed.

Sikorsky helicopter at Wright Field

Research and development were sharply curtailed with the end of the war in September 1945. Postwar demobilization substantially reduced the engineering workforce. Some laboratories, like Materials, were reduced to their prewar manpower level within a year. Research and development funding was likewise cut, though not as severely as manpower. This led to more contracting-out of work, which, in turn, increased the paper workload of in-house laboratory personnel.[14]

Within a year of war's end, ATSC was reorganized as the Air Materiel Command (AMC). AMC consolidated ATSC's five technical divisions into three directorates: the Directorate of Production and Industrial War Plans, the Directorate of Supply and Maintenance, and the Directorate of Research and Development (R&D). The Directorate of R&D comprised the Engineering Division (the laboratories), the Flight Test Division, and the All-Weather Flying Division.[15]

Hardly had the postwar reorganization of the command taken place than the advocates of R&D began to lobby for institutional changes, including even a separate command for R&D. There were several highly placed advocates of R&D. One of the principal advocates was Dr. Theodore von Karman, chairman of the Air Force's Scientific Advisory Board (SAB, previously the Scientific Advisory Group). Von Karman had served as principal scientific advisor to Army Air Forces (AAF) Commanding General Henry H. "Hap" Arnold during the war.[16] In 1944, General Arnold had commissioned von Karman to prepare a report on the R&D advances of America's wartime allies and opponents and to make recommendations for a postwar AAF R&D program. Von Karman's report, entitled *Toward New Horizons*, became the charter for those advocating a more aggressive Air Force R&D program.[17]

The first significant institutional change was the establishment, at von Karman's urging, of the Office of Air Research (OAR) in the Engineering Division. OAR laid the foundation for the Air Force's later program in *basic* research that gave rise to Wright Field's Aerospace Research Laboratories (ARL) and the Air Force Office of Scientific Research (AFOSR).[18]

The second and even more significant institutional change, the establishment of a command for R&D, resulted from lobbying by von Karman and the SAB, as well as senior officers like Major General James H. "Jimmy" Doolittle and Major General Donald L. Putt. A Wright Field veteran, Putt and his followers, or "Junior Indians" (among whom was Colonel Bernard A. Schriever), prevailed upon Air Force Chief of Staff General Hoyt S. Vandenberg to commission a study concerning the advisability of separating R&D from AMC and constituting it an independent command. Von Karman appointed Dr. Louis Ridenour of the Massachusetts Institute of Technology (MIT), to form a subcommittee of the SAB for this purpose. This group is known to history as the "Ridenour Committee" and its report, published in 1949, the

General Don Putt and Dr. Theodore von Karman advocated a vigorous post-World War II research and development program for the Air Force.

DR. THEODORE VON KARMAN

Professor von Karman *(National Aeronautics and Space Administration)*

Dr. Theodore von Karman was born in Budapest and spent most of his life as a professor of aerodynamics, first in Europe and subsequently in the United States. His contributions to the scientific community were significant and continued to influence modern aerodynamic theory and practice into the twenty-first century. He developed many theories of aeronautical and space science, such as the effects of forces and currents on aircraft. He was instrumental in developing supersonic aircraft and intercontinental ballistic missiles.

Von Karman also was involved in the institutional side of developmental breakthroughs in aviation. He helped establish the world's largest rocket corporation, Aerojet-General, and was instrumental in founding the Jet Propulsion Laboratory to develop rocket propulsion. Responsible for the formation of the Advisory Group for Aerospace Research and Development (AGARD), the aeronautical research arm of the North Atlantic Treaty Organization (NATO), Dr. von Karman served as the organization's first chairman.

In 1939 General "Hap" Arnold asked von Karman to advise on the design and construction of a 20-foot, 40,000-horsepower, wind tunnel for Wright Field. This was the first facility of its kind and allowed the Air Corps to make major advances in flight. In 1944, also at General Arnold's request, von Karman established the Scientific Advisory Group (SAG) to develop a plan for future air research. (The SAG later became the Air Force Scientific Advisory Board.) Von Karman and other members of the SAG went to Europe in 1945 to question German scientists and engineers about their rapid progress in aviation during the war. The group presented its findings in a report titled *Toward New Horizons*, which laid out a blueprint for future Air Force research and development. In line with the objectives of *Toward New Horizons*, von Karman protégé Dr. Frank L. Wattendorf proposed a center for the study and development of jet propulsion, supersonic aircraft, and ballistic missiles. Ground was broken for the new facility in 1951. In honor of General Arnold, it was named the Arnold Engineering Development Center (AEDC). In 1959 AEDC's Gas Dynamics Facility was named for von Karman, who was then the chief scientific advisor to the Air Force.

Theodore von Karman died in 1963.

Sources: "Dr. Theodore von Karman, 1881-1963," AEDC (Arnold Air Force Base, Tennessee) biography, online at http://www.arnold.af.mil/aedc/karman.htm.

Last known photograph of von Karman (far left) during a visit to Wright-Patterson. Frank Wattendorf is seated far right.

"Ridenour Report." Simultaneously, General Vandenberg appointed Major General Orvil Anderson of Air University to head a similar committee of senior officers. Both committees' reports strongly recommended that the Air Force create an R&D command. Air Force Vice Chief of Staff General Muir S. Fairchild agreed with the recommendation and directed its implementation.[19]

In January 1950, the Research and Development Command was established. The new command consisted essentially of AMC's Directorate of R&D. In September 1950, the command was redesignated the Air Research and Development Command (ARDC).[20]

In March 1951, AMC created the Air Development Center (Provisional) at Wright-Patterson Air Force Base. The center consisted of the Wright Field elements of AMC's former Directorate of R&D, including the 12 laboratories and the laboratory elements of OAR; the Flight Test Division, and the All-Weather Flying Division. In April 1951, the Air Development Center was transferred to ARDC and initially designated the Air Development Force and finally, in June 1951, the Wright Air Development Center (WADC).[21]

At the establishment of WADC the laboratories included: the Aircraft Laboratory, Power Plant Laboratory, Propeller Laboratory, Equipment Laboratory, Armament Laboratory, Photographic (reconnaissance) Laboratory, Aircraft Radiation (radar) Laboratory, Components and Systems (electronic devices) Laboratory, Communication and Navigation Laboratory, Aero Medical Laboratory, Computation and Simulation Laboratory, and Materials Laboratory.[22] The laboratories were reorganized several times during the 1950s. In 1952, the Computation and Simulation Laboratory (formed from the experimental elements of OAR) was redesignated the Flight Research Laboratory and, one year later, the Aeronautical Research Laboratory (ARL).[23] In 1955, the Flight Controls Laboratory was established from elements of the Aircraft Laboratory.[24] The same year, the Armament Laboratory was disestablished. Its munitions work was transferred to Eglin Air Force Base, Florida, and its guidance research was organized as the Weapons Guidance Laboratory of WADC and remained at Wright Field.[25] In 1958, the Propeller Laboratory was merged with the Power Plant Laboratory to form the Propulsion Laboratory.[26] The next year, the Propulsion Laboratory's rocket motor work was transferred to Edwards Air Force Base, California.[27]

In 1959, ARDC headquarters initiated a major reorganization of its science and engineering workforce at Wright Field. The reorganization was undertaken primarily to accelerate the transition of technology from the laboratories to weapon systems and to make the development of systems more efficient.[28] As a result of this reorganization, WADC became the Wright Air Development Division (WADD).

WADD consisted of three directorates: the Directorate of Systems Management, the Directorate of Systems Engineering, and the Directorate of Advanced Systems Technology. This last directorate was comprised of four divisions: the Aero-Mechanics Division (Flight Dynamics and Propulsion), Avionics Division, Materials Central, and the Aerospace Medical Division. The directorates of Systems Engineering and Advanced Systems Technology were formed by dividing in half the science and engineering (S&E) workforce of the WADC laboratories. These two directorates likewise divided the functions of the older labs: Systems Engineering provided dedicated engineering support to project offices for weapon systems under development while Advanced Systems Technology concentrated primarily on conducting *applied research* to enlarge the Air Force's future technology options.[29] Meanwhile, the Aeronautical Research Laboratory was reassigned to a new Air Force Research Division, Washington, D.C., directly under ARDC headquarters.[30]

In 1961, the Air Force reorganized its acquisition and logistics functions by establishing two new commands: Air Force Systems Command (AFSC) and Air Force Logistics Command (AFLC).[31] Unlike ARDC, which was responsible only for R&D, AFSC was responsible for both R&D and procurement and production. As a result of the command reorganization, at Wright Field WADD was merged with AMC's Aeronautical Systems Center (ASC), which had managed AMC's aeronautical procurement and production, to form the Aeronautical Systems Division (ASD).[32] Under ASD, the Directorate of Advanced Systems Technology, became the Deputy for Technology, and the Directorate of Systems Engineering became the Deputy for Systems Engineering. Meanwhile, WADD's Aerospace Medical Division became the Aerospace Medical Laboratory and was realigned under the new Aerospace Medical Division headquartered at Brooks Air Force Base, Texas.[33]

The reorganization of the Air Force's S&E corps continued in 1963 with the establishment of the Research and Technol-

LIEUTENANT GENERAL DONALD L. PUTT

Major General Donald L. Putt, 1952

One of the worst airplane disasters in the history of Wright Field occurred on an October morning in 1935. Boeing's Model 299, which had previously flown nonstop from Seattle to Dayton, had just taken off for a test flight. Shortly after becoming airborne and before clearing the field, however, it fell back to earth in a fiery crash. Emerging from the wreckage were five men, including a young lieutenant, Donald L. Putt.

Putt had reported to Wright Field two years before and had been assigned to the Flying Branch as a test pilot. Like many of his fellow pilots, he had an engineering degree—a bachelor of science degree in electrical engineering from the Carnegie Institute of Technology, Pittsburgh, Pennsylvania. While at Wright Field he attended the Air Corps Engineering School and was then sent to the California Institute of Technology. At that time Dr. Theodore von Karman headed up Cal Tech's Guggenheim Aeronautical Laboratory (GALCIT) and held court both on and off campus for aspiring protégés. At Cal Tech Putt earned a master of science degree in aeronautical engineering. In 1938 he returned to Wright Field where he was assigned to the Materiel Division's Aircraft Project Group and then, in 1939, to the Production Engineering Division.

Von Karman remembered meeting Putt and Major General Frank Carroll, wartime chief of the Engineering Division, early in 1943 to discuss the possibilities of supersonic flight. Of Putt, von Karman remarked that he was "a very progressive officer, who was later to become a good friend." Von Karman also recollected a more immediate concern of Carroll and Putt as the war neared its end: modification of the B-29 to carry the atomic bomb.

After serving with U.S. troops in Europe from 1944 to 1945, Putt returned to Dayton to become assistant chief of staff for Intelligence at Air Technical Service Command headquarters, Patterson Field. In 1946, he became deputy chief of the Engineering Division. During this period, he helped organize the transfer of German scientists and engineers to the United States under the aegis of Project Paperclip. Two years later, Putt was on his way to Washington, D.C., to become director of Research and Developement in the Office of the Deputy Chief of Materiel, U.S. Air Force. As director of R&D, Putt and a group of junior officers—Putt's "Junior Indians"—played a key role, along with von Karman and others, in the bureaucratic maneuverings to create an independent command for R&D, the Air Research and Development Command (ARDC).

In 1951, Putt became assistant deputy chief of staff for Development and then acting chief of staff for Development. The following year, Putt was named vice commander of ARDC and concurrently the commander of the Wright Air Development Center (WADC). He held this dual appointment until Major General Albert Boyd was named WADC commander in June 1952. In 1953, Putt became commander of ARDC and in 1954 deputy chief of staff for Development, the position from which he retired in 1958.

Lieutenant General Don Putt died in November 1988.

Sources: Biography of Donald L. Putt in ASC History Office Archive; Theodore von Karman and Lee Edson, *The Wind and Beyond: Theodore von Karman, Pioneer in Aviation and Pathfinder in Space* (Boston, 1967).

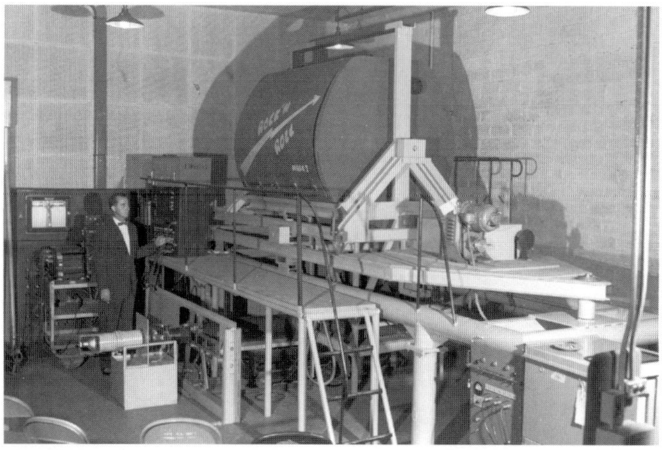

Jim Haley of the Avionics Laboratory and his Dynamic Analyzer constructed from a Snark missile. "Haley's Comet" simulated flight conditions for testing advanced reconnaissance systems on the ground.

Atomic power for the Air Force: During the 1950s, the Air Force made a heavy investment in nuclear power, including plans for an atomic-powered, long-range bomber. To assist in this work, the Air Force built a nuclear reactor at Wright Field, called the Nuclear Engineering Test Facility (shown above under construction in 1958). The photograph below shows an interior view of the facility.

ogy Division (RTD) under AFSC headquarters. RTD was headquartered at Bolling Air Force Base, D.C. As a result, the Deputy for Systems Engineering and the laboratories of the Deputy for Technology were realigned under RTD, although both remained at Wright Field. The laboratories were further consolidated and renamed the Air Force Materials Laboratory, the Air Force Avionics Laboratory, the Air Force Aero Propulsion Laboratory, and the Air Force Flight Dynamics Laboratory. The Deputy for Systems Engineering was renamed the Systems Engineering Group (SEG) of RTD.[34]

In 1967, the Air Force disestablished RTD. As a result, the applied research laboratories were placed under a Director of Laboratories at AFSC headquarters (AFSC/DL). Elements of the SEG at Wright Field were returned to ASD as the Deputy for Engineering (ASD/EN). At the same time, the SEG functions of preliminary aircraft design and cost analysis were constituted as a separate functional organization under ASD called the Deputy for Development Planning (ASD/XR).[35]

The downsizing of the military following the U.S. withdrawal from Vietnam in the early 1970s led, among other things, to a consolidation of the Air Force's laboratories. At Wright Field, the four applied research laboratories for Materials, Avionics, Aero Propulsion, and Flight Dynamics were realigned under a new umbrella organization, the Air Force Wright Aeronautical Laboratories (AFWAL).[36] Simultaneously, ARL was disestablished and its personnel and facilities distributed among the other laboratories, where they continued to pursue basic research projects. Meanwhile, the funding and overall direction of the Air Force's basic research program was directed by AFOSR.[37]

From 1975 to 1982, AFWAL reported to AFSC/DL. However, in 1982, AFSC realigned AFWAL under ASD in an attempt to improve technology transition from AFWAL's laboratories to ASD's system program offices.[38] To further this goal, ASD and AFWAL established the Senior Engineering (EN) Technical Assessment Review (SENTAR) process. Under SENTAR, laboratory projects were regularly reviewed by a panel made up of experts from ASD/EN and ASD/XR, which determined their maturity for transitioning to future weapon systems and systems under development.[39]

In 1988, AFWAL was reorganized as the Wright Research and Development Center (WRDC). This reorganization was begun

Air Force Wright Aeronautical Laboratories (AFWAL) was established July 1, 1975. The research laboratories for propulsion, avionics, flight dynamics, and materials reported to AFSC headquarters until 1982, when they returned to ASD.

EZRA KOTCHER

WRIGHT FIELD'S FATHER OF SUPERSONIC FLIGHT

After nearly a decade that saw some of the best and brightest scientists and engineers leave McCook and Wright fields for academe and industry, the Air Corps finally received permission from the Army, in the late 1920s, to hire new recruits. Among the newcomers was a young bachelor of engineering from the University of California named Ezra Kotcher, a native New Yorker born only three months before the Wright brothers' first powered flight. While on the West Coast, Kotcher met the peripatetic Professor John E. Younger, who divided his time between teaching aeronautics at the university and performing hands-on consulting work for the Materiel Division at Wright Field. So it was that, in July 1928, the 25-year-old Kotcher found himself in Dayton, too, and on his way, like Wilbur and Orville, to making history.

After a short stint as a junior aeronautical engineer in the Experimental Engineering Section, Kotcher was assigned to the Air Corps Engineering School at Wright Field as "professor of higher mathematics." Over the next 10 years young Professor Kotcher lectured such students as Benjamin W. Chidlaw, Orval R. Cook, Laurence C. Craigie, Donald L. Putt, Muir S. Fairchild, Frederick R. Dent, and Bernard A. Schriever, a veritable who's who of future Air Force general officers and R&D leaders. (Kotcher worked both sides of the lectern, earning a master's degree in aeronautical engineering from the University of Michigan during summers between 1935 and 1938.)

The classroom fell silent in 1939 as the Air Corps prepared for war and every available engineer was assigned to active projects at Wright Field. Kotcher became chief of the Aircraft Laboratory's Vibration and Flutter Unit, an appointment that allowed him to follow up on an idea that had intrigued him since the mid-1930s: overcoming the effects of "compressibility" in high-speed flight. As high-performance aircraft like the Lockheed P-38 Lightning and the Republic P-47 Thunderbolt approached Mach 1 in high-speed dives, their propellers lost efficiency and the aircraft themselves underwent terrific vibrations, sometimes resulting in their destruction. Wind-tunnel data was lacking for this transonic flight regime. Some paper studies even suggested the impossibility of ever overcoming the so-called "sound barrier." Kotcher drafted a proposal in August 1939 for a series of flight test vehicles, powered either by rocket or turbine engines, to experimentally probe this unexplored frontier.

The exigencies of world war prevented Kotcher's proposal from being acted upon for nearly five years while he kept busy devising aerial refueling techniques for long-range bombers and designing the new jet aircraft to withstand the aerodynamics of high-subsonic flight. However, in 1944, General Hap Arnold began to turn the sights of the Army Air Forces (AAF) to the future, and Wright Field entered into discussions with the National Advisory Committee for Aeronautics (NACA), whose own John Stack had similarly dreamed of achieving supersonic flight since the late 1920s. Meanwhile, Kotcher enlisted the Aircraft Laboratory's design branch for preliminary designs of experimental vehicles, one using a rocket and the other a jet engine. Armed with these studies, the AAF approached Bell Aircraft for the design and construction of a rocket-powered, flight test aircraft. Together with the NACA and Bell, the AAF undertook a series of top-secret test flights at Muroc Field, California. On October 14, 1947, Air Force test pilot Captain Chuck Yeager piloted the X-1 past the sound barrier and into the history books.

Following the war, Kotcher became the director of Wright Field's engineering school, renamed the Air Force Institute of Technology (AFIT). After the Wright Air Development Center (WADC) was established in the early 1950s, Kotcher became technical director, first of WADC's Aeronautics Division and later of the center's Directorate of Laboratories. When WADC became the Wright Air Development Division (WADD) in 1959, Kotcher became technical director of WADD's Directorate of Advanced Systems Technology. He spent the 1950s as a leading advocate of the systems approach to aircraft development and acquisition. He retired in 1961. Ezra Kotcher died in 1990.

Sources: Biography of Ezra Kotcher in the ASC History Office Archive; Jay Miller, *The X-Planes* (Arlington, Texas, 1988).

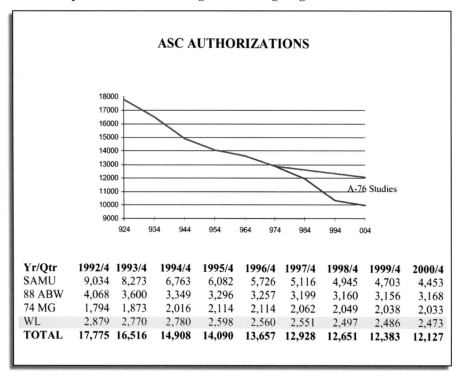

ASC AUTHORIZATIONS

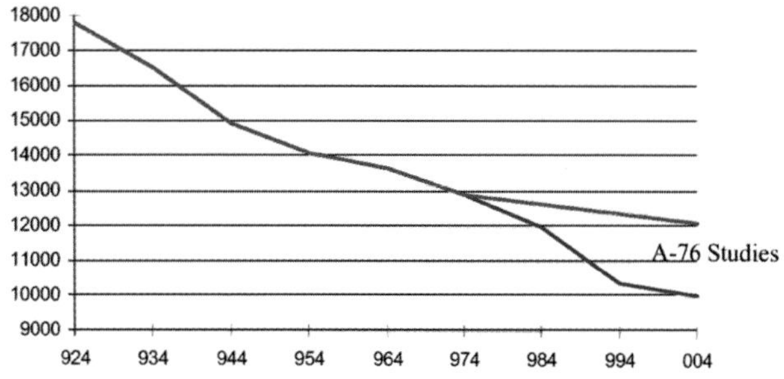

Yr/Qtr	1992/4	1993/4	1994/4	1995/4	1996/4	1997/4	1998/4	1999/4	2000/4
SAMU	9,034	8,273	6,763	6,082	5,726	5,116	4,945	4,703	4,453
88 ABW	4,068	3,600	3,349	3,296	3,257	3,199	3,160	3,156	3,168
74 MG	1,794	1,873	2,016	2,114	2,114	2,062	2,049	2,038	2,033
WL	2,879	2,770	2,780	2,598	2,560	2,551	2,497	2,486	2,473
TOTAL	**17,775**	**16,516**	**14,908**	**14,090**	**13,657**	**12,928**	**12,651**	**12,383**	**12,127**

Downsizing ASC's personnel from 1992 to 2000. Totals are broken down by the Systems Acquisition Mission Unit, the 88th Air Base Wing, the 74th Medical Group, and the Wright Laboratory .

Dr. Vincent J. Russo served as director of the Materials Laboratory (1988-1998) and executive director of the Aeronautical Systems Center (1998 -). Before becoming ASC's executive director, he played a key role in establishing the Air Force Research Laboratory (1997).

as a means of consolidating administrative staff at the direction of AFSC headquarters. However, as the process got under way, the opportunity was taken to reorganize several areas of laboratory work. Thus, in addition to the four laboratories under AFWAL, WRDC constituted a new Electronic Technology Laboratory (WRDC/EL) by taking the Electronic Technology Division from the Avionics Laboratory. At the same time, four new directorates were created, for Signature Technology (low-observables R&D), Cockpit Integration, Manufacturing Technology, and Technology Exploitation (technology planning).[40]

WRDC had operated for barely two years when it was caught up in another major reorganization and consolidation of the Air Force laboratories. Under this reorganization, directed by AFSC headquarters, the Air Force's 14 laboratories nationwide were consolidated into four "super labs." At Wright Field, WRDC was reorganized and redesignated the Wright Laboratory (WL). Under WL, WRDC's five laboratories were redesignated "directorates." In addition, the Electronic Technology Laboratory was renamed the Solid State Electronics Directorate (WL/EL). At the same time, WL acquired management of the Armament Laboratory, Eglin Air Force Base, Florida, upon the disestablishment of the Munitions Systems Division (MSD) and the realignment of its programs under ASD. Of the four WRDC directorates, only that for Manufacturing Technology survived the reorganization as an independent line organization. Elements of Cockpit Integration were realigned under Avionics and Flight Dynamics, and the Signature Technology Directorate's programs returned to Avionics. The Technology Exploitation Directorate became WL's Plans and Programs Directorate.[41]

The decade of the 1990s was a period of defense downsizing with declining budgets and manpower reductions-in-force. Wright Laboratory's directorates were reduced, in many areas, to "core" activities. One response to this downsizing was a consolidation of commands. In 1992, AFSC and AFLC merged to form the Air Force Materiel Command (AFMC). Under AFMC, ASD became the Aeronautical Systems Center (ASC) with expanded responsibilities that included operation of Wright-Patterson Air Force Base. As part of its own downsizing activity, ASC attempted to reduce the duplication of support activities base-wide. This reduction involved combining duplicative organizations and the outsourcing (A-76) of a number of functions, including those in support of WL, such as the technical library.

WL also consolidated many functions and activities internally. One result was the disestablishment in 1996 of the Solid State Electronics Directorate and the realignment of its elements once more under the Avionics Directorate.[42]

At the close of 1995, the Air Force released its latest science and technology forecasting report by the Air Force Scientific Advisory Board (SAB) called *New World Vistas*. Among the report's recommendations was the separation of the Air Force's laboratories from AFMC's product centers.[43] The SAB's recommendation reflected the belief among many in the R&D community that the laboratories were becoming too focused on the near-term needs of the system program offices instead of looking "over the horizon" in their research programs. This recommendation, as well as further laboratory consolidation, was studied by the Air Force's senior leaders and AFMC's Director of Science and Technology (AFMC/ST) during 1996. At the end of the year, the secretary of the Air Force and the Air Force chief of staff agreed to the formation of one Air Force Research Laboratory (AFRL).[44] As a result, the four Air Force super labs were detached from their respective product centers and realigned under AFRL (provisional) during the first half of 1997. The laboratories' technology directorates were reorganized and redesignated. Manufacturing technology and materials were once more combined into a single directorate, for Materials and Manufacturing. The Aero Propulsion and Power Directorate was assigned rocket motor work conducted at Edwards Air Force Base, California, and was renamed the Propulsion Directorate. The Avionics Directorate exchanged part of its technology portfolio with the Rome Laboratory (AFRL's Information Directorate) and was redesignated the Sensors Directorate. The Flight Dynamics Directorate ceded cockpit research to the Armstrong Medical Research Laboratory and was redesignated the Air Vehicles Directorate. Finally, the Armstrong Laboratory was redesignated the Human Effectiveness Directorate. A support organization for the six AFRL technical directorates at Wright Field was formed and designated the Wright Site. On the formation of the Wright Site in October 1997, the Wright Laboratory was formally deactivated. Finally, in 1998, AFRL's headquarters was transferred from AFMC headquarters in Area A of Wright-Patterson Air Force Base to Area B (Wright Field) and housed in Building 15 across the street from ASC headquarters.[45]

Model of jet being tested in the vertical wind tunnel at Wright Field

FLIGHT VEHICLES

The center of the Air Force's research and development of flight vehicles has been Dayton, Ohio, almost from the very beginning of military aviation. Indeed, it was Dayton businessmen Wilbur and Orville Wright who developed and sold the U.S. Army its first airplane, the first military airplane developed for any nation. Research and development of flight vehicles at Wright-Patterson originated in the Plane Design Office of the U.S. Army Signal Corps' Aviation Section in the years before World War I. The office's staff transferred to Dayton, Ohio, in the autumn of 1917 and took up quarters at McCook Field. In 1919, the design office and a number of small laboratories that had supported it, laboratories for structures testing, wind-tunnel testing, and propellers, were consolidated as the Airplane Section of the Engineering Division. In 1926, the Airplane Section became the Airplane Branch when the Engineering Division became part of the new Materiel Division at McCook. In 1932, the Materiel Division's Lighter-than-Air Branch merged with the Airplane Branch to form the Aircraft Branch. In 1939, the Aircraft Branch's propeller work was constituted an independent laboratory. At the same time, the Aircraft Branch was redesignated the Aircraft Laboratory.

The Aircraft Laboratory was one of the most important organizations at McCook and early Wright Field. In the mid-1920s, the Air Service discontinued the Laboratory's work of designing and testing its own in-house aircraft. However, the Laboratory continued to pursue in-house projects on aircraft components and other research problems of interest to the Army Air Corps and industry.

The main work of the Laboratory during the interwar years, however, was in preparing performance specifications and testing prototype and initial service aircraft prior to their procurement by the Air Corps. Testing consisted of both ground and flight testing (not always in that order). Ground testing concentrated on dynamic and static structural testing of the fuselage, wing, tail, canopy, and landing chassis. Wind tunnels also were employed to determine the aerodynamics of airfoils and the effects of drag induced by an airplane's contour.

In addition to testing experimental, prototype, and service aircraft, the Laboratory also sponsored a number of significant experimental projects during this period. Two of the most important were a 50-foot, all-metal wing, which demonstrated the possibilities and limitations of all-metal, cantilevered, stressed-skin construction; and the first successful, pressurized-cabin aircraft for high-altitude cruising. The first project, undertaken in the late 1920s, gave Wright Field engineers the knowledge and confidence needed to guide industry in developing all-metal monoplane aircraft. The second project, undertaken in the mid-1930s, resulted in the XC-35, which won for the Air Corps the Collier Trophy in 1937 and led, ultimately, to the development of the B-29 and all subsequent aircraft, both military and commercial, that employ pressurized cabins.

World War II dramatically increased the number of Laboratory employees and vastly expanded the Laboratory's experimental facilities. Prior to the war, the Wright Field complex included office space in buildings 11 and 16, the Aircraft

STRUCTURES TESTING

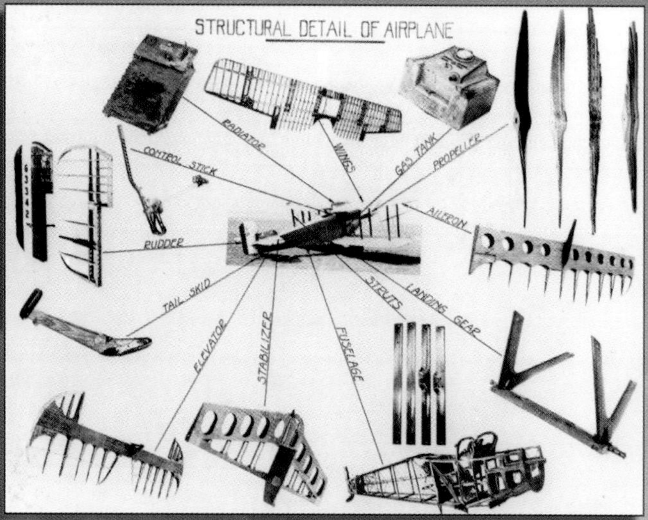

Pictured here are various airplane structures that were tested and evaluated by McCook Field engineers.

Building 65 under construction

Wing and fuselage of a C-74 undergoing static test inside Building 65

The testing of aircraft structural components has been a central feature of aeronautical research and development since the establishment of McCook Field. Beginning with sand loading tests in 1918, structures testing increased in scale and sophistication, as did the testing facilities. In the 1930s, Building 23 was the first facility at Wright Field erected specifically for structural tests. Building 65 was built during World War II to accommodate tests on large intercontinental bomber aircraft such as the B-36. Completed in 1946, Building 65 has remained the home of structures testing at Wright Field to the present day.

Final Assembly Building (Building 31) and (after 1934) the Static Test Building (Building 23). The war added an enormous, new, wind-tunnel complex that made the Laboratory one of the nation's leading tunnel centers for over two decades, as well as a number of other structures, including an office building for the Laboratory director and support staff.

Wartime projects included designing and testing aircraft modifications (including structural modifications to B-29s for carrying atomic bombs) and early research on the design of transonic and supersonic aircraft, including initial design work for what became the X-1, the world's first supersonic airplane.

The war years also saw the Laboratory expand beyond manned aircraft to research and development of unpiloted aircraft and missiles.

Much of this work continued into the 1950s. Since manpower was substantially reduced after the war, it was often difficult for the Laboratory to perform all the work that came its way. This was especially true since Laboratory engineers were often burdened with research, developmental engineering, and in-service engineering workloads in support of both experimental research and weapon system project office efforts.

During the 1950s, the Aircraft Laboratory assisted all of WADC's aircraft and missile project offices, offering technical and engineering expertise in the development of the Century Series fighters, the B-52 and B-58 bombers, the C-130 transport, and the KC-135 tanker. The Laboratory also assisted in helicopter work for the U.S. Army. In addition, the Laboratory conducted numerous experimental projects. These included support to the X-5 "swing-wing" aircraft, the X-6 "atomic powered" airplane, and all other X-plane programs that the Air Force conducted together with the Army, Navy, and the NACA. Perhaps the most spectacular of these experimental programs was the X-20 Dyna Soar at the end of the decade and plans for an aerospace plane.

In addition to man-rated aircraft, the Laboratory assisted in the development of air-to-air and air-to-ground guided missiles and, until the mid-1950s, ballistic missiles and rockets. Meanwhile, the Laboratory continued to conduct research into aircraft characteristics and to update and issue manuals to industry. Finally, it maintained the library of all military aircraft standards and specifications for the Air Force.

From World War II to the mid-1950s, the Aircraft Laboratory also directly sup-

First flight of the X-13 Vertijet. The X-13 demonstrated the feasibility of vertical takeoff and landing (VTOL) using jet thrust alone.

Aircraft Laboratory buildings, early 1950s

The X-18, developed during the 1950s by the Hiller Aircraft Corporation under contract with the Air Force and Navy, pioneered technologies for vertical/short takeoff and landing (V/STOL) using a tilt-wing concept. It foreshadowed development of the V-22 Osprey.

ported the development of intercontinental ballistic missiles. In 1954, the Air Force transferred this work to a new organization, the Western Development Division (WDD). However, for some time after the establishment of WDD, the Laboratory continued to lend its expertise to WDD and its engineering contract organization, the Ramo-Wooldridge Corporation.

The Laboratory also transferred other missions during the 1950s. Most prominent was aircraft flight controls, which was transferred from the Laboratory in 1955 and constituted the Flight Controls Laboratory, an independent laboratory under WADC.

When the laboratory and engineering functions were reorganized under the Wright Air Development Division (WADD) in 1959, the Aircraft Laboratory lost over half its engineering personnel to the new Systems Engineering Directorate. The remaining half was renamed the Flight Dynamics Laboratory and was initially associated with the Propulsion Laboratory under the Aero-Mechanics Division of the Directorate of Advanced Systems Technology.

After the formation of ASD in 1961, the Aero-Mechanics Division was dissolved and the Propulsion and Flight Dynamics laboratories were made co-equal with the new Avionics and Materials laboratories. In 1963, the Flight Dynamics Laboratory became the Air Force Flight Dynamics Laboratory and included portions of the Aero-Mechanics Division, including the Flight Control Laboratory. The Air Force Flight Dynamics Laboratory was thereupon transferred from ASD to the Research and Technology Division (RTD), to which it reported until 1967, when the latter was discontinued and the Laboratory was placed under the Director of Laboratories, Air Force Systems Command headquarters (AFSC/DL).

In technology development, the Flight Dynamics Laboratory, after its formation in 1962-1963, conducted applied research in areas of structures, flight controls (including flight-fire controls), aerodynamics and aeromechanics, fuel tanks, landing gear, aircraft canopies, and experimental diagnostic technologies. It also continued to troubleshoot problems of in-service flight vehicles.

In the area of *structures,* the Laboratory explored acoustic fatigue at elevated temperatures (1970-1974); advanced metallic structures (1975-1979); aeroelastic tailoring in forward swept wings (1975-1979); primary, adhesively bonded structures technology (1975-1979); cast aluminum structures technology (CAST) (1980-1984); superplastic formed/diffusion bonded (SPF/DB) titanium structures (1980-1984); and carbon-carbon, two-dimensional exhaust nozzles (1985-1990).[46] The Laboratory put considerable resources into researching applications of advanced composite materials—defined as composite materials capable of forming major aircraft structures.

The Laboratory began exploring the uses of advanced composites in the late 1960s and early 1970s. In the first half of the 1970s, it developed graphite-epoxy landing gear, a boron-epoxy rudder for the F-4, a graphite-epoxy wing and forward fuselage, and a graphite-epoxy speed brake

THE SADDEST WORDS: IT MIGHT HAVE BEEN

Celebrated in music (by Quincy Jones) and science fiction (*Mike Mars Flies the Dyna Soar*), the X-20 Dyna Soar was an idea ahead of its time. It was designed by Wright Field engineers to be the world's first space plane, a reusable vehicle capable of long-range reconnaissance and satellite observation. General Bernard Schriever, commander of the Air Force Systems Command, planned for the Dyna Soar to be the most ambitious Air Force project ever. After being boosted into space by a Titan rocket and performing its appointed mission, the Dyna Soar, unlike the National Aeronautics and Space Administration's (NASA's) space capsules, would have the ability to glide down to earth in a traditional landing under the control of a pilot. One of the pilots who participated in the X-20 program was Neil Armstrong, who flew approaches and abort maneuvers based on possible Dyna Soar scenarios.

Unfortunately for the U.S. Air Force, Secretary of Defense Robert S. McNamara clipped the Dyna Soar's wings before it ever got the chance to fly. In December 1963, McNamara cancelled the Air Force's X-20 program in favor of the civilian space program. Not all the hard work that had gone into the X-20 went to waste, however; NASA used the tremendous amount of research and development inspired by the Dyna Soar to build the space shuttle.

Sources: Quincy Jones, *Hip Hits* (Mercury 60799), online at http://www.eclipse.net/~fitzgera/rahsaan/hiphits.htm; "Neil A. Armstrong," NASA Biographical Data, Dryden Flight Research Center, online at http://www.dfrc.nasa.gov/PAO/PAIS/HTML/bd-dfrc-p001.html; Donald A. Wollheim, *Mike Mars Flies the Dyna Soar* (New York: 1962). Image of Dyna Soar created by and used with permission of Dan Roam, www.deepcold.com.

In the shadow of future flight: Dyna Soar engineers examine their craft.

William E. Lamar with model of Dyna Soar

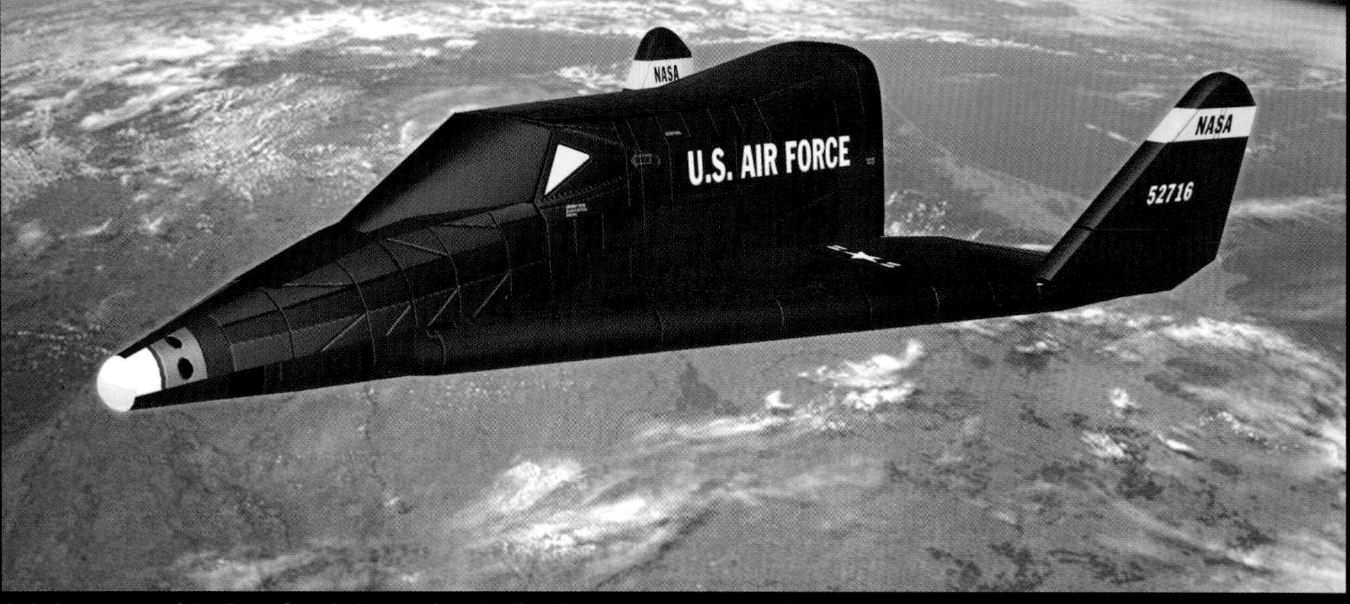

Artist's concept of the Dyna Soar in low earth orbit *(Dan Roam)*

WILLIAM E. LAMAR

William E. "Bill" Lamar

William E. "Bill" Lamar began his government service in 1941 as a second lieutenant in the Army Air Corps, serving as a project engineer in the Air Materiel Command at Wright Field. His subsequent five years of military experience included flight research, flight test engineering, and duty as a group engineering officer in China with the 14th Air Force, where he reached the rank of major.

After returning to Wright Field in 1946 as a civilian, he held key positions in experimental aircraft project engineering, advanced study and planning, new system development, systems management, systems engineering, and exploratory and advanced development. He served as assistant chief project engineer for the XB-36 and as chief project engineer for the XB-46 during the final development and flight test phase. He was closely associated with the conceptual and preliminary design, development, and later production of new bombardment aircraft such as the XB-52, B-58, RB-57D, KB-50J, B-52G/H and B-70. He pioneered Air Force hypersonic flight vehicle work in the early 1950s and was subsequently deeply involved in research and development activities for Air Force hypersonic vehicles and lifting-reentry spacecraft. From 1960 to 1964, he served as director of engineering for the X-20 Dyna Soar program, and the National Aeronautics and Space Administration (NASA) later used a substantial portion of the research and development that had gone into Dyna Soar to build the first space shuttle.

Lamar became deputy director of the Air Force Flight Dynamics Laboratory in April 1964, and applied system design and analysis techniques that led to such technological developments as fly-by-wire, wherein electrical impulses replaced hydraulic aircraft controls. In July 1975, Lamar assumed the position of deputy director, Technology Integration, Air Force Wright Aeronautical Laboratories, and led the formation of multi-laboratory program thrusts. Because Lamar was a staunch proponent of system simulation, the Large Amplitude Multimode Aerospace Research Simulator (LAMARS) was named in his honor. Bill Lamar retired from government service in January 1979. In retirement, he continued to serve as a consultant on numerous aerospace technology programs, including the Strategic Defense Initiative, the X-31, the X-29, the X-wing, other advanced flight vehicle and subsystems technologies, and military critical technologies.

After the Space Shuttle Enterprise successfully completed its approach and landing tests at Dryden Flight Research Center in 1977, officials from NASA presented Bill Lamar with a framed photograph of the Enterprise making its historic descent to earth. Director of Flight Operations George W. S. Abbey, autographed the photograph with the inscription: "To Bill Lamar, whose efforts made all this happen…," acknowledging Lamar's invaluable contribution to the knowledge base that was used to create the first space shuttle.

Source: William E. Lamar Collection, ASC History Office Archive.

Secretary of Defense Donald Rumsfeld visited the new LAMARS facility in the 1970s.

for the F-15. The Laboratory also made use of advanced composites in fabricating aircraft transparencies having greater resistance to bird impact.[47]

In the second half of the 1970s, the Laboratory developed advanced composite structures for the B-1; design methods for aeroelastic tailoring of advanced composites and application to forward swept wings (making possible the X-29); and a precision-mounting, platform structure for space satellites.[48] In the early 1980s, the Laboratory explored interactive, composite, joint design; the design of a composite wing box for fighters; thermoplastic composites; the effect of service environment on advanced structures; and the repair of composite structures. During the same period, the Laboratory developed a composite deployment module for the MX ballistic missile; composite substructure for the Advanced Ballistic Reentry Vehicle (ABRV); an equipment support module of advanced composites for the Global Positioning Satellite (GPS); and a composite outer wing panel for the A-7D aircraft.[49]

In the mid to late 1980s, the Laboratory explored development and application of metal-matrix composite structures and the use of plastic resins in fabricating frameless aircraft transparencies. The Laboratory also gave increased attention to detection and repair of service defects in composite structures. It conducted programs in damage tolerance of composites, the high-energy impact physics of composites, and delamination due to high-speed airflow over composite structures.[50] Among the applications of composite structures developed during this period were an F-111 horizontal stabilizer's leading edge and low-observable, engine front frames for the B-2 "stealth" bomber.[51]

In the 1990s, the Laboratory explored a number of new composites and their applications. These included titanium-matrix composites for landing gear and ceramic composites for thrust-vectoring nozzles for jet engines. The Laboratory also explored sonic fatigue design criteria and life prediction of advanced, carbon-carbon composites for hypersonic vehicle structures and next-generation launch vehicles.[52] The Laboratory also began developing materials property data, manufacturing processes, and the design of thermoplastic composite structures for potential use on the F-22.[53]

Finally, the Laboratory continued to address the issue of making composite structures more affordable. Efforts were undertaken in cooperation with Wright Field's manufacturing technology experts.

BIRD-STRIKE-RESISTANT CANOPIES

Between the years 1912 and 2000, more than 300 people died in bird collisions with aircraft. In 2000 alone, the Air Force reported the occurrence of more than 3,000 bird strikes that caused significant damage to its aircraft. The Air Force took a new look at the problem during the Vietnam War when the increase in low-level/high-speed missions led to an increase in the number of bird-strike instances. Engineers at Aeronautical Systems Division (ASD), Ohio, and at Arnold Engineering Development Center (AEDC), Tennessee, constructed the "Chicken Gun," which they used to shoot the carcasses of dead chickens at the windshields and canopies of Air Force aircraft. ASD maintained one such gun for research purposes, while another was constructed for systems work at AEDC. The guns were used to test windshields, canopies, and other high-potential impact areas of the A-7, A-10, F-15, F-16, T-37, B-1, C-130, and the new T-6A aircraft. In 1977, the ASD gun was given to the University of Dayton Research Institute (UDRI), Dayton, Ohio, for continuance of the tests. UDRI abandoned chicken carcasses in favor of a gelatin cylinder that simulated the weight and size of the birds.

Throughout the 1980s and early 1990s, the Vehicle Subsystems Division (VSD) of the Flight Dynamics Laboratory continued research related to bird strikes. Building upon the design knowledge from thorough testing (including use of the "chicken gun") of the canopies and windshields of the F-111 aircraft in the 1970s, the VSD developed safer bird-strike-resistant windshields used on the B-1B, F-4, F-15, and F-16. The windshields of the B-1B's were designed to withstand the impact of a four-pound bird at aircraft flight speeds up to 560 knots.

The B-2, C-17, and F-22 also benefited from the VSD's efforts with computer-aided designs for bird-strike-resistant windshields. Throughout the 1980s, division engineers led an international team in the development of the Materially and Geometrically Nonlinear Analysis (MAGNA) computer program. The program could assess the strength and bird-strike-resistant capabilities of prospective windshields before fabrication, thereby saving the Air Force millions of dollars and years of testing and developing each new windshield.

Sources: Frank Bokulich, "Birdstrikes Remain a Concern For Pilots," *Aerospace Engineering Online*, March 2000, at http://www.sae.org/aeromag/techupdate_3-00/05.htm; Flight Dynamics Directorate, Wright Laboratory, *Success Stories, October 1990 – September 1992* (Wright-Patterson Air Force Base, n.d.), p 25; Marcelle Size Knaack, *Post-World War II Fighters, 1945-1973* (Washington, D.C., 1986), p 240; Karaline Jackson, "Planes Get Safer With Chicken Gun," *The Flyer News* (University of Dayton), November 9, 1999, at http://www.ccsf.edu/Events_Pubs/Guardsman/f991108/uwire06.shtml.

An aircraft that benefited from the Flight Dynamics Laboratory's research on bird-strike-resistant windshields was the A-7 attack aircraft. The new windshield (left) was designed to resist bird strikes at up to 500 knots, as compared to 200 knots for the earlier windshield.

Goals included a 50 percent reduction in the acquisition cost of fabricated and assembled composite structures and a 25 percent reduction in maintenance cost.[54]

In the area of *aerodynamics and aeromechanics*, the Laboratory worked with the Aero Propulsion Laboratory in the latter's Advanced Propulsion Subsystems Integration (APSI) program for optimizing airframe-engine inlet interface.

The Laboratory continued its longstanding research of flutter phenomena, exploring subsonic and transonic flutter prediction (1965-1969); flutter safety evaluation for aircraft with external stores (1970-1974); and active-flutter-suppression, wind-tunnel-testing technology (1975-1979).[55]

The Laboratory explored the advantages of a smooth variable wing camber in the Advanced Fighter Technology Integration (AFTI)/F-111 Mission Adaptive Wing program (1975-1979 and 1985-1990). It also explored high-angle-of-attack maneuvers using an aircraft with a forward swept wing in the X-29 program (1985-1990).[56]

The Laboratory's research in *cockpits* included developing better cockpit display technology, including multimode matrix displays (1975-1979); energy management display evaluation (1975-1979); and flat-dimensioned, electronic display instruments (1980-1984). The Laboratory also conducted considerable research into developing better *aircraft canopies* and transparencies, especially those capable of surviving bird strikes. This included research to improve the windshields of the F-4 (1980-1984) and F-111 (1985-1990) aircraft, among others.[57]

The Laboratory's *landing gear* research included developing replaceable tread tires (1965-1969), including those for the C-130 (1975-1979). The Laboratory conducted research to develop graphite-epoxy landing gear (1970-1974) and conducted adaptive-landing-gear tests (1975-1979). From 1975 to 1979 the Laboratory also developed high-pressure landing gear struts and successfully demonstrated an electric brake (1985-1990).[58]

An area of revolutionary advance by the Laboratory was in *flight controls*. In this area, perhaps the greatest single development was that of fly-by-wire.

The Laboratory's interest in fly-by-wire began in the mid-1950s when Laboratory engineers saw it as a viable alternative to complex, mechanical flight control systems. Over the next decade and a half, the Laboratory pursued work in fly-by-wire by a combination of contracted and in-house efforts. The fly-by-wire concept was first

THE GRUMMAN X-29A

Joining the ranks of the distinguished group of "X" planes, the Grumman-built X-29A was one of the more unusual test aircraft that underwent flight testing between 1982 and 1992. The aircraft was designed for the exploration of state-of-the-art technologies in flight controls, airframe structure, and aerodynamics. The Grumman Corporation built two X-29A's for a jointly funded project for the Defense Advanced Research Projects Agency (DARPA) and the National Aeronautics and Space Administration (NASA). The Flight Dynamics Laboratory at Wright-Patterson Air Force Base managed the program for DARPA.

To reduce costs, many of the X-29A parts were off-the-shelf components, such as an F-5A forward fuselage and nose gear and an F-16 main landing gear. The most innovative component was the forward swept wings covered with advanced composite materials to counteract bending forces experienced at high speeds.

The trailing edges of the wings possessed aileron-like devices that worked independently of one another to alter wing shape, to increase maneuverability, and to reduce the drag characteristics of the X-29A's flight envelope. The front-mounted canards, constructed of conventional aluminum alloy, made the aircraft aerodynamically unstable. This in turn made the X-29A a formidable foe in any dogfight due to its amazing agility. The final advanced technology incorporated on the X-29A was the experimental fly-by-wire flight control system that allowed the pilot to make minor adjustments to flight control surfaces to keep the aircraft stable and provide optimum flight characteristics.

These advancements in technology allowed the X-29 to propel itself into history by being the first forward-swept-wing aircraft to travel at the speed of sound. The X-29A program provided invaluable data on advanced technology that shaped the way aircraft systems evolved.

Sources: John W.R. Taylor, ed., *Jane's All the World's Aircraft, 1983-1984* (New York, 1984), p 394; Fact Sheet, Grumman Corporation, X-29 Advanced Technology Demonstrator, n.d.

X-29 in flight showing forward swept wings and canards

The Flight Dynamics Laboratory and the Ames Dryden Flight Research Facility (of NASA) developed the mission adaptive wing (MAW) to study advanced fighter technologies. The new wing made its first flight on the AFTI/F-111 aircraft in October 1985 at Edwards Air Force Base. Unlike conventional wings with hinged flaps and spoilers, the MAW had a smooth surface that could change shape in flight. Variable-camber mechanisms and digital flight-control computers regulated the contour of the wing providing the aircraft with extended range, improved fuel economy, increased maneuverability, and decreased structural stress.

This 1968 photograph shows the team members of the B-47E fly-by-wire program in front of their aircraft. Team members are (left to right): Dale Bazil, Gavin Jenney, William Talley, Harry Shreadley, Charles Black, Vern Schmidt, and Lieutenant Jim Ramage. (Gavin Jenney)

F-4D aircraft on which the Flight Dynamics Laboratory successfully demonstrated fly-by-wire technology in the 1970s. The technology was first transitioned to the YF-16 and later to production F-16s. By allowing active control of unstable vehicles, the technology contributed to the successful development of the F-117, B-2, and C-17 aircraft.

successfully demonstrated in 1962. In 1967, the Laboratory undertook a flight test program using the B-47 as test bed. This was followed in the early 1970s with testing a complete fly-by-wire system on an F-4E, which successfully demonstrated improved combat survivability and performance. Fly-by-wire technology was transitioned to the YF-16 Lightweight Fighter, which became the Air Force's first airplane to use, as its primary flight control system, a quad-redundant, analog, fly-by-wire system without mechanical backup. The technology then was transitioned to production F-16s in the 1970s.[59]

At the same time it was developing analog fly-by-wire controls, the Laboratory also was exploring the potential of fly-by-wire systems using digital computation and signal transmission. Digital technology allowed for total integration of control systems with avionics, propulsion, fire control, navigation, and weapon-delivery subsystems. The most significant Laboratory program in the 1970s was the Digital Tactical Aircraft Control (DIGITAC), which demonstrated the flexibility of digital control with a task-oriented, selectable, multimode control system, which incorporated multimode control laws specifically tailored for weapons delivery and fail-operate capability using dual-control system configuration. It was followed in the 1980s with the AFTI/F-16 program, which demonstrated multimode control laws, triplex fault tolerant redundancy management, integration with fire control and sensor systems, and an advanced display avionics suite. Other programs that exploited digital flight control concepts included the AFTI/F-111 Mission Adaptive Wing, the X-29, and the Short Takeoff and Landing (STOL)/F-15 Maneuver Technology Demonstrator (MTD). Operational aircraft, besides the F-16, benefiting from fly-by-wire technologies included the F-15, F-22, F-117, B-2, and C-17.[60]

Overlapping the development of fly-by-wire were the Laboratory's efforts in developing fly-by-light (FBL) controls. These efforts began in the mid-1970s when a prototype fly-by-wire control system was modified to incorporate fiber optics in one of four redundant channels. The DIGITAC II implemented a digital flight control system employing dual-channel multiplex data buses with the capability of electrical or optical operation. More than a thousand flight tests were performed between 1982 and 1991 using fiber-optic communications. During the 1990s, efforts were under way to develop a complete systems-level approach and design for full exploitation of fly-by-light technology on military and commercial aircraft.[61]

Finally, the Laboratory also was developing multi-ship control technology in anticipation of exploiting the full potential of unmanned (or uninhabited) aerial vehicles (UAVs) flying alone, in formation, or with manned vehicles.[62]

Another Laboratory program that exploited fly-by-wire technology was the Variable Stability In-Flight Simulator Test Aircraft (VISTA). In-flight simulator aircraft were modified with alternate control systems that could be programmed to cause the host aircraft to fly like the aircraft to be simulated. They were essential tools in the research and development process, providing the capability to realistically and safely evaluate new aircraft flying qualities and flight systems before their first flight and before the decision to go into production. VISTA was developed in the late 1980s/early 1990s to replace the NT-33A that had performed the function of an in-flight simulator since the late 1950s.[63]

In addition to the Laboratory's successful advocacy and development of fly-by-wire technology, it conducted research into load alleviation, mode stabilization, and direct-lift control (1965-1969). It developed a functionally integrated throttle-control system (1970-1974) and conducted research into control-configured-vehicle (CCV) ride improvement (1970-1974). The Laboratory developed multi-function inertial reference assembly (MIRA) (1975-1979) and developed an ADA computer language-programmed reconfiguration strategy (1985-1990).[64]

Finally, the Laboratory developed technologies and facilities for conducting *diagnostic experimentation*. This included the Reentry Nose Tip (RENT) Test Facility (1965-1969); the Total In-Flight Simulator (1970-1974); and the Combined Environmental Reliability Test Facility (1975-1979).[65]

The Laboratory also pioneered development and application of one of the most revolutionary, experimental diagnostic tools since the invention of the wind tunnel in the nineteenth century: computational fluid dynamics (CFD). CFD proved to be a powerful instrument in the designing and troubleshooting of aerial vehicles, supplementing calculations based on wind-tunnel tests.

CFD techniques were pioneered in the 1960s and 1970s to assist the Laboratory in the development of several aerospace demonstration craft, including the X-24.

THE AFTI/F-16

The Advanced Fighter Technology Integration (AFTI)/F-16 was one of the most successful flight demonstrator aircraft programs ever undertaken by the Air Force. Nearly every new or derivative aircraft since the 1970s, from later models of the F-15 to the Joint Strike Fighter, benefited from technologies first tested and proven on the AFTI/F-16. Officially begun in 1978, the aircraft was one of the original Lockheed F-16A Fighting Falcons that was modified for studying the feasibility of advanced technologies. The research program was a joint venture between the Air Force and the National Aeronautics and Space Administration, with most flight tests conducted at Edwards Air Force Base, California.

The first phase of the program was a test of the Fly-By-Wire Flight Control System that was so successful it was incorporated into the entire F-16 fleet, as well as the F-22 and F-117 fighters, the B-2 bomber, and the C-17 transport. Between 1980 and 2000, the AFTI/F-16 also was used for the evaluation of automated maneuvering; automated, ground-collision-avoidance systems; voice-activated controls; helmet-mounted, target-designation sights; sensors; and close air support and battlefield-air-interdiction systems. In 1987, the AFTI/F-16 program received the Theodore von Karman Award for the most outstanding achievement in science and engineering in recognition of its work with the Automated Maneuvering Attack System for the close air support mission.

One of the aircraft's most audacious tests was for the Automatic Ground Collision Avoidance System (Auto-GCAS), during which the pilot flew the aircraft directly at the ground while trusting the automatic system to conduct an escape maneuver via autopilot and bring the aircraft back to level flight. The tests indicated that the GCAS system activated when minimum terrain clearance was between 50 and 150 feet. In the late 1990s, a ground-proximity warning system derived from the AFTI's GCAS was installed in commercial airliners throughout the world.

Sources: History of Aeronautical Systems Division, January–December 1988, pp 338-342; History of Aeronautical Systems Division, January–December 1989, pp 302-304; National Aeronautics and Space Administration, "F-16 Movie Gallery," viewed online February 5, 2002, at http://www.dfrc.nasa.gov.

AFTI/F-16, first flight test of automated maneuvering attack system, July 31, 1984

The F-15 STOL/MTD program began in 1983 as a study of improved short takeoff and landing and maneuver technology capabilities for future fighter aircraft. Working toward the goal of a supersonic fighter capable of taking off and landing in 1,500 feet or less in all weather conditions, engineers developed a two-dimensional, thrust-vectoring and reversing exhaust nozzle. The first test flight on May 10, 1989, indicated that the nozzles reduced takeoff and landing roll distances by 35 and 65 percent, respectively.

The Air Force used the C-45, B-26, T-33A, and X-22A as in-flight simulators. Between 1957 and the early 1990s, the Air Force operated the NT-33A simulator (pictured here), making it the oldest flying aircraft in the Air Force inventory. It simulated many fighter aircraft including the A-9, A-10, YF-17, F-18, the JAS Grippen (Sweden), and the Lavi (Israel). In addition, it was used to test the flying qualities of the X-15, X-24, and AFTI/F-16. The NT-33A averaged over 350 flight hours per year.

In 1982, the Air Force designed and built a new in-flight simulator because of the increasing complexity of high-performance military aircraft. VISTA, a modified F-16D, was designed to simulate not only Air Force developmental aircraft, but also those of the Navy and NASA. Use of the F-16 VISTA began in the 1990s.

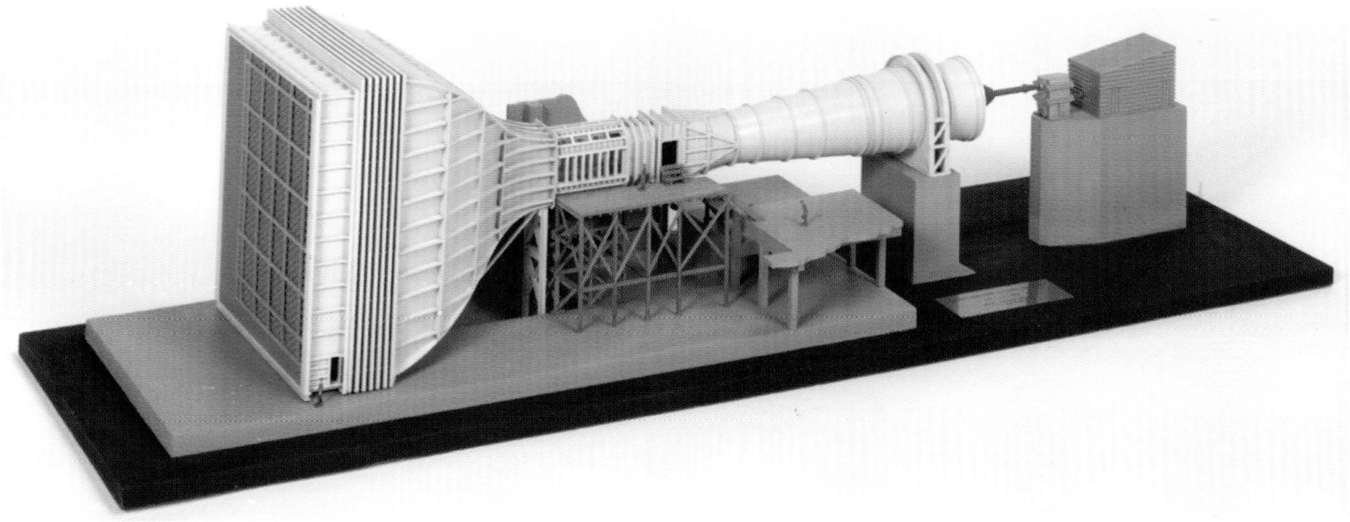

Model of the Philip P. Antonitos Subsonic Aerodynamic Research Laboratory (SARL). The SARL, which became operational in 1989, was designed to test high-angle-of-attack and vertical/short takeoff and landing (V/STOL) technologies and conduct studies in super-maneuverability, improvements in laser velocimetry, and code evaluation for computational fluid dynamics.

THE X-24B RESEARCH AIRCRAFT

In the 1960s and 1970s, a joint Air Force and National Aeronautics and Space Administration program studied the feasibility of an advanced lifting-body aircraft to make a high-speed descent and unpowered precision landing on a conventional runway. The proposed application for this concept was the reentry of space vehicles into the earth's atmosphere. The aircraft used for these tests was the Martin Marietta X-24. The X-24A made its first flight in March 1970. The second aircraft in the series was the X-24B—the X-24A rebuilt with a more stable external configuration that provided twice as much lift. The Flight Dynamics Laboratory designed this new configuration.

Beginning in August 1973, the X-24B was launched from a B-52 for a number of test flights and landings at Edwards Air Force Base, California. On August 15, 1975, the X-24B became the first lifting-body aircraft to make a landing on a conventional runway. Prior to this time, lifting-body aircraft had landed only on the dry lakebed at Edwards. The X-24B, along with the X-24A, validated the precision approach and landing techniques later employed by the space shuttle. The X-24B was the last rocket-powered research aircraft flown, with its 36th and final flight conducted on November 26, 1975. It was shipped to the United States Air Force Museum the following year.

Source: Richard P. Hallion and John L. Vitelli, "The Piloted Lifting Body Demonstrators: Supersonic Predecessors to Hypersonic Lifting Reentry," in *The Hypersonic Revolution: Eight Case Studies in the History of Hypersonic Technology*, Vol. II, ed. Richard P. Hallion (Wright-Patterson Air Force Base, 1987), pp 923, 928-930.

X-24A

X-24B

Laboratory scientists refined applications of Euler, Navier-Stokes, and Parabolized Navier-Stokes equations. Using Navier-Stokes equations, for instance, the Laboratory computed, for the first time ever, the flow field around a complete, three-dimensional, aerospace-craft configuration, the X-24C-10D hypersonic reentry vehicle. Likewise, the Laboratory provided experimental and analytical technology to the Ballistic Missile Office for the design and evaluation of maneuvering reentry vehicles and decoys. The Laboratory used CFD techniques to compute spike-tipped body buzz of reentry nosetips; axisymmetric nozzles in supersonic external stream; computation of airfoil stall characteristics; numerical simulation of autorotation; and the typology of unsteady wing-body juncture flows, among other applications. CFD was used to solve flow over the X-29's forward swept wing and the full-scale F-22, among many other applications.[66]

The applied research function and the overall operations of the Laboratory have endured since the reorganizations of 1959-1963. The organization of the Laboratory, however, has changed several times. In 1967, the Research and Technology Division was abolished, and the Laboratory was realigned under the Director of Laboratories at Air Force Systems Command headquarters (AFSC/DL).[67] In 1975, the Flight Dynamics Laboratory was federated with three other Wright Field laboratories under the Air Force Wright Aeronautical Laboratories (AFWAL).[68] When AFWAL became part of the Aeronautical Systems Division in 1982, it was the first time in 20 years that flight vehicle applied research was part of the product division.[69]

With the formation of the Wright Research and Development Center in 1988, the Flight Dynamics Laboratory lost its cockpit work to an Integrated Cockpit Directorate.[70] When Wright Laboratory was established in 1990, Flight Dynamics became a directorate and regained its cockpit work.[71] On the formation of the Air Force Research Laboratory (AFRL) in 1997, the Flight Dynamics Directorate was reorganized and renamed the Air Vehicles Directorate (AFRL/VA). At this time, cockpit work transferred to AFRL's Human Effectiveness Directorate (AFRL/HE), formerly the Armstrong Aeromedical Research Laboratory (AMRL), and air base technology work transferred to AFRL's Materials and Manufacturing Technology Directorate.[72]

One of the main jobs of the Power Plant Section (later Branch) at McCook and Wright fields from World War I through World War II was the test and evaluation of airplane engines. This was the pre-jet age and all engines were reciprocating engines designed to power propeller-driven airplanes. Engines were tested for torque and shaft power in Wright Field's torque stands and dynamometer laboratory, respectively. (Top) W-1-A liquid-cooled engine; (right) Wright Cyclone radial engine

PROPULSION AND POWER

Of the three major revolutions of the post-World War II period, the revolution in propulsion came first and was most decisive. Central to this revolution were the gas turbine (jet) engine and rockets. Both the jet engine and rocket motor were introduced to Wright Field during the war: the jet engine from Britain and the rocket motor from Germany.

Within a decade of its introduction, the jet engine had virtually supplanted the reciprocating engine as the principal power plant of advanced Air Force aircraft, including helicopters, and even propeller-driven, transport aircraft, which employed the so-called turboprop.

Much of the advance in jet-engine technology was due to the advocacy of Wright Field's engineering staff, which quickly apprehended the revolutionary implications of the jet engine and retooled accordingly. The principal organization at Wright Field that orchestrated the development of both jet engines and, until the late 1950s, rocket motors was Wright Field's Power Plant Laboratory. The Power Plant Laboratory was one of the most remarkable and dynamic organizations at Wright Field.

The Laboratory originated in the Engine Design Office of the Aviation Section, Washington, D.C., prior to World War I. Its staff assisted in the design of the Liberty engine for World War I even before transferring operations to McCook Field late in 1917.

The move to McCook substantially augmented the Engine Design Office's modest staff of engineers with other engine experts from around the nation and even several from Europe, such as British fuels and lubricants expert Samuel D. Heron. McCook also, for the first time, provided this staff with experimental facilities encouraging them to test not only designs developed by industry but to design, build, and test engines of their own invention.

In 1919, this group was formally constituted the Power Plant Section of the Engineering Division, McCook Field. In 1926, the section was renamed the Power Plant Branch of the Materiel Division (which had succeeded the Engineering Division) and, in 1939, was once again renamed, this time the Power Plant Laboratory, the designation that it carried for the next 20 years.

During the 1920s and 1930s, the Laboratory conducted rigorous tests of industry's reciprocating engines in its dynamometer laboratory and torque stands, noting defects and making recommendations to industry for improvements. The Laboratory contracted with industry for the development of such engine improvements as the turbosupercharger and developed standards and specifications for aviation fuels and lubricants in-house.

(The Laboratory was not responsible, however, for the entire propulsion system. The development of propellers was initially the responsibility of the Aircraft Laboratory until, in 1939, the group that conducted this work was constituted as the Propeller Laboratory. Ironically, only in 1958, when propeller research had taken a back seat to jet propulsion, was the Propeller Laboratory disestablished and its personnel and facilities transferred to the Power Plant Laboratory—see below.)

The Laboratory grew substantially during World War II. An entire complex (Building 18) was constructed around the old dynamometer laboratory, allowing the Laboratory's administrative staff to depart the old Wright Field laboratory building (Building 16). (Construction of the Building 18 complex continued through the 1950s, and modifications for different testing requirements continued into the twenty-first century.)

Throughout World War II, the principal activity of the Power Plant Laboratory was solving performance problems with reciprocating engines subject to all climes and combat conditions around the world, improving engines in development and production, and issuing performance specifications for new engines. However, the transferal of the first gas turbine engine to Wright Field from Great Britain in 1941 made clear to all that the days of the reciprocating engine were numbered.

In the 1940s and 1950s, the Power Plant Laboratory supported the development of all Air Force gas turbine engines by working closely with industry. Laboratory support included research into new engine technologies and engineering development and even in-service engineering. Throughout the 1950s, the Laboratory's Rotating Engine Branch (that developed turbine engines as opposed to the Nonrotating Engine Branch that developed rockets and ramjets) was organized by industry sup-

Among the earliest facilities set up at McCook were propeller test rigs for "whirling tests" that evaluated propeller durability. A number of larger, improved rigs were built at Wright Field, among them the largest and most powerful test rig in the world. In 1939, an independent Propeller Laboratory was established in the Materiel Division indicating the importance the Air Corps placed on propeller development. Propeller research did not become a part of the Power Plant Laboratory until 1958. (Above) Propeller workshop at McCook Field; (below) eight-blade dual propeller on test rig at Wright Field

Shown here is the nerve center of Air Force research and development for aircraft propulsion systems. These systems include gas turbine engines, ramjets, scramjets, propellers, helicopter rotors, and onboard electrical power.

Display of Power Plant Laboratory hardware at the end of World War II. In the center is a model of Hiero of Alexandria's steam engine. The model stood for many years in the vestibule of the Laboratory's headquarters in Building 18, Wright Field.

pliers: e.g., General Electric, Pratt & Whitney, and Allison.

Concurrent with developmental work (or, more properly, as an offshoot of it), the Laboratory also chalked up a number of impressive technical advances in state-of-the-art (in some cases "over-the-horizon") propulsion technology. These included:

- Development of the first practical, variable-area, convergent-divergent nozzle for turbine engines (with General Electric [GE], 1952)

- Testing the first air-cooled turbine engine, GE's J47 (1953)

- Qualifying the first dual-spool turbine engine, Pratt & Whitney's (P&W's) J57 (1953)

- Qualifying the first variable-geometry engine, GE's J79 (1954)

- Development of the first nuclear-powered turbine engine, GE's HTRE-1 (1956)

- Qualifying the first U.S. turbofan engine, P&W's TF33 (1959)

- Conducting in-house the first test of a liquid air cycle engine (1960)[73]

In addition to engine design and hardware, the Laboratory also developed specifications for all jet engine fuels and lubricants for the Air Force and U.S. Navy. Fuels developed during the decade included JP-4 (1950), which became the standard jet-engine fuel for the Air Force during the Cold War, and JP-5 for the Navy (1952).[74]

In addition, the Laboratory developed specifications for aircraft flying special missions. These included JP-TS fuel for the U-2/TR-1 aircraft (1956); JP-6 for the XB-70 supersonic (Mach 3) bomber; JP-7 for the SR-71 (1959); and RJ-1, the first fuel specification for ramjet engine applications (1960).[75]

Among the lubricant specifications developed in-house by the Laboratory were those for the first synthetic oil used in jet engines, MIL-L-7808 (1951) and MIL-L-9236 for the XB-70 (1956). The Laboratory also developed MIL-H-27601 hydraulic fluid for the SR-71 (1959).[76]

During the 1950s, the Laboratory also strongly advocated industry development of turbofan engines, which promised greater fuel efficiency over turbojets. Ultimately, the Laboratory's championing of turbofan technology led to development of the high-bypass turbofan engine by the mid-1960s. The high-bypass turbofan, in turn, made possible development of wide-body military airlifters, such as the C-5 (and later C-17), as well as, on the commercial side, the so-called "jumbo-jet," which nearly doubled cargo and passenger capacity over earlier airlift aircraft and airliners.[77]

When the Power Plant Laboratory became part of the Wright Air Development Center (WADC) during the latter's establishment in 1950-1951, its mission and *modus operandi* were very little altered from earlier decades. However, the 1950s were to usher in a number of significant organizational, mission, and func-

Gyroscopic Test Laboratory

AMERICA ENTERS THE JET AGE

In 1922, engineers at McCook Field were interested in pursuing the development of jet propulsion for aircraft, but were discouraged by a report published by the National Advisory Committee for Aeronautics which stated that jet-powered planes would never be able to fly as fast as planes with propellers. A few years after the personnel and facilities at McCook Field were moved to Wright Field, however, the idea was picked up again and Wright Field engineers completed their own study and wrote a report in 1936 entitled "The Gas Turbine as a Prime Mover for Aircraft." The following year General Electric sent Wright Field a paper called "Gas Turbine Power Plants for Aeronautical Applications," which explored the possibility of a turboprop engine. Less than five years later Wright Field and General Electric were working together to create the first American-built turbojet engine.

Major Donald J. Keirn of Wright Field was sent on a secret mission to England in October 1941 to bring back to the United States a W.1.X gas turbine engine designed by British jet engine inventor Frank Whittle. The engine was a copy of the one that had powered the Gloster E.28/39 that General Henry "Hap" Arnold had seen on a visit to England in April 1941, a disconcerting trip that convinced him the United States had to take immediate action or it would get left behind in this next stage of aviation. Arnold entrusted a handful of people—including Wright Field officers Brigadier General Oliver P. Echols, Lieutenant Colonel Benjamin W. Chidlaw, Major Ralph Swofford, and Major Keirn—with the mission of acquiring the technology needed to build the United States' first jet engine. Major Keirn took the first crucial step toward the creation of an American jet engine by transporting the W.1.X engine (and Whittle's drawings for a newer and better engine, the W.2.B) to the United States for American scientists to use as a guide while building their own engine. A new office at Wright Field was created to receive and analyze the technical data that General Electric engineers gleaned as they examined the engine and the drawings. One year later, on October 2, 1942, the Bell XP-59A took off from Muroc, California (later Edwards Air Force Base), under the power of two GE Type I-A turbojet engines. The United States had officially entered the jet age.

During World War II, several kinds of jet aircraft were flight tested at Wright Field, and it was not unusual to see Orville Wright hanging around the flight test hangar, eager to witness the birth of this new phase of flight. Wright Field flight test engineer Nathan R. Rosengarten received the Army Commendation Medal and Legion of Merit award for the pioneering jet propulsion work he did with the Bell XP-59, the Lockheed XP-80, the Republic XP-84, and the British Meteor. Chuck Yeager flew his first jet while stationed at Wright Field, and Ann Baumgartner became the first woman to fly a turbojet-powered plane while she was stationed at Wright Field. After World War II, Dr. Hans von Ohain, the German inventor of the first jet engine to successfully propel a plane, came to Wright Field as part of Project Paperclip and eventually became the chief scientist of the Aerospace Research Laboratories and of the Air Force Aero Propulsion Laboratory. In 1965, Wright-Patterson Air Force Base civilian engineer Cliff Simpson, an American jet engine pioneer, revolutionized the turbojet engine by developing the high-bypass turbofan engine, which gave subsonic jet planes greater thrust and fuel efficiency and made possible the development of heavy-lift aircraft such as the C-5. The Propulsion Directorate at Wright-Patterson continues to make significant contributions to jet engine technology with its development of more efficient compressors, engine oil, coolants, and jet fuel.

Sources: Ann B. Carl, *A Wasp Among Eagles: A Woman Military Test Pilot in World War II* (Washington, 1999); Margaret Conner, *Hans von Ohain: Elegance in Flight* (Reston, Virginia, 2001); Douglas J. Ingells, *They Tamed the Sky: The Triumph of American Aviation* (New York, 1947); James St. Peter, *The History of Aircraft Gas Turbine Engine Development in the United States . . . A Tradition of Excellence* (Atlanta, 1999); James O. Young, "Riding England's Coattails: The Army Air Forces and the Turbojet Revolution" in *Technology and the Air Force: A Retrospective Assessment,* ed. Jacob Neufeld, George M. Watson, Jr., and David Chenoweth (Washington, D.C., 1997); David M. Carpenter, *Flame Powered: The Bell XP-59A Airacomet and the General Electric I-A Engine* (New York, 1992); James St. Peter, ed., *The Memoirs of Ernest C. Simpson, Aero Propulsion Pioneer* (Wright-Patterson Air Force Base, 1987).

Orville Wright yearned to fly jets but, because he was in his seventies when the jet age dawned, he thought he was too old.

Major Donald J. Keirn (shown here when a brigadier general) was the Wright Field project officer in charge of the development of an American-made jet engine. For his contributions, he received the Legion of Merit, the Most Excellent Order of the British Empire, and the Thurman H. Bane Award.

Nathan R. Rosengarten received the Army Commendation Medal for the engineering work he performed that made possible the coast-to-coast speed record of the P-80 jet aircraft.

Although most Air Force and Department of Defense officials considered the jet engine a "done deal," Cliff Simpson showed them that major advancements were still possible by developing the high-bypass turbofan engine.

ADVANCED TURBINE ENGINE GAS GENERATOR PROGRAM

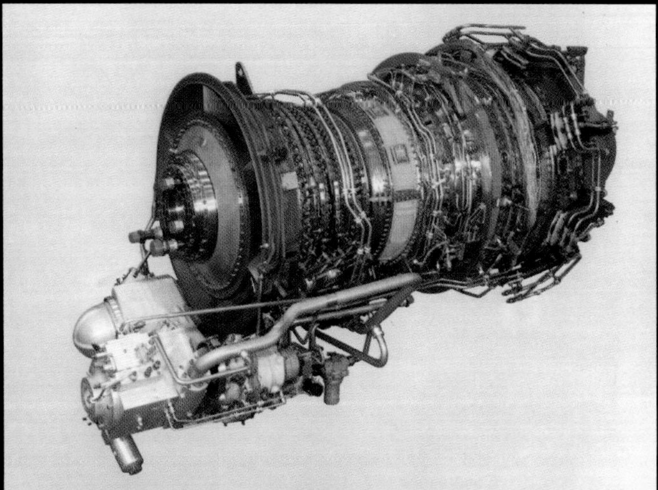

The heart of the gas turbine engine was the engine core consisting of compressor, turbine, and combustor. One key to improving engine performance was to improve engine core technologies. In the mid-1960s, the Aero Propulsion Laboratory initiated the Advanced Turbine Engine Gas Generator (ATEGG) program to improve engine core components and their operation. One of the longest ongoing programs in Laboratory history, ATEGG was an important part of the Integrated High Performance Turbine Engine Technology (IHPTET) initiative undertaken in the 1980s to double turbine engine performance by the early twenty-first century. Pictured here are (top) the Pratt & Whitney ATEGG PW 535, (middle) the Allison ATEGG, and (bottom) the General Electric ATEGG GE 23.

tional changes. The first occurred in 1957, when the Propeller Laboratory merged with the Power Plant Laboratory to form the Propulsion Laboratory. The following year, the Propulsion Laboratory disbanded the Propeller Division. Then, in 1959, the Laboratory transferred its Rocket Propulsion Division to the Air Force Flight Test Center (AFFTC), Edwards Air Force Base, California.

However, the change that redirected the entire future trajectory of propulsion research and development occurred in 1959 during the general reorganization of the laboratory and engineering functions at Wright Field. As part of this reorganization, the Propulsion Laboratory permanently transferred about half of its 800 engineers to the newly formed Directorate of Systems Engineering. Henceforth, the engineers of the Directorate of Systems Engineering interfaced directly with the system program offices. Meanwhile, the much-reduced Propulsion Laboratory was placed, together with the new Flight Dynamics Laboratory, Flight Controls Laboratory, and Flight Accessories Laboratory, under the Aero-Mechanics Division of the Wright Air Development Division's (WADD's) Directorate of Advanced Systems Technology.[78]

The reorganization did not stop there. In 1962, the Air Force decided to create a Research and Technology Division (RTD) that included both laboratories and systems engineering.[79] During the planning for RTD, the Aero-Mechanics Division was abolished and the Propulsion Laboratory was redesignated the Air Force Aero Propulsion Laboratory, a designation that it was to carry for more than 20 years.[80]

Even more fundamental than the changes in organization, manpower, and designation, however, was the change in mission focus. The Power Plant and Propulsion laboratories up to 1959 had been primarily concerned with assisting industry in developing and fielding (and, thereafter, troubleshooting) new propulsion equipment and components. After 1959, however, the new Propulsion Laboratory focused its efforts on *applied research*. The Laboratory still assisted ASD's program offices, often directly, in their development of turbine engines for aircraft and missiles; however, henceforth the Laboratory's principal mission was the development of new technology to improve and, where possible, revolutionize Air Force propulsion and power systems.[81]

In 1965, for instance, the Aero Propulsion Laboratory established the Advanced Turbine Engine Gas Generator (ATEGG) program to develop technologies centering on the core of the jet engine (turbine, compressor, and combustor). Under ATEGG, the Laboratory worked closely with jet-engine companies, suggesting ways in which engine cores could be designed for more durability, efficiency, and performance over their life cycles. The companies, in turn, developed experimental engine cores with one or several advanced features for testing. There were two main types of ATEGG diagnostic testing: *flowpath* testing, which measured engine core performance parameters, and *structures* testing, which determined core component durability and maintenance potential.[82]

The program proved to be one of the most successful in the history of Wright Field technology development and, indeed, continues to the present day. It is one of the principal reasons that the United States has remained the world's leader in gas turbine engine technology.

In 1968, the Aero Propulsion Laboratory established another "technology growth" program called the Aircraft Propulsion Subsystems Integration (APSI) program. APSI was initiated to resolve compatibility problems between airframes and propulsion systems. It concentrated on improving engine-inlet compatibility and had two main objectives: easier engine installation and removal and better aerodynamic performance for both airframe and engine. It achieved these objectives by better integrating inlets, fans, fan turbines, augmenters, controls, and exhaust nozzles with core engine components (see ATEGG, above). In addition, the program, like ATEGG, developed and refined analytical and design tools to assess and predict engine performance in different configurations.[83]

As an extension of the APSI program, in 1975 the Aero Propulsion Laboratory joined with the Navy in sponsoring tests of complete, large, gas turbine demonstrator engines under the Joint Technology Demonstrator Engine (JTDE) program. The demonstrator engines consisted of advanced, high-pressure components from the ATEGG program combined with advanced, low-pressure and adaptive components. The JTDE program subsequently provided the competitive base for all Air Force and Navy engines.[84]

The most recent gas turbine engine technology development program originating in the Aero Propulsion Laboratory achieved, in the last two decades of the twentieth century, truly national proportions. This was the High Performance Turbine Engine Technology (HPTET) program.

The Laboratory initiated the HPTET program in 1982. The program grew out of the attempt to disprove the belief in some government quarters that the gas turbine engine was nearing the end of its technological possibilities. An in-house study undertaken by the Laboratory determined that a 50 percent increase in turbine engine performance could be expected by 1995 with appropriate funding of advanced technology efforts.[85]

The Aero Propulsion Laboratory thereupon initiated the High Performance Turbine Engine Technology program. In 1984, the Materials Laboratory, whose work, particularly in high-temperature materials, was critical to the success of the effort, joined HPTET. At the same time, the time-frame for achieving HPTET's goals was shifted from the mid-1990s to the turn of the century to better realize long-term materials contributions.[86]

In 1985, six major U.S. gas turbine engine manufacturers, Allison, Garrett, General Electric, Pratt & Whitney, Teledyne, and Williams International, joined the Air Force team in developing corporate, long-term plans to achieve HPTET's objectives and schedule.[87]

In 1986, at the direction of the Department of Defense, the Air Force expanded HPTET to include the National Aeronautics and Space Administration (NASA), the Defense Advanced Research Projects Agency (DARPA), the Army, and the Navy to form the *Integrated* High Performance Turbine Engine Technology (IHPTET) program. Thereafter, IHPTET effectively guided nearly all military turbine engine exploratory and advanced development research in the United States with the goal of doubling engine thrust-to-weight performance through advances in engine aerothermodynamics, materials, and structures.[88]

While work on gas turbine engines consumed much of the Laboratory's resources and efforts, the Laboratory had a long tradition of performing leading-edge work in other areas, such

JOINT TECHNOLOGY DEMONSTRATOR ENGINE

An outgrowth of the Advanced Propulsion Subsystems Integration (APSI) program, the Joint Technology Demonstrator Engine (JTDE) was a joint test program conducted by the Air Force and Navy to test technologies on complete demonstrator engines. The program was inaugurated in the mid-1970s and became an important element of the Integrated High Performance Turbine Engine Technology initiative a decade later. Pictured are examples of JTDEs from the 1980s and early 1990s: (top) the JTDE XTE 65-1A, (middle) the JTDE XTE 43, and (bottom) the JTDE XTE 64.

In 1979, three of the original airplane hangars constructed at Wright Field were razed to make room for the new Fuels and Lubricants Laboratory. Construction was completed in 1982. The Laboratory developed and tested new fuels and oils for aircraft and missile systems, including the PF-1 priming fluid for the Air-Launched Cruise Missile and a high-temperature engine lubricant for the F-22 fighter. The state-of-the-art facility contains jet engine simulators and laboratories for chemical analysis, systems research, fuel combustion studies, and bearing fatigue and oil-deposition tests.

With the advent of cruise missiles in the 1970s, the Laboratory began developing technology for small, "expendable" gas turbine engines.

as high-speed, air breathing propulsion (ramjets and scramjets); fuels and lubricants; and aircraft and spacecraft power systems.

The Laboratory's Aircraft Power Division conducted research on aircraft electric and hydraulic power systems and components. In the 1930s and 1940s, hydraulic systems predominated due to their reliability and the limitations of onboard power available. However, with the increased use of gas turbine engines in the post-World War II period, aircraft flight control forces started to exceed the limits of the human-cable-pulley interface, and the criticality of onboard power generation increased.[89]

Modern aircraft, such as the F-16, F/A-18, and F/A-22, required continuous hydraulic and electric power to maintain control in flight. Modern transport aircraft, such as the C-5, C-141, and C-17, also required continuous power for primary flight control with rudimentary, mechanical backup for emergencies. In recent decades, aircraft power levels increased by an order of magnitude, and the weight of a typical aircraft power system was roughly equivalent to the weight of one engine, while the power system emitted nearly as much heat as an engine. Indeed, reduction of weight and vulnerability of hydraulic lines were among the principal reasons for the Laboratory to champion the "more electric aircraft" in the 1990s (see below).[90]

Much onboard electrical power could be generated by the aircraft's own turbine engines (in the same way that turbines drove dynamos for land-based power generation). However, improved aircraft batteries supplied additional onboard power. The Laboratory explored all these avenues of technical development in the decades following World War II.[91]

One important area of Laboratory focus was the development of aircraft auxiliary power units (APUs). APUs provided onboard electrical power, hydraulics, air-conditioning, avionics, pressurization, and main engine startup. Among the systems that benefited from the Laboratory's development of APU technologies were both U.S. Air Force aircraft and NASA's space shuttle. In the 1980s, the Laboratory sponsored development of APUs capable of cold-engine starting. In the 1990s, the Laboratory conducted research into lubrication-free APUs for increased reliability and easier maintenance.[92]

The Laboratory's work in aircraft electrical power development began in the pre-World War II period with small generators and batteries for aircraft lighting.[93] The Laboratory made significant advances on lighting and electric controls during the 1950s. During the decade, the Laboratory developed the first nickel-cadmium (NiCd) aircraft battery. More recently the Laboratory developed a NiCd battery that operated 15-20 years without maintenance.[94]

Meanwhile, advances in solid-state components led to significant weight reductions in power distribution and control wiring on the B-1 bomber. In 1971, the Laboratory demonstrated the first variable-speed, constant-frequency generator, which eliminated the mechanical, constant-speed drive. In the 1980s, the Laboratory sponsored work to further reduce the weight of electrical systems. The More Electric Aircraft (MEA) concept grew out of this work in which each function formerly controlled by hydraulics was to be replaced with an electric motor. The benefits of MEA technology included increased reliability, survivability, and reduced life cycle cost. Due to Laboratory backing, both the Department of Defense and industry adopted this concept.[95]

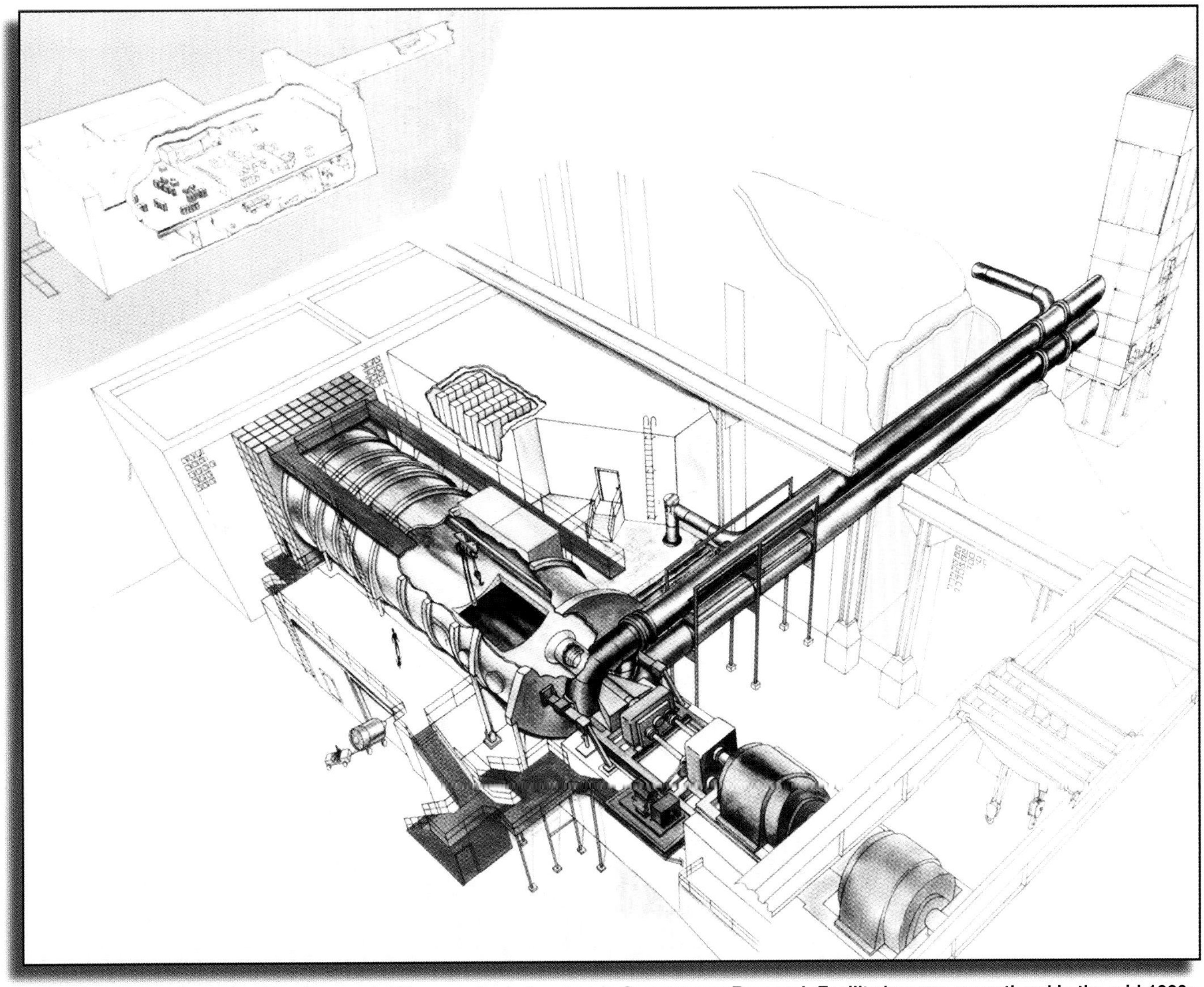

Under planning and construction for nearly 20 years, the Laboratory's Compressor Research Facility became operational in the mid-1980s, enabling in-depth assessments of advanced engine compressor aerodynamic performance and the resolution of operational compression system problems.

In 1975, the Aero Propulsion Laboratory federated along with Materials, Avionics, and Flight Dynamics laboratories as the Air Force Wright Aeronautical Laboratories (AFWAL), reporting to Air Force Systems Command's Director of Laboratories (AFSC/DL). In 1982, AFWAL was realigned under the Aeronautical Systems Division (ASD).

In 1988, AFWAL was reorganized as WRDC. As a result, the Aero Propulsion Laboratory was redesignated the Aero Propulsion and Power Laboratory. In 1990, WRDC became the Wright Laboratory and the Aero Propulsion Laboratory became the Aero Propulsion and Power Directorate. In 1997, when the Air Force Research Laboratory (AFRL) was formed, the Aero Propulsion Directorate combined with the (rocket) Propulsion Directorate at Edwards Air Force Base, California, to become the Propulsion Directorate (AFRL/PR).

ELECTRONICS AND AVIONICS

If propulsion was the first great technological development that revolutionized air warfare in the period beginning during World War II, electronics was the second and has had just as profound an impact on military aeronautics and space operations. The revolution began only three years after the war when scientists at Bell Laboratories invented the solid-state transistor.[96] Within a decade, the transistor was followed by the invention of the integrated circuit, and the world of microelectronics, as we know it today, was born.[97]

Microelectronics, as its name implied, made possible the miniaturization of electronic devices. In addition to being much smaller and more compact, microelectronic devices were also more durable and reliable, and generated considerably less heat than earlier electronic devices dependent on vacuum-tube technology for their operation.

From the very beginning, the military services played a key role in the development of microelectronic technology, where size, durability, and speed allowed the miniaturization of critical components of air and space vehicles. In the Air Force, the Wright Field laboratories were among the principal sponsors, advocates, and underwriters of the electronics revolution.

Within the Air Force, the electronics revolution involved not only the development of new devices, but also their integration into systems. It was in the years following World War II that the military airplane began to capitalize on the potentialities of electronic devices, whether based on vacuum-tube or solid-state technology. Indeed, it was in the postwar period that the term "avionics" (aviation electronics) gained currency, finally becoming for nearly four decades the designation of the principal laboratory organization for electronics development at Wright Field.

The largest complex of the Avionics Laboratory included a three-story concrete structure with a 13-story double tower built in 1967 and six additional buildings constructed between 1973 and 1989. The tower housed the Electronic Warfare Research Facility for countermeasures research. The Laboratory's anechoic chamber was used during the research of radar cross-section reduction that was applied to the F-117 "stealth" fighter and the B-2 bomber. The Electronic Technology Division of the Laboratory also used these facilities for development of the advanced microelectronic circuitry applied to fly-by-wire flight control.

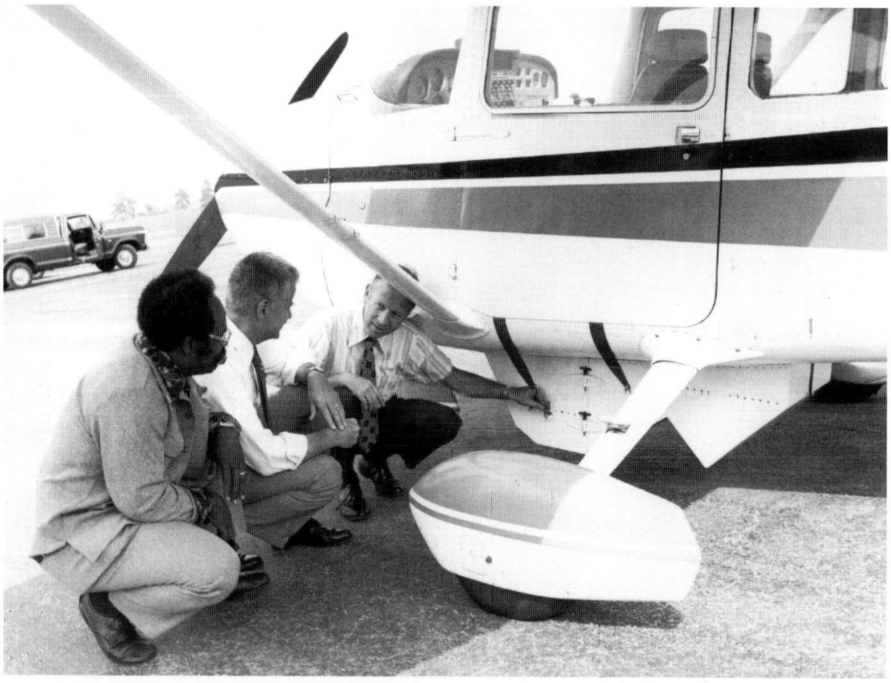

The Wright Field laboratories developed technologies for other government agencies in addition to the Air Force. The Enviro-pod, developed in the 1970s by the Avionics Laboratory, consisted of a 70-mm camera installed in a Cessna 172 airplane. It was used by the Environmental Protection Agency to obtain high-quality aerial photographs from medium altitudes. Enviro-pod team members included (left to right): Richard Freeman and Leonard Crouch of the Avionics Laboratory and Edward Fowle of the Mead Technology Laboratories, Dayton, Ohio.

Aviation electronics at Wright Field had its origins, beginning in the early 1920s, in work conducted by two separate organizations: the Aircraft Radio Laboratory, which reported to the Signal Corps but which was collocated with other technical sections of the Engineering Division at McCook and later Wright Field, and the Equipment Laboratory, part of the Air Corps' Materiel Division.

Early work conducted by these laboratories at McCook and Wright fields included the development of wiring, cockpit instrumentation, batteries, generators, and radio sets for the relatively simple aircraft of that era. Nor were the laboratories' staffs shy about promoting their work before the general public, as when the "radio dog" (a remotely-controlled vehicle that received wireless directions from a plane flying overhead) rode around the streets of Dayton one fine day in the early 1920s, turning corners and stopping for traffic signals at the tug of its "electronic leash" before astonished bystanders.[98] Work on radio, in turn, led to attempts during the 1930s at Wright Field to develop a form of primitive airborne radar.[99] However, it was not until the development of the cavity magnetron by the British during World War II—a development that they shared with their American allies—that airborne radar became practical.[100]

During World War II, aircraft electronics research continued to be conducted separately by the Equipment and Aircraft Radio laboratories until 1944 when the Radio Laboratory was assigned to the Materiel Command's Engineering Division. The division dissolved the Radio Laboratory and combined its personnel with electronics experts from the Equipment Laboratory to form several new laboratories for Radar, Communication and Navigation, and Electronic Components.[101]

With the formation of the Air Research and Development Command in 1951, these laboratories were transferred, along with the other laboratories of the Engineering Division, to the Wright Air Development Center (WADC) as the Aircraft Radiation Laboratory (radar), the Communication and Navigation Laboratory, and the Components and Systems Laboratory.[102]

During the course of the 1950s, WADC several times reorganized and sometimes redesignated its subordinate laboratory organizations. WADC's electronics laboratories were no exception. When WADC was first formed in 1951, the Aircraft Radiation Laboratory, the Communication and Navigation Laboratory, and the Components and Systems Laboratory were all located in WADC's Weapons Components Division.[103] In 1954, the Aircraft Radiation Laboratory was absorbed into the Aerial Reconnaissance Laboratory (previously the Photographic Reconnaissance Laboratory), and the Components and Systems Laboratory was renamed the Electronic Components Laboratory and transferred to the Directorate of Research.[104] In 1955, when the Armament Laboratory was disestablished, its munitions work transferred to Eglin Air Force Base, Florida, while its guidance work remained at Wright Field as the Weapons Guidance Laboratory, a future component of the Air Force Avionics Laboratory (see below).[105] In 1959 the Electronic Components Laboratory was renamed the Electronic Technology Laboratory.[106]

SOLID STATE PHASED ARRAY RADAR

The Air Force laboratories at Wright Field had pioneered the development of airborne radar since World War II. In the 1960s, the Air Force Avionics Laboratory, capitalizing on advances in solid-state electronics, inaugurated development of solid-state phased-array radar apertures. The success of the first program, Molecular Electronics for Radar Applications (MERA) undertaken in the mid-1960s, led to the Reliable Advanced Solid State Radar (RASSR) program within a few years and, a decade later, to the Solid State Phased Array (SSPA) program (1983-1988). The SSPA was an important component of the Laboratory's Ultra Reliable Radar (URR) program that led, in turn, to development of the radar for the F-22.

Source: James F. Aldridge, ed., *USAF Research & Development: The Legacy of the Wright Laboratory Science and Engineering Community, 1917-1997* [unpublished draft] (Wright-Patterson Air Force Base, 1997), pp 109-115.

Array aperture developed under the SSPA program (1983-1988) by Texas Instruments

Indeed, WADC's electronics engineers already had scored major successes in the late 1940s with the development of the first high-resolution, imaging radar and the invention of the evapograph infrared imaging detector.[107]

During the 1950s, aircraft and missile electronics underwent a profound transformation as a result of the emergence of solid-state devices.

In the course of the 1950s, WADC engineers sponsored development of the first military-standard transistor and silicon semiconductor technology. Going beyond development of devices based on silicon, with its limitations for military use, they also sponsored development of gallium arsenide (GaAs) semiconductor technology and the development of the first GaAs gun diodes at microwave frequencies.[108]

In the second half of the decade, WADC sponsored the development of the first silicon integrated circuit (IC) by Texas Instruments and the development of computers using ICs for the Minuteman II intercontinental ballistic missile.[109]

WADC's electronics engineers also developed the first optically pumped solid-state laser (ruby); the first orthicon/vidicon optical-image intensifiers; the coupled cavity traveling wave tubes (TWTs); optical processing of synthetic aperture radar; and coaxial magnetrons.[110]

WADC also developed and tested the first airborne anti-jam radio communications. This was a pseudo-noise, spread spectrum, anti-jam, ultra-high-frequency (UHF) radio system. It was first flown on aircraft in Germany shortly after the Berlin Airlift.[111]

One of the most momentous developments during the 1950s was an investigation into radar cross-section by a small group in the Aircraft Radiation Laboratory. This largely in-house work resulted in the discovery that shaping the radar's target in different ways could profoundly alter its cross-section. This discovery, in turn, led to the first investigations of low-observable or "stealth" techniques, such as air vehicle shaping, in addition to special paints and coatings.[112]

In the 1959 restructure of the laboratories and engineering functions at Wright Field, the Aerial Reconnaissance Laboratory, the Communication and Navigation Laboratory, the Electronic Technology Laboratory, and the Weapons Guidance Laboratory were consolidated under the new Wright Air Development Division (WADD). At the same time, they were reorganized and redesignated the Communications Laboratory, the Navigation and Guidance Laboratory, and the Reconnaissance Laboratory. The Electronic Technology Laboratory retained its former identity. All were placed together within the Avionics Division of WADD's Directorate of Advanced Technology.[113] These arrangements were initially little affected by the establishment of the Aeronautical Systems Division (ASD) under the Air Force Systems Command (AFSC), in 1961. The Avionics Division simply became part of ASD's Deputy for Technology.[114]

In 1963, ASD's Avionics Division was redesignated the Air Force Avionics Laboratory with four technical divisions corresponding to the Avionics Division's four laboratories: the Electronic Warfare Division, the Electronic Technology Division, the Navigation and Guidance Division, and the Reconnaissance Division.[115] Later in the year, the Avionics Laboratory was transferred from ASD and realigned under AFSC's new Research and Technology Division (RTD). In 1967, when RTD was abolished, the Laboratory was realigned under AFSC's Director of Laboratories (AFSC/DL), but remained at Wright Field.[116]

In the midst of the turmoil surrounding the latest reorganization, Wright Field's electronics scientists and engineers persevered in pursuing the accelerating electron-

DAIS

The DAIS program began in 1972 as an attempt to begin integrating the various avionics subsystems, so-called "black boxes," that had proliferated on modern military aircraft over the previous two decades. DAIS, which stood for Digital Avionics Information System, sought to develop and demonstrate emerging technologies in four areas that promised to provide significant improvements in mission processing of core avionics. These four areas included digital multiplex buses; higher order language (HOL) operational flight program designs; standard computer instruction set architecture (ISA) for multiplex federated processors; and integrated multi-function cockpit controls and displays based on multi-purpose cathode ray tube (CRT) screens and digital, programmable display generators. These technologies were tested in a ground-based integrated test bed (ITB) cockpit mock-up with man-in-the-loop mission simulation providing real-time demonstration of an actual mission scenario with computer-generated, out-of-window displays.

Although the DAIS program ended in 1981, its results subsequently influenced the integration of avionics subsystems on the F-15, F-16, B-52, B-1B, F-117, and C-17 aircraft.

Source: James F. Aldridge, ed., *USAF Research & Development: The Legacy of the Wright Laboratory Science and Engineering Community, 1917-1997* [unpublished draft] (Wright-Patterson Air Force Base, 1997).

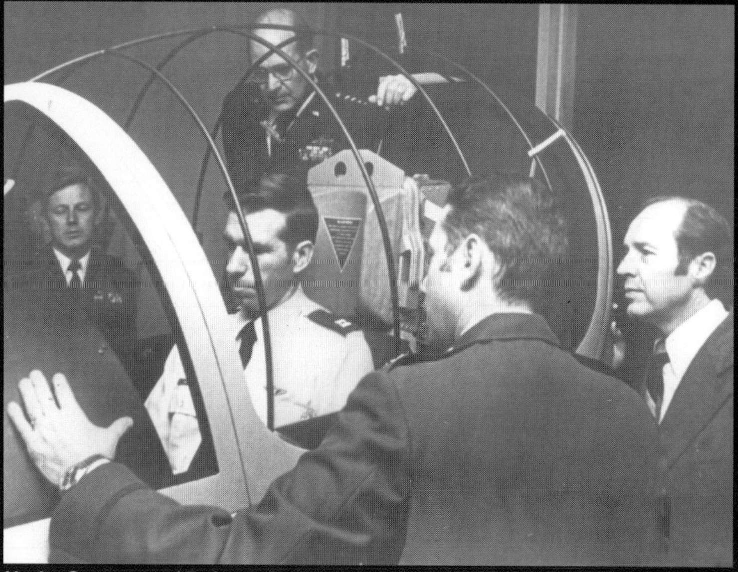

Under Secretary of Defense Dr. William J. Perry (far right) views DAIS mockup, November 10, 1977.

Artist's rendering of DAIS cockpit

ics revolution. During the first half of the 1960s, the Avionics Laboratory sponsored development of the carbon monoxide (CO) laser and developed low-power, complementary-metal-oxide-semiconductor (CMOS) technology; the scanning electron microscope; the first silicon bipolar transistors at microwave frequencies; concepts for the gas dynamic laser; the first continuous-wave, solid-state, visible laser (ruby); mercury cadmium telluride (HgCdTe) for use as an infrared (IR) detector; the first principal theory of holographic imaging; concepts for spotlight radar; and the first simulated Raman scattering.[117]

During the second half of the 1960s, the Laboratory continued its commitment to developing the electronics technology base. During this period, the Laboratory developed the first discrete, hybrid, microwave ICs; metal-nitride-oxide (MNO) nonvolatile memories; the first ICEM magnetron; the first holmium yttrium lithium fluoride laser (mid-IR); GaAs metal semiconductor, field-effect transistor (MESFET) for low noise and power amplification; and ring laser gyro technology. The Laboratory also invented hollow cathode lasers.[118]

The Laboratory developed a number of devices during the 1960s in response to Air Force needs in the Vietnam War. These included the first-generation, airborne, forward-looking infrared (FLIR) sensors for night attack from gunships; the first hand-held laser designators, airborne designators for forward air control (FAC) aircraft, and laser seekers on iron bombs; the first "smart weapons" to be used operationally; the first radar warning receivers used operationally; the first pod-mounted, electronic-warfare, countermeasures jammers used operationally; and the first "Wild Weasel" aircraft, a modified F-100F.[119] In addition, the Laboratory's Electronic Technology Division developed GaAs IR illuminators on gunships and guidance units for laser-guided bombs.[120]

In the 1960s, the Laboratory also began aggressively seeking applications for the new microelectronics technology that had emerged during the previous decade. One of the most important applications was solid-state, phased-array radar. The first program to develop a full-scale radar aperture was called the Molecular Electronics for Radar Applications (MERA) program (1964). Success with MERA encouraged the Laboratory to sponsor a follow-on effort, the Reliable Advanced Solid State Radar (RASSR), in 1969. Both the MERA and RASSR, while successful as technology demonstrators, were not deemed ready for operational use, in part due to the inadequate electrical properties of silicon as the principal substrate material for each radar's solid-state electronic components. The Laboratory spent the

In the 1980s, the Air Force joined with the Army and Navy to underwrite the development of very-high-speed integrated circuits (VHSICs). VHSIC incorporated improvements in performance several orders of magnitude over earlier integrated circuits. Shown here is the making of a VHSIC chip.

next decade studying both designs and materials before again sponsoring a full-size demonstration aperture.[121]

The Laboratory continued to pursue work on solid-state, phased-array radar as the new decade neared. It began exploiting the potentialities of laser and satellite technology. In the late 1960s, the Laboratory developed the first airborne laser communication technology for high-bit-rate satellite reconnaissance applications and airborne, high-powered-laser weapon technology.[122]

During the 1970s, the Laboratory developed an air-to-submarine, extremely high-frequency (EHF) satellite communications link. This was the first successful demonstration of a tri-service link providing a strategic communications capability for the nuclear equipment fleet.[123]

During the decade, the Laboratory also developed the design for a high, anti-jam Global Positioning Satellite (GPS) airborne receiver and null steering antenna technology. This technology was subsequently transitioned to the GPS System Program Office (SPO) for incorporation into airborne systems such as the C-130, F-15, and F-16.[124]

It was during the 1970s that the Laboratory also refined its earlier work on radar cross-section reduction and camouflage that was incorporated into the design of the F-117, B-2, and the Advanced Tactical Fighter (ATF, later the F/A-22).[125]

During the 1970s, the Laboratory performed extensive test and analysis of various techniques to provide effective countermeasures against monopulse radars employed as ground tracking radars and missile guidance.[126]

The Laboratory also added to the electronics technology device base during the 1970s. During the first half of the decade, the Laboratory developed the first charge-coupled device (CCD), magnetic bubble, and ferroelectric memories; the first GaAs gigabit/second logic circuits; the first Q-switched carbon monoxide laser (mid-IR); the first ultra-high-power, gas dynamic laser (carbon dioxide); the first solid-state, analog-to-digital converters; and single- and double-drift, GaAs read impact ionization avalanche transit time (IMPATT) diodes.[127]

In 1975, the Avionics Laboratory was aligned under a new organization, the Air Force Wright Aeronautical Laboratories (AFWAL), along with three other applied research laboratories at Wright Field. As a result of AFWAL's formation and the simultaneous disestablishment of the Aerospace Research Laboratories (ARL), the Avionics Laboratory acquired part of the Air Force's basic research mission along with basic research funding provided by the Air Force Office of Scientific Research (AFOSR).[128] When, in 1982, AFWAL was aligned under ASD, the Avionics Laboratory returned to the product division for the first time since 1963.[129]

Despite defense downsizing following the end of the Vietnam War, the Avionics Laboratory continued to make significant progress in developing basic and device technologies, particularly in the area of gallium arsenide (GaAs). This progress included development of the first leadless, controlled impedance chip carriers for GaAs. The Laboratory also pinpointed the lattice site of carbon (C) impurities in GaAs. The Laboratory, moreover, was the first to resolve photoluminescence of shallow donors in GaAs. The Laboratory also achieved the first molecular beam epitaxy (MBE) growth of aluminum gallium arsenide (AlGaAs) with arsine gas and the

PAVE PILLAR

The Pave Pillar program began in 1981 as a follow-on to part of the Digital Avionics Information System (DAIS) program. Pave Pillar continued research in advanced avionics architecture, particularly for integrated and automated computer-controlled aircraft subsystems in tactical aircraft and helicopters. The System Avionics Division of the Avionics Laboratory at Wright-Patterson Air Force Base evaluated an architecture that integrated all onboard electronic components, including communications, navigation, guidance, weapon delivery, target acquisition and tracking, terrain following and avoidance, threat detection, classification and avoidance, and electronic jamming systems. Integration was proposed to relieve problems with supply, maintenance, repair, and overall system cost associated with the growing complexity of electronic components. Pave Pillar concepts later were transitioned into the Air Force's F/A-22 Raptor and the Army's RAH-66 Comanche helicopter development programs.

Sources: History of Aeronautical Systems Division, January–December 1986, p 9; History of Aeronautical Systems Division, January–December 1986, Part II: The Air Force Wright Aeronautical Laboratories, 1984–1986, pp 100-103; History of Aeronautical Systems Division, January–December 1989, p 284; Fact Sheet, U. S. Air Force, "Automated Aircraft," October 1983.

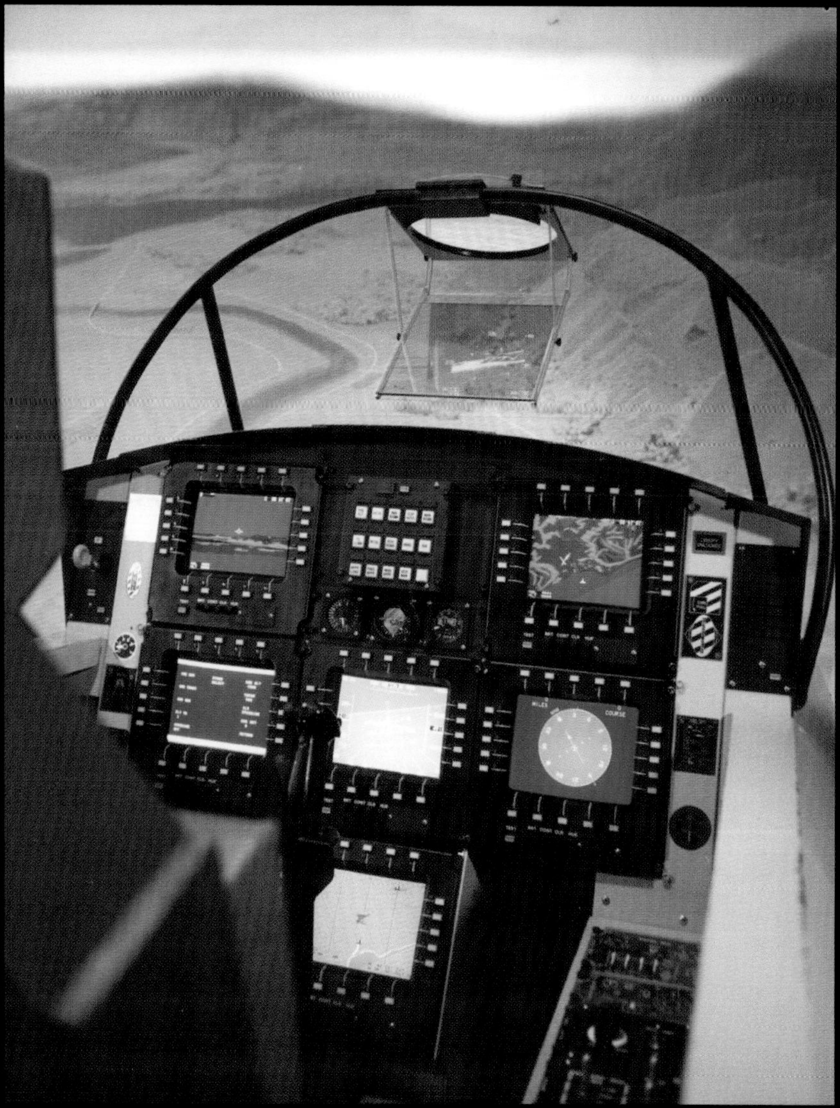

Pave Pillar cockpit

first MBE growth of GaAs with pure atomic arsenic gas cracker.[130]

One of the most important initiatives undertaken by the Avionics Laboratory during the 1970s, and which continued in the 1980s and 1990s, was the development of integrated avionics architectures. Until the early 1970s most avionics subsystems, called "black boxes," were stand-alone threads of functionality with limited digital computer processing capability. In addition, most avionics were analog with complex, signal-converter-box interface to a small, single-mission computer. Miles of point-to-point wiring connected various electronics boxes. It was up to the aircraft pilot to integrate the operation of these subsystems by manually operating their control heads and scanning their dedicated display gauges. Maintenance, too, was complex and laborious.[131]

The first attempt to develop an integrated avionics architecture was the Digital Avionics Information System (DAIS). DAIS demonstrated key technologies that promised to provide significant improvements in the mission processing of core avionics. These technologies included digital multiplex buses, higher order language (HOL) operational flight program design, standard computer instruction set architecture (ISA) for multiple federated processors, and integrated multi-function cockpit controls and displays based on multi-purpose cathode ray tubes (CRTs) and digital programmable display generators. The DAIS program resulted in the issuance of several key military standards (MIL-STD) that were subsequently applied to avionics systems on the F-15, F-16, B-52, B-1B, F-117, and C-17.[132]

Pave Pillar followed DAIS in the early 1980s. Under Pave Pillar, there were a number of related programs, including the Integrated Communication-Navigation-Identification Avionics (ICNIA) program, the Integrated Electronic Warfare System (INEWS), and a number of pilot-aiding system management programs, such as the Air-to-Air Battle Management program and the Pilot Associate. The enabling technologies for these programs included Very High Speed Integrated Circuits (VHSIC); fiber-optic, high-speed data buses; and ADA computer language. Pave Pillar also addressed availability and supportability issues of complex avionics systems, particularly at austere locations in the field. The technologies developed under Pave Pillar were to be applicable to the Army and Navy, as well as to Air Force weapon systems. The Joint Integrated Avionics

The Pilot's Associate was a collection of knowledge-based systems to assist pilots of modern fighter aircraft to cope with tasks like systems monitoring, threat assessment, and mission planning. In the illustration above, the Pilot's Associate is depicted as a "ghost" or second pilot in the cockpit.

Working Group (JIAWG) was the forum in which differences were discussed and worked out.[133]

The Progressive Avionics Concept Evaluation (Pave Pace) program followed Pave Pillar in the early 1990s. The purpose of Pave Pace was to develop integrated, affordable, supportable, and long-lived technologies for multi-role and multi-service applications. The success of Pave Pace depended on the maturing of Microwave and Millimeter Wave Monolithic Integrated Circuits (MIMICs); supercomputing, optical radio frequency (RF) and digital networks; and maintenance-free avionics concepts and supporting technologies. Pave Pace foresaw the need for open architecture specifications, commercial-off-the-shelf (COTS) and programmable network interfaces to allow for technology transparency, and several cycles of upgrades throughout the platform's lifetime.[134]

In the early 1980s, the Avionics Laboratory made another major effort to design, test, fabricate, and transition technologies leading to an operational, solid-state, phased-array radar for airborne combat operations. After the conclusion of the RASSR program in the early 1970s, the Laboratory had conducted a series of studies leading to the design, fabrication, and test of components using GaAs, whose electrical properties were superior to those of silicon. Encouraged, in 1983, the Laboratory awarded a contract to Texas Instruments for the design, fabrication, and testing of a full-scale, solid-state, phased array (SSPA). Despite some problems in manufacturing, schedule slippages, and cost overruns, the array performed as designed and was transitioned to the Laboratory's Ultra Reliable Radar (URR) program in 1988.[135]

The SSPA and URR programs were followed in the late 1980s and 1990s with a number of efforts to reduce the production cost of key radar components like the transmit-receive module. This was largely accomplished under the DARPA-funded Microwave and Millimeter Wave Monolithic Integrated Circuit (MIMIC) program.[136]

Also during the 1980s, the Laboratory successfully completed tests of a low-probability-of-intercept, high-data rate, air-to-air communication system for reconnaissance forces.[137]

The Laboratory also sponsored the first airborne test of a bistatic imaging radar in conjunction with a space shuttle, demonstrating the feasibility of space illumination (transmission) and airborne reception of radar information for low-observable aircraft applications.[138]

During the 1980s, the Avionics Laboratory and later the Electronic Technology Laboratory (see below) continued to underwrite efforts to improve electronic devices and the overall electronics technical base. In the first half of the decade, the Laboratory established the first international, standard, IC design language (VHDL). It also developed the first on-card MHz power converters; the first solid-state, ultraviolet photodiode; optical surface scatterometry; and the high-performance ring laser gyroscope. In the second half of the decade, the Laboratory developed the first 650° C silicon carbide (SiC) MESFET transistor for engine controls; the first 20-40 GHz, 100-watt traveling wave tubes (TWTs) for electronic countermeasures (ECM); the first 60 GHz, low-noise, high-electron mobility transistors (HEMTs) and monolithic ICs; and the first full wafer dislocation mapping for GaAs. In addition, the Laboratory demonstrated the world's fastest, 6-bit quantizer (3GSPS), GaAs heterojunction bipolar transistor (HBT), and set a performance record for AlGaAs/GaAs resonant tunneling diodes.[139]

A decade-long period of reorganizing and reprioritizing activity within the electronics and avionics community at Wright Field began in 1988. During the 1988 reorganization of the Wright Field laboratories that transformed AFWAL into the Wright Research and Development Center (WRDC), the Avionics Laboratory underwent the first substantial reorganization since the early 1960s when its Electronic Technology Division was constituted as a separate laboratory, the Electronic Technology Laboratory.[140] When WRDC, in turn, was reorganized as Wright Laboratory in 1990, the Avionics Laboratory became the Avionics Directorate, and the Electronics Technology Laboratory was renamed the Solid State Electronics Directorate.[141]

In 1995, the Solid State Electronics Directorate was once more assigned to the Avionics Directorate and ceased operation as an independent organization within Wright Laboratory.[142]

In the 1997 consolidation of the Air Force's laboratories into one Air Force Research Laboratory (AFRL), the Avionics Directorate was reorganized as the Sensors Directorate. In the process, it exchanged a portion of its technology portfolio with AFRL's Information Directorate (formerly the Rome Laboratory, Rome, New York), and, in turn, received a portion of Rome's portfolio.[143]

The 1990s began with Operation Desert Storm. During Desert Storm, the Air Force tested new technologies, sometimes for the first time under operational conditions. The use of new technologies pointed out shortcomings and confirmed other directions pursued by the Laboratory over the previous 30 years. It demonstrated the benefit of GPS navigation and the value of stealth technology and disruptive countermeasures. Above all, the Air Force confirmed the benefits of maintaining a qualified, in-house laboratory capable of responding quickly to contingency situations. During Desert Storm, many of the Laboratory's facilities were in use around the clock. Among the more important facilities employed during the war were those for foreign exploitation, target recognition, sensor evaluation, and communications.

The 1990s also posed new challenges to the Laboratory. Since the end of World War II, the Air Force's laboratories had led the nation in many areas of technology development. One of the most important areas of leadership was in electronics and avionics. However, with the downsizing of defense outlays and infrastructure, in addition to the maturing of the commercial electronics industry and markets, this began to change. As the decade advanced, it became increasingly clear that the Air Force's avionics systems would have to be more compatible with commercially available products and systems, or fall rapidly behind in capability. Indeed, by the end of the decade, the Air Force had mounted a full-fledged effort to "open up" the avionics of its air-and-space platforms and weapon systems.[144]

TARGETING AND WEAPON GUIDANCE

Historically, the Air Force's avionics researchers at Wright Field have sponsored two types of weapon guidance systems: those requiring a human operator to identify and designate a target and autonomous/automatic terrain or target recognition concepts using correlation or pattern-recognition processing.

In the late 1940s, Air Materiel Command's Engineering Division sponsored the Automatic Terrain Recognition and Navigation (ATRAN) system that became operational on the Mace and Matador cruise missiles. In the late 1950s, the Wright Air Development Division initiated development of the terrain-contour-matching (TERCOM) system. TERCOM, as modified during the following three decades, was incorporated on a number of Air Force and Navy missiles, including the Air Force's Air-Launched Cruise Missile (ALCM) and Advanced Cruise Missile (ACM) and the Navy's Tomahawk missile.

Beginning in the 1970s and continuing into the 1980s, the Defense Advanced Research Projects Agency (DARPA) sponsored the Autonomous Terminal Homing (ATH) program with the Air Force Avionics Laboratory as DARPA's principal technical agent. The ATH program led, in turn, to the Air Force's Cruise Missile Advanced Guidance (CMAG) program to develop a precision autonomous-terminal-guidance system for cruise missiles.

In addition to these efforts, the Avionics Laboratory also conducted work on laser sources and detectors beginning in the 1960s. This research resulted in the laser designation systems and laser-guided bomb units that were first used in Vietnam and which received high visibility during Operation Desert Storm. This work formed the foundation of such systems as the Pave-series and LANTIRN targeting pods.

Finally, the Avionics Laboratory also played a major role in the development of TV-like, electro-optical sensors and forward-looking infrared (FLIR) sensors for viewing scenes in total darkness.

Sources: James F. Aldridge, ed., *USAF Research & Development: The Legacy of the Wright Laboratory Science and Engineering Community, 1917-1997*, [unpublished draft] (Wright-Patterson Air Force Base, 1997), pp 89-94; History of Aeronautical Systems Division, January-December 1986, Part II: The Air Force Wright Aeronautical Laboratories, 1984-1986, vol. 1, pp 108-111.

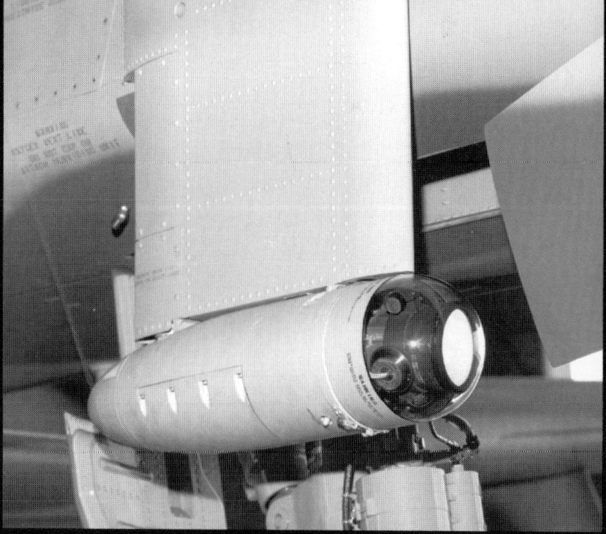

Pave Penny pod

F-16 equipped with LANTIRN pod on the left and Pave Penny pod on the right

MATERIALS

The Air Force's program in materials research and development originated in a collection of small laboratories for metallurgy, chemistry, textiles, and wood at McCook Field in 1917-1918. These laboratories were organized as the Materials Section of the Engineering Division in the spring of 1919.[145]

In 1926, when the Engineering Division became part of the larger Materiel Division, the Materials Section became the Materials Branch. Thirteen years later, in 1939, the Materials Branch was redesignated the Materials Laboratory, a designation that it carried, with one brief interruption (see below), until 1990.[146]

In the period before World War II, the Laboratory remained a relatively small outfit. Like most of the other McCook and Wright Field laboratories, it lost both manpower and experience after World War I. During the 1920s and early 1930s, the number of personnel barely exceeded 35. However, on the eve of World War II, manpower had climbed to nearly 100 personnel, and during the war this number nearly tripled.[147]

During World War I and the ensuing 20-year period leading up to World War II, the Laboratory's small staff worked hard in the midst of a materials revolution in aircraft design and construction, as wood-and-fabric biplanes gave way to all-metal, stressed-skin, monoplane aircraft. Much of the Laboratory's technical activity during this period was bound up with testing materials to ascertain their suitability for Air Corps aircraft and combat deployments and operations. In addition, Laboratory personnel frequently contributed to technical journals. Not a few issues of *Aviation* magazine, for instance, published articles bearing the by-line of J. B. Johnson, the Laboratory's chief from 1919 to the late 1940s,[148] as well as researchers like Charles J. Cleary, one of the Laboratory's much-honored research pioneers.

The move to Wright Field, in 1927, saw the Materials Laboratory leave behind its large wooden barracks at McCook Field[149] for a generous portion of the new concrete and glass accommodations under the immense, saw-tooth roof of the Wright Field laboratory building (Building 16), which housed a portion of most of the laboratories during the interwar years.[150]

World War II did much to accelerate and consolidate many of the gains of the previous decade. It also opened up research in developing alternatives to strategic materials in short supply. (It was during the war, for example, that plywood made a brief reappearance in aircraft structures, for the first time since World War I.)[151] The Laboratory also created, for the duration of the war, a special branch for the testing of aircraft coming off the production line.[152] Laboratory researchers also applied much effort into developing solutions to problems encountered in the field.[153]

To accommodate the expansion in the Laboratory's staff during the war, Laboratory personnel were moved from Building 16 to the old shops building across the street (Building 32).[154] (The shops had previously transferred to larger facilities in Building 5.)[155] This remained the Laboratory's home for much of the next four decades, until the construction of the multi-building laboratory complex at the top of the hill at Wright Field, a complex begun during the late 1960s and which continued to expand into the twenty-first century.[156]

In the aftermath of World War II, the number of personnel was drastically reduced to its immediate prewar level of around 100.[157] However, while the staff was reduced, the number of projects continued to increase in response to the burgeoning materials demands of the new jet-age Air Force. As a result, the Materials

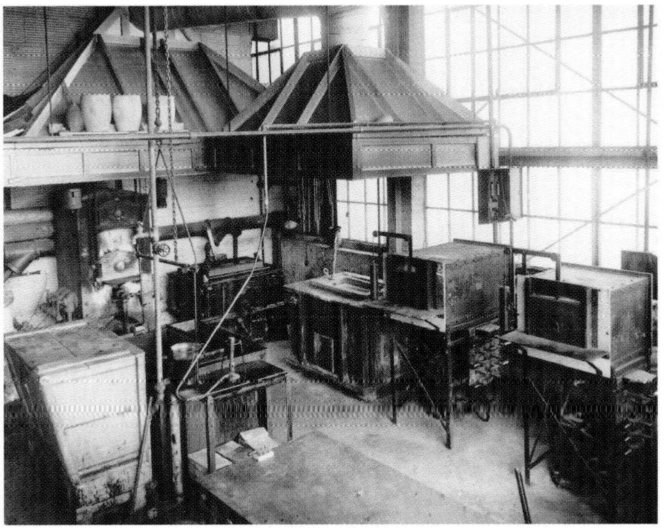

The research and development of materials by the Air Force began at McCook Field in 1917. Initially, several small laboratories for chemicals, metallurgy, and fabrics conducted materials work. These laboratories were organized into the Materials Section of the Engineering Division in the spring of 1919. The Materials Section was the forerunner of the Materials Laboratory (1939) and today's Materials and Manufacturing Directorate of the Air Force Research Laboratory. Picture here: (top) Chemistry laboratory at McCook Field, (middle) Metallurgy laboratory, and (bottom) McCook Field foundry

Laboratory substantially expanded the number of projects under contract with industry, academe, and other government research centers.[158]

The revolution in propulsion ushered in by the gas turbine (jet) engine, the scramjet, and the rocket motor, led to a complete redesign of the air vehicle and, indeed, pointed the way, within a decade, to *aerospace* vehicles, including intercontinental ballistic missiles, space booster rockets, and plans for an aerospace

In 1975, the Materials Laboratory moved into a new state-of-the-art, interconnected complex constructed specifically for its purposes. The first three buildings housed facilities for Electromagnetic Materials Survivability, Systems Support, and Materials and Manufacturing Technology. In 1985, a building for Nonmetallic Materials was added, and the final building for Metals and Ceramics was completed in 1986. Within the complex, researchers studied radiation-resistant materials, electro-luminescent lighted instrument panels, plastics, composites, fibers, camouflage coatings, high-temperature materials, and titanium and aluminum alloys.

plane. The demands for new, high-temperature, high-strength materials were, in some cases, literally out-of-this-world. Indeed, so challenging were materials requirements for some especially demanding applications that researchers compared their work to the search for "unobtainium."

As the dust settled from World War II and with the publication of Dr. von Karman's *Toward New Horizons*, however, no technical objective seemed unattainable. The Laboratory's researchers rolled up their sleeves and continued research in such areas as metals, textiles, rubber, and paints and other coatings. They forged ahead with initiatives to develop better aluminum alloys (one of which, designated ML, was named for the Laboratory) and pioneered the development and application of titanium, ceramics, and rare earth metals.[159] Meanwhile, the Laboratory continued its wartime pioneering work in

J. B. JOHNSON

MR. MATERIALS OF THE AIR FORCE

For nearly 30 years, from 1922 to 1949, materials research and development at McCook and Wright fields was synonymous with the name J. B. Johnson. Johnson was a "charter member" of the science and engineering cadre that first formed at McCook Field during the final year of World War I. It was a club that included, in addition to Johnson, D. M. Warner, C. J. Cleary, and R. R. Moore, among other outstanding individuals.

During that first year, no separate and distinct materials laboratory existed. Instead, several small workshops for metallurgy, chemistry, fabrics, and rubber supported the airframe and power plant engineers and the McCook Field shops as they tested, evaluated, designed, and built aircraft, engines, and aeronautical equipment for the Air Service.

In 1919, McCook reorganized its technical activity by forming six technical sections, one of which was for materials. The first two chiefs were military officers, Lieutenant Colonel H. C. K. Muhlenberg followed by Captain H. W. Flickinger, both of whom Johnson served as liaison to the rest of the section. By the end of 1922, "J. B." was himself in charge and remained very much in charge for nearly three decades.

These were decades that witnessed one materials revolution and the beginning of several others. In the 1920s, wood and fabric began to give way to metal structures in airplane construction, and by the mid-1930s, the most advanced transport, bomber, and fighter aircraft were all constructed of metal. Johnson and his group worked closely with industry in the test and evaluation of new steel and aluminum alloys and developed techniques for detecting and counteracting corrosion and metal fatigue, including ingenious non-destructive techniques using x-rays. Throughout these years, Johnson was more than an administrator. He was also actively involved in research and published his results in everything from Air Corps information circulars to articles in *Aviation* and other technical and trade magazines.

By the mid-1940s, still another revolution was under way—in fact, several revolutions. First was the challenge of developing substitute materials to help ration or replace scarce and strategic materials during World War II. Finding substitutes for metals was one such effort that resulted in the development and use of plastics, fiberglass, and other early composite materials. Second was the challenge of developing metals and other materials that could withstand the very high temperatures of vehicles traveling at transonic and supersonic speeds.

In 1949, the Air Force appointed a military officer, Colonel B. R. Lawrence, to head up the Materials Laboratory. J. B. Johnson was transferred to what became the Aeronautical Research Laboratory (ARL), first in a staff position. He was later named chief scientist of the laboratory. Johnson, known to all as "Mr. Materials of the Air Force," retired in 1958.

Source: James J. Niehaus, *Five Decades of Materials Progress, 1917-1967* (Wright-Patterson Air Force Base, 1967).

AIRCRAFT MODIFICATION SHOPS

When McCook Field was established in 1917, an integral part of the science and engineering activity were the in-house shops. Originally, there were three shops: a wood shop, metal shop, and machine shop. Together, they constituted what was called the "Factory." The Factory was responsible for fabricating nearly everything that McCook's engineers might need: wind-tunnel models and wind tunnels, propellers and propeller test rigs, airplane components and entire airplanes. When airplanes broke down, the shops fixed them. Indeed, so closely did the shops and engineering corps collaborate that, by the late 1930s, the shops were designated a "laboratory" along with the Materiel Division's other technical branches.

During World War I and the early 1920s, McCook Field's shops built experimental airplanes and engines. Shown here is fuselage assembly in McCook's "Factory."

In the 1920s, the factory designation was dropped, possibly to calm industry fears that the Air Service was attempting to establish an aircraft manufacturing organization along the lines of the Naval Aircraft Factory. However, the shops continued to fabricate experimental models and facilities and to repair aircraft damaged during ground and flight testing. In the 1930s, the Wright Field shops built the Air Corps' first centrifuge for testing multiple gravity forces on airmen.

The wood, metal, and machine shops at McCook Field were organized under the Factory Section. Shown here is the machine shop.

During World War II, the shops grew in size and extended the scope of their activities. In addition to the "central shops", there sprouted up a number of "zone shops." The central shops initially occupied three one-story buildings adjacent to the aircraft final assembly building (Building 31). During the war, they moved to a vast one-story structure (Building 5). The zone shops, meanwhile, were collocated with the technical activities they supported and were thus scattered around Wright Field.

After the war, the shops lost many personnel to reductions-in-force. In the 1950s, under the Wright Air Development Center, they also lost their laboratory designation. During the reorganizations of the laboratory and acquisition activities in the early 1960s, the shops were assigned to the Flight Test Directorate of the Aeronautical Systems Division (ASD). In 1971, Flight Test became the 4950th Test Wing. When the Test Wing was reorganized in the mid-1970s, the shops were restructured as the wing's Aircraft Modification Center, or "Mod Center" for short.

Throughout the Cold War, Wright Field's shops continued the tradition of precision craftsmanship of earlier decades, in support of the laboratories, flight test, and system program offices. They performed a particularly vital service during wartime and in support of contingency operations, as the Air Force's contribution to first-line industrial surge activity.

The end of the Cold War in 1989-1991 resulted in the closure and consolidation of numerous Air Force bases and facilities around the nation and the world. Among the units inactivated was the 4950th Test Wing, which transferred its flight test activities to the Air Force Flight Test Center (AFFTC), Edwards Air Force Base, California, in 1994. The Mod Center, however, remained at Wright-Patterson, where it was reorganized as the Developmental Manufacturing and Modification Facility (DMMF) and assigned to ASD. However, because of continued reductions in personnel authorizations across the Air Force, ASD reluctantly deactivated the DMMF in 1997, bringing to a close the era of in-house shop activity at Wright-Patterson.

Sources: *Against the Wind: 90 Years of Flight Test in the Miami Valley*, (Wright-Patterson Air Force Base, 1994); J. F. Aldridge, "ASC's Five Foot Wind Tunnel" Diana G. Cornelisse, et al.., (Wright-Patterson Air Force Base, 1997).

Beginning in the 1960s, the Materials Laboratory championed the development of carbon-carbon composites for very-high-temperature applications in airframe and engine hot structures. Shown here are various aerospace components made of carbon-carbon.

plastics and composite materials for application to both special aircraft structures, like radomes, and even major structural portions of the airframe.[160]

The Laboratory's program, meanwhile, was affected by two events that occurred in 1950-1951. The first was the Laboratory's realignment under the Air Research and Development Command's (ARDC's) Wright Air Development Center (WADC), which was completed in 1951. The second was the outbreak of the Korean War in June 1950. The first assured materials research and development—like all other technical areas—greater visibility and support in the Air Force. The second resulted in a modest expansion of the Laboratory's manpower and substantially larger expansion in the Laboratory's technical program, with an emphasis on *ad hoc* support of the war effort.

Thus, in the early 1950s, the Laboratory developed long-life rubber for aircraft tires, improved paints for aircraft markings and designations, lubricating oils for low-temperature aircraft operations, corrosion technology to preserve aircraft in salt and extreme operating environments, and better packaging techniques for war materiel shipped to the front. At the same time, however, the Laboratory was able to pursue more long-term R&D in such areas as improved aluminum alloys, the characteristics and uses of titanium alloys, and improvements in composite materials.[161]

So great was the increased number of projects, especially those on contract, both during the Korean War and after the armistice in 1953 that, by the end of the 1950s, Laboratory planners began to reconsider the organization and function of the Laboratory. The result was a concept called "Materials Central" that was to act as a sort of "clearinghouse" for materials developments across the aerospace industry, academe, and other government research centers. This model was no sooner unveiled, however, than it was subsumed under a much greater reorganization of the laboratory and engineering functions at Wright Field inaugurated in 1959 by ARDC Commander General Bernard Schriever and WADC Director of Laboratories Colonel Fred J. Ascani.[162]

Under this new structure, Materials Central became the Air Force Materials Laboratory in 1963, its mission and *modus operandi* little changed from the previous decade. Along with the Laboratory's new status came dedicated funding for longer-term efforts and opportunities to increase manpower substantially for the first time since the Korean War. As an Air Force constituted unit, moreover, the Laboratory had a visibility perhaps greater than at any time in its previous history with a mission centering on *applied research*.[163]

During the 1960s and following decades, the Laboratory continued and, where appropriate, redoubled its long-term efforts to develop more advanced metals and metal alloys, composite materials, and non-structural materials (paints, coatings, lubricants, hydraulic fluids, etc.), while inaugurating new lines of research in such areas as carbon-carbon composites and rare earth permanent magnets.[164]

In the area of *metals* research and development, for instance, the Laboratory, during the 1960s, conducted research in nickel-based "superalloys" and coated niobium alloys for high-temperature applications in jet engines. In the 1970s and 1980s, the Laboratory achieved a breakthrough in developing ductility in titanium-based intermetallics for advanced

Rare-earth permanent magnets were invented in the 1960s by a Materials Laboratory research team led by Dr. Karl J. Strnat. Such magnets were used in a variety of applications including traveling wave tubes; microwave circuits; inertial devices; motors, generators, and actuators; and spacecraft attitude control. By the mid-1990s, rare-earth magnets represented a $2 billion-a-year industry that included both military and commercial products.

turbomachinery. The Laboratory also sponsored the design and development of streamlined extrusion dies for producing aluminum components made from powder materials of aluminum-alloy-silicon-carbide whiskers. In the 1980s, the Laboratory pursued development of aluminum, titanium, and magnesium alloys. Research centered on molding metal powders under pressure and rapid solidification of molten metal. These techniques allowed metallurgists to develop alloys with highly refined microstructures for specific applications in aerospace vehicles and platforms.[165] Further, the Laboratory developed and transitioned to industry superplastic forming/diffusion bonding in the processing of titanium and its alloys.[166]

In the 1990s, the Laboratory's research continued in the development of lightweight, high-temperature metals and metal matrix composites based on titanium, aluminum, magnesium, and beryllium.[167]

As impressive as were the Laboratory's accomplishments in metals R&D, its work in the development of *advanced composite materials* was very nearly revolutionary and, to a large extent, dependent upon initial, in-house laboratory research and persistent sponsorship and advocacy.

The Laboratory's program in advanced composites R&D began during World War II at the behest of General Henry H. "Hap" Arnold, who was looking for substitutes for strategic metals. The Laboratory initiated programs to develop aircraft structures using reinforced plastics, which resulted in the flight test of aircraft with major structural components of composite make-up, including the aft fuselage of a Vultee BT-15 and an AT-6 sporting plastic sandwich wings.[168] However, the first operational use of composites during the war was in aircraft radomes made of glass-fiber-reinforced polyester.[169]

Following the war, the Laboratory continued exploring improvements and applications of glass-fiber-reinforced composites, including missile rocket motor cases.[170] However, to make composites truly competitive with aluminum alloys, the Laboratory, during the course of the 1950s, turned from glass fibers to fibers of boron, carbon, boron carbide, and beryllium oxide.[171]

Much of this research was conducted with internal Laboratory funds. The Laboratory's efforts were, therefore, greatly aided in 1963 when *Project Forecast* identified advanced composites as a critical technology. The resulting Air Force funding allowed the Materials Laboratory to design a long-term strategy for developing advanced composites. The Laboratory did this initially by demonstrating applications of available technology first, in order to develop Air Force confidence and industry interest. Some early demonstrated applications included an F-111 horizontal stabilizer and T-39 wing box of composite materials. Industry soon transitioned advanced composites to the F-14 and F-15 stabilizers[172] and the F-16 horizontal tail.[173] Subsequent experimental applications of composites to the F-15 wing and F-16 fuselage led to aggressive use of composites in the Navy's AV-8B and F-18. By the 1990s, advanced composites were in use on such aircraft as the B-2, F-117, C-17, and F-22. The most impressive use of composites was on the B-2, which had the largest primary composites structures fabricated and flown up to that time.[174] As a result of the successful use of composites on military aircraft, industry began incorporating them on commercial aircraft too, such as the Boeing 777.[175]

In addition to aircraft, the Materials Laboratory also began in the late 1960s to investigate applications of composites to spacecraft. Initially, this was done to save weight on space vehicles. Soon, however, other advantages were perceived, such as the very low coefficient of expansion of graphite-epoxy composites that allowed for the design of critical spacecraft components that might otherwise suffer from uneven heating. This application was first applied to the NATO III satellite. By the mid-1990s, most commercial satellites relied on advanced composites for most structural applications due to their high stiffness, low thermal distortion, and superior strength. Advanced composites also found military space applications as well, one of the most notable examples being the MX ballistic missile.[176]

Another class of composite material pioneered by the Materials Laboratory was *carbon-carbon composites*. Carbon-carbon composites were particularly suitable for very-high-temperature applications (above 2,500° F) over long periods of time. Laboratory advocacy and experimentation, in conjunction with several industrial partners, began in the early 1960s. Carbon-carbon composites very soon found uses in aircraft brake disks, solid rocket motor nozzle throats, exit cones, space battery sleeves, missile reentry vehicle nosetips, turbine engines, hypersonic flight vehicle nose caps and leading edges, semi-conductor manufacturing components, and electronic circuit board thermal planes.[177]

Another area pioneered by the Materials Laboratory in the post-World War II period was that of *electronic sensor materials*, i.e., those materials suitable for use in microelectronics, lasers, and related applications.

The era of microelectronics and solid-state physics was inaugurated with the invention of the transistor by Bell Laboratories in the late 1940s. A decade later, the Materials Laboratory laid the foundation for work in this area with the establishment of a Physics Laboratory (1957) and an Electronic and Magnetic Materials Section (1959). Later, in the 1970s, the Materials Laboratory added a Laser Windows Working Group (1971) and the Electromagnetic Materials Division (1974) with branches for Optical Materials and Laser Hardened Materials.[178]

The Laboratory's accomplishments in the area of sensor materials are many. In the mid-1960s, the Laboratory pioneered the invention and use by industry of *rare earth magnets*. In the 1970s, the Laboratory developed laser and infrared transparencies, prompted in part by the requirements for the Airborne Laser Laboratory.[179]

In the area of *infrared (IR) detector materials*, the Laboratory developed higher purity silicon that permitted exploitation of laser-guided bomb and missile technology, arsenic trisulfide coating for the Defense Support Program's (DSP) missile-launch-detection focal planes, and mercury-cadmium-telluride materials for use in DSP satellites and other space applications.[180]

In addition to developing high-purity silicon, the Laboratory also pioneered the development of other electronic materials including gallium arsenide (GaAs), indium phosphide (InP), silicon carbide, and gallium nitride (GaN). These materials enabled revolutionary advances in phased-array radar, communication systems, and electronic warfare, areas in which the Laboratory had cultivated breakthrough discoveries since the early 1960s.[181]

In the mid 1980s, *Project Forecast II* encouraged the Materials Laboratory to pursue research in *nonlinear-optical (NLO) materials*. The Laboratory undertook research in two NLO areas: NLO crystals for wavelength conversion in solid-state laser sources required primarily for infrared countermeasures (IRCM) to protect aircraft from IR missile threats, and electro-optic films for optoelectronic devices needed for optical communications and photonic architectures in such systems as phased-array radar. Research and development in the first area resulted in many new crystals available to military laser designers. One such crystal, zinc germanium phosphide (ZGP), contributed to the success of the Mid-Infrared Lasers program, undertaken jointly by the three services and the Defense Advanced Research Projects Agency (DARPA) in the 1990s; the Large Aircraft Multiband Source (LAMBS) laser (ca. 2000), sponsored by the Air Force; and the Laser Infrared Flight Experiment (LIFE), sponsored by the Air Force Research Laboratory. Work in the second NLO area led to successful development of significantly better electro-optical (EO) modulators and enabled the world's first demonstration of a modulator with an operating voltage of less than one volt. The Laboratory also undertook development of EO polymers and successfully demonstrated their suitability for space-based applications. The Laboratory investigated layered nanometer-scale composite materials for EO applications and developed, in collaboration with the Oak Ridge National Laboratory, Tennessee, a process for depositing single crystal films of barium titanate with an extremely large EO coefficient.[182]

Finally, the history of materials development at McCook and Wright fields included the detection of defects in materials and, where possible, their repair. The need for this line of research was evident very early as the Materials Section at McCook Field tested and evaluated problems like the delamination of wooden propellers used in airplanes stationed in Florida and Panama and other locations of high humidity and rainfall. The Materials Section likewise tested the durability of various fabrics, dopes, and paints used on early Air Service airplanes.

The increased use of metals in aircraft structures during the 1920s and 1930s opened up a new field of investigation, that of metal fatigue and corrosion. Indeed, the initial hesitancy with which the Air Corps greeted the prospect of all-metal aircraft was due in part to the lack of data on the durability and rate of deterioration of aluminum, aluminum alloys, and steel under various operating conditions. One solution adopted by the materials researchers at Wright Field in the mid-1920s was the introduction of x-rays to detect cracks and other evidence of metal fatigue.[183]

By the late 1950s, the Materials Laboratory had established a special branch for systems support and soon had collocated engineers in the various system program offices (SPOs) of the Aeronautical Systems Division. In the 1990s, with the creation of the Air Force Materiel Command, various systems support activities of the air logistics centers (ALCs) were assigned to the Materials Directorate's Systems Support Division. Members of the division, meanwhile, remained in close consultation with the ALCs, the operating commands, and units in the field, giving expert advice and solving problems, sometimes on an hour's notice.[184]

Among the recurrent challenges confronting system support engineers in the 1990s were the old bogies of metal fatigue, moisture-induced corrosion, and other factors affecting aircraft structural integrity.

LASER HARDENED MATERIALS LABORATORY

The development of the laser in the 1960s presented the Air Force with a number of remarkable opportunities and problems, both offensive and defensive. Depending upon their intensity and wavelength, laser beams were capable of impairing parts of aircraft and space vehicles, including structures, sensors, optical systems, and personnel. In response to these potential hazards, beginning in the mid-1970s, the Air Force undertook research into the development of materials "hardened" to the effects of laser beams. The Air Force Materials Laboratory was in the forefront of these efforts and, in the course of the 1970s and 1980s, developed laboratory facilities for testing laser-hardened materials, called the Laser Hardened Materials Evaluation Laboratory (LHMEL) I, which began operations in the late 1970s, and a LHMEL II facility constructed 10 years later.

Laser Hardened Materials Evaluation Laboratory II under construction. The two large vacuum spheres were transferred from other Wright Field facilities for use in the LHMEL II.

Sources: History of the Aeronautical Systems Division, January-December 1986, Part II: The Air Force Wright Aeronautical Laboratories, 1984-1986, vol. 1, pp 74-75; History of the Aeronautical Systems Division, January-December 1987, vol. 1, pp 266-269.

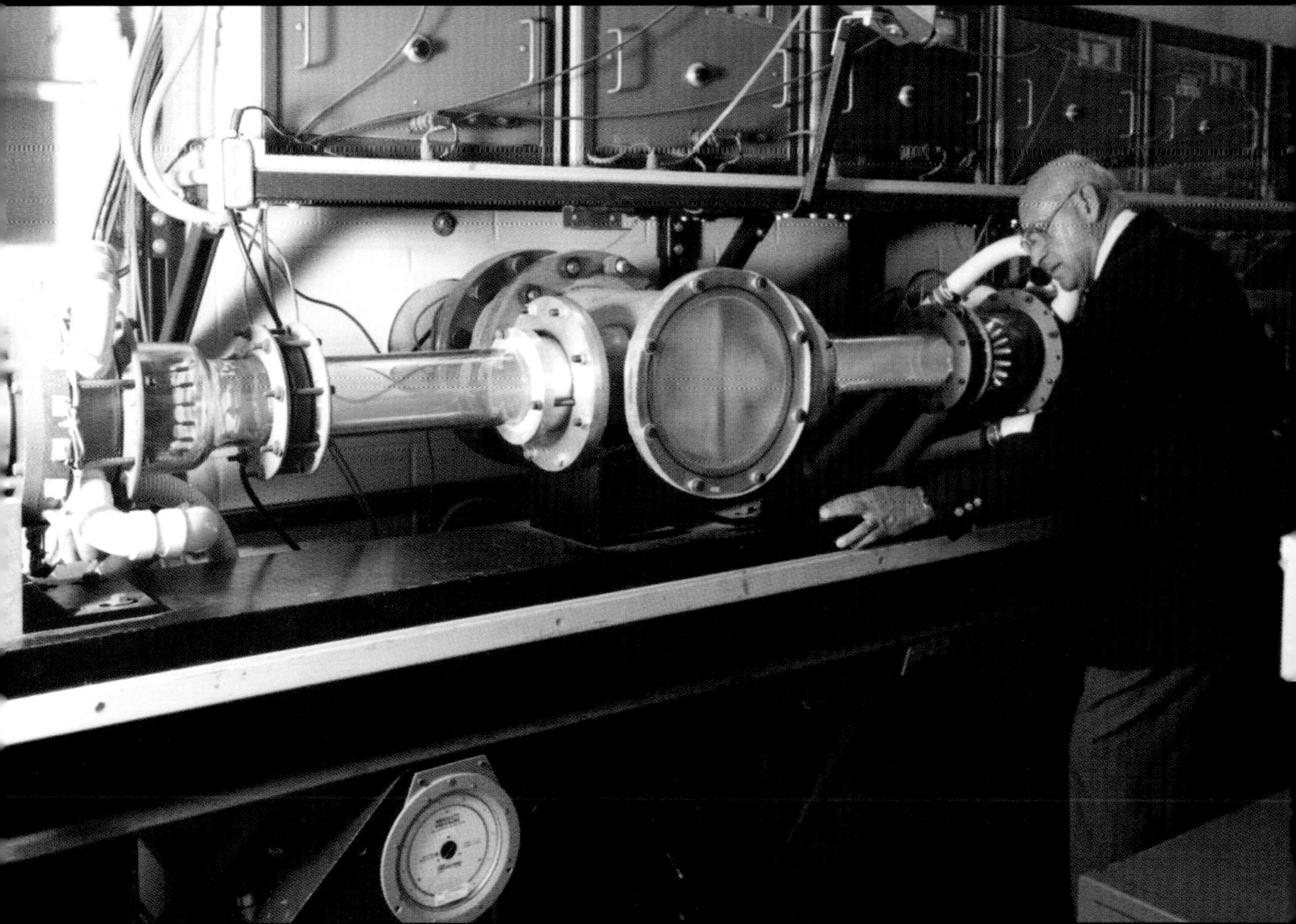

Interior view of Laser Hardened Materials Laboratory I in operation

Aircraft wiring, which had proliferated with the increase in avionics devices and systems on modern combat and transport aircraft, was also a major preoccupation of the Materials Laboratory's systems support specialists since wiring, as it aged, could degrade, causing false signals, loss of conductivity, subsystem or component failures, and fires. Indeed, all these problems were compounded by the increasing age of Air Force aircraft, many of which had exceeded their design lifetimes.[185]

Over the years, the Materials Laboratory's systems support personnel have continued to develop diagnostic inspection methods and decision support tools to aid field and depot maintenance personnel. In the early 1990s, for instance, cracks inside the wings of C-141 aircraft were observed emanating from "weep holes" in wing fuel tanks. The Laboratory's support engineers developed a repair method, conducted a demonstration of the procedure, and held classes for maintenance personnel at the Robins Air Logistics Center, Georgia. Their expertise was also called upon by the National Transportation Safety Board (NTSB) and the Federal Aviation Administration (FAA) to assist in the investigation of the crash of TWA 800 on July 16, 1996.[186]

In addition to developments in its technical program, the Materials Laboratory continued to evolve as an institution in the years after 1963. In 1975, the Laboratory was federated with the Aero Propulsion, Avionics, and Flight Dynamics laboratories in the Air Force Wright Aeronautical Laboratories (AFWAL).[187] The formation of AFWAL was coincident with the disestablishment of the Aerospace Research Laboratories (ARL) at Wright Field.[188] As a result, the Materials Laboratory inherited ARL's basic research mission in materials, along with its researchers, facilities, and funding through the Air Force Office of Scientific Research (AFOSR).[189]

When AFWAL was reorganized as the Wright Research and Development Center (WRDC) in 1988, the Materials Laboratory's Manufacturing Technology Division became an independent line organization called the Manufacturing Technology Directorate.[190] This separation continued when WRDC was reorganized two years later as the Wright Laboratory. Under the Wright Laboratory, the Materials Laboratory was itself redesignated a directorate, but otherwise remained intact.[191] Toward the end of the 1990s, the Air Force consolidated all its laboratories into one Air Force Research Laboratory (AFRL), and the materials and manufacturing technology missions were once more consolidated into AFRL's Materials and Manufacturing Directorate (AFRL/ML).[192]

MANUFACTURING TECHNOLOGY

An often overlooked aspect of transitioning technology to weapon systems and commercial products alike is manufacturing methods. One of the first great improvements in American arms manufacture was Eli Whitney's development of interchangeable parts for guns; likewise, Henry Ford's introduction of the assembly line revolutionized automobile manufacture. The introduction of the airplane posed a number of novel problems, not least the continuous and rapid introduction of new materials, designs, and structures of aircraft, particularly those for military use. The 1920s and 1930s witnessed the transition from wood and fabric to all-metal aircraft; World War II and the postwar period witnessed the gradual re-introduction of non-metallic components—including major structures—in airframes as well as revolutions in propulsion and electronic components and subsystems.

The Air Force's fostering of aircraft manufacture as a "technology" to be treated like other technology areas with a dedicated in-house cadre of engineers and budget line to coordinate efforts throughout industry developed slowly. During the 1920s and 1930s, engineers at McCook and Wright Field kept abreast of manufacturing problems confronting the aircraft industry, particularly during the transition from wood and fabric to all-metal construction. Interest centered on such problems as riveting, spot welding, and the design and manufacture of stressed-skin structures, from the standpoint of manufacturing, durability, inspection, and repair.[193] Aside from the Materials Laboratory, the Wright Field shops, which were themselves denominated a "laboratory" by the end of the 1930s, experimented with new methods of design and fabrication of aircraft components. Indeed, the shops issued at least one information circular to industry during this period.[194]

However, at the outset of World War II, American aircraft manufacturing enterprises were still largely organized as a craft industry. The war changed all this when, as early as 1940, President Franklin Roosevelt called upon American industry to supply the Army and Navy with 50,000 airplanes annually. The mass production of aircraft called for a revolution in aircraft manufacturing methods. Indeed, as the automobile industry won licenses to

Example of automated tape-laying process

The Air Force's Manufacturing Technology (Man Tech) program was one of the early champions of the application of robotics to manufacturing methods. Shown here are examples of robotics in the workplace underwritten by the Man Tech program: (top right) example of precision drilling using robotics, (right) demonstration of a robotics vision system, and (above) a forging press in the aircraft-engine-disk isothermal forging cell at United Technologies' Pratt & Whitney plant in Columbus, Georgia, loaded and unloaded by computer-controlled robotic systems.

produce airplanes, it became clear that aircraft manufacture would never be quite the same again.[195]

Before the end of the war, it became increasingly obvious to the Materiel Command, headquartered at Wright Field, that a more systematic approach would have to be taken to promote innovation in manufacturing methods of aircraft production. Thus was born the Air Force's program in manufacturing technology.

When the Air Materiel Command (AMC) was split up in 1950-1951 to create the Air Research and Development Command (ARDC), the manufacturing technology program remained within AMC, probably due to its close association with AMC's wartime planning and production responsibilities. However, when AMC and ARDC were reorganized in 1961 as the Air Force Systems Command (AFSC) and the Air Force Logistics Command (AFLC), manufacturing technology was transferred to AFSC. AFSC, in turn, made the Materials Laboratory at Wright Field responsible for conducting the manufacturing technology program, which was constituted a division within the Laboratory.[196]

Over the years the Air Force's manufacturing technology program made major contributions to modernizing the nation's defense manufacturing facilities and operations. The first significant project was the development of heavy forging presses for manufacturing large aircraft parts. The program also pioneered the development of numerically controlled machining.[197] More recently, the program sponsored efforts to improve the production of composite materials, electronics components, and packaging, and to develop new techniques for computer integrated manufacturing. In the 1990s, the Manufacturing Technology program recorded an estimated cost avoidance of over one billion dollars alone as a result of its Retirement for Cause program.

The growing importance of carbon-carbon composite materials, pioneered by Wright Field beginning in the 1960s, led the Manufacturing Technology Division over the following decade to undertake a program to improve carbon-carbon manufacturability, which had initially proved to be extremely long while exhibiting poor repeatability and high rejection rates.[198] Initially, the program aimed at reducing fabrication costs for three-dimensional nosetip and heat-shield applications. This resulted in the establishment of an industrial base consisting of two domestic sources that could supply components for full-scale heat shields and nosetips. The division also leveraged carbon-car-

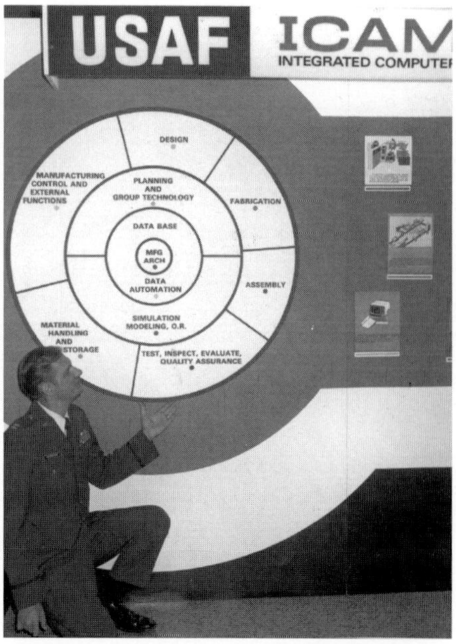

Integrated Computer Aided Manufacturing (ICAM) became a major thrust for Man Tech in the late 1970s and 1980s. As indicated in these photos, ICAM represented more than just computerization of machinery; ideally it implemented a change in business philosophy beyond the manufacturing floor.

bon technology developments from other government organizations, like the Defense Advanced Research Projects Agency (DARPA). In addition, the division focused on improving the producibility of oxidation-resistant, carbon-carbon composites for use in limited-life applications such as missile engine rotors.[199]

The Manufacturing Technology Division also tackled the problem of making the manufacture of advanced composite structures more efficient and affordable. Advanced composites came into their own beginning in the 1960s. Programs sponsored by the Materials and Flight Dynamics laboratories demonstrated their practicality in such structures as the F-111 and F-14 horizontal stabilizers, the F-16 vertical and horizontal stabilizers, and the F-15 speed brake.[200]

Thus, in the early 1970s, the Manufacturing Technology Division focused on reductions in manufacturing advanced composite structures through automation and improved quality. Tape laying, for instance, was automated. To make this practical, the quality and consistency of composite, pre-impregnated tape were improved. Subsequently, fiber placement technology, used on most modern Air Force weapon systems, was developed. Among the systems that benefited from these and other developments were the F-16, F-117, F/A-22, C-17, B-2, MX missile, and the Global Positioning System.[201]

Beginning in the 1970s, the Manufacturing Technology Division began sponsoring programs to apply computer technology to various manufacturing processes. This effort envisaged using computer technology to improve the technical efficiency and productivity of various manufacturing methods and processes.[202] One of the main efforts in this strategy was the Integrated Computer Aided Manufacturing (ICAM) program, inaugurated in 1976. ICAM provided guidance and seed money throughout the defense industrial base for the development of computer integrated manufacturing (CIM) prototype efforts. There were four major aspects of these CIM technologies: methods, tools, and techniques; information infrastructure; advanced engineering applications; and advanced manufacturing applications.[203]

Over the years, these and other applications of manufacturing technologies saved the Air Force hundreds of millions of dollars while rendering the nation's defense industrial base stronger and more competitive. Among specific recent beneficiaries of improved manufacturing technologies were the manufacture of infrared windows and domes;[204] transmit/receive modules for solid-state, phased-array radar;[205] and an affordable F-16.[206]

The manufacturing technology program remained a part of the Materials Laboratory until 1988 when, on the creation of the Wright Research and Development Center (WRDC), it was constituted an independent technology directorate.[207] However, in 1997, when the Air Force Research Laboratory (AFRL) was established, manufacturing technology was reintegrated with materials research in AFRL's Materials and Manufacturing Technology Directorate (AFRL/ML).[208]

THE HUMAN FACTOR

The systematic study of the human factor in flight was not undertaken at Wright Field until the arrival of Captain Harry G. Armstrong, M.D., at Wright Field in 1934. Within a year, Armstrong assembled a small research team, initially about four members strong, called the Physiological Research Laboratory, within the Materiel Division's Equipment Branch.[209]

The new laboratory team overhauled an old pressure chamber in the basement of the Wright Field laboratory building (Building 16) for use in altitude experiments on rabbits and students from Antioch College in Yellow Springs, Ohio, among others, and designed a small centrifuge (fabricated by the Wright Field shops from scrap metal and parts) for testing g forces on humans and goats.[210]

These early experiments bore immediate fruit in the design of the first pressure-cabin airplane, the XC-35. The XC-35 won the Collier Trophy for Wright Field in 1937; more importantly, it paved the way for the design and construction of the Air Corps' first truly long-range bomber, the B-29, as war clouds closed in on America from east and west.[211]

In 1940, Armstrong departed Wright Field, but not before writing and publishing a massive tome, *The Principles and Practice of Aviation Medicine* (1939), detailing the results of the Laboratory's experiments and systematically identifying and setting forth the basic elements that largely govern aerospace medicine to the present day.[212]

GENERAL HARRY G. ARMSTRONG, M.D.

The field of aviation medicine owes a great debt to one individual who did more throughout the 1930s, 1940s, and 1950s in this field than any other person, military or civilian. Harry Armstrong, born in 1899 in South Dakota, arrived at Wright Field in 1934 as a result of a letter he sent the air surgeon in Washington, D.C., regarding the inadequate protective equipment available for aircrews. The air surgeon's response was: "you are the one that complained and you are the logical man to try to solve it." Up to that point, Captain Armstrong had only been involved in the field of aviation medicine for five years and had no research or development background. He took the challenge, however, and the field of aviation medicine entered its prime.

Once at Wright Field, Armstrong established the Physiological Research Laboratory to study methods of protecting aircrew members from the extreme temperatures of high altitudes and winter climates. This unit later evolved into the Aero Medical Research Laboratory, with Armstrong at the helm. With a small staff, budget, and very little equipment, Armstrong implemented a variety of research projects, including studies of night vision; the effects of toxic gases; the fatigue aspects of flying; air-sickness prevention; and the development of protective equipment, aircraft first aid kits, tools for rescuing crash victims, aircraft carbon monoxide detectors, aircraft oxygen systems, soundproof flying helmets, color-blindness test equipment, shoulder-type safety belts, improved flight clothing and goggles, and cockpit lighting systems. Armstrong also constructed the first centrifuge in the United States, with which he conducted a number of studies on the effects of g forces on humans. Among his other accomplishments, he defined 63,000 feet as the altitude at which blood "boils" and wrote a textbook on aviation medicine that served as the leading word in the field for over 20 years.

Perhaps one of Armstrong's greatest contributions to aviation, however, was the development of the first successful, pressurized, passenger aircraft. In 1937, Armstrong prepared the specifications that led to the construction of the Lockheed XC-35. He also assisted Trans World Airlines (TWA) and Boeing in the development of the first pressurized-cabin stratocruiser (the Boeing Model 307 Stratoliner), the forerunner of today's commercial airliners. For its role in these developments, the Army Air Corps received the Collier Trophy.

Many of his admirers commented on his ability to forecast the wave of the future in aviation technology, often at the risk of personal ridicule. Armstrong attributed his vision to his admiration of General Billy Mitchell, who was court-martialed for his outspoken advocacy of the potential of air power. Armstrong remembered Mitchell telling him "...throughout history...there is continual progress in almost all lines and...that aircraft...would progress within the foreseeable future...and that anyone who failed to have that sort of vision was not very productive." Consequently, Armstrong determined that he "...should not deal just with the existing situation, but try to foresee what the future possibly held and to work to meet the problems of the future as well as those that existed at the present."

Armstrong's vision led to the establishment of the Department of Space Medicine at Randolph Field, Texas, in 1947, and the Aerospace Medical Center at Brooks Air Force Base, Texas, in 1959. He served as the surgeon general of the Air Force between 1949 and 1954 and retired from service in 1957 with the rank of major general. In 1998, General Armstrong was enshrined in the Aviation Hall of Fame, only the second physician to share that honor.

Sources: "Biographical Sketch of Major General Harry G. Armstrong, USAF (Ret)," n.d., Interview of Major General Harry G. Armstrong (Ret), U.S. Air Force, Medical Corps, conducted by John W. Bullard and T.A. Glasgow, Brooks Air Force Base, Texas, April 1976, for the United States Air Force Oral History Program.

Major General Harry G. Armstrong, M.D.

Captain Armstrong (left) with Dr. J. William Heim in their office at Wright Field. Armstrong personally recruited Heim from Harvard as his first civilian assistant.

View of the Wright Field Aero Medical Research Laboratory complex as it appeared in the late 1940s to early 1950s

During an assignment at Holloman Air Force Base, Captain Joseph W. Kittinger participated in high-altitude balloon projects initiated by the Aerospace Medical Laboratory at Wright Field. In the first of these, Project Man High, Kittinger set a balloon altitude record of 96,000 feet. Sealed inside a capsule about the size of a hot water heater, he survived by wearing a full pressure suit.

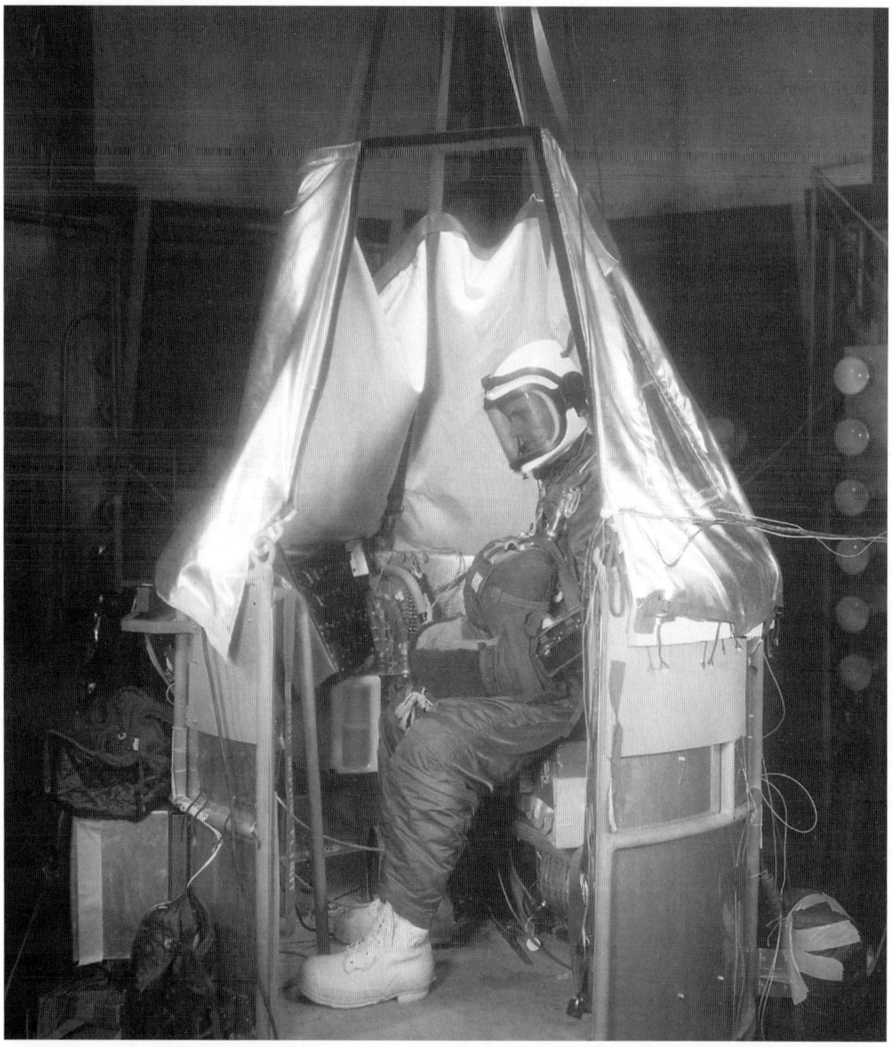

On August 16, 1960, Captain Kittinger jumped from a balloon-supported gondola at an altitude of 102,800 feet. Aerospace Medical Laboratory personnel designed and built the balloon and gondola that lifted Kittinger to heights never before achieved in a balloon, as well as the multi-stage parachute that prevented him from entering a life-threatening, uncontrollable flat spin during his four-minute free-fall. Project Excelsior proved the human capability to survive ejection from aircraft at high altitudes and contributed to potential escape methods for astronauts.

America's entry into World War II, in December 1941, vastly expanded the size and scope of the Wright Field laboratories and increased their number. The Equipment Laboratory spun off several of its units as separate laboratories within the Materiel Division. As early as 1939, its photographic section became the Photography Laboratory.[213] In July 1942, Armstrong's old group, now augmented by many new civilian and military recruits, became the Aero Medical Research Laboratory.[214]

During the war, the Aero Medical Research Laboratory continued to focus its research on human survival at high altitudes and high g-forces in combat maneuvering. This research included defining human tolerances to prolonged cold temperatures for cruising at high altitudes and the establishment of concomitant protective requirements in the design of flight clothing. Likewise, the Laboratory developed and standardized the first anti-g-force suits.[215]

The Laboratory also developed oxygen canisters and pressure-breathing equipment for both high-altitude flight and for bailing out at high altitudes, and established human tolerance limits to ejecting under conditions of severe windblast.[216] The Laboratory further continued to refine pressure-cabin characteristics for high-flying bomber and cargo aircraft, including human physiological limits in situations of explosive decompression.[217] The Laboratory also developed more mundane, but no

C-47 assigned to the Aero Medical Research Laboratory at Wright Field to conduct psychological research, 1950

less critical, medical evacuation facilities, supplies, and related equipment for the transport of the wounded.[218]

In January 1943, the Aero Medical Research Laboratory moved from the old laboratory building (Building 16) at Wright Field to a new facility constructed solely for the Laboratory's use.[219] A second centrifuge was constructed in May of that year for the testing of a new anti-g suit.[220]

Work in g-forces and high-altitude flight was not only immediately war-related but looked forward to the new age of truly high-speed, high-altitude flight that overtook the Air Force in the course of the war and the first postwar years. The Air Force's first jet airplane, the Bell P-59A, took to the skies over Muroc Field, California, on October 2, 1942. Only four years later, on October 14, 1947, Air Force Captain Chuck Yeager broke the "sound barrier" in the Bell X-1, heralding the age of supersonic flight.[221]

Significantly, at the end of the war, Dr. von Karman's study, *Toward New Horizons*, specifically recognized the importance of aviation medicine by including a volume on *Aviation Medicine and Psychology*.[222]

In the immediate postwar years, the Aero Medical Research Laboratory suffered the same substantial cuts in manpower as the other laboratories at Wright Field. Like some of the other laboratories, however, it, too, benefited from the influx of German scientists and engineers under the auspices of Project Paperclip. Altogether, around 15 German scientists and engineers joined the Laboratory beginning in May 1947, most coming from the Helmholtz Institute in Bavaria.[223]

These men, together with Laboratory veterans of the 1930s and war years (many of whom had been hired by Armstrong), led the Laboratory for the next several decades, well into the 1960s, even the 1970s and 1980s, in a few cases.

Four developments affected the operation of the Aero Medical Research Laboratory over the course of the next dozen years. The first was the establishment of an independent command for research and development, the Air Research and Development Command (ARDC) in 1950-1951. The second was the outbreak of the Korean War in June 1950. The third was the Air Force's push for flight at faster speeds and higher altitudes. And the fourth was the prospect of human exploration of the exoatmosphere—"outer space."

The realignment of the Aero Medical Research Laboratory from the Air Materiel Command's (AMC's) Directorate of Research and Development to ARDC's Wright Air Development Center (WADC) was perhaps, ironically, the least consequential for the Laboratory's overall organizational development or operations. It little affected the operation and technical thrust of the Laboratory's R&D program. The Laboratory continued its fruitful organizational association with the other Wright Field laboratories, all of which also transferred to WADC.[224]

The Korean War, on the other hand, prompted an increase in the number of projects and accelerated those already under way. More importantly in the long run perhaps, it substantially increased the Laboratory's manpower for the first time since the end of World War II.

Research in the late 1940s and 1950s addressed the human factors in both jet air craft and space flight. In the area of high-speed jet flight, the Laboratory established human tolerance limits and protective equipment requirements for ejection escape systems. The Laboratory also developed uniform flight clothing and protective clothing for Air Force pilots. This included development of the first operational pressure suits for Air Force pilots. The Laboratory also developed an operational, liquid-oxygen system for high-altitude jet flight.[225]

The Laboratory also explored human tolerance limits and established standards for bioacoustics environments for the Air Force. Related to this research was the first airfield noise survey and land-use program for the Air Force.[226]

The Aero Medical Research Laboratory underwent many of the same changes as the other Wright Field laboratories in the late 1950s and early 1960s. The first harbinger of change appeared in August 1959, when the Laboratory changed its name to the Aerospace Medical Laboratory. When WADC became WADD in December

CENTRIFUGES AND "G FORCE" RESEARCH

Modern pilots routinely experienced the effects of "g forces" (a force exerted upon an object by gravity or by reaction to acceleration or deceleration) and had to practice aerial maneuvers without endangering themselves and their aircraft. The g-forces pressed pilots into their seats and quickly drained oxygen from their brains. Left unchecked, g-forces could affect eyesight and ultimately cause total loss of vision.

Wright Field became involved with g-forces research in the 1930s when Captain Harry G. Armstrong, M.D., conducted experiments to determine aircrew tolerance limits. Specialists at Wright Field's shops fabricated the first centrifuge "to simulate the effect of gravity and accelerations by whirling a person or animal subject in a circle at fairly high speed." This simulator measured 20 feet in diameter, with a five-horsepower motor, and could generate a maximum of 20 g's. Operating with an equipment budget of only $100, Captain Armstrong arranged for construction of the centrifuge using a salvaged electric motor and aluminum aircraft tubing. Armstrong also saved funds by providing animal specimens for his research by raising a herd of goats at Wright Field!

At Wright Field, Captain Harry Armstrong studies man's tolerance to g forces in the first centrifuge built in the United States.

In May 1943, a second centrifuge was installed at Wright Field for the purpose of developing a new anti-g suit. The high-altitude air operations of World War II prompted the need for intense aeromedical research to adequately protect aircrews during flight. Armstrong guided his group of technicians in developing electric flight suits, pressure demand oxygen systems, armor for aircrews, high-altitude flight clothing, and anti-g suits. The new centrifuge at Wright Field and a centrifuge at the Mayo Clinic provided the Army Air Forces with the capability to perform highly specialized physiological experiments. Using volunteers, these experiments determined human tolerance to various rates of acceleration in developing the new g suit. Armstrong's researchers submitted themselves to grueling experiments to provide fliers the best and most advanced equipment for their protection—thereby making a significant contribution to the war effort.

The fourth and most recent centrifuge operated at Wright Field is the Dynamic Environmental Simulator (DES).

Following the war, the era of jet flight posed a series of challenges for the aeromedical community. This led to construction of a third centrifuge, in Building 33 at Wright Field, in 1948. The new simulator enabled scientists to test their theories about the effect of increased flight velocities, high acceleration forces, and high-altitude flight profiles on humans. This centrifuge established the human tolerance for normal and emergency space-flight trajectories—information vital to the United States at the dawn of the space age.

Ultimately, a fourth simulator became necessary as the Air Force became deeply involved in the space program. The Air Force completed the Dynamic Environment Simulator (DES) in early 1966. On December 19, 1969, Dr. Michael McCally completed the first human tests using the DES. A series of four runs completed the "man-rating" of the new centrifuge. In 1970 technicians modified the DES to provide closed-loop control up to 7.5 g man-rated simulation. This provided Wright Field researchers with new capabilities, especially in chemical defense, advanced flight-vehicle performance, and in testing technical problems in aircraft design and flight.

Jet-age fighter aircraft, such as the F-15 and F-16, pushed pilot physiology to the limit with their treacherous torque, power, and maneuverability. Scientists at the DES and at the simulator at Brooks Air Force Base, Texas, continued to develop technologies and techniques to improve fighter pilots' performance and their ability to survive high g forces. In 1991 aerospace medicine experts devised the Combat Edge positive-pressure breathing system that increased pressure in the subject's chest. This caused the blood pressure and oxygen flow to the brain to increase. Combat Edge helped pilots stay at higher g's for extended periods of time without tiring as quickly.

Both the DES and the Brooks centrifuges were certified to take subjects up to 12 g's, but all trips over nine g's required aeromedical approval. Recent centrifuge projects include studies to determine whether men or women can better tolerate simulated aerial combat; the effect of a dietary supplement on muscle fatigue and its ability to improve g tolerance; and the effects of sleep deprivation under high g conditions.

Sources: Charles A. Dempsey, *50 Years of Research on Man In Flight* (Air Force Aerospace Medical Research Laboratory, ca. 1985); James F. Aldridge, "Aerospace Medicine at Wright Field—Notes," ASC History Office; Edward B. Alcott and Robert C. Williford, *AMD: 25 Years of Excellence* (Aerospace Medical Division, Brooks Air Force Base, Texas, 1986); Interview of Major General Harry G. Armstrong (Ret), U.S. Air Force, Medical Corps, conducted by John W. Bullard and T.A. Glasgow, Brooks Air Force Base, Texas, April 1976, for the United States Air Force Oral History Program; "The Spin Doctors: Scientists prepare pilots to defy gravity,"*Airman*, http://www.af.mil/news/airman/0698/spin.htm.

The Aerospace Medical Laboratory at WADC participated in the astronaut selections for Project Mercury. Beginning in February 1959, the astronaut candidates underwent medical tests at the laboratory to shorten the long list of potential astronauts to just seven. The chosen Mercury astronauts (left to right): M. Scott Carpenter; L. Gordon Cooper, Jr.; John H. Glenn; Virgil I. Grissom; Walter M. Shirra, Jr.; Alan B. Shepherd, Jr.; and Donald K. Slayton. Behind them is an F-106B, January 20, 1961.

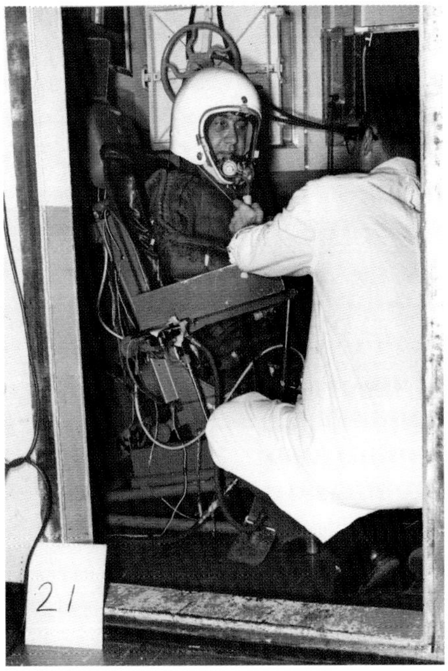

The seven Project Mercury astronauts returned to WADC several times to conduct training for their space flight, including mental, physical, and medical tests. Pictured here: Gus Grissom, in a pressure suit, spent one hour in a pressure chamber at a simulated altitude of 80,000 feet for Project Mercury.

1959, the Aerospace Medical Laboratory was renamed the Aerospace Medical Division under WADD's Directorate of Advanced Systems Technology.[227]

Less than a year later, in November 1960, however, the Aerospace Medical Division underwent two significant changes. First, it transferred from WADD to Air Research and Development Command's Assistant for Bioastronautics and was redesignated the Aerospace Medical Laboratory. Second, it lost responsibility for the engineering and development of end items to WADD's Directorate of Systems Engineering. As a result, the Laboratory transferred its Clothing Branch to Systems Engineering, as well as various other smaller organizations and personnel.[228]

One month after the Aeronautical Systems Division (ASD) was established, in April 1961, the Aerospace Medical Laboratory was reassigned to ASD. However, in November 1961, the Air Force established an Aerospace Medical Division (AMD) within Air Force Systems Command (AFSC), and in January 1962, the Aerospace Medical Laboratory was realigned under AMD as the 6570th Aerospace Medical Research Laboratory.[229] This arrangement lasted until the last decade of the century, when the Laboratory was reunited organizationally with the other Wright Field laboratories under the Air Force Research Laboratory (AFRL) in 1997 (see below).

Already during the 1950s, the Laboratory had pioneered America's new frontier in space. For instance, the Laboratory postulated the first physiological and psychological requirements for low earth orbit in outer space.[230] However, during the 1960s, the Laboratory increasingly turned its attention to space research. Both the Air Force and the National Aeronautics and Space Administration (NASA) benefited from the Laboratory's space-research programs.

For example, the Laboratory developed environmental control standards for space cabins. It also explored human performance and mobility in a weightless environment. For this purpose the Laboratory already had developed during the previous decade a method for simulating weightlessness by flying parabolas in cargo aircraft, outfitting the cargo bays with padded walls, floors and ceilings for this purpose. The laboratory also studied human movement during the rendezvous of two space vehicles in support of NASA's Apollo space program.[231]

The Laboratory also studied human tolerance to emergency thermal conditions (extremes of heat and cold) in space. This research included studies of human tolerance and performance during reentry flight and human tolerance to low-altitude, buffeting flight. The Laboratory studied and established nutritional requirements for long-term space flights and the toxicological requirements for space cabins. Closely related to the latter were studies conducted by the Laboratory for protecting humans from space radiation. Following on its development of pressure suits and other clothing for Air Force jet pilots the previous decade, the Laboratory performed operational validation of pressure suits for astronauts. Furthermore, the Laboratory studied the effects on astronauts of abrupt acceleration for the landing of manned space vehicles.[232] Finally, the Laboratory helped establish requirements and standards for training would-be astronauts, including the use of ground and flight simulators.[233]

During the 1970s and early 1980s, the Laboratory's emphasis began once more to shift from space-related research back to manned air vehicles. This redirection was due in part to the maturation of space technologies and experience—owing in not small degree to the Laboratory's contributions—and the development of computer technologies and their application to the human factor in aeronautics.[234]

The Laboratory studied fully automated cockpit technology and voice control of cockpit functions and also studied the ef-

THE "WEIGHTLESS WONDER"

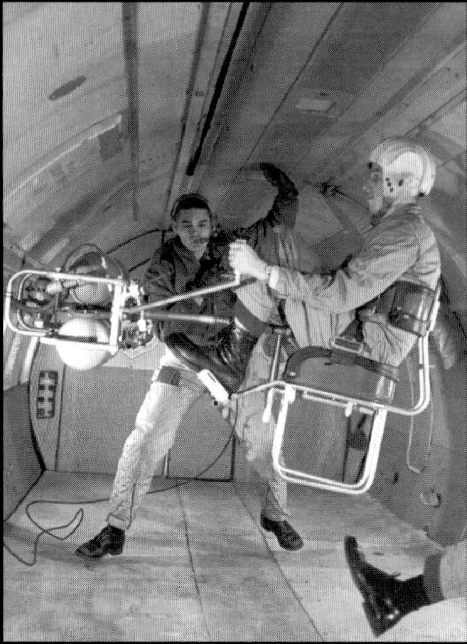

"Space Jeep" undergoes zero gravity tests.

Wright Air Development Center at Wright-Patterson Air Force Base began a Zero Gravity testing program in 1957 to measure the effects on humans of weightlessness during space flight. An aircraft flying Keplerian trajectories (parabolas) simulated weightlessness or reduced gravity for short periods of time. The aircraft first used was a modified C-131 transport (serial number 53-7823), which could produce 12 to 15 seconds of zero gravity during its parabolic flight path. In 1960, the first in a series of three modified KC-135s (serial number 55-3129) was acquired for weightlessness training. This aircraft, dubbed the "Weightless Wonder," could simulate zero or low gravity for 30-second intervals. The cargo compartment on the KC-135 was covered with protective padding and insulation to protect test subjects during their weightlessness, and cameras were mounted at waist height to document the test results. The other two C-135s modified for the program were C-135A number 60-0378 and KC-135A number 62-3536, both of which replaced the original Weightless Wonder in 1968 and continued in the zero gravity program until 1973 and 1970, respectively.

From the late 1950s through the early 1970s, the Aerospace Medical Laboratory and Flight Test Operations at Aeronautical Systems Division worked with the National Aeronautics and Space Administration (NASA) to perform tests for the astronauts who flew the Gemini, Apollo, and Skylab missions, as well as tests for full-scale cabin mock-ups of the spacecraft. Astronaut John Young, who flew six space missions, indicated that the weightlessness he experienced in the "Weightless Wonder" was identical to his actual space flights. Other test programs included egress-ingress techniques to prepare for the first "walk" in space; the use of self-maneuvering units; wheel development and crew training for the lunar roving vehicle; feasibility for crew transfer from the Gemini to an orbiting laboratory via a tunnel passing through the heat shield; and experiments with soil-sampling techniques for use on Mars.

By 1972, the Air Force's Zero Gravity program had flown 48,000 parabolas, the approximate equivalent of 15 days of space flight. In 1973 NASA took over the program with another modified KC-135, the "Weightless Wonder IV" (NASA's 930, serial number 59-1481). This aircraft flew more than 57,000 parabolas and also was used during the filming of the weightless scenes for the movie *Apollo 13*. It was retired in 1995 and was replaced by another KC-135A (serial number 63-7998).

DR. HENNING E. VON GIERKE

Henning von Gierke was born in 1917 in Karlsruhe, Germany. His early studies in Germany introduced him to the fields of electronics and acoustics, and he earned a doctorate in electrical engineering in 1944. Von Gierke worked as a research assistant at the Institute for Theoretical Electrical Engineering and Communications Techniques at the Technical University in Karlsruhe until 1947. At that time, he moved to the United States under Project Paperclip, a program through which a number of German aviation scientists and engineers were recruited to work in the United States following World War II. Initially, von Gierke signed a one-year contract, but decided to remain in the United States, becoming a citizen in 1977.

Von Gierke began work in the Biophysics Division of the Aerospace Medical Research Laboratory in 1947. He became director of the Biodynamics and Bioengineering Division at the laboratory in 1961. Through the years, he played a vital role in research and development programs to protect aircrews from a variety of hazards. Some of these programs included techniques to determine the effects on humans of ultrasonic noise from supersonic aircraft and the effects of acceleration and deceleration; studies of vibration and buffeting problems in high-speed, low-altitude aircraft; the development of upward, downward, and high- and low-altitude ejection systems; and the development of superior restraint systems. Some of this early research evolved into systems used outside the military, such as seat-belt restraints and airbags for automobiles and ultrasonic surgery and other techniques used in modern medicine.

The Biodynamics and Bioengineering Division also participated in programs that advanced knowledge of the effects of space travel on humans. Biospace experiments began as early as 1951, and in the 1960s the laboratory worked with the National Aeronautics and Space Administration (NASA) to establish safety and tolerance criteria for humans in space environments. Researchers in the laboratory studied the effects of impact landings and excessive vibration; developed dehydrated, frozen, freeze-dried, and stored foods; and assisted NASA in the selection of the final seven astronauts for Project Mercury. Dr. von Gierke also led the Biodynamics Division during studies of bionics, robotics (biocybernetics), and bioacoustics for the Air Force.

Sources: United States Air Force Biography of Dr. Henning E. von Gierke, September 1983, in the ASC History Office Archives; U.S. Air Force, News Release, "Bionics, Space Foods, Effects of Noise Made for Exciting Era," May 30, 1985; MSgt Lorenzo D. Harris, "It Runs in the Family," *Airman*, September 1984, pp 37-40.

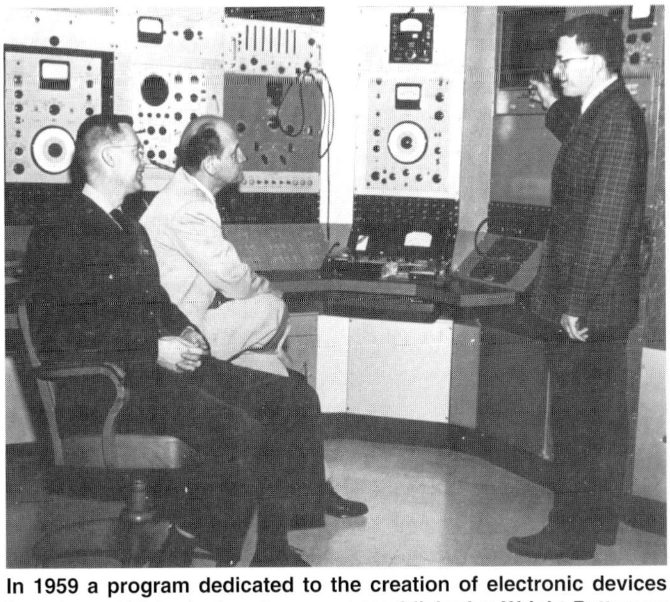

In 1959 a program dedicated to the creation of electronic devices based upon biological systems was established at Wright-Patterson Air Force Base, where Colonel Jack Steele created the word "bionics" (*bio*logy and electr*onics*) to describe this groundbreaking field of science. Scientists in the Aerospace Medical Laboratory are shown here performing word recognition experiments with an electronic model of the inner ear. In the mid-1970s the Biodynamics and Bionics Division changed its name because of the high volume of telephone calls it received after *The Bionic Woman* became a popular television series.

Shown here are the aural displays of the Bioacoustics Branch of the Human Effectiveness Directorate of the Air Force Research Laboratory, the branch that continues the pioneering acoustics work once performed by the Aerospace Medical Laboratory. The bionic experiments performed at Wright-Patterson Air Force Base on acoustical models led to the development of improved hearing aids, automatic speech recognition ability in computers, and the establishment of industrial and occupational noise standards by the Environmental Protection Agency for the protection of workers. (*Air Force Research Laboratory, Aural Displays and Bioacoustics Branch*)

fects of high acceleration for cockpit development. Further, the Laboratory established visual standards for aircraft windscreens.[235]

In the area of environmental concerns, the Laboratory investigated the toxicology of rocket fuels on humans and plants and chemical-defense modeling of human capability. The Laboratory also continued environmental noise modeling for land-use planning.[236]

The Laboratory established aircrew workload standards and conducted computer modeling of anthropometrics for workspace design. In addition, the Laboratory studied crew system design for strategic systems and developed a crew survivability/vulnerability model for weapon systems.[237] The Laboratory also used the computer to model escape-system performance and studied open ejection seat technology with protection to 1,600 Q (where Q equals incompressible dynamic pressure).[238]

The Laboratory studied secure tactical communications and explored human engineering design for command and control systems and developed a remotely piloted vehicle (RPV), multi-operator, real-time mission simulation.[239]

During the course of the 1960s, 1970s, and 1980s, the Laboratory underwent a number of internal reorganizations and two name changes. In 1979, the Laboratory changed its designation from the 6570th Aerospace Medical Research Laboratory to the Air Force Aerospace Medical Research Laboratory.[240] Then, in June 1985, the Laboratory was once again renamed, this time the Armstrong Aerospace Medical Research Laboratory, honoring, appropriately, its founder and the foremost pioneer of Air Force aerospace medicine, General Harry G. Armstrong.[241]

In 1982, the Laboratory's parent organization, the Aerospace Medical Division, headquartered at Brooks Air Force Base, Texas, was renamed the Human Systems Center upon the merger of Air Force Systems Command (AFSC) and Air Force Logistics Command (AFLC) to form Air Force Materiel Command (AFMC). Finally, when the Air Force established a consolidated Air Force Research Laboratory (AFRL) in 1997, the Armstrong Aerospace Medical Research Laboratory became AFRL's Human Effectiveness Directorate (AFRL/HE), receiving, in the process, responsibility for cockpit research from the former Wright Laboratory's Flight Dynamics Directorate.[242]

Scientists in uniform: researchers at WADC's Aeronautical Research Laboratory at work in the 1950s

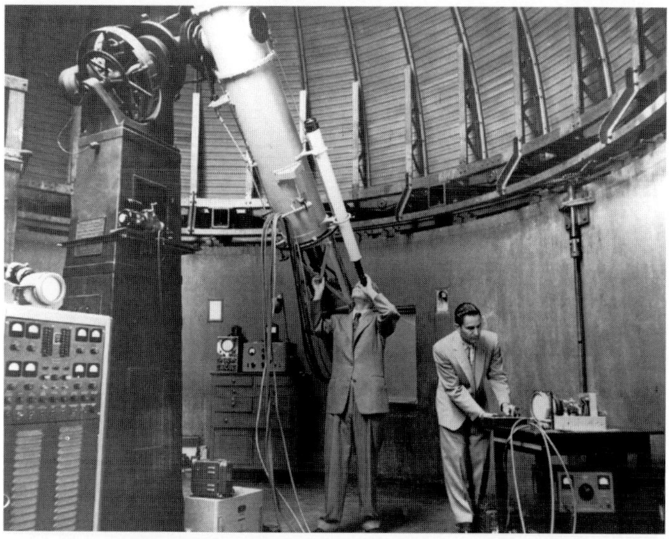

In the late 1950s, ARL scientist Ramdames K. H. Gebel invented the "Cat Eye," a light amplification system that had a sensitivity over 1,000 times that of an ordinary television camera. Used in conjunction with a telescope or other optical system, it could track missiles and satellites and allowed pilots to see the ground on moonless nights. Pictured here is a telescope equipped with the Cat Eye system.

BASIC RESEARCH

The importance of basic scientific research to better understand natural phenomena relating to flight vehicles was first recognized by the Wright brothers when they tested airfoil shapes in a homemade wind tunnel to determine for themselves their aerodynamic qualities. In order to undertake these experiments, the brothers had to educate themselves on aerodynamic theory and the necessary mathematics.[243] It was an accomplishment that impressed Theodore von Karman a quarter century later, when Orville Wright told him what he and brother Wilbur had done. Von Karman, like many others, had thought the brothers were essentially gifted tinkerers who had stumbled onto inventing the airplane. As he discovered to his "surprise and enormous interest" the invention of manned flight had had a thorough grounding in science from the very beginning.[244]

Research takes time and money. It is usually most successfully conducted by institutions, whether of higher learning or government research centers with a commitment to seeing things through the long term. As early as 1912, there were a few far-sighted individuals in the American aeronautical community who recognized the need for a national "aerodynamical" laboratory,[245] even as other countries such as Britain and Germany were establishing state-supported institutions to promote their domestic—primarily military—air-power needs.

However, it was not until the outbreak of World War I that the United States took steps for state sponsorship of aeronautical research. In 1915, Congress established the National Advisory Committee for Aeronautics (NACA) to conduct "scientific research on the fundamental problems of flight."[246] In 1917 the Army Signal Corps established a Science and Research Division, headquartered in Washington, D.C. Its director during the war was physicist Robert A. Millikan. (It was Millikan who in 1926 recruited Theodore von Karman to head up the Guggenheim Aeronautical Laboratory of the California Institute of Technology [GALCIT].[247]) Following the war, the Science and Research

Construction of the Physical Sciences Building at Wright-Patterson Air Force Base was completed in 1958. The Aeronautical Research Laboratory (later the Aerospace Research Laboratories) called the 100,000-square-foot structure "the most modern and best equipped research facility in the Air Force." It housed eight branches of the ARL: Chemistry, Engineering Physics, Modern Physics, Mechanics, Metallurgy, Applied Mathematics, System Dynamics, and Fluid Dynamics. Later, the building housed the Aero-Mechanics Division of the Flight Dynamics Laboratory.

Division was discontinued, and its remaining personnel were transferred to McCook Field, where they were integrated into the Engineering Division.[248]

The Army's basic research mission in aeronautics fell into desuctude during the interwar years. McCook's Engineering Division was intended primarily to conduct experimental engineering on aircraft prototypes, power plants, and equipment. During this period, the Army relied primarily on other government agencies and research centers, such as the NACA's Langley Memorial Laboratory or the laboratories of the National Bureau of Standards, for assistance in basic research problems. (This institutional division of labor did not prevent McCook and Wright Field scientists and engineers from occasionally performing basic research any more than it prevented NACA researchers from conducting projects, such as developing the NACA cowl, that might better be classified as developmental engineering.)

World War II substantially altered the Army Air Forces' (AAF) appreciation for aeronautical research. AAF Commanding General Henry H. "Hap" Arnold and his principal technical advisor, Dr. von Karman, were keen supporters of both basic and applied scientific research and engineering, including a substantial, in-house capability. Von Karman protégé, Dr. Frank L. Wattendorf,[249] was responsible for upgrading and vastly expanding the in-house facilities at Wright Field, including the construction of the most powerful wind tunnel then in existence and a smaller, transonic wind tunnel.[250]

Postwar demobilization and budget reductions slowed this program substantially. However, an intrepid band of scientifically

Air Force technology leaders meet in 1971. They are (left to right): Dr. Gorden A. Eckstrand, chief, Air Force Human Resources Laboratory; Mr. Lester J. Charnock, technical director, ASD Deputy for Engineering; Dr. Fred W. Berner, technical advisor to the 6570th Aerospace Medical Research Laboratory; Dr. Demetrius "Zip" Zonars, chief scientist, Air Force Flight Dynamics Laboratory; Dr. Bernard H. List, chief scientist, Air Force Avionics Laboratory; Dr. Hans J. P. von Ohain, chief scientist, Aerospace Research Laboratories; and Dr. William H. Heiser, chief scientist, Air Force Aero Propulsion Laboratory.

AIR FORCE WRIGHT AERONAUTICAL LABORATORIES FELLOWS PROGRAM

On August 3, 1987, the Air Force Wright Aeronautical Laboratories (AFWAL) at Wright-Patterson Air Force Base established the Fellows Program to recognize the outstanding accomplishments of its scientists and engineers. The laboratories nominated candidates based on several characteristics, including having national recognition in a scientific area; demonstrating productivity, creativity, and depth of insight; and being a team leader who contributed significantly to the solution of problems in national defense programs. A panel of academic, industrial, and government scientists reviewed the candidates and submitted recommendations to the AFWAL commander for final selections. The chosen candidates each received a grant of $100,000 per year for two consecutive years to continue their research goals. The program was a way for the laboratories to provide their excellent staff with monetary and management incentives to pursue state-of-the-art technologies that benefited the Air Force, as well as the scientific community.

Source: History of Aeronautical Systems Division, January–December 1987, pp 253-256.

At the October 27, 1987, banquet to honor the first four AFWAL Fellows, Dr. Harold Sorensen (center), U.S. Air Force chief scientist, was the guest speaker. The awardees were (left to right): Dr. Alan Garscadden (plasma physics), Dr. Joseph J. S. Shang (computational fluid dynamics), Dr. Arthur J. Wennerstrom (aerodynamics of turbine engines), and Dr. Nicholas J. Pagano (laminated composites).

minded officers, together with von Karman, who served as the chairman of the Air Force's Scientific Advisory Board throughout this period, pressed for a more aggressive research program. Due to their lobbying, the Air Force, in February 1947, established an Applied Research Section in the Air Materiel Command's (AMC's) Engineering Division at Wright Field.[251] In April 1949, the section was renamed the Office of Air Research (OAR).[252]

The new Air Force research organization operated on two levels. On one level, it included a nucleus of experienced scientists and engineers for conducting in-house experimentation. On the other, it also contracted extensively with university laboratories and research centers for work on projects for which it did not have the manpower or expertise. Indeed, the extensive use of university know-how was a major departure from prewar Air Corps practice and followed on the major utilization of university researchers during the war effort by the Office of Scientific Research and Development (OSRD). When OSRD was disestablished after the war, the military service laboratories, themselves severely reduced in manpower, continued OSRD's practice of contracting with academic institutions for work they themselves could not perform.

It was also during these years that the Air Force and Wright Field were enriched by the addition of German scientists and engineers under the auspices of Project Paperclip.[253] Over 100 Paperclip scientists came to Wright Field where many of them remained, some for several decades.[254] Among the most eminent was Dr. Hans von Ohain, the German inventor of the gas turbine engine, who rose to become the chief scientist of the Aerospace Research Laboratories (see below) at Wright Field in the 1960s and later served as chief scientist of the Aero Propulsion Laboratory.[255]

When the Air Research and Development Command (ARDC) was established in 1950-1951, some members of OAR were transferred to ARDC headquarters, Baltimore, Maryland; others remained at Wright Field, where they formed the Computation and Simulation Laboratory in ARDC's Wright Air Development Center (WADC).[256] In 1952, the Computation and Simulation Laboratory was renamed the Flight Research Laboratory and finally,[257] in 1953, the Aeronautical Research Laboratory (ARL).[258] Under WADC, the ARL was usually grouped together with the Materials Laboratory and the Aero Medical Research Laboratory, many of whose projects included a large measure of what today would be considered basic or early applied research (exploratory development). ARL's mission during these years is perhaps best summed up by former WADC director of laboratories, Major General Fred J. Ascani, who observed that its scientists were to "look in the smoke and see what you see."[259] At the end of the 1950s, ARL had research groups for chemistry, fluid dynamics, general physics, plasma physics, metals and ceramics, applied mathematics, thermomechanics, and solid-state physics.[260]

In the reorganization of the Air Force's laboratories at Wright Field in 1959-1963, ARL was transferred from WADC and realigned under a new Air Force Research Division (AFRD) within ARDC headquarters. In 1961, when ARDC was reorganized as the Air Force Systems Command (AFSC), AFRD was redesignated the Office of Aerospace Research (OAR) and made an independent operating agency of the Air Force.[261]

In 1962, the Aeronautical Research Laboratory, which had remained at Wright Field, was redesignated the Aerospace Research Laboratories (ARL) and continued to report to OAR.[262] The renamed ARL consisted of nine laboratories for research in chemistry, general physics, plasma physics, metallurgy and ceramics, applied

RESEARCH: A MATTER OF TEAMWORK

Ceramic composites

Combustion research

Computational fluid dynamics

Plasma physics

Epitaxial semiconductor films

High-temperature materials

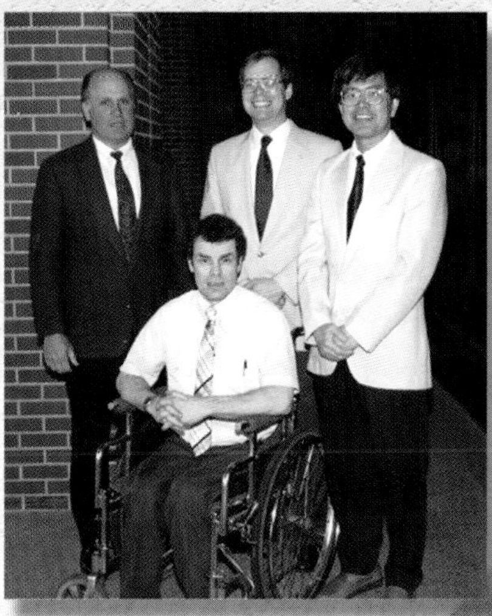

Polymers

While the popular imagination often conjures up the image of a lone (mad) scientist delving into nature's secrets with microscope and tweezers, real breakthroughs of a fundamental kind are more often the work of research teams assisted by supercomputers. Teamwork has been the hallmark of the Air Force's laboratories from the very beginning in areas of fundamental or "basic" research. Pictured here are several of the many research teams at Wright Field during the 1990s.

mathematics, thermomechanics, solid-state physics, fluid dynamics, and hypersonics.[263]

Like the other Air Force laboratories at Wright Field, ARL benefited from the Kennedy administration's attempt to build up the Air Force's in-house laboratory establishment.[264] Within a decade, however, the pendulum had begun to swing the other direction. By the mid-1970s, following defense reductions after the Vietnam War, the Department of Defense and the Air Force chose to shift more work to the private sector. This change in emphasis coincided with a reorganization of the laboratory structure at Wright Field. Under this reorganization, the Air Force's applied research laboratories at Wright Field were federated as the Air Force Wright Aeronautical Laboratories (AFWAL) in 1975.[265] Simultaneously, the Air Force disestablished ARL and transferred its buildings, facilities, and personnel to AFWAL's four "super" laboratories.[266]

The disestablishment of ARL did not, however, signify the end of the basic research mission at Wright Field. Henceforth, basic research fell under the purview of the four laboratory chief scientists, who met corporately in a Research Advisory Council.[267] Under AFWAL and its successor organizations, the basic research mission received primary funding and direction from the Air Force Office of Scientific Research (AFOSR), which, in 1975, was designated the Air Force's single manager for basic research. As the Air Force manager of basic research, AFOSR oversaw not only the Air Force's in-house efforts in basic research, but also a far larger contract program with various academic researchers and laboratories. Indeed, nearly 80 percent of the Air Force's basic research budget was devoted to research under contract with researchers and institutions outside the government.

In 1987, AFWAL established a Fellows Program to reward its top researchers and their teams with recognition and financial support. The Fellows Program was part of a wider Air Force effort to recognize its premier researchers nationwide. The first Fellows inductees were Dr. Alan Garscadden (plasma physics), Dr. Nicholas J. Pagano (laminated composites), Dr. Joseph J. S. Shang (computational fluid dynamics), and Dr. Arthur J. Wennerstrom (turbine engine aerodynamics).[268] In subsequent years, Wright Field recognized many more of its outstanding researchers in this way.

In 1990, AFOSR inaugurated a "star team" program. The purpose of the program was to recognize and lend financial support to outstanding research teams throughout the Air Force's laboratories. The star team approach complemented but did not supersede the laboratory Fellows Program.[269]

In 1989, the Air Force Systems Command directed its laboratories and centers to begin an aggressive program to increase the percentage of scientists and engineers with doctorates in their areas of expertise. AFWAL's successor organization, the Wright Research and Development Center (WRDC), developed a strategic plan for this purpose and in subsequent years added a substantial number of new PhDs to the in-house laboratory workforce, primarily through the Air Force's Palace Knight/Senior Knight program.[270] Indeed, during this period of personnel downsizing, this was one of the few programs that continued to allow hiring and renewal of the science and engineering workforce at Wright Field.

The consolidation of the Air Force's laboratories into four "super labs" in 1990 little affected the organization and functioning of the basic research program. In 1997, when the Air Force consolidated all of its laboratories nationwide into one Air Force Research Laboratory (AFRL), the Air Force Office of Scientific Research (AFOSR) became one of AFRL's 10 technical directorates, placing it on the same organizational level with the Air Force's nine consolidated, applied research organizations. However, it was the other nine directorates that continued to own the personnel and facilities dedicated to pursuing AFOSR's in-house research program.[271]

ENGINEERING

From the very beginning, engineering has played the central role in Air Force research and development at Wright-Patterson Air Force Base. This was obvious from the designation of successive organizations at McCook and Wright fields, from the Airplane Engineering Department in 1917 to the present-day Directorate of Engineering. Indeed, for the first 40 years, laboratory work at McCook and Wright fields was organized around what today would be called experimental or developmental engineering,[272] so that it is perhaps more accurate to call the laboratories of this period *engineering* laboratories.

What was the purpose of all this engineering activity? There are several core functions that have characterized aeronautical engineering over the years. These include translating Air Force requirements into performance specifications for aircraft, missiles, and various types of equipment; overseeing and assisting the contractor in developing new aircraft, missiles, and equipment; keeping apprised of technology advances for their incorporation into Air Force systems under development and future systems; test and evaluation of contractor products before they are acquired in quantity for operational use; and troubleshooting operational problems in cooperation with Air Force depots and operational forces.[273]

Indeed, engineering has historically been the vital link between the Air Force warfighter and mission accomplishment: for when, as the saying goes, the "rubber hits the ramp," it is the engineer who is ultimately responsible for having ensured that the tires do not blow out; that every nut and bolt of the undercarriage holds together; that the engines do not flame out or explode; that literally trillions of electrons course over hundreds of miles of wire to operate rudders and flaps, engine controls, and cockpit displays—all in proper sequence or simultaneously. It is the engineer, in short, who is responsible for the proper design integrity of all the systems and subsystems that the warfighter—and taxpayer—takes for granted, indeed, comes to expect of the finest and most complex aeronautical systems anywhere in the world today.

It is the aeronautical engineering organizations in Dayton, Ohio, that historically have stood at the center of this activity virtually since the days when Wilbur and Orville Wright corresponded with Benny Foulois on the operation, capabilities, and repair of his Wright Military Flyer.[274]

Engineering as it is organized and conducted today at Wright-Patterson, however, dates from 1959. In that year, as has been observed in other sections of this chapter, the Air Research and Development Command (ARDC) conducted a major reorganization of science and engineering functions throughout the command. The most significant impact of this reorganization occurred at Wright-Patterson in the constitution and function of its engineering cadres.

When the Wright Air Development Center (WADC) was established under the Air Research and Development Command in 1951, it essentially took over from the Air Materiel Command (AMC) its entire Di-

MAJOR GENERAL FRED J. ASCANI

WRIGHT FIELD'S FATHER OF SYSTEM ENGINEERING

The single most pivotal year in the history of Wright Field's science and engineering enterprise was 1959. In that year, Air Research and Development Command (ARDC) headquarters directed a complete reorganization of the Air Force's laboratory establishment. The man at the center of that reorganization at Wright Field was Colonel Fred J. Ascani, the Wright Air Development Center's director of Laboratories.

Fred J. Ascani, shown here when a brigadier general in charge of the XB-70 program

Ascani had been interested in flying since boyhood when he saw Lindbergh's *Spirit of St. Louis* fly over his hometown of Beloit, Wisconsin. When Ascani first visited Wright Field as a West Point cadet, even the fatal crash of a flight demonstration airplane on that occasion did not dissuade him from becoming an Air Corps officer and pilot. During World War II, Ascani flew bombing missions over Sicily and Italy. After his return from Europe in 1945, he joined the flight test organization at Wright Field, serving under Colonel Al Boyd, "the test pilot's test pilot." Ascani followed Boyd to Edwards Air Force Base, where he served as Boyd's deputy and fulfilled his dream of test piloting such aircraft as the X-1, X-4, X-5, and XF-92A. After piloting the F-86E for a record 635 mph at the National Air Show, he was awarded the Thompson Trophy that recognized high-speed advances in aircraft and the U.S. Air Force MacKay Trophy in 1951.

Following a number of assignments in Europe and the United States, Ascani was called on to head Wright Field's 12 laboratories in 1958. A year later, General Bernard A. Schriever, the commander of ARDC, initiated a reform of all the Air Force's laboratories to accelerate the transition of technology to weapon systems under development, including advanced fighters, bombers, ballistic missiles, and exotic aerospace vehicles.

The reform of the Wright Field laboratories required all of Ascani's considerable skills as a diplomat and his reputation for integrity and honest dealing. Within six months, Ascani and his top civilian advisors achieved the unthinkable: the complete transformation of a laboratory establishment, whose fundamental *modus operandi* had little changed since World War I, into one that could sustain the rapid technological advances of the Cold War. The Wright Field laboratories as they exist today still operate along the lines laid down by Ascani and his team in 1959. Just as significant as the new laboratories was the emergence of a separate systems engineering cadre from this reorganization. ASC's Engineering Directorate is a direct descendent of the Directorate of Systems Engineering established by Ascani's team.

Ascani went on to head the Directorate of Systems Engineering and its successor organization, the Systems Engineering Group, serving a stint as director of the B-70 Valkyrie program in between. By the time he departed Wright Field in 1965, Ascani had risen to the rank of major general.

After several other assignments in the Pacific, Wright-Patterson, and the Pentagon, Ascani retired from active duty in 1973, closing out a 32-year career in which he served his nation with courage, honor, and intelligence, and left at Wright Field a laboratory and engineering establishment that has stood the test of four decades.

Source: *A General Remembers: Major General Fred J. Ascani, Wright Field's Father of Systems Engineering*, ed. with narrative by James F. Aldridge (Wright-Patterson Air Force Base, 2001).

rectorate of Research and Development, including the Engineering Division. Under AMC, the Engineering Division was organized into a dozen or so laboratories. The laboratories had a dual function: to assist the project offices in the development of new airplanes, missiles, and equipment; and to conduct a limited degree of research for future, often "over-the-horizon," developments. Since the days of McCook Field, the developmental engineering function, consisting largely of the test and evaluation of contractor aircraft and equipment, had consumed most of the time and energy of the laboratories' limited technical staff.[275]

However, as the 1950s progressed, there were those who came to question whether this was the most efficient way to organize and conduct the engineering function in support of the project offices. It was during the 1950s that the "systems approach" to aircraft and weapons development came into favor. The systems approach called for planning and implementing the integration of all aspects of a new aircraft, including subsystems and components, from cradle to grave.[276]

However, the WADC laboratories were organized along the lines of an earlier model of aircraft development under which airframe, engines, instrumentation, armament, and controls were developed individually and then assembled by the airframe contractor.[277] Thus, the Aircraft Laboratory was responsible for the airframe, landing gear, cockpit, and flight controls; the Power Plant Laboratory, engines, fuels and lubricants, and onboard electrical power; the Equipment Laboratory, aircraft instrumentation, parachutes, and pilot clothing; the Aircraft Radiation

Laboratory, radar; the Photographic Reconnaissance Laboratory, cameras and other non-electromagnetic surveillance equipment; and so forth. There was, however, under this regime no dedicated engineering oversight of the process of systems integration, even for individual systems.

Compounding this problem was the dual role of most laboratory scientists and engineers. While engineers from the laboratories were routinely assigned to project offices to assist them in the technical aspects of overseeing the contractor's development of a new weapon system, they often were simultaneously working on research projects for the laboratory. To make matters worse, there were, in the end, not nearly enough scientists and engineers or funding to go around. Indeed, both advocates of systems development and advocates of applied research believed that their share of the mission was getting shortchanged.

In 1954, the Air Force, impatient with the progress on ballistic missile development at Wright Field, created the Western Development Division (WDD) in south ern California, and placed Major General Bernard A. Schriever in charge. Over the next five years, General Schriever's organization successfully developed the Atlas intercontinental ballistic missile, and Schriever was appointed commander of ARDC. He immediately set to work to reorganize his command to reflect his West Coast experience.[278]

At WDD, the Air Force contracted with the Ramo-Wooldridge Corporation to provide engineering support for product development. This was the first time that the Air Force had used engineers, contract or otherwise, solely to supply dedicated support for a system under development. (This was not the first time, however, that the Air Force had hired a contract organization to supply dedicated engineering support to operate a major engineering facility. In 1950, the Air Force had contracted with the Sverdrup Corporation to build and subsequently operate the Arnold Engineering Development Center (AEDC) in Tennessee.)

WDD was the model that General Schriever used to reorganize the Air Force's laboratories, primarily those at Wright Field. He assembled a team of senior colonels, including WADC's Director of Laboratories Colonel Fred J. Ascani, to develop an overall plan and strategy. In July 1959, their report was issued and the process of reorganization began.[279]

The result at Wright Field was the creation of a new organization in place of WADC: the Wright Air Development Division (WADD). The new division consisted of three line directorates: the Directorate of Systems Management, the Directorate of Advanced Systems Technology, and the Directorate of Systems Engineering. To create the last two, Colonel Ascani and his team literally divided up the old laboratories: half the laboratory engineering manpower went to Systems Engineering (around 2,500); the other half remained in the laboratories, which were further consolidated.

The purpose of the Systems Engineering Directorate was to provide dedicated engineering support to the system program offices (SPOs). To do this, the directorate collocated the bulk of its staff in the program offices while retaining a core that formed a "home office." The home office staff of several hundred was further subdivided into divisions for flight dynamics, propulsion, avionics, and studies and cost analysis. (The latter organization later formed the Directorate of Development Planning, see below.)

There were several subsequent reorganizations, mostly external to systems engineering, in ensuing years. In 1961, the Air Force united research and development with procurement and production in the Air Force Systems Command (AFSC). At Wright Field, WADD was merged with Air Materiel Command's (AMC's) Aeronautical Systems Center (ASC) to form the Aeronautical Systems Division (ASD), and WADD's Directorate of Systems Engineering became ASD's Deputy for Systems Engineering. In 1963, systems engineering was realigned, along with the laboratories, under the new Research and Technology Division (RTD). As a result, it was redesignated the Systems Engineering Group (SEG). When RTD was disestablished in 1967, the SEG was once more realigned under ASD as the Deputy for Engineering (ASD/EN). At Wright Field, to this day, "EN" means systems engineering.

The work of EN historically has been conducted by engineers collocated in the system program offices—the vast majority—and a smaller core contingent in a "home office." Indeed, very nearly every U.S. Air Force aircraft and aeronautical weapon system has been vetted at one or more stages in its development by EN's professionals. Among rated aircraft that Wright-Patterson's systems engineers have worked on since the formation of EN are

Lester J. Charnock, technical director of Systems Engineering (1960-1973). Major General Fred J. Ascani said of Charnock, "He was shrewd as could be... ."

EN assisted the C-17 SPO in determining paratrooper airdrop optimization.

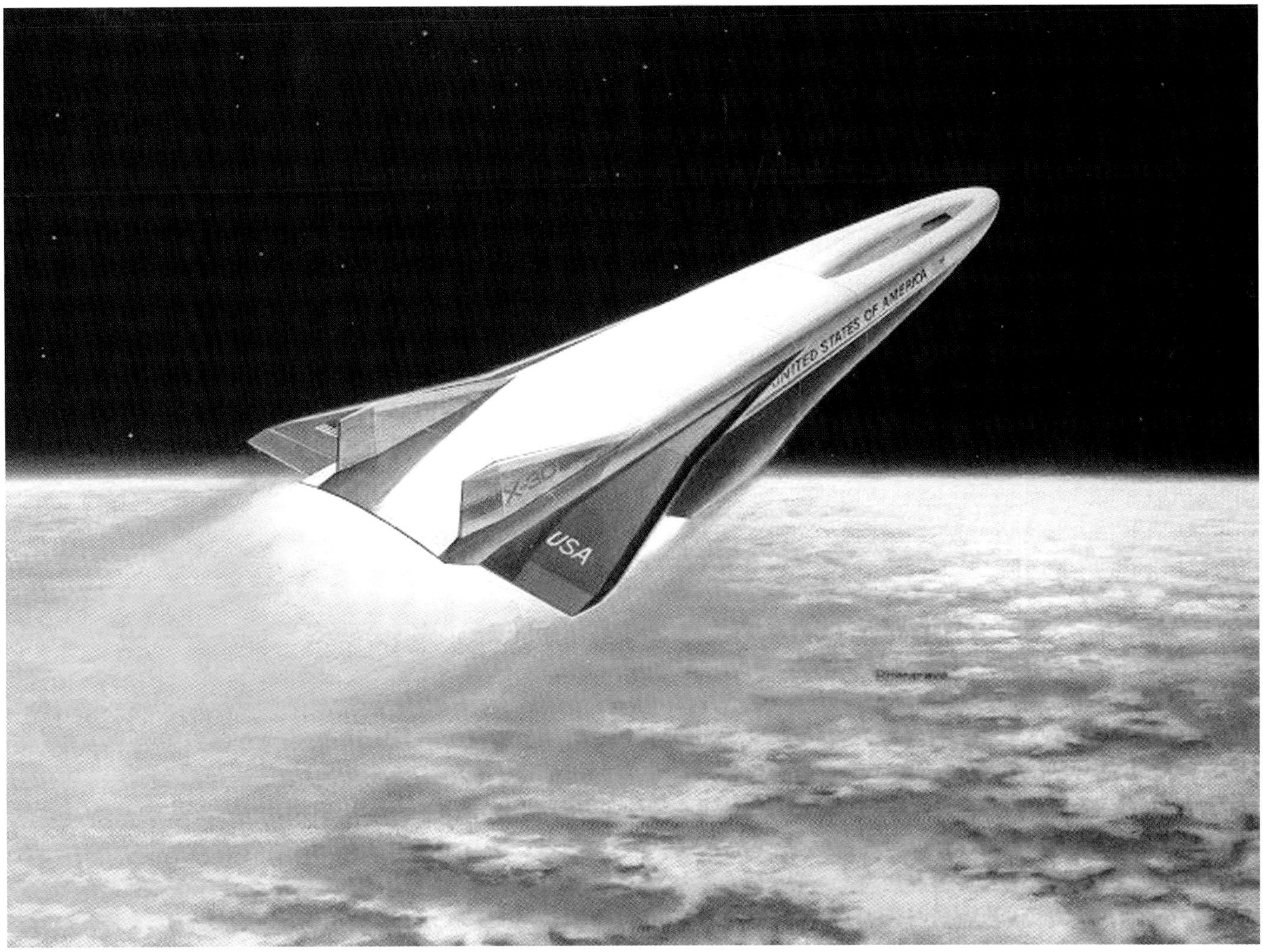

Artist's concept of the X-30, developed under the National Aerospace Plane (NASP) program from the mid-1980s to the mid-1990s. Although the NASP program never succeeded in building the X-30, it refocused national and world attention on hypersonic technologies and the potential of hypersonic flight.

the A-10, A-37, T-1, T-6, B-52 OAS, B-1A/B, C-5A/B, F-15, F-16, C-17, TR-1, KC-10, F-117, and F/A-22. In addition to these, EN has also contributed to the development of unmanned aerial vehicles, like Global Hawk and Predator, the Air-Launched Cruise Missile (ALCM), and the Maverick guided missile. Among the more exotic aircraft in which EN had a hand were the Have Blue stealth demonstrator and the National Aerospace Plane (NASP). In addition, at the component and subsystem level, EN has done everything from conducting studies on aircraft wiring to providing the technical expertise for the Air Force's Alternative Fighter Engine Competition, otherwise known as the "Great Engine War."

Wright-Patterson's systems engineers were instrumental from the very beginning in the development and maturation of the F-15 fighter aircraft. It was the SEG's Studies and Analyses Division that performed the initial studies for the F-X that led to the F-15 (see Development Planning below).[280] Once an F-15 program office was formed, it was EN's experts who provided dedicated technical support and ensured that aircraft development proceeded smoothly and on schedule. EN's support did not stop at system development, but continued long after the aircraft (and its upgrades) had been fielded. During the Gulf War, for instance, EN was called upon to solve a problem experienced by the main landing gear tires of the F-15E—which it did, successfully and expeditiously.[281]

Further examples of support, beyond program development, were provided by EN in the case of the F-16. Over recent years, EN's technical staff troubleshot and solved problems with the F-16's altimeter[282] and inertial navigation system.[283] EN also assisted the F-16 SPO and operators to reduce the cost of the aircraft's operational flight program software[284] and developed a low-cost alternative for the aircraft's low-level, high-speed, automatic, terrain-following system.[285] EN also provided technical and cost guidance concerning which of two electronic countermeasure (ECM) antennas to put on the F-16.[286]

In the development of the C-17, the Air Force's newest wide-body airlift aircraft, EN's contributions were numerous and noteworthy. EN's engineers conducted analyses of the core integrated processor;[287] cruise drag;[288] main landing gear;[289] fuel tank sealing;[290] multi-band radio system;[291] onboard, inert gas generation system;[292] and the wireless communication set.[293] Sometimes EN's results vindicated the contractor's designs; sometimes they led to less expensive alternative equipment and procedures. EN also performed tests and studies of the C-17's transportability of Army vehicles,[294] the airlifter's dual-row airdrop capability,[295] paratrooper airdrop optimization,[296] and strategic brigade airdrop formation spacing.[297] Indeed, EN's personnel often had a better understanding of the Army's (and other military operators') requirements than the contractor, and were thus able to advise the latter on development problems and "fixes" before they became program "show stoppers."

EN also provided developmental engineering support to the Air Force's F/A-22 Raptor. As in the case of all major weapon systems programs, EN dedicated a large contingent of engineers on a full-time basis to the F-22 SPO, where they were collocated with Air Force program managers and other functional support personnel. EN's support of the F-22 was typified by the SPO's preparations for first flight scheduled for 1997. A full year in advance, EN formed an independent review team (IRT) to carefully examine the aircraft's development in light of all first-flight requirements. The team identified a number of potential problems, all of which were subsequently addressed by SPO and contractor personnel, ultimately avoiding costly and unnecessary delays in the scheduling of the F-22's first flight. EN's formation and conduct of the IRT, as well as subsequently conducting a more formal, combined, government-contractor Executive Independent Review Team (EIRT), were recognized both by the ASC commander and the Air Force program executive officer for Fighters and Bombers as a "best practice."[298]

EN supplied technical support to unmanned aerial vehicles for over 30 years. Shown here are two recent representatives of the Air Force's UAV program: (above) DarkStar (which was cancelled in 1999) and (below) Predator (armed with two Army Hellfire missiles).

In the 1970s, EN compiled a historical database concerning low-observable (stealth) information to assist the Air Force in selection of the contractor to develop Have Blue, the nation's first stealth, flight-demonstrator aircraft. Since then, EN has continually updated this database for current and future low-observable program developments.[299] In the 1980s, EN provided substantial support to the NASP Joint Program Office (JPO), located at Wright Field, including a number of collocated engineers. EN was involved in numerous "sanity checks" of NASP design proposals. When the JPO had insufficient funding for its prime contractors to conduct testing, EN provided this support, in cooperation with the Wright Field laboratories and fabrication shops. This support included, for instance, wind-tunnel and water-tunnel testing of models designed and fabricated in-house. The result in the latter case was critical data provided to the contractor to modify the NASP design and improve low-speed, takeoff lift.[300]

In the 1990s, EN provided support to the Air Force's latest aerial weapon—unmanned aerial vehicles (UAVs). When the Air Force Operational Test and Evaluation Center (AFOTEC) requested advice on the advisability of flight testing the Predator UAV, EN was able to run an analysis and submit a report laying down guidelines not only for the Predator but also for other UAVs, such as DarkStar, Global Hawk, and others in development.[301]

EN also has actively supported the development and use of components and subsystems. When the U.S. Navy discontinued use of Kapton wiring in the 1980s due to concerns about cracking and carbon-arching due to hydrolysis, EN participated in a study to determine its suitability for Air Force use.[302]

EN's power plant experts also have played a major role in the development of gas turbine engines for U.S. Air Force airplanes and missiles. EN, for instance, developed the Engine Structural Integrity Program (ENSIP) to provide a structured approach to design, analysis, development, production, and life management of gas turbine engines. Among the engines developed under ENSIP guidelines are the F109, F100-PW-229, F110-GE-129, F119-PW-100, F120, and the engine for the Joint Strike Fighter (JSF). Existing engines also were assessed using ENSIP criteria to improve the design of the current fleet and provide better safety management. The major beneficiaries of ENSIP were the engines for the F-15 and F-16 fighters, which have since demonstrated substantially lower mishap rates in comparison with engines developed before ENSIP was adopted. As with many technical initiatives that served the needs of the modern Air Force, ENSIP was developed in partnership with industry. The U.S. Navy also has joined the program.[303] In addition to ENSIP, EN also conducted the Avionics Integrity Program (AVIP) and the Aircraft Structural Integrity Program (ASIP).[304]

ASIP began in 1958 in response to four catastrophic structural failures on B-47 aircraft. The program aimed to prevent fatigue failures in aircraft structures by defining a disciplined design and development process for new aircraft to increase system reliability. When shortcomings in the original ASIP approach surfaced in 1969 and the 1970s in structural failures on the F-111A and F-5A, EN revised ASIP by incorporating fracture mechanics theory

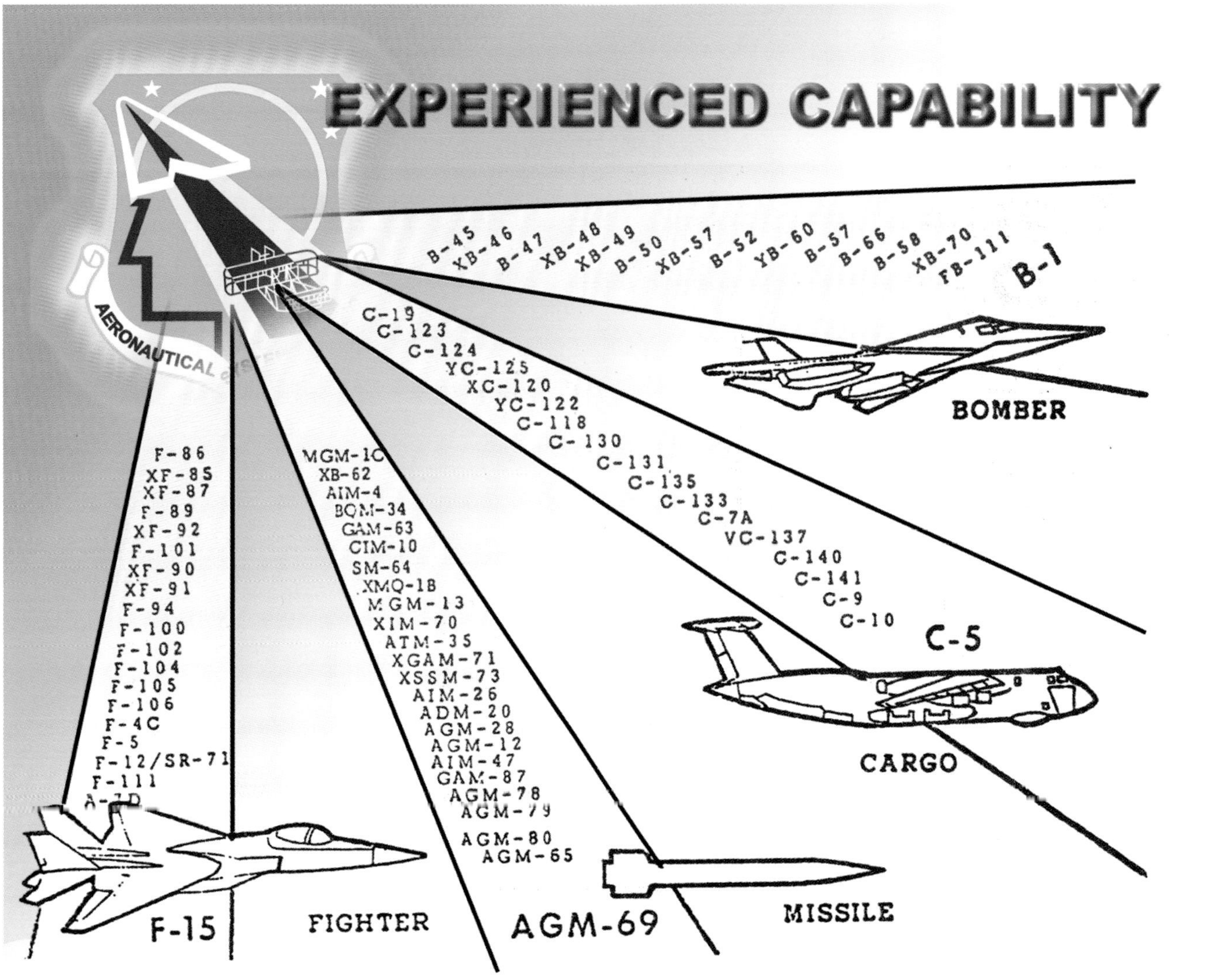

All this and more: aeronautical systems supported by EN in the 1970s

and damage tolerance design practices that had been employed in the space program during the 1960s. Since that time, ASIP has provided the Air Force with an unparalleled level of aircraft safety and has become the basis for the cradle-to-grave aircraft and engine structural force management for the Air Force, the Federal Aviation Administration, and several allied air forces.

In 1971, the Department of Defense (DOD) directed the establishment within EN of the Air Transportability Test Loading Agency (ATTLA). ATTLA served as the single organization in DOD authorized to approve non-standard cargo for airlift or airdrop using Air Force mission aircraft. ATTLA was staffed by acquisition certified engineers with experience in the development of cargo aircraft, including mechanical systems, aeronautics, parachute technology, aircraft structures, packaging, materials handling, and airdrop rigging. By the early twenty-first century, ATTLA's customer base included all branches of the federal government as well as humanitarian agencies such as Joint Relief International.

EN was a key driver in reducing the risk of injury to pilots in emergency situations. In the mid-1970s, the Advanced Concept Ejection Seat (ACES II) was developed at Wright Field as the first government-furnished escape system, providing significantly improved stability during low-level and high-speed ejections from aircraft. The ACES II was first placed in service in the A-10 aircraft in April 1978. In August of the same year, the first ejection using ACES II occurred with the successful recovery of the pilot, without injury, following a low-altitude emergency. Subsequently, a version of ACES II was installed on seven different types of aircraft and was credited with saving more than 500 lives worldwide.

In the 1980s, EN led a team of contractor and government participants to investigate enhancements to the standard oxygen system used on military aircraft. Primarily driven by cost and logistical support requirements, EN conducted a two-year feasibility study, including a six-month flight test program that demonstrated the capability of separating oxygen from ambient air through a system mounted on the aircraft. This onboard oxygen generation system evolved to become the system of choice for both newly designed aircraft and existing platforms during aircraft retrofit updates.

In the early 1980s, EN identified deficiencies in the F100-PW-100/200 engines that then exclusively powered the F-15 and F-16 fighters and established desirable characteristics for an improved engine, based on the F101 gas turbine that powered the B-1. EN then conducted a prototype program for an F101 derivative fighter engine as an engineering and manufacturing risk reduction effort. EN subsequently defined the technical requirements for the development and competition of the new F110-GE-100 engine with an extensively upgraded F100-PW-200. Both en-

FREDERICK T. RALL, JR.
CHIEF ENGINEER TO THE AIR FORCE

For nearly 20 years Frederick T. Rall, Jr., was technical director of ASD's Deputy for Engineering (ASD/EN). More than any other individual after Major General Fred Ascani, who established systems engineering at Wright Field in 1959, Fred Rall was responsible for making EN the organization that it is today, with the highest standards of professionalism, rigorous institutional discipline, and "can-do" *esprit de corps*.

Frederick T. Rall, Jr.

A native of Illinois, Rall began his professional career in 1950, armed with a bachelor of science degree in aeronautics from the Massachusetts Institute of Technology (MIT), first at the Cooperative Wind Tunnel, Pasadena, and then at the Douglas Aircraft Company, El Segundo, California. After leaving Douglas, he received a commission as second lieutenant in the Air Force and was assigned to the Wright Air Development Center's (WADC's) Aircraft Laboratory in 1953. In the Aircraft Laboratory, Rall became an expert in the internal aerodynamics of all Air Force aircraft and, on his separation from military service in 1955, he became chief of the Laboratory's Internal Aerodynamics Unit. Five years later he moved on to become chief of the Aerodynamics Branch of the B-70 Valkyrie Program Office.

The B-70 was Rall's first assignment as a member of the new Directorate of Systems Engineering after the breakup of the Aircraft Laboratory. In 1964, he became chief of the Aero-Mechanics Branch for the F-111 followed by chief of the Airframe Division, Deputy for F-15. (During this period, he also earned a master's degree in industrial engineering from MIT.)

Rall's outstanding managerial and technical skills in guiding these three high priority aircraft programs were rewarded in 1969 when he was appointed technical director of ASD's Deputy for Engineering. As technical director, Rall served as "chief engineer" to six commanders, including Lieutenant General James T. Stewart, General Lawrence A. Skantze, and General John M. Loh. He witnessed the development of the F-15, F-16, A-10, KC-10, C-5A/B, C-17, B-1B, B-2, F-117, and the Advanced Tactical Fighter (F/A-22). Among the many outstanding men and women who participated in the development of what amounts to the modern Air Force, Fred Rall was, in the words of an admiring General Stewart, "a giant among giants."

Rall's accomplishments were recognized many times over the years. Among the formal accolades he received were the Senior Executive Service Distinguished Executive Award, the Air Force Civilian of the Year for 1980, the Department of Defense Distinguished Civilian Service Award, the Air Force Exceptional Civilian Service Award, the first American Institute of Aeronautics and Astronautics (AIAA) Air Breathing Propulsion Award, and the AIAA Reed Aeronautics Award. On October 14, 1981, Fred Rall received a Presidential Rank Award at the White House from President Ronald Reagan. The accompanying program described Mr. Rall simply as "the Air Force's 'Chief Engineer.'"

Fred Rall retired on September 28, 1989.

Source: Biography of Frederick T. Rall, Jr., in the ASC History Office Archive.

President Ronald Reagan presented Fred Rall with a Presidential Rank Award in 1981.

Jon S. Ogg, director of Engineering (1999-), guided the organization through a period of Air Force transformation.

gines qualified for production, and the initial and follow-on buy decisions resulted in a split buy. The result was the Alternate Fighter Engine Competition otherwise known as the "Great Engine War," which ended Air Force reliance on a single engine design for its entire fighter force thereby promoting competition and a superior product at lower price.[305]

It should be pointed out that these are only a few, and not necessarily the most conspicuous, examples of EN's pervasive influence in the development of aerospace vehicles and weapon systems and subsystems for the Air Force.

In the course of the past three decades, EN has undergone a number of changes in organization and operations. These changes reflected an altered national defense posture, as well as shifting Air Force priorities.

One major change was the way in which technical requirements were stated by EN in standards and specifications for Air Force aircraft and subsystems. The first significant change, started in the late 1970s, was a migration from specifications communicating detailed "how-to" requirements to requirements that were performance-based. As the nature of the military aircraft business matured and less actual design work was performed by government engineers, industry advised the Air Force that achieving the state-of-the-art required more design freedom. Industry argued that detailed design requirements, based in part on the failures of the past, hindered its ability to innovate during the design process. As a result of adopting many of industry's suggestions, the Air Force implemented possibly the most innovative use of specifications ever undertaken within the DOD—a program and set of technical documents that EN dubbed "Mil-Primes."[306]

Mil-Prime specifications (so-called for combining military specifications with "prime item" specifications) contained not only performance requirements and verifications, but also an appendix for the user of the specification, whether government or industry, to gain insight into the rationale for the requirements; guidance on how to fill in the value-based blanks that were often inserted into Mil-Prime requirements; and lessons learned from prior experiences.[307]

The next major evolution in the use of technical requirements came with the appointment of Dr. William Perry as secretary of defense in 1994. Dr. Perry directed implementation of the recommendations that he had made to the DOD in a 1989 Defense Science Board report entitled "Use of Commercial Components in Military Equipment." As a result, the entire DOD underwent a complete analysis of its specifications and standards, cancelling many and converting many others to industry-consensus, non-government standards. ASC's Engineering Directorate, which managed the bulk of military aeronautical specifications, standards, and handbooks, was heavily involved in this effort and was a key contributor to the Air Force's lead on document conversions within DOD.[308]

As Dr. Perry's acquisition reforms took hold across DOD in the mid-1990s, the experience of EN, derived from earlier reforms of the late 1970s and early 1980s, proved beneficial. With a strong baseline of performance-based specifications used by the system program offices to help define program-peculiar requirements, the Mil-Prime program was adopted by the Joint Aeronautical Commander's Group (JACG) as a model to help define the requirements for joint programs. What had been called Air Force Guide Specifications (AFGS) grew into Joint Service Specification Guides (JSSG) and began to be developed and maintained by all the services. (And, in spite of the popular notion that *all* specifications and standards were "killed" by Dr. Perry, ASC's EN still managed or maintained cognizance over some 10,000 technical standards used to develop and sustain military aeronautical weapon systems.)[309]

In addition to managing technical specifications and standards and other technical process documentation, EN also continued to provide a library and database of standards and specifications and miscellaneous technical records of Air Force aircraft, missiles, and equipment. Indeed, it undertook a major effort to digitize its paper library in the mid-1990s, thereby making its contents more readily available to customers electronically.[310]

In fact, the identification and use of commercially available equipment and technologies became increasingly urgent, particularly in the area of electronics and avionics. In the late 1990s, EN undertook, on behalf of the Air Force, a major effort to develop an "open systems" approach to acquire and upgrade Air Force avionics systems. This was done to keep avionics upgrades and developments affordable and, indeed, possible, since many military-specific, avionics equipment and devices were becoming increasingly unavailable in a marketplace in which the military customer was no longer the principal financial player or innovator.[311]

Organizationally, EN also underwent a number of changes in the 1990s. At the end of the decade, EN's home office comprised six divisions: Avionics Engineering (ENA); Flight Systems Engineering (ENF); Systems Engineering (ENS); Engineering Operations and Support (ENO); Modeling, Simulation, and Analysis (ENM); and Acquisition Environmental, Safety, and Health (ENV). With the disestablishment of ASC's Development Planning Directorate (ASC/XR) in 1998-1999, EN acquired XR's air-vehicle design activity, which it placed under its Flight Systems Engineering Division (ENF) (see Development Planning below). The Modeling, Simulation, and Analysis Division (ENM) reflected the Air Force's commitment to explore the use of sophisticated computer analysis across the entire flight-vehicle acquisition cycle, from cradle to grave. Although still in its infancy at the beginning of the twenty-first century, the division showed much promise for the future development of aeronautical and aerospace systems. Today, ENM has a world-class capability for performing constructive analysis from physics to campaign level and executing virtual human-in-the-loop simulations in the Simulation and Analysis Facility (SIMAF) at Wright-Patterson Air Force Base.

Forty years after its creation, ASC's Engineering Directorate has repeatedly demonstrated the value of the Air Force maintaining an in-house government engineering cadre dedicated to full-time support of Wright Field's weapon system program of-

FRED D. ORAZIO, SR.
AN ENGINEER'S ENGINEER

When young Fred Orazio came to Dayton in 1939, Wright Field was a relatively small installation that had barely begun to gear up for World War II. When he retired, in the mid-1970s, Wright-Patterson Air Force Base was one of the epicenters of the Cold War's military-industrial complex. Fred Orazio lived through the greatest expansion in military aeronautics in history and played a central role in that development. He was intimately involved in the birth of the supersonic age, atomic propulsion for aircraft, the Air Force's man-in-space program, and the evolution of the systems approach to aircraft and weapons development.

Orazio was born in Sarver, Pennsylvania, in 1912—three years after the U.S. Army bought its first airplane from Wilbur and Orville Wright. Interested in engineering, Orazio attended the Carnegie Institute of Technology. Upon graduation, in 1934, he was commissioned a reserve second lieutenant in the U.S. Army Corps of Engineers and stationed in Detroit, where he went to work as a design engineer for the automobile industry.

Five years later, upon arriving at Wright Field, Orazio was assigned to the Aircraft Laboratory's Design Branch. There he worked on numerous projects during and after the war, including structural modifications to the B-29 for carrying the atomic bomb and preliminary design work on a jet airplane capable of exceeding the speed of sound. In the years following the war, Orazio studied nuclear engineering and participated in the Air Force's abortive attempt to design and build a long-range strategic bomber powered by atomic energy. Orazio also rose in the management ranks. As chief of the Wright Air Development Center's Directorate of Development, he encouraged the adoption of systems cost analysis in the development of ever more complex and costly aerospace vehicles and their support infrastructures. He also headed up a series of technical teams assigned to review such projects as the GAM (Ground-to-Air Missile)-87, the X-20 Dyna Soar, and the Air Force's man-in-space program. The latter made many contributions to the Project Mercury and Apollo programs managed by the National Aeronautics and Space Administration (NASA), just as the Dyna Soar explored technologies later incorporated in NASA's space shuttle.

In the 1960s, the Air Force made major organizational changes in its research and development corps. Orazio played a key role in these developments and went on to assume a series of senior positions, first in the Systems Engineering Group (later called the Aeronautical Systems Division's Deputy for Engineering) and the Deputy for Development Planning. By the time he retired from government service in 1975, ASD had laid the groundwork for many of today's weapon systems, including the B-1, F-15, F-16, A-10, and C-5A aircraft.

During his nearly 40-year career at Wright Field, Orazio was officially recognized for his many contributions to aerospace engineering and national security, receiving the Exceptional Civilian Service Award (1962), the Air Force's highest civilian citation, and the Air Force Association's Theodore von Karman Award (1971).

Despite his many aerospace achievements, however, Fred Orazio remained down-to-earth, never losing a life-long enthusiasm for automobiles, which he repaired in his spare time. "Fred wasn't afraid to get his hands dirty," remarked an admiring colleague. To the end of his life, Orazio remained an engineer's engineer.

Fred Orazio died on January 17, 1999.

Sources: Biography of Fred D. Orazio, Sr., in the ASC History Office Archive; Interview, Fred D. Orazio with J. F. Aldridge, ASC History Office, November 28, 1995.

fices. The experience of EN's career personnel is second to none in the "nitty-gritty" engineering essentials of developing and maintaining American air power.

DEVELOPMENT PLANNING

Development planning evolved from several different disciplines over many decades. The foremost and central discipline was aircraft design. Its origins were in the Plane Design Office of the Signal Corp's Aviation Section, Washington, D.C. The office and its technical staff transferred to McCook in 1917 and became the core around which other technical sections and laboratories of the Aircraft Engineering Division were organized.[312]

During World War I and the early 1920s, McCook's engineers designed and built their own prototype airplanes in addition to testing and evaluating industry models. McCook's premier airplane design engineer at that time was Alfred Verville.[313] Another veteran design engineer, Jean Roché, led the design group well into the 1930s.

McCook's design engineers discontinued the practice of designing prototype aircraft for in-house fabrication, test, and evaluation in the early 1920s. This was done by order of Air Service Chief Major General Mason Patrick, due to industry complaints of unfair competition by

In-house preliminary design of the F-15

McCook's aircraft design "brain trust" and fears that the Army intended to establish McCook along lines of an arsenal that would design and manufacture its own operational aircraft.[314] The Engineering Division continued, however, to develop designs for airplane structures like airfoils and small test specimens, such as gliders used in conducting experimental research. Most importantly for the later development planning function, however, the division's engineers continued the practice of drafting *preliminary* designs for all new aircraft to be developed and acquired by the Army. These preliminary designs incorporated Air Corps operational requirements and served as the basis for more detailed performance specifications issued to industry.

Back to the drawing board for ASD design engineers (left to right): Terry C. Dudley, Sr., Gordon A. Taylor, and Gary D. Stewart

The aircraft design group was part of McCook's Airplane Section, which became Wright Field's Aircraft Laboratory in 1939. There it remained until 1959, when the Wright Field laboratories were completely reorganized.

Development of more complex and expensive airplanes, beginning in the later 1930s and through World War II, led in the 1950s to the emergence of the second component of development planning: systems cost analysis. The foremost advocate of the need for performing cost analysis was Fred D. Orazio, the principal design engineer in the Aircraft Laboratory's Design Branch. In the 1950s, Orazio formed a group on the WADC staff that began to integrate weapon systems cost analysis with other aspects of WADC's planning functions.[315]

The reorganization of the Wright Field laboratories in the late 1950s and early 1960s resulted in placing cost analysis and weapon system design within the new systems engineering organization at Wright Field. There, as a result of a number of internal reorganizations in the course of the 1960s, they were more completely integrated with one another, first under the Directorate of Systems Engineering of the Wright Air Development Division (WADD) and, after 1961, in the Deputy for Systems Engineering of the Aeronautical Systems Division (ASD). In 1963, the engineering function was realigned under a new Research and Technology Division (RTD) as the Systems Engineering Group (SEG).[316]

The beginnings of computerization in the 1960s allowed many more possibilities in vehicle design and analysis to be investigated, and in greater detail, than were previously possible. Planning by mission area was also instituted around this time and several significant "mission analyses" were accomplished to determine the most cost-effective system solutions to existing needs.[317]

In 1967, RTD was abolished and the SEG once more became part of ASD as the division's Deputy for Engineering (ASD/EN). In August 1967, the Deputy for Development Planning (ASB) was officially formed by combining the SEG's Directorate of Studies and Analyses (SES) with ASD's Deputy for Advanced Systems Planning. Within a year, the new organization became known as the Deputy for Development Planning with the symbol XR. Development Planning would remain a central part of ASD's weapon systems planning and development for the next three decades.[318]

Both before and after Development Planning became an independent line organization within ASD, the design engineers, cost and mission analysis experts,

In-house preliminary design of the F-111

In-house preliminary design of the A-10

and others were involved in planning virtually every aircraft and missile system developed by WADC and ASD for the Air Force.

Development Planning historically had the critical function of supporting requirements development in the early stages (i.e., pre-Milestone I) and subsequent phases of the acquisition cycle of aeronautical weapon systems. In most cases, development planners worked closely with the Wright Field laboratories, and in some cases with the Defense Advanced Research Projects Agency (DARPA, established in 1958), during the synthesis process for new system starts. Additionally, development planners were involved in the evaluation of weapon systems major modifications (Milestone IV). A good example of the latter was the Dual Role Fighter (DRF) evaluation that led to the F-15E aircraft. In this case, Development Planning worked with the Wright Field laboratories and ASD's Engineering Directorate to perform a system assessment. Development planners also assisted in evaluating a number of proposed weapon systems that were either cancelled or not recommended for further development.[319]

The basis of this planning was almost always a preliminary design study, undertaken in-house by development planning engineers. These in-house designs served the purpose of sizing proposed flight vehicles and weapons to the Air Force's needs. As during the pre-World War II period, they served as the basis for vehicle performance specifications from which the contractor developed a final system design. As such, they allowed the Air Force to be a "smart buyer."[320]

Among the important post-World War II aircraft and missile systems that began as in-house conceptual design studies were

In-house preliminary design of the B-1A

the F-111, C-141, C-5, B-1, AGM-69 Short Range Attack Missile (SRAM), F-15, AGM-65 Maverick, A-10, AGM-86 Air-Launched Cruise Missile (ALCM), F-16, AGM-129 Advanced Cruise Missile (ACM), T-46, KC-10, C-17, and F/A-22.[321] Several examples of the role played by Wright Field's development planners follow.

One of the most notable combat aircraft in which Wright Field's design engineers played a leading role was the F-X, which became the F-15. In-house design and analysis studies were conducted under the direction of Fred D. Orazio, Deputy for Studies and Analysis, in the mid-1960s. Under Orazio's guidance, the deputate undertook three related efforts: F-X point design studies; a tactical air-to-air capability study for the Tactical Air Command (TAC); and cost/effectiveness analysis for the F-X point design. Aircraft tradeoffs included a fixed-wing design versus a variable sweep wing; radius versus maneuverability; and radius versus Mach number. The Air Force chose the fixed-wing concept developed by McDonnell Douglas, whose design was very close to that developed by Orazio's group.[322]

The Air-Launched Cruise Missile (ALCM) originated in studies of subsonic, turbine-powered missiles undertaken in-house in the late 1950s by the Aircraft Laboratory's Design Branch. The lack of efficient, small turbine engines, however, hindered the viability of a long-range missile until 1967, when preliminary design studies were initiated during the Bomber Penetration Mission Analysis chartered by Air Force Systems Command headquarters.[323] Early preliminary design studies of the ALCM included the Subsonic Cruise Attack Missile (SCAM), the Subsonic Cruise Armed Decoy (SCAD), and the Subsonic Cruise Unarmed Decoy (SCUD), the latter a replacement for the Quail decoy, all of which began as design studies by Wright Field's design engineers. ASD's Development Planning deputate worked with both the Air Force Avionics Laboratory and the Air Force Aero Propulsion Laboratory in developing the ALCM concept. Particularly vital was the projection of engine technologies for gas turbine power plants that were sufficiently small for use in a missile. After many years of further development studies in the Air Force and the Department of Defense, the AGM-86 ALCM achieved operational status in 1982.[324]

In addition to the F-15, development of the F-16 also was assisted by ASD's development planning engineers, who began defining a lightweight fighter (LWF) concept in 1969 and worked directly with a group within the Air Force Systems Command (AFSC) to define and evaluate program proposals. Subsequently,

In-house preliminary design of the Short Range Attack Missile

In-house preliminary design of the Air-Launched Cruise Missile

ASD's Development Planning deputate provided technical support to the LWF program office and conducted studies of potential production versions. This led to a unique, competitive, prototyping arrangement instituted in 1971 by which new technologies could be demonstrated at low cost but with no commitment to future production. In January 1975, General Dynamics' YF-16 was selected for full-scale development over Northrop's competing YF-17.[325]

The Development Planning deputate also conducted conceptual design and analysis for the follow-on to the ALCM, the AGM-129A Advanced Cruise Missile (ACM). The Defense Advanced Research Projects Agency (DARPA) initially funded the ACM under the project name "Teal Dawn." DARPA sought to develop a missile with better range, higher accuracy, and lower signature than the ALCM. The Development Planning deputate worked as agent for DARPA by evaluating many contractor designs, among other support activities. In 1983, the Air Force awarded a contract to General Dynamics for AGM-129A development. The production run of the ACM ended in 1993 with more than 400 missiles produced.[326]

Following the Arab-Israeli War in 1973, ASD's development planners were called upon to perform a series of preliminary studies of a proposed Advanced Tanker Cargo Aircraft (ATCA) to augment Boeing KC-135 tankers for the Military Airlift Command (MAC). XR studied a variety of potential ATCA solutions including derivatives of commercial transports. Based on these studies, the KC-X program was initiated to evaluate the Boeing 747 and the McDonnell Douglas DC-10. In December 1977, the DC-10 was selected for development and given the name KC-10 Extender.[327]

In 1972, XR helped establish performance parameters for the Advanced Medium Range Short Takeoff and Landing Transport (AMST). The AMST was intended to augment the C-130 for intratheater transport of troops and materiel. Two prototypes were built: the YC-14 by Boeing and the YC-15 by McDonnell Douglas. After flight testing the prototypes in 1975-1976, the Air Force cancelled the program in 1979 due to rising program costs and cuts in the Air Force's budget.

In 1979, ASD's development planning experts also worked with MAC to define requirements for a new tactical airlift aircraft, designated the C-X. The new airlifter was to be capable of carrying heavy and outsized payloads, such as the M-1 tank, into small, austere airfields near front-line troops. XR's studies allowed MAC to define the required aircraft and propulsion system size and set realistic performance requirements. In 1981, McDonnell Douglas's C-X design was selected and designated the C-17A. Following an extended development program, the C-17A became operational in 1995.[328]

One of the Air Force's most recent fighter aircraft, the F/A-22 Advanced Tactical Fighter (ATF), was the product of over 20 years of planning and analysis, beginning in 1969. ASD/XR played an early and continuing role in support of the ATF, and most major program decisions were based on information generated by XR. As early as 1976, XR advocated a supersonic cruise requirement for the ATF. Support included design trade offs for the Tactical Air Command's Director of Requirements (TAC/DR) to illuminate the impact of technology and performance variations on system cost. Included, during the early to mid-1980s, were studies of design, cost, and performance tradeoffs incorporating a menu of low-observable technologies. In addition were tradeoff studies of payload requirements. Indeed, when the ATF System Program Office (SPO) was formed in 1983, it was initially located in ASD/XR. The F-22 entered full-scale development in 1991.[329]

In the late 1980s, Development Planning engineers began looking at multi-role fighter designs for a replacement for the F-16.[330] In 1993 the Department of Defense launched the Joint Advanced Strike Technology (JAST) program to identify mature technologies for a future fighter aircraft whose variants among the Air Force, Navy, and Marine Corps would enjoy at least 70 percent common components and subsystems, such as engines and avionics. From the beginning, ASC's XR was actively engaged in studies in support of the JAST. These included studies of force and moments, weights reconciliation, and propulsion technology. These studies provided the basis of XR's analytical support of the JAST, which led to source selection for the Joint Strike Fighter (JSF) Concept Demonstrator conducted from May to October 1996. XR's team was selected to be the final authority for all "up-and-away" flight vehicle performance, while a Navy team addressed carrier suitability and the Marines were responsible for short takeoff and vertical landing (STOVL) performance. XR also performed a cost-and-operational performance study to ensure that the JSF program could deliver an affordable and effective solution that met tri-service requirements.[331] These activities supported the preparation of the interim requirements document and, finally, the Joint Operational Requirements Document (JORD) for the Joint Strike Fighter program.[332]

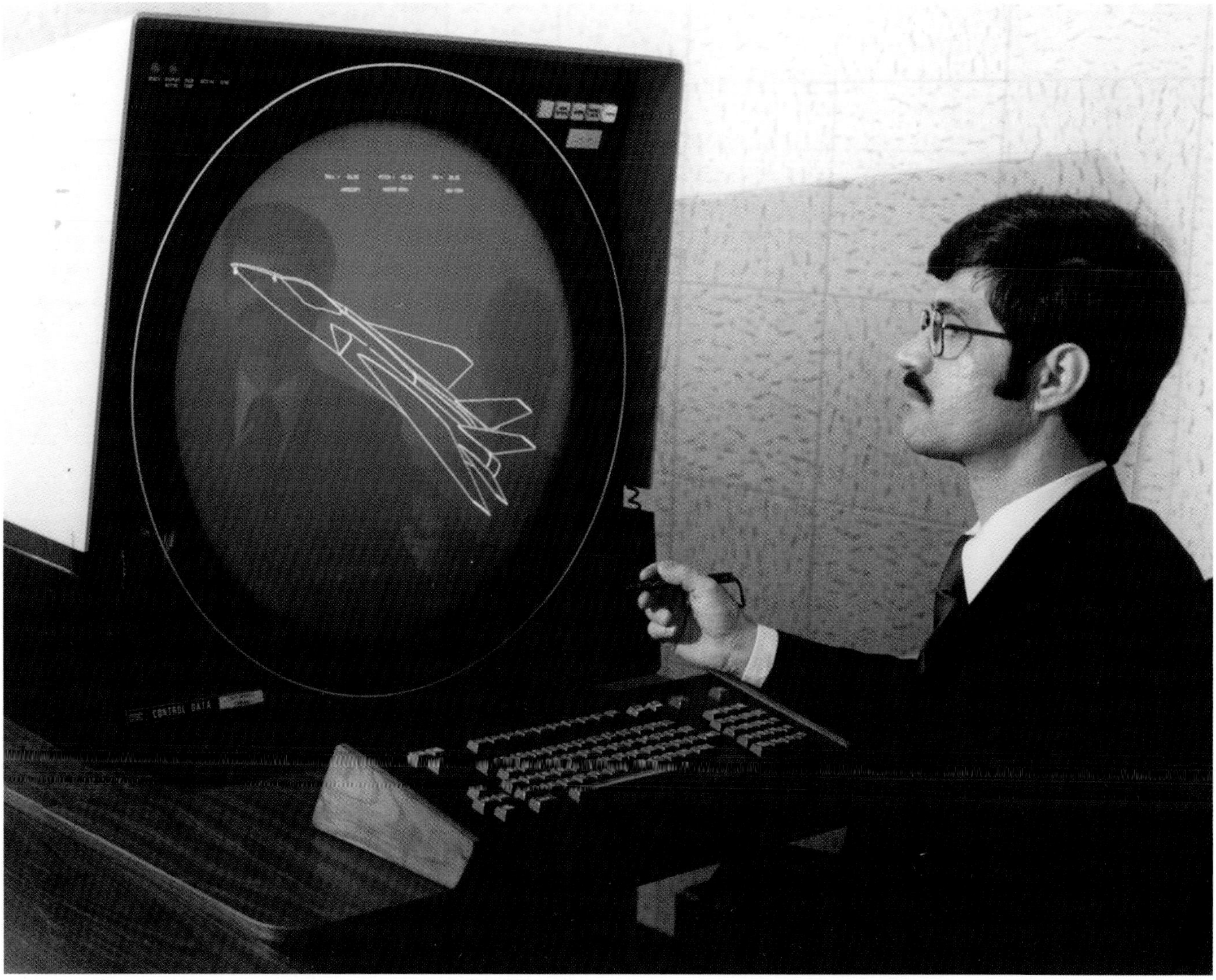

Design engineer Ed Brown illustrating the use of initial interactive computer aided design (CAD) capability

XR conducted alternative bomber studies in the early 1980s for a follow-on to the B-1. These studies considered, among other features, low observability and a flying-wing concept. The B-2 bomber, which was developed in a "black world" environment and built by Northrop, was finally unveiled in 1988.[333]

In the late 1990s, XR developed a comprehensive flight vehicle performance database for current Air Force aircraft. The database included tables of installed aerodynamics, propulsion, and weight-and-store loadings for developing mission and point maneuver performance. This performance database complemented the XR Pedigree Database and, when combined with cost, radar/infrared signature and sensor performance data, could be used as input to various mission engagement and campaign models supporting advanced concept studies for the Technical Planning Integrated Product Teams (TPIPTs) (see below).[334]

From its establishment as a functional organization within ASD in 1967, XR underwent a number of changes that affected both its internal organization and its relationship with organizations outside XR and even ASD. In the late 1970s, XR was reorganized and strategically reoriented to be even more responsive and "proactive" vis-à-vis the program offices, laboratories, and the operating commands.[335]

In 1990, ASD Commander Lieutenant General Thomas R. Ferguson, Jr., decided to consolidate the design activity of the Wright Laboratory's Flight Dynamics Directorate with XR. The laboratory group had originated in a number of personnel from XR, who had been transferred to the laboratory from XR in 1971. General Ferguson's transfer of personnel back to XR augmented and, to a certain extent, alleviated a slow but substantial loss in manpower and expertise that XR had experienced during the previous two decades.[336]

Beginning in 1992, within the formation of the Air Force Materiel Command (AFMC), XR pioneered attempts to bring the AFMC product centers, laboratories, industry, and the user community more closely together in a new "technology master process," with XR forming the critical nexus.[337] At the heart of the process were the TPIPTs. The TPIPTs were to provide development planning support for users through the development of roadmaps and investment recommendations for all Air Force mission areas. The TPIPTs gathered, organized, analyzed, and disseminated information relating user requirements to technology development and transition for current and future systems and for support infrastructure. A TPIPT consisted of a network of development planners, operational command users, technology planners from the Air Force laboratories, logistic center planners, system engineers, and representatives from test organizations, program offices, and intelligence agencies.[338]

Under the TPIPT model, XR performed analyses for upgrading and modernizing aircraft already in service. Among these efforts was modernizing the C-5A aircraft, an activity that XR had begun in the mid-

Bill J. Henkener and Joseph J. Lusczek, design engineers, taking the measure of the Air Force's future aerospace capabilities in the 1960s

1980s. XR worked with the San Antonio Air Logistics Center (ALC) to develop and price potential options to upgrade the C-5 with new subsystems to improve its mission capable and departure reliability rates. Among the options considered was purchasing and modifying other aircraft currently in production.[339]

In the late 1990s, XR conducted studies in parallel with several demonstration and development programs to improve infrared countermeasures (IRCM) for large aircraft, such as the new C-17 airlifter. Multiple TPIPTs, such as those for Aerospace Control, Mobility, Special Operations, and Electronic Warfare, identified IRCM deficiencies throughout the Air Force fleet. At the request of Military Airlift Command headquarters, the Electronic Countermeasures TPIPT prepared a programmed funding estimate for 1998. The TPIPT worked closely with the laboratories and industry to create a detailed system concept both to meet user's needs and to facilitate formal cost estimation.[340]

Despite the proven utility and successes of a consolidated development planning organization over a period of 30 years, ASC decided to disestablish XR early in fiscal year 1999. The action was undertaken to make way for a new Plans and Programs Directorate (ASC/XP). The Plans and Programs Directorate, whose function was aimed at *corporate* and business planning rather than *developmental* planning, had strong support from Air Force Materiel Command headquarters, which sought to establish similar planning functions across the command, in both its product centers and air logistics centers. As a result of this action, XR's TPIPTs and the manpower supporting them were transferred to the system program offices (SPOs), and XR's modeling, simulation, and analysis capability and its design and cost engineers were transferred to ASC's Directorate of Engineering.[341]

Today, ASC's design capability consists of about 20 engineers. This group includes experts in air vehicle design, aerodynamics, signature estimating, propulsion integration, mass-properties estimating, performance estimating, and avionics. It is the only organization currently in the Department of Defense that has a complete capability to accomplish aircraft design.[342] It is truly a *national* asset.

TECHNOLOGY FORECASTING

A prominent feature of the post-World War II Air Force has been the conduct at approximately 10- to 15-year intervals of exercises for assessing the current state of aerospace technology and forecasting future developments. The first such exercise was inaugurated by Commanding General of the Army Air Forces Henry H. "Hap" Arnold in 1944, when he commissioned his principal scientific advisor, Dr. Theodore von Karman, to lead a team to examine the technical advances of America's allies and enemies during the war and to sketch a technology development plan for the postwar U.S. Air Force. The published report, called *Toward New Horizons*, was published in December 1945. *New Horizons* comprised 34 individual studies that covered everything from guided missiles and "pilotless" aircraft to aviation psychology. Von Karman authored two of the reports, *Where We Stand*, which surveyed the current state of technology, and *Science: The Key to Air Superiority*, which recommended a vigorous postwar science and technology program for the Air Force.

The next major undertaking occurred in the early 1960s when Secretary of the Air Force Eugene M. Zuckert directed General Bernard A. Schriever, commander of Air Force Systems Command, to examine the Air Force's technology and weapon system options for the following 10 to 20 years. Called *Project Forecast*, the exercise was the largest in Air Force history, comprising 500 participants from the Air Force, other federal agencies, 26 institutions of higher learning, 70 corporations, and 10 non-profit organizations. *Project Forecast* focused on high-payoff technologies in the areas of materials, propulsion, flight dynamics, guidance, computers, and such ambitious systems as the C-X wide-body transport aircraft that became the C-5A.

In 1986, General Lawrence A. Skantze, commander of Air Force Systems Command and former Aeronautical Systems Division (ASD) commander, inaugurated *Project Forecast II*. *Forecast II* was largely modeled on its 1960s namesake and catalogued a host of technologies and systems under way and in planning by the Air Force's laboratories and product divisions.

The most recent technology forecasting activity occurred in the mid-1990s and consisted of two independent studies: *Air Force 2020*, undertaken by Air University, and *New World Vistas,* undertaken by the Air Force's Scientific Advisory Board. The latter study was significant for, among other things, recommending the separation of the Air Force's laboratories from the product centers, a recommendation that contributed, in part, to the establishment of the Air Force Research Laboratory (AFRL) in 1997.

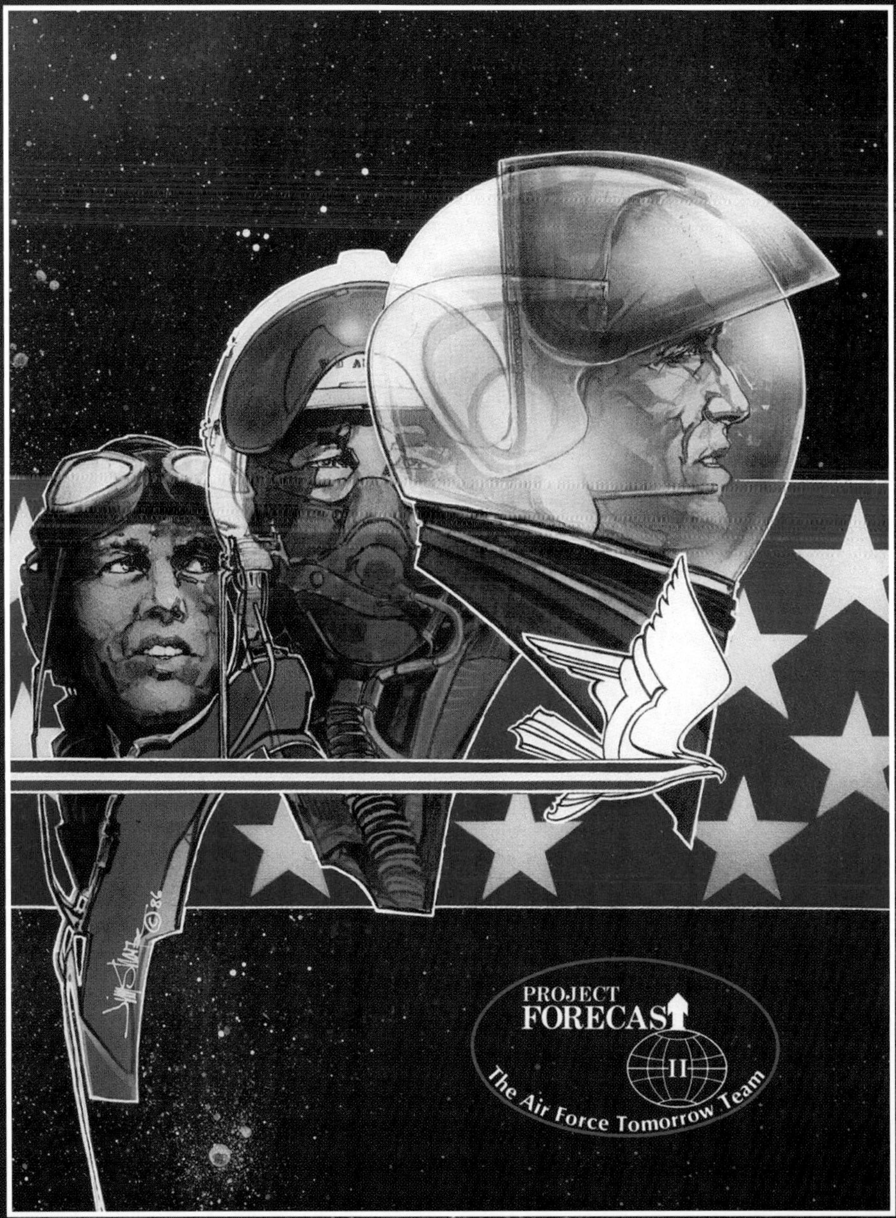

Sources: Michael H. Gorn, *Harnessing the Genie: Science and Technology Forecasting for the Air Force, 1944-1986* (Washington, D.C., 1988); *New World Vistas: Air and Space Power for the 21st Century*, summary volume ([Washington, D.C.], 1995).

ENDNOTES

ENDNOTES

Chapter 1. THE VIEW FROM HUFFMAN PRAIRIE–THE WRIGHTS AND THEIR FLYING MACHINE

1. Fred C. Kelly, *The Wright Brothers* (New York, 1950), p 72.
2. *Ibid.*
3. Arthur G. Renstrom, *Wilbur & Orville Wright: A Chronology Commemorating the Hundredth Anniversary of the Birth of Orville Wright, August 19,1871* (Washington, 1975), p 13. The acreage is variously described by other writers as 68, 80, or 90 acres.
4. Gilbert Guinn, "A Different Frontier: Aviation, the Army Air Forces, and the Evolution of the Sunshine Belt," *Aerospace Historian* 29 (Mar 1982), 34-35.
5. Marvin W. McFarland, ed., *The Papers of Wilbur and Orville Wright, Including the Chanute-Wright Letters and Other Papers of Octave Chanute*, Vol One; 1899-1905 (New York, 1972), p 441.
6. Renstrom, p 141.
7. Kelly, p 77.
8. Renstrom, p 142.
9. *Ibid.*, pp 140-145.
10. Charles H. Gibbs-Smith, "The World's First Practical Airplane," *NCR World* (Dayton, 1978), p 6.
11. Renstrom, p 17.
12. Kelly, p 131.
13. Charles deF. Chandler and Frank P. Lahm, *How Our Army Grew Wings: Airmen and Aircraft Before 1914* (New York, 1943), p 150.
14. Kelly, p 131.
15. Chandler and Lahm, p 153.
16. *Ibid.*, p 152.
17. *Ibid.*, p 153; Renstrom, pp 165-166.
18. Renstrom, p 166; Kelly, p 141.
19. Renstrom, p 176.
20. *Ibid.*, pp 42, 177.
21. Chandler and Lahm, pp 158-159.
22. Renstrom, pp 42, 178.
23. Chandler and Lahm, pp 295-298, citing Signal Corps Specification No. 486, Dec 23, 1907, "Advertisement and Specification for a Heavier than Air Flying Machine."
24. Elizabeth Fraterrigo, *Beyond Kitty Hawk: Inventing Flight at Huffman Prairie Flying Field* (WPAFB, 2000).
25. Brochure, *Wright Flyers* (Wright Aircraft Corporation, Dayton, Ohio, about 1915).
26. Henry H. Arnold, *Global Mission* (New York, 1949), p 17.
27. *Ibid.*, p 26.
28. Renstrom, p 204. Captain deF. Chandler had previously been qualified as a balloon pilot in 1907 and as a dirigible pilot in 1909.
29. Fraterrigo, *Beyond Kitty Hawk.*
30. Renstrom, p 206.

Chapter 2. THE CRADLE OF AVIATION–MCCOOK FIELD

1. Robert I. Curtis, John Mitchell, and Martin Copp, *Langley Field, the Early Years 1916-1946* (Langley AFB, 1977), p 11.
2. *Organization of Military Aeronautics 1907-1935* (AAF Historical Study 25, 1944), p 26.
3. Arthur Sweetser, *The American Air Service* (New York, 1919), p 66.
4. *Organization of Military Aeronautics*, p 28.
5. Sweetser, p 68.
6. *Ibid.*, p xxvii.
7. Curtis *et al.*, p 14.
8. Isaac F. Marcosson, *Colonel Deeds: Industrial Builder* (New York, 1947), pp 216-217.
9. *Ibid.*, p 221.
10. Sweetser, p 94.
11. Curtis *et al.*, p 22.
12. Marcosson, p 215.
13. *Ibid.*
14. *Ibid.*
15. George B. Smith, "History of North Dayton Property, Temporarily Called Wright Field, Now McCook Field" (unpublished recollections, n.d.).

16. Terence M. Dean, "The History of McCook Field, Dayton, Ohio, 1917-1927" (unpublished thesis, University of Dayton, 1969); Maurer Maurer, "McCook Field, 1917-1927," *The Ohio Historical Quarterly* 67 (Jan 1958): 23.
17. Memo, Brig Gen George O. Squier, Chief Signal Officer of the Army, to Adjutant General of the Army, subj: Approval of Buildings for Experimental Purposes, Dayton, Ohio, Sep 28, 1917.
18. J. K. Grannis, A.M.E.S.C., Superintendent of Construction, to Lt Col C. G. Edgar, Signal Corps, Subj: Experimental Field, Sep 28, 1917.
19. See Note 17.
20. Dean, p 13.
21. See Note 18.
22. Memo, Col E. A. Deeds, Signal Corps, to Lt Col Edgar (Construction Division), no subj., Oct 1, 1917.
23. Resolution Passed at Meeting of the Aircraft Production Board, Oct 1, 1917, submitted to Lt Col C. G. Edgar, Construction Division, Signal Corps.
24. Capt H. H. Blee, *History of Organization and Activities of Airplane Engineering Division, Bureau of Aircraft Production* (Misc. Report No. 220, McCook Field, 1919), p 82; Maurer, "McCook Field," p 23.
25. Dean, p 14.
26. R. M. McFarland, ed., *History of the Bureau of Aircraft Production*, Vol II (WPAFB, 1951), p 278.
27. Blee, p 82.
28. "Survey and History of McCook Field, Dayton, Ohio," History of McCook Field (Miscellaneous Correspondence) 1918-1926.
29. *Ibid.*
30. Blee, p 83.
31. *Ibid.*
32. *Ibid.*
33. Dean, p 10.
34. Marguerite Jacobs, "Flying Fields and Fashions Change" (unpublished recollections, 1928).
35. Dean, p 12.
36. McFarland, Vol II, p 279.
37. Dean, p 18.
38. McFarland, Vol II, p 280.
39. "History of the Air Corps Materiel Division,"(unpublished history), p 17.
40. Ltr, C. W. Nash, Assistant Director of Aircraft Production, to Col J. G. Vincent, Chief Engineer, Aircraft Production, subj: McCook Field, Nov 7, 1918.
41. Dean, p 16.
42. *Ibid.*, p 19.
43. Walt Boyne, "The Treasures of McCook Field," *Wings* 5 (Aug 1975): 8.
44. Walt Boyne, "The Treasure Trove of McCook Field," *Airpower* 5 (Jul 1975): 10.
45. Dean, p 47, Ltr, Director of Air Service to Chief, Engineering Division, Air Service, Dayton, Ohio, subj: Administration Matters Regarding Civilian Personnel and Telegraph Service, May 14, 1919.
46. Dean, p 15.
47. Rpt, C. R Simmons, Factory Manager, Airplane Engineering Division, *Organization and Activities of the Factory Department including Construction and Maintenance,* Nov 1917-Nov 1918, Serial No. 376.
48. Edward O. Purtee, *History of the Army Air Service, 1907-1926* (WPAFB, 1948), pp 42-44.
49. J. F. Curry, "What McCook Field Means to Aviation" (unpublished recollections, n.d.).
50. McCook Field, Engineering Division, Weekly Progress Reports No. 27 (Oct 22, 1918) and No. 29 (Nov 5, 1918).
51. Blee, p 84.
52. Maurer, "McCook Field," p 24.
53. See Note 28.
54. Record of Military Administration, Airplane Engineering Division, McCook Field, Ohio, Dec 16, 1918; *The Army's Order of Battle of the United States Land Forces in the World War (1917-1919)*, Vol 3, Part 1 (Washington, 1949), p 881.
55. Dean, p 20.
56. Alfred Goldberg, ed., *A History of the United States Air Force, 1907-1957* (Princeton, New Jersey, 1957), p 15.
57. Purtee, pp 101-102.
58. Dean, p 32.
59. Sweetser, pp 237-238.
60. McFarland, p 300.
61. Dean, p 45.
62. Purtee, p 107.
63. Telegram, War Department, McCook Field, Dayton, Ohio, to Division of Military Aeronautics, Washington, D.C., Executive Section, Dec 20, 1918.
64. Curtis *et al.*, p 16.
65. "Remembering the Forgotten Field," WPAFB *Skywrighter* (Oct 19, 1979), 17, 22.

66. Boyne, "Treasures," p 20.
67. Dean, p 98.
68. Purtee, p 128; Charles Worman, "McCook Field: A Decade of Progress," *Aerospace Historian* 17 (Spring 1970): 15.
69. Dean, p 110.
70. *Ibid.*, pp 72-76.
71. Maurer, "McCook Field," p 25.
72. Dean, pp 74-75.
73. *Ibid.*, p 73.
74. See Note 49.
75. T. C. McMahon, "Something About McCook Field" (unpublished recollections, n.d.).
76. Captain Sanders A. Laubenthal, *Yesterday, Today and Tomorrow* (WPAFB, 1979), pp 2, 4.
77. *Ibid.*, p 4.
78. *Ibid.*
79. *Ibid.*, p 7.
80. *Ibid.*, p 9.
81. Brig Gen William E. Gillmore, Chief, Materiel Division, "McCook Field Review 1926," Dec 20,1926, Doc. X in papers of George A. Biehn: *Indexed Documents Concerning McCook Field, Wright Field, 1929, and Air Service Progress through 1929.*
82. "Wright Field Today," Doc. XII, in *Indexed Documents*, p 4.
83. *Ibid.*
84. Dean, p 64.
85. "Valuation of Assets of Engineering Division Air Service, McCook Field, Dayton, Ohio" (unpublished financial report, Oct 31, 1923).
86. Maurer, "McCook Field," p 33.
87. *Ibid.*
88. See Note 49.
89. Maurer, "McCook Field," p 33.
90. Curtis *et al.*, p 16.
91. *Ibid.*, pp 44-45.
92. Memorandum for Chief of Staff, from Maj Gen Charles T. Menoher, Director of Air Service, subj: Purchase of Dayton-Wright Airplane Plant for Use as Air Service Engineering Experimental Station and Testing Field, Apr 11, 1919.
93. "Report of the Director of Air Service to the Secretary of War, 1920," War Department Annual Reports, Fiscal Year Ended Jun 30, 1920 (Washington, 1920), pp 1493-1494.
94. Charlotte Reeve Conover, ed., *Dayton and Montgomery County*, Vol I (New York, 1932), p 303.
95. *NCR Progress* (May 13, 1922), p 1.
96. Samuel Crowther, *John H. Patterson, Pioneer in Industrial Welfare* (New York, 1924), pp 363-364.
97. Conover, p 304.
98. Shelby E. Wickam, "Wright Field: Looking Back Over 50 Years of Aviation History," WPAFB *Skywrighter* (Oct 7, 1977), pp 6, 20.
99. *NCR Progress* (Nov 23, 1922), p 1.
100. *Ibid.*
101. *The Dayton Journal* (Oct 26, 1922), p 1.
102. *Ibid.*
103. *The Dayton News* (Oct 27, 1922), p 1.
104. See Note 99.
105. Conover, p 304.
106. See Note 99.
107. *Ibid.*
108. Ltr, 2750 ABW/DEIC (Real Estate, Cost Accounting Section), to 2750 ABW/HO, subj: History of Acquiring Fee Land, WPAFB (Your letter 16 Jul 1980), Jul 25, 1980, with attachment: Listing of Fee Land.
109. Warranty Deed, Dayton Air Service Incorporated Committee, to United States of America, Aug 9, 1924.
110. Deed, The Dayton Air Service Incorporated Committee, to The United States of America, Dec 18, 1924.
111. *Ibid.*
112. Photocopies of subject warranty deeds in 88 ABW/HO Archives.
113. *The Dayton Evening Herald* (Jan 5, 1923).
114. "Wright Field Today," Doc. XII in *Indexed Documents*.
115. Completion Report, "Wright Field, Dayton, Ohio," Vol I, Office Constructing Quartermaster, Dayton, Ohio, about Jul 1927, p 1.
116. War Department General Order 20, Aug 21, 1925.

Chapter 3. BUILDING A FIRM FOUNDATION–THE ESTABLISHMENT OF WRIGHT FIELD

1. "Dedication of Wright Field," *U. S. Air Services* 12 (Nov 1927): 32.
2. The most extensive contemporary account of the Wright Field dedication ceremonies is given in A. M. Jacobs, "The Dedication of Wright Field," *Air Corps News* XI (Nov 10, 1927).
3. First Annual Report of the Chief, Materiel Division, Air Corps, Fiscal Year 1927, pp 176-179. Also, A. M. Jacobs, general press release for publicity purposes and for the Air Corps newsletter, 1927.
4. First Annual Report, Chief, Materiel Division, Fiscal year 1927, p 179.
5. Third Annual Report, Chief, Materiel Division, Fiscal Year 1929, p 274.
6. James J. Niehaus, *Five Decades of Materials Progress, 1917-1967* (WPAFB, 1967), p 40.
7. First Annual Report, p 180.
8. Niehaus, p 40.
9. First Annual Report, p 23.
10. Second Annual Report, Chief, Materiel Division, Fiscal Year 1928, p 227.
11. Third Annual Report, p 274.
12. First Annual Report, pp 4-5; *U.S. Air Services* 11 (Oct 1926), p 24.
13. First Annual Report, p 26.
14. "Dedication of Wright Field in Honor of Wilbur Wright, Orville Wright, and The Citizens of Dayton Who Presented the Wright Field Site to the Government," Program, Dayton, Ohio, Oct 12, 1927, p 15. (Hereafter cited as Wright Field Dedication Program.)
15. Annual Reports, Chief, Materiel Division: Fiscal Year 1929, p 9; Fiscal Year 1930, p 9; Fiscal Year 1931, p 183; Fiscal Year 1932, pp 10-11; Fiscal Year 1933, p 10.
16. *Air Corps News Letter XX* (Special Materiel Division Number) (Jan 1, 1937), pp 4, 25.
17. First Annual Report, pp 183-184.
18. Eighth Annual Report, Chief, Materiel Division, Fiscal Year 1934, pp 12-13.
19. Sixth Annual Report, Chief, Materiel Division, Fiscal Year 1932, p 10.
20. Pamphlet, "Wright Field" (Materiel Division, U.S. Army Air Corps, Dayton, Ohio, 1938), p 9.
21. *Air Corps News Letter XX* (Jan 1, 1937), p 8.
22. Pamphlet, "Wright Field," p 12.
23. *Ibid.*, p 10.
24. *Ibid.*, p 14.
25. *Air Corps News Letter XX* (Jan 1, 1937), p 12.
26. *Ibid.*, p 12.
27. Pamphlet, "Wright Field," p 17.
28. *Ibid.*, p 18.
29. Seventh Annual Report, Chief, Materiel Division, Fiscal Year 1933, p 7; *Air Corps News Letter XX* (Jan 1, 1937), p 18.
30. *Air Corps News Letter XX* (Jan 1, 1937), pp 18-19.
31. David Gold, "The Parachute in Perspective: Looking Backward to 1931, circa A.I.A.A. Origin," paper presented to the A.I.A.A. 7th Aerodynamic Decelerator and Balloon Technology Conference, San Diego, California, Oct 21-23, 1981, pp 2-5, 8; David Gold, "Milestones in the History of Parachute Development," *SAFE* 9 (Spring 1979): 15.
32. Eleventh Annual Report, Chief, Materiel Division, Fiscal Year 1937, p 24.
33. *Air Corps News Letter XX* (Jan 1, 1937), p 17.
34. Eleventh Annual Report, p 25.
35. Pamphlet, "Wright Field," pp 24-25.
36. *Air Corps News Letter XX* (Jan 1, 1937), p 17.
37. Pamphlet, "Wright Field," p 26.
38. Niehaus, p 62.
39. *Ibid.*, pp 62, 65.
40. *Ibid.*, p 61; *Air Corps News Letter XX* (Jan 1, 1937), p 13.
41. Niehaus, p 61.
42. *Ibid.*, pp 59-60.
43. *Ibid.*, p 64.
44. Pamphlet, "Wright Field," p 16.
45. *Ibid.*, p 25.
46. Eleventh Annual Report, p 20.
47. *The Materiel Center and You* (Dayton, Ohio, Jan 1943), p 39.
48. Eleventh Annual Report, p 1.
49. First Annual Report, pp 198-199, 26.
50. Annual Reports, Chief, Materiel Division, Fiscal Years 1927 through 1940.
51. History of the Army Air Forces Materiel Command 1926-1941 (AMC Historical Study 281, 1943), p 39.

52. Niehaus, p 57.
53. Ninth Annual Report, Chief, Materiel Division, Fiscal Year 1935, p 5.
54. Thirteenth Annual Report, Chief, Materiel Division, Fiscal Year 1939, p 9.
55. Brig Gen W. E. Gillmore, "Industrial War Planning in the Army Air Corps," *U.S. Air Services* 14 (Mar 1929): 30-32.
56. Maj J. A. Mars, "Government Must Encourage Commercial Aviation," *U.S. Air Services* 10 (Jun 1925): 29.
57. Ninth Annual Report, p 15; Thirteenth Annual Report, p 55.
58. Eighth Annual Report, p 14; Ninth Annual Report, p 16.
59. Eleventh Annual Report, p 39.
60. *Ibid.*, p 40.
61. Fourteenth Annual Report, Chief, Materiel Division, Fiscal Year 1940, pp 30-31.
62. Alfred Goldberg, ed., *A History of the United States Air Force 1907-1957* (Princeton, New Jersey, 1957), pp 43-49.
63. "Wright-Patterson AFB Personnel Strength, 1918-2000," 88 ABW/HO Archives.
64. History of the Army Air Forces Materiel Command 1926-1941, pp 6-8.
65. *Ibid.*, p 9.
66. Hist, 2750 Air Base Wing, Jul 1974-Dec 1975, Vol II: Wright-Patterson AFB and 2750 Air Base Wing Heritage and Lineage 1917-1975, p 28.
67. History of the Army Air Forces Materiel Command 1926-1941, pp 58-59.
68. *Ibid.*
69. Interview with Mr. Harry S. Price Jr, Price Brothers Company, Dayton, Jan 3, 1984.
70. History of the Army Air Forces Materiel Command (Materiel Center) 1942 (AMC Historical Study 282, 1946), p 167.
71. Fourteenth Annual Report, p 3.
72. History of the Army Air Forces Materiel Command (Materiel Center), pp 167-71.
73. *Ibid.*, p 8.
74. History of the Army Air Forces Materiel Command 1926-1941, pp 39-40.
75. *Ibid.*, p 40.
76. *The Materiel Center and You*, p 10.
77. History of the Army Air Forces Materiel Command 1943 (AMC Historical Study 283, 1946), p 86.
78. "History of McCook and Wright Field" (WPAFB, n.d.), p 5.
79. Annual Report, Hq Wright Field, Part II: Wright Field Under the Materiel Command, Jan-Jun 1944, pp 6-7.
80. History of the Army Air Forces Materiel Command 1943, p 13; *The Materiel Center and You*, p 20.
81. *Flying and Popular Aviation XXIX* (Special U. S. Army Air Forces Issue) (Sep 1941): 84-85.
82. Administrative History of the Air Technical Service Command 1944 (AMC Historical Study 284, 1946), p 8.
83. *The Materiel Center and You*, pp 40-41.
84. *Flying and Popular Aviation XXIX*, p 119.
85. *Ibid.*, p 200.
86. History of the Army Air Forces Materiel Command 1926 through 1941, pp 86-89.
87. *Flying and Popular Aviation XXIX,* p 86.
88. *Ibid.*, p 200.
89. Administrative History of the Air Technical Service Command 1944, pp 39-40.
90. History of the Army Air Forces Materiel Command 1943, p 12.
91. *Ibid.*, pp 10-11.
92. *Air Force Logistics Command 1917-1992* (AFLC Historical Study 329, Dec 1996), p 10.
93. Administrative History of the Air Technical Service Command 1944, pp 103-104.
94. *The Wright-Patterson Post Script,* May 12, 1945, p 1.
95. "Thanks for the Memories," WPAFB *Skywrighter* (Jan 9, 1981), p 8.
96. *The Wright-Patterson Post Script*, 1945.
97. *The Wright-Patterson Post Script* (Aug 4, 1945), pp 1, 3.
98. *Ibid.* (Aug 18, 1945), pp 1, 3.
99. Frederic C. Lynch, "The 1945 Army Air Forces Fair—Forerunner of Today's Air Force Orientation Group," *Aerospace Historian* 28 (Jun 1981), pp 104-105.
100. Press release, "All in Readiness for Big Air Hit at Wright Field," Oct 16, 1945, Public Information Office files; History of the Air Technical Service Command 1945 (AMC Historical Study 285, 1951), p 89.
101. Lynch, p 107.
102. Bruce Ashcroft and Rob Young, *A Brief History of the Air Force Scientific and Technical Intelligence* (WPAFB, 2001).
103. History of the Air Technical Service Command 1945, p 19.
104. Herbert A. Shaw, "German Air Force Secrets Are Bared," *Dayton Daily News*, Nov 2, 1947.
105. History of the Air Materiel Command 1946 (AMC Historical Study 286, 1951), p 84.
106. The Wright [Field] Flyer, Aug 18, 1945, p 1.
107. *A Pictorial Review, Wright-Patterson Air Force Base, 1917-1967* (WPAFB, 1967), p 36; Goldberg, p 105.

108. For a discussion of the evolution and operation of the Air Force's post-World War II organizations and infrastructure see Karen J. Weitze, *Evolution of Air Force R&D and Logistics Installations During the Cold War: Command Lineage, Scientific Achievement, and Major Tenant Missions*, Vol I-II [draft, 2001].
109. *Ibid.*; History of the Air Technical Service Command 1945.
110. Weitze, *Evolution of Air Force R&D and Logistics Installations,* passim; History of the Air Materiel Command 1946, p 92.
111. Chronology, "35th Anniversary: Milestones."
112. *The Wright-Patterson Post Script*, Aug 30, 1946, p 1.
113. History of the Air Materiel Command 1946, p 93.
114. *Ibid.*, p 94; Weitze, *Evolution of Air Force R&D and Logistics Installations*, passim.
115. Weitze, *Evolution of Air Force R&D and Logistics Installations*, passim.
116. *Ibid.*; History of the Air Technical Service Command 1945.
117. Weitze, *Evolution of Air Force R&D and Logistics Installations,* passim; *A Pictorial Review, Wright-Patterson Air Force Base, 1917-1967*, p 37.
118. "Air Force Technical Achievements at Dayton," prepared by Richard D. Thomas, Historical Division, ASD, Jul 20, 1961, p 8.

Chapter 4. FORGING AN AIR FORCE–FLIGHT VEHICLE AND AERONAUTICAL MATERIEL, 1917-1951

1. Walt Boyne, "The Treasures of McCook Field," *Wings* 5 (Jul 1975): 8.
2. R. M. McFarland, ed., *The History of the Bureau of Aircraft Production*, Vol II, pp 280-281; Terence M. Dean, "History of McCook Field, 1917-1927," Master's Thesis (University of Dayton, 1969), pp 18-19.
3. Capt H. H. Blee, *History of Organization and Activities of Airplane Engineering Division, Bureau of Aircraft Production,* Aug 15, 1919, pp 5-14.
4. *Ibid.*, p 51.
5. *Ibid.*, pp 56-57.
6. Lt Harold H. Emmons, "U. S. Airplane Production, The Official History of Air Progress," *Motor Age* (Dec 5, 1918): 18-19, 30.
7. Air Force Pamphlet 70-7, *U. S. Air Force Historical Aircraft, Background Information*, Jun 1970, p 2. (Hereafter cited as AFP 70-7.)
8. Gordon Swanborough and Peter M. Bowers, *United States Military Aircraft Since 1908* (London, 1971), p 215.
9. *Ibid.*
10. *Ibid.*, pp 220-221.
11. Walt Boyne, "The Treasure Trove of McCook Field," *Airpower* 5 (Jul 1975): 18; Royal Frey, *Evolution of Maintenance Engineering 1907-1920*, Vol 1 (WPAFB, 1960), p 126.
12. Boyne, "Treasure Trove," p 18.
13. Swanborough and Bowers, pp 220-22; Frey, p 127; Blee, pp 42-44.
14. Blee, pp 42-44.
15. *Ibid.*, pp 43-44.
16. Ltr, C. W. Nash, Asst. Director, Aircraft Production, Airplane Engineering Dept., to Col J. G. Vincent, Chief Engineer, Bureau of Aircraft Production, subj: McCook Field, Nov 7, 1918.
17. Blee, p 44.
18. Peter Bowers, "Forgotten Fighters," *Air Progress* (Fall 1962): 42.
19. Walt Boyne, "Martin's Marvel," *Airpower* 2 (Jun 1972): 51.
20. According to Glenn L. Martin's biographer, the original contract called for 20 bombers to be constructed. See Henry Still, *To Ride the Wind: A Biography of Glenn L. Martin* (New York, 1964), p 133.
21. Still, p 139; Boyne, "Martin's Marvel," p 68.
22. Maurer Maurer, ed., *The U. S. Air Service in World War I*, Vol I: *The Final Report and A Tactical History* (Washington, 1978), pp 358-371.
23. Richard P. Hallion, *Test Pilots: The Frontiersmen of Flight* (New York, 1981), pp 62-63.
24. Maurer Maurer, "McCook Field, 1917-1927," *The Ohio Historical Quarterly 67* (Jan 1958): 24.
25. Boyne, "Treasure Trove," p 13.
26. Edward O. Purtee, *History of the Army Air Service 1907-1926* (WPAFB, 1948), pp 128-129.
27. Dean, p 79.
28. *Ibid.*, p 80.
29. Frey, p 190.
30. *Ibid.*, p 191.
31. Gardner W. Carr, "Organization and Activities of Engineering Division of the Air Service," *U. S. Air Services* 7 (Feb 1922): 22-25.
32. Boyne, "Treasures," p 10; Charles G. Worman, "McCook Field, A Decade of Progress," *Aerospace Historian* 17 (Spring 1970): 14.
33. Carr, p 23.

34. *Ibid.*
35. Worman, p 15.
36. Carr, p 25.
37. Marshall Lincoln, "The Barling," *Air Classics* 2 (Feb 1965): 29.
38. Earl H. Tilford, Jr., "The Barling Bomber," *Aerospace Historian* 26 (Jun 1979): 94.
39. Henry H. Arnold, *Global Mission* (New York, 1949), p 110.
40. *Ibid.*, p 120.
41. C. H. Hildreth and Bernard C. Nalty, *1001 Questions Answered About Aviation History* (New York, 1969), p 182; Joseph A. Ventolo, Jr., "Colonel John A. Macready," *Air Force Magazine* (Feb 1980): 76-78; Air Force Pamphlet 190-2-2, *A Chronology of American Aerospace Events from 1903 through 1964*, Sep 1965, p 22. (Hereafter cited as AFP 190-2-2.)
42. Dr. Robert F. Futrell, "The Development of Aeromedical Evacuation in the USAF 1909-1939," *AAHS Journal* 23 (Fall 1978): 216-218.
43. Paul Lambermont and Anthony Pirie, *Helicopters and Autogyros of the World* (New York, 1959), p 164.
44. Hallion, *Test Pilots*, p 147.
45. Carr, p 26.
46. Booklet, *A Little Journey to the Home of the Engineering Division, Army Air Service* (Hq Engineering Division, McCook Field, ca 1926), p 15.
47. Wright Field Dedication Program, Oct 12, 1927, p 12.
48. Brig Gen Ross G. Hoyt, "The Curtiss Hawks," *Air Force Magazine* (Oct 1976): 68-69.
49. C. G. Grey, ed., *Jane's All The World's Aircraft*, 1926 (London, 1926), p 240b.
50. Andrew W. Waters, *All the U. S. Air Force Airplanes, 1907-1983* (New York, 1983), p 285; James C. Fahey, ed., *U. S. Army Aircraft 1908-1946* (New York, 1946), p 21.
51. Hoyt, "The Curtiss Hawks," p 68.
52. *Ibid.*, pp 68-69; AFP 70-7, p 6.
53. Waters, p 215; Fahey, p 30.
54. *Ibid.*, p 63; Fahey, p 20.
55. C. G. Grey, ed., *Jane's All The World's Aircraft,* 1928 (London, 1928), p 212c; Waters, p 15.
56. C. G. Grey, ed., *Jane's All The World's Aircraft*, 1927 (London, 1927), pp 249b-250b.
57. Frederick P. Neely, "Army Makes Longest Overwater Flight," *U. S. Air Services* 12 (Aug 1927): 21-22, William B. Murphy, "The Flying Bird of Paradise," *Aerospace Historian* 26 (Mar 1979): 30-33.
58. John Goldstrom, *A Narrative History of Aviation* (New York, 1942), pp 235-236; Lloyd Morris and Kendall Smith, *Ceiling Unlimited: The Story of American Aviation from Kitty Hawk to Supersonics* (New York, 1953), pp 267-268.
59. Neely, p 20.
60. Murphy, p 33; AFP 190-2-2, p 25.
61. Third Annual Report, Chief, Materiel Division, Fiscal Year 1929, p 21.
62. Fourth Annual Report, Chief, Materiel Division, Fiscal Year 1930, pp 15-16.
63. Fifth Annual Report, Chief, Materiel Division, Fiscal Year 1931, pp 23-24.
64. Sixth Annual Report, Chief, Materiel Division, Fiscal Year 1932, Part II: Engineering Activities, pp 19-20; Fahey, p 20.
65. Seventh Annual Report, Chief, Materiel Division, Fiscal Year 1933, Part II: Engineering Activities, pp 13-14; Fahey, p 20; Waters, p 12.
66. Fifth Annual Report, pp 27-28.
67. AFP 70-7, p 6.
68. Sixth Annual Report, p 21; Waters, p 16, Fahey, p 22.
69. Seventh Annual Report, p 14.
70. Still, p 181.
71. AFP 70-7, p 7; Waters, p 16.
72. Waters, p 16.
73. AFP 190-2-2, p 30.
74. Third Annual Report, p 29.
75. *Ibid.*, p 30; Waters, p 378.
76. Fifth Annual Report, p 37.
77. Sixth Annual Report, p 25.
78. *Ibid.*
79. *Ibid.*, p 25; Seventh Annual Report, p 18.
80. Sixth Annual Report, p 26; Waters, p 379.
81. Waters, p 218.
82. Fahey, pp 30-31.
83. Sixth Annual Report, p 22.
84. AFP 70-7, p 5; Fahey, p 32.
85. Secretary of the Air Force, Office of Information, Photo Package No. 2, 1971, p 5.

86. Sixth Annual Report, p 23; Fahey, p 32.
87. Seventh Annual Report, p 16; Photo Package No. 2, p 5.
88. Seventh Annual Report, p 16.
89. Fourth Annual Report, pp 35-36.
90. Fahey, p 28.
91. Waters, p 284.
92. Sixth Annual Report, p 24.
93. Wesley F. Craven and James L. Cate, eds., *The Army Air Forces in World War II*, Vol I: *Plans and Early Operations* (Chicago, 1950), pp 54-71.
94. Ninth Annual Report, Chief, Materiel Division, Fiscal Year 1935, Part II: Engineering, p 13.
95. Douglas J. Ingells, *They Tamed the Sky* (New York, 1947), p 20.
96. Waters, p 68; AFP 70-7, p 11; Fahey, p 20.
97. Ninth Annual Report, p 14.
98. Lambermont and Pirie, pp 194-195; Fahey, p 28.
99. Waters, pp 203-204.
100. Craven and Cate, Vol I, pp 65-66.
101. Edward Jablonski, *Flying Fortress* (New York, 1949), p 155.
102. DeWitt S. Copp, *A Few Great Captains* (New York, 1980), p 328.
103. *Ibid.*
104. *Ibid.*, p 329.
105. Herbert Molloy Mason, Jr., *The United States Air Force: A Turbulent History* (New York, 1976), pp 120-121.
106. Jablonski, p 6; Copp, p 330.
107. Hallion, *Test Pilots*, pp 140-141; Jablonski, pp 12-13.
108. Tenth Annual Report, Chief, Materiel Division, Fiscal Year 1936, p 7.
109. Waters, p 16; AFP 70-7, p 8; Photo Package No. 2, p 6.
110. Tenth Annual Report, p 7; Hallion, *Test Pilots*, p 141; Jablonski, p 11.
111. Eleventh Annual Report, Chief, Materiel Division, Fiscal Year 1937, p 8.
112. Arnold, p 155.
113. Fahey, p 22.
114. Jablonski, pp 19-20; AFP 190-2-2, p 32.
115. Jablonski, p 128; AFP 190-2-2, p 33.
116. Craven and Cate, Vol VI: *Men and Planes*, pp 206-207.
117. *Ibid.*, pp 207-208; *U. S. Air Force Museum Photo Album*, (WPAFB, n.d.) p 44. (Hereafter cited as AFM Album).
118. Fahey, p 23; AFP 70-7, pp 12-13.
119. AFM Album, pp 40, 47.
120. Craven and Cate, Vol VI, pp 202-203.
121. *Ibid.*, pp 208-210; Steve Birdsall, *Saga of the Superfortress* (New York, 1980), p 323.
122. Craven and Cate, Vol VI, pp 210-211.
123. Waters, p 129.
124. Hist., 2750 Air Base Wing, Jul 1974-Dec 1975, Vol II, Wright-Patterson AFB and 2750 ABW Heritage and Lineage (WPAFB, 1976), pp 66-69.
125. Twelfth Annual Report, Chief, Materiel Division, Fiscal Year 1938, p 8.
126. Richard C. Hubler, *Big Eight: Biography of an Airplane* (New York, 1960), p 8.
127. Craven and Cate, Vol VI, p 224.
128. Waters, p 134.
129. Craven and Cate, Vol VI, p 224; Hubler, p 54.
130. Ninth Annual Report, p 15; AFM Album, p 31.
131. Twelfth Annual Report, pp 9-10.
132. Fahey, p 31.
133. Thirteenth Annual Report, Chief, Materiel Division, Fiscal Year 1939, pp 40-42; Fahey, p 31.
134. Waters, p 220.
135. Tenth Annual Report, p 6; Fahey, p 32; Waters, p 251.
136. AFP 70-7, p 10; AFM Album, p 27.
137. Craven and Cate, Vol VI, pp 212-214; Waters, pp 256-257.
138. Craven and Cate, Vol VI, pp 214-215; AFP 70-7, p 16; AFM Album, p 42.
139. Craven and Cate, Vol VI, pp 215-217; AFP 70-7, p 13; Photo Package No. 2, p 10; AFM Album, p 48.
140. Craven and Cate, Vol VI, pp 218-220; AFP 70-7, p 15; AFM Album, p 51.
141. Craven and Cate, Vol VI, pp 220-221; AFP 70-7, pp 15-16; AFM Album, p 60.
142. Waters, p 289; Fahey, pp 35-36.
143. Ninth Annual Report, p 17.
144. *Ibid.*; Waters, p 52.
145. Waters, p 289.

146. Thirteenth Annual Report, pp 41-42; AFP 70-7, pp 10-11; AFM Album, p 38.
147. Waters, p 291; Fahey, pp 21-22.
148. Photo Package No. 2, p 10; AFM Album, p 36.
149. Fahey, p 27; Waters, p 26.
150. Waters, p 28.
151. AFP 70-7, pp 17-19; Birdsall, p 233; AFP 190-2-2, p 48.
152. Alfred Goldberg, ed., *A History of the United States Air Force 1907-1957* (Princeton, 1957), p 124.
153. Craven and Cate, Vol VI, pp 243-245; AFP 70-7, p 18; Waters, pp 11-12; Lloyd S. Jones, *U. S. Bombers 1928 to 1980s*, 3rd ed. (Fallbrook, Ca., 1980), pp 121-223, 166-168.
154. Waters, p 176.
155. Grover Heiman, *Jet Pioneers* (New York, 1963), pp 52-67, 127-129; Hallion, *Test Pilots*, pp 168-172; Hildreth and Nalty, p 310.
156. Craven and Cate, Vol VI, pp 250-251; AFM Album, p 68.

Chapter 5. PIONEERING AIR FORCE ACQUISITION–A WORK IN PROGRESS

1. Juliette A. Hennessey, *The United States Army Air Arm, April 1861 to April 1917,* USAF Historical Study No. 98 (Washington, D. C., 1958; reprint ed., 1985), p 217.
2. *Ibid.*, p 25.
3. Hennessey, pp 28-33.
4. *Ibid.*, p 110.
5. I. B. Holley, Jr., *Ideas and Weapons: Exploitation of the Aerial Weapon by the United States during World War I; A Study in the Relationship of Technological Advance, Military Doctrine, and the Development of Weapons* (New Haven, 1953; reprint ed., Washington, D.C., 1983), Chapter 2, passim.
6. *Who's Who in American Aeronautics*, 3d ed., 1928, Compiled by Lester D. Gardner (New York City, 1928), p 71.
7. *Ibid.*, p 33.
8. Holley, *Ideas and Weapons*, p 30.
9. *Ibid.,* p 68.
10. H. H. Blee, *History of [the] Organization and Activities of [the] Airplane Engineering Division, Bureau of Aircraft Production* (McCook Field, 1919), pp 4, 11.
11. *Ibid.*, p 28.
12. *Ibid.*, p 29.
13. Lawrence R. Benson, *Acquisition Management in the United States Air Force and Its Predecessors* (Washington, D.C., 1997), p 6.
14. Blee, p 289.
15. Chronology, "Laboratories at Wright-Patterson AFB, Ohio, 1917-1975," p 1.
16. Albert E. Misenko and Philip H. Pollock, *Engineering History, 1917-1978: McCook Field to the Aeronautical Systems Division*, 4th ed. (WPAFB, 1979), Appendix A, chart 1.
17. Holley, *Ideas and Weapons*, p 105.
18. Albert E. Misenko, *Aero Propulsion* [draft, 1994], p 71.
19. Charles L. Lawrance, *Our National Aviation Program* (New York, 1932), pp 5-6.
20. Mason Patrick, *The United States in the Air* (Garden City, New York, 1928), pp 101-4.
21. Robert Frank Futrell, *Ideas, Concepts, Doctrine* (Maxwell AFB, Alabama, 1974; reprint ed., New York, 1980), p 29.
22. Benson, p 7.
23. Lawrance, pp 8-9; Benson, p 11.
24. John Kenneth Galbraith, *The Great Crash, 1929*, 3rd ed. (Boston, 1972), chapter 6.
25. Benson, p 11.
26. *Materiel Research and Development in the Army Air Arm, 1914-1945*, Army Air Forces Historical Studies, no. 50, AAF Historical Office, Headquarters, Army Air Forces, Nov 1946, p 49.
27. James J. Niehaus, *Five Decades of Materials Progress: Air Force Materials Lab, 1917-1967* (WPAFB, Ohio, 1967), p 56.
28. Benson, p 6.
29. Irving Brinton Holley, Jr., *Buying Aircraft: Materiel Procurement for the Army Air Forces, United States Army in World War II* (Washington, D.C., 1964), p 85.
30. Ronald Miller and David Sawers, *The Technical Development of Modern Aviation* (New York and Washington, 1970), pp 18-20.
31. C. G. Brown and Carl F. Greene, "Static-Test and Stress-Distribution Studies of the Materiel Division 55-Foot Cantilever All-Metal Wing," *Air Corps Information Circular*, Vol VII, no. 663, Feb 15, 1932 (Air Corps Technical Report, no. 3501).
32. "Pressure Cabin Investigations," *Air Corps Information Circular*, Vol VIII, no. 710, Oct 1, 1937 (Air Corps Technical Report no. 4220).

33. *R&D Contributions to Aviation Progress (RADCAP)*, Joint DoD-NASA-DoT Study (Aug 1972), Appendix 6, p 99.
34. Benson, p 12.
35. Bernard C. Nalty, ed., *Winged Shield, Winged Sword: A History of the United States Air Force*, Vol I: 1907-1950 (Washington, D.C., 1997), p 162.
36. Alfred Goldberg, ed., *A History of the United States Air Force, 1907-1957* (Princeton, New Jersey, 1957), p 48.
37. Dik Alan Daso, *Hap Arnold and the Evolution of American Airpower* (Washington, 2000), chapter 9.
38. James H. "Jimmy" Doolittle, *I Could Never Be So Lucky Again: An Autobiography*, with Carroll V. Glines (New York, 1991), pp 199ff.
39. Benson, p 16.
40. *Ibid.*, p 16.
41. *Ibid.*, p 16.
42. *Ibid.*, p 16.
43. *Ibid.*, p 16.
44. *Ibid.*, p 13.
45. *Ibid.*, p 13.
46. *Ibid.*, p 18; Bernard J. Termena, Layne B. Peiffer, and H. P. Carlin, *Logistics: An Illustrated History of AFLC and Its Antecedents, 1921-1981* (WPAFB, Ohio, 1981), p 93.
47. Diana G. Cornelisse, et al., *Against the Wind: 90 Years of Flight Test in the Miami Valley* (WPAFB, 1994), p 131.
48. Benson, pp 18-19.
49. *Ibid.*, p 18.
50. *Ibid.*, p 17.
51. *Ibid.*, p 18.
52. *Ibid.*, p 17.
53. Daso, chapter 9.
54. Theodore von Karman, *The Wind and Beyond: Theodore von Karman, Pioneer in Aviation and Pathfinder in Space*, with Lee Edson (Boston, 1967), pp 226-7.
55. James St. Peter, *The History of Aircraft Gas Turbine Engine Development in the United States: A Tradition of Excellence* (Atlanta, 1999), pp 32-34.
56. James F. Aldridge, ed., *USAF Research & Development: The Legacy of the Wright Laboratory Science and Engineering Community, 1917-1997* [draft, ASC/HO, 1996], pp 17f.
57. Theodore von Karman, *Toward New Horizons: Science, the Key to Air Supremacy*, Commemorative Edition, 1950-1992 (WPAFB, 1992), pp vii-ix.
58. Michael H. Gorn, *Prophecy Fulfilled: "Toward New Horizons" and Its Legacy* (Washington, D.C., 1994), pp 1-16.
59. Benson, p 13.
60. Roger E. Bilstein, *The Enterprise of Flight: The American Aviation and Aerospace Industry* (Washington, 2001), p 83.
61. Niehaus, *Five Decades of Materials Progress*, p 80.
62. Benson, p 19.
63. Misenko and Pollock, *Engineering History*, p 2.
64. *First Five Years of the Air Research and Development Command, United States Air Force* (Baltimore, Maryland, 1955), pp 18-19.
65. *Ibid.*, p 20.
66. *Ibid.*, p 21.
67. *Ibid.*, p 26.
68. *Ibid.*, pp 24-5.
69. Misenko and Pollock, *Engineering History*, p 16.
70. *Ibid.*, p 16.
71. Benson, p 29.
72. *Ibid.*, pp 24-5.
73. *Ibid.*, p 25.
74. Misenko and Pollock, *Engineering History*, pp 17-18; Benson, pp 25-6.
75. Benson, 26.
76. Misenko, *Engineering History*, pp 17ff.
77. See Lori S. Tagg, *On the Front Line of R&D: Wright-Patterson Air Force Base in the Korean War, 1950-1953* (WPAFB, 2001).
78. Jacob Neufeld, *The Development of Ballistic Missiles in the United States Air Force, 1945-1960* (Washington, D.C., 1990), pp 59-64.
79. Robert L. Perry, *System Development Strategies: A Comparative Study of Doctrine, Technology, and Organization in the USAF Ballistic and Cruise Missile Programs, 1950-1960,* The RAND Corporation, Santa Monica, California, Memorandum RM-4853-PR, Aug 1966, pp 48-53 and 82-5.

80. Lois E. Walker and Shelby E. Wickam, *From Huffman Prairie to the Moon: The History of Wright-Patterson Air Force Base, Ohio* (WPAFB, 1986), pp 382-3; Benson, pp 24-6.
81. Benson, pp 24-5.
82. Walker and Wickam, p 383.
83. Benson, pp 26-7.
84. *Ibid.*, p 27.
85. But see Perry, *System Development Strategies*, pp 112-138.
86. *A General Remembers: Major General Fred J. Ascani, Wright Field's Father of Systems Engineering,* ed. with narrative by James F. Aldridge (WPAFB, Ohio, 2001), p I-13.
87. Perry, *System Development Strategies*, pp 24-5; Misenko and Pollock, *Engineering History*, p 32.
88. *Major General Fred J. Ascani*, p I-12.
89. James F. Aldridge, *A Historical Overview of the Mission and Organization of the Wright Laboratory, 1917-1993* [draft, 1994], p 15.
90. Misenko and Pollock, *Engineering History*, pp 27-34.
91. *Major General Fred J. Ascani*, p I-15.
92. *Ibid.*, p I-16.
93. Chronology, p 10.
94. *Major General Fred J. Ascani*, p I-15.
95. Benson, p 29.
96. *Ibid.,* p 30.
97. *Ibid.*, p 31.
98. *Ibid.*, p 31.
99. Misenko and Pollock, *Engineering History*, pp 39-40.
100. *Ibid.*, p 32.
101. *Ibid.*, p 39.
102. *Ibid.*, p 34; Benson, p 30
103. *Ibid.*, Misenko and Pollock, *Engineering History*, p 34.
104. Benson, p 32.
105. Misenko and Pollock, *Engineering History*, pp 40-1.
106. *Major General Fred J. Ascani*, pp I-21 to I-22.
107. Chronology, p 16.
108. Misenko and Pollock, *Engineering History*, pp 42-4.
109. *Ibid.*, pp 48-53.
110. Michael H. Gorn, *Harnessing the Genie: Science and Technology Forecasting for the Air Force, 1944-1986* (Washington, 1988), chapter 3, *passim.*
111. Benson, pp 33-4.
112. Amos A. Jordan, William J. Taylor, Jr., and Lawrence J. Korb, *American National Security: Policy and Process*, 4th ed. (Baltimore, 1993), p 194.
113. *Ibid.*, pp 193-4.
114. Walker and Wickam, p 388; Benson, p 33.
115. Richard P. Hallion, *The Evolution of Commonality in Fighter and Attack Aircraft Development and Usage* (Edwards AFB, 1985), p. 5.
116. Walker and Wickam, p 388.
117. Written comments to ASC/HO by Mr. Ralph Johnson, Apr 2002.
118. Richard P. Hallion, *Storm over Iraq: Air Power and the Gulf War* (Washington, 1992), chapter 2.
119. *Ibid.*, p 391f.
120. *Ibid.*, p 390f.
121. Benson, p 38.
122. *Ibid.*, pp 34-5.
123. *Ibid.*, p 35.
124. *Ibid.*, p 38.
125. *Ibid.*, p 38.
126. Kenneth P. Werrell, *The Evolution of the Cruise Missile* (Maxwell AFB, 1985), p 177.
127. Benson, p 39.
128. J. S. Przemieniecki, *Acquisition of Defense Systems* (Washington, D.C., 1993), p 16.
129. Benson, p 39; Przemieniecki, p 16.
130. Przemieniecki, p 16.
131. Benson, p 40.
132. Przemieniecki, p 16.
133. Benson, p 39; Przemieniecki, p 16.
134. *History of the Aeronautical Systems Division (ASD), January-December 1987*, Vol I, p 84; Benson, pp 41-2.
135. *History of ASD, January-December 1984*, I: p 116; Benson, pp 40-41; Przemieniecki, pp 16-17.
136. Benson, p 41; Przemieniecki, p 17.

137. Benson, p 42.
138. *Ibid.*, p 42.
139. *Ibid.*, p 43.
140. *History of the Aeronautical Systems Division, January-December 1989,* 1989, Vol 1, pp 63-7.
141. Benson, p 44.
142. *Ibid.*, p 44.
143. *Ibid.*, p 38.
144. *Ibid.*, p 40.
145. *Ibid.*, p 44.
146. Aldridge, *Historical Overview*, p 23.
147. *History of the Aeronautical Systems Division, January-December 1990,* 1990, Vol 1, pp 20-21, 482.
148. *History of the Aeronautical Systems Center (ASC), January-September 1992*, Vol 1, pp 15-21.
149. For the implementation of TQM at ASC, see Albert E. Misenko, *Total Quality Management at the Aeronautical Systems Division, 1984-1992: The Road to Improvement* (WPAFB, Sep 1992).
150. Benson, p 48.
151. Robert W. Duffner, *Science and Technology: The Making of the Air Force Research Laboratory* (Maxwell AFB, Nov 2000).
152. Przemieniecki, p 263.
153. *History of the Aeronautical Systems Center, October 1997-September 1998,* Vol 1, pp 21-31.
154. *History of the Aeronautical Systems Center, October 1996-September 1997,* Vol 1, pp 85-88.
155. *Ibid.,* pp 54-56.
156. *Ibid.*, pp 52-53.
157. *Ibid.*, pp 48-51.
158. *History of the Aeronautical Systems Center, October 1999-September 2000,* Vol 1 [forthcoming]. (Hereafter cited as Hist, ASC, 1999-2000.)
159. Hist, ASC, 1999-2000, Vol 1 [forthcoming].
160. Donald H. Rumsfeld, "Transforming the Military," *Foreign Affairs*, Vol 81, no. 3 (May/Jun 2002): 20-32.

Chapter 6. FROM AIR POWER TO AEROSPACE DOMINANCE–AEROSPACE SYSTEMS DEVELOPMENT, 1951-2003

1. Richard P. Hallion, *Storm Over Iraq: Air Power and the Gulf War* (Washington, D.C., 1992), p 70.
2. Donald B. Rice, Secretary of Air Force, and General Merrill A. McPeak, Air Force Chief of Staff, *Fiscal Year 92 Air Force Posture Statement*, presented to House of Reps, Armed Services Committee, Feb 26, 1991; Dick Cheney, Secretary of Defense, *Defense Strategy for the 1990s: The Regional Defense Strategy*, Jan 1993.
3. Office of Information, Internal Information and Community Relations Division, *Aeronautical Systems Division* (WPAFB, 1961).
4. Marcelle Size Knaack, *Post World War II Bombers* (Washington, D.C., 1988), pp 21, 52, 169, 175.
5. *Ibid.*, pp 99-146; Hallion, *Storm Over Iraq*, p 66.
6. *History of Wright Air Development Center (WADC), 1 Jan – Jun 30, 1952*, Vol II, p 127. (Hereafter cited as Hist, WADC, 1952-1.)
7. Knaack, *Post-World War II Bombers*, pp 99-146.
8. William Elliott, *The Development of Fly-By-Wire Flight Control,* Air Force Materiel Command [AFMC] Historical Study No. 7 (WPAFB, 1996), pp 16-17.
9. Knaack, *Post-World War II Bombers*, pp 256, 268.
10. *Ibid.*, pp 205-290; ASC/HO, *Birthplace, Home, and Future of Aerospace* (WPAFB, 1999), p 48; "Chronology of Events Related to the Advanced Manned Strategic Aircraft Program, 1954-1965," in XB-70/AMSA File, Box 7000: History/Chronology, Topical A-J, ASC/HO Archive. See Walter Boyne, *Boeing B-52: A Documentary History* (London, 1981).
11. Mark A. Lorell, Alison Saunders, and Hugh P. Levaux, *Bomber R&D Since 1945: The Role of Experience* (Santa Monica, 1995), pp 20-21.
12. Knaack, *Post-World War II Bombers*, pp 351-378.
13. *Ibid.*, p 394.
14. *Ibid.*, p 386; Richard L. Atkins, *The B-58 Escape Capsule Indoctrination Brochure* (Fort Worth, Texas, 1962), pp 2-3, in B-58 File, Box 3219: History of the Development of the B-58 Bomber, Vols. I, II, and III, ASC/HO Archive.
15. Knaack, *Post-World War II Bombers*, pp 351-395; Lorell et al., *Bomber R&D*, pp 36-37.
16. Knaack, *Post-World War II Bombers*, pp 297-342.
17. *Ibid.*, pp 324-328.
18. *Ibid.*, pp 403-455; M.B. Rothman, *Aerospace Weapon System Acquisition Milestones: A Data Base* (Santa Monica, 1987), p 83.
19. Marcelle Size Knaack, *Post-World War II Fighters* (Washington, D.C., 1986), pp 242-246.

20. "Chronology of Events Related to the Advanced Manned Strategic Aircraft Program, 1954-1965;" Lorell et al., *Bomber R&D*, p 23.
21. Cecil H. Uyehara, "The B-70 Story (to summer 1959)" (Directorate of Systems Management, Headquarters Air Research and Development Command, 1959), pp 66, 71, in Box 3238: B-70 Bomber Files Box 2, ASC/HO Archive; Ward Lauren, "Riding the Shock Wave," *Skyline* 19 (1961): 21; Lorell et al., *Bomber R&D*, p 36.
22. "Chronology of Events Related to the Advanced Manned Strategic Aircraft Program, 1954-1965;" Uyehara, pp 75, 90.
23. Knaack, *Post-World War II Bombers*, pp 559-573; Rothman, p 85.
24. Knaack, *Post-World War II Bombers*, pp 575-579. North American Aviation merged with Rockwell Standard in 1967. Mark A. Lorell and Hugh P. Levaux, *The Cutting Edge: A Half Century of U. S. Fighter Aircraft R&D* (Santa Monica, 1998), p 107n.
25. "B-1/Long Range Combat Aircraft Program History Summary," in B-1 File, Box 7000: Reference, Chronology A-J, ASC/HO Archive; Kenneth P. Werrell, "The USAF and the Cruise Missile: Opportunity or Threat?" in *Technology and the Air Force: A Retrospective Assessment*, ed. Jacob Neufeld, George M. Watson, Jr., and David Chenoweth (Washington), p 149; Lorell et al., *Bomber R&D*, p 60.
26. Knaack, *Post-World War II Bombers*, p 587; Lorell et al., *Bomber R&D*, p 60.
27. *History of the Aeronautical Systems Center, October 1998 - September 1999*, Vol I, pp III-2, III-9. (Hereafter cited as Hist, ASC, 1998-1999.)
28. "B-2, Advanced Technology Bomber Program Chronology, 1978-1995," in Box 3193: B-2 Aircraft Miscellaneous Documents, ASC/HO Archive; Lorell et al., *Bomber R&D*, pp 55, 57.
29. Boeing Defense and Space Group, Military Airplanes Division, "Boeing B-2 History, 1993-1994" (1995), in Box 3190: B-2, Public Affairs Files, ASC/HO Archive; Lorell et al., *Bomber R&D*, p 57.
30. "B-2, Advanced Technology Bomber Program Chronology," p 12.
31. "B-2 Advanced Technology Bomber," Aeronautical Systems Division Fact Sheet (WPAFB, 1988), in Box 3190: B-2, PA Files, ASC/HO Archive.
32. Hist, ASC, 1998-1999, p III-25.
33. The Bell P-59 Airacomet was actually the first operational Air Force jet fighter. The XP-59 had its first flight in 1942, and the Air Force procured 66 P-59s. This aircraft was never used in combat, however, and was reserved primarily for training pilots destined to fly later jet fighters, such as the F-80. Walter J. Boyne, ed. *The Jet Age: Forty Years of Jet Aviation* (Washington, 1979), p 50.
34. *History of Wright Air Development Center (WADC), 1 January – 30 June 1953*, Vol II, pp 372-373 (Hereafter cited as Hist, WADC, 1953-1); Jacob Neufeld, "The F-15 Eagle: Origins and Development, 1964-1972," *Air Power History* 48 (Spring 2001), p 6. The late 1940s and early 1950s were notable for the proliferation of experimental fighter (as well as bomber) designs. For example, several escort designs (the XF-84, XF-88, XF-90, and YF-93) were made into flyable prototypes but were displaced in full-scale development by further improvement of the F-84 jet fighter. Some of the experimental designs were later refined into operational aircraft with different designations, such as the XF-88, which later became the F-101 escort.
35. On June 11, 1948, the Air Force revised its aircraft designations. At this time, all aircraft previously referred to as Pursuit with the P prefix were changed to an F prefix for Fighter. Knaack, *Post-World War II Fighters*, p 1n.
36. *Ibid.*, pp 23-50.
37. Knaack, *Post-World War II Fighters*, pp 38-45; Hist, WADC, 1952-1, p 220.
38. Knaack, *Post-World War II Fighters*, pp. 53-81; Hist, WADC, 1952-1, pp 183-184.
39. Knaack, *Post-World War II Fighters*, pp 60, 63, 72; Hist, WADC, 1952-1, pp 196, 205-206.
40. Knaack, *Post-World War II Fighters*, pp 83-98; *History of Wright Air Development Center (WADC), 1 January – June 30, 1955*, Vol II, pp 20, 23. (Hereafter cited as Hist, WADC, 1955-1.)
41. Knaack, *Post-World War II Fighters*, pp 101-104; Ray Wagner, *American Combat Planes* (New York, 1968), p 265.
42. Hist, WADC, 1952-1, pp 179, 204.
43. Knaack, *Post-World War II Fighters*, pp 101-111; F.G. Swansborough, *United States Military Aircraft Since 1909* (London, 1963), p 308.
44. Knaack, *Post-World War II Fighters*, pp 113-133.
45. The F-86 could fly supersonic in a dive, but the F-100 was the first aircraft to fly at supersonic speeds in straight and level flight.
46. Knaack, *Post-World War II Fighters*, pp 113-133; Lorell and Levaux, *The Cutting Edge*, p 67.
47. Knaack, *Post-World War II Fighters*, pp 135-157; Hist, WADC, 1952-1, pp 213-216; *History of Wright Air Development Center (WADC), 1 July – 31 December 1952*, Vol II, p 463 (Hereafter cited as Hist, WADC, 1952-2); Hist, WADC, 1955-1, p 35; Lorell and Levaux, *The Cutting Edge*, p 37. The F-88 was renamed the F-101 Voodoo in November 1951. Rothman, *Acquisition Milestones*, p 43.
48. Consolidated Aircraft merged with Vultee Aircraft to become Convair in 1943. Lorell and Levaux, *The Cutting Edge*, p 29.
49. The F-102 design competed against a more radical fighter design for the Ultimate Interceptor role—that of the Republic XF-103. The XF-103's design was challenging in that the airframe was to have been constructed primarily of titanium alloys that could withstand the high temperatures experienced at supersonic speeds better

than stainless steel. In order to achieve speeds in excess of Mach 3, the aircraft's propulsion system was a combination of turbojet and ramjet engines. The F-103 was "so radical, so advanced, and incorporated so many unproven components" that many engineers doubted it would ever reach production. By early 1953, the program had become an "experimental weapon system," and no fiscal year 1954 funds were allotted for an extended development program. In 1957 the program was cancelled altogether. Hist, WADC, 1952-1, pp 210-213; Hist, WADC, 1952-2, p 519; Hist, WADC, 1953-1, pp 236, 239; Knaack, *Post-World War II Fighters*, p 160, 329; Lorell and Levaux, *The Cutting Edge*, p 62.

50. The F-102 was also the first aircraft developed under the weapon system concept, which directed that research, development, and procurement should encompass a total vehicle or weapon system instead of a variety of individual components, ranging from airborne and ground equipment, to services, facilities, and trained personnel. This was a dramatic change from earlier procurement methods in which individual components were developed and procured independent of the aircraft and then "made to fit." A prime contractor, Convair in the case of the F-102, was chosen to oversee the design and system engineering of all components of the weapon system, and the Air Force's project engineer monitored the progress of development and production. This acquisition concept is discussed in more detail in Chapter 5. Lois E. Walker and Shelby E. Wickam, *From Huffman Prairie to the Moon: The History of Wright-Patterson Air Force Base* (WPAFB, 1986), p 382.
51. Hist, WADC, 1952-1, pp 207-210; Hist, WADC, 1952-2, p 508; Knaack, *Post-World War II Fighters*, pp 159-173; Swansborough *United States Military Aircraft Since 1909*, p 151.
52. Knaack, *Post-World War II Fighters*, pp 207-221.
53. The F-104 was the first aircraft in history to hold world records for both absolute speed and altitude (1,404.19 mph and 91,249 feet) simultaneously. Rothman, *Acquisition Milestones*, p 49.
54. Hist, WADC, 1953-1, p 324; Knaack, *Post-World War II Fighters*, pp 175-188.
55. Knaack, *Post-World War II Fighters*, pp 190-205; Swansborough, *United States Military Aircraft Since 1909*, p 420; Lorell and Levaux, *The Cutting Edge*, p 68.
56. The Air Force did study other advanced fighter designs during this period, such as the North American XF-108 Rapier, a high speed, long-range, all-weather interceptor. The F-108 was not ordered for production due to budget restrictions. Knaack, *Post-World War II Fighters*, pp 329-331.
57. The F-4, which drew heavily from McDonnell's F-101 program, was originally considered by the Air Force as an interim replacement for the F-106, F-105D, and RF-101 until the TFX (F-111) could be procured. Lorell and Levaux, *The Cutting Edge*, p 77.
58. Michael J.H. Taylor, ed., *Jane's Encyclopedia of Aviation* (New York, 1989), p 645; Neufeld, "The F-15 Eagle," p 10.
59. Taylor, *Jane's Encyclopedia of Aviation*, pp 645-646; Knaack, *Post-World War II Fighters,* pp 265-277.
60. News Release, Air Force News Service, "Phantom to Retire from AF Inventory," Nov 29, 1995.
61. *Ibid.*
62. Knaack, *Post World War II Fighters*, pp 287-291.
63. The F-111 did not receive an official name until the day in July 1996 when the last four were retired from Cannon Air Force Base, New Mexico. Known unofficially as the Aardvark for many years, the Air Force officially christened it at a retirement and naming ceremony at the Lockheed-Martin Tactical Aircraft Systems plant in Fort Worth, Texas. This facility was also the same plant (then General Dynamics) from which the first F-111 rolled out in 1964. News Release, Air Force News Service, "F-111 Officially Retires as the 'Aardvark'," Aug 5, 1996.
64. Knaack, *Post-World War II Fighters*, pp 223-261; Taylor, *Jane's Encyclopedia of Aviation*, p 417.
65. Knaack, *Post-World War II Fighters*, pp 238-256.
66. John W.R. Taylor, ed., *Jane's All The World's Aircraft, 1989-1990* (London, 1989), p 526; "F-111 Officially Retires as the Aardvark." Although ultimately the services agreed that it was unrealistic to develop a single aircraft to meet such differing requirements, the TFX program and resulting F-111 produced several "firsts" in aviation technology. It was the first production aircraft with variable sweep wings and the first with afterburning turbofan engines. It was also the first tactical fighter designed for unrefueled trans-oceanic flight. It could fly both low-altitude, supersonic interdiction and high-altitude, subsonic, air-superiority missions. Robert J. Art, *The TFX Decision: McNamara and the Military* (Boston, 1968).
67. Neufeld, "The F-15 Eagle," pp 8-9; Lorell and Levaux, *The Cutting Edge*, p 105.
68. Neufeld, "The F-15 Eagle," pp 13-14; John W.R. Taylor, ed., *Jane's All the World's Aircraft, 1970-1971* (London, 1970), p 394. McDonnell merged with Douglas Aircraft Company in 1967.
69. Taylor, *Jane's All The World's Aircraft, 1970-1971*, p 394; Neufeld, "The F-15 Eagle," pp 16, 19; Fact Sheet, U. S. Air Force, "F-15 Eagle," Sep 2000.
70. Neufeld, "The F-15 Eagle," p 19; Taylor, *Jane's All The World's Aircraft, 1989-1990*, p 450; Ron Dick, Reach and Power: *The Heritage of the United States Air Force in Pictures and Artifacts* (Washington, 1997), p 422; Hallion, *Storm Over Iraq*, p 292.
71. Fact Sheet, "F-15 Eagle."
72. General Dynamics was formed in 1952 with the merger of Electric Boat and Canadair. In 1954, they acquired Convair. Lockheed bought the Fort Worth Fighter Division of General Dynamics in 1993. Lorell and Levaux, *The Cutting Edge*, p 96n.

73. David C. Aronstein and Albert C. Piccirillo, "The F-16 Lightweight Fighter: A Case Study in Technology Transition," in *Technology and the Air Force: A Retrospective Assessment*, ed. Jacob Neufeld, George M. Watson Jr., and David Chenoweth (Washington, 1997), p 203; Taylor, *Jane's All the World's Aircraft, 1989-1990*, pp 412-413. The F-16 program also served to evaluate proposed acquisition reforms, such as competitive prototyping and performance-based requirements. Lorell and Levaux, *The Cutting Edge*, pp 113-114.
74. Fact Sheet, U. S. Air Force, "F-16 Fighting Falcon," Dec 2000. The Block 5, 10, and 15 F-16s came closest to the original concept of the austere daytime fighter. The Block 25 and 30 F-16 were developed as replacements for the F-4 fighter. These were equipped for long-range, radar-guided missile capability. The Block 40 has enhanced air-to-ground capability (with Maverick missiles) and is also equipped with LANTIRN. The most recent F-16s, the Block 50s, are described as "extremely versatile world-class multirole fighter-bombers." Lorell and Levaux, *The Cutting Edge*, p 115n.
75. Taylor, *Jane's All the World's Aircraft, 1989-1990*, p 413; Tressie Easterwood, F-16 System Program Office, personal communication with Lori S. Tagg, Feb 6, 2002.
76. Fact Sheet, "F-16 Fighting Falcon;" Paul Ferguson, ASC/HO, "F-16 Chronology," Mar 2000, p 17.
77. David C. Aronstein and Albert C. Piccirillo, *HAVE BLUE and the F-117A: Evolution of the "Stealth Fighter"* (Reston, Virginia, 1997), pp 87, 138; Mark Lambert, ed., *Jane's All The World's Aircraft, 1994-1995* (London, 1994), pp 563-565.
78. Aronstein and Piccirillo, *HAVE BLUE*, pp 144, 148-149.
79. Ronald C. Detmer, "Advanced Tactical Fighter: History of the Demonstration/Validation Phase, ASD/YF [ASD's Deputy for Advanced Tactical Fighter], 1986 through 1990," in *History of Aeronautical Systems Division (ASD) (Sanitized), January-December 1990,* Vol I, pp 418-439. (Hereafter cited as Hist, ASD, 1990.)
80. *History of Aeronautical Systems Division (ASD) (Sanitized), January-December 1991*, Vol I, p 328. (Hereafter cited as Hist, ASD, 1991.)
81. Hist, ASD, 1990, pp 364-368; Article, Boeing Company, "F-22 Air-Dominance Fighter," Apr 1997, viewed online Mar 30, 2001, at http://www.af.mil/news/Aprl1997/f22.html.
82. Secretary of the Air Force, Legislative Liaison, "F-22," in *1998 Air Force Congressional Issue Papers*, viewed online Mar 30, 2001, at http://www.af.mil/lib/afissues/1998/issue98.html; Article, "Lockheed Martin Awarded $818 Million Contract for F-22," *Aerospace Daily*, Sep 21, 2001.
83. John A. Tirpak, "Strike Fighter," *Air Force Magazine* 79 (Oct 1996): 22-28; Staff Sgt. A.J. Bosker, "Lockheed Martin Wins JSF Contract," *Air Force News*, Oct 26, 2001. Lockheed and Martin-Marietta merged in 1994 to become Lockheed-Martin. Boeing bought Rockwell's aerospace and defense divisions in 1996 and then merged with McDonnell-Douglas in 1997. Lorell and Levaux, *The Cutting Edge*, pp 149, 153.
84. The Air Force acquired many of the Navy's surplus Douglas A-1E, EA-1F, A-1G, A-1H, and A-1J Skyraiders in the early 1960s for use in Southeast Asia. These aircraft were developed during World War II, and the AD had its first flight in 1945. Production for the Navy continued until 1957. In 1962, the Navy's AD designation was changed to A-1. Leonard Bridgeman, ed., *Jane's All the World's Aircraft, 1956-1957* (New York, 1956), p 270; John M. Andrade, *U. S. Military Aircraft Designations and Serials Since 1909* (Leicester, England, 1979), pp 36, 180.
85. News Release, U. S. Air Force, untitled, May 28, 1968, in A-37 Photograph File, ASC/HO Archive; John W.R. Taylor, ed., *Jane's All the World's Aircraft, 1967-1968* (New York, 1967), pp 239-240; John W.R. Taylor, ed., *Jane's All the World's Aircraft, 1969-1970* (New York, 1969), p 302.
86. Neufeld, "The F-15 Eagle," pp 6, 8.
87. John W.R. Taylor, ed., *Jane's All the World's Aircraft, 1973-1974* (London, 1973), p 367. In the 1970s, an A-7D was used as a test bed for a "fly-by-light" Digital Tactical Aircraft Control (DIGITAC) system that demonstrated the feasibility of using fiber optics for flight control. John T. Carrell, "The Future Forms Up at ASD," *Air Force Magazine* (Jan1983): 40-50; News Release, U. S. Air Force, "A-7D Flies Via Single Glass Fiber Fly-By-Light," May 21, 1982, on file at ASC/HO Photographic Archive.
88. John W.R. Taylor, ed., *Jane's All the World's Aircraft, 1972-1973* (New York, 1972), pp 318, 388; Taylor, *Jane's All the World's Aircraft, 1973-1974*, p 326; Walker and Wickam, pp 391-392.
89. Taylor, *Jane's All the World's Aircraft, 1972-1973*, pp 318; Fact Sheet, U. S. Air Force, "A-10/OA-10 Thunderbolt II," Jun 2000.
90. William Head, "AC-47 Gunship Development," *Air Power History* (Fall 1990), pp 37-46.
91. Taylor, *Jane's All the World's Aircraft, 1969-1970*, p 324; John W.R. Taylor, *Jane's All the World's Aircraft, 1974-1975* (New York, 1974), p 333.
92. Taylor, *Jane's All the World's Aircraft, 1975-1976*, p 374; Taylor, *Jane's All the World's Aircraft,* 1989-1990, p 440.
93. Taylor, *Jane's All the World's Aircraft, 1989-1990*, p 441; Lambert, *Jane's All the World's Aircraft, 1994-1995*, pp 622-623; Fact Sheet, U. S. Air Force, "AC-130H/U Gunship," Oct 1999.
94. Eight other transport aircraft designs were in development at WADC in 1950: the Fairchild XC-120 Packplane with a detachable cargo compartment, the Fairchild XC-123 Provider assault transport, the Chase XG-20 glider, the Boeing KC-97 refueling tanker version of the C-97, the Chase YC-122A and B Avitruc, and the Douglas C-129 (a single Super DC-3, later redesignated the YC-47F). Only two of these (the C-123 and the KC-97) would enter production for the Air Force.

95. Marcelle Size Knaack, *Military Airlift and Aircraft Procurement: The Case of the C-5A* (Washington, 1998), pp 16, 22, 24; William Head, *Reworking the Workhorse: The C-141B Stretch Modification Program* (Robins AFB, 1984), p ix.
96. News Release, U. S. Air Force, Headquarters, CONAC, "C-119 Flying Boxcar", n.d., in untitled file, Box 3291: C-119 et al. Cargo Aircraft, ASC/HO Archive; U. S. Air Force, *Standard Aircraft Characteristics: C-119*, May 15, 1948 and Jan 11, 1950, ASC/HO Archive.
97. U. S. Air Force, *Standard Aircraft Characteristics: C-124,* May 15, 1948 and Aug 22, 1952, ASC/HO Archive.
98. Swanborough, pp 266-267; Bridgeman, *Jane's All the World's Aircraft, 1956-1957,* pp 279-280; Taylor, *Jane's Encyclopedia of Aviation*, pp 354-355.
99. Enzo Angelucci, *The Rand McNally Encyclopedia of Military Aircraft, 1914-1980* (New York, 1980), p 505; Taylor, *Jane's Encyclopedia of Aviation*, pp 582-583; Martin Caidin, *The Long Arm of America: The Story of the Amazing Hercules Air Assault Transport and our Revolutionary Global Strike Force* (New York, 1963), p 58.
100. Knaack, *Military Airlift and Aircraft Procurement*, p 117; Taylor, *Jane's Encyclopedia of Aviation*, pp 582-583; Fact Sheet, U. S. Air Force, "C-130 Hercules," Jul 2001; John W.R. Taylor, ed., *Jane's All the World's Aircraft, 1966-1967* (New York, 1966), p 275.
101. Fact Sheet, U. S. Air Force, "MC-130E/H Combat Talon I/II," Aug 2001; Fact Sheet, U. S. Air Force, "MC-130P Combat Shadow," Aug 2001.
102. Swanborough, pp 252-253; Bridgeman, *Jane's All the World's Aircraft, 1956-1957*, pp 265-266; *Taylor, Jane's Encyclopedia of Aviation*, p 346.
103. Rothman, *Acquisition Milestones*, p 96; Fact Sheet, U. S. Air Force, "C-141B Starlifter," Dec 2000; Taylor, *Jane's All the World's Aircraft, 1966-1967*, pp 277-278; Taylor, *Jane's Encyclopedia of Aviation*, p 583; Head, *Reworking the Workhorse*, p ix.
104. Head, *Reworking the Workhorse*, pp ix, xviii, 1, 10; Fact Sheet, "C-141B Starlifter."
105. Taylor, *Jane's All the World's Aircraft, 1966-1967*, p 279; Angeluzzi, *Rand McNally Encyclopedia of Military Aircraft,* p 507; Knaack, *Military Airlift and Aircraft Procurement,* pp 27-28, 97. Although the C-5 is enormous, it is not the largest aircraft in the world. That honor goes to the Ukranian AN-225 Mriya.
106. Knaack, *Military Airlift and Aircraft Procurement*, p 97; Fact Sheet, U. S. Air Force, "C-5 Galaxy," Nov 2000; Walker and Wickam, pp 388-389; Taylor, *Jane's All the World's Aircraft, 1989-1990*, pp 443-444.
107. John W.R. Taylor, ed., *Jane's All the World's Aircraft, 1975-1976* (New York, 1975), p 389; Fact Sheet, U. S. Air Force, "C-9A/C Nightingale," n.d.
108. Taylor, *Jane's All the World's Aircraft, 1975-1976*, pp 290, 394-395; John W.R. Taylor, ed., *Jane's All the World's Aircraft, 1976-1977* (New York, 1976), pp 249, 334; Knaack, *Military Airlift and Aircraft Procurement*, p 104; Dr. George M. Watson, *The Advanced Medium Short-Take-Off-And-Landing Transport (AMST) and the Implications of the Minimum Engineering Development (MED) Program* (Andrews AFB, 1983).
109. In 1997, the Air Force leased the YC-15 back to McDonnell-Douglas for use as a test bed for advanced technologies, such as active core exhaust control, autonomous landing, enhanced defensive systems, and advanced "inerting" in which the fuel tanks are filled with inert gases to make them less vulnerable to enemy ground fire. News Release, McDonnell Douglas, "McDonnell Douglas YC-15 to Fly Again as an Advanced Technology Demonstrator," Apr 11, 1997.
110. Hans M. Mark, Secretary of the Air Force, Memorandum for Assistant Secretary of Defense, Program Analysis and Evaluation: C-X Analysis, Mar 17, 1980, in C-X Queries and Clippings File, Box: Cargo/SST, ASC/HO Archive.
111. Taylor, *Jane's All the World's Aircraft, 1989-1990*, p 461; Fact Sheet, U. S. Air Force, "C-17 Globemaster III," n.d.; Knaack, *Military Airlift and Aircraft Procurement*, p. 105; Lambert, *Jane's All the World's Aircraft, 1994-1995*, pp 599-602; William T. Y'Blood, "From the Deserts to the Mountains," in *Winged Shield, Winged Sword: A History of the United States Air Force*, Volume II: 1950-1997, ed. Bernard C. Nalty (Washington, 1997), p 490.
112. Article, Rick Burnham, Tech. Sgt., "C-27s Fly Last Mission: To the Boneyard," *Air Force News* Jan 1999; News Release, ASC/PA, "Air Force Accepts Final C-27A Spartan," Feb 1, 1993; "Airlift Enhancement," *Backgrounder, Air Force Internal Information* (Kelly AFB, n.d.), p 5.
113. Tommy Thomason and Warren Lieberman, "The V-22 Osprey," *Horizons* (1985), pp 18-25; Director, Operational Test and Evaluation, "Combined Operational Test and Evaluation and Live Fire Test and Evaluation Report on the V-22 Osprey," Nov 17, 2000, pp I-1, I-3, I-6; Article, Gidge Dady, "First CV-22 Arrives at Edwards," *Air Force News* Sep 22, 2000. The V-22 program came under attack due to two fatal crashes in 2000 and evidence that Marines falsified maintenance records to give the troubled Osprey a boost in congressional decisions for full-scale production. Article, Mary Pat Flaherty, "Three Marines Guilty in Osprey Records Case," *Washington Post*, Sep 15, 2001.
114. Swanborough, pp 98-100; Hallion, *Storm Over Iraq*, p 64.
115. John W.R. Taylor, ed., *Jane's All the World's Aircraft, 1960-1961* (New York, 1960), pp 267, 270; Knaack, *Military Airlift and Aircraft Procurement*, p 97; Fact Sheet, U. S. Air Force, "KC-135 Stratotanker," Jul 2001; Fact Sheet, U. S. Air Force, "OC-135 Open Skies," Feb 2001.

116. Taylor, *Jane's All the World's Aircraft, 1989-1990*, pp 458-459; Fact Sheet, U. S. Air Force, "KC-10A Extender," Jul 2001; Knaack, *Military Airlift and Aircraft Procurement*, p 97; U. S. Air Force, *Airlift Master Plan*, Sep 29, 1983, in Box: Cargo/SST, ASC/HO Archive.
117. Notable was the revolutionary acquisition process for the C-32A during which the Air Force acted like any other customer buying a commercial aircraft. In the late 1990s, the C-32 was purchased from the existing Boeing production line instead of being designed and developed according to military specifications. It was then modified with military communications and navigation equipment. The C-32 replaced the aging VC-137s, which had been used to transport the vice president, cabinet members, and congressional delegations around the world since the early 1960s. Various newspaper articles and press releases on file in ASC/HO Archive.
118. Taylor, *Jane's All the World's Aircraft, 1989-1990*, p 392.
119. Leonard Bridgeman, ed., *Jane's All the World's Aircraft, 1951-1952* (London, 1951), pp 201c-203c, 249c, 250c, 261c, 280c, 288c-290c; Leonard Bridgeman, ed., *Jane's All the World's Aircraft, 1952-1953* (London, 1952), pp 198, 216, 237. Other programs in 1951 included the Bell YH-12, the Bell XH-15, the Piasecki XH-16 Transporter, the Kellett/Hughes XH-17 jet helicopter, the Sikorsky H-18, the McDonnell XH-20 ramjet helicopter, the Seibel YH-24 Skyhawk, and the Piasecki/Vertol H-25 Retriever/Army Mule. With the exception of the H-25, which both the Army and Navy acquired, these programs were terminated prior to 1960.
120. Leonard Bridgeman, ed., *Jane's All the World's Aircraft, 1953-1954* (New York, 1953), pp 240, 276; Leonard Bridgeman, ed., *Jane's All the World's Aircraft, 1954-1955* (New York, 1954), pp 295-295; Leonard Bridgeman, ed., *Jane's All the World's Aircraft, 1955-1956* (New York, 1955), p 219; Leonard Bridgeman, ed., *Jane's All the World's Aircraft, 1958-1959* (New York, 1958), p 320. These programs included the Doman YH-31 and the Hiller YH-32 Hornet. The YH-32 eventually became an Army/Navy program.
121. Bridgeman, *Jane's All the World's Aircraft, 1955-1956*, p 219; Bridgeman, *Jane's All the World's Aircraft, 1956-1957*, pp 233-234; Bridgeman, *Jane's All the World's Aircraft, 1958-1959*, p 259.
122. Taylor, *Jane's All the World's Aircraft, 1960-1961*, p 260; John W.R. Taylor, ed., *Jane's All the World's Aircraft, 1963-1964* (New York, 1963), pp 175-176.
123. Rothman, *Acquisition Milestones*, p 153; Fact Sheet, U. S. Air Force, "UH-1N Huey," Jun 1999; Fact Sheet, U. S. Air Force Space Command, "UH-1N Huey," Mar 2001; Fact Sheet, U. S. Air Force Space Command, "HH 1H Iroquois," May 1997.
124. Taylor, *Jane's All the World's Aircraft, 1960-1961*, p 332; John W.R. Taylor, ed., *Jane's All the World's Aircraft, 1964-1965* (London, 1964), p 240; Carl Berger, ed., *The United States Air Force in Southeast Asia, 1961-1973: An Illustrated Account* (Washington, 1984), pp 236, 280.
125. Taylor, *Jane's All the World's Aircraft, 1963-1964*, pp 277-278; John W.R. Taylor, ed., *Jane's All the World's Aircraft, 1965-1966* (New York, 1965), pp 295-296; Rothman, *Acquisition Milestones*, p 128.
126. Taylor, *Jane's All the World's Aircraft, 1970-1971*, pp 447-449; Taylor, *Jane's All the World's Aircraft, 1976-1977*, p 385.
127. Taylor, *Jane's All the World's Aircraft, 1970-1971*, p 452.
128. Taylor, *Jane's All the World's Aircraft, 1976-1977*, p 387; John W.R. Taylor, ed., *Jane's All the World's Aircraft, 1987 1988* (New York, 1987), p 513; Fact Sheet, U. S. Air Force, "MH-53J/M Pave Low," Jul 2000.
129. Taylor, *Jane's All the World's Aircraft, 1973-1974*, p 440; John W.R. Taylor, ed., *Jane's All the World's Aircraft, 1977-1978* (New York, 1977), p 407.
130. John W.R. Taylor, ed., *Jane's All the World's Aircraft, 1982-1983* (London, 1982), p 474; John W.R. Taylor, ed., *Jane's All the World's Aircraft, 1985-1986* (New York, 1985), p 510; Taylor, *Jane's All the World's Aircraft, 1987-1988*, p 514; John W.R. Taylor, ed., *Jane's All the World's Aircraft, 1988-1989* (New York, 1988), p 511; Mark Lambert, ed., *Jane's All the World's Aircraft, 1993-1994* (London, 1993), p 561; Fact Sheet, U. S. Air Force, "HH-60G Pave Hawk," Sep 2000.
131. Fact Sheet, U. S. Air Force, "T-37 Tweet," n.d.; James Klein, "T-37 Life Extension Study, Status 14 August 2000," in T-37 Documents File, Box: Trainers, ASC/HO Archive.
132. Various official and unofficial press releases and news articles posted on the Internet on *Air Force Link* and *Air Force News*, and printed in the *WPAFB Skywrighter*, *Aerospace Daily*, and *Defense Daily*, 1986-2001; Fact Sheet, U. S. Air Force, "T-38 Talon," Jun 2001.
133. Fact Sheet, U. S. Air Force, "T-43A," Jun 2001; *History of Aeronautical Systems Division (ASD), January – December 1986*, Vol I, pp 202-206 (Hereafter cited as Hist, ASD, 1986).
134. Article, "A Checklist of Major ASD Systems," *Air Force Magazine* (Jan 1989), p 57; Article, Karla Bickley, "JSUPT Track Select System Undergoes Changes," *Air Force News*, Apr 30, 1998; Fact Sheet, U. S. Air Force, "T-1A Jayhawk," Jun 2001.
135. Various official news stories printed on *Air Force News* web site, 1995-1999, on file at the ASC/HO Archive; Article, "A Checklist of Major Aeronautical Systems," *Air Force Magazine* (Jan 1991): 44. In 2001, the Academy began conducting its own flight training again, reverting back to the T-41D instead of the T-3.
136. Various official news stories printed on *Air Force News* web site, 1994-2000, on file at the ASC/HO Archive; Frank Oliveri, "A Trainer Built for Two," *Air Force Magazine* (Jun 1992), pp 38-43; Capt. Christa D'Andrea, "T-6 Flying Training Begins at Moody," *Air Force News*, Nov 26, 2001. LT-6G's, also known as "Mosquitos,"

were used as forward air control spotters in the Korean War. They directed allied aircraft to the locations of enemy targets and relayed requests between ground commanders and the Tactical Air Control Center.

137. Article, "A Checklist of Major ASD Systems," *Air Force Magazine* (Jan 1989): 57.
138. Randy Olson, Training Systems Product Group, ASC, "The Road to DMT," 2000, viewed online Dec 3, 2001, at http://dmt.wpafb.af.mil/Documents/DMT/road.htm; Article, John J. Lumpkin, "Logging on for Battle," *Albuquerque Journal* (Oct 25, 2000): 1; Sue Baker, "Power By the Hour," *Leading Edge* (Jun 2000).
139. History of the Engineering Division, Aircraft and Guided Missiles Section, Jul 1 – Dec 31, 1950, p 1.
140. Hist, WADC, 1952-2, p 734.
141. Knaack, *Post-World War II Bombers*, pp 403-450.
142. *Ibid.*, pp 403-455; Rothman, *Acquisition Milestones*, p 83.
143. Knaack, *Post-World War II Fighters*, pp 142-149; Berger, p 213.
144. Knaack, *Post-World War II Fighters*, pp 269-273; News Release, ASC/PA, "Air Force Creates Unmanned Aerial Vehicle System Program Office," Nov 13, 1995, in PA Files, Box 3329: Drones/RPVs, ASC/HO Archive.
145. Walton S. Moody, Jacob Neufeld, and R. Cargill Hall, "The Emergence of the Strategic Air Command," in *Winged Shield, Winged Sword*, pp 62-63; Geoffrey Oxlee, *Aerospace Reconnaissance*, Volume 9 of *Brassey's Air Power: Aircraft, Weapons Systems and Technology Series* (London, 1997), p 46; Taylor, *Jane's Encyclopedia of Aviation*, p 605.
146. Taylor, *Jane's Encyclopedia of Aviation*, p 605.
147. Fact Sheet, U. S. Air Force, "U-2S," Dec 2000.
148. Thomas P. McIninch, "The Oxcart Story," a secret study (now declassified) of the A-12 published in the Winter 1970-1971 issue of the CIA's internal publication *Studies in Intelligence*. McIninch was a collective pseudonym for several CIA analysts who authored the report. A condensed version was published in *Air Force Magazine* (Nov 1994): 40-47. Knaack, *Post-World War II Fighters*, pp 333-334.
149. Oxlee, pp 48-49; Richard H. Graham, Colonel USAF (Ret.), *SR-71 Revealed: The Inside Story* (Osceola, Wisconsin, 1996), pp 41-44; Fact Sheet, U. S. Air Force Museum, "Lockheed SR-71A," n.d.; Lorell and Levaux, *The Cutting Edge*, pp 132-133.
150. Fact Sheet, "Lockheed SR-71A," Graham, pp 215-217; McIninch, "The Oxcart Story." A second article condensed from this publication outlines the Black Shield mission in Vietnam. Thomas P. McIninch, "Black Shield," *Air Force Magazine* (Jan 1995): 66-71.
151. Berger, pp 218, 226-227; Walton S. Moody, Jacob Neufeld, and Bernard C. Nalty, "The Air Force and Operations Short of War," in *Winged Shield, Winged Sword*, Vol II, p 221; John Schlight, "The War in Southeast Asia, 1961-1968," in *Winged Shield, Winged Sword*, Vol II, pp 287, 292.
152. Fact Sheet, "OC-135 Open Skies."
153. Fact Sheet, U. S. Air Force, "RC-135V/W Rivet Joint," Mar 2000; Article, "Rivet Joint Intelligence Jets to Fly Higher, Faster," *Aviation Week and Space Technology* (May 14, 2001), pg. 32, Michael W. Patterson, RC-135 Deputy Program Manager, Personal Communication with Lori S. Tagg, Feb 14, 2002. In addition to the 16 RC-135 Rivet Joint aircraft in the fleet, the Air Force also had one operational Rivet Joint Trainer and a second trainer scheduled for delivery in 2003. These two trainers were used for cockpit training only; they had no sensors installed.
154. Air Chief Marshal Sir Michael Armitage, *Unmanned Aircraft* (London, 1988), pp xi, 1.
155. William Wagner, *Lightning Bugs and other Reconnaissance Drones* (Fallbrook, California, 1982), pp 10-12; Taylor, *Jane's All the World's Aircraft, 1960-1961*, p 469; Taylor, *Jane's All the World's Aircraft, 1970-1971*, pp 542-543; Hank Basham, "RPV's Make the Difference," *Air University Review* (Jan-Feb 1974): 40.
156. Susan H.H. Young, "Gallery of USAF Weapons," *Air Force Magazine* (May 1994): 132; Jeffrey P. Rhodes, "The Drone Pilots," *Air Force Magazine* (Mar 1991): 94-99.
157. John W.R. Taylor, ed., *Jane's All the World's Aircraft, 1981-1982* (London, 1981), p 670; Taylor, *Jane's All the World's Aircraft, 1985-1986*, p 819; Taylor, *Jane's All the World's Aircraft, 1987-1988,* p 861.
158. Andrade, pp 45, 54, 102, 108; Taylor, *Jane's All the World's Aircraft, 1960-1961*, p 342; Taylor, *Jane's All the World's Aircraft, 1977-1978*, pp 664, 671, Knaack, *Post-World War II Fighters*, pp 10, 170, 180.
159. Taylor, *Jane's all the World's Aircraft, 1966-1967*, p 374.
160. Major Christopher A. Jones, U. S. Air Force, "Unmanned Aerial Vehicles (UAVS): An Assessment of Historical Operations and Future Possibilities," pp 4, 10, Research Paper presented to the Research Department of the Air Command and Staff College, Mar 1997; William Wagner and William P. Sloan, *Fireflies and other UAVs* (Arlington, Texas, 1992), p 13; Taylor, *Jane's All the World's Aircraft, 1973-1974*, pp 529-530.
161. Taylor, *Jane's All the World's Aircraft, 1972-1973*, p 505; Jones, "Unmanned Aerial Vehicles," pp 55-56.
162. Fact Sheet, U. S. Air Force, "RPV," Sep 1974, in RPV (Remotely Piloted Vehicle), BGM-34 and Others File, Box 3329: Drones/RPVs, PA Files, ASC/HO Archive.
163. Taylor, *Jane's All the World's Aircraft, 1973-1974*, pp 530-531; Taylor, *Jane's All the World's Aircraft, 1972-1973*, p 505; Wagner and Sloan, *Fireflies*, pp 36, 38, 47.
164. Taylor, *Jane's All the World's Aircraft, 1973-1974*, pp 519, 533-534; Wagner and Sloan, *Fireflies*, pp 110-118.
165. Louis J. Rodrigues, Director, Defense Acquisitions Issues, National Security and International Affairs Division, "Unmanned Aerial Vehicles: DoD's Acquisition Efforts," Statement before the Subcommittee on Military

Research and Development and Military Procurement, Committee on National Security, House of Representatives, Apr 9, 1997, General Accounting Office Report No. GAO/T-NSIAD-97-138, p 1; Jones, "Unmanned Aerial Vehicles," pp 43-44; News Release, ASC/PA, "Air Force Creates Unmanned Aerial Vehicle System Program Office," Nov 13, 1995, in PA Files, Box 3329: Drones/RPVs, ASC/HO Archive.

166. Rodrigues, "UAVs: DoD's Acquisition Efforts," pp 5, 11; Louis J. Rodrigues, Director, Defense Acquisitions Issues, National Security and International Affairs Division, "Unmanned Aerial Vehicles: DoD's Demonstration Approach Has Improved Project Outcomes," Report to the Secretary of Defense, Aug 1999, General Accounting Office Report No. GAO/T-NSIAD-99-33, pp 3-4; Department of Defense, *UAV Annual Report, Fiscal Year 1996* (Washington, Nov 6, 1996), pp 18-19; John A. Tirpak, "The Robotic Air Force," *Air Force Magazine* (Sep 1997): 70-74.
167. Rodrigues, "UAVs: DoD's Acquisition Efforts," pp 6, 13; Rodrigues, "UAVs: DoD's Demonstration Approach," p 5; Department of Defense, *UAV Annual Report, Fiscal Year 1996*, pp 22-23.
168. Rodrigues, "UAVs: DoD's Acquisition Efforts," pp 5-6, 12; Rodrigues, "UAVs: DoD's Demonstration Approach," pp 5-6; Department of Defense, *UAV Annual Report, Fiscal Year 1996*, pp 20-21.
169. Wagner and Sloan, *Fireflies*, pp 98-100, 105-107; Taylor, *Jane's All the World's Aircraft, 1973-1974*, p 532; Taylor, *Jane's All the World's Aircraft, 1977-1978*, p 676.
170. In the Air Force Scientific Advisory Board's *New World Vistas: Air and Space Power for the 21st Century*, UCAVs are defined as "uninhabited" combat aerial vehicles as opposed to "unmanned," purportedly to distinguish vehicles employing new and constantly evolving information technologies of the future from those now in operation or planned. These vehicles operating in distant theaters would be linked via fiber and satellite communications networks to an Executive Control Center located in the continental United States.
171. News Release, ASC/PA, "Air Force Creates Unmanned Aerial Vehicle System Program Office," Nov 13, 1995, in PA Files, Box 3329: Drones/RPVs, ASC/HO Archive; Article, Adam J. Hebert, "Air Force Desire for UCAV Pushing Program Nearly As Fast As Possible," *Inside the Air Force*, Jun 22, 2001, p 1; Article, Sue Baker, "Predator Missile Launch Test Totally Successful," *Air Force Link*, Feb 27, 2001.
172. "MILNET: Air-to-Air Missiles," viewed online Dec 3, 2001, at http://www.milnet.com/milnet/aam.htm.
173. Jacob Neufeld, *The Development of Ballistic Missiles in the United States Air Force, 1945-1960* (Washington, 1990), pp 58, 62; Hist, WADC, 1952-1, p 232; Hist of WADC, 1952-2, pp 874-875; Knaack, *Post-World War II Fighters*, pp 93, 167.
174. Knaack, *Post-World War II Fighters*, p 97, Jeffrey P. Rhodes, "AIR-2 Genie," in *Gallery of Classics: A Flock of Warbirds from the Air Force's Past*, viewed online Dec 3, 2001, at www.afa.org/magazine/gallery/air-2.html (*Air Force Magazine*).
175. Fact Sheet, U. S. Air Force, "AIM-7 Sparrow," Oct 1999; Knaack, *Post-World War II Fighters*, pp 250-251, 266n, 273n; Hallion, *Storm Over Iraq*, p 48; Fact Sheet, U. S. Air Force, "AIM-9 Sidewinder," Oct 1999.
176. Jeffrey P. Rhodes, "The Next Round for Aerial Combat," *Air Force Magazine* (Feb 1991): 46-51; Fact Sheet, U. S. Air Force, "AIM-120 AMRAAM," Aug 1999.
177. "MILNET. Air-to-Ground Missiles (AGMs)," viewed online Dec 3, 2001, at www.milnet.com/milnet/agm.htm; "Air-to-Surface Missiles," viewed online Dec 3, 2001, at http://vectorsite.tripod.com/avbomb5.html (Greg Goebel's VectorSite).
178. Neufeld, *Ballistic Missiles*, pp 32, 62; Hist, WADC, 1953-1, p 507. The Shrike (X-9) was not intended to become operational as an air-to-ground missile. Its sole purpose was as a test vehicle to obtain aerodynamic information applicable to the Rascal. Hist, WADC, 1952-1, p 269.
179. *History of Wright Air Development Center (WADC), July 1 – December 31, 1957,* Vol I, p 167 (Hereafter cited as Hist, WADC, 1957-2); *History of Aeronautical Systems Division (ASD), April – December 1961,* Vol II, p II-74 (Hereafter cited as Hist, ASD, 1961); Knaack, *Post-World War II Bombers*, p 271; Kenneth P. Werrell, *The Evolution of the Cruise Missile* (Maxwell AFB, 1985), pp 121-123; "Cruise Missiles of the 1950s and 1960s," viewed online Dec 3, 2001, at http://vectorsite.tripod.com/avcruz3.html (Greg Goebel's VectorSite).
180. *History of Wright Air Development Division (WADD), January – June 1960*, Vol II: Space Systems and Strategic Systems, pp II-83, II-84 (Hereafter cited as Hist, WADD, 1960); *History of Aeronautical Systems Division (ASD), July – December 1962*, p 37 (Hereafter cited as Hist, ASD, 1962); Stephen I. Schwartz, ed., "Box 2-2: Weapons That Did Not Make the Cut," in Atomic Audit: The Costs and Consequences of U. S. Nuclear Weapons Since 1940, 1998, viewed online Dec 3, 2001, at http://www.brook.edu/fp/projects/nucwcost/box2-2.htm.
181. Hist, WADD, 1960, Vol III: Air Defense, Tactical, and Supporting Systems, p III-62; Knaack, *Post-World War II Fighters*, pp 124, 185n.
182. Hist, ASD, 1961, p II-169.
183. "Air-to-Surface Missiles," viewed online Dec 3, 2001, at http://vectorsite.tripod.com/avbomb5.html (Greg Goebel's VectorSite).
184. Hist, ASD, 1962, p 121; Knaack, *Post-World War II Fighters*, 266n.
185. The Z reportedly meant "in the planning stages." *History of Aeronautical Systems Division (ASD), January – December 1964*, pp 132-134 (Hereafter cited as Hist, ASD, 1964); *History of Aeronautical Systems Division*

(ASD), January – December 1965, Vol I-A, pp 93-97 (Hereafter cited as Hist, ASD, 1965); "AGM-62 Walleye," viewed online Dec 14, 2001, at http://www.wpafb.af.mil/museum/arm/arm0a.htm.

186. Robert Wall, "USAF to Update Maverick Missile," *Aviation Week and Space Technology* (Jun 29, 1998), p 62; Collie J. Johnson, "Maverick Airframe Team Scores Stunning Acquisition Reform Success," *Program Manager* (Sep/Oct 1998), pp 10-18; Hallion, *Storm Over Iraq*, p 285. The Maverick was acquired through the same Total Package Procurement program as the C-5 Galaxy transporter. Unlike the C-5, the Maverick program was successfully executed.
187. The Missile X Program also included plans for the Hitting Missile, a response to Project Forecast's requirement for a short-range missile with a 95 percent success rate of hitting a fixed target approximately 10 feet by 10 feet in size. This program lacked official recognition from Air Force Headquarters and the SPO was dissolved in late 1965. Hist, ASD, 1964, pp 136-139; Hist, ASD, 1965, Vol I-B, p 204. Like the Maverick, Total Package Procurement of the SRAM also was more successful than that experienced in the case of the C-5.
188. *History of Aeronautical Systems Division (ASD), January – December 1966*, Vol I, p 153 (Hereafter cited as Hist, ASD, 1966); *History of Aeronautical Systems Division (ASD), January – December 1984,* Vol I, p 171 (Hereafter cited as Hist, ASD, 1984); *History of Aeronautical Systems Division (ASD), January – December 1988*, p 164 (Hereafter cited as Hist, ASD, 1988); *History of Aeronautical Systems Division (ASD), January – December 1991,* Vol I, pp 291, 295-296 (Hereafter cited as Hist, ASD, 1991).
189. *History of Aeronautical Systems Division (ASD), January – December 1977*, Vol I, pp 244, 247 (Hereafter cited as Hist, ASD, 1977).
190. *History of Aeronautical Systems Division (ASD), July 1971 – June 1972*, Vol I, pp 108-109 (Hereafter cited as Hist, ASD, 1971-1972); *History of Aeronautical Systems Division (ASD), July 1974 – December 1975*, Vol I, p 264 (Hereafter cited as Hist, ASD, 1974-1975); Hist, ASD, 1977, pp 243-248; *History of Aeronautical Systems Division (ASD),* Oct 1980 – Sep 1981, Vol I, p 165 (Hereafter cited as Hist, ASD, 1980-1981); Werrell, *Evolution of the Cruise Missile*, pp 145, 149.
191. *History of Aeronautical Systems Division (ASD), October 1982 – December 1983,* Vol I, pp 166-167 (Hereafter cited as Hist, ASD, 1982-1983); Fact Sheet, U. S. Air Force, "AGM-86B/C Missiles," n.d.; Article, "Boeing Co. Today Will Celebrate its Program to Convert 322 ALCMs to the CALCM Configuration," *Aerospace Daily,* Nov 2, 1999.
192. Lt. Col. Craig McPherson, "Advanced Cruise Missile, 1982-1997," presentation at the Acquisition Staff Meeting, Mar 25, 1997; *History of Aeronautical Systems Division (ASD), January – December 1989,* Vol I, p 157 (Hereafter cited as Hist, ASD, 1989); *History of Aeronautical Systems Center (ASC), January – September 1992*, Vol I, pp 215-217 (Hereafter cited as Hist, ASC, 1992).
193. Hist, ASD, 1991, pp 367-368; *History of Aeronautical Systems Center (ASC), October 1992-September 1993,* Vol I, p 167 (Hereafter cited as Hist, ASC, 1992-1993); David A. Fulghum, "TSSAM Follow-On to Take Shape This Year," *Aviation Week and Space Technology* (Feb 27, 1995), pp 49-51.
194. *History of Aeronautical Systems Center (ASC) October 1994 – September 1995,* Vol I, pp 196-199 (Hereafter cited as Hist, ASC, 1994-1995); Director, Defense Operational Test and Evaluation, "Joint Air-to-Surface Standoff Missile," *Annual Report to Congress, Fiscal Year 2000.*
195. Rothman, *Acquisition Milestones*, p 199; John C. Lonnquest and David F. Winkler, *To Defend and Deter: The Legacy of the United States Cold War Missile Program* (Champaign, Illinois, 1996), pp 59-63; Hist, WADD, 1960, Vol III: System Development (Part 2), p III-2.
196. Neufeld, *Ballistic Missiles*, pp 61-87; Werrell, *Evolution of the Cruise Missile*, pp 108-112; Tom Compere, ed., *The Air Force Blue Book*, Vol I (New York, 1959), p 344.
197. Compere, *The Air Force Blue Book*, p 344; Werrell, *Evolution of the Cruise Missile*, pp 110-112; Rothman, *Acquisition Milestones*, pp 218-220; Hist, WADD, 1960, Vol III, p III-67; Karen J. Weitze, *Guided Missiles at Holloman Air Force Base: Test Programs of the United States Air Force in Southern New Mexico, 1947-1970* (Holloman AFB, 1997), p 67.
198. Neufeld, *Ballistic Missiles,* pp 2, 28, 87, 99; Werrell, *Evolution of the Cruise Missile,* pp 82-97, 100-101, 107-108; Lorell and Levaux, *The Cutting Edge*, p 62; Robert L. Perry, *System Development Strategies: A Comparative Study of Doctrine, Technology, and Organization in the USAF Ballistic and Cruise Missile Programs, 1950-1960* (Santa Monica, 1966), p 37; Schwartz, "Box 2-2: Weapons That Did Not Make the Cut." The Navaho program also contributed to North American's F-100 fighter design and the cancelled XB-70 bomber.
199. Lonnquest and Winkler, *To Defend and Deter*, pp 209, 215; Werrell, *Evolution of the Cruise Missile*, pp 107-108.
200. Hist, ASD, 1986, pp 157-158; *History of Aeronautical Systems Division (ASD), January – December 1987*, Vol I, p 143 (Hereafter cited as Hist, ASD, 1987); Werrell, *Evolution of the Cruise Missile*, pp 201-205; Greg Ogletree, "Ground Launched Cruise Missiles," viewed online Dec 3, 2001, at http://glcmhf.org/glcm/history.shtml (Ground Launched Cruise Missile Historical Foundation).

Chapter 7. WHETTING THE CUTTING EDGE–AEROSPACE SCIENCE AND ENGINEERING

1. Peter L. Jakab, *Visions of a Flying Machine: The Wright Brothers and the Process of Invention* (Washington, 1990).
2. Ronald Miller and David Sawers, *The Technical Development of Modern Aviation* (New York, 1970), chapter 2.
3. H. H. Blee, *History of the Organization and Activities of the Airplane Engineering Division, Bureau of Aircraft Production* (Aug 1919), p 1.
4. I.B. Holley, Jr., *Ideas and Weapons: Exploitation of the Aerial Weapon by the United States during World War I; A Study in the Relationship of Technological Advance, Military Doctrine, and the Development of Weapons* (New Haven, 1953; reprint ed., Washington, 1983), chapter 7.
5. Bruce Seeley, "Research, Engineering, and Science in American Engineering Colleges: 1900-1960," *Technology & American History: A Historical Anthology from "Technology and Culture,"* ed. by Stephen H. Cutcliffe and Terry S. Reynolds (Chicago, 1997), pp 345-87.
6. See "Index to Technical Reports of Engineering Division, Supply Group, Air Service, nos. 1-1300, January, 1918 – June, 1919," prepared by [the] Engineering Division, Air Service, McCook Field (Washington, 1920), *passim.*
7. Gardner W. Carr, "The Organization and Activities of the Engineering Division of the Army Air Service," *U.S. Air Service* (Mar 1922): 23; James F. Aldridge, *A Historical Overview of the Mission and Organization of the Wright Laboratory, 1917-1993* (WPAFB, 1994), p 11.
8. Mary L. McMurtrie and Paul N. Davis, *History of the Army Air Forces Materiel Command, 1926 through 1941,* AMC Historical Study No. 281 (Wright Field, 1943).
9. *The Engineering of Flight: Aeronautical Engineering Facilities of Area B, Wright-Patterson Air Force Base, Ohio*, ed. by Emma J. Dyson, Dean A. Herrin, and Amy E. Slaton, Historical American Buildings Survey/Historic American Engineering Record (Washington, 1993), *passim.*
10. Aldridge, *Mission and Organization,* p 10.
11. *Otto Peter Morgensen, Jr., Aeronautical Engineer, Wright Field, 1936-1970: Oral History Interview*, ASC/HO ([draft] 2001), pp 17-20.
12. David M. Carpenter, *Flame Powered: The Bell XP-59A Aeracomet and the General Electric I-A Engine, The Story of America's First Jet-Powered Aircraft* (n.p., 1992).
13. Theodore von Karman, *The Wind and Beyond: Theodore von Karman, Pioneer in Aviation and Pathfinder in Space*, with Lee Edson (Boston, 1967), p 298.
14. James J. Niehaus, *Five Decades of Materials Progress, 1917-1967* (WPAFB, 1967), p 78.
15. Albert E. Misenko and Philip H. Pollock, *Engineering History, 1917-1978: McCook Field to the Aeronautical Systems Division*, 4th ed. (WPAFB, 1979), p 2.
16. Dik Alan Daso, *Hap Arnold and the Evolution of American Airpower* (Washington, 2000), pp 141ff.
17. Michael H. Gorn, *The Universal Man: Theodore von Karman's Life in Aeronautics* (Washington, 1992), pp 100ff.
18. Robert M. Detweiler, "Air Force Research in Retrospect," *Air University Review*, Vol 28, no. 1 (Nov-Dec 1976): 3-14.
19. Detweiler, "Air Force Research," pp 11-12; "The First Five Years of the Air Research and Development Command, United States Air Force," Historical Division, Office of Information Services (Baltimore, 1955), pp 15ff.
20. "First Five Years of ARDC," pp 23-24.
21. Misenko and Pollock, *Engineering History*, p 16.
22. *Ibid.*
23. Chronology, "Laboratories at Wright-Patterson AFB, Ohio: 1917-1975," pp 4, 6.
24. *Ibid.*, p 8.
25. *Ibid.*
26. *Ibid.*, p 9.
27. *Ibid.*
28. *A General Remembers: Major General Fred J. Ascani, Wright Field's Father of Systems Engineering,* ed. with narrative by James F. Aldridge (WPAFB, Ohio, 2001), pp I-11 to I-15.
29. Misenko and Pollock, *Engineering History*, p 34.
30. Chronology, "Laboratories at WPAFB," p 10; Detweiler, "Air Force Research," pp 12-13.
31. Misenko and Pollock, *Engineering History*, p 39.
32. *Ibid.*
33. Edward B. Alcott and Robert C. Williford, *Aerospace Medical Division, Twenty-Five Years of Excellence, 1961-1986* (Brooks AFB, 1986), pp 28-29.
34. Misenko and Pollock, *Engineering History*, p 41.
35. *Ibid.*, p 59.
36. Aldridge, *Mission and Organization*, p 20.
37. Detweiler, "Air Force Research," p 13.
38. Aldridge, *Mission and Organization*, pp 23-24.
39. *History of the Aeronautical Systems Division (ASD), January-December 1986*, Part II: The Air Force Wright Aeronautical Laboratories, CY 1984-1986, Vol 1 (WPAFB, 1988), pp 62-63.

40. Hist, ASD, 1988, Vol 1, pp 253-60.
41. Hist, ASD, 1990, Vol 1, pp 489-93.
42. *History of the Aeronautical Systems Center (ASC), October 1995-September 1996,* Vol 1, p 185.
43. *New World Vistas: Air and Space Power for the 21st Century*, Summary Volume (Washington, 1995), p 68.
44. Robert W. Duffner, *Science and Technology: The Making of the Air Force Research Laboratory* (Maxwell AFB, Nov 2000), chapter 7.
45. Hist, ASC, 1996-1997, Vol 1, pp 247-50.
46. List, "Flight Dynamics Laboratory (WRDC/FI) Tech Base Accomplishments," pp 8, 11, 13, 13-14, 16, 16, and 19.
47. James F. Aldridge, ed., *USAF Research & Development: The Legacy of the Wright Laboratory Science and Engineering Community, 1917-1997* [draft, ASC/HO, 1996], pp 59-60.
48. *USAF R&D,* pp 60-61.
49. *Ibid.*, pp 63-64.
50. *Ibid.*, pp 66-67.
51. *Ibid.*, p 67.
52. *Ibid.*, p 68.
53. *Ibid.,* p 69.
54. *Ibid.*, p 68.
55. List, "FI Tech Base Accomplishments," pp 1, 6, and 8.
56. *Ibid.*, pp 13, 17, and 18.
57. *Ibid.*, pp 12, 9, 16a, 15, and 19.
58. *Ibid.*, pp 1, 11a, 8, 8-9, 13, and 16a.
59. *USAF R&D*, pp 71-72; see also James E. Tomayko, "Blind Faith: The United States Air Force and the Development of Fly-by-Wire Technology," in *Technology and the Air Force: A Retrospective Assessment*, ed. Jacob Neufeld, et al. (Washington, 1997), pp 163-185.
60. *USAF R&D*, pp 73-74.
61. *Ibid.*, pp 74-76.
62. *Ibid.*, p 77.
63. Hist, ASD, 1989, Vol 1, pp 312-316.
64. List, "FI Tech Base Accomplishments," pp 2, 3, 7, 12, and 20.
65. *Ibid.*, pp 1-2, 4, and 9.
66. *USAF R&D*, pp 79-86.
67. Aldridge, *Mission and Organization*, p 18.
68. *Ibid.*, p 20.
69. *Ibid.*, pp 23-24.
70. Hist, ASD, 1988, Vol 1, p 258.
71. Hist, ASD, 1990, Vol 1, p 492.
72. Hist, ASC, 1996-1997, Vol 1, p 249.
73. List, "Propulsion Tech Base Accomplishments," p 1
74. *Ibid.*
75. *Ibid.*, pp 1-2.
76. *Ibid.*
77. *The Memoirs of Ernest C. Simpson, Aero Propulsion Pioneer*, ed. by James J. St. Peter (WPAFB, 1987), and St. Peter, *The History of Aircraft Gas Turbine Engine Development in the United States: A Tradition of Excellence* (Atlanta, 1999).
78. Chronology, "Laboratories at WPAFB," p 10.
79. Aldridge, *Mission and Organization*, p 16.
80. Chronology, "Laboratories at WPAFB," pp 13-14.
81. Aldridge, *Mission and Organization*, pp 16-17.
82. Hist, ASD, 1986, Part II, Hist, AFWAL, 1984-1986, Vol 1, p 116.
83. *Ibid.*, I: 118.
84. *Ibid.*, I: 121.
85. Hist, ASD, 1986, Part II, Hist, AFWAL, 1984-1986, Vol 1, p 123.
86. *Ibid.*
87. *Ibid.*
88. *Ibid,* pp 123-125.
89. *USAF R&D*, p 47.
90. *Ibid.*
91. *Ibid.*
92. *Ibid.*, p 48.
93. *Ibid.*
94. *Ibid.*
95. *Ibid.*
96. Gerald Messadié, *Great Modern Inventions* (New York, 1991), p 84.

97. T. R. Reid, *The Chip: How Two Americans Invented the Microchip and Launched a Revolution* (New York, 1984).
98. Walter Boyne, "The Treasures of McCook Field: America's First Aero-Engineering and Testing Center, Part I," *The Best of "Wings": Great Articles from "Wings" and "Airpower" Magazines* (Washington, 2001), p 4.
99. Dulany Terrett, *United States Army in World War II, The Technical Services, The Signal Corps: The Emergency (to December 1941)* (Washington, 1956), pp 185-91.
100. *Ibid.*, pp 251-2.
101. Aldridge, *Mission and Organization*, p 11.
102. Chronology, "Laboratories at WPAFB," p 4.
103. *Ibid.*
104. *Ibid.*, p 8.
105. *Ibid.*
106. *Ibid.*, p 9.
107. List, "Forty-Three Years of Air Force Technology Base Accomplishments, 1947-1990, WRDC/EL," p 2.
108. *Ibid.*, p 2.
109. *Ibid*, p 2; Reid, *The Chip.*
110. List, "Electronic Technology Accomplishments," p 2.
111. List, "Avionics Tech Base Accomplishments," p 1.
112. William F. Bahret, "The Beginnings of Stealth Technology," *IEEE Transactions on Aerospace and Electronic Systems* Vol 29, no. 4 (Oct 1993): 1374-1385.
113. Chronology, "Laboratories at WPAFB," p 10.
114. *Ibid.*, p 12.
115. *Ibid.*, p 14.
116. *Ibid.*, p 18.
117. List, "Electronic Technology Accomplishments," *Forty-Three Years of Air Force Technology Base*, p 2.
118. *Ibid.*, p 1.
119. *Ibid.*
120. *Ibid.*
121. *USAF R&D*, pp 109-111.
122. List, "Avionics Tech Base Accomplishments," *Forty-Three Years of Air Force Technology Base*, p 1.
123. *Ibid.*, p 1.
124. *Ibid.*
125. *Ibid.*
126. *Ibid.*, p 2.
127. List, "Electronic Technology Accomplishments," *Forty-Three Years of Air Force Technology Base*, p 1.
128. See the section in this chapter on Basic Research.
129. Aldridge, *Mission and Organization*, pp 23-24.
130. List, "Electronic Technology Accomplishments," *Forty-Three Years of Air Force Technology Base*, p 1.
131. *USAF R&D*, p 97.
132. *Ibid.*
133. *Ibid.*, p 98.
134. *Ibid.*
135. *Ibid.*, p 111.
136. *Ibid.*, p 112.
137. List, "Avionics Tech Accomplishments," *Forty-Three Years of Air Force Technology Base*, p 2.
138. *Ibid.*, p 2.
139. List, "Electronics Technology Accomplishments," *Forty-Three Years of Air Force Technology Base*, p 1.
140. Hist, ASD, 1988, Vol 1, pp 253-260.
141. Hist, ASD, 1990, Vol 1, pp 489-493.
142. Hist, ASC, 1995-1996, Vol 1, p 385.
143. Hist, ASC, 1996-1997, Vol 1, p 247.
144. Hist, ASC, 1999-2000, Vol 1 [forthcoming].
145. Niehaus, *Five Decades of Materials Progress*, p 5.
146. Aldridge, *Mission and Organization*, p. 9.
147. Niehaus, *Materials Progress*, pp 56, 71, 80.
148. *Ibid.*, p 59.
149. For a photo identifying the location of the orginal Materials Section at McCook Field, see *ibid.*, p 12.
150. *Engineering of Flight*, pp 75-78.
151. Niehaus, *Materials Progress*, p 70.
152. *Ibid.*, p 68.
153. *Ibid.*, p 69.
154. Dyson, Herrin, et al, eds., *Engineering of Flight*, pp 164-166.
155. *Ibid.*, pp 48-50.
156. Hist, ASD, 1987, Vol 1, pp 260-266.

157. Niehaus, *Materials Progress*, p 80.
158. *Ibid.*, p 78.
159. List, "ML [Materiels Laboratory] Accomplishments," p 1; *USAF Research & Development: The Legacy of the Wright Laboratory Science and Engineering Community, 1917-1997,* James F. Aldridge, ed. [draft, ASC/HO, 1996], pp 1-34.
160. *USAF R&D*, pp 17-34.
161. Niehaus, *Materials Progress,* pp 78-110, and *passim*; list, "ML Accomplishments," p 1.
162. Misenko and Pollock, *Engineering History*, pp 27-42; *Major General Fred J. Ascani*, p I-12ff.
163. Albert E. Misenko, *History of the Air Force Materials Laboratory, July – December 1963*, AFSC Historical Publications Series 64-217-I, Feb 1965.
164. For rare earth magnets, see *USAF R&D*, pp 3-10; for carbon-carbon composites, see below.
165. Hist, ASD, 1986, part II, Hist, AFWAL, 1984-1986, Vol 1, pp 75-9.
166. List, "ML Accomplishments," pp 1-2.
167. *Materials Technology Area Plan, FY 92*, HQ Air Force Systems Command, DCS/Technology, Andrews AFB, MD, p 15.
168. *USAF R&D*, pp 17-18.
169. *Ibid.*, p 17.
170. *Ibid.*, p 18.
171. *Ibid.*, p 19.
172. *Ibid.*, p 21.
173. *Ibid.*, p 25.
174. *Ibid.*
175. *Ibid.*
176. *Ibid.*, pp 22-23.
177. *Ibid.*, p 11.
178. Background paper, AFRL/ML, "History of Sensor Materials Technology in ML and Its Predecessors," (ca., Jul 2002), p 1.
179. *Ibid.*
180. *Ibid.*, p 2.
181. *Ibid.*
182. *Ibid.*, p 3.
183. Niehaus, *Materials Progress*, p 37.
184. Background paper, AFRL/ML, "AFRL Systems Support: The Laboratory's Response for the Warfighter," (ca., Jul 2002), p 1.
185. *Ibid.*, *passim*.
186. *Ibid.*, p 4.
187. Aldridge, *Mission and Organization*, p 20.
188. *Ibid.*
189. See "Basic Research," below.
190. Hist, ASD, 1988, Vol 1, pp 255-258.
191. Hist, ASD, 1990, Vol 1, pp 489-493.
192. Hist, ASC, 1996-1997, Vol 1, p 247.
193. See, e.g., "Spot Welding and Its Application to Aircraft Structure," *Air Corps Information Circular*, Vol 7, no. 692 (Jul 10, 1934).
194. "Shop Practice—Working and Welding Stainless Steel—Tube Bending—Bending Radiator Cores Using High Melting Point Solder (A.C. Specification 11064)," *Air Corps Information Circular*, Vol 7, no. 696 (Sep 8, 1934).
195. Roger E. Bilstein, *The Enterprise of Flight: The American Aviation and Aerospace Industry* (Washington, 2001), pp 74-5.
196. *USAF R&D*, p 165; Niehaus, *Materials Progress*, p 112.
197. Niehaus, *Materials Progress*, pp 167-8; *R&D Contributions to Aviation Progress (RADCAP)*, Vol 1: Summary Report, Aug 1972, p III – 25.
198. *USAF R&D*, pp 137-140.
199. *Ibid.*, p 137.
200. *Ibid.*, pp 151-156.
201. *Ibid.*, p 151.
202. *Ibid.*, p 141-150.
203. *Ibid.*, pp 142-144.
204. *Ibid.*, pp 157-160.
205. *Ibid.*, pp 161-164.
206. *Ibid.*, p 165-175.
207. Hist, ASD, 1988, Vol 1, pp 255-258.
208. Hist, ASC, 1996-1997, Vol 1, p 247.

209. Charles A. Dempsey, *Air Force Aerospace Medical Research Laboratory: 50 Years of Research on Man in Flight* (WPAFB, 1985), p xxvii.
210. Biography, "Harry G. Armstrong," n.d.; *Interview with Harry G. Armstrong (Ret.), U.S. Air Force, Medical Corps*, United States Air Force Oral History Program, John W. Bullard and T. A. Glasgow, interviewers, Brooks AFB, Texas, Apr 6, 8, 13, and 20, 1976; presentation, Mr. Raymond Whitney, at Armstrong Aerospace Medical Research Laboratory, WPAFB, Ohio, 1996.
211. Background paper, "First Sealed Pressure Cabin Airplane, XC-35, Wright Field, 1935-1937," James F. Aldridge, ASC/HO, 25 Aug 1999.
212. Dempsey, *Aerospace Medical Research Laboratory*, p 6.
213. Aldridge, *Mission and Organization*, p 9.
214. Dempsey, *Aerospace Medical Research Laboratory*, p 27.
215. *Ibid.*, p 2.
216. *Ibid.*, p 28.
217. *Ibid.*
218. *Ibid.*
219. *Ibid.*, p 37.
220. *Ibid.*, pp 37, 39.
221. Jay Miller, *The X-Planes: X-1 to X-31* (Arlington, Texas, 1988), p 18.
222. Theodore von Karman, *Toward New Horizons: Science, the Key to Air Supremacy*, Commemorative Edition, 1950-1992 (Washington, 1992).
223. Dempsey, *Aerospace Medical Research Laboratory*, p 57.
224. *Ibid.*
225. *Ibid.*, p 58.
226. *Ibid.*
227. *Ibid.*, p 115.
228. *Ibid.*
229. *Ibid.*, p 116.
230. *Ibid.*, p 58.
231. *Ibid.*, p 117.
232. *Ibid.*
233. *Ibid.*
234. *Ibid.*, pp 158-159.
235. *Ibid.*
236. *Ibid.*
237. *Ibid.*
238. *Ibid.*
239. *Ibid.*
240. *Ibid.*, p 158.
241. Alcott and Williford, *Aerospace Medical Division*, p 148.
242. Hist, ASC, 1996-1997, Vol I, pp 241, 247-248.
243. Jakab, *Visions of a Flying Machine*, chapter 6.
244. Von Karman, *The Wind and Beyond*, pp. 128-29.
245. Roger E. Bilstein, *Flight in America: From the Wrights to the Astronauts*, rev. ed. (Baltimore, 1994), p 31.
246. Alex Roland, *Model Research: The National Advisory Committee for Aeronautics, 1915-1958*, Vol 1 (Washington, 1985), p 22.
247. Paul A. Hanle, *Bringing Aerodynamics to America* (Cambridge, Massachusetts, 1982), chapter 2.
248. Holley, *Ideas and Weapons*, p 117.
249. File, "Frank L. Wattendorf," ASC/HO Archive.
250. Von Karman, *Wind and Beyond*, p 226.
251. Chronology, "Laboratories at WPAFB," p. 5.
252. *Ibid.*, p. 5.
253. Clarence G. Lasby, *Project Paperclip: German Scientists and the Cold War* (New York, 1971).
254. File, "List of Paperclip Scientists and Engineers," ASC/HO Archive.
255. File, "Dr. Hans Joachim Pabst von Ohain," ASC/HO Archive.
256. Chronology, "Laboratories at WPAFB," p. 4.
257. *Ibid.*
258. *Ibid.*, p. 6.
259. *Major General Fred J. Ascani,* p II-49.
260. Chronology, "Laboratories at WPAFB," p. 13.
261. *Ibid.*, p. 11.
262. *Ibid.*, p. 12.
263. *Ibid.*, p. 13.
264. Carl Berger, *The Strengthening of Air Force In-House Laboratories, 1961-1962* (Washington, 1962).

265. Aldridge, *Mission and Organization*, pp. 19-23.
266. *Ibid.*, p. 20; James F. Aldridge, "The Research Mission at Wright Field: An Historical Sketch" [unpublished paper], pp. 5-6.
267. Hist, ASC, 1986, Part II, Hist, AFWAL, 1984-1986, Vol 1, p 50.
268. Hist, ASD, 1987, Vol 1, pp 253-256.
269. Hist, ASC, 1992, Vol 1, pp 433-434.
270. *Ibid.*, Vol 1, pp 432-433.
271. Duffner, *Making of the Air Force Research Laboratory*, pp. 117-118.
272. Robert L. Perry, *System Development Strategies: A Comparative Study of Doctrine, Technology, and Organization in the USAF Ballistic and Cruise Missile Programs, 1950-1960*, RAND Memorandum RM-4853-PR (Santa Monica, 1966), pp 22-28.
273. See also J. S. Przemieniecki, *Acquisition of Defense Systems* (Washington, 1993.)
274. John F. Shiner, "Benjamin D. Foulois: In the Beginning," *Makers of the United States Air Force*, ed. by John L. Frisbee (Washington, 1987), p 14.
275. Perry, *System Development Strategies*, pp 22-28.
276. *Ibid.*, pp 9-11 and 14-22.
277. *Ibid.*, p 19.
278. Michael H. Gorn, *Vulcan's Forge: The Making of an Air Force Command for Weapons Acquisition (1950-1986)* (Andrews AFB, 1987), chapter 2.
279. *Major General Fred J. Ascani,* pp I-12 to I-15..
280. Background paper, "F-X Concept Definition Studies (1964-65)," n.d.
281. Background paper, "F-15E Main Landing Gear (MLG) Tires," n.d.
282. Background paper, "F-16 CARA Performance Improvements," n.d.
283. Background paper, "F-16 INS Performance Anomalies at Aviano AB," n.d.
284. Background paper, "F-16 Operational Flight Program (OFP) Software Cost Reduction," n.d.
285. Background paper, "F-16 System Wide Integrity Management," n.d.
286. Background paper, "F-16 ECM Technique," n.d.
287. Background paper, "C-17 Core Integrated Processor," n.d.
288. Background paper, "C-17 Cruise Drag Projection Analysis," n.d.
289. Background paper, "C-17 Design for Manufacturing/Assembly (DFMA) Project Main Landing Gear Pod," n.d.
290. Background paper, "C-17 Fuel Tank Sealing Improvement Team," n.d.
291. Background paper, "C-17 Multi-Band Radio System," n.d.
292. Background paper, "C-17 On-Board Inert Gas Generation System (OBIGGS)," n.d.
293. Background paper, "C-17 Wireless Communication Set," n.d.
294. Background paper, "C-17 Air Transportability Analysis of Army Vehicles," n.d.
295. Background paper, "C-17 Dual Row Airdrop," n.d.
296. Background paper, "C-17 Paratrooper Airdrop Optimization (PAO) Phases I and II," n.d.
297. Background paper, "C-17 Strategic Brigade Airdrop (SBA) Formation Spacing," n.d.
298. Background paper, "F-22 Readiness for First Flight (FF)," n.d.
299. Background paper, "Have Blue RCS Signature Evaluation," n.d.
300. Background paper, "National Aerospace Plane (NASP) Wind Tunnel/Water Tunnel Tests," n.d.
301. Background paper, "Predator Data Link Analysis," n.d.
302. Background paper, "Kapton Wiring Study," n.d.
303. Background paper, "Engine Structural Integrity Program (ENSIP), n.d.
304. Comment, Andrew Kididis, ASC/EN.
305. Background paper, "Alternate Fighter Engine Competition," n.d.
306. Comments, Mr. Robert J. Kuhnen, ASC/EN.
307. *Ibid.*
308. *Ibid.*
309. *Ibid.*
310. Interview, Mr. Jon Ogg, ASC/EN, with Dr. James F. Aldridge, ASC/HO, Feb 7, 2000.
311. Interview, Mr. David A. Ardis, ASC/ENA, with Dr. James F. Aldridge, ASC/HO, Feb 7, 2000.
312. Blee, *Airplane Engineering Division.*
313. Article, "Alfred Victor Verville," *Who's Who in American Aeronautics*, 3d ed. (New York City, 1928), p 120.
314. Report, *The Engineering Division: A Consideration of Its Status with Respect to the Air Service and the Aeronautical Industry in the United States and Abroad*, revised, Nov 20, 1924.
315. File, "Fred D. Orazio, Sr," ASC/HO Archive.
316. Misenko and Pollock, *Engineering History*, pp 40ff.
317. Comment, Mr. J. J. Lusczek, ASC/ENFD, Jul 19, 2002.
318. Background paper, J. Lusczek, "The Origins of the F-15," 29 Jun 92.
319. Draft ATF History, "ASD/XR Involvement in the History of the Advanced Tactical Fighter (ATF) Analysis," Jul 31, 1991.
320. Point paper, "SOR-182 (C-141) Airlift Systems Studies (1959-60)," n.d.

321. Briefing (excerpt), "XRED Accomplishments—Historical Perspective," n.d.
322. Point paper, "F-X Concept Definition Studies (1964-65)," n.d.; background paper, Joe Lusczek, ASD/XRX, "The Origins of the F-15," Jun 29, 1992.
323. Comment, Mr. J. J. Lusczek, ASC/ENFD, Jul 19, 2002.
324. Background paper, "Justification of [Pioneer] Award [to Joseph J. Lusczek, Jr.]"
325. Background paper, "LWF/F-16," n.d.
326. Background paper, "Teal Dawn/AGM-129 ACM," n.d.
327. Background paper, "KC-X/SC-10," n.d.
328. Background paper, "C-X/C-17," n.d.
329. Background paper, "ATF/F-22," n.d.; background paper, Wayne O'Connor, ASC/LUC, "Design Analysis Directorate (ASD/XRH ATF Team Activities)," Mar 25, 1998.
330. Comment, Mr. J. J. Lusczek, ASC/ENFD, Jul 19, 2002.
331. Memo, J. Lusczek, to John Griffin, ASC/XR, "Continued Support to JSF," Jan 15, 1997.
332. Comment, Mr. J. J. Lusczek, ASC/ENFD, Jul 19, 2002.
333. Background paper, "ATB/B-2," n.d.
334. Memo, Luszcek to Griffin, "Continued Support to JSF," Jan 15, 1997.
335. Intvw, Mr. Stanley A. Tremaine with Dr. James F. Aldridge, ASC/HO, and Mr. Joseph Lusczek, ASC/ENFD, Nov 7, 2001.
336. Intvw, Mr. Joseph Lusczek, ASC/ENFD, with Dr. James F. Aldridge, ASC/HO, Apr 12, 2002.
337. Biography, "Mr. John M. Griffin," Mar 1993.
338. *Guide to the Technology Master Process*, DCS/Science & Technology (HQ AFMC, Oct 30, 1992, p 2-2.
339. Background paper, "TPIPT Success Stories," n.d.
340. Background paper, "TPIPT Success Stories," n.d.
341. *History of the Aeronautical Systems Center (ASC), October 1997 – September 1998*, I: 54-56.
342. Intvw, Mr. J. J. Lusczek, ASC/ENFD, with Dr. James F. Aldridge, ASC/HO, 2000-2001.

APPENDICES

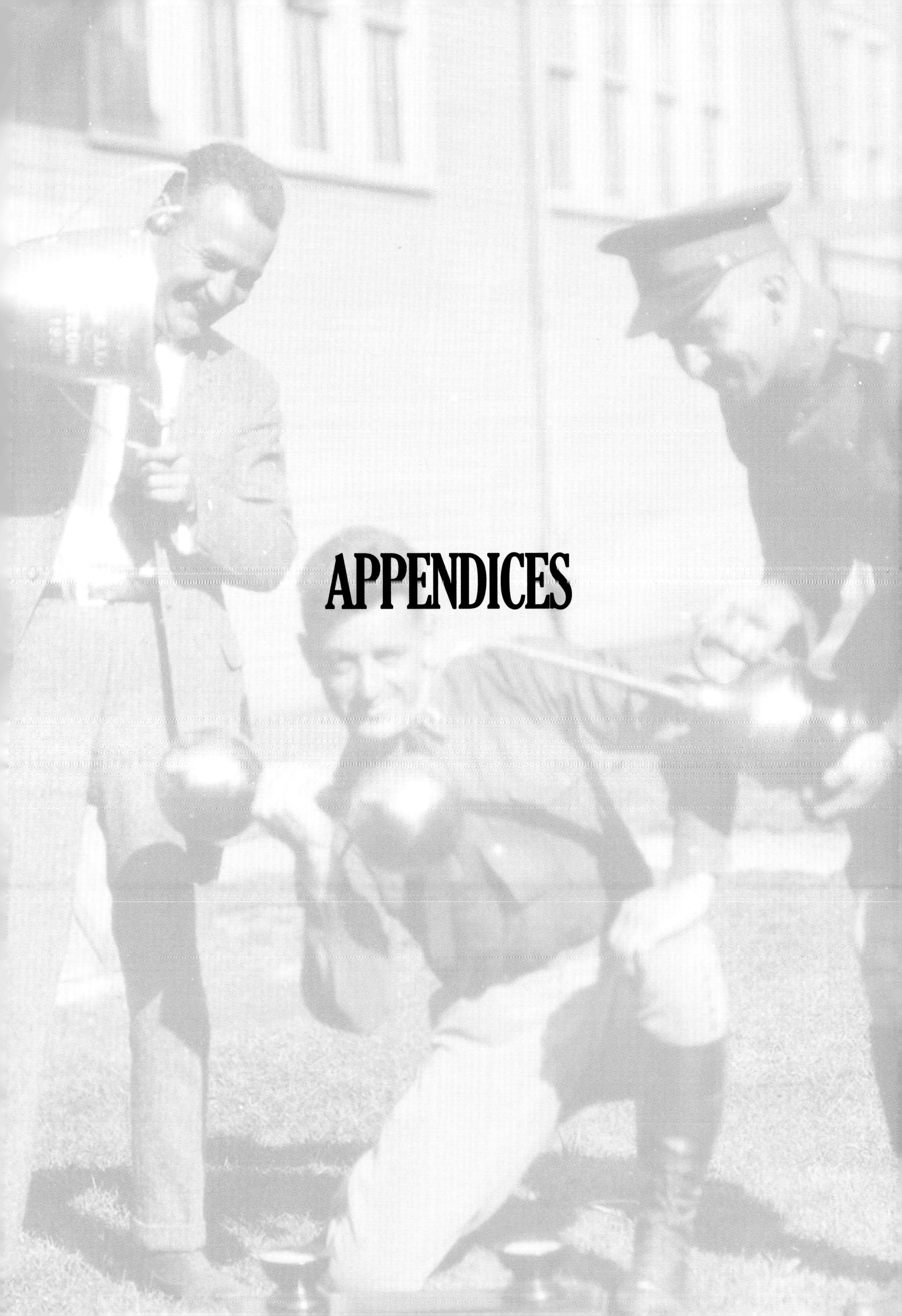

APPENDIX 1
ORGANIZATIONAL EVOLUTION OF THE ACQUISITION & LOGISTICS FUNCTIONS AT WRIGHT-PATTERSON AIR FORCE BASE AND ITS PREDECESSORS

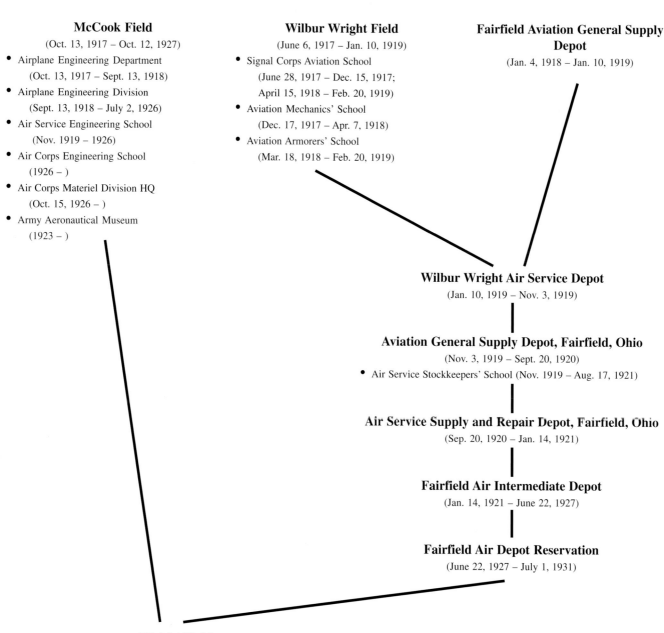

McCook Field
(Oct. 13, 1917 – Oct. 12, 1927)

- Airplane Engineering Department
  (Oct. 13, 1917 – Sept. 13, 1918)
- Airplane Engineering Division
  (Sept. 13, 1918 – July 2, 1926)
- Air Service Engineering School
  (Nov. 1919 – 1926)
- Air Corps Engineering School
  (1926 –)
- Air Corps Materiel Division HQ
  (Oct. 15, 1926 –)
- Army Aeronautical Museum
  (1923 –)

Wilbur Wright Field
(June 6, 1917 – Jan. 10, 1919)

- Signal Corps Aviation School
  (June 28, 1917 – Dec. 15, 1917;
  April 15, 1918 – Feb. 20, 1919)
- Aviation Mechanics' School
  (Dec. 17, 1917 – Apr. 7, 1918)
- Aviation Armorers' School
  (Mar. 18, 1918 – Feb. 20, 1919)

Fairfield Aviation General Supply Depot
(Jan. 4, 1918 – Jan. 10, 1919)

Wilbur Wright Air Service Depot
(Jan. 10, 1919 – Nov. 3, 1919)

Aviation General Supply Depot, Fairfield, Ohio
(Nov. 3, 1919 – Sept. 20, 1920)

- Air Service Stockkeepers' School (Nov. 1919 – Aug. 17, 1921)

Air Service Supply and Repair Depot, Fairfield, Ohio
(Sep. 20, 1920 – Jan. 14, 1921)

Fairfield Air Intermediate Depot
(Jan. 14, 1921 – June 22, 1927)

Fairfield Air Depot Reservation
(June 22, 1927 – July 1, 1931)

Wright Field
(Oct. 12, 1927 – July 1, 1931)

- Air Corps Materiel Division HQ (Oct 15, 1926 –)
  Field Service Section
  Fairfield Air Depot Reservation
  Air Corps Engineering School
  Army Aeronautical Museum

Wright Field

(July 1, 1931 – Dec. 15, 1945)

- Air Corps Materiel Division (– Oct. 2, 1939, transfer to D.C.)
    - Army Aeronautical Museum (– June 1, 1940)
    - Air Corps Engineering School (– Aug. 1941)
    - Army Air Forces Engineering School (Aug. 1941 – Dec. 9, 1941)
- Materiel Center (Mar. 16, 1942 – Apr. 1, 1943)
- Materiel Command, transferred from D.C (Apr. 1, 1943 – Aug. 31, 1944)
    - Army Air Forces Engineering School (Mar. 17, 1944 – Dec. 15, 1945)
- Air Technical Service Command (Aug. 31, 1944 – Mar. 9, 1946)*
- Army Air Forces Institute of Technology (Dec. 15, 1945 –)

Patterson Field

(July 1, 1931 – Dec. 15, 1945)

- Provisional Air Corps Maintenance Command (Mar. 15, 1941 – Apr. 29, 1941)
- Air Corps Maintenance Command (Apr. 29, 1941 – Dec. 15, 1942)
    - Fairfield Air Depot (July 1, 1931 – Feb. 1, 1943)
        - Air Corps Weather School (July 1, 1937 – June 1, 1940)
        - Autogiro School (Apr. 20, 1938 – unknown)
- Air Service Command (Dec. 15, 1942 – Aug. 31, 1944)
    - Fairfield Air Depot Control Area Command (Feb. 1, 1943 – May 17, 1943)
    - Fairfield Air Service Command (May 17, 1943 – Dec. 6, 1944)
- Fairfield Air Technical Service Command (Dec. 6, 1944 –)

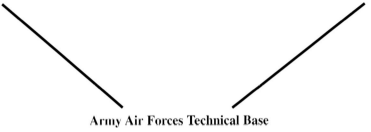

Army Air Forces Technical Base

(Dec. 15, 1945 – Dec. 9, 1947)

- Air Materiel Command (Mar. 9, 1946 –)
- Fairfield Air Technical Service Command (– Jan. 1, 1946)
- Air Force Institute of Technology (Dec. 5, 1947 –)

Air Force Technical Base

(Dec. 9, 1947 – Jan. 13, 1948)

- Air Materiel Command
- Air Force Institute of Technology

Wright-Patterson Air Force Base

(January 13, 1948 – Present)

- Air Materiel Command (– Apr. 1, 1961)
    - Aeronautical Systems Center (Sept. 1958 – Apr. 1, 1961)
- Air Research and Development Command (Apr. 2, 1951 – June 1951, transferred to Baltimore)
    - Wright Air Development Center (Apr. 2, 1951 – Dec. 15, 1959)
    - Wright Air Development Division (Dec. 15, 1959 – Apr. 1, 1961)
- Air Force Logistics Command (Apr. 1, 1961 – July 1, 1992)
- Air Force Systems Command (Apr. 1, 1961 – July 1, 1992, headquarters at Andrews Air Force Base, Maryland)
    - Aeronautical Systems Division (Apr. 1, 1961 – July 1, 1992)
- Air Force Materiel Command (July 1, 1992 – Present)
    - Aeronautical Systems Center (July 1, 1992 – Present)
- Air Force Institute of Technology (– Present)
- National Air Intelligence Center (May 21, 1951 – Present)
- United States Air Force Museum (Apr. 1954 – Present)
- United States Air Force Medical Center (July 1, 1969 – Present)
- 88th Air Base Wing (Apr. 1, 1944 – Present)

*The headquarters of the Air Technical Service Command originally was located on Patterson Field. When Air Service Command and Air Materiel Command merged in 1944, the acting commander of Air Service Command incorporated the part of Patterson Field occupied by headquarters into Wright Field. The headquarters portion of Wright Field then became known as Area A and the original Wright Field was known as Area B. The remainder of Patterson Field became Area C when it merged with Wright Field in 1948.

APPENDIX 2

Form No. 13.

Signal Corps, United States Army.

These Articles of Agreement entered into this-------tenth--------- day of February---, nineteen hundred and-eight--, between----Chas. S. Wallace----, Captain------------------, Signal Corps, United States Army, of the first part, and

Wilbur and Orville Wright, trading as Wright Brothers, of 1127 West Third Street, Dayton,

in the county of--------Montgomery----------, State of------Ohio-----------, of the second part, Witnesseth, that in conformity with copy of the advertisement, specifications, and proposal hereunto attached, and which, in so far as they relate to this contract, form a part of it, the said--------------------Chas. S. Wallace, Captain,----------------- Signal Corps, United States Army, for and in behalf of the United States of America, and the said ---------------------------Wright Brothers------------------------- (hereinafter designated as the contractor) do covenant and agree, to and with each other, as follows, viz:

Article I. That the said contractor shall manufacture for and deliver to the United States of America,

One (1) heavier-than-air flying machine, in accordance with Signal Corps Specification No. 486, dated December 23, 1907.

Art. II. That the deliveries of the supplies and materials herein contracted for shall be made in the manner, numbers, or quantities, and for each number or quantity, on or before the date specified therefor, as follows, viz:

That complete delivery shall be made on or before August 28, 1908.

Art. III. All supplies and materials furnished and work done under this contract shall, before being accepted, be subject to a rigid inspection by an inspector appointed on the part of the Government,

3—1100

and such as do not conform to the specifications set forth in this contract shall be rejected. The decision of the Chief Signal Officer, United States Army, as to quality and quantity shall be final.

ART. IV. That for and in consideration of the faithful performance of the stipulations of this contract, the contractor shall be paid at the office of -----the Chief Signal Officer-------------of the Army---------, at-----Washington, D. C.---, for all supplies and materials delivered in conformity with the requirements of this contract, on or before the dates above specified (Article II, *supra*) *and accepted*, the following prices, viz:

One (1) heavier-than-air flying machine at a total cost of twenty-five thousand (25,000) dollars.

to be paid as soon as practicable after the acceptance of the same, in funds furnished by the United States for the purpose, reserving per cent from each payment until final settlement, on completion of the contract or otherwise.

ART. V. It is further agreed that for all supplies and materials which shall not be delivered in conformity with the requirements of this contract on or before the dates prescribed therefor in Article II, above, but which shall be subsequently delivered and accepted, the prices shall be as follows:

3—1100

Art. VI. That in case of the e of the said contractor to perf he stipulations of this contract within the time and in the manner specified above, Articles I to III, inclusive, the said party of the first part may, instead of waiting further for deliveries under the provisions of the preceding article, supply the deficiency by purchase in open market or otherwise, at such place as may be selected (the articles so procured to be the kind herein specified, as near as practicable); and the said contractor shall be charged with the increased cost of the supplies and materials so purchased over what they would have cost if delivered by the contractor on the date they were received under such open-market purchase.

Art. VII. It is further agreed by and between the parties hereto that until final inspection and acceptance of, and payment for, all of the supplies and materials and work herein provided for, no prior inspection, payment, or act is to be construed as a waiver of the right of the party of the first part to reject any defective articles or supplies or to require the fulfillment of any of the terms of the contract.

Art. VIII. The contractor further agrees to hold and save the United States harmless from and against all and every demand, or demands, of any nature or kind for, or on account of, the use of any patented invention, article, or process included in the materials hereby agreed to be furnished and work to be done under this contract.

Art. IX. Neither this contract nor any interest herein shall be transferred to any other party or parties, and in case of such transfer the United States may refuse to carry out this contract either with the transferor or the transferee, but all rights of action for any breach of this contract by said contractor are reserved to the United States.

Art. X. No Member of or Delegate to Congress, nor any person belonging to, or employed in, the military service of the United States, is or shall be admitted to any share or part of this contract, or to any benefit which may arise therefrom.*

Art. XI. That it is expressly agreed and understood that this contract shall be noneffective until an appropriation adequate to its fulfillment is made by Congress and is available.

Art. XII. That this contract shall be subject to approval of the Chief Signal Officer, United States Army.

IN WITNESS WHEREOF the parties aforesaid have hereunto placed their hands the date first hereinbefore written.

Witnesses:

John J. Mullaney as to Chas. M. Allen
Albert Larrere as to C..., Signal Corps, U. S. Army.

C. E. Taylor as to
H. G. Hoffman as to Wright Brothers
by Orville Wright

Approved: FEB 28 1908, 190

Brigadier General,
Chief Signal Officer of the Army.

*Here add to any contract made with an incorporated company for its general benefit the following words, viz: "But this stipulation, so far as it relates to Members or Delegates to Congress, is not to be construed to extend to this contract." See section 3740, Revised Statutes.

(EXECUTED IN QUINTUPLICATE.)

8—1100

SIGNAL CORPS SPECIFICATION, NO. 486.

ADVERTISEMENT AND SPECIFICATION FOR A HEAVIER-THAN-AIR FLYING MACHINE.

TO THE PUBLIC:

Sealed proposals, in duplicate, will be received at this office until 12 o'clock noon on February 1, 1908, on behalf of the Board of Ordnance and Fortification for furnishing the Signal Corps with a heavier-than-air flying machine. All proposals received will be turned over to the Board of Ordnance and Fortification at its first meeting after February 1 for its official action.

Persons wishing to submit proposals under this specification can obtain the necessary forms and envelopes by application to the Chief Signal Officer, United States Army, War Department, Washington, D. C. The United States reserves the right to reject any and all proposals.

Unless the bidders are also the manufacturers of the flying machine they must state the name and place of the maker.

Preliminary.—This specification covers the construction of a flying machine supported entirely by the dynamic reaction of the atmosphere and having no gas bag.

Acceptance.—The flying machine will be accepted only after a successful trial flight, during which it will comply with all requirements of this specification. No payments on account will be made until after the trial flight and acceptance.

Inspection.—The Government reserves the right to inspect any and all processes of manufacture.

GENERAL REQUIREMENTS.

The general dimensions of the flying machine will be determined by the manufacturer, subject to the following conditions:

1. Bidders must submit with their proposals the following:

(*a*) Drawings to scale showing the general dimensions and shape of the flying machine which they propose to build under this specification.

(*b*) Statement of the speed for which it is designed.

(*c*) Statement of the total surface area of the supporting planes.

(*d*) Statement of the total weight.

(*e*) Description of the engine which will be used for motive power.

(*f*) The material of which the frame, planes, and propellers will be constructed. Plans received will not be shown to other bidders.

2. It is desirable that the flying machine should be designed so that it may be quickly and easily assembled and taken apart and packed for transportation in army wagons. It should be capable of being assembled and put in operating condition in about one hour.

3. The flying machine must be designed to carry two persons having a combined weight of about 350 pounds, also sufficient fuel for a flight of 125 miles.

4. The flying machine should be designed to have a speed of at least forty miles per hour in still air, but bidders must submit quotations in their proposals for cost depending upon the speed attained during the trial flight, according to the following scale:

40 miles per hour, 100 per cent.
39 miles per hour, 90 per cent.
38 miles per hour, 80 per cent.
37 miles per hour, 70 per cent.
36 miles per hour, 60 per cent.
Less than 36 miles per hour rejected.
41 miles per hour, 110 per cent.
42 miles per hour, 120 per cent.
43 miles per hour, 130 per cent.
44 miles per hour, 140 per cent.

5. The speed accomplished during the trial flight will be determined by taking an average of the time over a measured course of more than five miles, against and with the wind. The time will be taken by a flying start, passing the starting point at full speed at both ends of the course. This test subject to such additional details as the Chief Signal Officer of the Army may prescribe at the time.

6. Before acceptance a trial endurance flight will be required of at least one hour during which time the flying machine must remain continuously in the air without landing. It shall return to the starting point and land without any damage that would prevent it immediately starting upon another flight. During this trial flight of one hour it must be steered in all directions without difficulty and at all times under perfect control and equilibrium.

7. Three trials will be allowed for speed as provided for in paragraphs 4 and 5. Three trials for endurance as provided for in paragraph 6, and both tests must be completed within a period of thirty days from the date of delivery. The expense of the tests to be borne by the manufacturer. The place of delivery to the Government and trial flights will be at Fort Myer, Virginia.

8. It should be so designed as to ascend in any country which may be encountered in field service. The starting device must be simple and transportable. It should also land in a field without requiring a specially prepared spot and without damaging its structure.

9. It should be provided with some device to permit of a safe descent in case of an accident to the propelling machinery.

10. It should be sufficiently simple in its construction and operation to permit an intelligent man to become proficient in its use within a reasonable length of time.

11. Bidders must furnish evidence that the Government of the United States has the lawful right to use all patented devices or appurtenances which may be a part of the flying machine, and that the manufacturers of the flying machine are authorized to convey the same to the Government. This refers to the unrestricted right to use the flying machine sold to the Government, but does not contemplate the exclusive purchase of patent rights for duplicating the flying machine.

12. Bidders will be required to furnish with their proposal a certified check amounting to ten per cent of the price stated for the 40-mile speed. Upon making the award for this flying machine these certified checks will be returned to the bidders, and the successful bidder will be required to furnish a bond, according to Army Regulations, of the amount equal to the price stated for the 40-mile speed.

13. The price quoted in proposals must be understood to include the instruction of two men in the handling and operation of this flying machine. No extra charge for this service will be allowed.

14. Bidders must state the time which will be required for delivery after receipt of order.

JAMES ALLEN,
Brigadier General, Chief Signal Officer of the Army.

SIGNAL OFFICE,
WASHINGTON, D. C., *December 23, 1907.*

APPENDIX 3

THE UNITED STATES AIR FORCE AND ITS PREDECESSORS

Aeronautical Division, U.S. Signal Corps	August 1, 1907 – July 18, 1914
Aviation Section, U.S. Signal Corps	July 18, 1914 – May 20, 1918
Division of Military Aeronautics	May 20, 1918 – May 24, 1918
Air Service	May 24, 1918 – July 2, 1926
Air Corps	July 2, 1926 – September 18, 1947*
Army Air Forces	June 20, 1941 – September 18, 1947
United States Air Force	September 18, 1947 – Present

* On June 20, 1941, the Air Corps became a subordinate element of the Army Air Forces. It continued to exist as a combat arm of the Army until 1947.

August 1, 1907 – July 18, 1914

The Army pursued its growing interest in "all matters pertaining to military ballooning, air machines, and all kindred subjects" by establishing the **Aeronautical Division, U.S. Signal Corps,** on August 1, 1907. The Army purchased its first airplane from the Wright brothers in 1909.

July 18, 1914 – May 20, 1918

After successfully demonstrating aviation's capabilities through strafing, bombing, and photography, Congress established the **Aviation Section, U.S. Signal Corps**. The new unit absorbed the Aeronautical Division's assets consisting of six aircraft, 19 officers, 101 enlisted men, and one squadron.

May 20, 1918

A presidential executive order on May 20, 1918, removed the aviation responsibilities assigned to the Signal Corps. The president created two co-equal agencies: the Division of Military Aeronautics (DMA) and the Bureau of Aircraft Production (BAP). On May 24, 1918, the War Department officially recognized these two Army agencies as comprising the Air Service. On August 28, 1918, John D. Ryan was appointed as second assistant secretary of war and director of the **Air Service** to supervise both the DMA and the BAP.

July 2, 1926 – September 18, 1947

Congress established the **Air Corps**, on July 2, 1926, thereby creating an aviation arm with a significant degree of autonomy within the Army. This action elevated the service to an equal status alongside the infantry and artillery, thus making it an offensive force.

March 1, 1935 – June 20, 1941

The **General Headquarters (GHQ) Air Force** assumed control of all Army aviation combat units within the continental United States. The GHQ Air Force reported directly to the chief of staff of the Army.

June 20, 1941 – September 18, 1947
On June 20, 1941, the Air Corps and the Air Force Combat Command (the GHQ Air Force was so redesignated effective this date) combined to form the **Army Air Forces**. Major General Henry H. Arnold, chief of the Air Corps, assumed command of the new organization that provided virtual autonomy to the air arm for the first time. The Air Corps became a subordinate element of the Army Air Forces. It continued to exist as a combat arm of the Army until 1947.

September 18, 1947 – Present
The National Security Act of 1947 established the **Department of the Air Force** and the **United States Air Force**. W. Stuart Symington became the first secretary of the Air Force and General Carl A. Spaatz served as the first Air Force chief of staff.

The United States Air Force Symbol honors the heritage of our past and represents the promise of our future. It retains the core elements of our Air Corps heritage—the "Arnold" wings and star with circle — and modernizes them to reflect our aerospace force of today and tomorrow.

Sources: "The Lineage of the United States Air Force," Air Force History Support Office, http://www.airforcehistory.hq.af.mil/PopTopics/lineage.htm; "United States Air Force Seal," Air Force History Support Office, http://www.airforcehistory.hq.af.mil/PopTopics/usafsealhist.htm; I.B. Holley, Jr., *Ideas and Weapons* (Washington, D.C., 1997), pp 68-69; Robert F. Futrell, *Ideas, Concepts, Doctrine: Basic Thinking in the United States Air Force 1907-1960* (Maxwell Air Force Base, Alabama, 1989), pp 28, 104; Juliette A. Hennessy, *The United States Army Air Arm April 1861 to April 1917* (Washington, D.C., 1985), p 217; Stephen L. McFarland, *A Concise History of the U.S. Air Force* (Washington, D.C., 1997), pp 2, 5, 13; Bernard C. Nalty, ed., *Winged Shield, Winged Sword: A History of the United States Air Force* (Washington, D.C., 1997) Volume I 1907-1950, pp 50-51, 126-130, 181; George M. Watson, Jr., *Secretaries and Chiefs of Staff of the United States Air Force* (Washington, D.C, 2001), p 1; Air Force Link, Useage Guidlines, online at www.af.mil/airforcestory/guidelines.shtml; Charles A. Ravenstein, *The Organization and Lineage of the United States Air Force* (Washington, D.C., 1986), pp 1-9.

APPENDIX 4

AIRCRAFT COLORS AND NATIONAL INSIGNIA

A comprehensive review of aircraft colors and paint schemes would fill several volumes. In brief, aircraft colors have changed frequently throughout the history of the United States Air Force and its predecessor organizations. The varnish applied to early aircraft gave their fabric-covered surfaces a white or light buff appearance, but they were not painted. In 1918, during World War I, American aircraft sported their first color scheme consisting of olive drab (O.D.) painted over all surfaces. This scheme lasted until 1927 with the advent of chrome yellow wing and tail surfaces for increased visibility (the remainder of the aircraft remained O.D.). The advent of the Ford Trimotor in 1929 brought natural metal into vogue.

In the 1930s, some aircraft received a coat of water-based camouflage paint that could be removed after participation in "War Games" or other activities. In 1933, Technical Order 07-01-1, *Aircraft Markings, Insignia and Camouflage*, established two divisions: ground camouflage and sky camouflage. By 1936, light blue replaced the O.D. scheme. With the likelihood of war increasing in 1940, the Air Corps reverted to O.D. top and side surfaces and gray under surfaces. This remained the predominant paint scheme until 1944 when the changing tactical situation dictated a return to natural metal finishes (a variety of paint schemes existed in the various theaters). As the U.S. air offensive stretched deep into Germany and Japan, bombers and fighter escorts could not afford the extra weight and drag produced by camouflage paint. As the war drew to a close, local commanders had the authority to retain/apply camouflage or strip the planes to bare metal.

Following World War II, most aircraft retained their natural metal finish but new color standards also came into effect. The first Federal Specification in 1950, TT-C-595, assigned four-digit numbers grouped by degree of gloss, with 200 color chips. Consequently, some aircraft in the Korean War sported camouflage. For example, some B-29 bombers featured natural metal upper surfaces with black under surfaces for night bombing missions. United States Air Force aircraft sometimes displayed special coloring. For example, some desert aircraft were sand colored (such as B-24 bombers during World War II), while arctic aircraft reflected bright markings (red wings in some cases) to aid search-and-rescue operations. Orange or fluorescent "day-glo" allowed easy identification of some special test or research aircraft. In the late 1940s, air-sea rescue paint schemes included yellow wing tips and a wide yellow band outlined in black around the fuselage.

During the 1950s, the Air Force adopted Technical Manual T.O. 1-1-4, *Exterior Finishes, Insignia and Markings Applicable to Aircraft and Missiles*. The widening conflict in Vietnam brought the return of camouflage paint. The need to maintain a flexible capability throughout the Cold War and especially during its aftermath, forced the Air Force to apply a variety of finishes to its aircraft. Major commands such as Strategic Air Command, Tactical Air Command, and Aerospace Defense Command, each implemented its own color standards based on mission requirements.

Some missions, especially those providing humanitarian relief, frequently necessitated the use of aircraft without the ready-for-war appearance implied by camouflage. Conflicts, such as the Persian Gulf War and actions in the Balkans, again made camouflage necessary. Other aircraft, such as the SR-71 and F-117, presented an all-black appearance because of the nature of their missions. Serving virtually around the globe, in all kinds of climates, and operating in all types of terrain, the Air Force adapted its insignia, markings, and colors to each situation.

1916
Used during the Mexican Punitive Expedition in 1916. Also used without the white background circle.

1917, 1919
Aircraft initially deployed to France in 1917 carried this insignia. It was replaced by the concentric circles insignia until after the war. U.S. military aircraft resumed using the insignia in May 1919.

1918
This became the official American insignia to enable easier recognition in combat during World War I.

1942
The red center was removed from the star to reduce confusion with Japanese insignia during World War II. Some aircraft based in England and North Africa sported a yellow border surrounding the national insignia for a brief period beginning in late 1942.

1943
On June 29, 1943, the national insignia was changed to include a white rectangle or bar on each side of the blue circle. It also featured a red border surrounding the entire insignia.

1943
On August 14, 1943, the red border was replaced with a blue border.

1947
The current national insignia was adopted on January 14, 1947. The insignia features horizontal red bars added to the white blocks on either side of the circle.

Sources: Ross Whistler, *USAAF Camouflage 1933-1969* (Dover, Massachusettes, 1969), pp 1-4, 6, 13-24; F. G. Swansborough, *United States Military Aircraft Since 1909* (London, 1963), pp 23-30; Dana Bell, *Air Force Colors Volume I 1926-1942* (Carrollton, Texas, 1995), pp 6, 21, 54; Dana Bell, *Air Force Colors Volume 3 Pacific and Home Front, 1942-47* (Carrollton, Texas, 1997), pp 15; Robert F. Futrell, *The United States Air Force in Korea* (Washington, D.C., rev 1983), p 520; "Evolution of USAF Insignia 1947," on line at www.wpafb.af.mil/museum/research/insig11.htm; Bill Yenne, *The History of the U.S. Air Force* (New York, 1984), p 222.

APPENDIX 5
AIRCRAFT DESIGNATIONS

When the Army first acquired military aircraft they referred to them only by the manufacturer's model number. The few aircraft acquired before World War I mainly were used for observation purposes, so there was no need to identify them by function. During the war, aircraft functions became more specialized and a precise system of aircraft identification was needed; however, a new system was not developed until after the war.

The 1919 Identification System

The system introduced in September 1919 described aircraft according to Types, assigning a numeral to each. The following year, the Engineering Division at McCook Field instituted a series of letter designations to supplement the Type series; these two or three letter designations served as an abbreviation of the function of the aircraft. Sequential numbers were added to these letters to further identify aircraft, thus creating an identification system familiar today.

Type I	PW	Pursuit, water-cooled
Type II	PN	Pursuit, night
Type III	PA	Pursuit, air-cooled
Type IV	PG	Pursuit, ground attack
Type V	TP	Pursuit, two-place
Type VI	GA	Ground attack
Type VII	IL	Infantry liaison
Type VIII	NO	Night observation
Type IX	AO	Artillery observation, surveillance
Type X	CO	Corps observation
Type XI	DB	Day bomber
Type XII	NBS	Night bombardment, short distance
Type XIII	NBL	Night bombardment, long distance
Type XIV	TA	Training, air-cooled
Type XV	TW	Training, water-cooled

Between 1919 and 1924, the Engineering Division added nine more letter designations. The letters proved to be more flexible and descriptive than the Type numerals, and the Type series was dropped.

A	Ambulance
COA	Corps observation, amphibian
G	Glider
M	Messenger
MAT	Messenger, aerial torpedo
PS	Pursuit, special alert
R	Racer
S	Seaplane
T	Transport

The 1924 Revision

The first major revision occurred in May 1924. Once the Roman-numerated Type designations were abandoned, identification was entirely by function of the aircraft. It was during this period that the prefix X was first used to designate experimental aircraft, prototypes, and temporary test aircraft. Y denoted service test aircraft; and Z designated obsolete models. As the years passed and additional functions for military aircraft were realized, more letter codes were added, especially during World War II. Following is a partial listing of aircraft designations in use between 1924 and 1947:

A	Attack	1926-1947
AT	Advanced trainer	1925-1947
B	Bomber	1925 to date
BC	Basic combat	1936-1940
BLR	Bomber, long range	1935-1936
BT	Basic trainer	1930-1947
C	Transport	1925 to date
CG	Transport Glider	1941-1947
F	Photographic	1930-1947
FM	Fighter, multi-place	1936-1941
G	Gyroplane	1935-1939
HB	Heavy bomber	1925-1927
L	Liaison	1942-1962
LB	Light bomber	1925-1932
O	Observation	1924-1942
P	Pursuit (fighter)	1925-1947
PT	Primary trainer	1925-1947
R	Rotary wing	1941-1947

The 1948 System

By the end of World War II, nearly 40 code letters had been used to describe aircraft. In 1948, the designations were again revised to streamline the identification system. The two-letter symbols were replaced by one-letter designations, and families of aircraft were grouped under a single letter code. This system formed the basis for the one currently in use.

A	Amphibian
B	Bomber
C	Transport
F	Fighter
G	Glider
H	Helicopter
L	Liaison
Q	Aerial target
R	Reconnaissance*
T	Trainer
U	Utility
V	Convertiplane (V/STOL)
X	Research

*The R designation for aircraft with an exclusive reconnaissance function was used for only a short time. With the increasing research and development in unmanned aircraft, the R was appropriated to identify Rockets and the M designation was used for Missiles.

The 1962 Tri-Service System

In 1962, the Department of Defense unified the Army, Navy, and Air Force systems of aircraft identification, with the intention of bringing the other services' designations more in line with those used by the Air Force. The revision resulted in only a few changes to the 1948 Air Force listing, and many of the new designations were for Navy aircraft types.

A	Tactical support
E	Electronic surveillance
O	Observation
P	Patrol
S	Anti-submarine
Z	Airship

In addition to this type letter, popularly known military aircraft designations had three other parts: a status/role prefix, a type sequence number, and a suffix model letter. The type sequence number indicated the aircraft's place in the type series, (i.e. B-**50**, B-**52**, B-**57**), and the model letter (beginning with A) indicated the variant of the aircraft (i.e., B-52A, B-52B). The status/role prefix identified an aircraft's secondary role or its stage of development or deployment. These prefixes are listed below. Military designations also included a manufacturer identification (typically a two letter abbreviation of the company name), as well as any applicable block numbers to identify modifications to aircraft within the same model series.

A	Tactical support (e.g., AC-130)
D	Drone director
E	Electronics
F	Fighter (e.g., FB-111)
G	Permanently grounded
H	Search and rescue (e.g., HH-60)
J	Temporary special tests
K	Tanker
M	Special operations
N	Permanent special tests
O	Observation
Q	Radio-controlled drone
R	Reconnaissance
V	Staff transport
X	Experimental
Y	Service test
Z	Project

Over the years, a few aircraft have had non-standard designations. The SR-71 was a prominent example. The SR indicated "strategic reconnaissance" and its type sequence number was within the bomber series.

Sources: John M. Andrade, *U.S. Military Aircraft Designations and Serials Since 1909* (Leicester, 1979), pp 6-9; F.G. Swanborough, *United States Military Aircraft Since 1909* (London, 1963), pp 8-20.

APPENDIX 6
NATIONAL DEFENSE LEADERSHIP

U.S. President Commander-In-Chief	Secretary of War (1904 - 1947)/ Secretary of Defense (1947 - Present)	Military Air Chief (1907 - 1947)/ U.S. Air Force Chief of Staff (1947 - Present)	Secretary of the Air Force (and Antecedents)
Theodore Roosevelt 1901 - 1909	William H. Taft 1904 - 1908	Capt Charles DeF. Chandler 1907 - 1911	
	Luke Edwar Wright 1980 - 1909		
William H. Taft 1909 - 1913	Jacob McGavock Dickinson 1909 - 1911	Capt Arthur S. Cowan 1910 - 1911	
	Henry L. Stimson 1911 - 1913	Capt Charles DeF. Chandler 1911 - 1912	
		Lt Henry H. Arnold 1912 - 1913	
Woodrow Wilson 1913 - 1921	Lindley Miller Garrison 1913 - 1916	Col Samuel Reber 1914 - 1916	
	Newton D. Baker 1916 - 1921	Brig Gen George O. Squier 1916 - 1917	
		Lt Col John B. Bennet 1917	
		Brig Gen Benjamin D. Foulois 1917	
		Brig Gen Alexander L. Dade 1917 - 1918	John D. Ryan (Chief, Bureau of Aircraft Production) 1918
		Maj Gen Charles Menoher 1919 - 1921	John D. Ryan (Director, Air Service) 1918
Warren G. Harding 1921 - 1923	John W. Weeks 1921 - 1925	Maj Gen Mason M. Patrick 1921 - 1927	
Calvin Coolidge 1923 - 1929	Dwight Filley Davis 1925 - 1929	Maj Gen James E. Fechet 1927 - 1931	F. Trubee Davison (Assistant Secretary of War for Air) 1926 - 1932
Herbert Hoover 1929 - 1933	James W. Good 1929	Maj Gen Benjamin D. Foulois 1931 - 1935	
	Patrick J. Hurley 1929 - 1933		
Franklin D. Roosevelt 1933 - 1945	George H. Dern 1933 - 1936	Maj Gen Oscar Westover 1935 - 1938	
	Harry Hines Woodring 1936 - 1940	Gen Henry H. Arnold 1938 - 1946	
	Henry L. Stimson 1940 - 1945		Robert A. Lovett (Assistant Secretary of War for Air) 1941 - 1946
Harry S. Truman 1945 - 1953	Robert Porter Patterson 1945 - 1947	Gen Carl A. Spaatz 1946 - 1947	
	Kenneth Royall 1947	Gen Carl A. Spaatz 1947 - 1948	W. Stuart Symington (Assistant Secretary of War for Air) 1947
	James V. Forrestal 1947 - 1949	Gen Hoyt S. Vandenberg 1948 - 1953	W. Stuart Symington 1947 - 1950
	Louis A. Johnson 1949 - 1950		

	George C. Marshall 1950 - 1951		Thomas K. Finletter 1950 - 1953
	Robert A. Lovett 1951 - 1953		
Dwight D. Eisenhower 1953 - 1961	Charles E. Wilson 1953 - 1957	Gen Nathan F. Twining 1953 - 1957	Harold E. Talbott 1953 - 1955
	Neil H. McElroy 1957 - 1959	Gen Thomas D. White 1957 - 1961	Donald A. Quarles 1955 - 1957
	Thomas S. Gates Jr. 1959 - 1961		James H. Douglas, Jr. 1957 - 1959
			Dudley C. Sharp 1959 - 1961
John F. Kennedy 1961 - 1963	Robert S. McNamara 1961 - 1968	Gen Curtis E. LeMay 1961 - 1965	Eugene M. Zuckert 1961 - 1965
Lyndon B. Johnson 1963 - 1969	Clark M. Clifford 1968 - 1969	Gen John P. McConnell 1965 - 1969	Harold Brown 1965 - 1969
Richard M. Nixon 1969 - 1974	Melvin R. Laird 1969 - 1973	Gen John D. Ryan 1969 - 1973	Robert C. Seamans, Jr. 1969 - 1973
	Elliott L. Richardson 1973	Gen George S. Brown 1973 - 1974	John L. Lucas 1973 - 1975
Gerald R. Ford 1974 - 1977	James R. Schlesinger 1973 - 1975	Gen David C. Jones 1974 - 1978	James W. Plummer 1975 - 1977
	Donald H. Rumsfeld 1975 - 1977		
Jimmy Carter 1977 - 1981	Harold Brown 1977 - 1981	Gen Lew Allen, Jr. 1978 - 1982	John C. Stetson 1977 - 1979
			Hans Mark 1979 - 1981
Ronald W. Reagan 1981 - 1989	Caspar Weinberger 1981 - 1987	Gen Charles A. Gabriel 1982 - 1986	Verne Orr 1981 - 1985
	Frank C. Carlucci 1987 - 1989	Gen Larry D. Welch 1986 - 1990	Russell A. Rourke 1985 - 1986
			Edward C. Aldridge, Jr. 1986 - 1988
			James F. McGovern (acting) 1988 - 1989
George H.W. Bush 1989 - 1993	Richard B. Cheney 1989 - 1993	Gen Michael J. Dugan 1990	John J. Welch (acting) 1989
		Gen Merrill A. McPeak 1990 - 1994	Donald B. Rice 1989 - 1993
			Michael B. Donley (acting) 1993
			Merrill A. McPeak (acting) 1993
William J. Clinton 1993 - 2001	Les Aspin 1993 - 1994	Gen Ronald R. Fogleman 1994 - 1997	Shelia E. Widnall 1993 - 1997
	William J. Perry 1994 - 1997	Gen Michael E. Ryan 1997 - 2001	F. Whitten Peters 1997 - 2001
	William S. Cohen 1997 - 2001		Dr. Lawrence J. Delaney (acting) 2001
George W. Bush 2001 - Present	Donald H. Rumsfeld 2001 - Present	Gen John P. Jumper 2001 - Present	Dr. James G. Roche 2001 - Present

Sources: George M. Watson, Jr., *Secretaries and Chiefs of Staff of the United States Air Force: Biographical Sketches and Portraits* (Washington, D.C., 2001); Tamar A. Mehuron, ed., "The U.S. Air Force in Facts and Figures," *AIR FORCE Magazine* 77:5 (May 1994), p 27.

APPENDIX 7
AVIATION AWARDS, 1911-2000

ROBERT J. COLLIER TROPHY

Robert J. Collier, a prominent American publisher and aviator who was the first person to purchase an airplane from the Wright brothers for personal use, established the most prestigious award in American aviation. Originally known as the Aero Club of America Trophy, the award was first presented in 1911 to Glenn Curtiss. After Mr. Collier's death in 1918, the trophy was renamed in his honor. The Collier Trophy is currently awarded by the National Aeronautic Association to recognize the "greatest achievement in the performance, efficiency, and safety of air or space vehicles." The bronze trophy, designed by sculptor Ernest Wise Keyser, depicts man rising in triumph over gravity and other forces of nature. The original trophy weighs 525 pounds and is on permanent display at the National Air and Space Museum, Washington D.C., The name of each winner is engraved on the original, and each honoree receives a small replica of the trophy.

1911 **Glenn H. Curtiss**—development of the hydroplane

1912 **Glenn H. Curtiss**—development of the flying boat

1913 **Orville Wright**—development of the automatic stabilizer

1914 **Elmer A. Sperry**—development of gyroscopic control

1915 **W. Sterling Burgess**—development of the Burgess-Dunne hydroplane

1916 **Elmer A. Sperry**—development of the Sperry drift indicator

1917-1920 No awards presented on account of World War I

1921 **Grover C. Loening**—development of his aerial yacht

1922 **U.S. Air Mail Service**—providing a year's operation without a single fatal accident

1923 **U.S. Air Mail Service**—night flying in commercial transportation

1924 **U.S. Army Air Service**—first aerial flight around the world

1925 **Sylvanus Albert Reed**—development of the metal airplane propeller

1926 **Major Edward L. Hoffman, Engineering Division, McCook Field, U.S. Army Air Service**—development of the first practical parachute

1927 **Charles L. Lawrance**—development of radial, air-cooled aircraft engines

1928 **Aeronautics Branch, Department of Commerce**—development of airways and air navigation facilities

1929 **National Advisory Committee for Aeronautics**—development of cowling for radial, air-cooled engines

1930 **Harold F. Pitcairn and his associates**—development and application of the autogiro

1931 **Packard Motor Car Company**—development of the diesel aircraft engine

1932 **Glenn L. Martin**—development of a high-speed, weight-carrying airplane

1933 **Hamilton Standard Propeller Company and Frank Walker Caldwell, chief engineer**—development of a controllable pitch propeller

1934 **Captain A. F. Hegenberger, Materiel Division, Wright Field, U.S. Army Air Corps**—development of a successful, blind-landing system

1935 **Donald W. Douglas and his technical and production personnel**—development of an outstanding, twin-engine transport airplane

1936 **Pan American Airways**—establishment of the transpacific airplane and the successful execution of extended, over-water navigation

1937 **U. S. Army Air Corps**—development, construction, and equipage of the first successful, pressure-cabin airplane, the XC-35

1938 **Howard Hughes and his associates**—completion of their round-the-world flight in 91 hours 14 minutes

1939 **Airlines of the United States**—establishment of their safety record in air travel. Special recognition: Drs. Walter M. Boothby and W. Randolph Lovelace II, both of the Mayo Foundation for Medical Education and Research, and Captain Harry G. Armstrong, Wright Field, U.S. Army Air Corps, for their contributions "to this safety record through their work in aviation medicine in general and pilot fatigue in particular"

1940 **Dr. Sanford A. Moss and the U.S. Army Air Corps**—development of the turbosupercharger

1941 **U.S. Army Air Forces and the airlines of the United States**—"pioneering world-wide air transportation vital to immediate defense and ultimate victory" in World War II

1942 **General Henry H. Arnold, United States Army**—in recognition of his organization and leadership of the Army Air Forces

1943 **Captain Luis De Flores, U.S. Navy Reserve**—contributions to safe and rapid training of combat pilots and crews

1944 **General Carl A. Spaatz, U.S. Army Air Forces**—demonstration of the air power concept through employment of American aviation in the war against Germany

1945 **Dr. Luis W. Alvarez**—"for his conspicuous and outstanding initiative in the concept of, and his contribution to, the construction, adaptation and effective use of the ground-control approach system for safe landing of aircraft under all weather and traffic conditions"

1946 **Lewis A. Rodert, Chief of the Flight Research Branch at the Cleveland Laboratory of the National Advisory Committee for Aeronautics**—pioneering research and guidance in the development and practical application of a thermal ice-prevention system for aircraft

1947 **Captain Charles E. Yeager (U.S. Air Force), John Stack (National Advisory Committee for Aeronautics), and Lawrence D. Bell (Bell Aircraft Corporation)**—research, design and test work culminating in the first flight (in the Air Force's Bell X-1) to exceed the sound barrier, on October 14, 1947

1948 **The Radio Technical Commission for Aeronautics**—establishment of a guide plan for the development and implementation of a system of air navigation and traffic control to facilitate safe and unlimited aircraft operations under all weather conditions

1949 **William P. Lear**—development of the F-5 automatic pilot and automatic, approach-control-coupler system

1950 **The Helicopter Industry, the Military Services, and the U.S. Coast Guard**—development and use of rotary-wing aircraft for air rescue operations

1951 **John Stack and Associates at Langley Aeronautical Laboratory, National Advisory Committee for Aeronautics**—conception, development, and practical application of the transonic wind-tunnel throat

1952 **Leonard S. Hobbs of United Aircraft Corporation**—design, development, and production of the J57 jet engine

1953 **James H. Kindelberger**—development of the land-based, North American F-100 fighter
Edward H. Heinemann—development of the carrier-based, Douglas F4D

1954 **Richard Travis Whitcomb, National Advisory Committee for Aeronautics research scientist**—discovery and experimental verification of the area rule, a contribution that led to significantly higher airplane speeds and greater range with same power

1955 **General Nathan F. Twining, Air Research and Development Command, U.S. Air Force, and William M. Allen, Boeing**—development and operational use of America's first, all-jet, long-range bomber, the Boeing B-52 Stratofortress

1956 **Charles J. McCarthy and Associates of Chance-Vought Aircraft Incorporated and Vice Admiral James S. Russell & Associates of the U.S. Navy Bureau of Aeronautics**—conception, design, and development of the carrier-based F-8U fighter, the first operational aircraft capable of speeds exceeding 1,000 mph

1957 **Edward P. Curtis**—completion of his report "Aviation Facilities Planning," a dramatic advance in the field of long-range planning to meet the complex problems involved in aircraft using our air space

1958 **The U.S. Air Force and the Industry Team**—development of the F-104 interceptor. Special recognition: Clarence L. Johnson (Lockheed) for design of the airframe; Neil Burgess and Gerhard Neumann (Flight Propulsion Division, Wright Air Development Center); General Electric Company for development of the J79 turbojet engine; and U.S. Air Force pilots Major Howard Johnson and Captain Walter W. Irwin for establishing a world, land-plane altitude record of 91,243 feet and for establishing a world, straightaway speed record of 1,404.09 mph, respectively

1959 **U.S. Air Force, Convair Division of General Dynamics Corporation, and Space Technology Laboratories Inc.**—development, test, production, and deployment of the Atlas, America's first intercontinental ballistic missile "so vital to the security and space exploration needs of the United States and the free world"

1960 **Vice Admiral William F. Raborn, U.S. Navy**—"under whose direction the United States Navy, Science and Industry created the operational fleet ballistic missile weapon system, Polaris"

1961 **Major Robert M. White, U.S. Air Force; Joseph A. Walker, National Aeronautics and Space Administration; A. Scott Crossfield, North American Aviation; and Commander Forrest Petersen, U.S. Navy**—invaluable technological contributions to the advancement of flight and for great skill and courage as test pilots of the X-15

1962 **Lieutenant Commander Malcolm Scott Carpenter, U.S. Navy; Major L. Gordon Cooper, U.S. Air Force; Lieutenant Colonel John H. Glenn, Jr., U.S. Marine Corps; Major Virgil I. Grissom, U.S. Air Force; Commander Walter M. Schirra, Jr., U.S. Navy; Commander Alan B. Shepard, Jr., U.S. Navy; Major Donald K. Slayton, U.S. Air Force**—pioneering manned space flight in the United States

1963 **Clarence L. "Kelly" Johnson**—design and development of the U.S. Air Force A-11 Mach 3 aircraft

1964 **General Curtis E. LeMay, U.S. Air Force**—development of high-performance aircraft, missiles, and space systems, "which in 1964 significantly expanded the frontiers of American aeronautics and astronautics"

1965 **James E. Webb and Hugh L. Dryden**—representing all of the Gemini program teams which significantly advanced human experience in space flight

1966 **James S. McDonnell**—leadership and perseverance in advancing aeronautics and astronautics exemplified by the F-4 Phantom aircraft and the Gemini space vehicles

1967 **Lawrence A. Hyland**—"representing the Surveyor Program Team at Hughes Aircraft Company, the Jet Propulsion Laboratory, and associated organizations that put the eyes and hands of the United States on the Moon"

1968 **Colonel Frank Borman, U.S. Air Force; Captain James A. Lovell, Jr., U.S. Navy; and Lieutenant Colonel William A. Anders, U.S. Air Force, the crew of Apollo 8 and representing the entire United States space flight team**—successful and flawless execution of the first manned lunar orbit mission in history

1969 **Neil A. Armstrong, Colonel Edwin E. Aldrin, Jr., and Colonel Michael Collins, U.S. Air Force**—for the epic flight of Apollo 11 and the first landing of man on the surface of the moon, July 20, 1969

1970 **The Boeing Company, leader of the industry-airline-government team**—successful introduction of the 747 aircraft into commercial service, with particular recognition to Pratt & Whitney Division of United Aircraft Corporation and to Pan American World Airways

1971 **Colonel David R. Scott, Colonel James B. Irwin, and Lieutenant Colonel Alfred M. Worden, U.S. Air Force—**demonstration of superb skill and courage; and Dr. Robert T. Gilruth—as representative of the engineering genius of the manned space flight team, culminating in Apollo 15, man's most prolonged and scientifically productive lunar mission

1972 **The officers and men of the 7th Air Force and 8th Air Force of the U.S. Air Force and Task Force 77 of the U.S. Navy**—successful operation of Linebacker II missions, "the air campaign against North Vietnam in December 1972 which through precise, accurate, and determined attacks on key military targets in the face of unprecedented defenses, brought about a cease fire under terms which attained United States objectives in Southeast Asia"

1973 **The Skylab Program, with special recognition to William C. Schneider, program director, and the three Skylab astronaut crews**—proving beyond question the value of man in future explorations of space and the production of data of benefit to all the people on Earth

1974 **Dr. John F. Clark, National Aeronautics and Space Administration, and Daniel J. Fink, General Electric Company, representing the NASA/Industry Team responsible for the Earth Resources Technology Satellite Program, LANDSAT**—proving the value of U.S. space technology in the management of the Earth's resources and environment for the benefit of all mankind, with special recognition to Hughes Aircraft Company and RCA

1975 **David S. Lewis, General Dynamics Corporation, and the F-16 Air Force-Industry Team**—significant advancements in aviation technology leading to innovative fighter aircraft effectiveness

1976 **U.S. Air Force, Rockwell International Corporation, and the B-1 Industry Team—**successful design, development, management, and flight test of the B-1 strategic aircraft system

1977 **General Robert J. Dixon, commander, and the Tactical Air Command, U.S. Air Force**—development and implementation of Red Flag, an unprecedented combat-simulated, flight-training program for aircrews of the U.S. Armed Forces, a significant contribution to national defense

1978 **Sam B. Williams, chairman and president of Williams Research Corporation**—conception and development of the world's smallest, high-efficiency, turbofan engine, which was selected to power U.S. cruise missiles

1979 **Dr. Paul B. MacCready**—conception, design, and construction of the Gossamer Albatross, which made the first man-powered flight across the English Channel, with special recognition to Bryan Allen, the pilot

1980 **The Voyager Mission Team, represented by its chief scientist, Dr. Edward C. Stone**—for the spectacular fly-by of Saturn and the return of basic new knowledge of the solar system

1981 **National Aeronautics and Space Administration, Rockwell International, Martin Marietta, Thiokol, and the entire Government/Industrial Team**—improvement of the concept of manned, reusable spacecraft, with special recognition to astronauts John Young, Robert Crippen, Joe Engle, and Richard Truly

1982 **T. A. Wilson and the Boeing Company**—private development of two advanced technology transports, the 757 and the 767, with the support of the Federal Aviation Administration, industry and the airlines

1983 **U.S. Army, Hughes Aircraft Helicopters, and the Industry Team**—development of the AH-64A Apache advanced technology helicopter weapon system

1984 **National Aeronautics and Space Administration and Martin Marietta Corporation**—development of the NASA industry satellite-rescue team, and Astronaut Bruce McCandless, NASA's Charles E. Whitsett, Jr., and Martin Marietta's Walter W. Bollendonk

1985 **Russell W. Meyer, Cessna Aircraft Company, and Cessna's Line of Citation Business Jet Aircraft**—for an unparalleled passenger safety record during the past 14 years since the Citation's introduction

1986 **Jeana L. Yeager, Richard G. Rutan, Elbert L. Rutan, and the Voyager Aircraft Team of Volunteers**—ingenious design and development of the Voyager aircraft and skillful execution of the first nonstop, non-refueled flight around the world

1987 **National Aeronautics and Space Administration Lewis Research Center and the NASA/Industry Advanced Turboprop Team**—development of advanced turboprop-propulsion concepts for single-rotation, gearless-counter-rotation, and geared-counter rotation inducted fan systems

1988 **Rear Admiral Richard H. Truly, U.S. Navy**—for his assistance in the successful return of America to space

1989 **Mr. Benjamin R. Rich, Lockheed Aircraft Corporation, and the U.S. Air Force Team (Aeronautical Systems Division)**—development of the F-117A stealth aircraft

1990 **The Bell Boeing Team**—development of the V-22 Osprey Tiltrotor, the world's first large-scale, tiltrotor aircraft

1991 **The Northrop Corporation, the Industry Team, and the U.S. Air Force (Aeronautical Systems Division)**—design, development, production, and flight test of the B-2 aircraft, which has contributed significantly to America's enduring leadership in aerospace and the country's future national security

1992 **The Global Positioning System Team, the U.S. Air Force, the U.S. Naval Research Laboratory, the Aerospace Corporation, Rockwell International Corporation, and IBM Federal Systems Company**—development of the most significant, safe, and efficient navigation and surveillance of air and spacecraft since the introduction of radio navigation 50 years ago

1993 **The Hubble Space Telescope Recovery Team**—for outstanding leadership, intrepidity, and the renewal of public faith in America's space program by the successful orbital recovery and repair of the Hubble Space Telescope

1994 **U.S. Air Force, the McDonnell Douglas Corporation, the U.S. Army, and the C-17 Industrial Team of Subcontractors and Suppliers**—design, development, test, production, and deployment of the C-17 Globemaster III, whose performance and efficiency make it the most versatile airlift aircraft in aviation history

1995 **The Boeing Company and the 777 Team**—design, manufacture, and introduction into service of the world's most advanced, commercial airplane transport, the Boeing 777

1996 **Cessna Aircraft Company and the Citation X Design Team**—design, test, certification, and introduction into service of the Citation X, the first commercial aircraft in U.S. aviation history to achieve a cruising speed of Mach .92

1997 **Gulfstream Aerospace Corporation and the Gulfstream V Industry Team**—successful application of advanced design and efficient manufacturing techniques, together with innovative international business partnerships to place into customer service the Gulfstream V, the world's first ultra-long-range business jet

1998 **Lockheed Martin Corporation, General Electric Aircraft Engines, National Aeronautics and Space Administration, Air Combat Command of the U.S. Air Force, and the Defense Intelligence Agency**—design, manufacture, and operation of the U-2S/ER-2 high-altitude, all-weather, multi-functional, data-collection aircraft, which serves as America's "Sentinel of Peace" around the world

1999 **The Boeing Company, General Electric Aircraft Engines, Northrop Grumman Corporation, Raytheon Company, and the U.S. Navy**—design, manufacture, test, and deployment of the F/A-18E/F multi-mission strike fighter aircraft, the most capable and survivable carrier-based combat aircraft

2000 **Northrop Grumman Corporation, Rolls-Royce, Raytheon Company, L-3 Communications, U.S. Air Force, and the**

Defense Advanced Research Projects Agency—design, manufacture, test, and operation of Global Hawk, the first fully autonomous, operationally demonstrated, and most capable surveillance and reconnaissance unmanned aerial vehicle in the world

2001 **Pratt & Whitney, Rolls-Royce, Lockheed Martin Corporation, Northrop Grumman Corporation, BAE Systems, and the Joint Strike Fighter Program Office (U.S. Air Force)**—design, development, and demonstration of the Integrated Lift Fan Propulsion System, the next generation in aviation propulsion performance, efficiency and safety.

Sources: "Awards—Robert J. Collier Trophy," National Aeronautic Association, online at http://www.naa-usa.org/website/html/awardsset.html; "The Robert J. Collier Trophy," *AIR FORCE Magazine* 77:5 (May 1994), pp 110-111

CLARENCE M. MACKAY TROPHY

The Mackay Trophy is the oldest award presented exclusively to flying officers of the U.S. Air Force. Awarded annually by the National Aeronautic Association, it recognizes "the most meritorious flight of the year" by an Air Force person, persons, or organization. The award was created in 1912 by Clarence M. Mackay, a prominent American industrialist, philanthropist, and aviation enthusiast. The three-foot-tall silver trophy rests on a mahogany base and features four winged figures surrounding the cup, each holding a different pusher-type biplane. Winners' names are engraved onto silver shields affixed to the base. The trophy is now on permanent display at the National Air and Space Museum of the Smithsonian Institution, Washington, D.C. Each recipient of the Mackay Trophy receives an engraved gold medal to commemorate his achievement.

1912 **2nd Lieutenant Henry H. Arnold**

1913 **2nd Lieutenant Joseph E. Carberry and 2nd Lieutenant Fred Seydel**—reconnaissance

1914 **Captain Townsend F. Dodd and Lieutenant S. W. Fitzgerald**—reconnaissance

1915 **Lieutenant B. W. Jones**—American duration record during a one-man flight, 8 hours 53 minutes, San Diego, and a world's record for three men (two passengers) of 7 hours 5 minutes, San Diego

1916-1917 No Award Presented

1918 **Captain Edward V. Rickenbacker**—official record in bringing down 16 enemy aircraft

1919 **Lieutenant Belvin W. Maynard, Lieutenant Alexander Pearson, Jr., Lieutenant R. S. Worthington, Captain John O. Donaldson, Captain Lowell H. Smith, Lieutenant Colonel Harold E. Hartney, Lieutenant E. H. Manzelman, Lieutenant R. G. Bagby, Lieutenant D. B. Gish, Captain F. Steinle**—flights between the Atlantic and Pacific and return

1920 **Captain St. Clair Streett, 1st Lieutenant Clifford C. Nutt, 2nd Lieutenant Eric H. Nelson, 2nd Lieutenant C. H. Crumrine, 2nd Lieutenant Ross C. Kirkpatrick, Sergeant Edmond Henriques, Sergeant Albert T. Vierra, Sergeant Joe E. English**—flights to Nome, Alaska, and return

1921 **Lieutenant John A. Macready**—world altitude record of 34,509 feet flying a Fokker T-2

1922 **Lieutenant John A. Macready and Lieutenant Oakley G. Kelly**—world air endurance record, staying aloft for 36 hours 4 minutes 32 seconds

1923 **Lieutenant John A. Macready and Lieutenant Oakley G. Kelly**—first nonstop, transcontinental flight from New York to California at an average speed of 94 mph

1924 **Captain Lowell H. Smith, 1st Lieutenant Leslie P. Arnold, 1st Lieutenant Leigh Wade, 1st Lieutenant Eric H. Nelson, 2nd Lieutenant Henry H. Ogden**—first round-the-world flight

1925 **Lieutenant James H. Doolittle and Lieutenant Cyrus K. Bettis**—winners of the Schneider and Pulitzer races, respectively. Doolittle flew 232.573 mph in a seaplane.

1926 **Major Herbert A. Dargue, Captain Ira C. Eaker, Captain Arthur B. McDaniel, Captain C. F. Wolsey, 1st Lieutenant J. W. Benton, 1st Lieutenant Charles McRobinson, 1st Lieutenant Muir S. Fairchild, 1st Lieutenant Bernard S. Thompson, 1st Lieutenant Leonard D. Weddington, 1st Lieutenant Ennis C. Whitehead**—Pan-American Goodwill Flyers

1927 **Lieutenant Albert F. Hegenberger and Lieutenant Lester J. Maitland**—Hawaiian flight, June 28, 1927, in a Fokker C-2

1928 **Lieutenant Harry A. Sutton**—demonstration of quiet bravery, intelligence, skill, and spirit while performing spinning tests of observation planes

1929 **Captain A. W. Stevens**—demonstrated mastery of the upper air and his use of long-range photography

1930 **Major Ralph Royce**—"Arctic Patrol" flight of the 1st Pursuit Group from Selfridge Field, Michigan, to Spokane, Washington, and return in January 1930, during a period of extreme cold, snow, and other poor flying and operating conditions, which resulted in valuable information being gathered concerning airplanes, equipment, and the survival of flying personnel under severe, winter operating conditions.

1931 **Brigadier General Benjamin D. Foulois, commander of 1st Air Division (Provisional)**—approximately 40,000 hours total flight time without loss of life or serious injury to any participating personnel during exercises in May 1931

1932 **11th Bombardment Squadron of March Field, California, 1st Lieutenant Charles H. Howard, commanding officer**—air relief mission to the snowbound Navajo and Hopi Indian reservations in January

1933 **Captain Westside T. Larson**—pioneering flights in connection with the development of methods and procedure of Aerial Frontier Defense during the year 1933

1934 **Brigadier General Henry H. Arnold, commanding officer**—Alaskan Flight (from Bolling Field, D.C., to Fairbanks, Alaska) of 10 B-10 bombers

1935 **Captain A. W. Stevens and Captain O. A. Anderson**—world balloon record, stratosphere flight to 72,395 feet

1936 **Captain Richard E. Nugent, 1st Lieutenant Joseph A. Miller, 1st Lieutenant Edwin G. Simenson, 2nd Lieutenant William P. Ragsdale, Jr., 2nd Lieutenant Burton W. Armstrong, 2nd Lieutenant Herbert Morgan, Jr., Tech Sergeant Gilbert W. Olson, Staff Sergeant Howard M. Miller, Corporal Air Mechanic 2/c Frank B. Conner**—demonstration of expert instrument flying and navigation, and the will to overcome obstacles to accomplish their mission under exceptionally adverse weather conditions during a flight of three B-10s from Langley Field, Virginia, to Allegan, Michigan

1937 **Captain Carl J. Crane and Captain George V. Holloman**—successful development and demonstration flights of the automatic landing system

1938 **Lieutenant Colonel Robert Olds and the 2nd Bombardment Group of the Air Corps**—Goodwill flight to Buenos Aires, Argentina, and return

1939 **Major Caleb V. Haynes, Major William D. Old, Captain John A. Samford, Captain Richard S. Freeman, 1st Lieutenant Torgils G. Wold, Tech Sergeant William J. Heldt, Tech Sergeant Henry L. Hines, Tech Sergeant David L. Spicer, Staff Sergeant Russell E. Junior, Staff Sergeant James E. Sands, Master Sergeant Adolph Cattarius**—flight in the B-15 from Langley Field, Virginia, via Panama and Lima, Peru, at the request of the American Red Cross, for the purpose of placing without delay, urgently needed vaccines and other medical supplies in areas of Chile devastated by an earthquake. Elasped time: 40 hours 18 minutes; flying time: 29 hours 53 minutes; great circle distance: 4,933 statue miles

1940–1946 No Awards Presented

1947 **Captain Charles E. Yeager**—first supersonic flight in the Bell XS-1

1948 **Lieutenant Colonel Emil Beaudry**—rescue of 12 marooned airmen from the Greenland Icecap

1949 **Captain James G. Gallagher and flight crew of the Lucky Lady II**—first round-the-world, nonstop flight

1950 **27th Fighter Wing**—planning and executing the mission of Fox Able Three involving the movement of 180 jet fighter aircraft across the Atlantic

1951 **Colonel Fred J. Ascani**—establishment of a new world's record of 635.686 mph in the 100-kilometer, closed-course event at the National Air Races

1952 **Major Louis H. Carrington, Jr., Major Frederick W. Shook, Captain Wallace D. Yancey**—first nonstop, transpacific flight of a multi-engine RB-45 jet-bomber aircraft, a distance of 3,460 nautical miles in 9 hours 50 minutes, with two aerial refuelings

1953 **40th Air Division, Strategic Air Command**—deployment of 25 F-84G jet fighter aircraft, utilizing air refueling under adverse conditions, flying nonstop from the continental United States to bases in the United Kingdom and North Africa

1954 **308th Bombardment Wing (M), 38th Air Division, Strategic Air Command**—successful completion of a leapfrog intercontinental maneuver, a milestone in expanding and proving the combined operational capabilities of the B-47 bombardment aircraft and in determining fatigue limits of combat crews

1955 **Colonel Horace A. Hanes**—establishment of a world speed record of 822.135 mph in an F-100C aircraft at the National Air Show

1956 **Captain Iven C. Kincheloe, Jr., Air Research and Development Command, U.S. Air Force**—outstanding contributions to the science of aviation by flying the Bell X-2 aircraft to an altitude considerably higher than had ever been reached before in a piloted aircraft

1957 **93rd Bombardment Wing, Strategic Air Command**—execution of Operation Powerflight, the first jet, round-the-world, nonstop, record-breaking flight by three B-52 aircraft

1958 **Tactical Air Command's Air Strike Force, X-Ray Tango**—rapid and effective deployment to the troubled Far East during the fall of 1958

1959 **4520th Aerial Demonstration Team (U.S. Air Force Thunderbirds)**—Goodwill tour of the Far East

1960 **6593rd Test Squadron**—first aerial recovery of an object from space orbit

1961 **Lieutenant Colonel William R. Payne, Major William L. Polhemus, and Major Raymond R. Wagener, 43rd Bomb Wing, Strategic Air Command**—historic nonstop flight from Carswell Air Force Base, Texas, to Paris, France, which culminated in the establishment of two international speed records

1962 **Major Robert G. Sowers, Captain Robert MacDonald, and Captain John T. Walton**—the most meritorious flight of the year as members of the Strategic Air Command B-58 crew who established three transcontinental speed records

1963 **Crew of C-47 *Extol Pink*: Captain Warren P. Tomsett, Captain John R. Ordemann, Captain Donald R. Mack, Tech Sergeant Edsol P. Inlow, Staff Sergeant Jack E. Morgan, and Staff Sergeant Frank C. Barrett**—evacuation of wounded troops in Vietnam at night under enemy fire

1964 **464th Troop Carrier Wing, Tactical Air Command**—participation in the humanitarian airlift of some 1,500 hostages and refugees from rebel-held territory in the Republic of Congo during November 1964

1965 **YF-12A/SR-71 Test Force: Colonel Robert L. Stephens, Lieutenant Colonel Daniel Andre, Lieutenant Colonel Walter F. Daniel, Major Noel T. Warner, and Major James P. Cooney**—the most meritorious flight of the year in the YF-12A aircraft, which culminated in the establishment of nine new world speed and altitude records

1966 **Lieutenant Colonel Albert R. Howarth**—demonstration of exemplary courage and airmanship as a pilot in a combat strike mission in Southeast Asia under the most hazardous conditions of darkness and intense enemy fire

1967 **Major John J. Casteel, Captain Dean L. Hoar, Captain Richard L. Trail, and Master Sergeant Nathan C. Campbell, Strategic Air Command**—demonstration of exemplary courage and outstanding aerial accomplishments by performing the first multiple aerial refueling between a KC-135 aircraft and an A-3 Navy tanker which simultaneously refueled a Navy F-8 Crusader under emergency fuel shortages and combat conditions

1968 **Lieutenant Colonel Daryl D. Cole**—demonstration of conspicuous gallantry as a C-130 pilot in the emergency evacuation of personnel in the Republic of Vietnam

1969 **49th Tactical Fighter Wing**—flawless deployment of 72 F-4D aircraft from Spangdahlem Air Base, Germany, to Holloman Air Force Base, New Mexico, without a single abort, completing 504 successful aerial refuelings on the 5,000-mile trip

1970 **Captain Alan D. Milacek, Captain James A. Russell, Captain Roger E. Clancy, Captain Ronald C. Jones, Captain Brent C. O'Brien, Tech Sergeant Albert A. Nash, Staff Sergeant Adolfo Lopez, Jr., Staff Sergeant Ronald R. Wilson, Sergeant Kenneth E. Firestone, and Airman First Class Donnell H. Cofer**—demonstration of valor and perseverance in accomplishing a vital mission and returning their aircraft to its base despite severe damage.

1971 **Lieutenant Colonel Thomas B. Estes and Major Dewain C. Vick**—operation of the SR-71 aircraft that established new world records for duration and distance covered, thereby proving the extended, supersonic, reconnaissance capability of this aircraft

1972 **Captain Richard S. Ritchie, Captain Charles B. DeBellevue, and Captain Jeffrey S. Feinstein**—demonstration of extraordinary gallantry, superb airmanship, and intrepidity in the face of the enemy

1973 **Operation Homecoming, Military Airlift Command aircrews**—demonstration of diligent and dynamic efforts during the return of the prisoners of war to United States control

1974 **Major Roger J. Smith, Major David W. Peterson, and Major Willard R. MacFarlane**—extraordinary achievement while participating in aerial flight as F-15 Advanced Tactical Fighter test pilots during Operation Streak Eagle, during which time eight world-class, time-to-climb records were established

1975 **Major Robert W. Undorf**—demonstration of conspicuous gallantry, initiative, and resourcefulness during the joint military operation to rescue and ensure the return of the SS *Mayguez* crew from an opposing armed force on Koh Tang, an island in the Gulf of Thailand

1976 **Captain James W. Yule**—demonstration of gallantry and unusual presence of mind while participating in a flight as an instructor pilot of a B-52D aircraft

1977 **Captain David M. Sprinkel and crew of C-5 Aircrew Mission AAM 1962-01, composed of members from the 436th Military Airlift Wing and the 512th Military Airlift Wing**—completion of the airlift of a large, super-conducting electromagnet, support equipment, and personnel in support of the joint United States-Soviet energy research program

1978 **Members of C-5 Aircrew Mission AM 770021: Lieutenant Colonel Robert F. Schultz and crew, and Captain Todd H. Hohberger and crew, members from the 436th Military Airlift Wing**—conduct of a historic flight into Africa, the first C-5 airlift mission in support of the free world effort against rebel forces in Zaire

1979 **Major James E. McArdle, Jr.**—demonstration of professional competence and aerial skill in rescuing 28 Taiwanese seamen from a sinking cargo ship

1980 **Crews S-21 and S-31, 644th Bombardment Squadron, Strategic Air Command**—executing a nonstop, round-the world mission with the immediate objective of locating and photographing elements of the Soviet Navy operating in the Arabian Gulf

1981 **Captain John J. Walters**—demonstration of extraordinary achievement while participating in aerial flight as HH-3 helicopter commander in the rescue of 61 persons, in adverse conditions, from the burning cruise ship *Prinsendam*

1982 **B-52 Crew E-21, Strategic Air Command: Captain Richard L. Cavendish, 2nd Lieutenant Frank A. Boyle, Captain Ronald D. Nass, 1st Lieutenant James D. Gray, 1st Lieutenant Michael J. Connor, Tech Sergeant Ronald B. Wright, and 1st Lieutenant Gerald E. Valentini**—successful landing of their crippled B-52, under almost impossible conditions, thereby saving their lives and a valuable aircraft

1983 **KC-135A Crew E-113, Strategic Air Command: Captain Robert J. Goodman, Captain Michael F. Clover, Captain Karol F. Wojcikowski, and SSgt Douglas D. Simmons**—demonstration of outstanding achievement while on a routine aerial refueling mission involving an F-4E aircraft, saving a valuable aircraft from destruction and its crew from possible death

1984 **Lieutenant Colonel James L. Hobson, Jr.**—aircraft commander of the lead MC-130E during the Grenada rescue mission

1985 **Lieutenant Colonel David E. Faught**—demonstration of heroism and outstanding airmanship thus saving the lives of eight crewmembers and preventing the loss of an irreplaceable aircraft

1986 **Captain Marc D. Felman, Captain Thomas M. Ferguson, Master Sergeant Clarence Bridges, Jr., Master Sergeant Patrick S. Kennedy, Master Sergeant Gerald G. Treadwell, Tech Sergeant Lester G. Bouler, Tech Sergeant Gerald M. Lewis, Staff Sergeant Samuel S. Flores, Staff Sergeant Scott A. Helms, and Staff Sergeant Gary L. Smith**—flawless demonstration of the impressive capabilities and outstanding professionalism of the U.S. Air Force during an unprecedented and highly demanding mission to the nuclear test site at Semipalatinsk, Soviet Central Asia

1987 **Detachment 15, Air Force Plant Representative Office, and the B-1B System Program Office, Aeronautical Systems Division, Air Force Systems Command**

1988 **Military Airlift Wing C-5 Crew, Military Airlift Command**

1989 **B-1B Crew, 96th Bombardment Wing: Captain Jeffrey K. Beene, Captain Vernon B. Benton, Lieutenant Colonel Joseph G. Day, and Captain Robert H. Hendricks**—completion of the first-ever, gear-up emergency landing of a B-1B aircraft

1990 **Crew of AC-130H, mission #1J1600GA354, 16th Special Operations Squadron, Air Force Special Operations Command**—demonstration of airmanship and outstanding professionalism during an aerial flight over the Republic of Panama during Operation Just Cause

1991 **MH-53J Pave Low Crew, 20th Special Operations Squadron, Hurlburt Field, Florida, Air Force Special Operations Command: Captain Thomas J. Trask, Major Michael Homan, Master Sergeant Timothy B. Hadrych, Tech Sergeant Gregory Vanhyning, Tech Sergeant James A. Peterson, Jr., Staff Sergeant Craig Dock, and Sergeant Thomas W. Bedard**—demonstration of extraordinary heroism and self-sacrifice during the rescue of a downed, U.S. Navy F-14 pilot in Iraq

1992 **C-130 Aircrew, 310th Airlift Squadron, Howard Air Force Base, Panama, Air Combat Command: Captain Peter B. Eunice, Captain Daniel G. Sobel, Captain Robert K. Stich, Major Christopher J. Duncan, Master Sergeant Joseph C. Beard, Jr., Master Sergeant Carl V. Wilson, Tech Sergeant John H. Armintrout, Tech Sergeant Charles G. Bolden, Tech Sergeant Rory E. Calhoun, Tech Sergeant Ray A. Fisher, Tech Sergeant Peter J. Paquette, Tech Sergeant Andrew W. Toth, Tech Sergeant Darren R. Tresler, and Staff Sergeant Ronald P. Hetzel**—demonstration of extraordinary resourcefulness and unusual presence of mind during an unprovoked attack in international airspace

1993 **Crew E-21, 668th Bomb Squadron, Griffiss Air Force Base, New York: Captain Jeffrey R. Swegel, Major Peter B. Mapes, Captain Charles W. Patnaude, Lieutenant Glen J. Caneel, and Captain Joseph D. Rosmarin**—demonstration of quick thinking, immediate reaction, and astute situational awareness enabling them to return a crippled B-52 aircraft to stable flight and safe landing

1994 **Crew of Air Force Rescue 206: Captain John W. Blumentritt, Captain Gary W. Henderson, Senior Airman Jeffrey M. Frembling, Staff Sergeant Matthew A. Wells, and Senior Airman Jesse W. Goerz; Crew of Air Force Rescue 208: Lieutenant Colonel James A. Sills, Lieutenant Colonel Gary L. Copsey, Lieutenant Richard E. Assaf, Tech Sergeant Gregory M. Reed, and Senior Airman William R. Payne**—demonstration of extraordinary heroism and self-sacrifice during the rescue of six Icelandic sailors who were stranded when their ship foundered in heavy seas and strong winds

1995 **Crew of BAT-01: Lieutenant Colonel Doug Raaberg, Captain Gerald Goodfellow, Captain Kevin Clotfelter, Captain Rick Carver, Captain Chris Stewart, Captain Steve Adams, Captain Kevin Houdek, and Captain Steve Reeves**—conduct of the history-breaking, aerial achievement flight of the decade demonstrating the B-1B's Global Power combat capability with live bombing activity at three bombing ranges on three continents in two hemispheres

1996 **Crew of Duke 01 Flight**—performance of the first combat employment of the B-52H in history

1997 **Crew of Whick-05: Lieutenant Colonel Frank J. Kisner, Major (Dr.) Robert S. Michaelson, Captain John C. Baker, Captain Reed Foster, Captain Mark J. Ramsey, Captain Robert P. Toth, Master Sergeant Gordon H. Scott, Tech Sergeant Tom L. Baker, Staff Sergeant John D. Hensdill, and Staff Sergeant Jeffrey A. Hoyt**—overcoming hostile gunfire, three heavyweight aerial refuelings, and over 13 hours flying 3,179 nautical miles to their objective to insert a European Survey and Assessment Team and extract 56 people from the carnage and wanton violence in Brassaville, Republic of Congo, achieving this goal while on the ground for less than 23 minutes

1998 **Crew of Air Force Rescue 470**—conduct of a daring, mountaintop rescue of six survivors trapped inside an airplane that had crashed on a glacier during a near-zero visibility approach in winds gusting to 45 knots

1999 **Captain Jeffrey G. J. Hwang**—in recognition of an exceptionally meritorious F-15C flight during combat operations in support of Operation Allied Force when he simultaneously destroyed two enemy aircraft during a single intercept

2000 **E10E1 Mission: Lieutenant Colonel Marlon Nailling, Major John Andrus, Major Kathryn Drake, Major David Sellars, Captain Richard Hunt, Captain Kevin Keith, Captain Karey Dufour, Captain Karin Petersen, Captain Donna Fournier, 1st Lieutenant Lucas Jobe, Staff Sergeant Edward Franceschina, Staff Sergeant Heather Robertson, Staff Sergeant Bradley Atherton, Staff Sergeant Ryan Reller, Senior Airman Chad Schusko, and Staff Sergeant Brian Hoffmeyer**

E10E2 Mission: Colonel Byron Hepburn, Lieutenant Colonel Linda Torrens, Major Jonas Allman, Major Thomas Jenkins, Major Lola Casby, Major Jeffrey Davis, Captain Raymond Chehy, Captain Natalie Sykes, Captain Michael Smith, Captain Tim Carter, 1st Lieutenant Jennifer Bagozzi, Staff Sergeant Alan Wooldridge, Staff Sergeant Kelly Pollard, Staff Sergeant Trent Arnold, Staff Sergeant Juan Garza, Senior Airman Anna Duffner

Critical Care Air Transport Team: Colonel David Welling, Captain Raymond M. Nudo, Captain Andrew J. Reynolds, Captain Bernd T. Wegner, Staff Sergeant Chyrise M. Jenkins, Staff Sergeant Christopher E. Whited, U.S. Air Force; and Major Stephan A. Alkins, U.S. Army

2001 **20th Special Operations Squadron KNIFE 04**

Sources: "Awards—Clarence M. Mackay Trophy," National Aeronautic Association online at http://www.naa-usa.org/website/html/awardsset.html; "The Mackay Trophy," *AIR FORCE Magazine* 77:5 (May 1994), pp 112-113.

DAEDALIAN WEAPON SYSTEM AWARD
COLONEL FRANKLIN C. WOLFE MEMORIAL TROPHY

The Order of Daedalians was founded in 1934 to honor aviators who served in World War I. The Daedalian Foundation now recognizes excellence in all areas of aviation with numerous awards and scholarships. The Daedalian Weapon System Award, one of 18 Daedalian Awards, was first presented in 1970 by Colonel Franklin C. Wolfe, who served as assistant chief and then chief of the Armament Laboratory of the Army Air Forces Materiel Command at Wright Field from 1939 until 1944. It is presented annually, in turn, to organizations in the Air Force, Army, and Navy for development of the most outstanding weapon system operating, in whole or in part, in the aerospace environment. The Daedalian Weapon System Award is a large silver cup featuring the emblem of the Order of Daedalians. The original Daedalian Trophy resides at Daedalian headquarters in San Antonio, Texas, and each honoree receives a small replica copy. Air Force awardees of the Daedalian Trophy are listed below.

1972 AGM-65 Maverick Missile Program Office, Aeronautical Systems Division, Wright-Patterson Air Force Base, Ohio

1975 F-15 System Program Office, Aeronautical Systems Division, Wright-Patterson Air Force Base, Ohio

1978 F-16 System Program Office, Aeronautical Systems Division, Wright-Patterson Air Force Base, Ohio

1981 Air-Launched Cruise Missile and B-52 Offensive Avionics System/Cruise Missile Integration programs, Strategic Systems Program Office, Aeronautical Systems Division, Wright-Patterson Air Force Base, Ohio

1984 B-1B System Program Office, Aeronautical Systems Division, Wright-Patterson Air Force Base, Ohio

1987 Low Altitude Navigation & Targeting Infrared system for Night (LANTIRN) Program Office, Aeronautical Systems Division, Wright Patterson Air Force Base, Ohio

1990 B-2 Weapon System Team, Aeronautical Systems Division, Wright-Patterson Air Force Base, Ohio

1993 Joint STARS, U.S. Air Force

1996 C-17 System Program Office, Aeronautical Systems Center, Wright-Patterson Air Force Base, Ohio

1999 F-22 System Program Office, Aeronautical Systems Center, Wright-Patterson Air Force Base, Ohio

THEODORE VON KARMAN AWARD
AERONAUTICAL SYSTEMS CENTER AWARD WINNERS

The Theodore von Karman Award is named for the renowned Hungarian-American aerodynamacist and visionary strategic planner who, together with General Henry H. "Hap" Arnold, forged modern Air Force research and development. In 1945 he completed two landmark studies, *Where We Stand* and *Toward New Horizons: Science, the Key to Air Supremacy*, in which he analyzed air power during the World War II era, assessed current technology, and provided a roadmap for aerospace development in the postwar era. The von Karman Award is now presented yearly by the Air Force Association to honor the most outstanding contribution to national defense in the field of science and engineering. Six Aeronautical Systems Center personnel and organizations have been honored with the award.

1971 **Mr. Fred D. Orazio, Sr., scientific director, Aeronautical Systems Division**—distinguished service in the field of aerospace science and engineering

1982 **Aeronautical Systems Division and its more than 8,000 personnel**—development, test, and procurement of Air Force aircraft, simulators, and related subsystems

1986 **Lieutenant General Thomas H. McMullen, U.S. Air Force, Retired** —leadership as commander of Aeronautical Systems Division

1987 **Advanced Fighter Technology Integration (AFTI)/F-16 Program**—dramatic demonstration of new combat capabilities achievable through a highly automated and integrated weapon system

1990 **B-2 Test Team**—test and evaluation of the B-2 design, validating 10 years of simulation and ground testing

1994 **B-2 System Program Office, Oklahoma Air Logistics Center, B-2 Combined Test Force, Air Force Flight Test Center, Site Activation Task Force, and the B-2 Mission Planning System Development Office**—management of the B-2 stealth bomber program, surpassing sustainability goals, and dramatically improving production efficiency and schedules

GLOSSARY

GLOSSARY

A

A	Ambulance airplane
	Amphibian
	Attack airplane
	Tactical support airplane
A-76	Outsourcing
AAC	Air Armament Center
	Army Air Corps
AAF	Army Air Forces
AAFIT	Army Air Forces Institute of Technology
AAFTB	Army Air Forces Technical Base
AAHS	American Aviation Historical Society
AAM	Air-to-Air Missile
ABC/M	Activity Based Costing and Management
ABM	Antiballistic Missile
ABRV	Advanced Ballistic Reentry Vehicle
ABW	Air Base Wing
ACC	Air Combat Command
ACES	Advanced Concept Ejection Seat
ACM	Advanced Cruise Missile
ACTD	Advanced Concept Technology Demonstration
ADD	Air Documents Division
ADP	Advanced Development Project
AEC	Atomic Energy Commission
AEDC	Arnold Engineering Development Center
AF	Air Force
AFB	Air Force Base
AFBMD	Air Force Ballistic Missile Division
AFFTC	Air Force Flight Test Center
AFGS	Air Force Guide Specifications
AFIT	Air Force Institute of Technology
AFLC	Air Force Logistics Command
AFMC	Air Force Materiel Command
AFMC/ST	Air Force Materiel Command, Director of Science and Technology
AFOG	Orientation Group, United States Air Force
AFOSR	Air Force Office of Scientific Research
AFOTEC	Air Force Operational Test and Evaluation Center
AFP	Air Force Pamphlet
AFRD	Air Force Research Division
AFRL	Air Force Research Laboratory
AFRL/HE	Air Force Research Laboratory, Human Effectiveness Directorate
AFRL/ML	Air Force Research Laboratory, Materials and Manufacturing Directorate
AFRL/PR	Air Force Research Laboratory, Propulsion Directorate
AFRL/VA	Air Force Research Laboratory, Air Vehicles Directorate
AFSAC	Air Force Security Assistance Center
AFSARC	Air Force Systems Acquisition Review Council
AFSC	Air Force Systems Command
AFSC/DL	Air Force Systems Command, Director of Laboratories
AFTB	Air Force Technical Base
AFTEC	Air Force Test and Evaluation Center
AFTI	Advanced Fighter Technology Integration
AFWAL	Air Force Wright Aeronautical Laboratories
AGARD	Advisory Group for Aerospace Research and Development
AGM	Air-to-Ground Missile
AIAA	American Institute of Aeronautics and Astronautics
ALC	Acquisition Logistics Center
	Air Logistics Center
ALCM	Air-Launched Cruise Missile
ALD	Acquisition Logistics Division
AlGaAs	Aluminum gallium arsenide
ALSS	Advanced Location Strike System
AMC	Air Materiel Command
	Air Mobility Command
AMD	Aerospace Medical Division
AMRAAM	Advanced Medium-Range Air-to-Air Missile
AMRL	Armstrong Aeromedical Research Laboratory
AMSA	Advanced Manned Strategic Aircraft
AMST	Advanced Medium Short Takeoff and Landing Transport
ANP	Aircraft Nuclear Propulsion
AO	Two-seat Army/Coast Guard Artillery Observation Airplane
APSI	Advanced Propulsion Subsystems Integration
APU	Auxiliary Power Unit
ARDC	Air Research and Development Command
ARL	Aeronautical Research Laboratory
	Aerospace Research Laboratories
ARM	Anti-Radiation Missile
ARPV	Advanced Remotely Piloted Vehicle
AS	Air Service
ASARS	Advanced Synthetic Aperture Radar
ASB	Deputy for Development Planning
ASC	Air Service Command
	Aeronautical Systems Center
ASC/HO	Aeronautical Systems Center History Office
ASC/XP	Aeronautical Systems Center Plans and Programs Directorate
ASC/XR	Aeronautical Systems Center Development Planning Directorate
ASD	Aeronautical Systems Division
ASD/EN	Aeronautical Systems Division, Deputy for Engineering
ASD/XR	Aeronautical Systems Division, Deputy for Development Planning
ASIP	Aircraft Structural Integrity Program
ASPA	Advanced Strategic Penetrating Aircraft
AT	Advanced Training airplane
ATB	Advanced Technology Bomber
ATC	Advanced Technology Council
ATCA	Advanced Tanker Cargo Aircraft
ATD	Advanced Technology Demonstration
ATEGG	Advanced Turbine Engine Gas Generator
ATF	Advanced Tactical Fighter
ATH	Autonomous Terminal Homing
ATRAN	Automatic Terrain Recognition and Navigation
ATSC	Air Technical Service Command
ATTLA	Air Transportability Test Loading Agency

Avionics	Aviation electronics
AVIP	Avionics Integrity Program
AWACS	Airborne Warning and Control System

B

B	Bomber airplane
BAP	Bureau of Aircraft Production
BC	Basic Combat
Bionics	Biology and Avionics
BLR	Bomber, Long Range
Bomarc	Boeing and the Michigan Aeronautical Research Center
BSD	Ballistic Systems Division
BT	Basic Trainer airplane

C

C	Carbon
	Cargo airplane
	Transport
C2	Command and Control
CALCM	Conventional Air-Launched Cruise Missile
CAST	Cast Aluminum Structures Technology
CBS	Columbia Broadcasting System
CCD	Charge-Coupled Device
CCV	Control-Configured-Vehicle
CEO	Chief Executive Officer
CFD	Computational Fluid Dynamics
CG	Transport Glider
CGS	Common Ground Segment
CIA	Central Intelligence Agency
CIM	Computer Integrated Manufacturing
CMAG	Cruise Missile Advanced Guidance
CMI	Cruise Missile Integration
CMOS	Complementary Metal Oxide Semiconductor
CMUP	Conventional Mission Upgrade Program
CO	Carbon monoxide
	Two-seat Corps Observation airplane
	Commanding Officer
COA	Corps Observation, Amphibian
COMINT	Communications Intelligence
COO	Chief Operating Officer
COTS	Commercial-Off-The-Shelf
CRT	Cathode Ray Tubes
CX-HLS	Cargo Experimental-Heavy Logistics System

D

D	Drone director
DAC	Designated Acquisition Commander
DAE	Defense Acquisition Executive
DAIP	Defense Acquisition Improvement Program
DAIS	Digital Avionics Information System
DAMS	Defensive Anti-Missile Subsystem
DARPA	Defense Advanced Research Projects Agency
DB	Two-seat Day Bomber
DC	Douglas Commercial
DCS	Deputy Chief of Staff
DES	Dynamic Environmental Simulator
DH	DeHavilland airplane, i.e., DH-4
DIGITAC	Digital Tactical Aircraft Control
DMA	Division of Military Aeronautics
DMMF	Developmental Manufacturing and Modification Facility
DMR	Defense Management Review
DMRD	Defense Management Review Decision
DMSP	Defense Meteorological Satellite Program
DMT	Distributed Mission Training
DOD	Department of Defense
DOT	Department of Transportation
DRF	Dual Role Fighter
DSARC	Defense Systems Acquisition Review Council
DSP	Defense Support Program

E

E	Electronic surveillance airplane
ECM	Electronic Countermeasures
EHF	Extremely High-Frequency
EIRT	Executive Independent Review Team
ELINT	Electronic Intelligence
EMR	Electromagnetic Reconnaissance System
EN	Engineering
ENA	Avionics Engineering Division
ENF	Flight Systems Engineering Division
ENM	Modeling, Simulation, and Analysis Division
ENO	Engineering Operations and Support Division
ENS	Systems Engineering Division
ENSIP	Engine Structural Integrity Program
ENV	Acquisition Environmental, Safety, and Health Division
EO	Electro-Optical
ESC	Electronic Systems Center

F

F	Fighter airplane
	Photographic airplane
FAA	Federal Aviation Administration
FAC	Forward Air Control
FAD	Fairfield Air Depot
FADR	Fairfield Air Depot Reservation
FBL	Fly-by-light
FDL	Flight Dynamics Laboratory
FEAF	Far East Air Force
FFAR	Folding Fin Air Rocket
Ficon	Fighter Conveyor
FLIR	Forward-Looking Infrared
FM	Fighter, Multi-place
FOUO	For Official Use Only
FYDP	Five-Year Defense Program

G

G	Autogiro airplane
	Glider
	Gyroplane
	Permanently Grounded
GA	Two-seat Ground Attack airplane
GaAs	Gallium arsenide
GALCIT	Guggenheim Aeronautical Laboratory of the California Institute of Technology
GAM	Ground-to-Air Missile
GaN	Gallium nitride
GAO	General Accounting Office

GAR	Ground-to-Air Rocket
GAX	Ground Attack experimental airplane
GBU	Guided Bomb Unit
GCAS	Ground Collision Avoidance System
GE	General Electric
GEBO	Generalized Bomber [Studies]
GHQ	General Headquarters
GLCM	Ground-Launched Cruise Missile
GMB	Glenn Martin Bomber
GOCO	Government-Owned, Contractor-Operated
GPS	Global Positioning System
	Global Positioning Satellite

H

H	Helicopter
	Search and Rescue
HAE	High Altitude Endurance
HAHST	High Altitude High Speed Target
HALE	High Altitude Long Endurance
HARM	High Speed Anti-Radiation Missile
HB	Heavy Bomber
HBT	Heterojunction bipolar transistor
HEMT	High-electron mobility transistor
HgCdTe	Mercury Cadmium Telluride
HMTT	Hurricane Mesa Test Track
HO	History Office
HOL	Higher Order Language
HPTET	High Performance Turbine Engine Technology
HQ	Headquarters
HSC	Human Systems Center
HSW	Human Systems Wing
HVAR	High Velocity Aircraft Rocket

I

IC	Integrated Circuit
ICAM	Integrated Computer Aided Manufacturing
ICBM	Intercontinental Ballistic Missile
ICNIA	Integrated Communication-Navigation-Identification Avionics
IHPTET	Integrated High Performance Turbine Engine Technology
IL	Two-seat Infantry Liaison airplane
IMPATT	Impact Ionization Avalanche Transit Time
INEWS	Integrated Electronic Warfare System
INF	Intermediate-Range Nuclear Forces
InP	Indium Phosphide
IPD	Integrated Product Development
IPT	Integrated Product Team
IR	Infrared
IRADS	Infrared Acquisition and Designation System
IRBM	Intermediate Range Ballistic Missile
IRCM	Infrared Countermeasures
IRT	Independent Review Team
ISA	Instruction set architecture
ITB	Integrated Test Bed
IWSM	Integrated Weapon System Management

J

J	Temporary special tests
JACG	Joint Aeronautical Commander's Group
JAFE	Joint Advanced Fighter Engine
JASSM	Joint Air to Surface Standoff Missile
JAST	Joint Advanced Strike Technology
JCMPO	Joint Cruise Missile Program Office
JDAM	Joint Direct Attack Munitions
JIAWG	Joint Integrated Avionics Working Group
JORD	Joint Operational Requirements Document
JPATS	Joint Primary Aircraft Training System
JPO	Joint Project Office
JSCMPO	Joint Service Cruise Missile Program Office
JSF	Joint Strike Fighter
JSSG	Joint Service Specification Guides
JTDE	Joint Technology Demonstrator Engine
JVX	Joint VTOL Experimental

K

K	Tanker
KB	Bomber modified as aerial tanker

L

L	Liaison airplane
LAMARS	Large Amplitude Multimode Aerospace Research Simulator
LAMBS	Large Aircraft Multiband Source
LANDSAT	Land Remote Sensing Satellite
LANTIRN	Low-Altitude Navigation and Targeting Infrared system for Night
LB	Light Bomber
LHMEL	Laser Hardened Materials Evaluation Laboratory
LIFE	Laser Infrared Flight Experiment
LTV	Ling-Temco-Vought
LUSAC	LePere United States Army Combat [aircraft], i.e. LUSAC-11
Lusty	Luftwaffe Secret Technology
LWF	Lightweight Fighter

M

M	Messenger
	Special Operations
	Missile
MAC	Military Airlift Command
MAG	Mission Area Group
MAGNA	Materially and Geometrically Nonlinear Analysis
MAP	Military Assistance Program
MARS	Mid-Air Retrieval System
MAT	Messenger, Aerial Torpedo
MATS	Military Air Transport Service
MAW	Mission Adaptive Wing
MBE	Molecular Beam Epitaxy
MDS	Mission Design Series
MEA	More Electric Aircraft
MED	Manhattan Engineering District
	Minimum Engineering Development
MERA	Molecular Electronics for Radar Applications
MESFET	Metal Semiconductor, Field-Effect Transistor
MIL-STD	Military standards
MIMIC	Microwave and Millimeter Wave Integrated Circuit
	Microwave and Millimeter Wave Monolithic Integrated Circuit

MIRA	Multi-function Inertial Reference Assembly
MIT	Massachusetts Institute of Technology
MLG	Main Landing Gear
MNO	Metal-nitride-oxide
MSD	Munitions Systems Division
MTC	Mission Training Center
MTD	Maneuver Technology Demonstrator

N

N	Permanent special tests
NACA	National Advisory Committee for Aeronautics
NAIC	National Air Intelligence Center
NARA	National Archives & Records Administration
NASA	National Aeronautics and Space Administration
NASP	National Aerospace Plane
NASTC	National Aerospace Systems and Technology Conference
NATO	North Atlantic Treaty Organization
NBL	Multi-seat Night Bomber—Long Distance
NBS	Multi-seat Night Bomber—Short Distance
	National Bureau of Standards
NCR	The National Cash Register Company
n.d.	No date
NDRC	National Defense Research Council
NEPA	Nuclear Energy for the Propulsion of Aircraft
NETF	Nuclear Engineering Test Facility
NGT	Next Generation Trainer
NiCd	Nickel-Cadmium
NLO	Nonlinear-Optical
NO	Two-seat Night Observation airplane
NRL	Naval Research Laboratory
NTA	Nuclear Test Aircraft
NTSB	National Transportation Safety Board
NVIS	Night-Vision Imaging System

O

O	Observation, Corps and Army airplane
OA	Observation, Amphibian airplane
OAR	Office of Aerospace Research
	Office of Air Research
OAS	Offensive Avionics System
O.D.	Olive Drab
OLR	Observation, Long Range airplane
OMB	Office of Management and Budget
OSA	Operational Support Aircraft
OSRD	Office of Scientific Research and Development
OSU	Ohio State University
OT&E	Operational Test and Evaluation

P

P	Patrol airplane
	Pursuit, mono-place airplane
P&W	Pratt & Whitney
PA	Pursuit, air-cooled engine
Pace	Progressive Avionics Concept Evaluation
PB	Pursuit, Biplace airplane
PEO	Program Executive Officer
PG	Single-seat Pursuit, Ground attack
PLSS	Precision Location Strike System
PM	Program Manager
PMRT	Program Management Responsibility Transfer
PN	Single-seat Pursuit, Night attack
PPBS	Planning, Programming, and Budgeting System
PS	Pursuit, special alert
PSO	Product Support Office
PT	Primary Trainer airplane
PW	Single-seat Pursuit airplane with Water-cooled engine

Q

Q	Aerial target
	Radio-controlled drone

R

R	Racer
	Reconnaissance
	Rocket
	Rotary Wing
R&D	Research and Development
RAF	Royal Air Force
RADCAP	R&D Contributions to Avionics Progress
RAND	Research and Development
RASSR	Reliable Advanced Solid State Radar
RCS	Radar Cross-Section
RDT&E	Research, Development, Test, and Evaluation
RENT	Reentry Nose Tip
RF	Radio Frequency
RFP	Request for Proposals
RIF	Reduction-in-Force
RPV	Remotely Piloted Vehicle
RTD	Research and Technology Division

S

S	Anti-submarine
	Seaplane
S&E	Science & Engineering
S&T	Science & Technology
SAAD	San Antonio Air Depot
SAB	Scientific Advisory Board
SAC	Strategic Air Command
SAD	Sacramento Air Depot
SAE	Service Acquisition Executive
SAG	Scientific Advisory Group
SAGE	Semi-Automatic Ground Environment
SAM	Surface-to-Air Missile
SAMSO	Space and Missile Systems Organization
SAMU	Systems Acquisition Mission Unit
SARL	Subsonic Aerodynamic Research Laboratory
SCAD	Subsonic Cruise Armed Decoy
SCAM	Subsonic Cruise Attack Missile
SCUD	Subsonic Cruise Unarmed Decoy (U.S.-made)
Scud	SS-1 (Surface-to-Surface) Ballistic Missile (Soviet-made)
SEAD	Suppression of Enemy Air Defenses
SEG	Systems Engineering Group
SENTAR	Senior Engineering Technical Assessment Review
SES	Systems Engineering Group, Directorate of Studies and Analyses
SiC	Silicon carbide

SIGINT	Signals Intelligence
SIMAF	Simulation and Analysis Facility
SLBM	Submarine-Launched Ballistic Missile
SLCM	Sea-Launched Cruise Missile
SMART	Supersonic Military Air Research Track
SOR	Specific Operational Requirement
SPF/DB	Superplastic formed/diffusion bonded
SPO	System Program Office
SR	Strategic Roconnaissance, i.e., SR-71
SRAM	Short Range Attack Missile
SSD	Space Systems Division
SSM	Surface-to-Surface Missile
SSPA	Solid-State Phased Array
SST	Supersonic Transport
STOL	Short Takeoff and Landing
STOVL	Short Takeoff and Vertical Landing
SUPT	Specialized Undergraduate Pilot Training

T

T	Trainer airplane Transport airplane
TA	Trainer, Air-cooled engine
TAC	Tactical Air Command
TAC/DR	Tactical Air Command, Director of Requirements
TEDS	Tactical Expendable Drone System
TEL	Transporter Erector Launcher
TELINT	Telemetry Intelligence
TERCOM	Terrain-Contour-Matching
TEWS	Tactical Electronic Warfare System
TFR	Terrain-Following Radar
TFX	Tactical Fighter Experimental
T.O.	Technical Order
TP	Two-seat Pursuit airplane
TPIPT	Technology Planning Integrated Product Team
TPP	Total Package Procurement
TQM	Total Quality Management
TSSAM	Tri-Service Standoff Attack Missile
TTTS	Tanker-Transport Training System
TW	Trainer, Water-cooled engine
TWA	Trans World Airlines
TWT	Traveling wave tubes

U

U	Utility airplane
UAV	Unmanned (or Uninhabited) Aerial Vehicle
UC	Utility/Cargo airplane
UCAV	Unmanned (or Uninhabited) Combat Aerial Vehicle
UDRI	University of Dayton Research Institute
UFO	Unidentified Flying Object
UHF	Ultra-high-frequency
UR	Unsatisfactory Report
URR	Ultra Reliable Radar
USA	United States Army
USAC	United States Army Combat [aircraft], i.e., USAC-1
USAF	United States Air Force
USAFE	United States Air Forces in Europe
USN	United States Navy
USSR	Union of Soviet Socialist Republics
USXB	United States Experimental Bomber, i.e., USXB-1
UTTAS	Utility Tactical Transport Aircraft System

V

V	Convertiplane Staff Transport
V-E	Victory in Europe
V-J	Victory in Japan
VHB	Very Heavy Bomber
VHDL	VHSIC Hardware Description Language
VHSIC	Very High Speed Integrated Circuits
VISTA	Variable Stability In-Flight Simulator Test Aircraft
VLCEHV	Very Low Cost Expendable Harassment Vehicle
VLO	Very Low Observable
VLR	Very Long Range
VSD	Vehicle Subsystems Division
VTOL	Vertical Takeoff and Landing
VVHB	Very Very Heavy Bomber

W

WADC	Wright Air Development Center
WADD	Wright Air Development Division
WASP	Women Airforce Service Pilots
WDD	Western Development Division
WFTD	Women's Flying Training Detachment
WL	Wright Laboratory
WL/EL	Wright Laboratory, Solid State Electronics Directorate
WPA	Works Progress Administration
WPAFB	Wright-Patterson Air Force Base
WRDC	Wright Research and Development Center
WRDC/EL	Wright Research and Development Center, Electronic Technology Laboratory
WS	Weapon System
WSPO	Weapon System Project Office
WST	Weapon Systems Trainers

X

X	Experimental airplane Research
XST	Experimental Survivable Testbed

Y

Y	Service test airplane

Z

Z	Airship Obsolete type airplane Project aircraft
ZGP	Zinc germanium phosphide

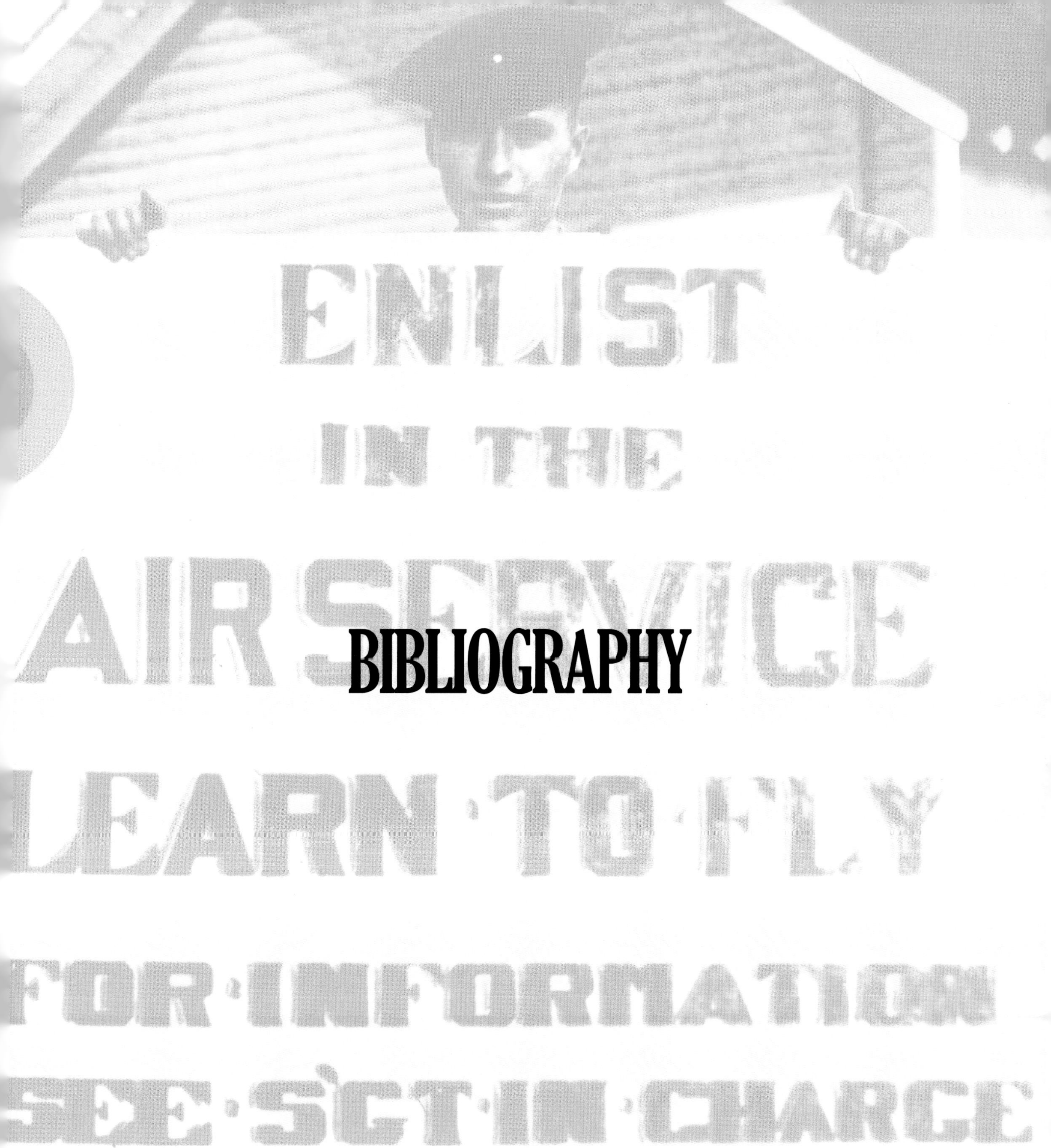

BIBLIOGRAPHY

BIBLIOGRAPHY

BOOKS

Aircraft Year Book for 1924. New York: Aeronautical Chamber of Commerce, 1925.

Alcott, Edward B. and Robert C. Williford. *Aerospace Medical Division: 25 Years of Excellence*. Brooks AFB, Texas: Aerospace Medical Division, History Office, 1986.

Andrade, John M. *U.S. Military Aircraft Designations and Serials Since 1909.* Leicester, England: Midland, 1979.

Angelucci, Enzo. *The Rand McNally Encyclopedia of Military Aircraft, 1914-1980.* New York: Military Press, 1980.

Armitage, Air Chief Marshal Sir Michael. *Unmanned Aircraft.* London: Brasseys, 1988.

The Army's Order of Battle of United States Land Forces in the World War (1917-1919). Vol. 3, Part 1. Washington: Government Printing Office, 1949.

Arnold, Henry H. *Global Mission*. New York: Harper and Bros., 1949.

Aronstein, David C., and Piccirillo, Albert C. *HAVE BLUE and the F-117A: Evolution of the "Stealth Fighter."* Reston, Virginia: AIAA, 1997.

Art, Robert J. *The TFX Decision: McNamara and the Military*. Boston: Little, Brown, 1968.

Bell, Dana. *Air Force Colors.* Vol. 1: 1926-1942. Carrollton, Texas: Aviation Book Co., 1995.

____. *Air Force Colors*. Vol. 3: Pacific and Home Front, 1942-47. Carrollton, Texas: Aviation Book Co., 1997.

Benson, Lawrence R. *Acquisition Management in the United States Air Force and Its Predecessors*. Washington: Air Force History and Museums Program, 1997.

Berger, Carl, ed. *The United States Air Force in Southeast Asia, 1961-1973: An Illustrated Account*. Washington: Office of Air Force History, 1984.

Bilstein, Roger E. *The Enterprise of Flight: The American Aviation and Aerospace Industry*. Washington: Smithsonian, 2001.

_____. *Flight in America: From the Wrights to the Astronauts*. Rev. ed. Baltimore: John Hopkins UP, 1994.

Birdsall, Steve. *Saga of the Superfortress*. New York: Doubleday, 1980.

Blee, H. H. *History of [the] Organization and Activities of [the] Airplane Engineering Division, Bureau of Aircraft Production*. N.p., 1919.

Boyne, Walt. *The Best of "Wings": Great Articles from "Wings" and "Airpower" Magazines.* Washington: Brasseys, 2001.

_____. *Boeing B-52: A Documentary History*. London: Jane's Publishing Co., 1981.

Boyne, Walter J., ed. *The Jet Age: Forty Years of Jet Aviation*. Washington: Smithsonian, 1979.

Bridgeman, Leonard, ed. *Jane's All the World's Aircraft, 1951-1952*. London: Jane's Publishing Co., 1951.

______. *Jane's All the World's Aircraft, 1952-1953*. London: Jane's Publishing Co., 1952.

______. *Jane's All the World's Aircraft, 1953-1954*. New York: McGraw-Hill, 1953.

______. *Jane's All the World's Aircraft, 1954-1955*. New York: McGraw-Hill, 1954.

______. *Jane's All the World's Aircraft, 1955-1956*. New York: McGraw-Hill, 1955.

______. *Jane's All the World's Aircraft, 1956-1957*. New York: McGraw-Hill, 1956.

______. *Jane's All the World's Aircraft, 1958-1959*. New York: McGraw-Hill, 1958.

Caidin, Martin. *The Long Arm of America: The Story of the Amazing Hercules Air Assault Transport and our Revolutionary Global Strike Force*. New York: E.P. Dutton, 1963.

Carl, Ann B. *A Wasp Among Eagles: A Woman Military Test Pilot in World War II.* Washington: Smithsonian, 1999.

Carpenter, David M. *Flame Powered: The Bell XP-59A Aeracomet and the General Electric I-A Engine, The Story of America's First Jet-Powered Aircraft*. N.p., 1992.

Chandler, Charles deF. and Lahm, Frank P. *How Our Army Grew Wings: Airmen and Aircraft Before 1914*. New York: Ronald Press, 1943.

Compere, Tom, ed. *The Air Force Blue Book*. Vol. I. New York: Bobbs-Merrill Co., 1959.

Conner, Margaret. *Hans von Ohain: Elegance in Flight*. Reston, Virginia: AIAA, 2001.

Conover, Charlotte Reeve, ed. *Dayton and Montgomery County*. Vol. 1. New York: Lewis Historical Publishing Co., 1932.

_______. *Dayton, Ohio: An Intimate History*. Dayton: Landfall Press, 2000.

Copp, DeWitt S. *A Few Great Captains*. Garden City, New York: Doubleday, 1980.

Craven, Wesley F. and Cate, James L., eds. *The Army Air Forces in World War II*. Vol. I: *Plans and Early Operations*; Vol. VI: *Men and Planes*. Chicago: University Press, 1950.

Crouch, Tom D. *The Bishop's Boys: A Life of Wilbur and Orville Wright*. New York: Norton, 1989.

______. *The Giant Leap: A Chronology of Ohio Aerospace Events and Personalities, 1815-1969*. Columbus: Ohio Historical Society, 1971.

Crowther, Samuel. *John H. Patterson, Pioneer in Industrial Welfare*. New York: Doubleday, 1924.

Curtis, Robert I.; Mitchell, John; and Copp, Martin. *Langley Field, the Early Years, 1916-1946*. Langley AFB, Virginia: Historical Office, 4500th ABW, 1977.

Daso, Dik Alan. *Hap Arnold and the Evolution of American Airpower*. Washington: Smithsonian, 2000.

Delury, George E., ed. *The World Almanac and Book of Facts, 1980*. New York: Newspaper Enterprise Association, 1979.

Dempsey, Charles A. *Air Force Aerospace Medical Research Laboratory: Fifty Years of Research on Man in Flight*. WPAFB: Air Force Aerospace Medical Research Laboratory, 1985.

_______. *Heritage of the Flight Dynamics Laboratory: Evolution of an Engineering Miracle*. WPAFB: Flight Dynamics Laboratory, 1988.

Dick, Ron. *Reach and Power: The Heritage of the United States Air Force in Pictures and Artifacts*. Washington: Air Force History and Museums Program, 1997.

Doolittle, James H. *I Could Never Be So Lucky Again: An Autobiography*. With Carroll V. Glines. New York: Bantam, 1991.

Duffner, Robert W. *Science and Technology: The Making of the Air Force Research Laboratory*. Maxwell AFB, Alabama: Air University, 2000.

DuFour, Howard R. *Charles E. Taylor: The Wright Brothers Mechanician*. New Carlisle, Ohio: DuFour, 1997.

Dyson, Emma J. H.; Herrin, Dean A.; and Slaton, Amy E., eds. *The Engineering of Flight, Aeronautical Engineering Facilities of Area B, Wright-Patterson AFB, Ohio*. Washington: National Park Service, 1993.

Fahey, James C., ed. *U.S. Army Aircraft, 1908-1946*. New York: Ships and Aircraft, 1946.

Fisk, Fred C. and Todd, Marlin W. *From Bicycle to Biplane: An Illustrated History of the Wright Brothers*. West Milton, Ohio: Miami Graphics, 1990.

Futrell, Robert Frank. *Ideas, Concepts, Doctrine: Basic Thinking in the United States Air Force, 1907-1960*. Maxwell AFB, Alabama: Air University, 1974; reprint edition, 1980.

_____. *The United States Air Force in Korea*. Rev. ed. Washington: Air Force History and Museums Program, 1983.

Galbraith, John Kenneth. *The Great Crash, 1929*. 3d ed. Boston: Houghton Mifflin, 1972.

Goldberg, Alfred, ed. *A History of the United States Air Force, 1907-1957*. Princeton, New Jersey: D. Van Nostrand, 1957.

Goldstrom, John. *A Narrative History of Aviation*. New York: Macmillan Co., 1942.

Gorn, Michael H. *Harnessing the Genie: Science and Technology Forecasting for the Air Force, 1944-1986*. Washington: Government Printing Office, 1988.

____. *Prophecy Fulfilled: "Toward New Horizons" and Its Legacy*. Washington: Government Printing Office, 1994.

____. *The Universal Man: Theodore von Karman's Life in Aeronautics*. Washington: Smithsonian, 1992.

____. *Vulcan's Forge: The Making of an Air Force Command for Weapons Acqusition (1950-1986)*. Washington: Office of History, Air Force Systems Command, 1987.

Graham, Richard H., Colonel (Ret.). *SR 71 Revealed: The Inside Story*. Osceola, Wisconsin: Motorbooks International, 1996.

Grey, C. G., ed. *Jane's All The World's Aircraft*. London: Sampson Low, 1926.

____. *Jane's All The World's Aircraft*. London: Sampson Low, 1927.

____. *Jane's All The World's Aircraft*. London: Sampson Low, 1928.

Haining, Peter. *The Jules Verne Companion*. New York: Baronet, 1979.

Hallion, Richard H. *The Evolution of Commonality in Fighter and Attack Aircraft Development and Usage*. Edwards AFB, California: Air Force Flight Test Center History Office, 1985.

_____. *The Hypersonic Revolution: Eight Case Studies in the History of Hypersonic Technology*. 2 vols. Bolling AFB: Air Force History and Museums Program, 1987.

_____. *Storm Over Iraq: Air Power and the Gulf War*. Washington: Smithsonian, 1992.

_____. *Test Pilots: The Frontiersmen of Flight*. New York: Doubleday, 1981.

Hanle, Paul A. *Bringing Aerodynamics to America*. Cambridge, Massachusetts: MIT, 1982.

Head, William. *Reworking the Workhorse: The C-141B Stretch Modification Program*. Robins AFB, Georgia: Air Logistics Center Office of History, 1984.

Heiman, Grover. *Jet Pioneers*. New York: Duell, Sloan and Pearce, 1963.

Hennessey, Juliette A. *The United States Army Air Arm, April 1861 to April 1917*. Washington: Office of Air Force History, 1958; reprint edition, 1985.

Hildreth, C. H. and Nalty, Bernard C. *1001 Questions Answered About Aviation History*. New York: Dodd, Mead & Co., 1969.

Holley, Irving Brinton, Jr. *Buying Aircraft: Materiel Procurement for the Army Air Forces*. Washington: Office of the Chief of Military History, 1964.

_____. *Ideas and Weapons: Exploitation of the Aerial Weapon by the United States during World War I; A Study in the Relationship of Technological Advance, Military Doctrine, and the Development of Weapons*. New Haven, Connecticut: Yale University Press, 1953; reprint edition, Washington: Office of Air Force History, 1983.

Hopkins, Robert S., III. *Boeing KC-135 Stratotanker: More Than Just a Tanker*. England: Midland Publishing Ltd, 1997.

Hubler, Richard C. *Big Eight: Biography of an Airplane*. New York: Duell, Sloan & Pearce, 1960.

Ingells, Douglas J. *They Tamed the Sky*. New York: D. Appleton-Century, 1947.

Jablonski, Edward. *Flying Fortress*. Garden City, New York: Doubleday, 1949.

Jakab, Peter L. *Visions of a Flying Machine: The Wright Brothers and the Process of Invention*. Washington: Smithsonian, 1990.

Jones, Lloyd S. *U.S. Bombers, 1928 to 1980s*. 3rd ed. Fallbrook, California.: Acro Publishers, 1980.

Jordan, Amos A.; Taylor, William J.; and Korb, Lawrence J. *American National Security: Policy and Process*. 4th ed. Baltimore: John Hopkins University Press, 1993.

Karman, Theodore von, and Edson, Lee. *The Wind and Beyond: Theodore von Karman, Pioneer in Aviation and Pathfinder in Space*. Boston: Little Brown, 1967.

Kelly, Fred C. *The Wright Brothers*. New York: Farrar, Straus and Young, 1950.

Knaack, Marcelle Size. *Military Airlift and Aircraft Procurement: The Case of the C-5A*. Washington: Air Force History and Museums Program, 1998.

______. *Post-World War II Bombers*. Washington: Office of Air Force History, 1988.

______. *Post-World War II Fighters*. Washington: Office of Air Force History, 1986.

Lambermont, Paul and Pirie, Anthony. *Helicopters and Autogyros of the World*. New York: Philosophical Library, 1959.

Lambert, Mark, ed. *Jane's All the World's Aircraft, 1993-1994*. London: Jane's Publishing Co., 1993.

______. *Jane's All The World's Aircraft, 1994-1995*. London: Jane's Publishing Co., 1994.

Lasby, Clarence G. *Project Paperclip: German Scientists and the Cold War*. New York: Atheneum, 1971.

Lawrance, Charles L. *Our National Aviation Program*. New York: Aeronautical Chamber of Commerce of America, 1932.

Lonnquest, John C. and Winkler, David F. *To Defend and Deter: The Legacy of the United States Cold War Missile Program*. Champaign, Illinois: Defense Publishing Service, 1996.

Lorell, Mark A. and Levaux, Hugh P. *The Cutting Edge: A Half Century of U.S. Fighter Aircraft R&D*. Santa Monica: RAND, 1998.

Lorell, Mark A.; Saunders, Alison; and Levaux, Hugh P. *Bomber R&D Since 1945: The Role of Experience*. Santa Monica: RAND, 1995.

Marcosson, Isaac F. *Colonel Deeds, Industrial Builder*. New York: Dodd, Mead & Co., 1947.

Mason, Herbert Molloy, Jr. *The United States Air Force: A Turbulent History*. New York: Mason/Charter, 1976.

McFarland, Marvin W., ed. *The Papers of Wilbur and Orville Wright, Including the Chanute-Wright Letters and Other Papers of Octave Chanute*. Vol. 1: 1899-1905. New York: Arno Press, 1972.

McFarland, Stephen L. *A Concise History of the United States Air Force*. Washington: Government Printing Office, 1997.

Messadié, Gerald. *Great Modern Inventions*. New York: Chambers, 1991.

Miller, Jay. *The X-Planes: X-1 to X-31*. Arlington, Texas: Aerofax, 1988.

Miller, Ronald, and Sawers, David. *The Technical Development of Modern Aviation*. New York: Praeger, 1970.

Morris, Lloyd and Smith, Kendall. *Ceiling Unlimited: The Story Of American Aviation from Kitty Hawk to Supersonics*. New York: Macmillan Co., 1953.

Nalty, Bernard C., ed. *Winged Shield, Winged Sword: A History of the United States Air Force*. 2 vols. Washington: Air Force History and Museums Program, 1997.

Neufeld, Jacob. *The Development of Ballistic Missiles in the United States Air Force, 1945-1960*. Washington: Office of Air Force History, 1990.

Neufeld, Jacob; Watson, George M.; and Chenoweth, David; eds. *Technology and the Air Force: A Retrospective Assessment*. Washington: Air Force History and Museums Program, 1997.

New World Vistas: Air and Space Power for the 21st Century. Summary Volume. Washington: USAF, 1995.

Oxlee, Geoffrey. *Aerospace Reconnaissance*. Vol. 9 of *Brassey's Air Power: Aircraft, Weapons Systems and Technology Series*. London: Chrysalis Books, 1997.

Patrick, Mason. *The United States in the Air*. Garden City, New York: Doubleday, 1928.

A Pictorial Review, Wright-Patterson Air Force Base, 1917-1967. WPAFB: 2750th Air Base Wing, 1967.

Przemieniecki, J. S. *Acquisition of Defense Systems*. Washington: AIAA, 1993.

Ravenstein, Charles A. *The Organization and Lineage of the United States Air Force*. Washington: Air Force History Support Office, 1986.

Reid, T. R. *The Chip: How Two Americans Invented the Microchip and Launched a Revolution*. New York: Random House, 1984.

Renstrom, Arthur G. *Wilbur & Orville Wright: A Chronology Commemorating the Hundredth Anniversary of the Birth of Orville Wright, August 19, 1871.* Washington: Library of Congress, 1975.

Roland, Alex. *Model Research: The National Advisory Committee for Aeronautics, 1915-1958.* 2 vols. Washington: Government Printing Office, 1985.

Ryan, Daniel Joseph. *The Civil War Literature of Ohio, A Bibliography with Explanatory and Historical Notes.* Cleveland: Burrows Brothers, 1911.

St. Peter, James. *The History of Aircraft Gas Turbine Engine Development in the United States: A Tradition of Excellence.* Atlanta: American Society of Mechanical Engineers, 1999.

Simpson, Ernest C. *The Memoirs of Ernest C. Simpson, Aero Propulsion Pioneer.* James St. Peter, ed. WPAFB: Aeronautical Systems Division, 1987.

Still, Henry. *To Ride the Wind: A Biography of Glenn L. Martin.* New York: Julian Messner, 1964.

Swanborough, F. G. *United States Military Aircraft Since 1909.* London: Putnam, 1963.

Swanborough, Gordon and Bowers, Peter M. *United States Military Aircraft Since 1908.* London: Putnam, 1971.

_____. *United States Military Aircraft Since 1909.* Washington: Smithsonian, 1989.

Sweetser, Arthur. *The American Air Service.* New York: Appleton, 1919.

Taylor, John W.R., ed. *Jane's All the World's Aircraft, 1960-1961.* New York: Jane's Publishing Co., 1960.

_____. *Jane's All the World's Aircraft, 1963-1964.* New York: Jane's Publishing Co., 1963.

_____. *Jane's All the World's Aircraft, 1964-1965.* London: Jane's Publishing Co., 1964.

_____. *Jane's All the World's Aircraft, 1965-1966.* New York: Jane's Publishing Co., 1965.

_____. *Jane's All the World's Aircraft, 1966-1967.* New York: Jane's Publishing Co., 1966.

_____. *Jane's All the World's Aircraft, 1967-1968.* New York: Jane's Publishing Co., 1967.

_____. *Jane's All the World's Aircraft, 1969-1970.* New York: Jane's Publishing Co., 1969.

_____. *Jane's All the World's Aircraft, 1970-1971.* London: Jane's Publishing Co., 1970.

_____. *Jane's All the World's Aircraft, 1972-1973.* New York: Jane's Publishing Co., 1972.

_____. *Jane's All the World's Aircraft, 1973-1974.* London: Jane's Publishing Co., 1973.

_____. *Jane's All the World's Aircraft, 1974-1975.* New York: Jane's Publishing Co., 1974.

_____. *Jane's All the World's Aircraft, 1975-1976.* New York: Jane's Publishing Co., 1975.

_____. *Jane's All the World's Aircraft, 1976-1977.* New York: Jane's Publishing Co., 1976.

_____. *Jane's All the World's Aircraft, 1977-1978.* New York: Jane's Publishing Co., 1977.

_____. *Jane's All the World's Aircraft, 1981-1982.* London: Jane's Publishing Co., 1981.

_____. *Jane's All the World's Aircraft, 1982-1983.* London: Jane's Publishing Co., 1982.

_____. *Jane's All the World's Aircraft, 1983-1984.* London: Jane's Publishing Co.,1983.

_____. *Jane's All the World's Aircraft, 1985-1986.* New York: Jane's Publishing Co., 1985.

_____. *Jane's All the World's Aircraft, 1987-1988.* New York: Jane's Publishing Co., 1987.

_____. *Jane's All the World's Aircraft, 1988-1989.* New York: Jane's Publishing Co., 1988.

_____. *Jane's All The World's Aircraft, 1989-1990.* London: Jane's Publishing Co., 1989.

Taylor, Michael J.H., ed. *Jane's Encyclopedia of Aviation.* New York: Portland House, 1989.

Terrett, Dulany. *United States Army in World War II, The Technical Services, The Signal Corps: The Emergency (to December 1941).* Washington: Government Printing Office, 1956.

Thomas, Lowell J. *The First World Flight.* Boston: Houghton, Mifflin Co., 1925.

Thomas, Lowell J. and Thomas, Lowell, Jr. *Famous First Flights That Changed History.* Garden City, New York: Doubleday, 1968.

Thompson, Wayne. *To Hanoi and Back: The United States Air Force and North Vietnam, 1966-1973.* Washington: Smithsonian, 2000.

Trester, Delmer J. *History of Project Brass Ring.* Vol. I. WPAFB: WADC, 1953.

U.S. Air Force Museum Photo Album. WPAFB: Air Force Museum Foundation, n.d.

Wagner, Ray. *American Combat Planes.* New York: Doubleday, 1968.

Wagner, William. *Lightning Bugs and other Reconnaissance Drones.* Fallbrook, California: Aero, 1982.

Wagner, William, and Sloan, William P. *Fireflies and Other UAVs.* Arlington, Texas: Aerofax, 1992.

Walker, Lois E. and Wickam, Shelby E. *From Huffman Prairie to the Moon: The History of Wright-Patterson Air Force Base.* WPAFB: Office of History, 2750th Air Base Wing, 1986.

Waters, Andrew W. *All the U.S. Air Force Airplanes, 1907-1983.* New York: Hippocrene Books, 1983.

Watson, George M., Jr. *Secretaries and Chiefs of Staff of the United States Air Force: Biographical Sketches and Portraits.* Washington: Air Force History and Museums Program, 2001.

Weitze, Karen J. *Guided Missiles at Holloman Air Force Base: Test Programs of the United States Air Force in Southern New Mexico, 1947-1970.* Holloman AFB, New Mexico: 1997.

Werrell, Kenneth P. *The Evolution of the Cruise Missile*. Maxwell AFB, Alabama: Air UP, 1985.

Whistler, Ross. *USAAF Camouflage, 1933-1969*. Dover, Massachusetts: N.p., 1969.

Who's Who in American Aeronautics. 3d ed. Compiled by Lester D. Gardner. New York: Aviation Publishing, 1928.

Wollheim, Donald A. *Mike Mars Flies the Dyna Soar.* New York: Doubleday, Paperback Library, 1962.

Yeager, Chuck, and Janos, Leo. *Yeager: An Autobiography*. New York: Bantam, 1985.

Yenne, Bill. *The History of the U.S. Air Force*. New York: Exeter Books, 1984.

ARTICLES

"AGM-62 Walleye." Online at http://www.wpafb.af.mil/museum/arm/arm0a.htm.

"An Air Force Almanac." *Air Force Magazine* (May 1982): 171.

"Air Force Logistics Command." *Air Force Magazine* (May 1983): 78-79.

Air Force Museum Foundation *Friends Bulletin* 6 (Fall 1983): 17-20.

"Air-to-Surface Missiles." Greg Goebel's VectorSite, online at http://vectorsite.tripod.com/avbomb5.html.

Alumni Homepage. Air Force Institute of Technology, online at http://www.afit-aog.org/ag.html.

Aronstein, David C. and Piccirillo, Albert C. "The F-16 Lightweight Fighter: A Case Study in Technology Transition." *Technology and the Air Force: A Retrospective Assessment*. Jacob Neufeld et al., eds. Washington: Air Force History and Museums Program, 1997.

"Aviation at Indianapolis Motor Speedway." *Indiana Historian* (Indiana Historical Bureau), online at http://www.statelib.lib.in.us/www/ihb/tiharch-jun98.html.

Bahret, William F. "The Beginnings of Stealth Technology." *IEEE Transactions on Aerospace and Electronic Systems*. Vol. 29, No. 4 (Oct 1993): 1374-1385.

Baker, Sue. "Power By the Hour." *Leading Edge* (Jun 2000).

Basham, Hank. "RPV's Make the Difference." *Air University Review* (Jan-Feb 1974): 40.

Boeing Company, "F-22 Air-Dominance Fighter," online at http://www.af.mil/news/Aprl1997/f22.html.

Bokulich, Frank. "Birdstrikes Remain a Concern For Pilots." *Aerospace Engineering Online* (Mar 2000), at http://www.sae.org/aeromag/techupdate_3-00/05.htm.

Bowers, Peter. "Forgotten Fighters." *Air Progress* (Fall 1962): 38-61.

Boyne, Walt. "The Man Who Built the Missiles." *Air Force Magazine* (Oct 2000), online at http://www/afa.org/magazine/Oct2000/1000bennie.html.

_____. "Martin's Marvel." *Airpower* 2 (Jun 1972): 51-67.

_____. "The Treasure Trove of McCook Field." *Airpower* 5 (Jul 1975): 6-25.

_____. "The Treasures of McCook Field: America's First Aero-Engineering and Testing Center, Part I." *Wings* 5 (Aug 1975): 8-25.

Butrica, Andrew J. "Outline of *Volume IV: From the Reagan Buildup to the End of the Cold War, 1981-1990*." Defense Acquisition History Project Newsletter, Summer 2001, Vol. I, Issue 3, online at http://www.army.mil/cmh-pg/acquisition/acq1-3.htm.

Carr, Gardner W. "Organization and Activities of Engineering Division of the Air Service." *U.S. Air Services* 7 (Jan-Mar 1922): 9-12; 22-27.

Carrell, John T. "The Future Forms Up at ASD." *Air Force Magazine* (Jan 1983): 40-50.

Casari, Robert. "Number of U.S. Aircraft WWI." *American Aviation Historical Society Journal* 20 (Spring 1977): 36-38.

"Charles Edward Taylor—1965." National Aviation Hall of Fame Enshrinees, online at http://www.nationalaviation.org/enshrinee/taylor.html.

"Charles Stark Draper Prize." National Air and Space Museum, online at http://nasm.edu/nasm/aero/trophy/draper.htm.

"A Checklist of Major ASD Systems." *Air Force Magazine* (Jan 1989): 57.

"A Checklist of Major Aeronautical Systems." *Air Force Magazine* (Jan 1991): 44.

Christy, Joe. "The First Round-the-World Flight." *Air Force Magazine* 57 (Mar 1974): 53-59.

"Colonel Joseph W. Kittinger, Jr." Air Force Space Command, online at http://www/spacecom.af.mil/hqafspc/history/kittinger.htm.

"Cruise Missiles of the 1950s and 1960s." Greg Goebel's VectorSite, online at http://vectorsite.tripod.com/avcruz3.html.

"Dedication of Wright Field." *U.S. Air Services* 12 (Nov 1927): 32.

"Designating and Naming Defense Military Aerospace Vehicles—Air Force Joint Instruction 16-401." U.S. Air Force, online at http://afpubs/hq/af/mil.

Detweiler, Robert M. "Air Force Research in Retrospect." *Air University Review*, Vol. 28, No. 1 (Nov-Dec 1976): 3-14.

"Dr. Theodore von Karman, 1881-1963." Arnold AFB Biography, online at http://www.arnold.af.mil/aedc/karman.htm.

"Eddie Rickenbacker." International Motorsports Hall of Fame, online at http://www.mortorsportshalloffame.com/halloffame/1992/Eddie_Rickenbacker_main.htm

Emmons, Lt Harold H. "U.S. Airplane Production, The Official History of Air Progress." *Motor Age* (Dec 5, 1918): 18-19, 30.

"F-16 Movie Gallery." National Aeronautics and Space Administration, online at http://www.dfrc.nasa.gov.

"Frank C. Carlucci, November 23, 1987-January 20, 1989, 16th Secretary of Defense." DefenseLINK. U.S. Department of Defense, online at http://www.defenselink.mil/specials/secdef_histories/bios/carlucci.htm.

Futrell, Dr. Robert E. "The Development of Aeromedical Evacuation in the USAF 1909-1939." *American Aviation Historical Society Journal* 23 (Fall 1978): 212-25.

Geisenheyner, Stefan. "Air Force of Tomorrow." *Aerospace International* 8 (Jul-Aug 1972): 2-11.

"General Henry H. Arnold." United States Air Force Biography, online at http://www.af.mil/news/biographies/arnold_hh.html.

"General Lawrence A. Skantze." United States Air Force Biography, online at http://www.af.mil/news/biographies/skantze_la.html.

Gibbs-Smith, Charles H. "The World's First Practical Airplane." *NCR World* (4th Qtr, 1978): 5-6.

Gillmore, Brigadier General W. E. "Industrial War Planning in the Army Air Corps." *U.S. Air Services* 14 (Mar 1929): 30-32.

Gold, David. "Milestones in the History of Parachute Development." *SAFE* 9 (Spring 1979): 10-17.

Golightly, Glen. "Vomit Comet Finds a Home." Mar 15, 2000. Online at http://www.space.com/news/spaceagencies/comet_retired_000515.html.

Guinn, Gilbert S. "A Different Frontier: Aviation, the Army Air Forces, and the Evolution of the Sunshine Belt." *Aerospace Historian* 29 (Mar 1982): 34-35.

Hall, R. Cargill. "The Air Force Agena: A Case Study in Early Spacecraft Technology." *Technology and the Air Force: A Retrospective Assessment.* Jacob Neufeld et al., eds. Washington: Air Force History and Museums Program, 1997.

Hall, R. Cargill. "Civil-Military Relations in America's Early Space Program." *The U.S. Air Force in Space: 1945 to the Twenty-First Century,* R. Cargill Hall and Jacob Neufeld, eds. Washington: United States Air Force, 1998.

Harris, Lorenzo D. "It Runs in the Family." *Airman* (Sep 1984): 37-40.

Head, William. "AC-47 Gunship Development." *Air Power History* (Fall 1990): 37-46.

"The Honorable Donald Rumsfeld: Secretary of Defense." DefenseLINK. U.S. Department of Defense, online at http://www.defenselink.mil/specials/secdef_histories/.

House, Walter D. "Warbird Tech Data." *American Aviation Historical Society Journal* 26 (Fall 1981): 206-208.

Hoyt, Brigadier General (Ret.) Ross G. "The Curtiss Hawks." *Air Force Magazine* (Oct 1976): 68-69.

Jackson, Karaline. "Planes Get Safer With Chicken Gun." The Flyer News (University of Dayton), Nov 9, 1999. Online at http://www.ccsf.edu/Events_Pubs/Guardsman/f991108/uwire06.shtml.

Jacobs, A. M. "The Dedication of Wright Field." *Air Corps News* XI (Nov 10, 1927): 1.

Johnson, Collie J. "Maverick Airframe Team Scores Stunning Acquisition Reform Success." *Program Manager* (Sep/Oct 1998): 10-18.

Justus, Graham, ed. "Aircraft Production in Dayton." *NCR World* (Sep-Oct 1970): 20-25.

Kinney, William A. "Under the Dome at Wright-Pat." *The Airman* (Feb 1966): 16-18.

Kittinger, Joseph W., Jr. "The Long, Lonely Leap." *National Geographic* 118 (Dec 1960).

Lauren, Ward. "Riding the Shock Wave." *Skyline* 19 (1961): 21.

Lincoln, Marshall. "The Barling." *Air Classics* 2 (Feb 1965): 28-32.

Lynch, Frederic C. "The 1945 Army Air Forces Fair--Forerunner of Today's Air Force Orientation Group." *Aerospace Historian* 28 (Jun 1981): 104-5.

"The Mackay Trophy." *Air Force Magazine* 77:5 (May 1994): 112-113.

"Major General Franklin O. Carroll." United States Air Force Biography, online at http://www.af.mil/news/biographies/carroll_fo.html.

Mars, Major J. A. "Government Must Encourage Commercial Aviation." *U.S. Air Services* 10 (Jun 1925): 29.

Maurer, Maurer. "McCook Field, 1917-1927." *The Ohio Historical Quarterly* 67 (Jan 1958): 21-34.

McIninch, Thomas P. "The Oxcart Story." *Air Force Magazine* (Nov 1994): 40-47.

_______. "Black Shield." *Air Force Magazine* (Jan 1995): 66-71.

McMaster, R. K., ed. "The Adventures of a Junior Military Aviator: Extracts from the Diary of Leo G. Heffernan." *Aerospace Historian* 25 (Jun 1978): 92-102.

Mehuron, Tamar A., ed. "The U.S. Air Force in Facts and Figures." *Air Force Magazine* 77:5 (May 1994): 27.

"MILNET: Air-to-Air Missiles." Online at http://www.milnet.com/milnet/aam.htm.

"MILNET: Air-to-Ground Missiles (AGMs)." Online at www.milnet.com/milnet/agm.htm.

Mohr, Col George C. "AMRL Biotechnology Research and Development Activities." *Medical Service Digest* (Summer 1983): 1-3.

Moody, Walton S.; Neufeld, Jacob; and Nalty, Bernard C. "The Air Force and Operations Short of War." *Winged Shield, Winged Sword: A History of the United States Air Force.* Vol. II: 1950-1997. Bernard C. Nalty, ed. Washington: Air Force History and Museums Program, 1997.

Moody, Walton S.; Neufeld, Jacob; and Hall, R. Cargill. "The Emergence of the Strategic Air Command." *Winged Shield, Winged Sword: A History of the United States Air Force.* Vol. II: 1950-1997. Bernard C. Nalty, ed. Washington: Air Force History and Museums Program, 1997.

Murphy, William B. "The Flying Bird of Paradise." *Aerospace Historian* 26 (Mar 1979): 30-33.

"NF-15B." Edwards AFB, online at http://www.edwards.af.mil/gallery/html_pgs/miscaircra1.htm.

National Aeronautic Association Review 2, Special Air Race Edition (Sep 18, 1924).

Neely, Frederick P. "Army Makes Longest Overwater Flight." *U.S. Air Services* 12 (Aug 1927): 18-22.

"Neil A. Armstrong." NASA Biographical Data, Dryden Flight Research Center, online at http://www.dfrc.nasa.gov/PAO/PAIS/HTML/bd-dfrc-p001.html.

Neufeld, Jacob. "The F-15 Eagle: Origins and Development, 1964-1972." *Air Power History* 48 (Spring 2001).

"New World's Records." *Aviation* 16 (Feb 11, 1924): 147.

Ogletree, Greg. "Ground Launched Cruise Missiles." Ground Launched Cruise Missile Historical Foundation, online at http://glcmhf.org/glcm/history.shtml.

Oliveri, Frank. "A Trainer Built for Two." *Air Force Magazine* (Jun 1992).

"Project Excelsior." United States Air Force Museum, online at http://www/wpafb.af.mil/museum/history/coldwar/pe.htm.

Rhodes, Jeffrey P. "AIR-2 Genie." Gallery of Classics: A Flock of Warbirds from the Air Force's Past. *Air Force Magazine*, online at www.afa.org/magazine/gallery/air-2.html.

_____. "The Drone Pilots." *Air Force Magazine* (Mar 1991): 94-99.

_____. "The Next Round for Aerial Combat." *Air Force Magazine* (Feb 1991): 46-51.

"The Robert J. Collier Trophy." *Air Force Magazine* (May 1994): 110-111.

Rumsfeld, Donald H. "Transforming the Military." *Foreign Affairs*, Vol. 81, No. 3 (May/Jun 2002): 20-32.

Schlight, John. "The War in Southeast Asia, 1961-1968." *Winged Shield, Winged Sword: History of the United States Air Force.* Vol. II: 1950-1997. Bernard C. Nalty, ed. Washington: Air Force History and Museums Program, 1997.

Schwartz, Stephen I., ed. "Box 2-2: Weapons That Did Not Make the Cut." *Atomic Audit: The Costs and Consequences of U.S. Nuclear Weapons Since 1940.* 1998. Brookings Institute, online at http://www.brook.edu/fp/projects/nucwcost/box2-2.htm.

Scott, Phil. "Watson's Whizzers." *Air & Space* 12 (Oct-Nov 1997): 66-73.

Scott, William B. "Lantirn Gives Tomcat Night Attack Role." *Aviation Week and Space Technology* (Jun 10, 1996): 40-43.

Seeley, Bruce. "Research, Engineering, and Science in American Engineering Colleges: 1900-1960." *Technology & American History: A Historical Anthology from "Technology and Culture."* Stephen H. Cutcliffe and Terry S. Reynolds, eds. Chicago: University Press, 1997.

Shiner, John F. "Benjamin D. Foulois: In the Beginning." *Makers of the United States Air Force*. John L. Frisbee, ed. Washington: Office of Air Force History, 1987.

"The Spin Doctors: Scientists Prepare Pilots to Defy Gravity." *Airman*, online at http://www.af.mil/news/airman/0698/spin.htm.

Thomason, Tommy and Lieberman, Warren. "The V-22 Osprey." *Horizons* (1985): 18-25.

Tilford, Earl H., Jr. "The Barling Bomber." *Aerospace Historian* 26 (Jun 1979): 91-97.

Tirpak, John A. "Strike Fighter." *Air Force Magazine* 79 (Oct 1996): 22-28.

_____. "The Robotic Air Force." *Air Force Magazine* (Sep 1997): 70-74.

Tomayko, James E. "Blind Faith: The United States Air Force and the Development of Fly-by-Wire Technology." *Technology and the Air Force: A Retrospective Assessment*. Jacob Neufeld et al., eds. Washington: Air Force History and Museums Program, 1997.

U.S. Air Services (Oct 1926): 24.

Van Inwegen III, Earl S. "The Air Force Develops an Operational Organization for Space." *The U.S. Air Force in Space: 1945 to the Twenty-First Century.* R. Cargill Hall and Jacob Neufeld, eds. Washington: United States Air Force, 1998.

Ventolo, Joseph A., Jr. "Col. John A. Macready." *Air Force Magazine* (Feb 1980): 76-78.

Weaver, Richard L., Colonel. "Report of Air Force Research Regarding the 'Roswell Incident.'" Jul 1994. Online at http://www.af.mil/lib/roswell.html.

Werrell, Kenneth P. "The USAF and the Cruise Missile: Opportunity or Threat?" *Technology and the Air Force: A Retrospective Assessment.*" Jacob Neufeld et al., eds. Washington: Air Force History and Museums Program, 1997.

"Women Pilots in WWII, WASP Class 43-W-5," United States Air Force Museum, online at http://www.wpafb.af.mil/museum/history/wasp/wasp26.htm.

Worman, Charles G. "McCook Field, A Decade of Progress." *Aerospace Historian* 17 (Spring 1970): 12-16, 35-36.

Y'Blood, William T. "From the Deserts to the Mountains." *Winged Shield, Winged Sword: A History of the United States Air Force*. Vol. II: 1950-1997. Bernard C. Nalty, ed. Washington: Air Force History and Museums Program, 1997.

_____. "Peace Is Not Always Peaceful." *Winged Shield, Winged Sword: A History of the United States Air Force*. Vol. II: 1950-1997. Bernard C. Nalty, ed. Washington: Air Force History and Museums Program, 1997.

Young, James O. "Riding England's Coattails: The Army Air Forces and the Turbojet Revolution." *Technology and the Air Force: A Retrospective Assessment.* Jacob Neufeld et al., eds. Washington: Air Force History and Museums Program, 1997.

Young, Susan H.H. "Gallery of USAF Weapons." *Air Force Magazine* (May 1994): 132.

OFFICIAL USAF UNIT HISTORIES

ARMY AIR FORCES HISTORICAL STUDIES

Army Air Forces Historical Study No. 25, *Organization of Military Aeronautics 1907-1935,* 1944.

Army Air Forces Historical Study No. 50, *Materiel Research and Development in the Army Air Arm, 1914-1945*, 1946.

USAF HISTORICAL STUDIES

Hennessey, Juliette A. USAF Historical Study No. 98, *The United States Army Air Arm, April 1861 to April 1917*, 1958.

USAF HISTORIES

Maurer, Maurer, ed. *Air Force Combat Units of World War II.* Maxwell AFB, Alabama: Albert F. Simpson Historical Research Center, 1960.

_____. *Aviation in the U.S. Army, 1919-1939.* Washington: Office of Air Force History, 1987.

_____. *Combat Squadrons of the Air Force During World War II.* Maxwell AFB, Alabama: Albert F. Simpson Historical Research Center, 1969.

_____. *The U.S. Air Service in World War I.* Vol. 1: *The Final Report and a Tactical History*. Washington: AF Historical Office, 1978.

COMMAND HISTORICAL STUDIES

AFLC Historical Study No. 329, *Air Force Logistics Command 1917-1992*, 1996.

AMC Historical Study No. 281, *History of the Army Air Forces Materiel Command 1926-1941*, 1943.

AMC Historical Study No. 282, *History of the Army Air Forces Materiel Command (Materiel Center) 1942*, 1946.

AMC Historical Study No. 283, *History of the Army Air Forces Materiel Command 1943*, 1946.

AMC Historical Study No. 284, *Administrative History of the Air Technical Service Command 1944*, 1946.

AMC Historical Study No. 285, *History of the Air Technical Service Command 1945*, 1951.

AMC Historical Study No. 286, *History of the Air Materiel Command 1946*, 1951.

AMC Historical Study No. 329, *AMC and Its Antecedents 1917-1960*, 1960.

Elliott, William. *The Development of Fly-By-Wire Flight Control.* Air Force Materiel Command (AFMC) Historical Study No. 7. WPAFB: AFMC, 1996.

McMurtrie, Mary L. and Davis, Paul N. *History of the Army Air Forces Materiel Command, 1926 through 1941.* AMC Historical Study No. 281. Wright Field: Army Air Forces Materiel Command, 1943.

COMMAND HISTORIES

Baker, Doris A. *History of AMC Field Organization 1917-1955*. Historical Office, Air Materiel Command, 1956.

Frey, Royal. *Evolution of Maintenance Engineering 1907-1920*. Historical Office, Air Materiel Command, 1960.

Histories of the Air Force Logistics Command
Fiscal Year 1986; Fiscal Year 1987; Fiscal Year 1988; Fiscal Year 1989.

History of the AMC Contract Airlift System (LOGAIR) 1954-1955. Historical Office, Air Materiel Command, 1956.

History of Fairfield Air Depot Control Area Command (FADCAC) and Fairfield Air Service Command (FASC), 1 Feb 1943-1 Oct 1944. Historical Office, Air Materiel Command, n.d.

McFarland, R. M., ed. *History of the Bureau of Aircraft Production*. Historical Office, Air Materiel Command, 1951.

Pendergast, 1st Lt Frank J. *History of the Air Depot at Fairfield, Ohio 1917-1943*. Historical Office, Fairfield Air Service Command, 1944.

Purtee, Dr. Edward O. *History of the Army Air Service 1907-1926*. Historical Office, Air Materiel Command, 1948.

Termena, Bernard J.; Peiffer, Layne B.; and Carlin, H.P. *Logistics: An Illustrated History of AFLC and Its Antecedents, 1921-1981*. WPAFB: Air Force Logistics Command, 1981.

AERONAUTICAL SYSTEMS CENTER HISTORIES AND STUDIES

Aldridge, James F. *Wright Field's Five Foot Wind Tunnel*. WPAFB: ASC History Office, 1997.

Aldridge, James F. *Wright from the Start: Contributions of Dayton's Science and Engineering Community to American Air Power in the 20th Century*. WPAFB: ASC History Office, 1999.

Birthplace, Home and Future of Aerospace: The Evolution of Aeronautical Development at the Aeronautical Systems Center. WPAFB: ASC History Office, 1999.

Cornelisse, Diana G., et al., *Against the Wind: 90 Years of Flight Test in the Miami Valley*. WPAFB: ASC History Office, 1994.

An Encounter between the Jet Engine Inventors Sir Frank Whittle and Dr. Hans von Ohain, 3-4 May 1978. WPAFB: ASC History Office, 1986.

Histories of the Aeronautical Systems Center
Jan-Sep 1992; Oct 1992-Sep 1993; Oct 1993-Sep 1994; Oct 1994-Sep 1995; Oct 1995-Sep 1996; Oct 1996-Sep 1997; Oct 1997-Sep 1998; Oct 1998-Sep 1999; Oct 1999-Sep 2000.

Narducci, Henry M. *A Century of Growth: The Evolution of Wright-Patterson Air Force Base*. WPAFB: ASC History Office, 1999.

Romesburg, Laura N. *An Extraordinary Century for Women: Wright-Patterson Air Force Base During World War II*. WPAFB: ASC History Office, 2000.

Tagg, Lori S. *On the Front Line of R&D: Wright-Patterson Air Force Base in the Korean War, 1950-1953*. WPAFB: ASC History Office, 2001.

AERONAUTICAL SYSTEMS DIVISION HISTORIES AND STUDIES

Detmer, Ronald C. "Advanced Tactical Fighter: History of the Demonstration/Validation Phase." *History of the Aeronautical Systems Division, Fiscal Years 1986-1990*. Vol. I. WPAFB: Aeronautical Systems Division History Office, 1990.

Histories of the Aeronautical Systems Division
Apr-Dec 1961; Jul-Dec 1962; Jan-Dec 1964; Jan-Dec 1965; Jan-Dec 1966; Jul 1971-Jun 1972; Jul 1974-Dec 1975; Jan-Dec 1977; Oct 1978-Sep 1979; Oct 1980-Sep 1981; Oct 1982-Dec 1983; Jan-Dec 1984; Jan-Dec 1985; Jan-Dec 1986; Jan-Dec 1987; Jan-Dec 1988; Jan-Dec 1989; Jan-Dec 1990, Jan-Dec 1991.

Misenko, Albert E. *History of the Air Force Materials Laboratory, July – December 1963*. AFSC Historical Publications Series 64-217-I. WPAFB: Aeronautical Systems Division, Historical Division, Information Office, 1965.

_____. *Total Quality Management at the Aeronautical Systems Division, 1984-1992. The Road to Improvement*. WPAFB: Aeronautical Systems Division History Office, 1992.

Misenko, Albert E. and Pollock, Philip H. *Engineering History, 1917-1978, McCook Field to the Aeronautical Systems Division*. 4th ed. WPAFB: Aeronautical Systems Division History Office, 1979.

Wolf, Bruce R. *Peace Pearl* (U-FOUO). WPAFB: Aeronautical Systems Division History Office, 1991.

NATIONAL AIR INTELLIGENCE CENTER HISTORIES AND STUDIES

Ashcroft, Bruce, and Young, Rob. *A Brief History of the Air Force Scientific and Technical Intelligence*. WPAFB: National Air Intelligence Center History Office, 2001.

WRIGHT AIR DEVELOPMENT CENTER HISTORIES

Histories of the Wright Air Development Center
Jan 1-Jun 30, 1952; Jul 1-Dec 31, 1952; Jan 1-Jun 30, 1953; Jan 1-Jun 30, 1954; Jul 1-Dec 31, 1954; Jan 1-Jun 30, 1955; Jul-Dec 1957; Jan-Dec 1958; Jan-Jun 1960.

Wright Air Development Center, Aero Medical Laboratory
Semiannual History, 1 Jan-30 Jun 1959.

WRIGHT AIR DEVELOPMENT DIVISION HISTORIES

Histories of the Wright Air Development Division
Jan-Jun 1960.

WING HISTORIES AND STUDIES

Histories of the 2750th Air Base Wing
Jan-Jun 1948; Jul-Dec 1948; Jan-Jun 1949; Jul-Dec 1949; Jan-Jun 1950; Jul-Dec 1950; Jan-Jun 1951; Jul-Dec 1951; Jan-Jun 1952, Jul-Dec 1952; Jan-Jun 1953; Jul-Dec 1953; Jan-Jun 1954; Jul-Dec 1954; Jan-Dec 1955; Jan-Jun 1956; Jul-Dec 1956; Jan-Dec 1957; Jan-Jun 1958; Jul-Dec 1958; Jan-Jun 1959; Jul 1959-Jun 1960; Jul 1960-Jun 1961; Jul 1961-Jun 1962; Jul 1962-Jun 1967; Jul 1967-Jun 1969; Jul 1969-Jun 1971; Jul 1971-Jun 1972; Jul 1972-Jun 1974; Jul 1974-Dec 1975; Jan-Dec 1976; Jan-Dec 1977; Jan-Dec 1978; Oct 1978-Sep 1979; Oct 1979-Sep 1980.; Oct 1980-Sep 1984; Oct 1989-Sep 1990; Oct 1990-Sep 1991; Oct 1991-Jun 1992.

Strength Through Support: The 2750th Air Base Wing and Wright-Patterson AFB in Operations Desert Shield and Desert Storm. WPAFB: 2750th Air Base Wing, 1993.

Walker, Lois E. and Wickam, Shelby E. *From Huffman Prairie to the Moon: The History of Wright-Patterson Air Force Base.* WPAFB: Office of History, 2750th Air Base Wing, 1986.

OTHER HISTORIES

Annual Historical Report, Air Force Aero Propulsion Laboratory
1 Jul 1973-30 Jun 1974; 1 Jul 1974-30 Jun 1975.

Histories of the Engineering Division, Aircraft and Guided Missiles Section
1 Jul-31 Dec 1950.

REPORTS

Annual Report, Air Force Human Resources Laboratory, FY 1982, AFHRL Technical Paper 83-15.

Annual Report, Air Force Logistics Command, FY 1982, Feb 1, 1983.

Annual Report, Defense Institute of Security Assistance Management, FY 1982, Feb 25, 1983.

Annual Report, Hq Wright Field, Part II: Wright Field Under the Materiel Command, Jan-Jun 1944.

Annual Report, Signal Corps Aviation School, Wilbur Wright Field, Fairfield, Ohio, May 31, 1918.

Annual Reports, Chief, Materiel Division, Fiscal Years 1927 through 1940.

Archeological and Historical Consultants, Inc., *Documenting the Cold War Significance of Wright Laboratory Facilities.* WPAFB: 88th Air Base Wing Office of Environmental Management, 1996.

Army Air Forces Technical Base Planning Board, Preliminary Master Plan Report, approved Mar 18, 1947.

Base and Tenant Strength Report, 2750 ABW Base Plans Division, Oct 1, 1982.

Blee, Capt. H. H. *History of Organization and Activities of Airplane Engineering Division, Bureau of Aircraft Production.* Miscellaneous Report 220, McCook Field, Aug 15, 1919.

Brown, C.G. and Greene, Carl F. "Static-Test and Stress-Distribution Studies of the Materiel Division 55-Foot Cantilever All-Metal Wing." *Air Corps Information Circular*, Vol. VII, No. 663, Feb 15, 1932. Air Corps Technical Report, No. 3501.

Completion Report, "Wright Field, Dayton, Ohio." Vol. 1. Office of Constructing Quartermaster, Dayton, Ohio, ca. Jul 1927.

"Cultural Landscape Report, Wright Brothers Hill, Wright-Patterson Air Force Base, Ohio." National Park Service, Sep 1997.

The Engineering Division: A Consideration of Its Status with Respect to the Air Service and the Aeronautical Industry in the United States and Abroad. Rev. ed. Dayton, Ohio: McCook Field, Engineering Division, U.S. Army Air Service, Nov 20, 1924.

Guide to the Technology Master Process. WPAFB: Deputy Chief of Staff for Science and Technology, Headquarters, Air Force Materiel Command, Oct 30, 1992.

HAER No. OH–103, *Wright-Patterson Air Force Base Officers' Brick Quarters.* Historic American Engineer Record, National Park Service, 1996.

Hammer, Lois R. "Aeronautical Systems Division Studies in Weightlessness, 1959-1960." Wright Air Development Division Technical Report 60-715, WPAFB, 1961.

"Hardlines Design & Delineation." *History of the Wright-Patterson Air Force Base Railroad Network.* WPAFB: 88th Air Base Wing Office of Environmental Management, Apr 11, 1995.

"Index to Technical Reports of Engineering Division, Supply Group, Air Service, Nos. 1 – 1300, January 1918 – Jun 1919." Washington: Engineering Division, Air Service, McCook Field, 1920.

"Joint Air-to-Surface Standoff Missile." *Annual Report to Congress, FY 2000*. Director, Defense Operational Test and Evaluation.

Karman, Theodore von. *Toward New Horizons: Science, the Key to Air Supremacy*. Commemorative Edition, 1950-1992. WPAFB: Headquarters Air Force Systems Command History Office, 1992

Materials Technology Area Plan, FY 92. Andrews AFB, Maryland: Headquarters, Air Force Systems Command, DCS/Technology, 1992.

McCook Field, Engineering Division, Weekly Progress Reports, Numbers 27 (Oct 22, 1918) and 29 (Nov 5, 1918).

New World Vistas: Air and Space Power for the 21st Century. Washington: U.S. Air Force Scientific Advisory Board, Dec 15, 1995.

"Pressure Cabin Investigations." *Air Corps Information Circular*, Vol. VIII, No. 710, Oct 1, 1937. Air Corps Technical Report, No. 4220.

R&D Contributions to Aviation Progress (RADCAP). Joint Department of Defense-NASA-Department of Transportation Study, Aug 1972.

RDB Project Card: Special Carrier (MX-1457) (Nickname: Brass Ring) Termination Report, Aug 23, 1954. Brass Ring Termination Report File, Box 3197: AC/B-47, Box 1, ASC History Archive.

"Report of the Commission to Assess United States National Security Space Management and Organization," online at http://www.defenselink.mil/pubs/space20010111.html.

"Report of the Director of Air Service to the Secretary of War, 1920." *War Department Annual Reports.* Fiscal Year Ending Jun 30, 1920.

Report, Historical Data, Maintenance Division, Fairfield Air Service Command, Patterson Field, May 1, 1944.

Rodriques, Louis J., Director, Defense Acquisitions Issues, National Security and International Affairs Division. "Unmanned Aerial Vehicles: DoD's Acquisition Efforts." General Accounting Office Report No. GAO/T-NSIAD-97-138: Statement before the Subcommittee on Military Research and Development and Military Procurement, Committee on National Security, House of Representatives, Apr 9, 1997.

_____. "Unmanned Aerial Vehicles: DoD's Demonstration Approach Has Improved Project Outcomes." General Accounting Office Report No. GAO/T-NSIAD-99-33: Report to the Secretary of Defense, Aug 1999.

Rothman, M.B. *Aerospace Weapon System Acquisition Milestones: A Data Base*. N-2599-ACQ. Santa Monica: RAND Corporation, 1987.

Shiman, Philip. *Forging the Sword: Defense Production During the Cold War.* CERL Special Report 97/77. Washington: Construction Engineering Research Laboratory, 1997.

"Shop Practice—Working and Welding Stainless Steel—Tube Bending—Bending Radiator Cores Using High Melting Point Solder (A.C. Specification 11064)." *Air Corps Information Circular*, Vol. 7, No. 696, Sep 8, 1934. Air Corps Technical Report, No. 3820.

Simmons, C. F., Factory Manager, Airplane Engineering Division, *Organization and Activities of the Factory Department Including Construction and Maintenance, Nov 1917-Nov 1918*. Serial No. 376.

"Spot Welding and Its Application to Aircraft Structure." *Air Corps Information Circular*, Vol. 7, No. 692, Jul 10, 1934. Air Corps Technical Report, No. 3901.

Technical Report: AFFDL-TR-79-3071. Boggs, Bernard C. *History of Static Test and Air Force Structures Testing*. WPAFB: Air Force Flight Dynamics Laboratory, Structures Test Branch, 1979.

UAV Annual Report, FY 1996. Department of Defense, Washington, Nov 6, 1996.

USACERL Technical Report 98/98, *Archeological, Geophysical, and Remote Sensing Investigations of the 1910 Wright Brothers' Hangar at Wright-Patterson Air Force Base, Ohio*. U.S. Army Corps of Engineers, Jul 1998.

Watson, Dr. George M. *The Advanced Medium Short-Take-Off-And-Landing Transport (AMST) and the Implications of the Minimum Engineering Development (MED) Program*. Andrews AFB, Maryland: 1983.

UNPUBLISHED MATERIALS

Aldridge, James F. *A Historical Overview of the Mission and Organization of the Wright Laboratory, 1917-1993*. Unpublished draft. WPAFB: ASC History Office, 1994.

_____. "The Research Mission at Wright Field: An Historical Sketch." Unpublished paper. WPAFB: ASC History Office, n.d.

_____. *USAF Research & Development: The Legacy of the Wright Laboratory Science and Engineering Community: 1917-1997*. Unpublished draft. WPAFB: ASC History Office, 1996.

"ASD/XR Involvement in the History of the Advanced Tactical Fighter (ATF) Analysis." ATF History (draft). ASC History Office Archive, Jul 31, 1991.

"B-1/Long Range Combat Aircraft Program History Summary." In B-1 File, Box 7000: Reference, Chronology A-J. ASC History Office Archive.

"B-2, Advanced Technology Bomber Program Chronology, 1978-1995." In Box 3193: B-2 Aircraft Miscellaneous Documents. ASC History Office Archive.
Background paper. "AFRL Systems Support: The Laboratory's Response for the Warfighter," AFRL/ML, ca. Jul 2002.
Background paper. "ATB/B-2," ASC History Office Archive, n.d.
Background paper. "ATF/F-22," ASC History Office Archive, n.d.
Background paper. "Alternate Fighter Engine Competition," ASC History Office Archive, n.d.
Background paper. "C-17 Air Transportability Analysis of Army Vehicles," ASC History Office Archive, n.d.
Background paper. "C-17 Core Integrated Processor," ASC History Office Archive, n.d.
Background paper. "C-17 Cruise Drag Projection Analysis," ASC History Office Archive, n.d.
Background paper. "C-17 Design for Manufacturing/Assembly (DFMA) Project Main Landing Gear Pod," ASC History Office Archive, n.d.
Background paper. "C-17 Dual Row Airdrop," ASC History Office Archive, n.d.
Background paper. "C-17 Fuel Tank Sealing Improvement Team," ASC History Office Archive, n.d.
Background paper. "C-17 Multi-Band Radio System," ASC History Office Archive, n.d.
Background paper. "C-17 On-Board Inert Gas Generation System (OBIGGS)," ASC History Office Archive, n.d.
Background paper. "C-17 Paratrooper Airdrop Optimization (PAO) Phases I and II," ASC History Office Archive, n.d.
Background paper. "C-17 Strategic Brigade Airdrop (SBA) Formation Spacing," ASC History Office Archive, n.d.
Background paper. "C-17 Wireless Communication Set," ASC History Office Archive, n.d.
Background paper. "C-X/C-17," ASC History Office Archive, n.d.
Background paper. "Design Analysis Directorate (ASD/XRH ATF Team Activities)," Wayne O'Connor, ASC/LUC, Mar 25, 1998.
Background paper. "Engine Structural Integrity Program (ENSIP)," ASC History Office Archive, n.d.
Background paper. "F-15E Main Landing Gear (MLG) Tires," ASC History Office Archive, n.d.
Background paper. "F-16 CARA Performance Improvements," ASC History Office Archive, n.d.
Background paper. "F-16 ECM Technique," ASC History Office Archive, n.d.
Background paper. "F-16 INS Performance Anomalies at Aviano AB," ASC History Office Archive, n.d.
Background paper. "F-16 Operational Flight Program (OFP) Software Cost Reduction," ASC History Office Archive, n.d.
Background paper. "F-16 System Wide Integrity Management," ASC History Office Archive, n.d.
Background paper. "F-22 Readiness for First Flight (FF)," ASC History Office Archive, n.d.
Background paper. "First Sealed Pressure Cabin Airplane, XC-35, Wright Field, 1935-1937," James F. Aldridge, ASC History Office, Aug 25, 1999.
Background paper. "F-X Concept Definition Studies (1964-65)," ASC History Office Archive, n.d.
Background paper. "Have Blue RCS Signature Evaluation," ASC History Office Archive, n.d.
Background paper. "History of Sensor Materials Technology in ML and Its Predecessors," AFRL/ML, ca. Jul 2002.
Background paper. "Justification of [Pioneer] Award [to Joseph J. Lusczek, Jr.]," ASC History Office Archive, n.d.
Background paper. "KC-X/SC-10," ASC History Office Archive, n.d.
Background paper. "Kapton Wiring Study," ASC History Office Archive, n.d.
Background paper. "LWF/F-16," ASC History Office Archive, n.d.
Background paper. "National Aerospace Plane (NASP) Wind Tunnel/Water Tunnel Tests," ASC History Office Archive, n.d.
Background paper. "The Origins of the F-15," J. J. Lusczek, ASC/XR, Jun 29, 1992.
Background paper. "Pioneers and Heroes," ASC History Office Archive, n.d.
Background paper. "Predator Data Link Analysis," ASC History Office Archive, n.d.
Background paper. "TPIPT Success Stories," ASC History Office Archive, n.d.
Background paper. "Teal Dawn/AGM-129 ACM," ASC History Office Archive, n.d.
Biography. "Harry G. Armstrong," ASC History Office Archive, n.d.
Biography. "Henry Harley ('Hap') Arnold," Laura Romesburg, ASC History Office, Jul 19, 1994.
Biography. "George W. Goddard," ASC History Office Archive, n.d.
Biography. "Mr. John M. Griffin," ASC History Office Archive, n.d.
Biography. "Ezra Kotcher," ASC History Office Archive, n.d.
Biography. "Fred D. Orazio, Sr.," ASC History Office Archive, n.d.
Biography. "Donald L. Putt," ASC History Office Archive, n.d.
Biography. "Frederick T. Rall, Jr.," ASC History Office Archive, n.d.
Biography. "Bennie Thomas," ASC History Office Archive, n.d.
Boeing Defense and Space Group, Military Airplanes Division. "Boeing B-2 History, 1993-1994" (1995). In Box 3190: B-2, PA Files. ASC History Office Archive.
Briefing. "XRED Accomplishments—Historical Perspective." ASC History Office Archive. N.d.

Chronology. "35th Anniversary: Milestones."
Chronology. "Laboratories at Wright-Patterson AFB, Ohio, 1917-1975." ASC History Office Archive. N.d.
"Chronology of Events Related to the Advanced Manned Strategic Aircraft Program, 1954-1965." In XB-70/AMSA File, Box 7000: History/Chronology, Topical A-J. ASC History Office Archive.
Curry, J. F. "What McCook Field Means to Aviation." Unpublished recollections, n.d.
Dean, Terence M. "The History of McCook Field, Dayton, Ohio, 1917-1927." Masters thesis, University of Dayton, 1969.
"Dedication of the General James H. Doolittle Acquisition Management Complex and the Lieutenant General James T. Stewart Hall." Program. WPAFB: Sep 16, 1994.
"Dedication of the Lieutenant General Kenneth B. Wolfe Hall, Major General William L. Mitchell Hall, and the Frederick T. Rall, Jr. Hall." Program. WPAFB: Apr 30, 1997.
"Dedication of the Major General Franklin Otis Carroll Hall." Program. WPAFB: Jun 1, 2001.
"Dedication of Wright Field in Honor of Wilbur Wright, Orville Wright, and The Citizens of Dayton Who Presented the Wright Field Site to the Government." Program. Dayton, Ohio: Oct 12, 1927.
Deutrich, Mabel E. "History of the Decimal Filing System in the War Department." National Archives Seminar on Record Keeping Practices. Paper. College Park: National Archives Library, Sep 14, 1956.
"Enlisted Firsts: MSgt Ralph Bottriell." Air Force Enlisted Heritage Research Institute, File 19-10.
Ferguson, Paul. "F-16 Chronology," ASC History Office, Mar 2000.
File. "Foreign Aircraft," ASC History Office Archive, Box 5873.
File. "Hans Joachim Pabst von Ohain," ASC History Office Archive, n.d.
File. "[List of] Paperclip Scientists and Engineers," ASC History Office Archive, ca. late 1940s.
File. "Jules Verne," ASC History Office Archive, n.d.
File. "Frank L. Wattendorf," ASC History Office Archive, n.d.
Gold, David. "Early Development of the Manually Operated, Personnel Parachute, 1900-1919." Paper presented to the A.I.A.A. 2nd Aerodynamic Deceleration Systems Conference, El Centro, California, Sep 23-25, 1968.
____. "The Parachute in Perspective: Looking Backward to 1931, circa A.I.A.A. Origin." Paper presented to the A.I.A.A. 7th Aerodynamic Decelerator and Balloon Technology Conference, San Diego, California, Oct 21-23, 1981.
"Historical Sketch, Supply Division, FASC, 1917-1938," ASC History Office Archive, n.d.
"History of the Air Corps Materiel Division." Unpublished history. ASC History Office Archive, n.d.
"History of McCook and Wright Field," ASC History Office Archive, n.d.
Jacobs, Marguerite. "Flying Fields and Fashions Change." Unpublished recollections. ASC History Office Archive,1928.
Johnson, Ralph. Written comments on draft of Chapter 5 of *Splendid Vision, Unswerving Purpose*. ASC History Office, Apr 2002.
Jones, Christopher A., Major, USAF. "Unmanned Aerial Vehicles (UAVS): An Assessment of Historical Operations and Future Possibilities." Research paper presented to the Research Department of the Air Command and Staff College, Mar 1997.
Kididis, Andrew S. "The Art of Drag, A History of U.S. Air Force Parachute Technology Development." Manuscript, 2002.
Klein, James. "T-37 Life Extension Study, Status 14 August 2000." In T-37 Documents File, Box: Trainers. ASC History Office Archive.
Lamar, William E. Papers and Archives. WPAFB: ASC History Office Archive.
List. "Flight Dynamics Laboratory (WRDC/FI) Tech Base Accomplishments." ASC History Office Archive, ca. 1990.
List. "Forty-Three Years of Air Force Technology Base Accomplishments, 1947-1990, WRDC/EL." ASC History Office Archive.
List. "ML [Materials Laboratory] Accomplishments." ASC History Office Archive, ca. 1990.
List. "Propulsion Tech Base Accomplishments." ASC History Office Archive, n.d.
McMahon, T. C. "Something About McCook Field." Unpublished recollections, n.d.
McPherson, Lieutenant Colonel Craig. "Advanced Cruise Missile, 1982-1997." Presentation at the Acquisition Staff Meeting, Mar 25, 1997.
Memo. [Joseph J.] Lusczek to [John] Griffin, ASC/XR. "Continued Support to JSF." ASC History Office Archive. Jan 15, 1997.
Misenko, Albert E. *Aero Propulsion*. Draft, ASC History Office, 1994.
Niehaus, James J. *Five Decades of Materials Progress: Air Force Materials Lab, 1917-1967*. WPAFB: 1967.
Perry, Robert L. *History of the Nuclear Engineering Test Facility* (unpublished final draft). WPAFB: Aeronautical Systems Division, Historical Division, Information Office, n.d.
Point paper. "Acquisition Management Complex," Mike Bauman, ASC History Office Archive, Nov 13, 2001.
Point paper. "F-X Concept Definition Studies (1964-65)," ASC History Office Archive, n.d.
Point paper. "The National Air Intelligence Center's Legacy," Rob Young, National Air Intelligence Center, n.d.
Point paper. "SOR-182 (C-141) Airlift Systems Studies (1959-60)," ASC History Office Archive, n.d.

Pollock, P.H. "Data Related to Lt. Col. Henry E. Warden During 1945-1950 Assignment." WPAFB: Aeronautical Systems Division Historical Division, 1964.

Smith, George B. "History of North Dayton Property, Temporarily Called Wright Field, Now McCook Field." Unpublished recollections, n.d.

"Success Stories, Oct 1999 – Sep 1992." WPAFB: Flight Dynamics Directorate, Wright Laboratory, n.d.

Thomas, Richard D. "Air Force Technical Achievements at Dayton." Aeronautical Systems Division, Historical Division, Jul 20, 1961.

U.S. Air Force. *Airlift Master Plan*. In Box: Cargo/SST, ASC History Office Archive, Sep 29, 1983.

U.S. Air Force. *Standard Aircraft Characteristics: C-119*. ASC History Office Archive, May 15, 1948, and Jan 11, 1950.

U.S. Air Force. *Standard Aircraft Characteristics: C-124*. ASC History Office Archive, May 15, 1948, and Aug 22, 1952.

Uyehara, Cecil H. "The B-70 Story (to summer 1959)." Directorate of Systems Management, Headquarters Air Research and Development Command, 1959. In Box 3238: B-70 Bomber Files Box 2. ASC History Office Archive.

Weitze, Karen J., *Evolution of Air Force R&D and Logistics Installations During the Cold War: Command Lineage, Scientific Achievement, and Major Tenant Missions*. 2 vols. (Draft), 2001.

Whitney, Raymond. Presentation at Armstrong Aerospace Medical Research Laboratory, WPAFB, Ohio, 1996.

Wright Air Development Center. "Physical Resources of the Aeronautical Research Laboratory." WPAFB, 1956.

DOCUMENTS

Boom to Drogue Adaptors, KC-135. Memorandums to File, Dec 17, 1956 and Mar 12, 1957. Air Refueling File, Box 8081: Subsystems/Refueling Box 1: ASC History Office Archive.

Cheney, Dick, Secretary of Defense. *Defense Strategy for the 1990s: The Regional Defense Strategy*, Jan 1993.

Copy of Lease, Purchase Request A-6951, Order No. 50214, between the Miami Conservancy District and Lt Col C. G. Edgar, Signal Corps, Jul 1, 1917.

The Dayton Air Service Incorporated Committee. Deed to The United States of America, Dec 18, 1924.

The Dayton Air Service Incorporated Committee. Warranty Deed to The United States of America, Aug 9, 1924.

Deeds, Col E. A., Signal Corps. Memo to Lt Col Edgar (Construction Division), no subj., Oct 1, 1917.

Director of Air Service. Letter to Chief, Engineering Division, Air Service, Dayton, Ohio, subj: Administration Matters Regarding Civilian Personnel and Telegraph Service, May 14, 1919.

Director, Operational Test and Evaluation. "Combined Operational Test and Evaluation and Live Fire Test and Evaluation Report on the V-22 Osprey." Nov 17, 2000.

GRB-36 Aircraft (FICON), Revision of Test Requirements. Memorandum to File, Mar 15, 1956. GB-36 File, Box 3195: Aircraft/Bombers/B-36, Box 1, ASC History Office Archive.

Gilmore, Brigadier General William E., Chief, Materiel Division. "McCook Field Review 1926." Dec 20, 1926, Doc. X. Indexed Documents Concerning McCook Field, Wright Field, 1929, and Air Service Progress through 1929. Papers of George A. Biehn.

Grannis, J. K., A.M.E.S.C., Superintendent of Construction. Letter to Lt Col C. G. Edgar, Signal Corps, U.S.R., subj: Experimental Field, Sep 28, 1917.

LeRoy, Amos Swan Collection, U.S. Air Force Museum Archives.

Mark, Hans M., Secretary of the Air Force. Memorandum for Assistant Secretary of Defense, Program Analysis and Evaluation: C-X Analysis, Mar 17, 1980. In C-X Queries and Clippings File, Box: Cargo/SST. ASC History Office Archive.

Menoher, Major General Charles T., Director of Air Service. Memorandum for Chief of Staff, subj: Purchase of Dayton-Wright Airplane Plant for Use as Air Service Engineering Experimental Station and Testing Field, Apr 11, 1919.

Nash, C. W., Assistant Director, Aircraft Production, Airplane Engineering Dept. Letter to Col J. G. Vincent, Chief Engineer, Bureau of Aircraft Production, subj: McCook Field, Nov 7, 1918.

_____. Assistant Director of Aircraft Production. Letter to Col J. G. Vincent, Chief Engineer, Aircraft Production, subj: McCook Field, Nov 7, 1918.

Office of Chief of Air Service. Memo to Engineering Division, no subj., Feb 12, 1925.

Olson, Randy, ASC/YWI. "The Road to DMT," 2000. Online at http://dmt.wpafb.af.mil/Documents/DMT/road.htm.

Pennewill, Mr. E.E., Vice President and General Manager, Standard Aircraft Corp. of Elizabeth, New Jersey. Letter to Dept. Military Aeronautics, Technical Section, Dayton, Ohio. Subj: Performance of Airplanes, Sep 7, 1918.

Perry, Robert L. *System Development Strategies: A Comparative Study of Doctrine, Technology, and Organization in the USAF Ballistic and Cruise Missile Programs, 1950-1960* (For Official Use Only). RAND Technical Memorandum RM-4853-PR. Santa Monica: RAND Corporation, 1966.

Record of Military Administration. Airplane Engineering Division, McCook Field, Ohio. Dec 16, 1918.

Records of the United States Air Force Commands, Activities, and Organizations. Record Group 342, online at http://www.nara.gov/guide/top.

Registrar Yale College [University], New Haven, Conn. Letter to Frank S. Patterson, no subj., Apr 27, 1918; Certificate of Enlistment, ERC (AGO Form 422-1).

Resolution Passed at Meeting of the Aircraft Production Board, Oct 1, 1917, submitted to Lt Col C. G. Edgar, Construction Division, Signal Corps.

Rice, Donald B., Secretary of Air Force, and McPeak, General Merrill A., Air Force Chief of Staff. *FY92 Air Force Posture Statement.* Presented to House of Representatives, Armed Services Committee, Feb 26, 1991.

Secretary of the Air Force, Legislative Liaison. "F-22." *1998 Air Force Congressional Issue Papers*. Online at http://www.af.mil/lib/afissues/1998/issue98.html.

Squier, Brigadier General George O., Chief Signal Officer of the Army. Memo to Adjutant General of the Army, subj: Approval of Buildings for Experimental Purposes, Dayton, Ohio, Sep 28, 1917.

"Survey and History of McCook Field, Dayton, Ohio." History of McCook Field (Miscellaneous Correspondence) 1918-1926.

2750th ABW/DEIC (Real Estate, Cost Accounting Section). Letter to 2750th ABW/HO, subj: History of Acquiring Fee Land, WPAFB (Your ltr 16 Jul 1980), Jul 25, 1980, with attachment: Listing of Fee Land.

"Valuation of Assets of Engineering Division Air Service, McCook Field, Dayton." Financial report, Oct 31, 1923.

War Department. General Order 20, Aug 21, 1925.

War Department. Telegram from McCook Field, Dayton, Ohio, to Division of Military Aeronautics, Washington, Executive Section, Dec 20, 1918.

Wilbur Wright Field Armorers School Commanding Officer (Maj H. C. K. Muhlenberg). Letter to Director of Military Aeronautics, Technical Section, Washington, subj: Report on Accident to DeHavilland Four Plane No. 32098, Jun 26, 1918.

NEWSPAPERS AND PERIODICALS

Air Corps News Letter

Jan 1, 1937, Vol. XX (Special Materiel Division Number).

Air Service News Letter

Jul 19,1923, Vol. VII
Nov 22, 1923, Vol. VII
Feb 1, 1924, Vol. VIII
Jul 31, 1924, Vol. VIII
Oct 31, 1924, Vol. VIII

"Airlift Enhancement." *Backgrounder, Air Force Internal Information*. Kelly AFB, Texas, n.d.

Baker, Sue. "Predator Missile Launch Test Totally Successful." *Air Force Link*, Feb 27, 2001.

Bickley, Karla. "JSUPT Track Select System Undergoes Changes." *Air Force News*, Apr 30, 1998.

"Boeing Co. Today Will Celebrate its Program to Convert 322 ALCMs to the CALCM Configuration." *Aerospace Daily,* Nov 2, 1999.

Bosker, Staff Sergeant A.J. "Lockheed Martin Wins JSF Contract." *Air Force News*, Oct 26, 2001.

Burnham, Tech. Sergeant Rick. "C-27s Fly Last Mission: To the Boneyard." *Air Force News*, Jan 1999.

Dady, Gidge. "First CV 22 Arrives at Edwards." *Air Force News*, Sep 22, 2000.

D'Andrea, Captain Christa. "T-6 Flying Training Begins at Moody." *Air Force News*, Nov 26, 2001.

The Dayton Evening Herald, Jan 5, 1923, n.p.

The Dayton Journal, Oct 26, 1922, p 1.

The Dayton News, Oct 27, 1922, p 1.

Flaherty, Mary Pat. "Three Marines Guilty in Osprey Records Case." *Washington Post*, Sep 15, 2001, n.p.

Flying and Popular Aviation, Sep 1941, Vol. XXIX (Special U.S. Army Air Forces Issue).

Fulghum, David A. "TSSAM Follow-On to Take Shape This Year." *Aviation Week and Space Technology*, Feb 27, 1995, pp 49-51.

Hebert, Adam J. "Air Force Desire for UCAV Pushing Program Nearly As Fast As Possible." *Inside the Air Force*, Jun 22, 2001.

"Lockheed Martin Awarded $818 Million Contract for F-22." *Aerospace Daily*, Sep 21, 2001.

Lumpkin, John J. "Logging on for Battle." *Albuquerque Journal*, Oct 25, 2000.

NCR Progress, May 13, 1922, Vol. 3, No. 3; Nov 23, 1922, Vol. 3, No. 8.

"New Post Hospital Open." *Patterson Field Postings*, May 20,1942, p 1.

"Remembering the Forgotten Field." *WPAFB Skywrighter*, Oct 19, 1979, pp 17, 22.
"Rivet Joint Intelligence Jets to Fly Higher, Faster." *Aviation Week and Space Technology*, May 14, 2001, p 32.
"Service Awards to Civilian Employees Authorized by WD." *Patterson Field Postings*, Nov 5, 1943, p 2.
Shaw, Herbert A. "German Air Force Secrets Are Bared." *Dayton Daily News*, Nov 2, 1947, n.p.
"Speedway has ties to Air Force." *WPAFB Skywrighter*, Aug 10, 2001, p 11.
"Thanks for the Memories." *WPAFB Skywrighter*, Jan 9, 1981, p 8.
"Von Ohain, 86, Dies." *Dayton Daily News*, Mar 14, 1998, p 2B.
Wall, Robert. "USAF to Update Maverick Missile." *Aviation Week and Space Technology*, Jun 29, 1998.
"When Pilots Flew on Two Wings." *WPAFB Skywrighter*, May 15, 1981, pp 16, 19.
Wickam, Shelby E. "Wright Field: Looking Back Over 50 Years of Aviation History." *WPAFB Skywrighter*, Oct 7, 1977, pp 6, 20.
"Wing innovation takes NASA back to future." *Dayton Daily News*, Mar 27, 2002, pp 1E, 6E.
The Wright[Field] Flyer, Aug 18, 1945.
Wright-Patterson Air Force Base Skywrighter
Jun 17, 1960
Jun 9, 1961
Jun 9, 1967
Aug 18, 1967
Sep 26, 1969.
Wright-Patterson Post Script
May 12, 1945
Aug 4, 1945
Aug 18, 1945
Sep 21, 1945
Sep 28, 1945
Nov 16, 1945
Nov 21, 1945
Dec 14, 1945
Dec 28, 1945
Aug 30, 1946.

INTERVIEWS

Mr. David A. Ardis, ASC/ENA, Interview with Dr. James F. Aldridge, ASC History Office, Feb 7, 2000.
Brigadier General Harry G. Armstrong. *Interview with Harry G. Armstrong (Ret.), U.S. Air Force, Medical Corps.* By John W. Bullard and T. A. Glasgow, interviewers. Brooks AFB, Texas: United States Air Force Oral History Program, Apr 1976.
Major General Fred J. Ascani. *A General Remembers: Major General Fred J. Ascani, Wright Field's Father of Systems Engineering*. Edited with narrative by James F. Aldridge. WPAFB: ASC History Office, 2001.
Mr. John Bauer, Air Force Materiel Command, Logistics Information Support, Personal Communication with Robin Smith, Jan 30, 2002.
Ms. Virginia Brown, Peace Pearl Program, Personal Communication with Jim Ciborski, Mar 8, 2002.
Mr. Donald Davidson, Indianapolis Motor Speedway Museum, Personal Communications with Robin Smith, Jun 18, 2002 and Jul 15, 2002.
Mr. D. Adam Dickey, Interviews, Dayton, Ohio, Sep 2, 1983; Sep 16, 1983.
Mrs. Darlene Gerhardt, Interviews, Dayton, Ohio, 1983-1984.
Mrs. Alice Hanks, Personal Communication with Robin Smith, Jul 22, 2002.
Mr. Joseph Lusczek, ASC/ENDF, Interviews with Dr. James F. Aldridge, ASC History Office, Nov 7, 2001, and Apr 12, 2002.
Mr. Otto Peter Morgensen, Jr. *Otto Peter Morgensen, Jr., Aeronautical Engineer, Wright Field, 1936 – 1970: Oral History Interview*. Interview by Laura N. Romesburg; edited with notes by James F. Aldridge. WPAFB: ASC History Office, 2001.
Mr. Jon Ogg, ASC/EN, Interview with Dr. James F. Aldridge, ASC History Office, Feb 7, 2000.
Mr. Fred D. Orazio, Sr., Interview, WPAFB: ASC History Office, Nov 28, 1995.
Mr. Harry S. Price, Jr., Price Brothers Company, Interviews, Dayton, Ohio, Jan 3, 1984; Jun 22, 1984.
Mr. Dick Ralstin, Dick Ralstin's Racing Home Page, Personal Communication with Robin Smith, May 9, 2002.

Lieutenant General James T. Stewart. *A Man for the Time: An Oral History Interview with Lieutenant General James T. Stewart.* WPAFB: 1990.

Mr. Stanley A. Tremaine, Interview with Dr. James F. Aldridge, ASC History Office, Nov 7, 2001.

OTHER

"AFHRL." Pamphlet published by the Air Force Human Resources Laboratory Office of Public Affairs, 1982.

"Aeronautical Systems Division." WPAFB: Office of Information, Internal Information and Community Relations Division, Air Force Systems Command, ca. 1961.

Air Force Institute of Technology Graduate School of Engineering and Management: Academic Year 2001-2002 Catalog.

Air Force Pamphlet 70-7, *U.S. Air Force Historical Aircraft, Background Information*, Jun 1970.

Air Force Pamphlet 190-2-2, *A Chronology of American Aerospace Events from 1903 through 1964,* Sep 1965.

Air Force Security Assistance Center Web Site. Online at https://rock.afsac.wpafb.af.mil/.

Aldridge, James F. "Aerospace Medicine at Wright Field—Notes." ASC History Office, n.d.

"Ann Baumgartner Carl on: Her Interest in Flying," Fly Girls, American Experience, PBS, online at http://www.pbs.org/wgbh/amex/flygirls/filmmore/reference/interview/carl01.html.

Atkins, Richard L. *The B-58 Escape Capsule Indoctrination Brochure*. Fort Worth, General Dynamics, 1962. In B-58 File, Box 3219: History of the Development of the B-58 Bomber. 3 vols. ASC History Office Archive.

"Awards—Clarence M. Mackay Trophy." National Aeronautic Association, online at http://www.naa-usa.org/website/html/awardsset.html.

"Awards—Robert J. Collier Trophy." National Aeronautic Association, online at http://www.naa-usa.org/website/html/awardsset.html.

Base Guide, 1956. WPAFB: 2750th Air Base Wing, 1956.

Berger, Carl. "The Strengthening of Air Force In-House Laboratories, 1961-1962." Washington: USAF Historical Division Liaison Office, 1962.

Case History of Air-to-Air Refueling. Historical Office, Air Force Materiel Command, Mar 1949. Air Refueling File, Box 8081: Subsystems/Refueling Box 1, ASC History Office Archive.

"Comprehensive History of Patterson and Wright Field Planning, Nov 1942-Feb 1945." ASC History Office Archive.

Dick Ralstin's Racing Home Page. Online at http://home.flash.net/~dralstin/.

Doolittle's Tokyo Raiders 60th Anniversary Reunion. Online at http://www.thestateonline.com/doolittle/doolittle.htm.

Drones/RPVs, Public Affairs Files, ASC History Office Archive.

"Evolution of USAF Aircraft Insignia 1947." Online at http://www.wpafb.af.mil/museum/research/insig11.htm.

Fact Sheet, Aeronautical Systems Division. "B-2 Advanced Technology Bomber," WPAFB: 1988, in Box 3190: B-2, PA Files, ASC History Office Archive.

Fact Sheet, U.S. Air Force. "A-10/OA-10 Thunderbolt II," Jun 2000.

Fact Sheet, U.S. Air Force. "AC-130H/U Gunship," Oct 1999.

Fact Sheet, U.S. Air Force. "AGM-86B/C Missiles," n.d.

Fact Sheet, U.S. Air Force. "AIM-7 Sparrow," Oct 1999.

Fact Sheet, U.S. Air Force. "AIM-9 Sidewinder," Oct 1999.

Fact Sheet, U.S. Air Force. "AIM-120 AMRAAM," Aug 1999.

Fact Sheet, U.S. Air Force. "The Air Force Institute of Technology," n.d.

Fact Sheet, U.S. Air Force. "Automated Aircraft," Oct 1983.

Fact Sheet, U.S. Air Force. "C-5 Galaxy," Nov 2000.

Fact Sheet, U.S. Air Force. "C-9A/C Nightingale," n.d.

Fact Sheet, U.S. Air Force. "C-17 Globemaster III," n.d.

Fact Sheet, U.S. Air Force. "C-130 Hercules," Jul 2001.

Fact Sheet, U.S. Air Force. "C-141B Starlifter," Dec 2000.

Fact Sheet, U.S. Air Force. "F-15 Eagle," Sep 2000.

Fact Sheet, U.S. Air Force. "F-16 Fighting Falcon," Dec 2000.

Fact Sheet, U.S. Air Force. "HH-60G Pave Hawk," Sep 2000.

Fact Sheet, U.S. Air Force. "KC-10A Extender," Jul 2001.

Fact Sheet, U.S. Air Force. "KC-135 Stratotanker," Jul 2001.

Fact Sheet, U.S. Air Force. "LANTIRN," Jun 2001.

Fact Sheet, U.S. Air Force. "MC-130E/H Combat Talon I/II," Aug 2001.

Fact Sheet, U.S. Air Force. "MC-130P Combat Shadow," Aug 2001.

Fact Sheet, U.S. Air Force. "MH-53J/M Pave Low," Jul 2000.

Fact Sheet, U.S. Air Force. "OC-135B Open Skies," Feb 2001.
Fact Sheet, U.S. Air Force. "RC-135V/W Rivet Joint," Mar 2000.
Fact Sheet, U.S. Air Force. "RPV," Sep 1974. In RPV, BGM-34 and Others File, Box 3329: Drones/RPVs, PA Files, ASC History Office Archive.
Fact Sheet, U.S. Air Force. "T-1A Jayhawk," Jun 2001.
Fact Sheet, U.S. Air Force. "T-37 Tweet," n.d.
Fact Sheet, U.S. Air Force. "T-38 Talon," Jun 2001.
Fact Sheet, U.S. Air Force. "T-43A," Jun 2001.
Fact Sheet, U.S. Air Force. "U-2S," Dec 2000.
Fact Sheet, U.S. Air Force. "UH-1N Huey," Jun 1999.
Fact Sheet, U.S. Air Force. "Unidentified Flying Objects and Air Force Project Blue Book," Jun 2000. Online at http://www.af.mil/news/factsheets/Unidentified_Flying_Objects_a.html.
Fact Sheet, U.S. Air Force. "X-29 Advanced Technology Demonstrator," n.d.
Fact Sheet, U.S. Air Force Museum. "Lockheed SR-71A," n.d.
Fact Sheet, U.S. Air Force Space Command. "HH-1H Iroquois," May 1997.
Fact Sheet, U.S. Air Force Space Command. "UH-1N Huey," Mar 2001.
First Around the World. Santa Monica: Douglas Aircraft Corp., 1974.
First Five Years of the Air Research and Development Command, United States Air Force. Baltimore: Historical Division, Office of Information Services, Headquarters, Air Research and Development Command, 1955.
"The 500-Mile Adventure." *Rare Sportsfilms, Inc.*, online at http://www.raresportsfilms.com/1957indian.html.
Fraterrigo, Elizabeth. *Beyond Kitty Hawk: Inventing Flight at Huffman Prairie Flying Field.* WPAFB: Dayton Aviation Heritage National Historical Park, 2000.
Hanley, Tim. *Space and Missile Systems Organization: A Chronology, 1954-1979.*
The Historic Brick Quarters of Wright-Patterson Air Force Base. Brochure produced by the Historic American Buildings Survey/ Historic American Engineer Record, National Park Service, 1996.
History of the United States Air Force. ATC Pamphlet 190-1. Randolph AFB, Texas, 1961.
Jones, Quincy. *Hip Hits* (Mercury 60799). Online at http://www.eclipse.net/~fitzgera/ rahsaan/hiphits.htm.
"LANTIRN." Brochure produced by Martin Marietta Electronics and Missiles, Jul 1994.
Laubenthal, Capt Sanders A. *Yesterday, Today, and Tomorrow*. WPAFB: Air Force Institute of Technology, Office of Public Affairs, 1979.
The Legacy of Wright Field. Brochure published by the National Park Service, 1993.
"The Lineage of the United States Air Force," Air Force History Support Office, online at http://www.airforcehistory.hq.af.mil/PopTopics/lineage.htm.
A Little Journey to the Home of the Engineering Division, Army Air Service. McCook Field, Hq Engineering Division, ca.1926.
"The Materiel Center and You." Wright Field, Jan 1943.
McDonnell Douglas F-4G "Wild Weasel." Online at http://www.wpafb.af.mil/museum/research/fighter/f4g.htm.
"The Mid-60s and the Aeronautical Systems Division." WPAFB: Aeronautical Systems Division, n.d.
News Release. "A-7D Flies Via Single Glass Fiber Fly-By-Light." United States Air Force, May 21, 1982, on file at ASC History Office Photographic Archive.
News Release. "Air Force Accepts Final C-27A Spartan." ASC/PA, Feb 1, 1993.
News Release. "Air Force Creates Unmanned Aerial Vehicle System Program Office." ASC/PA, Nov 13, 1995, in PA Files, Box 3329: Drones/RPVs, ASC History Office Archive.
News Release. "Air Force selects 8 senior NCOs for AFIT." Air Force Print News, Jul 2, 2002.
News Release. "C-119 Flying Boxcar." U.S. Air Force, Headquarters, CONAC, n.d., in untitled file, Box 3291: C-119 et al. Cargo Aircraft, ASC History Office Archive.
News Release. "F-111 Officially Retires as the 'Aardvark'." Air Force News Service, Aug 5, 1996.
News Release. Joy, Lieutenant Ron. "Bionics, Space Foods, Effects of Noise Made for Exciting Era." Aeronautical Systems Division, Office of Public Affairs, WPAFB, PAM #85-095, May 30, 1985.
News Release. "McDonnell Douglas YC-15 to Fly Again as an Advanced Technology Demonstrator." McDonnell Douglas, Apr 11, 1997.
News Release. "Phantom to Retire from AF Inventory." Air Force News Service, Nov 29, 1995.
News Release. "Propelled Decoy Successfully Flight Tested." Aeronautical Systems Division, Nov 7, 1974. Systems/ Drones, 1972-98, Propelled Decoy Successfully Flight Tested file, Box 3316, ASC History Office Archive.
News Release. Untitled. Aeronautical Systems Division, Nov 25, 1969. Systems/Drones, 1972-98, Subsonic Cruise Armed Decoy file, Box 3316, ASC History Office Archive.
News Release. Untitled. Lockheed Missiles and Space Company. U.S. Air Force, Space Systems Division, Information Kit,

n.d., Space Related Miscellaneous Documents, Box 9086, ASC History Office Archive.

News Release. Untitled. U.S. Air Force, May 28, 1968, in A-37 Photograph File, ASC History Office Archive.

"1957 Belond Exhaust Special," online at http://www.indycals.com/Museum/winners/1957.html.

"Photograph of Wright-Patterson Air Force Base and its Master Plan," 1948.

Press Release. "All in Readiness for Big Air Hit at Wright Field," Oct 16, 1945.

Press Release. Gillmore, Brigadier General W. E. "Review of Air Corps Developments in 1927," Headquarters, Materiel Division, Wright Field, Jan 31, 1928.

Secretary of the Air Force, Office of Information, Photo Package No. 2, 1971.

Seek Spinner File, Box 3316, ASC History Office Archive.

Shows, H. R. and Hackney, D. I. *Staff Study of the Aerial Refueling Program.* WADC, May 1957. Box 8081: Subsystems/ Refueling Box 1: ASC History Office Archive.

60th Doolittle Raiders Reunion. Online at http://www.doolittleraidersreunion.com/attend.html.

Story of the Miami Conservancy District. Brochure, Dayton, Ohio, n.d.

U.S. Air Force, Standard Aircraft Characteristic Charts and Characteristic Summaries. ASC History Office Archive.

"The U.S. Air Force Symbol—Guidelines for Use." Air Force Link, Useage Guidelines, online at http://www.af.mil/ airforcestory/guidelines.shtml.

United States Air Force Biographies. Online at http://www.af.mil/news/biographies.html.

"United States Air Force Seal." Air Force History Support Office, online at http://www.airforcehistory.hq.af.mil/ PopTopics/usafsealhist.htm.

User's Manual, United States Air Force Smart Track. Los Angeles: Coleman Engineering, n.d. ASC History Office Archive.

Wild Weasel. Online at http://www.boeing.com/defense-space/military/f4/wildweasel.htm.

Women Pilots in WWII, WASP Class 43-W-5. United States Air Force Museum, online at http://www.wpafb.af.mil/ museum/history/wasp/wasp26.htm.

"Wright Field." Pamphlet published by the Materiel Division, U.S. Army, Air Corps, 1938.

Wright Field and World War I. Brochure published by the National Park Service, 1993.

Wright Field Five-Foot Wind Tunnel. Brochure published by the American Society of Mechanical Engineers, Mar 22, 1995.

Wright Flyers. Brochure published by the Wright Aircraft Corporation, Dayton, Ohio, ca. 1915.

"Wright-Patterson AFB Personnel Strength, 1918-2000," 88 ABW/HO Archives.

INDEX

INDEX

A

B

C

D

E

F

G

H

I

J

K

N

O

P

T

U

X

Y

Z

In Memoriam

This book is dedicated to the memory of Mr. Donald R. Yates, of the Aeronautical Systems Center Public Affairs Office. Don served for 10 years at Wright-Patterson Air Force Base as a printing liaison with the Government Printing Office (GPO). He was responsible for communicating Wright-Patt's needs to the GPO and became the corporate knowledge on the subject, offering invaluable information and insight. Don wrote specifications for this book and was in good spirits as he helped deliver the completed files for publication to the GPO in Columbus, Ohio. The next day, he passed away. Don's many friends and colleagues in the ASC History Team, the GPO, and Wright-Patterson Air Force Base deeply mourn his loss. His friendship, professionalism, and expertise will be sorely missed.

☆ U.S. Government Printing Office 2002 Jacket 753-429